A Companion to the Anthropology of Europe

The *Blackwell Companions to Anthropology* offer a series of comprehensive syntheses of the traditional subdisciplines, primary subjects, and geographic areas of inquiry for the field. Taken together, the series represents both a contemporary survey of anthropology and a cutting edge guide to the emerging research and intellectual trends in the field as a whole.

1. *A Companion to Linguistic Anthropology*, edited by Alessandro Duranti
2. *A Companion to the Anthropology of Politics*, edited by David Nugent and Joan Vincent
3. *A Companion to the Anthropology of American Indians*, edited by Thomas Biolsi
4. *A Companion to Psychological Anthropology*, edited by Conerly Casey and Robert B. Edgerton
5. *A Companion to the Anthropology of Japan*, edited by Jennifer Robertson
6. *A Companion to Latin American Anthropology*, edited by Deborah Poole
7. *A Companion to Biological Anthropology*, edited by Clark Larsen
8. *A Companion to the Anthropology of India*, edited by Isabelle Clark-Decès
9. *A Companion to Medical Anthropology*, edited by Merrill Singer and Pamela I. Erickson
10. *A Companion to Cognitive Anthropology*, edited by David B. Kronenfeld, Giovanni Bennardo, Victor C. de Munck, and Michael D. Fischer
11. *A Companion to Cultural Resource Management*, edited by Thomas King
12. *A Companion to the Anthropology of Education*, edited by Bradley A. Levinson and Mica Pollock
13. *A Companion to the Anthropology of the Body and Embodiment*, edited by Frances E. Mascia-Lees
14. *A Companion to Paleopathology*, edited by Anne L. Grauer
15. *A Companion to Folklore*, edited by Regina F. Bendix and Galit Hasan-Rokem
16. *A Companion to Forensic Anthropology*, edited by Dennis Dirkmaat
17. *A Companion to the Anthropology of Europe*, edited by Ullrich Kockel, Máiréad Nic Craith, and Jonas Frykman
18. *A Companion to Border Studies*, edited by Thomas M. Wilson and Hastings Donnan
19. *A Companion to Rock Art*, edited by Jo McDonald and Peter Veth
20. *A Companion to Moral Anthropology*, edited by Didier Fassin
21. *A Companion to Gender Prehistory*, edited by Diane Bolger
22. *A Companion to Organizational Anthropology*, edited by D. Douglas Caulkins and Ann T. Jordan
23. *A Companion to Paleoanthropology*, edited by David R. Begun
24. *A Companion to Chinese Archaeology*, edited by Anne P. Underhill
25. *A Companion to the Anthropology of Religion*, edited by Janice Boddy and Michael Lambek
26. *A Companion to Urban Anthropology*, edited by Donald M. Nonini
27. *A Companion to the Anthropology of the Middle East*, edited by Soraya Altorki
28. *A Companion to Heritage Studies*, edited by William Logan, Máiréad Nic Craith, and Ullrich Kockel
29. *A Companion to Dental Anthropology*, edited by Joel D. Irish and G. Richard Scott

Forthcoming

A Companion to Witchcraft and Sorcery, edited by Bruce Kapferer
A Companion to Anthropological Genetics, edited by Dennis H. O'Rourke
A Companion to Anthropology and Environmental Health, edited by Merrill Singer
A Companion to South Asia in the Past, edited by Gwen Robbins Schug and S. R. Walimbe
A Companion to Oral History, edited by Mark Tebeau

A Companion to the Anthropology of Europe

Edited by
Ullrich Kockel,
Máiréad Nic Craith,
and Jonas Frykman

WILEY Blackwell

This paperback edition first published 2016

Edition history: Blackwell Publishing Ltd (hardback, 2012)

Registered Office
John Wiley & Sons Ltd, The Atrium, Southern Gate, Chichester, West Sussex, PO19 8SQ, UK

Editorial Offices
350 Main Street, Malden, MA 02148-5020, USA
9600 Garsington Road, Oxford, OX4 2DQ, UK
The Atrium, Southern Gate, Chichester, West Sussex, PO19 8SQ, UK

For details of our global editorial offices, for customer services, and for information about how to apply for permission to reuse the copyright material in this book please see our website at www.wiley.com/wiley-blackwell.

Library of Congress Cataloging-in-Publication Data

A companion to the anthropology of Europe / edited by Ullrich Kockel, Máiréad Nic Craith, and Jonas Frykman.

p. cm.

Includes bibliographical references and index.

ISBN 978-1-4051-9073-2 (hardcover : alk. paper) ISBN 978-1-119-11162-7 (papercover)

1. Anthropology—Europe. 2. Ethnology—Europe. 3. Ethnic groups—Europe. I. Kockel, Ullrich. II. Nic Craith, Máiréad. III. Frykman, Jonas, 1942–

GN17.3.E85C66 2012

301.094—dc23

2011038090

A catalogue record for this book is available from the British Library.

Cover image: A Red Figure Attic krater depicting the kidnapping of Europa by Jupiter diguised as a bull. The Berlin Painter, cca. 500-490 B.C. Photograph © Christel Gerstenberg/CORBIS; One Euro Coin © Zoran Kolundzija / iStockphoto; European Parliament, Brussels © Alan Copson City Pictures / Alamy

Set in 10/12.5pt Galliard by SPi Global, Pondicherry, India
Printed and bound in Malaysia by Vivar Printing Sdn Bhd

1 2016

Contents

Notes on Contributors

Elisenda Ardévol is a senior lecturer in the Arts and Humanities Department at the Open University of Catalonia. She also collaborates with the Autonomous University of Barcelona. Her doctoral dissertation focused on visual anthropology and ethnographic cinema. During her career, she has taught courses and seminars in different Spanish universities and cultural institutions, and she also has been visiting scholar at the Center for Visual Anthropology, at the University of Southern California, Los Angeles. She carried out fieldwork among the gypsy community of Granada, in Afro-American religious communities of Los Angeles, and in the Courts of Justice in Barcelona. She is currently doing research about the Internet, new media, online sociability, and digital cultures. Elisenda is also involved in the Master of Creative Documentary program at the University of Barcelona. She has a strong publishing record.

Hugh Beach studied anthropology at Harvard College and as a young man participated in a year of study and travel with Gregory Bateson. He has lived among Sámi reindeer herders for many years in Sweden, Norway, and the Kola Peninsula of Russia. In Swedish Sápmi, he has studied changes in reindeer herding practices and also the effects of the Chernobyl nuclear disaster. He has worked as a reindeer herder in Alaska with the Inuit NANA Regional Corporation herd, and is specialized in the study of indigenous circumpolar peoples. He has been Chairman of the Swedish Minority Rights Group and expert adviser on Sámi affairs to Sweden's first two ombudsmen against ethnic discrimination. He is now Professor of Cultural Anthropology at Uppsala University, Sweden. He has led and been engaged in a number of interdisciplinary and international research projects. Currently he is principal investigator for the American NSF funded IPY project Dynamics of Circumpolar Land Use and Ethnicity (CLUE): Social Impacts of Policy and Climate Change.

Michał Buchowski is Professor of Social Anthropology at the University of Poznań and Professor of Comparative Central European Studies at European University Viadrina in Frankfurt (Oder). He also lectured as a visiting professor at Rutgers University and Columbia University. His scientific interest is in anthropological theories and in Central European postsocialist cultural and social transformations. He has published several articles in reviewed journals and edited volumes as well as books, among them in English *Reluctant Capitalists* (1997), *The Rational Other* (1997), *Rethinking Transformation* (2001), and in Polish, *To Understand the Other* (2004). He is also the coeditor of *Poland Beyond Communism* (with Eduard Conte and Carole Nagengast, 2001) and *The Making of the Other in Central Europe* (with Bożena Chołuj, 2001). Currently he serves as a Head of the Department of Ethnology and Cultural Anthropology in Poznań.

Reginald Byron, born in 1944, is University of Wales Professor Emeritus of Sociology and Anthropology and Research Professor of Anthropology at Union College, Schenectady, New York. He is the author, editor, or coeditor of 12 books on economic, political, social, and cultural anthropology including *Irish America* (1999), *Music, Culture, and Experience* (1995), *Retrenchment and Regeneration in Rural Newfoundland* (2003), *Migration and Marriage* (with Barbara Waldis, 2006), and *Negotiating Culture* (with Ullrich Kockel, 2006).

Marion Demossier Head of Department and Professor of French and European Studies at the University of Southampton. Her research focuses on how global forces and policies impact on specific groups and "communities" in French and European societies, and she has just published a monograph entitled *Wine and National Identity: Drinking Culture in France* with the University of Wales Press. She has also published extensively on rural societies (*terroir*), and European and French politics.

Adolfo Estalella is a researcher working in the field of science and technology studies with an anthropological perspective. He has been working on the topic of technological hopes and expectations around the Internet and on the intersection of art, science, and technology. His theoretical approach is based on actor-network theory with an ethnographic orientation. His research topics are cyberculture, digital method for social science research, and ethics of Internet research.

Elena Filippova is an anthropologist and senior researcher in the Institute of Ethnology and Anthropology at the Russian Academy of Sciences (Moscow). She earned her Diploma in History and PhD in Ethnology and Anthropology from Lomonossoff Moscow State University. Elena publishes on migration and identity issues, with a particular interest in French society. Her research topics include cross-national comparison of ethnic and racial classification practices on censuses worldwide, scientific concepts of ethnicity, nationality, and citizenship.

Norbert Fischer holds an MA in cultural anthropology from the University of Hamburg, and has a PhD in social history. He completed his habilitation in 2008. He was appointed as an associate professor at University of Hamburg. His research interests include landscape history and theory, regional studies, spatial change, and urbanization processes in the twentieth century, the history of death, and the development of the cemetery and funeral culture. His many publications include *Inszenierungen der Küste* (2007, ed., with B. Schmidt-Lauber and S. Müller-Wusterwitz),

Vom Hamburger Umland zur Metropolregion (2008), and *Landschaft als kulturwissenschaftliche Kategorie* (2008).

Jonas Frykman is Professor II at Agderforskning, Norway, and Professor emeritus of European Ethnology at Lund University. His publications include *Identities in Pain* (with Nadia Seremitakis, 1997), *Articulating Europe: Local Perspectives* (with Peter Niedermüller, 2003), and *Sense of Community: Trust Hope and Worries in the Welfare State* (with Bo Rothstein et al., 2009).

Christina Garsten is Professor of Social Anthropology in the Department of Social Anthropology, Stockholm University. Her research interests are oriented toward the anthropology of organizations, with focus on the globalization of corporations and markets and on emerging forms of governance in transnational trade. In this vein of research, she has studied the perspectives of corporate managers in Sweden and in the United States on accountability and ethics as well as the models for social accountability that are expressed in codes of conduct, soft law, policies, and other voluntary forms of regulation. Her current research engagement is focused on the study of the role of international think tanks in the fashioning of global markets.

Christian Giordano holds a doctorate in sociology from the University of Heidelberg. His habilitation in anthropology was completed at the University of Frankfurt am Main. Christian is Full Professor of Social Anthropology at the University of Fribourg, Switzerland and holds many other honors and positions. These include a Dr Honoris Causa from the University of Timisoara: a permanent guest professorship at the Universities of Bucharest, Murcia, and Bydgoszcz; and guest lectureships at the Universities of Naples, Asuncion, Berlin (Humboldt University), Moscow (Russian State University for Humanities), Torun, Zürich and Kuala Lumpur (University of Malaya). His main research interests include political anthropology, economic anthropology, historical anthropology and his geographical foci include Southeast Europe, Mediterranean societies, and Southeast Asia (Malaysia, Singapore).

Valdimar Tr. Hafstein is an Associate Professor in the Department of Folkloristics/ Ethnology and Museum Studies at the University of Iceland, and he is currently a visiting researcher in the Department of Conservation at the University of Gothenburg and a KNAW visiting professor at the Meertens Institute in Amsterdam. His publications from recent years focus on cultural heritage as a concept, category, and social dynamic, and on intellectual property in traditional expression. His book on the making of intangible cultural heritage in UNESCO is forthcoming from the University of Illinois Press and he is presently involved in a European collaborative research project, Copyrighting Creativity.

Chris Hann is a founding director of the Max Planck Institute for Social Anthropology, Halle, Germany, where his research group has recently concluded a large-scale project on religion after socialism (www.eth.mpg.de). He is coeditor of *Eastern Christians in Anthropological Perspective* (with Hermann Goltz, 2010). Other research foci include theories of ethnicity and nationalism, and economic anthropology. His publications include *Economic Anthropology: History, Ethnography, Critique* (with Keith Hart, 2011).

Gabriela Kiliánová, PhD CSc, is a senior research fellow and the director of the Institute of Ethnology of Slovak Academy of Sciences. Her main research interests involve collective identity and memory, oral traditions, modernization processes, burial rituals, and history of ethnology. She has conducted field work in Slovakia and Central Europe (Hungary, Austria). Along with E. Krekovičová and E. Kowalská, she recently (2009) published *My a tí druhí v modernej spoločnosti: Konštrukcie a transformácie kolektívnych identít* [Us and the others in modern society: Constructions and transformations of collective identities].

Ullrich Kockel is Professor of Culture and Economy at Heriot-Watt University Edinburgh and Visiting Professor of Social Anthropology, Vytautas Magnus University Kaunas. In the 1980s and 1990s, following an earlier career in industry, he held research and teaching appointments in Germany, Ireland, England, and Scotland, including at the University of Liverpool's Institute of Irish Studies and University College Cork's Department of Geography. The author and editor of more than 10 books and an Academician of the UK's Academy of Social Sciences, he is currently editor of the *Anthropological Journal of European Cultures* and President of the Société Internationale d'Ethnologie et de Folklore.

Sabrina Kopf is a doctoral student and lecturer at the University of Vienna, Department of Social and Cultural Anthropology. She has studied EU projects and their impact on local Roma communities in Slovakia. Currently, she is working on her doctoral thesis on urban activism and grassroot movements in Belgrade.

Orvar Löfgren is Professor Emeritus of European Ethnology at Lund University. His main field is the cultural analysis of everyday life. He has worked with studies of media and consumption, tourism and travel, as well as studies of national identities and transnational processes. Among his recent books are *Magic, Culture and Economy* (ed., with Robert Willim, 2005), *Off the Edge: Experiments in Cultural Analysis* (ed., with Richard Wilk, 2006), and *The Secret World of Doing Nothing* (with Billy Ehn, 2010).

Sharon Macdonald is Alexander von Humboldt Professor in the Institute of European Ethnology at the Humboldt University of Berlin. She has carried out anthropological fieldwork in Scotland, England, and Germany, and worked on topics including museums, heritage, science, and identity. Her publications include *Inside European Identities* (ed., 1993); *Reimagining Culture: Histories, Identities and the Gaelic Renaissance* (1997); *Behind the Scenes at the Science Museum* (2002); *A Companion to Museum Studies* (ed., 2006); and *Difficult Heritage: Negotiating the Nazi Past in Nuremberg and Beyond* (2009). Her next book is entitled *Memorylands: Heritage and Identity Complexes in Europe.*

Peter Jan Margry is an ethnologist. He studied history at the University of Amsterdam, and was awarded his PhD by the University of Tilburg (2000) for his dissertation on the religious culture war in nineteenth-century Netherlands. He is a senior research fellow at the Meertens Institute, a research center on the culture and language of the Royal Netherlands Academy of Arts and Sciences in Amsterdam. He is Professor of European Ethnology at the University of Amsterdam. His work focuses on contemporary religious cultures, on rituals and on cultural memory. Recent books are *Shrines and Pilgrimage in the Modern World: New Itineraries into the Sacred* (2008) and *Grassroots Memorials: The Politics of Memorializing Traumatic Death* (with Cristina Sánchez-Carretero, 2011).

Gabriele Marranci is a visiting senior fellow at the National University of Singapore, Department of Sociology as well as honorary professor at the Centre for the Study of Islam in the United Kingdom, University of Cardiff. He is an anthropologist by training, working on Muslim societies. His main research interests concern youth identity, religion, extremism, fundamentalism, political Islam, secularization processes. He is the author of four monographs: *Jihad Beyond Islam* (2006); *The Anthropology of Islam* (2008); *Understanding Muslim Identity: Rethinking Fundamentalism* (2009); and *Faith, Ideology and Fear: Muslim Identities Within and Beyond Prisons* (2009). He is the founding editor of the journal *Islam: Dynamics of Muslim Life*, and the book series *Muslims in Global Societies.*

Maryon McDonald is Fellow in Social Anthropology at Robinson College, Cambridge, and has long engaged with the anthropology of Europe. She has both studied and advised the European Commission. In Cambridge, she has run courses on European Anthropology, Medical Anthropology, and Science and Society, and is a member of the Royal Anthropological Institute's Medical Anthropology Committee in the United Kingdom and of the European ELPAT group (Ethical, Legal, and Psychosocial aspects of Organ Transplantation). Along with Marilyn Strathern, she founded and ran a research group on Comparative Issues in Biotechnology and Accountability (CBA) from 2002–2008, and is just completing a Leverhulme-funded research project examining changing understandings of the human body.

David Murphy is the Communications and Research Officer with INVOLVE / Travellers' Voice magazine in Ireland. In 2005 he was awarded the John Hume Scholarship for his PhD research into the Serbian and wider Slavic black metal music scene. His research interests include the Balkans, anthropology of the body, new social movements, neo-paganism, neo-nationalism, musicology, and contemporary sovereignty. David is currently a board member of the Centre for the Study of Wider Europe, and public relations officer with the Anthropological Association of Ireland.

Catherine Neveu is Director of Research at the IIAC-LAIOS (Institut Interdisciplinaire d'Anthropologie du Contemporain, Laboratoire d'Anthropologie des Institutions et des Organisations Sociales), CNRS-EHESS, Paris. She studies citizenship processes in different contexts in Europe. Her main research topics are political subjectivation, cultural dimensions of citizenship, and relationships between citizenship(s), space(s) and sites.

Máiréad Nic Craith is Professor of European Culture and Heritage at Heriot-Watt University Edinburgh. As the author or editor of 14 books, she was joint winner of the 2004 Ruth Michaelis-Jena Ratcliff research prize for folklife. In 2006, she was awarded a Senior Distinguished Research Fellowship at the University of Ulster, and in 2009 she was elected to the Royal Irish Academy. She served as a panel member for the 2008 Research Assessment Exercise in the United Kingdom and is again involved in the 2013 Research Excellence Framework audit. In 2011, she was invited by the United Nations as an expert on heritage and human rights.

Maja Povrzanović Frykman is Professor of Ethnology at the Department of Global Political Studies, Malmö University and Senior Researcher at Agder Research. Her dissertation in *Ethnology, Culture and Fear: Wartime Everyday Life in Croatia 1991–1992* was defended at the University of Zagreb. Her main areas of research include concepts and practices within the semantic domains of diaspora and transnationalism, relations between place and identity, labor- and refugee-migrants in Sweden, experiences of war and exile, and war-related identification processes. Her major publications include the edited volumes *War, Exile, Everyday Life: Cultural Perspectives* (with Renata Jambrešc Kirin, 1996), *Beyond Integration: Challenges of Belonging in Diaspora and Exile* (2001), and *Transnational Spaces: Disciplinary Perspectives* (2004).

Christiane Schwab is currently working on a project on literary journalism and social observation in the 19th century at Humboldt-University, Berlin. She holds a PhD in European Ethnology from the Ludwig-Maximilian University of Munich and has worked as a visiting scholar at the University of California at Berkeley. Her research interests center on urban anthropology, Spanish cultural history, and historical anthropology.

Martin Skrydstrup holds a PhD in cultural anthropology from Columbia University and is currently a postdoctoral research fellow at the Department of Food and Resource Economics, University of Copenhagen. In his doctoral research, Martin sought to understand repatriation claims by way of intersecting exchange theory and postcolonial theory. Most generally, his publications address the relationships between culture and property departing from various repatriation claims set in Greenland, Hawaii, Ghana, and Iceland with their various postcolonial and postimperial entanglements.

Justyna Straczuk is an assistant professor at the Polish Academy of Science in Warsaw. She has conducted long-term fieldwork in the borderland of Poland, Belarus, and Lithuania, and has produced many publications on the region, including two books: *Język i tożsamośd człowieka w warunkach społecznej wielojęzyczności: Pogranicze polsko-litewsko-białoruskie* [Language and identity in multilingual communities: Polish-Lithuanian-Belarusian borderland] (1999) and *Cmentarz i stół: Pogranicze* *prawosławno-katolickie w Polsce i na Białorusi* [A cemetery and a table: Catholic-Orthodox borderland in Poland and Belarus] (2006). Her current research interests are border issues, Eastern Christian spirituality, and anthropology of emotions.

Elka Tschernokoshewa was head of the Department of Empirical Cultural Studies and Anthropology at the Sorbian Institute, Bautzen, Germany, until retiring in 2015. She was born in Sofia, Bulgaria, and went on to study cultural studies and aesthetics in Berlin. She received her doctorate from Humboldt University Berlin and post-doctorate from Sofia. She has held a number of visiting professorships at the Universities of Bristol, Basel, Tübingen, Leipzig, Bremen, and Sofia. Elka is a founding member of the European Research Institute for Culture and the Arts (ERICarts) and a board member of the European Association of Cultural Researchers (ECURES). Her main research interests are cultural diversity, minorities, gender and comparative studies, and Eastern–Western Europe. She is editor of the book series *Hybride Welten*.

Ksenija Vidmar Horvat completed her PhD in sociology at the University of California, Davis, USA and is full professor at the Department of Sociology, Faculty of Arts, University of Ljubljana, Slovenia. Her research interests include questions of cultural identity, social theory of Europe, cosmopolitanism, and multiculturalism. Most recent publications and articles include "Mitteleuropa and the European Heritage" (with Gerard Delanty, 2008); *Maps of In-betweeness: Essays on European Culture and Identity After the End of the Cold War* (2009), and "Multiculturalism in Time of Terrorism: Re-imagining Europe Post-9/11" (2010).

Gisela Welz was appointed Professor and Chair of Cultural Anthropology and European Ethnology at Goethe University Frankfurt am Main, Germany in 1998. As a research fellow and visiting professor, she has taught at UCLA, NYU, the University of Cyprus, ISCTE Lisbon, and the University of Manchester. Most of her recent publications and research projects address Europeanization issues, with a focus on Cyprus as a case study. In 2006, she coedited, with Yiannis Papadakis and Nicos Peristianis, an anthology titled *Divided Cyprus. Modernity, History, and an Island in Conflict*. In 2009, she published the essay collection *Projekte der Europäisierung* in cooperation with Annina Lottermann.

Lisanne Wilken, DPhil is an anthropologist from Copenhagen University and associate professor at the Department for European Studies at Århus University. She has conducted extensive research on cultural aspects of European integration including research on institutional support for linguistic minorities, minorities' strategies toward integration in the EU, everyday life and food consumption in Europe, and on media representations of "other" Europeans. She is currently working on a project on exchange students and integration.

Thomas M. Wilson is Professor of Anthropology in the Department of Anthropology at Binghamton University, State University of New York. He has conducted ethnographic research in Ireland, the United Kingdom, Hungary, and Canada.

Among his most recent books are *The Anthropology of Ireland* (with Hastings Donnan, 2006), *Drinking Cultures* (ed., 2005), *Europeanisation and Hibernicisation: Ireland and Europe* (ed., with Cathal McCall, 2010), and *The Blackwell Companion to Border Studies* (ed., with Hastings Donnan, in press). In 2008–2010 he was President of the Society for the Anthropology of Europe.

Terence Wright is Professor of Visual Arts at the University of Ulster. His films include *The Firemen of Dolní Roveň* (45 mins) 2006; *Migrations*, 2006 (gallery installation); and *The Interactive Village*, 2007 (non-linear digital ethnography). For 10 years he worked for BBC Television News and Current Affairs, and Independent Television News (ITN). He has written widely on the subject of visual anthropology and is the author of *Visual Impact: Culture and the Meaning of Images* (2008) and *The Photography Handbook* (1999). Formerly he was senior research officer at the Refugee Studies Centre, University of Oxford where he ran the project Moving Images: The Media Representation of Refugees. He taught at the UK's National Film and Television School from 1989–1997.

Helena Wulff is Professor of Social Anthropology at Stockholm University. Her current research engages with expressive cultural forms in a transnational perspective and questions of place, mobility, the emotions, visual culture, and recently of writing as process and form focusing on Irish contemporary writers. Her major publications include *Ballet across Borders* (1998) and *Dancing at the Crossroads* (2007). She was editor of *The Emotions* (2007) and coeditor of *Youth Cultures* (with Vered Amit-Talai, 1995), *New Technologies at Work* (with Christina Garsten, 2003), and *Ethnographic Practice in the Present* (with Marit Melhuus and Jon P. Mitchell, 2009).

CHAPTER 1

Introduction: The Frontiers of Europe and European Ethnology

Ullrich Kockel, Máiréad Nic Craith, and Jonas Frykman

This *Companion to the Anthropology of Europe* offers a survey of contemporary Europeanist anthropology and European ethnology, and a guide to emerging trends in this geographical field of research. Given the diversity of approaches within Europe to the anthropological study of Europe, the book is intended to provide a synthesis of the different traditions and contemporary approaches. Earlier surveys – whether in German (e.g. Drackle and Kokot 1996), French (e.g. Jeggle and Chiva 1992), or English (e.g. Macdonald 1993; Goddard et al. 1996) – have approached the subject through regional ethnographic case studies, mostly concentrating on Western Europe, or focusing on specific aspects, such as European integration (e.g. Bellier and Wilson 2000); the present volume is different in that its approach is both thematic and fully cross-European.

Any reader picking up this book may well do so on the assumption that the terms that frame it, "Europe" and "anthropology," are reasonably straightforward and that their meaning is more or less clear. This must surely be why such a volume has been produced: to summarize and reflect on the engagement of an agreed discipline with its (more or less) self-evident subject matter. As editors, we have approached this project in a different spirit, considering that neither "anthropology" (or its cousin, European ethnology) nor "Europe" are intellectual *terrae firmae* – historically and conceptually, both can be described as "moving targets": in a constant process of transformation since their first inception – and perhaps, as some would argue, so elusive that it is doubtful whether they have any reality at all outside the imagination.

The idea that "Europe" may be elusive or indeed nonexistent might strike the unsuspecting reader as rather strange. Are the origins of Europe not located in Greek mythology (Tsoukalas 2002)? Is this not the Continent that lays claim to having been the cradle of (at least Western) civilization? From where the major global empires were built and administered, and where two world wars originated? And are we not

A Companion to the Anthropology of Europe, First Edition. Edited by Ullrich Kockel, Máiréad Nic Craith, and Jonas Frykman.

witnessing, in our own lifetime, the coming together of diverse European nations to build a peaceful European Union (EU), aspiring to be a major global economic power? Is not this list of stereotypes, for all its brevity, full of questionable assumptions?

Anthropologists have looked critically at these and other themes for some time, and have even engaged in debates about them with other disciplines. "Europe" as a sociocultural construct has increasingly come under the magnifying glass and one cannot help the impression that the keener the gaze, the deeper the subject recedes into a haze. Part of the problem with the definition of – the drawing of boundaries around – Europe is that its frontiers to the south and east are rather fuzzy. Is Russia part of Europe, or where does Europe's eastern boundary run? Both Turkey and Israel regularly compete in the Eurovision Song Contest, as do various former Soviet Republics whose geographical Europeanness depends rather on where one draws an arbitrary line on the map and whose cultural Europeanness is every bit as debatable, from the hegemonic point of view, as that of Turkey, nevertheless a long time candidate for membership of the EU. Turkey is also a long-standing member of the North Atlantic Treaty Organization (NATO), which has been an important component of Europe's defenses. But are matters any clearer in the north and west? And what about those who argue that geographically Europe is not a continent at all but merely a component in a landmass more accurately named as Eurasia? (See Hann, Chapter 6 in this volume.)

For most of the latter half of the twentieth century, "Europe" was usually conflated with "Western Europe," while "Eastern Europe" was at best considered a debatable land. With the decline of Communism we have witnessed the fragmentation of Eastern Europe, and that concept has become increasingly fuzzy. It now appears that there could be a threefold division between East Central Europe, the Balkans, and Eastern Europe "proper" (i.e. Belarus, Ukraine, and Russia; see Burgess 1997:23).

It has always been problematic to delineate the spatial boundaries of Europe precisely, perhaps because Europe is more a conceptual than a geographical entity. Even before the emergence of Benedict Anderson's (1983) notion of "imagined community," it had become customary to think about Europe in terms of an "imagined space" (Said 1978), and ideas of Europe have varied considerably between different geographical locations (Malmborg and Stråth 2002; Nic Craith 2006).

And yet, in much of western and northern Europe, "Europe" is considered to be somewhere else. Looking "over one of their cultural shoulders," Russians have always perceived Europe as on their doorstep, while the German and French perspective on Europe has been tempered by centuries of bloody conflict – for them "Europe could be just about anywhere they could live peacefully alongside one another" (Kockel 2003:53). From the traditional Danish perspective, Europe was located between their southern border and the Dolomites, and Danes crossing the German border are "going to Europe," as do English people crossing the Channel. Irish people used to snigger at this as a typically English idiosyncrasy until they discovered, following the IMF bailout in 2010, that they never belonged to Europe either. And even the center of the Continent is hard to locate.

A large number of places, as far apart as the German Rhineland and the Lithuanian-Belarusian frontier, are laying claim to the honor, and definitions of "Central Europe" range from "the German-speaking former Prussian and Habsburg lands" to a group of contemporary states that do not even include any of the latter. Part of that particular discrepancy lies, of course, in the way language prevalence is defined – whether it is measured according to the official language of state administration or the language spoken by the majority of the population in their everyday lives.

At the turn of the twenty-first century, the concept of Europe has frequently become confused with that of the EU, and the term "Europe" is often used as shorthand when journalists make references to EU administrative and political decision-making bodies (Phillipson 2003:29). Yet the two are not coterminous. Many states, such as Switzerland and Norway, form part of historical, geographical Europe but have no representation in the European parliament.

All of this makes interesting study for anthropologists and others concerned with aspects of culture, history, and society, and so the vagueness of Europe as a concept and cultural actuality can be intriguing and inspiring rather than being an obstacle to rigorous research. However, for a book such as this, vagueness of its subject matter constitutes a certain quandary – which regions to include or exclude, whether to focus on the common perception that equates Europe and the EU, and so on. It is important to recognize that Europe is not a fixed entity, and as an analytical category it remains in historical flux.

Similarly, the discipline of anthropology, perhaps marginally more so than other fields, remains in flux. A generation ago, it was claimed (Kosuth 1991) that anthropologists were not suited to the scientific study of their own society – at a time when anthropologists were increasingly getting ready to "come home" from colonial and otherwise exotic outposts and do just that. The anthropology of Europe has, nevertheless, remained very much "in the shadow of a more proper anthropology elsewhere," as Nigel Rapport (2002:4) put it with reference to the anthropology of Britain. Most European regions have at some stage developed the study of their own culture, usually in association with the respective project of "nation-building." Regional and national differences have led to a proliferation of labels for these approaches, and while the designation "European ethnology" has been extensively used since it was proposed by Sigurd Erixson in the 1930s, practice in this field remains firmly focused on the local and regional, with quite limited references to any wider "Europe" of sorts. In one sense, this is a good thing because its acute awareness of the "Local" is a key strength of European ethnology; in another sense, the lack of a decidedly European perspective has made the designation a bit of a misnomer that causes confusion outside the immediate field (and often enough within it). Many of the departments and institutes of European ethnology have since the 1970s aligned themselves thematically, theoretically, and methodologically with cultural anthropology. Many of the authors in this volume would be *Grenzgänger*, scholars who cross the boundaries between an anthropology "proper" and those other approaches gathered under the label of "European ethnology."

Rather than providing a simple, straightforward answer to the question of how "Europe" should be delineated for the purpose of this book, we have chosen a somewhat shamanic approach, beginning this exploration of the anthropology of Europe with journeys toward Europe's cardinal directions. The chapters in the first section seek to locate Europe with reference to its various – real or imagined – geographical frontiers. Christian Giordano reviews the original regional field of Europeanist anthropology from a perspective encompassing the Mediterranean region as a whole, identifying current issues and future research directions. He highlights the fluidity of Europe's borders by exploring the idea of the Mediterranean space as historical region which spans over three continents. This critiques some Eurocentric visions concerning both the external and internal boundaries of Europe. In a contribution on circumpolar anthropology, Hugh Beach addresses social science issues and deals with indigenous peoples and their relations to the environment.

Reginald Byron looks westward across the Atlantic, contrasting American and European perspectives. He argues against "neat tidy categories" such as multiculturalism, which are useful for the purposes of control but which can result in cultural boundaries that are unhelpful for society at large. Major issues and controversies relating to the transformations in the ethnoanthropological study of Eastern Europe since 1989 are discussed by Michał Buchowski, who explores disciplinary boundaries in the work of scholars in postsocialist Europe. This contribution reviews the achievements of academics in the fields of ethnology and anthropology with a view to bridging the gap between one group and the other and breaking down an inappropriate hierarchical division in favor of more egalitarian area studies. Chris Hann also attempts to break down geographical and conceptual boundaries. Traveling further east, he ponders the boundaries of geographical Europe as well as its cultures and society. He considers the case for a wider geocultural perspective in the context of debates about the Eurocentric nature of much of anthropology.

The concept of *Mitteleuropa* or Central Europe has proved fascinating for scholars in many disciplines (for example: Ash 1989, Bauman 1989, Kundera 1984, Miłosz 1989, Schöpflin 1989, Schwarz 1989). In the final contribution in this section, Gabriela Kiliánová compares and contrasts the polycentric discipline of European ethnology with social/cultural anthropological approaches originating from or studying Central Europe. She concludes that contemporary ethnology in Central Europe finds itself on the frontiers between the historical and social disciplines. Although ethnologists in Central Europe draw on different methodological approaches, they remain strongly orientated toward cultural anthropology and the social sciences.

Following this conceptual triangulation of an anthropology and ethnology of Europe, the remainder of the volume is organized according to thematic rather than regional foci. Because the political project of European integration continues to attract a relatively large amount of anthropological research on Europe, we begin with a thematic section reviewing key aspects of EU policy, practice, and everyday lived experience. Lisanne Wilken opens the section, considering how a specific "European" identity is being constructed by European, national, regional, and local agencies. She explores three different anthropological approaches to questions of culture and identity in relation to EU integration and suggests that all three contribute to our understanding of the idea of European integration and its implications for identity construction.

Since borders are a major issue for European integration, this aspect is addressed by several of the contributors. Ksenija Vidmar Horvat examines how consumer culture affects processes of European integration especially since the EU enlargements in 2004 and 2007. Locating her enquiry in postsocialist regions, she asks how we will envison a post–Cold War, post-Western and post-national Europe. She believes that the postsocialist experience has central relevance for any understanding of Europe and argues that the problem of Eurocentrism will not be dismantled until the collective perceptions of Europe in postsocialist countries are fully appreciated.

The concept of a "Europe of the Regions," from the perspective of the lived experience of internal and external border regions in particular, is discussed by Thomas M. Wilson. Pointing to the significance of these border regions for the European Commission itself, as well as for national and subnational governments, he argues that a "regional Europe" is thriving both in the cores and peripheries of every country on the European continent. Catherine Neveu and Elena Filippova reflect on issues of mobility and security in the context of the Schengen acquis and the question of a European citizenship. Drawing on their own research in France and Russia, these contributors focus on the need to distinguish between different conceptions of citizenship across the continent and in particular of its specific connections with issues of (national) identities.

Turning a spotlight on what may well be the geographical center of Europe but is currently the Eastern frontier of the EU, Justyna Straczuk discusses issues at the interface of identity and policy. Suggesting that the new eastern border of the EU may well be a very strong symbolic sign of a divided Europe, Straczuk examines the implications of a sealed political border in a particular region which traditionally enjoyed an open borderland mentality. The chapter explores the contradictions and full implications of a political border which orientalizes and excludes near neighbors while promoting the idea of a "unified Europe" which can appear very illusory. Marion Demossier concludes this section with a discussion of how EU policies are experienced, negotiated, and sometimes subverted at the grass roots level. This chapter highlights the contribution that anthropology can make to an understanding of social and cultural processes in Europe and argues for anthropological expertise at the core of debates on the relationship between culture and politics in the EU.

In years to come, readers might expect to find in this part of the book a discussion of anthropological perspectives on the Eurozone crisis. That crisis escalated at a time when this volume was almost ready (these lines are written as the cancellation of the Greek referendum on the latest EU bailout of the Greek economy is being announced on the radio), and so has become one of the inevitable lacunae that occur when events overtake analysis and publication schedules; a subsequent edition may well take up this topic, perhaps in the context of a broader evaluation of the cultural foundations of European social economy and its post-Capitalist transformations.

Culture and identity have always been difficult issues for the EU and the concept of EU cultural identity usually refers to the sum total of national icons and identities. The Preamble to the Charter of Fundamental Rights (European Convention 2003:75) suggests that the Union "contributes to the preservation and to the development of these common values while respecting the diversity of the cultures and traditions of the peoples of Europe as well as the national identities of the Member States." Inevitably, there are difficulties associated with this process. Cultural elements such as memory, shared heritage, and history, which unify identities at the national level tend to divide them at European level (Shore 2000:18). The overarching principle of unity in diversity has proved very difficult to carry through. "Diversity is a wild and chameleonic animal with thousands of heads that can hardly be kept imprisoned in the case of one legal principle" (Toggenburg 2004:18). The motto "unity in diversity" could be construed in many different ways. Obviously, it could be regarded as an acknowledgment and affirmation of the diverse range of European (national) identities and cultures, as well as including the various regional and minority cultures. However, it could also be viewed as an appropriation of power and symbolism to the center – as if "Europe's 'mosaic of cultures' was but a multiplicity of smaller units in a greater European design." From that viewpoint, European culture is characterized as the "over-arching, encapsulating and transcendent composite of national cultures; a whole greater than the sum of its discordant parts" (Shore 2000:54).

Chapters in the third section of this volume focus on whether there is such a thing as a single European heritage or collective identity. Sharon Macdonald, looking at how Europeans have been dealing with their past, both publicly and privately, introduces the concept of *past presencing* to avoid the problematic categorization of "history" versus "memory." Taking the breakup of Yugoslavia as a case study, Maja Povrzanović Frykman considers aspects of conflict and recovery on the continent. She argues for the importance of fieldwork as a basis for an anthropology of "state-building" that can draw on the anthropology of "transition," the anthropology of state, and the anthropology of violence and recovery. Peter Jan Margry reviews the significance of belief systems in Europe, past and present, with particular reference to popular religion today. Significantly, he explores the relationship between changes in the history of Europe and the way in which individual and collective developments have been inspired by Europe's (Christian) past. Continuing with the theme of religion and its political aspects, Gabriele Marranci reviews the study of Muslims in Europe and the challenges that anthropologists face in engaging with such issues, not least of which are questions of definition, especially how one defines Muslims in Europe. With this, Marranci is highlighting a critical aspect of European ethnic ascription. Challenging conventional definitions of "European," Sabrina Kopf takes up the theme of "othering" in her study of Roma and Sinti, who represent the largest ethnic minority within the EU, with an estimated population of 10–12 million. Finally, Norbert Fischer examines if and how a specific European sense of place may be founded in visions of landscape. People have always invested landscapes with meaning and the idea of a European perspective on landscape is not necessarily new. However, the definition of the concept of landscape has changed and there is greater recognition of its dynamic and fluid nature as well as its significance for understanding people and society.

Identity and heritage are inextricably linked to cultural practice, but not all such practice is explicitly aimed at establishing identity and defining heritage. In the fourth section, contributors offer ethnoanthropological perspectives on key aspects of cultural practice in European everyday life. Orvar Löfgren deals with tourism as a specific form of mobility and its potential contribution to European integration "from below." Exploring the institutionalization of travel and the routines of holiday making, Löfgren examines the ways in which the tourist Europeanizes Europe. This exploration is not confined to the continent itself but also to the way European models of tourism have been exported to other regions of the globe.

In a contribution that takes up threads from the second and third sections, Gisela Welz discusses aspects of diversity, regulation, and heritage production in relation to

European food cultures. Since European Union policies impact directly on food products and on the process of production, it follows that that European consumption habits are strongly shaped by such policies. Welz introduces the concept of "foodscape" and explores the impact of sometimes contradictory EU policies on what we eat and drink at the beginning of the new century.

Different cultural perspectives and traditions are an ongoing issue for the EU, and one of its most difficult challenges is the management of the range of languages and dialects spoken on the Continent. The changing role of languages in the context of intercultural identity politics and the challenges that this diversity poses for Europe are assessed in a contribution by Máiréad Nic Craith. The treatment of cultural rights by various agencies is a difficult issue, and one of direct relevance for states that query the right of women to wear a burqa or the right, for example, of Somali migrants to circumcise their female children according to traditional customs. Valdimar Hafstein and Martin Skrydstrup explore different ways of telling stories of cultural rights and the different appeals to tradition or human dignity which can be used to support such claims. Christina Garsten compares and contrasts different approaches to corporate social responsibility (CSR), assessing their relevance for contemporary Europe. Arguing that CSR is a concept which impacts on larger issues such as globalization, Garsten proposes that it has relevance for the relativity or universality of human rights and values. David Murphy takes us into the dark heart of Europe with his examination of the Far Right music scene as an aspect of cultural identity. Murphy's argument is that in some instances music scenes have offered an alternative avenue of belonging for young people who are not particularly interested in ideals of nationalism. Finally in this section, Christiane Schwab takes a critical look at urban life through an anthropological lens. In 2005, more than half of the world's population lived in urban environments, and this proportion is on the increase. Schwab's contribution explores relationships between anthropologists and cities and the theoretical and methodological responses to urban issues.

The fifth and final section deals with areas where disciplinary boundaries are explicitly and deliberately being crossed. This may seem a strange notion, given our earlier pointer toward the blurred disciplinary boundaries of anthropology. It may be said with some justification that many anthropologists are less concerned with the maintenance of canonical disciplinary purity than some of their academic peers in disciplinary ivory towers, and that this willingness to engage is perhaps a result of the anthropologists' greater experience of cross-cultural perspectives. There is, of course, also the "four fields" view of anthropology – physical, cultural (or ethnological), linguistics, and archaeology – especially in the US-American tradition, which in itself constitutes a multiple boundary-crossing.

The chapters in this section raise issues in interdisciplinary developments with reference to key areas of cross-disciplinary collaboration, beginning with Maryon McDonald's discussion of the role of anthropology in relation to medicine and science, both as a contributor to and a critical perspective on these disciplines, which to some extent connects with that "four fields" tradition. Elisenda Ardévol and Aldofo Estalella examine the growing uses of the Internet in ethnographic research. They draw an important distinction between the Internet as a tool of research versus the Internet as an object of study, which illustrates the complexities of conceptions of the Internet for anthropological research and the challenges and opportunities it poses for fieldwork.

The rise of interactive media and its implications for ethnography is explored by Terence Wright from the perspective of visual culture. Traditionally, the relationship between anthropology and the visual arts has not been easy, but in highlighting the significance of the visual in contemporary culture, Wright emphasizes the pertinence of visual culture and visual representations of culture for anthropologists. Elka Tschernokoshewa reviews theoretical and practical implications of the increasing realization that cultural worlds are hybrid rather than pure. Citing Ina-Maria Greverus (2002:26), she suggests that anthropologists themselves are becoming more and more hybrid. The hermeneutic value of creative writing for anthropological inquiry is evaluated by Helena Wulff with reference to an Irish case study. Engaging with texts is not a new practice for anthropologists. In 1973, Clifford Geertz proposed the notion of culture as text. He suggested that the "culture of a people is an ensemble of texts, themselves ensembles, which the anthropologist strains to read over the shoulders of those to whom they properly belong" (Geertz 1977[1973]:452). He compared the process of doing ethnography with "trying to read (in the sense of 'construct a reading of') a manuscript." Wulff notes that anthropologists have become more reflexive regarding their own writing, and she raises the provocative question: Can writing be taught?

Ullrich Kockel concludes this section with an ethnoecological meditation on issues of place and displacement, opening up critical viewpoints for an ethnotopology that has to grapple with the contentious politics of belonging.

In the concluding essay to this companion, Jonas Frykman takes stock of European ethnology and the anthropology of Europe at this historical juncture, and locates European ethnology in the wider field of anthropology, especially the anthropology of Europe, at the beginning of the twenty-first century.

It is inevitable with a project of this scope that one has to be selective with regard to issues and aspects to be included. There are gaps in the coverage of regions and themes. Moreover, some of the topics we had originally hoped to cover in the volume could not be included for various reasons. A different editorial team may well have chosen a different set of foci and approached the treatment of the overall theme differently. In the context of a discipline and subject matter in considerable flux, that can only be a good thing, engendering debate and further development of the field. With this in mind, we invited contributions to this volume from both well-established scholars and emerging researchers, who are, after all, the future of the discipline, and who will be shaping the agenda for such debate and development. Although this is a European volume, we did not confine ourselves to scholars located on that continent, but aimed instead to present a list of contributors who are experts in Europeanist anthropology/ethnology – regardless of their location. Moreover, we have encouraged contributors not to confine themselves to English-language material and resources, instead taking a broad perspective which would embrace the multilingual nature of the European experience. Our aim with this collection has been to be comprehensive, but not exhaustive, explorative but not definitive. In due course, we hope to complement this volume with a reader that will cover some of the topics that could not be included here and provide further food for thought on those that could.

ACKNOWLEDGMENTS

We would like to thank the contributors for making this volume possible. As well as providing a synthesis of current scholarship and scholarly debates, each of them was invited to present his or her own research. All contributions were subject to peer review, and we are grateful to the many colleagues from different traditions of Europeanist anthropology and European ethnology who engaged with that vital review process. Our institutions, the University of Ulster and the University of Lund, supported this project in various ways. Last but by no means least, we are grateful to the editorial staff at Wiley-Blackwell, especially to Rosalie Roberston for commissioning and enthusiastically supporting the project, Julia Kirk who patiently coordinated the whole process, and Annabelle Mundy and Alec McAulay who dealt with copyediting issues during the final, hectic months.

REFERENCES

Anderson, Benedict
1991[1983] Imagined Communities: Reflections on the Origin and Spread of Nationalism. London: Verso.
Ash, Timothy Garton
1989 "Does Central Europe Exist?" *In* In Search of Central Europe. George Schöpflin and Nancy Wood, eds. pp. 191–215. Cambridge: Polity.
Bauman, Zygmunt
1989 Intellectuals in East-Central Europe: Continuity and Chance. *In* In Search of Central Europe. George Schöpflin and Nancy Wood, eds. pp. 70–90. Cambridge: Polity.
Bellier, Irene, and Thomas M. Wilson, eds.
2000 An Anthropology of the European Union: Building, Imagining and Experiencing the New Europe. Oxford: Berg.
Burgess, Adam
1997 Divided Europe: The New Domination of the East. London: Pluto.
European Convention
2003 Draft Treaty Establishing a Constitution for Europe, submitted to the European Council Meeting in Thessaloniki. Luxembourg: Office for Official Publications of the European Communities.
Geertz, Clifford
1977[1973] Interpretation of Cultures: Selected Essays. New York: Basic Books.
Goddard, Victoria, Joseph Llobera, and Cris Shore, eds.
1996 The Anthropology of Europe: Identities and Boundaries in Conflict. Oxford: Berg.
Greverus, Ina-Maria
2002 Anthropologisch Reisen. Münster: LIT.
Jeggle, Utz, and Isac Chiva, eds.
1992 Ethnologies en miroir. La France et les pays de langue allemande. Paris: Mission Patrimoine.
Kockel, Ullrich
2003 EuroVisions: Journeys to the Heart of a Lost Continent. Journal of Contemporary European Studies, 11(1):53–66.

Kokot, Waltraud, and Dorle Dracklé, eds.
1996 Ethnologie Europas. Grenzen–Konflikte–Identitäten. Berlin: Reimer.
Kosuth, Joseph
1991 Art After Philosophy and After. Collected Writings 1966–1990. pp. 117–119. Cambridge, MA: MIT Press.
Kundera, Milan
1984 The Tragedy of Central Europe. New York Review of Books, April 26: 35.
Macdonald, Sharon, ed.
1993 Inside European Identities. Ethnography in Western Europe. Oxford: Berg.
Malmborg, Mikael af, and Bo Stråth, eds.
2002 The Meaning of Europe: Variety and Contention Within and Among Nations. Oxford: Berg.
Miłosz, Czesław
1989 Central European Attitudes. *In* In Search of Central Europe. George Schöpflin and Nancy Wood, eds. pp. 116–136. Cambridge: Polity.
Phillipson, Robert
2003 English-Only Europe: Challenging Language Policy. London: Routledge.
Rapport, Nigel
2002 "Best of British!" An Introduction to the Anthropology of Britain. *In* British Subjects: An Anthropology of Britain. N. Rapport, ed. pp. 3–23. Oxford: Berg.
Said, Edward
1978 Orientalism. Harmondsworth: Penguin.
Schöpflin, George
1989 Central Europe: Definitions Old and New. *In* In Search of Central Europe. George Schöpflin and Nancy Wood, eds. pp. 7–29. Cambridge: Polity.
Schwarz, Egon
1989 Central Europe – What It Is and What It Is Not. *In* In Search of Central Europe. George Schöpflin and Nancy Wood, eds. pp. 143–155. Cambridge: Polity.
Shore, Cris
2000 Building Europe: The Cultural Politics of European Integration. London: Routledge.
Toggenburg, Gabriel N.
2004 "United in Diversity": Some Thoughts on the New Motto of the Enlarged Union. Paper presented at Mercator International Symposium: Europe 2004; A New Framework for All Languages? Taragona, Catalonia, February 27–28. Available at http://www.ciemen.org/mercator/pdf/simp-toggenburg.pdf (accessed November 3, 2011).
Tsoukalas, Constantine
2002 The Irony of Symbolic Reciprocities: the Greek Meaning of "Europe" as a Historical Inversion of the European Meaning of "Greece." *In* The Meaning of Europe: Variety and Contention within and among Nations. Mikael af Malmborg and Bo Stråth, eds. pp. 27–50. Oxford: Berg.

PART I Europe's Cardinal Directions

CHAPTER 2

The Anthropology of Mediterranean Societies

Christian Giordano

The Discovery of Mediterranean Societies as an Anthropological Subject

In comparison with other more distant and hard-to-reach geographical areas, anthropologists discovered Mediterranean societies, especially the Mediterranean societies of continental Europe, as a subject of study, fairly recently.[1] This is not fortuitous, but neither can it be traced back to negligible and superficial reasons, as some critics would have it (Moreno Navarro 1972; Gilmore 1979:38). Any claim that it was the mild climate, the pleasant company of easy-going, amusing, and generous contacts or, worse still, the proverbial fine dining, that drove northern-European anthropologists (British and Dutch especially, but also French) to choose the Mediterranean as a *locus amoenus* for their researches, would be tendentious. In fact, if this hypothesis were true, we would then need to wonder why these societies were not studied sooner. But, as John Cole pointed out, the rationale behind this choice is far less banal and conceals political reasons (Cole 1979).

Aside from the groundbreaking and isolated research carried out by Charlotte Gower-Chapman in the small Sicilian agro-town of Milocca at the end of the 1920s, but discovered only in the 1970s (Gower-Chapman 1971), the anthropology of Mediterranean societies, according to authoritative opinions, made its first appearance in 1954 with the publication of Julian Pitt-Rivers' monograph *The People of the Sierra* (Boissevain 1979:81). Along with this study of an Andalusian rural community, we also need to mention *A Turkish Village* by Paul Stirling (Stirling 1965) and *Honour, Family and Patronage* by John Campbell (Campbell 1974) centered on the Sarakatsani community in Epirus (northwestern Greece).

All of these field researches in the Mediterranean area were carried out in the late 1940s and the 1950s – that is during a period of great transformations and upheavals in extra-European countries. In fact, colonial empires – those territories where

A Companion to the Anthropology of Europe, First Edition. Edited by Ullrich Kockel, Máiréad Nic Craith, and Jonas Frykman.

anthropologists, especially British, French, and Dutch ones, had carried out their researches, were disintegrating. India and Indonesia by then had attained independence, while many future new nations in Africa and Asia were slowly breaking away from colonial dominion and were on the brink of independence. It is a well-known fact that decolonization processes were marked by tensions and conflicts. This epoch was characterized by nonviolent protests (as in India), nativist revolts (e.g. Mau Mau in Kenya) guerrilla warfare (e.g. Indonesia), and full-blown wars (e.g. French Indochina), all followed by the colonial powers' brutal repressions. In this world in turmoil, anthropological field research became increasingly problematic, if not impossible; difficulties were made greater because anthropologists were no longer under the umbrella of the colonial order, with whom most of them had at least collaborated. Without this protection, finding a place to study the allegedly untouched traditions of "savage societies," as they had been termed by Bronisław Małinowski and Alfred Reginald Radcliffe-Brown, was a nearly unthinkable endeavor in such an endemically unstable situation. Moreover, in countries that had attained independence, anthropologists were increasingly viewed with disfavor and were often considered *personae non gratae*, since they were suspected of being agents of the former colonial power.

In all likelihood, these specific political circumstances, occurring precisely in the years just mentioned, played a major role in the rise and development of the anthropology of Mediterranean societies. At first, however, researchers did not change their methodological paradigm. Indeed, we can trace several continuities between what we shall call colonial anthropology and the newborn anthropological research in the Mediterranean region. In the first place, Pitt-Rivers, Stirling, and Campbell chose extremely peripheral and highly isolated locations for their field researches. Thus, there is a clear correspondence between field choices in colonial anthropology and in Mediterranean societies. Moreover, we cannot fail to notice a more or less overt equivalence between African, Asian, and American "primitives" on the one hand and southern European shepherds and peasants on the other. In itself, this would be sufficient proof of the link between the earliest anthropologists of Mediterranean societies and the classic researches of colonial anthropology. Yet, there is also another interesting correspondence in the nearly identical use of monographs made by Pitt-Rivers, Stirling, and Campbell, as well as other researchers who followed in these three authors' footsteps. In this first phase of studies on Mediterranean societies, the monographic study of a village, located in the most out-of-the-way area possible, was still seen as the sole legitimate standard for serious anthropological research.

The monograph approach, based on studies of a single and generally marginal rural community (and thus one that could be regarded as a virtuous example of an authenticity still untouched by modernity's influence) was soon subject to criticism. Even so, this approach remained prevalent up to the 1980s, notwithstanding due exceptions such as the pioneering multisided research by Caroline White (White 1980) who studied two neighboring but historically different townships in the Fucino basin in Abruzzi (south-central Italy). This more or less explicit connection with the methodology developed by colonial anthropology and its field research was pointed out by Jeremy Boissevain in particular. Boissevain questioned whether persisting with the study of Mediterranean societies, and European societies in general, by means of monographic researches could still be appropriate, since these were based on the assumption that the communities examined were actually isolated, thus as truly autonomous as they appeared to be (Boissevain 1975, 1979). Boissevain's criticism, which exposes the tribalization of Mediterranean societies (and of European societies in general), presents two fundamental arguments. In the first place, the choice of field investigation sites located in areas known for their socioeconomic marginality highlights how anthropologists at the time sought out societies in the Mediterranean area, especially the European one, that were as akin as possible to the segmentary ones of the "primitives" that had been studied overseas during the colonial epoch. Second, any monograph research centered almost exclusively on the social life occurring within a purported community microcosm tends to overlook the significance of the historical dimension, and thus also to underestimate phenomena such as the presence and incorporating role of the state, the more or less enforced processes of bureaucratization and national integration, the dynamics of urbanization and finally, the power relationships and class conflicts between those within the little community and those outside (Boissevain 1975:11). Accordingly, the condition of subservience, and thus the structural asymmetries in relation to the hegemonic outer world, is hardly examined. Identifying ways to surpass the tribalistic and intrinsically ahistorical viewpoint inherent in village monographs, a crucial goal for the anthropology of Mediterranean societies, was precisely the most noteworthy contribution of the volume *Beyond the Community: Social Process in Europe*, edited by Jeremy Boissevain and John Friedl (Boissevain and Friedl 1975).

In fact, from the mid-1970s up to the great crisis of the anthropology of Mediterranean societies in the second half of the 1980s, monographs were still published, but their nature underwent a significant change, since they became less generalistic and impressionistic. There was no longer that eagerness to describe and interpret the entire social life of a little community as if withdrawn into itself. The subjects and the questions involved, as the titles of the publications indicate, became increasingly specific and targeted. Moreover, history as a long-term process and not as a historicist vision, that is, a pedantic event-based sequence, began to emerge in the narration's background. Amongst the various studies, those by Anton Blok, *The Mafia of a Sicilian Village: 1860–1960* (Blok 1974), Jane and Peter Schneider, *Culture and Political Economy in Western Sicily* (Schneider and Schneider 1976), David Gilmore, *People in the Plain* (Gilmore 1980) and Caroline White, *Patron and Partisans* (White 1980), notwithstanding their different theoretic approaches, are probably the most representative of this initial shift, not least because their new methodological approach was explicitly thematized in their books' introductions.

Finally, we need to add that essays such as those by John Davis (1977) and David Gilmore (1982) began to appear in print during this highly fruitful phase of the anthropology of Mediterranean societies. Thanks to a professedly more to-the-point approach, thus greeted with keen interest for comparisons, these essays went beyond both the narrow scope of monograph studies and the apparently comparative, yet ultimately rather fragmentary, character of some miscellaneous texts on specific themes such as honor and patronage (Peristiany 1965; Gellner and Waterbury 1977), which will be examined later. In fact, Davis's main concern seems to be this disregard for, and unwillingness to undertake, comparison, as he underscores right from the introduction of his book:

> the reader may think he is in a luxuriant field, but gradually sees there is no controversy; he may think he is in the company of scientists, but find they do not compare their results. It is a constant theme of this book that Mediterraneanists have failed in their plain duty to be comparative and to produce even the most tentative proposition concerning concomitant variations, and so it need not to be elaborated here: one example will suffice. (Davis 1977:5)

Admittedly, though Davis's appeal did not go unheeded, it would be followed only by some and those, moreover, much later (Giordano 1992). Christian Bromberger also pointed up these misgivings about comparisons in his closing remarks to the volume of the conference proceedings in Aix-en-Provence in 2001. Bromberger, going back to Davis's remarks, confirmed that they were still pertinent and could very well apply to the new miscellany work (Bromberger and Durand 2001:740). Maybe we ought to wonder whether other regional anthropologies, such as those of societies in Southeast Europe or Southeast Asia, are just as unheeding of comparison.

The Anthropology of Mediterranean Societies: Major Themes

The anthropology of Mediterranean societies is characterized by a remarkable variety of themes, as the previously mentioned studies by Davis and Gilmore also show (Davis 1977; Gilmore 1982). However, we can identify some topics that were particularly debated in the past and which, beyond the circumscribed Mediterranean area, have lost none of their relevance. Under this aspect, we shall consider three main themes:

- honor, status, and gender relationships;
- patronage and political practices;
- history and the past in the present.

Honor, status, and gender relationships

It is widely known that in anthropology the theme of honor in Mediterranean societies was propagated by two authors in particular: John G. Peristiany (Peristiany 1965; Peristiany and Pitt-Rivers 1992) and Julian Pitt-Rivers (Pitt-Rivers 1968, 1977; Peristiany and Pitt-Rivers 1992). However, before, and contemporaneous with, these two anthropologists Mediterranean honor had been a very popular subject amongst leading literary and cinematography figures, and, due to some aspects linked to criminal law, jurisprudence, and criminology experts, too. We need to add, though, that all of the above have to do with works of art or strictly juridical, thus normative, reasoning, the concern of which is not discovering ways to delineate and identify the various facets of honor.

With reference to Mediterranean societies, Pitt-Rivers was the first to attempt a structured and thorough characterization that would encompass the various dimensions of honor.

Paraphrasing Jean-Jacques Rousseau's *Nouvelle Héloïse*, Pitt-Rivers begins by distinguishing between two key aspects of honor, the inner and the outer:

- Honor can be understood as a feeling or, more precisely, as a specific state of consciousness. This consists of a conviction that there is nothing one should reproach oneself for, and that consequently one can claim, and indeed has, a right to pride (Pitt-Rivers 1968:503, 1977:1). This point of view considers the individual aspect only, since the sole judge of one's own honor is the individual – that is, oneself.
- The second aspect refers to concrete behavior as a manifestation of this state of mind. This state, therefore, is exclusively relevant if courses of action are regarded in relation to their reception and their appraisal by the society to which the actor belongs. Consequently, honor is strictly linked to what may be broadly defined as public opinion. Pitt-Rivers emphasizes, therefore, that honor felt becomes honor claimed, and honor claimed becomes honor paid (Pitt-Rivers 1977:2). Thus, personal expectation is not enough: to be guaranteed, honor requires a social status validation from a collectivity (Pitt-Rivers 1977:21). Peristiany holds the same opinion when he highlights that honor is dependent on specific *social evaluations* (Peristiany 1965:11).

Based on the foregoing rather general observations, researchers have analyzed the various expressions of honor in Mediterranean societies. The focus has been on exploring the singly ascribed and acquired qualities as well as the visible and assessable ones that attribute honor to individuals and groups, since honor in the Mediterranean area is not based exclusively on personal status. The qualities that bestow honor, thus ensuring the collectivity's recognition, also define reputation and position on the social ladder.

Yet, the most authoritative experts confirm nearly in unison that the above qualities are not the same for all and that a gender divide is crucial: the prerequisite qualities for men are different from those for women. There is a male honor and a female honor, thus there is also a rather marked and strict division of social roles. Male honor is essentially dependent on its visible will and the ability to shield one's own and one's family's reputation from possible attacks from potential rivals (Pitt-Rivers 1977:22). Qualities that have been attested and verified by public opinion, such as nearly heroic courage and valor (Pitt-Rivers 1977:22; Kaser 1992), composure, presence of mind, readiness to fight, feeling of pride (Campbell 1976:269) as well as generosity, hospitality, and even mildness of character and patience, are essential to be acknowledged as a true *uomo d'onore*.

Female qualities are mainly related to modesty, which most authors believe to be the cornerstone of women's honor. Consequently, female honor is strictly linked to sexual behavior: premarital virginity and absolute fidelity to one's spouse are the imperative hallmarks of purity, together with modesty, shyness, self-restraint, and obedience.

According to some authors however, this difference between the two roles does not imply an actual social disparity between genders, since the status of the powerful is counterbalanced by the virtue of the weak (Lisón-Tolosana 1966:108).

Moreover, male and female honor are not two separate, individual phenomena, but must be considered jointly, since honor is also a collective issue. This led Pitt-Rivers to state that between the two genders there is a moral division of labor guaranteeing the honor of the entire family (nuclear or extended) and in some cases of the entire kinship group (Pitt-Rivers 1977:78).

The concept of honor and shame societies is based precisely on the above-mentioned division of roles and corresponding social practices in accordance with gender. This label was created and used to characterize Mediterranean societies' specifically, and, despite criticisms of an anthropological nature that we shall discuss further on, is still in use to some extent in social science parlance.

One of the most outstanding features of the purported honor and shame societies in the Mediterranean area, in addition to the ones previously mentioned, was their agonistic character by which groups would vie fiercely for honor, thus triggering an unremitting competition for recognition, respect, and ultimately reputation and social status. Yet, in this case as well, we can observe a tendency to substantiate the egalitarian and harmonious nature of honor and shame societies. In fact, the agonism linked to honor was ultimately regarded as a social strategy to remain equal and not as a set of practices aimed at reaffirming the disparity between individuals and groups.

Credit for calling into question the theoretical framework based on the notion of honor and shame societies goes to Michael Herzfeld in particular. He criticizes anthropologists, especially those of Anglo-Saxon origin, for their ethnocentric viewpoint tainted by both heterophilic and heterophobic stereotypes about the concept of honor and honor-related beliefs and actions (Herzfeld 1984:440, 1987a:9).

For these researchers, the discussion of Mediterranean honor ultimately proves to be a fatal trap because they project on to the "alien" reality which confronts them with their own fear of, and longing for, an archaic world, which constantly appears to them as an ambivalent allegory. Thus, Mediterranean societies are made "archaic" both artificially and arbitrarily.

The reader gets the impression that these societies are a relic of past epochs, admittedly characterized by violent and bloodthirsty barbarism, along with a primitive purity, and finally by an earthy simplicity of ways of life and social relationships. What emerges, therefore, is that the "archaization" of Mediterranean societies by Anglo-Saxon anthropologists simultaneously and always implies an "exoticization" of these cultures (Herzfeld 1980, 1987a:64). One can hardly challenge the fact that the manifest penchant of North American and northern-European researchers for the theme of honor evokes an "alien," hence an "exotic," image of Mediterranean societies. The entire Mediterranean region is thereby presented as an appendix of the "wilderness" in both its positive and negative form. Further, the Euro-Mediterranean space is staged as being nearly unrelated to Europe. According to Herzfeld, the most serious consequence of the "archaization" and "exoticization" of Mediterranean countries is the artificial separation of Euro-Mediterranean societies from other European cultures, so that "Mediterranean Studies" ends up regarding the region as an accumulation of autonomous, yet socioculturally homogeneous primitive societies.

To support his thesis, Herzfeld adds that while the national ethnologies of this region do not entirely deny honor and shame, neither do they regard it as a central element in the study of Mediterranean values. This is in pleasant contrast to the reports of travelers and researchers from northern Europe and the United States, because local folklorists strive to resist this explicit or implicit "exoticization" (Herzfeld 1987a:64). Though recognizing their parochial approach (Herzfeld 1987a:13), Herzfeld is rather lenient with the various versions of Mediterranean folklore studies since we cannot fail to notice that nearly all of them provided welcome material for the construction and development of nationalist, separatist, populist, and localist ideologies precisely via the "archaization" and "exoticization" of their own lower strata, particularly the rural ones. In doing so, there was a clear will to create far too idyllic an image of the Mediterranean peasant's world.

Aside from Herzfeld's contentions, there are further criticisms regarding the anthropology of honor in Mediterranean societies. In the first place, we need to highlight the implicit communitarian vision by which, notwithstanding the previously mentioned agonism, the single actors have a strong sense of solidarity and reciprocity. Still, the term *agone*, that is "contest," in itself, as used by anthropologists of Mediterranean societies, brings to mind loyal competitions, if not between socially equal persons, at least between people with a similar social status. This construction of the subject-matter downplays both the importance of social disparity and of the conflicts and tensions between individuals and groups, while emphasizing the social harmony of the communities examined. As Jacob Black-Michaud proposed, in several cases the term "feuding societies," in which the struggles for recognition, thus honor contentions, are much more violent, would be more suitable (Black-Michaud 1975).

The point that appears to be particularly questionable – and this is true also of Herzfeld's suggestion to replace the notion of honor with other terms such as hospitality (Herzfeld 1987b) – is the tendency to believe that coercive systems of norms and values mirroring specific forms of morality underpin the idea of honor and its social practices. We feel quite skeptical about this rather idealistic and perhaps somewhat naive vision.

Given these criticisms, should we then believe that everything that has been researched and published by anthropology on the subject of honor and shame societies in the Mediterranean area ought to be regarded as outmoded, unreliable and unrealistic, thus scientifically irrelevant and not fit to be used? This would definitely be too drastic, considering that in recent years other social sciences, such as sociology and social history, have reintroduced the theme of honor and shame societies, drawing on and reinterpreting anthropologists' highly criticized results and analyses. Nowadays, however, the interest in honor goes beyond the limited space of Mediterranean societies and extends to other social configurations, such as specific societies in the Near and Middle East (Husseini 2009) and the Indian subcontinent, as well as immigration societies in north-central Europe. Obviously, this rediscovery is also strictly linked to the rising number of honor killing cases and of the far less frequent but not less shocking blood revenge in this area of the Old Continent (Wikan 2008).

Most likely Unni Wikan is right when she questions the current validity of the term honor and shame societies. This is due mainly to the ambiguity of the term shame, which may convey both the idea of disgrace as in impudence, indignity, and infamy, and of decency as in modesty, propriety, and purity. It would probably be more suitable to speak simply of honor and dishonor. Under this aspect, we should mention the terminological question, that is, honor's semantic differences from one society to another in the Mediterranean area. Without going into much detail, there seems to be a far more marked variety of concepts in the Arab and Turkish world (we need only refer to the difference between the notions of *namus* and *sheref*) than in Greece, Spain, and Italy, though all these various representations with dissimilar connotations always involve reputation, prestige, esteem, standing, saving face, and good name.

Personally, I believe that we ought to revise those previously mentioned concepts of honor steeped in romanticism and resume a more transactional approach, as suggested by Bailey (Bailey 1971:19). Honor in general, thus also honor in the Mediterranean societies, is not merely a moral code comprising values, norms, representations, and a set of practices, but rather a cultural idiom and a combination of social strategies found in several public arenas. Thus, honor in its various expressions in terms of representations and social practices alike is a phenomenon set up to highlight social differences (class and gender especially), and maintain, increase or restore status and reputation in order to define (better yet, redefine) the social identifications and auto-comprehensions of individuals and groups (Brubaker and Cooper 2000). Therefore, as my experience as expert witness in criminal court cases confirms, an agent acts in accordance with the social logic of honor not so much because he feels duty-bound by a culturally-defined moral obligation, but rather because he fears being sanctioned and stigmatized by his significant others.

With specific reference to the Mediterranean, but also elsewhere, the person who reacts to an alleged or actual offence to his honor (even in a criminally indictable way), does so because he fears the annihilation of his social status and personal reputation, including the good name of his primary group (family and relatives) with the reference community. This loss of status and good repute often implies negative economic consequences, too. Honor and its social practices are not so much a nearly genetically set cultural legacy, as much as a system of concrete strategies intentionally put to use in everyday life. Thus, honor in this specific case stops being a static entity that the actor cannot escape and becomes a pliant and flexible phenomenon. It proves to be a cultural knowledge, and consequently an adequate action know-how. Therefore, honor is a social resource for individuals who will both put it to use to assess their own social situation and activate it in specific constellations in order to achieve what is regarded as an opportune goal. To conclude: in line with Max Weber and Pierre Bourdieu we can state that the actors abide by a given rule to the extent that their interest in doing so exceeds their interest in not conforming to said rule (Weber 1956; Bourdieu and Wacquant 1996:147). If, on the one hand, interests and rules are not universal and ought to be regarded, in a sense, as cultural products, on the other hand, actors are not trapped in their social and cultural habitus, which must be regarded as a socially acquired disposition and not as a strictly binding behavior dictated by a coercive morality.

Patronage and political practices

In anthropology, the debate concerning forms of patronage cannot be properly conducted without mentioning what was and still is the most renowned, though probably the most criticized, study on the political culture of Mediterranean societies, and

Euro-Mediterranean ones in particular (Pizzorno 1976; Silverman 1968; Davis 1970; Schneider and Schneider 1976; Pitkin 1985; Herzfeld 1987a). We allude to the book written by American political scientist Edward C. Banfield, *The Moral Basis of a Backward Society* (Banfield 1958). Banfield had carried out field research in the small community of Montegrano in Basilicata (southern Italy) and, by applying a typically anachronistic stance borrowed from North American political studies, believed he observed a lack of civic culture in this town on the margins of Italian society.

His key argument, taken up even recently by two rather ideologically opposed authors Francis Fukuyama (Fukuyama 1995) and Robert Putnam (Putnam et al. 1993), was that there was no awareness of the common good in this southern Italian society, and that in the public sphere its inhabitants were only pursuing the interests of their own family group. Their attitude was summarized as an "amoral familism," which highlighted a condition of moral, social, and economic backwardness. Clearly, this vision was so blatantly ethnocentric that we need not comment further. Banfield's fundamental error lay not so much in this vision distorted by ethnocentrism, as much as in reducing Montegrano into an atomistic society consisting solely of family units with the possible addition of nearest kin members. According to Banfield, beyond this quasi-segmentary sociability there was only a structural desert. On his quest for an unlikely American-style civil society, this author had practically disregarded the social complexity based on highly personalized relationships within the community and beyond the family and closest relatives. Wide of the mark, he had focused exclusively on his search for formal and permanent organizations (such as voluntary associations, cooperatives, or trade unions) and had utterly overlooked the less apparent, yet also more informal, changeable, and flexible existence of quasi-groups and networks.

Anthropological researches on Mediterranean societies have tried to remedy this serious theoretical and empirical deficit and have provided ample evidence that the single family units extend their social relationships beyond the limited range of their own members, including closest relatives and in-laws. Therefore, Mediterranean societies cannot be likened to fictitious and improbable atomistic societies (Galt 1973; Gilmore 1975).

The family's role is definitely central, yet its interests, as Italian anthropologist Carlo Tullio-Altan highlighted, are managed by its own members through skillful strategies that may often be in contrast with the proper administration of the state or to the detriment of the common good (Tullio-Altan 1986). But, in order to effectively guarantee advantages for the family, the single members need to extend their network of social relationships by joining extrafamilial coalitions of various types and dimensions. By means of the asymmetrical and often vertical relationships of symbolic kinship, such as godparenthood for example, and the rather symmetrical and horizontal ones of friendship, the anthropologists of Mediterranean societies (Pitt-Rivers 1977:54; Gilmore 1980; Piselli 1981) were able to observe two principal forms of extending cooperation relationships beyond the inner circle of parents, relatives, and in-laws. Neighborhood ties, instead, would seem to be less important and at times rather trouble-ridden (Davis 1973:68; Du Boulay 1979).

Probably though, with his study *Friends of Friends* (1974), which drew inspiration from the concept of network developed by the Manchester School, Jeremy Boissevain revealed the significance of extrafamilial personalized coalitions in Mediterranean societies, thus indirectly confirming the flimsiness of Banfield's analysis.

Anthropological researches on the crucial role of patronage relationships and coalitions in Mediterranean societies' political and bureaucratic fabric stem precisely from this debate and the subsequent study of personalized and barely formalized forms of social organization. Relationships between patrons and clients on which all these networks are based were defined as personalized, asymmetrical, and vertical dyadic links rooted in the reciprocal exchange of qualitatively unbalanced favors (Foster 1963; Mühlmann and Llaryora 1968). The asymmetry was determined by the fact that the client was more dependent on the patron than vice versa, while the verticality was due to the palpable social gap between patron and client – the latter belonged to a lower social class. Therefore, the relationship between patron and client was characterized by a clear social disparity between the two contracting parties.

With good reason, anthropologists of Mediterranean societies were revealing that, apart from a few exceptions (White 1980), patronage coalitions permeated the political systems of the societies studied (Signorelli 1983). Consequently, personalized patron–client relationships were typical between political entrepreneurs and electors, wherein the latter would provide their vote in exchange for a previous or subsequent counter-favor from the former to their own exclusive advantage. The term "political entrepreneurs" included both aspirants to a political position and brokers, that is, middlemen who mobilized the single client for the candidates using door-to-door strategies. In Sicily, for example, prominent members of Mafia networks would take on the role of broker.

Yet, the situation described by most anthropologists was typical of the so-called "clientele system of the notables." An outmoded and declining form of patronage, this was a local elite that would disappear from the political scene during the 1960–1970 decade. In place of the old notables, full-time professional politicians emerged, especially in Euro-Mediterranean countries (Italy, Spain, and Greece) and what political scientists call party clientelism or mass clientelism set in (Weingrod 1968; Belloni et al. 1979; D'Amico 1993). This brought about a substantial change in patronage policies, which, moreover, has seldom been studied by the anthropologists of Mediterranean societies. The professional politician in his role of party official, or his broker, no longer aimed at obtaining the single client's vote, but rather at controlling entire blocks of votes (Blok 1974:222). From then on, the role played by the old notables was taken on by the managers of so-called secondary associations, such as trade unions, cooperatives, youth, professional and sports associations. The management can include both professional politicians who control these electoral clusters directly as well as socially influential persons who, though not directly involved in politics, can tender the electoral potential at their disposal. Contrary to the old clientele system of the notables, the current forms of patronage policies are based mainly on the systematic capture and control of votes obtained by exploiting civil society institutions. However, the personalization of social relationships is also essential in this case.

The main, as well as the most pertinent, criticism of anthropological researches on patronage in Mediterranean societies is that they produced, perhaps unintentionally, a deficit theory. Patronage strategies and policies have been regarded as a systemic deficiency or, worse still, as a sociocultural pathology. Thus, patronage has been held responsible for weakening the state, for subverting the political system based on democracy, for hindering the construction of a civil society, for corrupting the bureaucratic organization and, in Marxist terms, for undermining class solidarity. In brief, either directly or indirectly through this perspective developed in northern Europe and North America, patronage has been held to be the origin of all political and administrative malfunctions in the public sphere of Mediterranean societies and in particular of southern-European ones. At first glance, these interpretations appear to be unexceptionable and may seem likely. However, they provide cursory explanations that reveal an ethnocentric vision oblivious to the social rationale of the actors involved and to the historical context in which the various forms of modern patronage emerged and took root.

Perhaps we ought to reverse the perspective and wonder whether the state's fundamental and repeated failure to monopolize the use of physical force, thus also to guarantee peacemaking within its territory, may have engendered what we may call a clientelistic reaction. From this viewpoint, it was the weakness of the state's political and administrative institutions that favored the rise and development of patronage rather than the other way around. However, national states in the Mediterranean area that rose in high hopes from the ashes of centuries-old misgovernment regimes, greedy foreign rulers and rapacious colonial domination lacked the ability, in turn, to be acknowledged as legitimate by their own citizens due precisely to their permanent institutional shortcomings. Given these circumstances, the emergence of societies guided by the principle that the only reliable form of trust is a personalized one – that is, the only one that can counter the activities of a state that neither protects nor respects its citizens – is not surprising. These are not out-and-out low-trust societies, as Francis Fukuyama thinks (Fukuyama 1995), but rather public distrust societies, in which patronage becomes a rational strategy to neutralize or influence to one's own advantage the state's activity that most times is regarded as unfair and detrimental.

With this reversed perspective, patronage becomes a fitting and rational strategy employed to remedy the state's failure or shortcomings. It can no longer be regarded as a set of social practices, nor as a hallmark of sociocultural backwardness or stagnation, nor as the expression of a parasitic attitude, nor, worse still, as the sign of a mentality lacking public spirit. As Alessandro Pizzorno aptly points up, one cannot expect people to believe in the state's legitimacy, to comply with the proper governance of its institutions, to have a positive attitude toward politics, to organize themselves in civil society organizations and thus to forgo patronage practices, when it stands to reason that it would be pointless (Pizzorno 1976:243). This is neither fatalism nor exotic immobilism, nor organizational inefficiency, but simply a rational choice within the context of a permanent failing statehood in which the state's lawfulness falls short of the requisite legitimacy, that is, the citizen's recognition and thus their trust (Pardo and Prato 2011).

Clearly we have to avoid viewing the patronage system and its specific practices – which disconcert anthropologists since willingly or not they have been brought up to believe in the universality of the values of enlightenment, *civitas* and citizenship – as a nearly exclusive peculiarity characterizing practically all Mediterranean societies.

This would truly mean exoticizing patronage and disregarding the fact that it can be found to varying degrees in virtually all societies, including those of the Western world that are too often hastily extolled as the most civilized, and thus free from such crude practices.

Indeed, thanks to a broader anthropological outlook we can aim at a fresh assessment of researches on patronage in Mediterranean societies. Under this aspect, anthropological researches on political practices in this part of the world have been very useful, since they stimulated research in other sociocultural contexts. The fall of the Berlin Wall and the investigation of Eastern Europe's postsocialist societies by social scientists and anthropologists provided paradigmatic evidence that the patronage practices and networks first observed in the Mediterranean region showed unmistakable similarities to analogous action strategies and forms of social organization found in postsocialist scenarios. Moreover, the diffusion of these social facts showed on the one hand that the Mediterranean could not be reduced to a culture area, and on the other that there were other social configurations in which a corresponding personalization of social relationships was crucial in a failing statehood context (Giordano and Kostova 2002; Giordano 2007; Georgiev 2008). This provided an opportunity to observe, in line with researches on Mediterranean societies, that the activity of the state (presocialist, socialist, and often also postsocialist) was considered inadequate, detrimental, or even unfair, and practically lacking any legitimacy by most citizens. Therefore, given this situation of deep-seated, yet justified, mistrust in public institutions, patronage was a possible and legitimate strategy (along with others, such as corruption) to neutralize a state that often treated its own citizens like subjects.

History and the past in the present

Aside from the early monographs on villages, in which the historical dimension is virtually nonexistent, the anthropologists writing about Mediterranean societies had quite quickly to face the fact that an ahistorical perspective was rather naive and inadequate in terms of both theoretical and empirical approach, since it led not only to an exoticizing vision of the societies in question but also to an extremely reductive one. The absence of history significantly hindered an adequate understanding of the present, giving rise in particular to interpretations warped by serious oversimplifications with the consequent construction of stereotypes. As previously mentioned, however, we can observe that Carmelo Lisón-Tolosana (Lisón-Tolosana 1966), Anton Blok (Blok 1974), and later John Davis (Davis 1977, 1982) along with other authors (Schneider and Schneider 1976; Gilmore 1980), highlighted the shortcomings of a purely synchronic perspective and stressed the importance of a diachronic analysis, thus acknowledging the significance of past history to explain the present of Mediterranean societies. Under this aspect, probably the most revealing study is Caroline White's, in which she aimed to show how two neighboring towns in south-central Italy, which at the time of the research were also economically similar, developed two different if not indeed opposite political cultures due precisely to two parallel but fundamentally different histories (White 1980). Through her field research the author had noticed a predominance of vertical and asymmetrical patronage relationships in Trasacco, while in Lugo de' Marsi socially equal individuals interacted within more horizontal and symmetrical cooperative structures. According to the author, the different pasts of these two communities needed to be taken into account in order to explain this apparently baffling circumstance. This historically determined difference lay mainly in the fact that for centuries land distribution had been more unequal in the former community than in the latter. Thus for centuries the inhabitants of Trasacco had been more vulnerable and dependent on feudal lords and agrarian capitalists than those of Lugo, and therefore the former were more inclined to accept patronage relationships than the latter.

As this further example shows, these researchers' concept of history, though no longer event-based and albeit taking into account long-term conjunctures, is still strongly biased by the principle of causality. Consequently, the relationship between past and present is explained in a rather mechanical and decontextualized way. In fact, there is an attempt to determine past and present facts, circumstances, and objective processes and simply correlate them via a direct or nearly automatic cause-and-effect relationship.

To round off this rather fruitful way of conceiving history's role, we need to highlight the importance of an interpretative turning-point in the analysis of Mediterranean societies, until now seldom employed, which could better thematize, from a hermeneutical viewpoint, the meaning given by the actors themselves to their past in the present. Therefore, the aim is not only to determine objective events, but mainly to observe how they are perceived by those who are touched by these events. When Paul Ricoeur talks about the efficiency of history, he is referring specifically to that close connection between the interpreting present and the interpreted past (Ricoeur 1985, 3:320). In order to move beyond a too-positivistic notion of history we must be prepared to examine the spaces of experience as well as the horizons of expectation of a given society as they are constructed and perceived by its members (Koselleck 1979). Therefore, as Jean Pouillon maintains, history is composed of all the versions that the members of a present-day collectivity regard as having actually occurred (Pouillon 1975). Accordingly, all the various revisions of a social aggregation's collective memory merge with the official or established version of the past. Thus, history means above all reviewing past events, including their manipulation and misrepresentation. To exemplify the above we might consider the bandit Salvatore Giuliano in Sicily. Current official history states that he was an outlaw in conflict with the state. According to the memory of the inhabitants of Montelepre, his native town, Giuliano is to this day a hero worthy of commemorations and celebrations. For the inhabitants of Piana degli Albanesi, in contrast, he remains a bloodthirsty murderer, because he led the Portella della Ginestra massacre on May Day 1947, in which peasants of this town were killed. If we were to analyze the historical interpretations from a political viewpoint we would find further contrasting versions regarding this figure (Giordano 1992).

The intention of the latter somewhat abstract paragraph is to highlight the significance of moving beyond the dimension of history as a universal objective truth, especially in the context of anthropological studies on the Mediterranean area where societies or segments thereof have often been, and to some extent still are, violently antagonistic. Concurrently, reconstructing the plurality of history and its efficiency in the present by means of interpretative analyses is essential.

Conclusion: The Mediterranean Space – from Culture Area to Historical Region?

Perhaps the most incisive, and probably the most legitimate, criticism is the one that held the anthropology of Mediterranean societies responsible for pigeonholing these societies into a flat, uniform, and thus homogeneous culture area (Llobera 1986:33). There has been an effort to substantiate the existence of artificial sociocultural constants, invariably present in the entire Mediterranean space, mainly through the themes of honor and, to a lesser extent, patronage (Gilmore 1987; Bromberger and Durand 2001:742). Given these observations, it may seem that anthropologists of Mediterranean societies have put forward only simplistic and reductionist stereotypes. So, should we forgo this type of anthropology? I don't think so.

In the first place, we need to stress that the idea of dividing the Mediterranean space into separate and probably more homogenous zones, as Llobera and Pina-Cabral once suggested, seems hardly productive (Llobera 1987; Pina-Cabral 1989). Maybe this course of action could enhance the comparative approach, but the division would also imply a downscale, and would be tantamount to creating a series of equally artificial and no less stereotyped culture areas.

Instead, building on the notion of historical regions (Giordano 2001) and considering the Mediterranean space in such terms would seem to be more fruitful. The Mediterranean space cannot be described as a clearly defined unit (Braudel 1985:10) so much as a mosaic of societies and cultures that are very different from each other yet that have had to coexist with each other during millennia of ongoing contacts and clashes. Despite countless conflicts and constant tensions, they influenced each other, often mingling with the aid of the sea. This leads these societies to define themselves and define others through a recurrent complementary relationship with their neighbors. Consequently, identifications and auto-comprehensions are the outcome of a permanent, long-term, mirror effect (Brubaker and Cooper 2000; Bromberger and Durand 2001:746).

However, any attempt to map out clear-cut, unchangeable, and thus static borders would be specious because the Mediterranean space in terms of a historical region does not coincide with the limited geographical area. In fact, contacts with other neighboring societies and their influence were not sporadic. As such, considering this historical region as a discrete and closed entity would be a misconception (Davis 1977:11). Besides this Mediterranean core that includes coastal peninsulas and the islands, there are a variety of very fluid transitory zones with shifting borders (Braudel 1982, 1:21, 155). Therefore, we can speak of interpenetrations between the Mediterranean space and the other more or less neighboring historical regions.

This notion of historical region would prevent anthropology from underestimating the importance of the single spaces of experience, rooted in the past but active in the present, which, despite shared reference points, should never be considered identical. As Bromberger and Durand keenly comment, it is not so much the similarities as much as the historically-shaped differences that determine a system in the Mediterranean space (Bromberger and Durand 2001:743). This perspective would allow the anthropology of Mediterranean societies to avoid the tendency to seek impossible uniformities and to insist instead on the cognate differences, or better yet, paraphrasing Ludwig Wittgenstein, on the family resemblances between societies (Wittgenstein 1958:par. 66–67; Albera and Blok 2001; Bromberger and Durand 2001:743).

This way of conceiving the Mediterranean space also allows us to forgo the idea of uniqueness specific to this part of the world and begin to observe, interpret, and compare the family resemblances with those of other historical regions (such as Eastern Europe, the Middle East, or the Caucasus) where the social representations of honor or patronage practices, for example, play a major role in several social fields of these societies.

Finally, the idea of the Mediterranean space as a historical region spanning three continents allows us to highlight the fluidity of Europe's borders. Another strong point is that it will bring into question certain increasingly widespread Eurocentric visions concerning both the external boundaries of the Old Continent and its internal demarcations.

NOTES

1 In dealing with the anthropology of Mediterranean societies we shall be largely referring to researches carried out by Anglo-Saxon, French, and, to some extent, German scholars associated with specific anthropological schools that some critics hold to be hegemonic (Llobera 1986:30f.; Bromberger and Durand 2001). Accordingly, our presentation will not include most of the so-called national ethnologies of Mediterranean countries, such as *tradizioni popolari*, *studi demologici* or *studi folklorici* in Italy, or *laographia* in Greece. This partial omission is due essentially to the fact that, unlike the anthropology of Mediterranean societies, these disciplines lack a comparative project and their research is focused solely on their own national societies without taking into consideration other countries.

REFERENCES

Albera, D., and A. Blok
2001 The Mediterranean as a Field of Ethnological Study. A Retrospective. *In* L'anthropologie de la Méditerranée. D. Albera, A. Blok, and Chr. Bromberger, eds. pp. 15–37. Paris: Maisonneuve et Larose; Maison méditerranéenne des sciences de l'homme.
Albera, D., A. Blok, and Chr. Bromberger, eds.
2001 L'anthropologie de la Méditerranée. Paris: Maisonneuve et Larose; Maison méditerranéenne des sciences de l'homme.
Bailey, F. G.
1971 Gifts and Poison: The Politics of Reputation. Oxford: Blackwell.
Banfield, E. C.
1958 The Moral Basis of a Backward Society. Glencoe, IL: Free Press.
Belloni, F., M. Caciagli, and L. Mattina
1979 The Mass Clientelism Party: The Christian Democratic Party in Catania and in Southern Italy. European Journal of Political Research 7:253–275.
Black-Michaud, J.
1975 Feuding Societies. Oxford: Blackwell.

Blok, A.
1974 The Mafia of a Sicilian Village 1860–1960: A Study of Violent Entrepreneurs. Oxford: Blackwell.
Boissevain, J.
1974 Friends of Friends: Networks, Manipulators and Coalitions. Oxford: Blackwell.
1975 Introduction: Towards a Social Anthropology of Europe. *In* Beyond the Community: Social Process in Europe. J. Boissevain and J. Friedl, eds. pp. 9–17. The Hague: Information Department of the Ministry of Education.
1979 Towards a Social Anthropology of the Mediterranean. Man, New Series, 3(4):542–556.
Boissevain, J. and J. Friedl, eds.
1975 Beyond the Community: Social Process in Europe. The Hague: Information Department of the Ministry of Education.
Bourdieu, P., and L. J. D. Wacquant
1996 Réponses pour une anthropologie reflexive. Paris: Editions du Seuil.
Braudel, F.
1982 La méditerranée et le monde méditerranéen à l'époque de Philippe II, vol. 2. Paris: Armand Colin.
Braudel, F., ed.
1985 La méditerranée. L'espace et l'histoire. Paris: Flammarion.
Bromberger, Chr., and J.-Y. Durand
2001 Conclusion: Faut-il jeter la méditerranée avec l'eau du bain? *In* L'anthropologie de la Méditerranée. D. Albera, A. Blok, and Chr. Bromberger, eds. pp. 733–752. Paris: Maisonneuve et Larose; Maison méditerranéenne des sciences de l'homme.
Brubaker, R., and F. Cooper
2000 Beyond Identity. Theory and Society 20:1–47
Campbell, J. K.
1976 Honour, Family and Patronage: A Study of Institutions and Moral Values in a Greek Mountain Community. Oxford: Oxford University Press.
Cole, J. W.
1979 Gemeindestudien der Cultural Anthropology in Europa. *In* Gemeinde im Wandel: Volkskundliche Gemeindestudien in Europa. G. Wiegelmann, ed. pp. 15–31. Münster: F. Coppenrath.
D'Amico, R.
1993 La "cultura elettorale" dei siciliani. *In* Far politica in Sicilia: Deferenza, consenso, e protesta. M. Morisi, ed. pp. 211–257. Milan: Feltrinelli.
Davis, J.
1970 Morals and Backwardness: Comparative Studies in Society and History 12(3):340–353.
1973 Land and Family in Pisticci. London: Athlone Press.
1977 People of the Mediterranean: An Essay in Comparative Social Anthropology. London: Routledge and Kegan Paul.
1982 History in the Making. *In* Europäische Ethnologie: Theorie und Methodendiskussion aus ethnologischer und volkskundlicher Sicht. H. Nixdorff and T. Hauschild, eds. pp. 291–298. Berlin: Reimer.
Du Boulay, J.
1979 Portrait of a Greek Mountain Village. Oxford: Clarendon Press.
Foster, G. M.
1963 The Dyadic Contract in Tzintzuntzan: Patron–Client Relationship. American Anthropologist, 65:1280–1294.

Fukuyama, F.
1995 Trust: The Social Virtues and the Creation of Prosperity. New York: Free Press.
Galt, A.
1973 Carnival on the Island of Pantelleria: Ritualized Community Solidarity in an Atomistic Society. Ethnology, 12:325–339.
Gellner, E., and J. Waterbury
1977 Patrons and Clients in Mediterranean Societies. London: Duckworth.
Georgiev, P. K.
2008 Corruptive Patterns of Patronage in South East Europe. Wiesbaden: VS Verlag für Sozialwissenschaften.
Gilmore, D.
1975 Friendship in Fuenmayor: Patterns of Integration in an Atomistic Society. Ethnology 14:311–324.
1979 CA Comment. Current Anthropology 20:87–88.
1980 The People of the Plain: Class and Community in Lower Andalusia. New York: Columbia University Press.
1982 Anthropology of the Mediterranean Area. Annual Review of Anthropology 11:175–205.
Gilmore, D., ed.
1987 Honor and Shame and the Unity of the Mediterranean. AAA Special Publication 22. Washington, DC: American Anthropological Association.
Giordano, Chr.
1992 Die Betrogenen der Geschichte, Überlagerungsmentalität und Überlagerungsrationalität in mediterranen Gesellschaften. Frankfurt am Main: Campus.
2001 Europe: Sociocultural Overview. *In* International Encyclopedia of the Social and Behavioral Sciences, vol. 7. pp. 4917–4923. Oxford: Pergamon.
Giordano, Chr., and D. Kostova
2002 The Social Production of Mistrust. *In* Postsocialism: Ideals, Ideologies and Practices in Eurasia. C. Hann, ed. pp. 74–91. London: Routledge.
Giordano, Chr.
2007 Privates Vertrauen und informelle Netzwerke: Zur Organisationskultur in Gesellschaften des öffentlichen Misstrauens. *In* Soziale Netzwerke und soziales Vertrauen in den Transformationsländern. Freiburger Sozialanthropologische Studien 15. K. Roth, ed. pp. 21–49. Münster: LIT.
Gower-Chapman, C.
1971 Milocca: A Sicilian Village. Cambridge, MA: Schenkman.
Herzfeld, M.
1980 Honour and Shame: Problems in the Comparative Analysis of Moral Systems. Man, New Series 15:339–351.
1984 The Horns of the Mediterraneanist Dilemma. American Ethnologist 11:439–454.
1987a Anthropology through the Looking Glass: Critical Anthropology in the Margins of Europe. Cambridge: Cambridge University Press.
1987b "As in your own House": Hospitality, Ethnography, and the Stereotype of Mediterranean Society. *In* Honor and Shame and the Unity of the Mediterranean. AAA Special Publication 22. D. Gilmore, ed. pp. 75–89. Washington, DC: American Anthropological Association.
Husseini, R.
2009 Murder in the Name of Honour. Oxford: Oneworld.
Kaser, K.
1992 Hirten, Kämpfer Stammeshelden, Ursprünge und Gegenwart des balkanischen Patriarchats. Vienna: Böhlau Verlag.

Koselleck, R.
1979 Vergangene Zukunft. Zur Semantik geschichtlicher Zeiten. Frankfurt am Main: Suhrkamp.
Lisón-Tolosana, C.
1966 Belmonte de los Caballeros: A Sociological Study of a Spanish Town. Oxford: Clarendon Press.
Llobera, J. R.
1986 Fieldwork in Southwestern Europe: Anthropological Panacea or Epistemological Straitjacket? Critique of Anthropology 6(2):25–33.
1987 The Anthropology of Southwestern Europe: The Way Forward. Critique of Anthropology 7(2):101–118.
Moreno Navarro, I.
1972 El trabajo de campo etnólogico en España y el problema de la selecció de comunidad. Ethnica 3:163–180.
Mühlmann, W. E., and R. J. Llaryora
1968 Klientschaft, Klientel und Klientelsystem in einer sizilianischen Agro-Stadt. Tübingen: J. C. B. Mohr.
Pardo, I., and G. B. Prato
2011 Citizenship and the Legitimacy of Governance: Anthropology in the Mediterranean Region. Farnham: Ashgate.
Peristiany, J. G.
1965 Honour and Shame: The Values of Mediterranean Societies. London: Weidenfeld and Nicolson.
Peristiany, J. G., and J. Pitt-Rivers
1992 Honour and Grace in Anthropology. Cambridge: Cambridge University Press.
Pina Cabral, J. de
1989 The Mediterranean as a Category of Regional Comparison: A Critical View. Current Anthropology 3:399–406.
Piselli, F.
1981 Parentela ed emigrazione: Mutamenti e continuità in una comunità calabrese. Torino: Einaudi.
Pitkin, D.
1985 The House that Giacomo Built. Cambridge: Cambridge University Press.
Pitt Rivers, J.
1954 The People of the Sierra. London: Weidenfeld and Nicolson.
1968 Honour. *In* International Encyclopaedia of the Social Sciences, vol. 6. pp. 503–510. New York: Macmillan.
1977 The Fate of Shechem or the Politics of Sex. Essays in the Anthropology of the Mediterranean. Cambridge: Cambridge University Press.
Pizzorno, A.
1976 Familismo amorale e marginalità storica ovvero perché non c'è niente da fare a Montegrano. *In* Le basi morali di una società arretrata. Nuova edizione di Edward C. Banfield Una comunità del Mezzogiorno. D. De Masi, ed. pp. 237–252. Bologna: Il Mulino.
Pouillon, J.
1975 Fétiches sans fétichisme. Paris: Maspéro.
Putnam, R., with R. Leonardi, and R. Y. Nanetti
1993 Making Democracy Work: Civic Traditions in Modern Italy. Princeton, NJ: Princeton University Press.
Ricoeur, P.
1985 Temps et récit. Paris: Editions du Seuil.

Schneider, J., and P. Schneider
1976 Culture and Political Economy in Western Sicily. New York: Academic Press.
Signorelli, A.
1983 Chi può e chi aspetta. Giovano e clientelismo in un'area interna del Mezzogiorno. Napoli: Liguori.
Silverman, S.
1968 Agricultural Organization, Social Structure and Values in Italy: Amoral Familism Reconsidered. American Anthropologist 70(1):1–20.
Stirling, P.
1965 A Turkish Village. London: Weidenfeld and Nicolson.
Tullio-Altan, C.
1986 La nostra Italia. Arretratezza socioculturale, clientelismo e ribellismo dall'Unità ad oggi. Milan: Feltrinelli.
Weber, M.
1956 Wirtschaft und Gesellschaft. Tübingen: J. C. B. Mohr.
Weingrod, A.
1968 Patrons, Patronage, and Political Parties. Comparative Studies in Society and History 10:377–400.
White, C.
1980 Patrons and Partisans: A Study of Politics in Two Southern Italian "Comuni." Cambridge: Cambridge University Press.
Wikan, U.
2008 In Honor of Fadime: Murder and Shame. Chicago: University of Chicago Press.
Wittgenstein, L.
1958 Philosophical Investigations. Oxford: Blackwell.

CHAPTER 3 Nordic Reflections on Northern Social Research

Hugh Beach

This chapter provides an introduction to some of the more pressing concerns of contemporary social science research in the North.[1] In the pages ahead, points will be illustrated from cases derived primarily from the Nordic countries, while contrasting and confirming cases will be drawn from a much broader base. What follows is an anthropological discourse derived from qualitative data and field experience, making no pretense at representative sampling procedures or the stringency of quantitative data methodology. It is hoped that the discourse of patterns and trends will prove to hold validity that transcends the regional confines used to introduce them.

This effort to address social science issues and research will deal largely with so-called (and so-contestably-defined) indigenous peoples (Kuper 2003) and their relations to the environment both as encultured space, landscape (seascape), and also as what we in the West would define as "resource," a dis-encultured, and despiritualized, concept of so-called "material substance" needed for food and other material goods. Despiritualized lands are the more easily plundered, despiritualized animals the more easily commoditized for wealth rather than just sustenance, and the more we despiritualize our world, the more too we despiritualize ourselves. Hence, it is plain that we are dealing with variable views of the universe and humankind's place in it, as well as with the concrete policies and regulations controlling access to *it* or allocating *it* among those given access. Equally plain is the fact that in today's world no adequate description of Northern conditions and no attempted description of any of its native peoples can be remotely considered without involving the dominating presence (even when present at a distance) of the ambient, "White" majority (Csonka and Schweitzer 2004).

Finally, it should be emphasized that just as social science study in the North is generated through the relations of various peoples and cultures, indigenous and immigrant, minority and majority, peripheral local and central removed, rural and urban, so is there a decidedly relational aspect between the pursuit of social

A Companion to the Anthropology of Europe, First Edition. Edited by Ullrich Kockel, Máiréad Nic Craith, and Jonas Frykman.

science research and the pursuit of natural science research. While some might claim that it is of no significance to the specific "truths" discovered by natural science research *per se*, there is no denying that the mere activity of natural science research, its funding, its inclusion or exclusion of local participation, and not least the policy impacts of its results, have significant dimensions for indigenous peoples, some of them liberating, many of them, unfortunately, colonizing. It will not only affect how they live (often with improvements) and where they live, but also how they think, how their cosmologies are affected and how they identify. These are certainly social matters, many of which we still barely understand.

Social science research among peoples of the North is flourishing as never before. At least three relatively recent major developments are arguably responsible for increased interest and activity in Northern social science. First, globalization has brought with it growing mutual awareness and collaboration among the indigenous peoples of the North. Second, the dissolution of the Soviet Union has opened the Eurasian continent all the more to Western researchers (even if the wealth and democratic freedoms of the Western world have reciprocated poorly in the hosting of Russian scholars to carry out social research in northern North America and Europe). Third, the threats posed by rapid climatic change have opened the coffers of politicians and the eyes of scientists eager to use funds, previously scant, to protect Northern landscapes and their inhabitants. Yet, the same climatic changes, estimated to occur with twice the speed in the Arctic as they do in the world in general (Broadbent and Lantto 2009:341), which have brought about the melting of glaciers and Arctic sea ice, have also opened the door to the exploitation of new mineral and oil resources, together with new transportation routes. These have predictably stirred a rash of economic and geopolitical interests often (but not at all always nor in every respect) counter to those of Northern local inhabitants, particularly those of indigenous origin. Social scientists sometimes eagerly rally to, and sometimes find themselves unavoidably dragged into, the fray, as the goals of environmental protection, ethnic and cultural indigenous rights, and national economic and political interests butt heads.

Adopting a wider historical perspective, and thereby shifting the scale of what we might consider as relatively recent, one should not fail to recognize that compared to the habitation of indigenous peoples in the North, the huge influx of peoples from the core, with their dominance of governance, law, social welfare, education, resource exploitation, and all the other accoutrements of colonization (much of it a boon to those impacted), is of recent origin. The creation of the new nations of Canada and the United States must be regarded in this wider historical frame as part and parcel of the same European blitz. We need only consider the languages spoken today by the peoples of the northern regions of the so-called New World. Besides the variety of indigenous languages spoken by them, the inhabitants of lands stretching along at least one half of the circumpolar rim speak also, and sometimes only, a European language, notably English. To the east, with the Russification of the Eurasian continent, we see an analogous situation, but one which, from an indigenous perspective (for better in some respects, or worse in others) has followed its own course with variable colonial intensity according to a number of radically shifting ideologies.

Paradoxical as it may seem, cutting across all these themes has been the continued decolonialization of the anthropological discipline – at times optimistically but mistakenly believed to have been completed with the mere removal of European colonial regimes from the lands they have ruled in the South – which has brought with it the recognition of, and inevitable debates about, traditional knowledge as opposed to any other knowledge. Not surprisingly, the anthropological discipline has become immersed in a hermeneutic revolution about how we interpret, evaluate, and present any such knowledge, the so-called data of our science, be it traditional, Western, phenomenological, or otherwise. As with the struggles over accessibility to and usage of concrete resources of the sea, of the land, and their subsurface riches within the indigenous/colonial context, so are there struggles over the authenticity of tradition, whose voice can represent it, who "owns" traditional knowledge, what it actually might be, and if its content can be separated from its original purpose while still maintaining its traditional status (Krupnik and Jolly 2002). Is, for example, the knowledge of ecological relationships couched in cultural myths, structuring the identity of a clan group or supporting the survival of its youth by teaching useful skills by oral traditions, really the same so-called Traditional Ecological Knowledge (TEK) when used to produce skin creams for European markets?

The mere facile appendage of indigenous data on to the scientific repertoire fails fundamentally to embrace the essence of indigenous knowledge. So-called "indigenous knowledge" may not be uniform among, or universal to, indigenous peoples, but it often comprises far more than scientifically proven, ineffectual superstitions on the one hand, or detailed and accurate environmental observations on the other; it often contains deep understanding of the balance required by humankind to maintain a place in nature. Most importantly, it can hold a metamessage for us beyond the scientific truth of its details, through a purposiveness perspective dedicated to the survival and veneration of life/spirit which goes beyond that of any human ethnic group or any species alone, to embrace the Whole.

Obviously, these issues are not confined at all to Arctic social science. The Arctic, like every region of the world, hosts unique cultures and ways of securing a livelihood, but it also shares many of the same basic general trends of social change and social problems with the rest of the world. Many differences will be matters of degree rather than kind, and yet, due to the unique confluence of elements of extreme temperature ranges, geophysical location, and vulnerability of biotopes composed of relatively few species, Arctic environmental degradation and its social impacts will tend to adumbrate developments elsewhere, later.

Colonialism, Yesterday and Today

With the partitioning of the northern regions of Europe, Asia, and North America into various nation-states, native peoples as well as immigrants have come to be ruled by different legal frameworks with different policies of resource access and allocation. Peoples united by culture and livelihood have been divided by national borders and colonial policies. Some states, for example, have come to reserve reindeer-herding rights for their native minority alone, the Reindeer Herding Act of 1971 (Sweden), while others have shunned any racial criterion in favor of an eligibility system linked to ownership of land. One finds many different criteria for herding eligibility, even distinctions made between reindeer herders and reindeer owners, and a variety of definitions specifying who qualifies as a native under the law. The resources tapped by hunters and fishers will commonly fall under regulatory regimes quite distinct from those controlling pastoralists. This latter group owns real property, and hence domestic stock (lending to the term "stock" a social, and not merely a biological significance), whereas the animal resources of hunters and fishers are not owned until killed or caught (Paine 1971; Ingold 1980) and hence are commonly considered "wild" even if their future harvest, their kill or catch quotas, might be commoditized, owned, and sold (Einarsson 2011). As one might anticipate, the negotiations between environmentalists and resource users can have a distinctly different character depending on the status of the resource in question. Owners of domestic property are prone to enjoy legal protections which the hunters of a wild resource might not, as wild animals are generally thought to be totally within the environmentalist domain. Predators, especially, epitomize the wild no matter how managed their every movement, their reproduction, and survival, in a globalized world traumatized by the awareness of rapid climatic change and environmental degradation. Native minority policies of different countries have evolved, often over hundreds of years. With increasing population growth, globalization, global warming, discovery of oil in Northern regions, and increasing conflict over Northern resources, the laws governing ethnic definitions and the regulation of livelihoods accruing to them, evolve all the more rapidly along paths blazed by their fundamental, though often conflicting, premises.

It would be simplistic to view colonialism merely as a dominating "Southern" or "Western" agent exerting its will upon protesting "Northern" victims. Nor does the character of any constraint or possibility remain fixed; possibilities will shift with time and context and become constraints in different ways in different degrees to different parts of any local population. Indigenous peoples, like everyone else, will adapt to change and adopt creatively, internalizing some of the colonizers' ways while repudiating the rest. Unlike the situation for many other indigenous peoples, the native peoples of the North American and European circumpolar rim find themselves within highly developed First World nations that espouse the doctrines of democracy, liberal market economy, social welfare ideology, and solidarity with international covenants on human rights. While the core principles of these same practices and ideals can certainly be found within traditional indigenous societies, the inclusion of these societies as minority subunits in the frame of the far larger ambient society and nation-state will necessarily change the conditions of power and all variable relations. As external social categories become created and imposed upon other groups by intercultural contact, be it by colonization or any more benign form of globalization, and as resources become allocated according to them as the result of new pressures and possibilities, forms of allocation according to traditional social categories become shifted. A resulting new array of winners and losers, and subsequent new divisions, will be generated internally and unavoidably.

Indigenous peoples might certainly bemoan the (forced) loss of traditional ways on the one hand while demanding the right to develop (voluntarily) with new technologies and education on the other. This is no different from the song sung by people in general; the distinction between what is forced and what is voluntary is not always easily drawn, even for an individual, and all the more so for a group. Yet, when sung by indigenous peoples, this refrain often arouses deep indignation among members of the dominant society. The indigenous are accused of wanting their cake and eating it too – an understandable and not always unjustified attitude by members of the dominant society – for the "cake" often involves special rights over land and resources which the nonindigenous, many with long generational depth of permanent local residency, do not share. During the last 50 years (especially since the discovery of vast oil and gas resources in the North), social science in the North has been very much concerned with consideration of what is, or should be, the indigenous "cake." The degree to which this question is considered to be ruled either by national historical legality (e.g. treaties or courtroom precedent) or by newly devised political policies varies among the Northern nations, and also within each nation over time.

Nonetheless, the last half of the last century witnessed the birth of the Sámi parliaments, the revision of Sámi herding laws, the establishment of Greenlandic Home Rule (and more recently Greenlandic Self Rule), the creation of Nunavut (and other comprehensive land claims acts in Canada), and, in the United States, the passage of the Alaskan Native Claims Settlement Act (ANCSA) for Alaska. The Russian Association of Indigenous Peoples of the North, (RAIPON) born as the Soviet Union dissolved – since 1993 officially called the Association of Indigenous Peoples of the North, Siberia and Far East of the Russian Federation – has been exceptionally dramatic and, especially at first, surprisingly effective, although beset with the most dire conditions following upon the abandonment of Soviet infrastructure. Social scientists have been active both in the processes involved in the creation of these milestones and in following the impacts these changes have generated.

Of course, such proclamations and land-claims settlements do not erase by any means the ongoing debates and struggles over resources in the North. They do shift the balance of power of certain forces, and they do introduce some new and important players with new rules of negotiation. In the last decades of the twentieth century, with the dissolution of the Soviet Union, much of the European map was reshaped and Cold War power structures were realigned. The reach of the central authority of the Russian Federation, emanating from Moscow, cannot be maintained with the same force following the withdrawal of Soviet infrastructure and economic support from the more isolated interior regions and the far-flung borderlands. State-run collective farms have been closed or abandoned to fend for themselves, and the populations of the small towns and villages these state farms once sustained have either been decimated or forced to accept heavy industrial resource extraction and ravaged landscapes. In Alaska, extensive areas given protection as parklands under one regime come under new threat of exploitation as protections are lifted by the next regime. In Sweden, court cases contesting the immemorial right of Sámi herders to utilize winter grazing on lands in forested areas owned by settlers have become frequent, since the state has to date refused to pass general legislation on Sámi resource rights (as opposed to the rights of herders) and still will not ratify ILO Convention 169 concerning indigenous and tribal peoples in independent countries. Article 14 of this convention supports indigenous peoples' ownership claims to land. Instead, in 1993 the Swedish state confiscated, without due process or just compensation, exclusivity of Sámi small-game hunting rights, on the grounds that game was in sufficient abundance for the state to assert a parallel hunting right and to sell its own licenses. The Sámi have fared far better in Norway during the last decades, among other things with the acceptance in 2005 of the *Finnmarksloven*, the Finnmark Law, in which the state specified the resource rights of the Sámi while at the same time securing the well-defined rights of non-Sámi in the Finnmark area.

Although indigenous land claims have become increasingly respected, even if by no means fully settled, in the North, further influx of Southern peoples, further globalized integration, and recognition of the worldwide holism of environmental impacts have led to an unavoidable (and easily exploited) condition whereby environmental concerns – including those misguided in good faith, or even purposefully falsified or exaggerated – trump native rights. Indigenous peoples generally share the unenviable position of being pressed to the wall by colonial policies, economic rationalization, and market integration, with ensuing commoditization of their own cultures and lifestyles, only to find themselves being accused of being ecological "fallen angels" who therefore do not warrant the special resource privileges once accepted to preserve their traditional cultures and sustainable environmental relationships (Beach 1997:127).

Conceptions of Ethnicity

A burning issue in the North (as elsewhere) concerns the criteria by which one is to identify the eaters of the "cake," that is, to identify those considered to be members of the group that is recognized to possess special land and resource rights. Within this realm of discourse, the Nordic nations hold to a relatively peculiar position. In Norway, Sweden, and Finland the Sámi constitute the sole autochthonous indigenous people. When considered from the bygone perspective of a Danish colony or protectorate, Greenland is also the domain of one indigenous people, the Greenlanders. Today Greenlanders on the home front are politically active in the quest for statehood rather than equitable treatment as a minority or disempowered indigenous group under the control of others (Nuttall, personal communication 2011; cf. Nuttall 2009:295). The immemorial rights of land ownership or use for indigenous peoples might not be recognized to the full degree of their original conception by the dominant societies of the Nordic nations today, of course a hotly contested matter of interpretation, but the complexity of the legal issues controlling such rights is made yet more problematic by the superimposition of claims of a number of different indigenous peoples (perhaps but not necessarily using different resources or the same resources differently) for the same lands. Situations like this are not unusual in North America or Eurasia with a great number of indigenous peoples. In the case of Iceland one can question the validity of the indigenous/colonizer distinction at all, for in a sense all are indigenous, while by other characteristics, none are. In either case no special rights result.

When defining the holders of special indigenous rights, Sweden, Norway, and Finland have been moving away from the kind of essentialist models used in many other countries where people are identified for eligibility according to forms of biological inheritance. For example, access to resources rights of the Sámi in Sweden (notably the practice of reindeer herding) has been, and largely still is, determined by congenital credentials of "Sámi ancestry" (see the Reindeer Herding Act 1971). Until 1971, sex could also figure into the equation, for a Sámi herding woman who married a non-Sámi would lose her right to utilize Crown grazing lands, although a Sámi herding man who married a non-Sámi would not. Essentialist criteria such as these, acquired at birth and impossible to change, can take a number of forms – variable blood quotients, for example – and can also be combined with other kinds of criteria for resource use. Residency in defined areas is a common criterion for resource use, as is also the historical practice (with variable degrees of generational depth) of a particular form of livelihood. Until 1993 the right to herd reindeer in Sweden could be held only by those of Sámi ancestry who also had a parent or grandparent who had herded as a steady livelihood. This latter constraint formed a kind of phase-out clause over the generations, especially when combined with government policies of structural rationalization of the herding industry (Beach 1983). Its purpose was to reduce the number of herders to accommodate welfare ideologies for improved living standards for herding families. By reducing the number of herders, the number of reindeer available to each remaining herder within the total allowable limit would increase as would, it was thereby argued, the herders' living standard. The phase-out clause received severe international criticism, for it hindered Sámi from the right to pursue cultural traditions as specified in the United Nations Covenant for Civil and Political Rights, ratified by Sweden. This livelihood criterion was revoked with new legislation which established a Swedish Sámi parliament (*Sameting*), but little on this score has changed in practice, since the demand to adhere to total allowable herd-size limits for each designated year-round grazing zone gives those herders already members of the group permitted to graze there, so-called *sameby* members, the ability to close out those that seek admission. In effect, arguments of environmental sustainability are invoked to control Sámi livelihoods and hence govern Sámi cultural sustainability even though the reindeer-grazing resource itself is not otherwise utilized. It is the mineral deposits over which the grazing grows, the electricity-producing rivers which flow through the grazing lands, and the forests which dot and merge with them which cause modern states to show such concern for (the control over) Sámi reindeer grazing and accruing rights.

The establishment of Sámi parliaments in Norway 1989 and Sweden 1993 (Finland had one in place about 20 years earlier) finally forced the states to consider a true definition for Sámihood. The Sámi parliaments are organizations for the representation of an ethnic group, with an ethnically based electorate. Hence there must be criteria defining who is a Sámi, not merely a definition stating who can herd. The bestowal of rights on those of Sámi ancestry fails to address the more fundamental question of who is Sámi. From whom can one count Sámi ancestry? In reaction to the terrible genocide of the Second World War, Nordic countries have generally been opposed to ethnic registration in any formal documents. In Sweden, for example, while old church books have records of those listed as "nomads," people who were therefore surely Sámi as opposed to the expanding settled Swedish agrarian population, such distinctions have been blurred over and, for a long time now, not maintained. There is no record permitted in the Swedish census concerning ethnicity of any kind. Security measures against ethnic negative discrimination, however, also block positive discrimination, and Sweden has found itself in a difficult position when designing policies concerning its Sámi parliament and defining the Sámi electorate. This dilemma underpins the move away from ascribed to voluntary ethnic designation, while for the category of voluntary designees, new forms of ascribed nonessentialist criteria are devised to hinder the registration of so-called Sámi "wannabes" as opposed to the enforced essentialist ascription of "gottabes."

> In the spirit of Nordic harmonization of Saami policies, the governments of Norway and Sweden (following the Finnish precedent) have instituted a combination of subjective and objective criteria defining those Saami who, if they so desire, can register themselves to vote in their respective Saami Parliament elections. In order to join the Saami electorate, one must feel oneself to be a Saami (subjective criterion), and one must have used the Saami language in the home or had a parent or grandparent for whom Saami was a home language (objective criterion). In Norway the descent requirement was extended in 1997 to at least one great-grandparent. (Beach 2007:10–11)

A couple of concrete cases have tested the possibility of someone lacking Sámi ancestry to transit to sufficient Sámi identity classification to gain the right to herd reindeer on the basis of cultural competency (for example learning to speak the Sámi language), but to date success for wannabes has been limited when it comes to access to or use of resources. While the objective criterion (language proficiency) for Sámi parliament electorate membership has proved to be so vague as to be satisfied by the most minimal degree of competence, and thereby to be hardly distinguishable from the subjective requirement (feeling oneself to be Sámi), the Swedish state will not confer reindeer-herding rights on someone with only a constructivist form of Sámi identity, lacking any biological Sámi ancestry. However, it has proven sufficient to gain entrance into the Sámi parliament electorate. This in turn has caused the recent development whereby members of the existing Sámi parliament electorate have gained the option of questioning the Sámi credentials both of wannabes and even of other current Sámi parliament electoral members (Beach 2007).

The number of herding Sámi constitute only about 15% of the Sámi ethnic group, and one can expect that the Sámi parliament will, over time, increasingly reflect this proportion. Hence, as the Sámi parliament comes to gain increasing responsibilities over Sámi-related issues, so too will the non-herding Sámi assume greater power over Sámi affairs. The gradual shift toward more constructivist sway over Sámi political power probably carries with it greater acceptance from the ambient majority population for special Sámi rights as a matter of cultural preservation. Yet it also carries with it the danger of further loss of historically based Sámi land rights, which today are linked almost exclusively to reindeer herding and legislated on the basis of an essentialist ancestry criterion.

The case of the Sámi in Sweden is but one of the many varieties of ways in which group categorization (such as ethnicity) is correlated with special resource rights in the North. With the Alaska Native Claims Settlement Act of 1971, native-American residents of 12 demarcated regions were made shareholders in their respective regional corporations. According to this scenario, while future native generations might inherit corporation stock, their native status and residency are not in themselves sufficient to become a stockholding member of the regional corporations.

Russia presents its own mix of criteria and formal census list for determining which groups qualify for the legal status necessary for special resource rights. Such criteria determine where those who qualify can access such resources and how they must utilize them in order to maintain these rights. Besides residency in specific areas, and the pursuit of a traditional livelihood, population size is also an important factor in this equation. The maximum size of a population to qualify for status as one of the so-called "indigenous small-numbered peoples of the Far North, Siberia and the Far East," and thereby be given special rights, is 50 000. Yet, what we in the West might class as indigeneity might be neither necessary nor sufficient for a family in the forests of Siberia engaged in a traditional lifestyle to enjoy special resource privileges (Donahoe et al. 2008). The interpretation of the regulations and the emphasis given to any of the criteria mentioned can be quite variable from region to region when determining resource use.

With the dissolution of the Soviet Union, new policies were introduced for all citizens of Russia so that ethnic identity was no longer to be noted in newly issued passports. Yet, according to a wide array of ordinances, ethnic categorization remains determinative for access to and utilization of natural resources for numerous indigenous peoples in designated areas of the country. For many elderly people, old and even invalid passports might come to serve the vital purpose of establishing ethnic identity, but this is not an option for the young or for those obtaining passports for the first time. The matter of justifying or denying special resource use for individuals claiming indigenous heritage in Russia is handled in a variety of ways, often involving ethnic designation registered on birth certificates by parents, or sometimes by community consensus and membership in ethnic heritage societies with adherence to distinctive ethnic cultural idioms and their performative resurgence and reinvention (Beach et al. 2009).

Political Ecology

Issues concerning resource rights, conceptions of ethnicity, and so-called traditional ecological knowledge, all of which are cultural as well as material, from the local to the global, are enveloped in spheres of power and lend themselves, therefore, to the rapidly developing anthropological subdiscipline called political ecology. Of course, studies of political ecological content have been ongoing long before the term was coined. There has been no dearth of studies related to struggles for resources both material and cultural, the exercise and distribution of power, indigenous rights or environmental protection since the dawn of social science. Enlightened academic discourse has moved to overcome much of colonial bias, Western bias, and to some extent, gender bias, even if these linger and are all too evident in a real world. Features of Northern indigenous struggles for resource rights can range from the well-intentioned but misdirected efforts of some external NGOs to the worst of suppressive national minority policies and brutal armed conflicts, fostered not infrequently by ruthless international economic organizations. Yet, with the advent of rapid globalization and the perception of rapid climatic change in tandem, there has been a change along the western circumpolar rim in the premises of negotiation with respect to the resource "cake," notably land.

With all the bells and whistles alerting us now to climatic threats (that have actually been impending since the industrial revolution) to the survival of our species, it is little wonder that the social sciences, and Arctic social science in particular, have become preoccupied with practical matters concerned largely with issues such as resource sustainability and social resilience. Both of these concepts, sustainability and resilience, relate to the management of change, and both are predicated upon the recognition of some entity, be it an ecosystem, a species, or a society, by whose fate we are to measure the success or failure of such management. The core premise of ecological consciousness, however, rests upon the realization of the complex relations of hierarchically embedded survival entities. Each individual species, any survival-oriented entity, at any level, is also a part of a larger organism, ecological system, or so-called unit of mind (to use Batesonian terminology), and hence, any narrow focus for sustainability or resilience on one part of the system alone is not only theoretically bogus, but also likely to jeopardize the relations within which the part is embedded, resulting in *unsustainability* for its most immediately encompassing environment and thereby paradoxically, but naturally, for itself as well.

In systems of hierarchically and embedded homeostatic "units," *adaptive change on one level occurs to keep unchanged more primary relationships* (Bateson, personal communication 1971). This raises immediately the question at what level resilience is sought. What is the unit of purposive survival? This crucial political and moral question, the recognition of which forms the *sine qua non* for approaching the problem, is often camouflaged by a misconceived devotion to pure science and the notion that one need simply note the rise of temperature to understand that it must be brought down. But for whom? How far down? At what expense? From whose pocket? While some Northern natives have launched an initiative to lobby for "the right to be cold," in the effort to maintain traditional livelihoods, others sense positive effects by a slight temperature shift which might, for example, increase access to subterranean ore deposits. In the Greenlandic case under self rule, the Greenlanders should be positioned to draw advantage from access to "thawed resources" which their Inuit brethren in Canada or Alaska might gain little from in relation to their losses (Nuttall 2009).

It might be argued that scientists should not engage in such questions and should not promote the survival of one group over another. It can also be claimed that to the scientist such positioning becomes meaningless when *all* embedded units will surely perish in the furnace if the continual temperature increase is not reduced. Yet, when humans discuss ecology, we must be upfront with the admission that we are primarily concerned with our *human* survival within this complexity, and far too many of us are more concerned with the survival of our nation, group, ethnicity or personal comforts for which thousands of other humans (not to mention whales or gorillas) might be sacrificed to misfortune or death with lip service given to ecological concern.

Cultures have bravely faced extinction before, nor is this the first time that humankind has seriously reflected on the end of its kind or even of all species by flood or fire and brimstone. These thoughts of The End are not new, but the ways in which humankind perceives it, the moral retribution read into it, or the possible role of human agency to avert it can be quite different and far from uniform. To those who hold an animistic worldview, there may be comfort in the knowledge that modern systems theory supports astounding similarities of worldview. Even if couched in different metaphoric language, both ancient epistemologies and much of cutting-edge modern science hold that should the human experiment fail, the world will still turn, and the astounding relational integration between that which constitutes supposedly "dead" atomistic material and "living" evolving organism will still prevail. According to this view, the miracle whereby life is created out of dead matter occurs each time we consume food. Speed of informational feedback is not necessarily of prime significance to the measure of adaptation, evolution, and other forms of communication which constitute the life principle in any logical sense. Life, like matter – or rather with and in matter, for the two are inseparable – has never been created nor can it be destroyed. It might be more appropriate to conclude that if and when matter was created, so in that instant was life in its most rudimentary form. What has evolved since the origin of our universe was not the eventual spark of life, but rather the ever increasing complexity of relation of the mind–matter unity. Yet, many indigenous people feel that the enlightened truths of modern science go unheeded by most of modern people who find themselves in a spiritual "Dark Ages" where God, not humankind, has been expelled from Eden. To make matters worse, modern Western science powers an enormous propaganda machine, and launches massive missionary activity which, intentional or not, generates an understanding of the world devoid of immanent spirituality.

Reflections like these may seem totally misplaced in a scientific essay, but they are relevant to our discussion of social science research in the North. We must try to grasp alternative cosmologies in terms that make sense to us, not only as strange superstitions that make sense to others. How otherwise can we possibly perceive what we are really asking non-Christian, non-Western, indigenous persons who see no distinction between God and his *ongoing* creation when we question their perceptions of climatic change, their understanding of such change, and suggest what they should do to help counteract it, or what externally imposed human regulations they should accept to "save the environment"? Informants who have grasped such meanings have already converted to our scientific ideology of disjuncture between humankind and nature. We assume their complicity in the belief in a true lack of divinity in the agency of world change.

> On the spiritual level, the moral imperative of rationalization obviates the role of the Animal Masters. It is no longer they who give freely or perhaps withhold whimsically; it is we who take according to our own ecology. *Our* ecology, even if supposedly sustainable, is dramatically distinct from any ecology dreamed of as universal or abiding to the holistic morality of equity among the purposive "needs and greeds" of all species. (Beach and Stammler 2006:16)

For many Northern indigenous peoples following traditional lifestyles and adhering to traditional worldviews related to hunting and gathering and reindeer hunting or herding, the process of rationalization within the paradigm of sustainability and scientific perspectives on "ecology" implies a positioning of humankind in the world which is fundamentally different from their own. Immersed as we are in our own worldviews, we can be unaware of the ideological pressures imposed on others by our vision of ecology.

The biases of our own scientific epistemology are commonly hidden under the appeal to "pure science," which might better be termed the "capitalistic ecological metaphor." According to this metaphor, one should live off of the "interest" of any resource, without tapping its "capital." While useful at times to strike a rudimentary point against overuse of resources, by its reduction of politics and its moral issues to mere arithmetic this metaphor is useless in helping to navigate the treacherous waters of political ecology. It is a kind of vulgar ecology, for there are an infinite number of long-term sustainable ecosystems that can be promoted in a given region; *which*, is a political question. Supposedly, if one follows the capitalist-metaphor rule of thumb, nature (or whatever ecosystem has been targeted by human purposiveness, for example "wetlands") will be sustained. However, in this monetary metaphor, even if amounts of it change, money is a qualitative constant. One is sustaining *it*, increasing *it* or depleting *it*. However, a balanced bank account says nothing about the content of your investment portfolio. Most importantly, ecosystems do not work this way at all. In whatever way they are being preserved or utilized and to whatever degree, they also thereby alter *character* (not just quantity; Beach 2004:122).

If we pursue this metaphor further, we find that it is not only inadequate, but that it also promotes a most unhealthy ecological condition, that which occurs when the precept of economic rationalization is added to the arithmetic equation. Its most destructive manifestation can be witnessed in the Nordic countries with their highly centralized governments and developed welfare ideologies, as these assert the rationalization paradigm on indigenous livelihoods, notably reindeer management.

> Rationalization is the prescriptive ideology that one should use resources fully in order to provide the greatest benefit to users (humans) as long as one does not thereby endanger the continuation of this process. Logically, wastage, according to the precepts of rationalization, becomes synonymous with *not* being utilized for human benefit if it could be, without injuring sustainability. It is wastage if a deer which could be killed, without injury to the sustainability of the deer species, is not killed for the benefit of humankind. It is against the precepts of rationalization if grazing is not utilized (sustainably) which could have nurtured that reindeer. If "sustainability" means do not overuse, "rationalization" means not only do not overuse, but also use maximally up to the ceiling of sustainability. (Beach and Stammler 2006:15)

Note that rationalization is not simply a new, independent concept, but the necessary logical conclusion and practical solution to the capitalistic metaphor of resource sustainability when no restraints are imposed on the sustainable *development* of the resource *user* category. Rationalization positions resource use at the brink of overuse. Unless social mechanisms are in place to react swiftly and with force enough to curb a runaway depletion of resources, for example grazing depletion due to a runaway population increase of reindeer, sustainability is forfeit. It is a scenario as logically compulsive and potentially as destructive as the renowned tragedy of the commons. Yet tragedy of the commons differs from rationalization tragedy in significant ways. The former is driven by the cumulative maximizing schemes of individual players, while the latter is commonly fostered by a centralized authority. The former builds off of an acceptable condition, until it has gone too far, whereas for the latter the situation (i.e. even the *under*use of resources) is unacceptable to the authorities until use has expanded almost too far and teeters on the edge of unsustainability. In the former case, social mechanisms to circumvent tragedy have often evolved within the society of users, while in the latter case the players look to the promoting centralized authority for the implementation of controls (and are on the one hand often disappointed by their lack, or on the other hand infuriated by the permits, quotas, or restructuring of property imposed upon them).

Most significantly, the individualistic strategies of property ownership under the paradigm of the tragedy of the commons make no pretense at environmental sustainability, whereas the rationalization tragedy paradigm includes this goal as part of its manifesto. It is all the more tragic not only for perching the resource category of users it is designed to benefit on the brink of overuse. Should this user category increase to the point where the need for acceptable living standards pushes members beyond sustainable use (not necessarily through increasing numbers of consumers, but through reduced flexibility by any means of the relation between consumers and resource capacity), then it can also impose mechanisms to address the problem and to redistribute resources and access to them from above. While one must recognize that the problems borne of resource and consumer pressure are not necessarily *caused* by the rationalization paradigm, which is, rather, devised to relieve them, and even traditional indigenous mechanisms for adjustment can be a painful and bloody business, the mechanism imposed by a strongly centralized state according to its own welfare ideology has hardly evolved within the society of users themselves, is of colonial rather than native social fabric, and of necessity therefore is open to purposive aims for the use of those same resources which extend beyond indigenous sociocultural benefit.

As its name implies, the research of those involved in the political ecology of the circumpolar North concerns the relations of power over the resources of Northern landscapes. Such resources are not simply material, but are also anchored in the historical, symbolic, and epistemological ways of knowing the world and constructing oneself as a social being. Not only are we interested in the physical realities of industrial encroachment in the North, we are very much concerned with the *discourses* employed by extractive industry, local people, those granted by various criteria "indigenous status," and environmentalists. The circumpolar North provides a fascinating comparative field, for on the one hand it encompasses enormous variation with respect to legal systems of resource governance, while on the other hand it is an area which still maintains in part and to degrees an epistemology essentially different from that of our own western, urban norms.

Domesticating the Wilderness

Ownership rights to land or rights to land resource use for indigenous people (variously defined) are often predicated upon physical remains or landscape alteration as proof of land occupancy according to specific degrees of intensity and time. However, should the indigenous "footprint" be considered too large, they face exclusion from their traditional landscapes according to the self-righteous environmental concern of the empowered majority. For indigenous peoples, finding a sustainable space between the existential mark for resource rights without triggering environmentalist condemnation can prove difficult. Moreover, any such position once found, can never be secure, as the laws and lobbies which frame it are themselves often in motion.

The justification often invoked by colonial powers for denying special indigenous resource rights has commonly hinged on the concept of "*terra nullius*," alluding to land "untouched by humans" even when human habitation (by non-Western humans) has been recognized. The simple concept of land as "untouched" not only conflates a number of analytical possibilities but also rarely does justice to the historical context of the term when coined. One can argue for a distinction between (i) untouched meaning never even trodden by human feet; (ii) untouched in the sense that humans may have walked over it but departed, having left (supposedly) no trace at all; or (iii) untouched in the sense that human presence is to compare with that of birds and bears, an impact which composes rather than opposes (or scars) nature. Naturally, the categories are not necessarily firmly bounded. As noted, colonial powers employing the concept of *terra nullius* have commonly been interested in demanding "proof" of land-use and occupancy for granting land claims, evidence of land use in the form of fixed alteration and enduring human impact, indicating sustained resource extraction. Weightier than the mere matter of being "touched" or not has been indication of human "progress," a point which, after all, was thought to distinguish humans from animals. Increasing recognition of indigenous land rights and various forms of protection for indigenous landscapes since the latter half of the twentieth century has not merely resulted from better acquaintance with traditional forms of indigenous land-use; there has also been a marked change in the criteria by which states entertain such rights and grant such protective status.

There has been a strong trend toward the acknowledgment of cognitive rather than simply physical human–land relations, together with international harmonization of policies. The dramatic proliferation of World Heritage Sites, bestowing protected status on areas of unique natural or cultural value from a global perspective is one example. Another example is the bestowal of protected status on land areas which host identified and mapped religious sites. This has forced some indigenous people whose sacrificial sites are considered desecrated if revealed to "sacrifice" some sacrificial sites to the public domain in order to protect the lands containing other undisclosed sacrificial sites. A current and most extreme case is the granting of protected status to certain land areas in Russia where it can be demonstrated that particular places figure in traditional indigenous folklore. Opponents of the new policy claim that it has brought about a proliferation of supposedly traditional place-oriented folklore. Authenticity becomes a vital point in the negotiation of such policies, but with the realization that almost all land "touched" by human presence at all has figured in authentic folkloristic motifs and naming traditions, one can speculate that the decisive point for the bestowal of protected land status will most likely in time come to settle on the evaluation of what might be termed the "continuity of memory," that is, memories with unbroken pedigree of authenticity. In this case, the cognitive aspect of landscaping, like naming practices, comes to share the same sort of dilemma as that discussed above concerning material resource usage and observable environmental "footprint." While landscaping is recognized as a creative cultural process, establishing legal claims, too much creativity can become counterproductive.

At the root of this dilemma seems to be the flawed concept of "wilderness" as that utmost realm of nature which embodies a primeval condition of lands bereft of both cognitive name and human physical impact. We can easily imagine wilderness as composed of millions of other species, but when it comes to humankind we mark a halt. Other primates may be VIPs of the wilderness world, but somewhere along the evolutionary path from hominid to human we have excluded ourselves. Admittedly we are distinctive in many ways, but if both wilderness and humankind are encompassed by nature, than wilderness must hold commonality even with humans. If nothing else, this discussion must underscore that the concept of "wilderness" is indeed precisely a concept, a *human* construct. Human attempts to preserve it and manage it, especially when trying to do so without allowing for human presence, become absurdly futile.

As one might expect, with world attention turning northward to the threat of melting ice and the lure of thawing riches and new transportation possibilities, pressures mount to harness Northern resources under various flags. Just as, predictably, the various nations will collaborate, not so much with regard to limiting the environmental impacts of what they take, but with regard to the relatively small areas they are willing to exclude from exploitation, Northern residents worry that the carving of parks and nature reserves out of nature, in the effort to shield fragments of the natural world as symbolic icons of the pristine, is in fact nothing other than a new form of colonization. It constitutes a domestication of lands which, as in so many previous cases, will lead to their commoditization as tourist goals. When forced to keep their traditional livelihoods operational at low-tech, low-income levels to avoid (purported) stress to the environment, indigenous peoples will come to sustain their societies increasingly through external subsidies in return for their environmental compliance. In effect, maintenance of both landscape cognitive continuity (and spirituality) and also a legal right based on the continuity of usage becomes commoditized through state support (perhaps in time international support, for example, by "elevating" indigenous residents to the status of World Heritage Site "Rangers"). Just what it is that constitutes a subsidy, what is actually subsidized, and who the recipients of such subsidies should be, are elusive, as they are grounded in our perceptions of what we consider to be nature's norm, or the way things have the right to be.

What can be termed here as a domestication of a wilderness with respect to land is precisely analogous to the domestication of "wild" animals like the wolf when, as mentioned above, their every movement, their reproduction, and survival, become matters of human legislation. In fact, so stubborn is the essentialist, self-contained perception of wolves as wild, that when Sámi herders are forced to feed them reindeer without interference, the compensation provided the herders for their lost reindeer is often conceived of as a subsidy to reindeer herding. More logical would be to class it as a subsidy to wolf herding (Beach 2004), for under Swedish wolf governance, the destruction they cause is no longer an uncontrollable act of nature, but a consequence of human legal construction. The wolf may be unaware of his domestication by such process, just as parklands might be conceived of as unaltered in their pristine nature by the regulations that enclose them, but in fact, both have been changed to their core and, in a sense, domesticated.

My general point is that in order to understand the determinants which influence a herder's knowledge, desire, and practical ability to implement any given form of livelihood, one must grasp his or her situation in a broad social context, encompassing not only the given family's own economy, but also the economic situation of one's herding partners, the economy of the sameby (a Sámi social and territorial grazing unit) in question as well as the relative labor capacities of these units. The combined determinants of herding law, taxation policy, predator policy, and other regulatory constraints on the one hand, combined with the possibilities occasioned by such things as new technological developments and government catastrophe aid for starving reindeer on the other, shape the variable responses of herders when it comes to labor investment and animal-handling techniques. For example, among the Swedish samebys, there is a wide variety of methods to drive reindeer, and even within a single sameby different herders hold widely different philosophies about what is stressful for the animals. On the collective sameby level, the gradually advancing implementation of the wage system funded by membership herding fees has resulted in greater labor efficiency, but also altered settlement patterns and, on occasion, increased herding extensivity (meaning less control over and contact with the reindeer), loss of skills, and reduced internal sameby solidarity. We have at hand discourses of indigenous rights, welfare policies, environmental sustainability, biodiversity, collective labor solidarity, rationalization for increased efficiency, maintenance of traditional skills, and humane animal care. In comparison to these discourses, awareness of rapid climatic change has been sudden and by its nature globally compelling. Not only will rapid climatic change itself alter the physical living situation of Northern indigenous peoples, but its power as discourse integrates in various ways with the delicate alliances and contentions which constantly develop among the major discourses noted above.

For example, despite obvious differences, there are also close parallels between what happened in Sweden following upon the Chernobyl disaster of 1986 and what we encounter today with rapid climatic change. While both are very real, they are also subject to dramatically variable *perceptions* and *interpretations* making politics out of what is to be considered nature or natural enough. Swedish Sámi herders might never have known about the effects of Chernobyl, or been made to feel them, had it not been for the scientists who informed them, tested their reindeer meat and read values off of strange instruments. In the first slaughter season after Chernobyl, reindeer meat was to be confiscated in Sweden if it held cesium-137 at a concentration above 300 Bq/kg, while in Norway at the same time the confiscation threshold value was 6000 Bq/kg. What does either value really mean with respect to human health? The following year, Sweden raised the marketability level of reindeer meat to 1500 Bq/kg. Herders who had meat in the freezer from the slaughter season before Chernobyl submitted that for testing too and found that it was already above the 300 Bq/kg limit due to the atmospheric nuclear bomb tests in the Soviet Union during the 1950s (Beach 1990). How long had global warming been going on before we became (at least somewhat) aware of its impact? Where should we position the thermostat of our worries?

Climate change will bring new pressures to bear on the relationships between ethnic groups, their forms of land-use, and what the majority ambient population is willing to accept as "traditional" and thereby warranting special rights. Are indigenous peoples to become barred from access to their traditional resources and land "privileges" because climate change forces them to alter livelihood? Key to this moral discourse on land-use is the variable interpretation of Sámi immemorial right. Do Sámi have an immemorial right to herd because their ancestors herded on the land, and an immemorial right to fish in a specific lake because their ancestors fished there (the Swedish model)? Or is it not a generalized right to use the land used by one's ancestors as one pleases, with the same ability to be entirely flexible as they had been? (This latter interpretation has been applied by the Norwegian court in the Black Forest case.) Exactly how and to what extent the Sámi have used the land are issues raised during the famous Taxed Mountain case in Sweden (Supreme Court verdict 1981), and they have only gained in importance with a rash of new court cases contesting immemorial right.

The increasing scope of human power, heated by population growth and rapid technological change – occurring at a rate far faster than that of rapid climatic change – gives humankind the *potential* to do more than ever before to the environment even if it chooses not to. Regardless of whether or not this power is actually exercised in fact, even if it *is* exercised to *remove* specific regions from forms of human influence (for example, by the creation of parks, nature reserves, or World Heritage Sites), nonetheless it signifies a form of human colonization of the world. The condition of the world becomes increasingly a matter governed by the exercise of *human choice*. Even when the choice taken is one for environmental preservation, either with a "hands off" policy (forcibly removing people from their homelands) or all the more with policies of active repair, wilderness becomes tamed. It becomes *our* nature preserve, *our* environment. Ironically, the very struggle by which we attempt to preserve our environment and maintain sustainable systems envelope the world in yet further forms of control and modern forms of colonization. Perhaps the best we can do for the world is nothing different from what we can do for ourselves as individuals. We must accept our certain demise, someday, but with neither despondent resignation nor with manic environmental restorative fanaticism. Instead, we must first learn to appreciate our world as it is today and can become, even with the demise of our species tomorrow.

The perspective captured in the photograph of the earth, the Blue Planet, from a manned vehicle in orbit in outer space has been regarded as the starting shot of the global environmental movement. A necessary companion of this photo and the environmental movement it has fostered is carried in the positioned perspective of the photographer who took it. In a sense, it is the culmination of humankind's evolutionary path, which, once put in orbit, embodies significance no less profound than the Copernican Revolution. While we have known forever that the fate of humankind is in the hands of the World, we now perceive that the fate of the world is in *our* hands. Both perspectives are inadequate. Without the humility to match the hubris inspired by technological feats such as human planetary orbit, this "new" perspective, new in evolutionary time, can become the ticket to ultimate colonization and the destruction of both ourselves and the environment. Still, the end of humankind is decidedly not the end of the World, and there could be no more exciting challenge to the evolution of life forms and the Whole in which they are embedded than if humans could come to exercise the self-control and the wisdom necessary to live on.

NOTES

1 Some of the thoughts presented here have developed from the remarks I made at the IPY meeting in Oslo, 2010 and recently published in the newsletter of the Arctic Studies Center, Smithsonian Institute under the title "When Push Comes to Shove: The Political and Moral Discourse of Rapid Climate Change."

REFERENCES

Beach, H.

1983 A Swedish Dilemma: Saami Rights and the Welfare State. Production Pastorale et Société 12:9–17.

1990 Perceptions of Risk, Dilemmas of Policy: Nuclear Fallout in Swedish Lapland. Social Science and Medicine 30(6):729–738.

1997 Negotiating Nature in Swedish Lapland: Ecology and Economics of Saami Reindeer Management. *In* Contested Arctic: Indigenous Peoples, Industrial States, and the Circumpolar Environment. E. Smith, ed. pp. 122–149. Seattle: University of Washington Press.

2004 Political Ecology in Swedish Saamiland. *In* Cultivating Arctic Landscapes: Knowing and Managing Animals in the Circumpolar North. D. Anderson and M. Nuttall, eds. pp. 110–123. Oxford: Berghahn.

2007 Self-determining the Self: Aspects of Saami Identity Management in Sweden. Acta Borealia 24(1):1–25.

Beach, H., and F. Stammler

2006 Human–Animal Relations in Pastoralism. *In* Humans and Reindeer on the Move. F. Stammler and H. Beach, eds. Theme issue. Nomadic Peoples 10(2):6–30.

Beach, H., Funk, D., and L. Sillanpää, eds

2009 Post-Soviet Transformations: Politics of Ethnicity and Resource Use in Russia. Acta Universitatis Upsaliensis (Uppsala Studies in Cultural Anthropology) vol. 46. Uppsala: University of Uppsala.

Broadbent, N., and P. Lantto

2009 Terms of Engagement: An Arctic Perspective on the Narratives and Politics of Global Climate Change. *In* Anthropology and Climate Change: from Encounters to Actions. S. Crate and M. Nuttall, eds. pp. 341–355. Walnut Creek, CA: Left Coast Press.

Csonka, Y., and P. Schweitzer

2004 Societies and Cultures: Change and Persistence. *In* AHDR (Arctic Human Development Report) pp. 45–68. Akureyri, Iceland: Stefansson Arctic Institute.

Donahoe, B., J. Habeck, A. Halemba, and I. Santha

2008 Size and Place in the Construction of Indigeneity in the Russian Federation. Current Anthropology 49(6):993–1020.

Einarsson, N.

2011 Culture, Conflict and Crises in the Icelandic Fisheries: An Anthropological Study of People, Policy and Marine Resources in the North Atlantic Arctic. Acta Universitatis Upsaliensis (Uppsala Studies in Cultural Anthropology), 48. Uppsala: University of Uppsala.

Ingold, T.

1980 Hunters, Pastoralists and Ranchers. Cambridge: Cambridge University Press.

Krupnik, I., and D. Jolly

2002 The Earth is Faster Now: Indigenous Observations of Arctic Environmental Change. Fairbanks, AL: Arctic Research Consortium of the United States.

Kuper, A.

2003 The Return of the Native. Current Anthropology 44(3):389–395; with comments pp. 395–402; and further discussion Current Anthropology 45(2):261–267.

Nuttall, M.

2009 Living in a World of Movement: Human Resilience to Environmental Instability in Greenland. *In* Anthropology and Climate Change: from encounters to actions. S. Crate and M. Nuttall, eds. pp. 292–310. Walnut Creek, CA: Left Coast Press.

Paine, R.

1971 Animals as Capital: Comparisons among Northern Nomadic Herders and Hunters. Anthropological Quarterly 44:157–172.

CHAPTER 4

Multiculturalism in North America and Europe

Reginald Byron

> Between the politics of recognition and the politics of compulsion, there is no bright line.
>
> (Appiah 1994)

> the logic of the war of recognition presses the combatants to absolutize the difference: it is difficult to eradicate the "fundamentalist" streak in any claim that makes recognition demands . . .
>
> (Bauman 2001)

Twenty years ago, it was apparent that the scale of immigration into Europe from non-European countries was becoming a phenomenon of a new order. Developments in North America current at that time provided intellectual inspiration in a number of European countries including the United Kingdom, Germany, the Netherlands, Denmark, and Sweden. Assimilationism, the ideology blind to cultural difference that had until then predominated, was coming to be regarded as illiberal and outmoded; the new thinking, influenced by civil rights legislation in the United States and the French-language question in Canada, favored multiculturalism, a political philosophy whose buzzwords were "culture," "ethnicity," and "identity." These three words have long histories in the social sciences, far antedating the rise of popular ideas and public discussion about multiculturalism and the political programs in which these words also figured, and still figure, so prominently today. In this chapter, I ask how these words are used in this discourse, how their meanings differ from our social scientific understandings of them, and whether multiculturalism – as it has played out in practice in North America and in those European countries that have been influenced by North American ideas about it – has proved as benign and liberating as it promised to be 20 years ago.

A Companion to the Anthropology of Europe, First Edition. Edited by Ullrich Kockel, Máiréad Nic Craith, and Jonas Frykman.

I

My current field research is in the United States, among the descendants of nineteenth-century European immigrants. My particular interest is in people of Irish ancestry, and how – nowadays – they see themselves. I am myself an American more or less, having spent the first 25 years of my life in that country, and being myself the descendant of immigrants from Europe. Although I have now spent well over half of my life living on the European side of the Atlantic, my background is otherwise very much like those of the people among whom I have been working for the last twenty years. Like most of my informants, as indeed like nearly all Americans whose ancestors were nineteenth-century immigrants, I have a mixed pedigree. I have English, Scottish, and German ancestors. I suppose you could say that I am a living example of multiculturalism, as are tens of millions of other Americans of mixed ancestry, most of whom have pedigrees that are more mixed than mine.

Having mixed ancestries like this is the result of a particular set of social conditions: these conditions brought about the decline and disappearance of cultural differences between people that were once quite distinct. My immigrant ancestors spoke different languages and professed different religions. The weakening of such cultural differences over time is both the precondition for, and consequence of, the kind of intermingling and intermarriage that results in mixed-ancestry individuals like me. This is, however, not what multiculturalism is about or what it has become, at least in the United States.

An illustration of what it does concern comes from a newspaper story that appeared in February 1996 in the place in New York State where I do my fieldwork. This was a report about a bill sponsored by Irish-American ethnic activists that was being put to the state legislature. The bill, if passed, would make it a state law that children in New York's schools be taught that the Great Famine in Ireland was a crime against humanity of the same order as the enslavement of Africans and the Jewish Holocaust, with which it would be bracketed in school curricula on human rights issues.[1] They were to be taught that mass starvation was deliberately planned by the British government to rid the country of indigent Catholics, and that this was the main cause of emigration from Ireland to the United States in the nineteenth century. The bill was a clear attempt to use the law to make official and legally binding the view that Irish people were involuntary migrants, by nature attached to their nation of birth, and to the religion and culture handed down to them by their forefathers – things held to be deeply rooted, authentic, and morally satisfying, things that they would never have abandoned unless forced to do so by political oppression.

Analytically, there are a number of points that one might tease out of this example. I shall mention six. The first is that there was no grass-roots movement behind this bill; it was not the result of popular demand (nor even – as far as I can tell, based on the research I have done with several hundred Americans of Irish ancestry – are these the views a reflection of majority opinion within this category of people). The second point, therefore, is that the main protagonists are not the people themselves, but elites who claim to speak for them, and presume to educate them as to who they are and what they ought to believe. The third point to note is the attempt by these protagonists to use the legal system to transform a vague category of people into an officially recognized group having a set of defining attributes or properties. The fourth concerns the nature of these properties: common descent and a common religion (the two are tied together), and a narrative about historical injustice. The fifth is the circular nature of the proposition: we are a group because of our common descent and historical experience, and because of that descent and historical experience we are a group. The sixth concerns the field or platform upon which this claim to recognition is made: an obviously political one, involving the state legislature and educational institutions (in this case, every school in the State of New York).

By October 1996, the newspapers were quoting the following press release:

> Governor George E. Pataki today signed into law legislation that requires the state Board of Regents to devote particular attention to the study of mass starvation in Ireland from 1845 to 1850 when establishing mandatory courses of instruction in human rights issues.
>
> "History teaches us the Great Irish Hunger was not the result of a massive failure of the Irish potato crop but rather was the result of a deliberate campaign by the British to deny the Irish people the food they needed to survive," Governor Pataki said.
>
> "More than one million men, women and children died as a result of this mass starvation, and millions more were forced to flee their native land to avoid certain death, while large quantities of grain and livestock were exported from Ireland to England," the Governor said. "This tragic event had dramatic implications on the United States, where millions of Irish immigrants had significant impacts on every facet of American life and culture."
>
> The legislation adds the study of the mass starvation to existing law that requires the Board of Regents to prescribe courses of instruction in patriotism, citizenship and human rights issues, with particular attention to be devoted to the study of genocide, slavery and the Holocaust. The law takes effect immediately. (Office of the Governor, Press release, October 9, 1996)

We might note here that although Governor Pataki did not actually say that the Great Famine was an act of genocide, the word "genocide" is mentioned in this press release along with the words "slavery" and "Holocaust," inviting his readers and listeners to make the connections themselves. The responsibility for this tragic event is, however, made perfectly explicit: it was, he says, "the result of a deliberate campaign by the British." Anyone familiar with the history of Irish nationalism will recognize in Governor Pataki's statement echoes of the rhetoric used by John Mitchel (1815–1875), the radical Young Irelander who, following his emigration to the United States, sought to mobilize American support for Irish independence and is famously quoted as having said "The Almighty, indeed, sent the potato blight, but the English created the Famine" (see, e.g., Miller 1985:306).[2]

Governor Pataki's words are even more exaggerated, flatly – and quite breathtakingly – denying that a potato blight was to blame (saying that it "was not the result of a massive failure of the Irish potato crop"), thus implying that the Famine was a calculated act of malign human intention, leaving no room for bad luck, plant pathology, or the Almighty. In other words – although he was careful not to use them – this was a case of expulsion and mass murder, comparable to the Jewish Diaspora and the Holocaust. A century of Irish historical scholarship has had rather different things to say about the causes and consequences of the Famine, overwhelmingly holding it to be a natural disaster of unprecedented magnitude, not a man-made one, although it is generally agreed that its effects were exacerbated by unpreparedness, ineptitude, mistakes, misunderstandings, ignorance, and confusion at all levels of government in Ireland and Britain, along with some policy responses by parliamentarians in London that seemed harsh and wrong-headed even by the rather less humanitarian moral standards prevailing in the Western world at that time (see Byron 1999 for references). Yet had this disaster, under all the same objective conditions, happened in the United States rather than in Ireland, it is open to question whether the public authorities of the day would have been any better able to deal with it, or any more generous or consistent in their policy responses.

The bill was designed to appeal to a narrow, carefully chosen audience. This was not the public at large, for the bill was never put to a popular vote (as through a referendum or a party manifesto proposal), but rather the intended audience was the State Assembly itself, many of whose members were of Irish ancestry or had large numbers of Irish-ancestry electors in their constituencies, and New York State has the greatest number of Irish-ancestry electors in America. Remarkably, the bill was passed within *three hours* of its presentation in the legislative schedule: this was highly expeditious. It was not referred to a committee; there were no public hearings, and there was no opportunity for international and scholarly opinion to be heard by the legislators. Thus an ideological position taken by militant ethnic activists – supported by little or no academically respectable evidence, with scarcely any debate, and without a direct public mandate of any kind – became the sole officially recognized version of Irish history to be taught in the State of New York.

The bill was quickly passed into law by the Governor, who put his own populist interpretation on the significance of the new law in the press release quoted above. Only then, after the bill had passed into law, was there much public discussion of the matter. A number of high-profile objections to Governor Pataki's statement appeared in the press in October 1996 (see Archdeacon 2002 for details), pointing out that this was not what historians in Ireland have had to say about their own history. These objections were casually swept aside. It was too late anyway, and in any case by then the issue was not about truth or historical accuracy – if, indeed, it had ever been – but about votes.

II

The origin of multiculturalism as it has developed in the United States lies in the civil rights movements of the 1950s and 1960s, which attempted to correct the historical wrongs suffered by Americans of African ancestry by recognizing them as a category of people deserving of restorative justice. No one would dispute the moral rectitude of this. Yet, as has been observed: "Once [officially recognized] minority status has been granted to a group, there is an inherent likelihood of proliferation. The recognition of a minority group divides the world into three segments: majority, recognized minorities, and not-yet-minorities" (Joppke and Lukes 1999:12).

In other words, the politics of multiculturalism encourages competition between ethnies or would-be ethnies. In practice, in the United States, those who have been able to sustain their claims to have endured the most suffering and injustice through their ethnic advocates have won the contests for recognition. The success of these claims has not been lost on all those other interested parties seeking to advance their interests or even just to avoid losing ground relative to the rest. There are political goods to be won for being a wronged and exploited minority, but none for being part of the comfortable, middle-class majority. Political expediency thus influences what kinds of stories come to fill the spaces within the ethnic boundaries (Byron 1999:291; cf. Turner 1993).

And, as we see in my example, even the advocates of people of Irish descent have joined in, despite their being– along with the people of English and German ancestry with whom they have freely intermarried for more than a century – by a wide margin the most highly educated, prosperous, assimilated, and middle-class people in America.[3] Nonetheless, some Irish-American ethnic activists seem to have felt the need to make the same kinds of claims of historical victimhood in order – one surmises – to distance themselves from the suspicion that the people for whom they presume to speak might have been (and still be) part of the oppressive middle-American majority that was, and is, complicit in keeping others in their places, such as, notably, Native American Indians, Blacks, Jews, Chinese, Italians, Poles, Muslims, Hispanics, women, and gays, all of whom, at one or another place and historical moment have suffered maltreatment at the hands of "the Irish" – and even suffered attempted genocide, if the efforts of a considerable number of Irish-born, Catholic young men who volunteered for duty in the US Army cavalry in the latter part of the nineteenth century to "pacify" the native peoples of the American West are included.[4]

In the United States, and increasingly in Europe, multiculturalism has come to be generally accepted as a kind of diffuse, positive moral principle. Most people think it is a good thing to recognize people's cultural differences, and that these differences should in some way be respected. This much, at least, seems uncontentious. Yet, at the same time, the idea continues to provoke heated debate, and the terms used in this debate are often difficult, complex, and ambiguous (see, e.g., Kuper 1999 and Watson 2000 for British anthropological views on the usages of "culture" in this debate). There seem to be two main dimensions of this debate: first, philosophical arguments about particularism versus universalism and the rights of the individual versus those of the group (see especially Taylor 1994); and second, more practical and pragmatic arguments about which groups are deserving of recognition in what ways, and how multicultural policy works, or should work (e.g. Baumann 1996).

The reason for some of this confusion must surely lie in the tension between *phenotype* (or "race") and *culture*. In American interpretations of multiculturalism (which have been exported to Europe and elsewhere through the dominance, on this topic, of American opinion, both scholarly and popular) the word "culture" is prominently implicated in the term "multiculturalism," but the first successful case of recognition, that of African Americans, concerned a phenotypical difference, not a cultural one, as have other successful cases since then. This is a point to which we shall return later in this chapter. However, multiculturalism is not just a matter of these ambiguities, tensions, and unresolved arguments. In one way or another, normally by means of piecemeal affirmative action, antidiscrimination, and equal opportunities legislation, it is already legally established in many countries; if not in name as multiculturalism (as in Canada), then – in variable degrees – in effect.

And, because multiculturalism is at a certain level popularly accepted as a positive moral principle (confused and ill-defined as it may be) it has also become an everyday practice. There are many thousands of people involved in the practice of multiculturalism in these countries: in education, in employment policy and administration, in social welfare, and in the justice system; and there are also the media, all trying hard to put some sort of multicultural ethos into practice. Those groups who have achieved recognition as minorities, or are attempting to do so, or have been identified by others as potential groups of a recognizable kind, may of course have their own advocates, spokespersons, or friends at court. Some of the words used in these discourses about multiculturalism, and everyday multicultural practice, such as "culture," "ethnicity," and "identity," are ubiquitous and figure in almost every argument about multiculturalism, or discussion about multicultural practice. They are used by hundreds of thousands of people, and are drawn from same lexicon as anthropology draws its terms, but their meaning can be very different. What I am going to argue is that, in popular, and some scholarly, discourses, these words and concepts may be – and frequently are – used in ways that may be completely incompatible with our anthropological understandings of them. I am going to focus on three interrelated problems: ethnocentrism, essentialism, and primordialism.

III

Ethnocentrism

In the scientific tradition in which I was trained, lesson number one is the idea that while it is a common human propensity to see the world through the medium of your own culture, and to judge other people by your own moral standards, as anthropologists we try not to do this. We adopt a position of cultural and ethical relativism. We accept that other people – or peoples – have different ways of seeing the world, and that it is worth making the effort to understand how they do so. Only then can we begin to appreciate why they think and behave as they do. This relativistic approach is an ideal that is not always easy to live up to in practice because we are just as much creatures of culture as anyone else, and it is often difficult to avoid making moral judgments about the things we witness. Nonetheless, a commitment to cultural relativism and ethical neutrality are among the fundamental precepts of social anthropology, and they are also among the main things that define the discipline.

Ethnocentrism is not just judging others by the standards of "the majority," as is often thought by the proponents and practitioners of multiculturalism. Anyone, anywhere, can be ethnocentric. Ethnocentrism, in its most stripped-down form, is to privilege any cultural belief, or practice, over another. What is implicit here is the likelihood that this will also involve a value-judgment or a moral position: if something has been privileged, it is probably because the speaker feels that one cultural belief, or practice, is better or worse, more true or false, or more or less authentic and worthy of our attention and respect.

In an effort to distance themselves from their own perceived propensity to be ethnocentric – of which they are keenly aware – the proponents and practitioners of multiculturalism are, all too often, prepared to accept at face value what people of other cultural backgrounds say about themselves, and to privilege these others' understandings over their own; or to accept at face value what people who themselves are not of the cultural background in question but who nonetheless presume to "speak for" or "interpret" such a "culture" say about it. To my mind, this is a sort of half-baked understanding of cultural relativism. If the matter of "culture" is approached with the idea that all our ideas and observations about others are false, and these others' accounts are true, we are headed for trouble, and bound to make matters worse rather than better. This is because, in so doing, we are not attempting to negotiate some common ground of mutual understanding, but simply exchanging our subjectivities for their subjectivities (or what we, or their "interpreters," imagine their subjectivities to be).

The principle of cultural relativism demands that all viewpoints be accorded equal weight, and that we do not judge some of them – our own, for example – to be less true or morally less worthy, and other viewpoints – theirs, or purportedly theirs – as more true and morally more worthy. We are entitled to have a view of ourselves as well as them and what they do, just as they are entitled to have a view of us and what we do, as well as of themselves. As social scientists we have an obligation to accord equal weight to both parties' points of view, and to be equally skeptical and enquiring of both. Genuinely relativistic and objective approaches to questions of ethnicity, culture, and identity recognize that ignorance and self-interest, or prejudice and racism, can – and do – work *both* ways.

Essentialism

Essentialism has to do with the essence of things; their fundamental nature. Just as it is a common human propensity to see the world through one's own cultural lenses – something that we, as anthropologists, try to avoid – it is also a common human propensity to see the world in terms of categories and meanings. We tend to divide up and classify our cognitive and material worlds into manageable bits and pieces, and to imbue these bits with certain characteristics by which we can recognize them and think and act in appropriate ways. Among the things in our material and cognitive worlds which we classify and attribute typical or essential characteristics are other people: men and women, us and them, people like us and people not like us. There is nothing wrong with this: all of us do this, all the time. It is the way our brains are programmed. It is called analogical thinking. It is what makes our kind of languages possible, and distinguishes us from other primates.

When psychologists use the term "identity," or Anglo-American sociologists speak of "ethnicity," or French historians describe "mentalities," or ethnologists and anthropologists talk about "culture," what they have in mind are limited general statements based upon bodies of empirical evidence which have been, or are capable of being validated through the accepted scientific procedures of the discipline. When we hear politicians, journalists, ethnic spokespersons, and militant multiculturalists use these words, however, they can mean anything the speaker wants them to mean. Sometimes they are used in ways that are beyond time and space. They assert that the real essence of being, for example, Irish, is to have inherited and unconsciously to embody the true spirit of Celticness. If something is beyond time and space, like a transcendent "true spirit of Celticness," of which its human embodiments are not conscious and so are unable to talk about to us, it is highly unlikely to be capable of testing or validation by means of our normal scientific procedures. What would count as empirical evidence? How would we collect it? Who would we talk to, or what would we measure? Such an assertion is simply a statement of someone's belief, and no more; in turn, it demands *your* belief: it has to be taken on trust, or not, according to your inclinations.

The absence of any verifiable or independent evidence that is congenial to the position they wish to take frequently tempts multiculturalists to accept, as substitutes, the assertions of persons who are not social scientists – so-called ethnic experts or spokespersons, who may be anything from footballers to poets to theologians, to say nothing of those who take it upon themselves explicitly to advocate the political interests of "their" group, or that of another set of people for whom they presume to speak. The claims made by these persons about the existence and qualities of the cultural attributes that are supposed to characterize the group are more often based upon personal anecdote; interpretations of historical, theological, or literary sources; or idealized or wished-for states of affairs, than upon anything resembling representative, academically respectable evidence. And, the idea that these qualities – so asserted – can then be said to inform the identities of the individual members of that group is simply accepted without any additional justification as a self-evident corollary of the previous statement: that this further claim is a reification, unsupported by any sort of evidence pertaining to these individuals' actual identity-choices, is unnoticed or conveniently ignored.

The authors of such claims do not normally stop here, however, but go on to make *normative prescriptions*: that is, to make ethical or moral statements about what the people of a certain category ought to believe about themselves, and how they ought to behave in respect of these beliefs. Persons of the category who do not believe these things, or behave in these ways, are not "proper" members of the category: they are ignorant of the "true" meaning of their culture, and have to be educated; or they are revisionists, heretics, or traitors who have to be denounced, disciplined, or excluded. We should note well that the strategic deployment of essentialisms is a highly effective tool in the creation of moral solidarities. Their use is frequently quite deliberate.

Orthodoxies and fundamentalisms – in various kinds and degrees – seem to be the consequence of this procedure, depending upon how far it is taken. The words "orthodoxy" and "fundamentalism" are, of course, associated most closely with theological ideologies and their corresponding social movements. There would seem to be close parallels with ethnic ideologies and their corresponding social movements. One could call certain kinds of ethnic representations secular theologies, if they are concerned (as most of them are) with the true, transcendent essence of being, believing, and behaving; in other words, they are concerned not merely with *describing difference*, but with *prescribing moral values.* In this multicultural world, in which spokespersons for ethnic interests jostle and compete for attention, it is not enough simply to say – for example – that most Irish and Welsh people speak the same language and except for a few small details have pretty much the same ways of life as people in England; there must also be a narrative about what Irishness or Welshness *means*, a narrative that is bound to involve judgments about the rights and wrongs of history; things that can be construed as making Irish or Welsh people different, in a moral sense, from the English.

PRIMORDIALISM

> Ethnic identity and its practical upshot, ethnopolitics, base their authority on bonds of blood and descent, and even the bonds of language and culture are treated as if they were natural facts. . . . Far from being a natural identity, ethnicity is a carefully cultivated, and not seldom a manipulated, strategy of social action led by unelected elites who often exploit or mislead their supposed beneficiaries. (Baumann 1999:136–137)

For our purpose, primordialism may be defined as the intellectual position which asserts that ethnic identity is a more-or-less immutable – permanent and unchangeable – aspect of the person. Lesson two of the kind of anthropology that I was taught as a first-year undergraduate was contained within the words of Edward Burnett Tylor's definition of culture, written in 1871, that culture is "learned by man as a member of society." That is, culture is a matter of social propinquity: one grows up to speak, think, and behave like the people who are nearest to you, and with whom you have the most social traffic. Thus "culture" is a phenomenon of society, and not of nature. One does not inherit culture genetically. One acquires it environmentally. How one becomes cultured, and what one become cultured as, is a matter of one's socialization and immediate social environment. There is nothing here about deep or true essences, or inheritance, or genetics.

Primordialism, however, frequently takes the form of asserting that culture is mainly a matter of nature – of "blood," parentage, or inherited essence – rather than of social learning. If, say, your parents are Ethiopians, someone taking a primordialist position would claim that you have acquired or inherited the deep essence of Ethiopianness, even though you might have been adopted as an infant by Danes and brought up in Denmark only among Danes. A primordialist interpretation would say that you still embody this essence of Ethiopianness, which is buried deep within you, and which defines your "real" or "true" identity: an identity that it is "unnatural" for you to deny. You will find yourself classified and treated by people holding these views as "really" an Ethiopian, and "not really" a Dane. Since you look physically different from most Danes, the attribution of Ethiopianness to you may well be a form of racism (even otherwise well-intentioned middle-class people often assume that someone who looks different must be culturally different, if not on the surface then somewhere deep down in their psyche).

This form of primordialism merges and confounds questions of genetics with questions of culture. It relies on myths and folk theories of blood and essence that do not distinguish between inherited physical characteristics (e.g. phenotypes) and cultural characteristics transmitted through socialization (e.g. language and religion). The ethos of multiculturalism has revitalized and given new veneer of legitimacy to these folk theories of blood and essence, because they usefully reinforce difference, and difference is what multicultural politics are about. Let me say that again: multicultural politics are concerned with establishing and emphasizing difference: things that make the group uniquely recognizable and distinct from all others. This is the vital principle.

It is significant here that multiculturalism in the United States was founded upon a phenotypic distinction (Black African), not a cultural one, and the monitoring of minorities under later American antidiscrimination legislation has been largely concerned with phenotypical categories – people who are visibly different from the White, Euro-American majority. The issue of phenotype established the paradigm case, the standard criterion of difference against which all subsequent claims to recognition have been judged, not only in the United States but also in other countries that have been influenced by American ideas and practices. Nowadays, no group can enter the political arena, or hope to achieve public recognition, unless its advocates can persuade journalists, educators, legislators, and the public at large that it is different in some quite distinctive and demonstrable ways from other groups, and that at least some of these differences are – or can be treated as if they were – of a genetic kind: that is, that they can be asserted to be involuntarily and permanently embodied, implanted through inheritance in one's persona, if not actually in one's phenotype.

As social scientists, we know that languages, religious practices, and social customs are contingent phenomena *par excellence*: they are matters of social environment and learned behavior that are highly variable from one individual to another, and change over time in response to a whole range of conditions. For generations, we have been pointing this out. We have emphasized that culture changes over time, and how it changes is a matter of its contexts. Where contexts change, cultural practices can be expected to change along with them. Yet, contrarily, multiculturalist spokespersons routinely respond to any criticism of a cultural practice that is unpalatable to the majority (e.g. the mutilation of children's genitals, slavery, the sequestration of women, kidnapping and forced marriage, the public utterance of death-threats, sororicide and filicide: all of which can be found as traditional practices among some groups of recent immigrants to Great Britain) by tactically invoking the most powerful rhetoric available to them: that of "race." In doing so they are blurring the distinction between immigrants' non-European origins on the one hand (which are unlikely to be the source of much British disquiet), and, on the other hand, some of their old-country social customs (murder and kidnap, among them), which certainly *are* matters of widespread public concern, directly challenging the modern nation-state's constitutional responsibility to safeguard the lives and liberties of its citizens, whoever they might be.

That social phenomena are normally matters of degree and contingency is soon ignored, once the debate heats up. In Britain, ethnic activists and "anti-racist" spokespersons regard questions about the compatibility of some new-immigrant cultural practices with the predominant values of contemporary British society not as matters of public interest in which it might be possible to explore questions of degree and contingency, but as evidence of "race hate." Since "race" is about phenotype, not culture, this kind of exaggerated defensive reaction is, in effect, to claim that people are born with sets of genes that involuntarily make them God-fearing Pentecostalists, wife-beaters, vegetarians, or Francophones. Taken literally, as they are often meant to be, such claims are preposterous, by turns comical in their naive sanctimoniousness and dispiriting in their willful obscurantism, yet many people – including those in the spheres of educational and community-relations policy, who ought to be more critical – have come to believe that they must not dismiss or question these claims, however silly or pernicious; it is too risky: they are afraid that they might, themselves, be branded as racists. So, British schoolteachers, aware that eleven- or twelve-year-old girls are being abducted by their families and taken to Somalia to be forcibly subjected to clitoral amputation and infibulation, or to Bangladesh to be sold into rural servitude, say nothing.

To complicate things even more, "ethnic" is often used nowadays as a euphemism for "race." People in the Anglophone world have come to think that the word "race" is impolite, insulting, and scientifically inappropriate. "Ethnic" refers to *ethnos*, to a people having common kinship and common customs – in other words, to both biology *and* culture. To use it to refer mainly to physical differences encourages the belief that culture is an emergent or secondary property of genotype (that is, that you have "a culture" by virtue of your parentage, or that your culture is an inseparable part of your ancestral inheritance). This thoroughly muddles two quite separate things, confounding what is genetically inherited with what is not. Again, emphatically, human beings are not "born with" any particular culture, language, or religion: they are socialized into ways of thinking, speaking, believing, and behaving by the people around them.

Inevitably, it seems, the politics of multiculturalism encourages the absolutization and concretization of "culture," or at least those cultural attributes that are held to be the vital stigmata of difference. In order that it may be recognized at all, each group must have a set of essential characteristics that makes it distinguishable from others and which defines its boundaries. These stigmata have a marked tendency to become irreducible, fixed, and sacralized. They must not change, except to become purer, more clearly defined, and more universally inculcated and displayed. The continued maintenance of these characteristics becomes a crucial matter, at least to the elites who purport to represent the group and to educate its members about who they are and what they ought to believe. These characteristics must be made as permanent and transcendent as possible, by whatever means can be devised. Subjecting them to any sort of objective scrutiny comes to be regarded as a kind of blasphemy. If the cultural stigmata melt away over time, through individuals choosing to believe and behave as they choose, or as they may, the integrity of the group will dissipate and its recognizability will eventually disappear. The insistent assertion that people are born into, or born with, "a culture" attempts to transform things that are contingent matters of sociality into things that are determinate matters of genetics, fixed forever by biology. Rhetorical and symbolic devices that treat "race" and "culture" as inseparable are, thus, highly effective tools in the hands of people who have a material or political interest in policing the boundaries, keeping insiders in and outsiders out.

Gatekeeping of this kind, which relies among other things upon specious claims that one's culture is inseparable from one's genetic inheritance, hinders the discussion and negotiation of things that ought to be discussed and negotiated in an open and liberal democracy like Britain, a country that values the integrity and capacity for self-actualization of the individual. It promotes a kind of apartheid in which some people (the "nonethnics") may have the freedom to choose how to dress, who to marry, or what to believe, and others (the "ethnics") – since they are expected to have, by virtue of their origins, "their own culture" – may not. For instance, young British-born and British-educated women of immigrant parentage are still coerced into arranged marriages under threat of violence or death, a constraint upon individual liberty that is all but inconceivable among nonethnics. There is a real risk that, by failing to dispute primordialist claims, well-meaning people in positions of responsibility are inadvertently endorsing limits on other people's freedoms in the belief that they are protecting their rights to express their ancestral cultures, a belief frequently based upon nothing more than the gatekeepers' assurances that this is what the people in question would choose, and what is "natural" or "good" for them.

This future-world is already with us: Quebec's Law 101 states that Francophones and immigrants must bring up their children as French-speakers; neither the parents nor the children are given any choice.[5] Where people actually are given the choice, what they choose is not always what the proponents of multiculturalism would choose for them: in Oakland, California, Black parents concerned about their children's future employability rejected a proposal that their children should be taught in Black English dialect as the official language of instruction for Black children in the city's schools. In Britain, social workers and adoption agency officials (who themselves were mostly White), influenced by ideas about multiculturalism, routinely refused to place Black Afro-Caribbean children with White families on the grounds that the children would be denied their "natural" (i.e. biological) "culture" of Blackness and so would be confused about their "identity," a practice that was formally repudiated by the government's ministry for social affairs only when it came to public attention through the popular press.

In California, once again, Hispanic parents overturned a proposal by multiculturalist educators that their children should be taught mainly in Spanish rather than in English. In other states, however, children with Hispanic surnames are routinely placed in bilingual classes regardless of their fluency in either language or their parents' wishes. Some of these children are from monolingual English-speaking households. Nonetheless, Spanish is clearly perceived by their educators as these children's "natural" language, essential to their "identity" as Latinos or Latinas. Political decisions have been made that any child with a Hispanic surname ought to be treated as an ethnic Latin and inculcated with that which is deemed to be their birthright by those who have taken it upon themselves to define and police the Latinness of other people's children.

These things have happened and continue to happen because the well-meaning people who propose, legislate, and administer multicultural policies have allowed themselves to be persuaded by the ethnicists' insistent rhetorical claim that biology and culture are inseparable, at least as far as *other people* are concerned, and more particularly other *ethnic-type* people (who it is believed can be readily recognized and classified by their phenotypical features or, if not, by some convenient substitute like their surnames), while as individuals they themselves are well aware that having, say, blond hair, blue eyes, and an Americanized German surname passed down from their paternal grandfather, their other grandparents having been of English and Irish ancestry, does not make them ethnic Germans nor does it create an expectation among their social peers that they should speak German and take particular pleasure in a plate of pig's trotters and sauerkraut.

Looked at this way, multiculturalism is far from benign, and far from challenging the hegemony of the established elites: it is just another naive and crude means of stereotyping people – potentially (and actually) as pernicious and degrading as any other – and just another means of defining and reinforcing social and cultural hierarchies, with the difference that these crude distinctions are no longer merely the folk beliefs of people who are regarded as prejudiced, ignorant, and wrong-headed, but the gospel of people who regard themselves as enlightened, intelligent, and socially responsible and who have by virtue of their social positions the power to make *their* folk beliefs the policy of their local school board and the law of the land.

IV

The tragedy of multiculturalism, as a political phenomenon, has been to encourage the belief that cultural categorizations are "natural" (rather than merely social, or political), and that they are permanent (rather than context-dependent and subject to change). And that the world of people can be neatly divided up into such categories into which everyone can be fitted, ignoring people of mixed or indeterminate background, and disregarding the willingness of individuals to be classified, spoken for, and have their cultural loyalties put under surveillance and continually policed. Ethnic boundaries have been drawn where none existed previously, or have been reinforced: cultural differences have been politicized: sharpened up, and claims made about their essence, their immutability, and their power to define the "identity" of individual human beings. Ironically, the possibility that we might all become one big happy family of cultural mongrels recedes into the distance, instead of being brought closer to reality.

As one such cultural mongrel, I do not feel that I have been denied anything in not having a clear, singular sense of ethnic identity. In fact, I have a mixed set of cultural options that is unique to me and which I can exercise as I choose, or as I may. The idea that my psychic well-being demands that I embody only one true ethnic identity, and that this essence must be awakened within me so that I know who I really am and so can believe and behave appropriately, and so that other people can know what my identity is and what I signify, is an idea that I find deeply offensive. It is an idea inimical to my liberty and integrity as an individual. I might as well be obliged to wear a sign around my neck, or be forced to sew a yellow, blue, or green star on my sleeve.

No social scientist worth reading or quoting could possibly think in this way. Yet it is precisely this absurdly reductive idea that the proponents and practitioners of multiculturalism often succeed in turning into political and social reality, whether intentionally or not.

That we should all strive to get along with one another is an ideal to which all of us can subscribe, and to some extent the ethos of multiculturalism has had positive effects in encouraging us to be more tolerant and understanding of others. But we should be aware that some of the cultural politics that go on under the banner of multiculturalism, perversely, serve only to create, reinforce, and perpetuate ethnic sectarianism. These pressures come from the inside as well as from the outside: they are not always forced upon minorities by majorities; just as often they are forced on majorities by minorities, or their spokespersons.

Perhaps the greatest failing of multiculturalism has been the inability of its advocates and practitioners to distinguish between, on the one hand, the political ideology of assimilation (that is, the absorption of a minority into the majority), to which they are implacably opposed, and, on the other, the process of societal integration: the culturally unpredictable outcome of individuals freely choosing to marry one another over the generations. Culturally unpredictable it certainly is, since no one can predict whether a child of a Somalian and a Swede bought up in the Netherlands will choose to "be" Somalian, or Swedish, or Dutch, or all three, or two of them, or none; or vacillate between any of these "identities" or bits and pieces of them from situation to situation over the course of a lifetime. Should this child choose to marry a Dutch or Swedish person of similarly mixed ancestry it will no longer be a heterogenous marriage, but a homogenous one because the parties in question are no longer culturally dissimilar.

The outcome, and the measure, of societal integration – whether across socioeconomic, cultural, or racial boundaries – has always been, and forever more will be, intermarriage; and the rates at which individuals can, and do, choose to marry others of dissimilar background. Marriage is the truest test of the capacity of people to tune into each other's cultural wavelengths, and to accept one another in the most intimate, voluntary, long-term relationships. It is the fundamental social mechanism of societal integration. Without it, societal integration does not and cannot happen.

In a free and open society, without politically defined and actively managed cultural boundaries, one would expect to see, over the generations, as an effect of social mixing, a regression to the mean. That is, all else equal, over time the statistical outliers tend to become less extreme, and eventually lose their salience. Cultural differences become less marked, and over time matter less and less in the choice of a marriage partner until the statistical salients between them have disappeared completely, as they have now between Protestants, Catholics, and Jews in the United States. This is a long-term outcome of social mixing; it took four or five generations to arrive at this point. Is it also, in effect, "assimilation"? I doubt whether sociologically rigorous evidence could be found to support a hypothesis that as people in the United States have come increasingly over the generations since their ancestors' arrival to speak English and no other language that they have been absorbed headlong, and unwillingly, into an Anglican, tea-and-cricket English ethnie. In fact, according to the US Census, nearly three times as many monoglot English-speaking Americans "identify" with being German or Irish than with being English.

Thus the final paradox: multiculturalists like neat, tidy categories whose devices (and people) they can define and manipulate, not unpredictability and indeterminacy which they cannot. Any political ideology or program that, despite good intentions, has the effect of shoring up cultural boundaries which would otherwise have crumbled away in the fullness of time, such that people in positions of authority are led to believe that the children in their care are different from others in ways that cannot easily be reconciled, and so act to discourage them from acquiring the social competences and forming the kinds of close social associations which ultimately lead to marriage across boundaries, can only slow down societal integration or prevent it from happening altogether.

Multiculturalism, as an ideology or as a political practice, is in itself neither better nor worse than assimilationism. It is what people say and do in its name that makes it better or worse. Although popular discourses about multiculturalism have freely borrowed words from our scientific vocabulary, very few anthropologists have focused upon multiculturalism as a political phenomenon in the modern world which might, in itself, be an object of scientific investigation and analysis. More anthropological voices need to be heard, if we are to learn the lessons of history. As anthropologists, it is our duty to ensure that multiculturalism is, and remains, a topic of open and critical debate about the means and ends of tolerance, in which the policing of cultural boundaries – by anyone, insider or outsider, teacher, priest, or politician – has no place.

NOTES

1 The bill sought to amend Section 801, Paragraph 1, of the Education Law of the State of New York, to read as follows (I have italicized the added words): "In order to promote a spirit of patriotic and civic service and obligation and to foster in the children of the state moral and intellectual qualities which are essential in preparing to meet the obligations of citizenship in peace or in war, the Regents of The University of the State of New York shall prescribe courses of instruction in patriotism, citizenship, and human rights issues, with particular attention to the study of the inhumanity of genocide, slavery (including the freedom trail and underground railroad), the Holocaust, *and the mass starvation in Ireland from 1845 to 1850*, to be maintained and followed in all the schools of the state. The boards of education and trustees of the several cities and school districts of the state shall require instruction to be given in such courses, by the teachers employed in the schools therein. All pupils attending such schools, over the age of eight years, shall attend upon such instruction."

2 Governor Pataki also paraphrases Mitchel's emotive claim that food was still being exported from Ireland during the Famine. True enough, food was indeed being exported, but Mitchel omitted to mention – as do those who quote him – that this "food" was mainly unmilled grain, for which there was insufficient milling capacity in Ireland; nor did Mitchel – nor do his followers – choose to acknowledge that vastly more food (including among other foodstuffs the same Irish-grown grain, having been milled in England) was simultaneously being imported into Ireland in the largest relief effort undertaken anywhere in the world up to that time.

3 See Alba 1990, Waters 1990, and Lieberson 1988, for discussions of the significance of the 1980 US Census statistics and the contemporary social dynamics of European ancestral

categories. The 1980 census was the first to ask an "ethnicity" question and thus to permit broad-scale socioeconomic comparisons and studies of marital preference to be made of national-origin and racial categories.

4 The 1870 and 1880 US Census manuscripts give long lists of Irish-born men, with distinctively Catholic names, in remote US Army outposts on the western frontier; in some of these barracks, they predominated in the ordinary ranks and outnumbered all others (see Byron 2006:162).

5 There have been court challenges to this law. Most recently, in March 2005, the Supreme Court of Canada denied an application filed by French-speaking parents who wanted to enroll their children in English-language schools. The court upheld Law 101, which prevents Francophones from placing their children in English schools, and stated that the law was reasonable. It said that linguistic majorities have no constitutional right to receive education in minority languages (Canadian Broadcasting Corporation News Online, March 30, 2005).

REFERENCES

Alba, Richard D.

1990 Ethnic Identity: The Transformation of White America. New Haven: Yale University Press.

Appiah, K. Anthony

1994 Identity, Authenticity, Survival: Multicultural Societies and Social Reproduction. *In* Multiculturalism: Examining the Politics of Recognition. Charles Taylor, ed. pp. 149–164. Princeton: Princeton University Press.

Archdeacon, Thomas J.

2002 The Irish Famine in American School Curricula. Eire-Ireland (Spring–Summer):119–29.

Bauman, Zygmunt

2001 The Great War of Recognition. Theory, Culture and Society 18(2–3):137–150.

Baumann, Gerd

1996 Contesting Culture: Discourses of Identity in Multi-Ethnic London. Cambridge: Cambridge University Press.

1999 The Multicultural Riddle: Rethinking National, Ethnic, and Religious Identities. London: Routledge.

Byron, Reginald

1999 Irish America. Oxford: Oxford University Press.

2006 The Case of the Mail-Order Brides: Marriage Strategies among Irish Migrants in Nineteenth-Century America. *In* Migration and Marriage: Heterogamy and Homogamy in a Changing World. Barbara Waldis and Reginald Byron, eds. pp. 161–178. Münster: LIT.

Joppke, Christian, and Steven Lukes, eds.

1999 Multicultural Questions. Oxford: Oxford University Press.

Kuper, Adam

1999 Culture: The Anthropologists' Account. Cambridge, MA: Harvard University Press.

Lieberson, Stanley

1988 From Many Strands: Ethnic and Racial Groups in Contemporary America. New York: Russell Sage.

Miller, Kerby A.
1985 Emigrants and Exiles: Ireland and the Irish Exodus to North America. New York: Oxford University Press.
Office of the Governor, George E. Pataki
1996 Press release, October 9. Electronic document. http://www.ny.gov/governor/press/index.php (accessed November 5, 2011).
Taylor, Charles, ed.
1994 Multiculturalism: Examining the Politics of Recognition. Princeton: Princeton University Press.
Turner, Terence
1993 Anthropology and Multiculturalism: What Is Anthropology that Multiculturalists Should Be Mindful of It? Cultural Anthropology 8(4):411–429.
Waters, Mary C.
1990 Ethnic Options: Choosing Identities in America. Berkeley: University of California Press.
Watson, C. W.
2000 Multiculturalism. Buckingham: Open University Press.

CHAPTER 5

Anthropology in Postsocialist Europe

Michał Buchowski

The Ethnoanthropology of (Post)socialism

Writing about anthropology in postsocialist Europe is not easy, since the multiplicity of research practices is complicated by intradisciplinary politics.[1] Divergent traditions of doing anthropology have been practiced in the region for decades. On the one hand, anthropology is a well-established multilingual tradition, comprising both ethnology and folklore. On the other, anthropology is a discipline practiced by people from the West. Although no single mainstream socialist ethnological enterprise could have been considered "empire building" (cf. Stocking 1982), a rich tradition of doing research on other continents in countries like Poland, Czechoslovakia, and Yugoslavia must be mentioned. Moreover, a "surprising feature of ethnography (ethnology) in . . . Central and Eastern European countries is that there has never been an absolute dichotomy between home investigations and research on distant territories" (Sárkány 2002:562). Though Eastern European scholarship is still perceived by some as descriptive and nationalist (see Kuper 1996:192), the "anthropologization of ethnology," that is, the practice of conducting fieldwork outside one's own culture and applying recent anthropological theories, was in full swing in the 1970s and 1980s. Thus, the myth of nationalist ethnology in (post)socialist Central and Eastern Europe must be dispelled. This kind of ethnoanthropology that combines "anthropology at home," history, and ethnology, appears less commonly in the Anglo-American world, but is quite common in several continental countries. These studies should today be seen as matching inquiries carried out by Eastern European anthropological luminaries coming from the West, who conducted research that was revealing, insightful, and referred to the ideas of local historians, sociologists, and political scientists (see Hann 1994:232–237).

In what follows, I try to paint a picture that takes into account the achievements of scholars practicing ethnology and anthropology of postsocialism both as "outsiders" and "insiders." It is an attempt to take "a step toward bridging the dichotomy

A Companion to the Anthropology of Europe, First Edition. Edited by Ullrich Kockel, Máiréad Nic Craith, and Jonas Frykman.

of Us versus Them and loosening the boundaries of the world's hierarchical division into area studies. Fostering an equality of learning and sharing by the two groups" should break down "the offensive borders of 'post-Soviet' and 'Western' anthropology" (Buyandelgeriyn 2009:241). So far, despite many declarations like this, in all past and recent summaries of postsocialist anthropology (cf. Hann 2002; Brandtstädter 2007; Buyandelgeriyn 2008; Hörschelmann and Stenning 2008), Central European scholars' contributions have been systematically ignored.

The key question regarding postsocialism is: what makes it a specific phenomenon and anthropological studies on it a distinct field of study? One can say that an old diagnosis of Bettelheim's has apparently become true in Central Europe today: "Inside social formations in which capitalism is predominant, this domination mainly tends to expand reproduction of the capitalist mode of production, that is to dissolution of the other modes of production . . ." (1969:297). The introduction of capitalism in former socialist countries in the era of globalization is complex and affects not only modes of production, but also differently influences various spheres of life and categories of social actors. People confronted with capitalism react according to their own conceptions of it that are partially rooted in traditionally defined meanings. In other words, implemented strategies become transformed by the capitalist relationships of production, but also alter capitalism at the local level, leading to what Marshall Sahlins calls the "indigenization of modernity" (1999:410) in response to globalization.

The variety of phenomena addressed in postsocialist studies forces us to focus on select issues and to choose key notions around which to weave the story. First, I will discuss concepts of socialism and postsocialist transition. Second, I will attempt to deconstruct orientalizing occidental views on Central–Eastern Europe, such as an image of civil society, nationalism, and anthropological scholarship, and to follow a thread of transforming identities in the sphere of property, labor, class, and gender relations. Third, I will also show that postsocialist changes are most often rendered within a paradigm that contrasts East to West, or in other words, always considers (post)socialism in its relationship to and divergence from Western models. To make reading easier I follow this strategy of representation, although in undermining dominant images a deconstructive accent is present. Fourth, I will argue that in all these issues, cultural determinism in the form of "postsocialist mentalities and habits" does not explain historical processes that are propelled by currently emergent relations of power. Finally, I will show that in these power-dependent worlds, individual and collective actors are active social agents.

What Was Socialism? And What Is Postsocialism?

The very term "postsocialism" evokes controversy. Within contemporary public and scholarly rhetoric, the notion is confined in practice to the pre-1989 Soviet bloc countries characterized by "really existing socialism" (Bahro 1977). Therefore, I will address the state of anthropological art in the European space of these former socialist countries, comprising most of Central Europe and stretching from the Baltic Sea to the Balkans. Caroline Humphrey (2002:12) justifies use of the term "postsocialism" by arguing that socialism-related practices were deeply embedded in these societies, and have not been replaced by new ones overnight. Just as there were commonalities in the socialist experience, it follows that there must be some degree of unity in the postsocialist experience.

However, these socialist and postsocialist unities are simultaneously relative and ambiguous (Buchowski 2001a:9–13). Communist countries, for instance, had distinct systems of property relations, ranging from collectivized agricultural land in most of them to privately owned farms in Yugoslavia and Poland. While state property dominated in the industrial sector, in the Yugoslav model cooperative companies and workers' councils were common. In both these countries, and in Hungary, private entrepreneurship was encouraged in "late socialism." Political regimes exercised different forms of authoritarian domination and ideological hegemony. In general, and especially since the 1970s, all three countries enjoyed various forms of freedom. Restrictions on travel were systematically lifted; freedom of religious practice in Poland was practically unhindered. A relative freedom of speech, culture, and social-scientific publication ensued.

As Humphrey writes, "the divergences between the former socialist countries have been accentuated over the last decade" (2002:12). These differences become visible when comparing Central European to Central Asian or Caucasian variants of post-socialism. In Central Europe itself, some regions (e.g. the northern tier) experienced smooth sociopolitical transformation, while in others (i.e. former Yugoslavia) bloody wars erupted. Still, the combination of the modern capitalist global regime with past forms has brought about some degree of unity, as has the current membership of ten postsocialist countries in the European Union. These realities find their reflection in anthropological production.

Postsocialist Transformations

The mental division of Europe into East and West has a long tradition that reaches back to the Enlightenment (Wolff 1994; Todorova 1997). Historians (cf. Chirot 1989) reassured the public that the partition of the continent into center and periphery reflected "real" phenomena. Such dualism was strengthened during Cold War. For many, the collapse of state socialism meant the "end of history," or the inevitable transformation of postsocialist nations into modern, Western-like societies, and the universal domination of capitalism. Indeed, new spaces opened for capital and transnational connections have been intensified. But this does not imply a homogenization of social forms or the modes of thought nurtured by them. There is no end to history.

In order to "naturalize" transformation processes, neoliberal experts invented theories to fit these master images. Katherine Verdery's writing best describes the situation:

> A number of the stories of post-socialism have the knights of Western know-how rushing to rescue the distressed Eastern Europe. . . . The rescue scenario has two common variants: "shock therapy" and "big bang." The first compares the former socialist bloc with

> a person suffering from mental illness – that is, socialism drove them insane, and our job is to restore their sanity. The second implies that . . . history is only now beginning . . ." (1996:205)

The category of "the West" is given, fixed, and transhistorical, while all other possible forms are treated as aberrant. The East should be absorbed by the West for its own – and the greater – good.

These schemes are reminiscent of 1960s modernization theories. This progressive view also recalls communist leaders' faith in the superiority of socialism to capitalism, which now paradoxically appears as a prefiguration of post-1989 Western triumphalism. Besides, "the idea of transition . . . responds to a unilinear, evolutionary vision expounded by Comte and Spencer. Societies are purported to develop according to a 'universal law of stages' or, in other words, to a pre-established succession deemed inevitable . . ." (Conte and Giordano 1999:6). Current transformations present a kind of reversal of history, thanks to which, societies are put back on the legitimate track of development. From another perspective, transformation could be seen as a rite of passage from socialism to capitalism, in which the transitory stage is analogous to a liminal period in Victor W. Turner's (1967:93–111) scheme. However, history is again conceptualized as proceeding from one clearly defined juncture, socialism, to an equally determined destination, capitalism (Buchowski 2001a:100–116).

Anthropologists prefer to understand postsocialism as that which emerges at the interface of the social structural framework, which is produced by various social actors, and those individuals acting within such structures. Grasping all these phenomena is a strenuous task. Meanwhile, ready-made neoliberal models have engendered the academic industry of "transitology." Anthropologists should contest analyses that explain failures of transformation by " 'socialist legacies' or 'culture'. Repeatedly, we find that what may appear as 'restorations' of patterns familiar from socialism are something quite different: direct *responses* to the new market initiatives, produced *by* them, rather than remnants of an older mentality" (Burawoy and Verdery 1999:1–2; emphases in original). Because ethnographers understand grass-roots perspectives and local meanings to be central, they analyze people's experiences in an attempt to understand native conceptualizations and how they are conditioned by relations of power between social actors.

Anthropologists have also argued against neoliberal views that history can be erased by applying "shock therapy," which demolishes old institutions, and that economic problems are caused by the "malfeasance and intransigence" (Lampland 2002:36) of ordinary people. Such neoliberal perspectives can lead to path-dependency theory (cf. Stark and Bruszt 1998), a version of which is the institutional economists' view that destroying previous institutions caused difficulties in absorption of postsocialist reforms. This argument also demonstrates that "path-dependent causation . . . is not just retrospective. Prior conditions . . . shape tools for improvisation in contemporary daily practice, in here and now of an unmapped and insecure terrain that joins past with possible future" (Kalb 2002:323). Therefore we should conceptualize postsocialism within an analytic perspective that connects local reactions and places to global processes. Moreover, postsocialism should be viewed in a wider context of post–Cold War geopolitical economic power relations in which strands of (post)-socialism, (post)colonialism and (neo)imperialism are interconnected (Chari and Verdery 2009).

Thus, anthropologists have tried to undermine stereotypical accounts of transformation. Two scholars from Hungary and the Czech Republic critically write: "Assumptions that all socioeconomic and political difficulties are attributable to the transitional period have so permeated research on East–Central Europe, that it is difficult to break free with their premises and legacies . . . it is timely that these assumptions were rigorously and entirely deconstructed" (Kürti and Skalník 2009:2). Therefore, anthropologists must contest the view that undesired phenomena, such as poverty, unemployment, and other collective and individual afflictions that emerged in postsocialism can be either attributed to the heritage of socialism itself or deficiencies of capitalism. In evaluating the outcomes of transformation some differences are visible between foreign and domestic perspectives. Most Western anthropologists have been extremely critical about the social consequences of economic reforms. As Kürti and Skalník argue, certainly, there are many social groups that have "lost out" during transformation, and anthropologists should unmask the mechanisms by which they have suffered and been marginalized. However, not all changes have brought poverty and dissatisfaction.

Anthropologists' deconstruction of clichéd images of postsocialism can be seen across various domains of practice and analysis. Next, I will consider such attempts to dispel stereotypes regarding the political sphere.

Civil Society

The first Western anthropologists who ventured into Central Europe during the socialist period wanted to deny entrenched and distorted representations of socialism. This was a difficult task, since phenomena there were sometimes incomprehensible even to anthropologists. To deny ethnocentrism, they attempted to present local life as complex and often highly sociable, even if not all Western liberal notions had their counterparts in the socialist East.

One such mistaken idea held by many in the West was that civil society did not exist during socialism. Therefore, in the rush to implement a new Western-like social order, a whole civil-society-building industry developed. Consultants flooded the region and helped to organize NGOs. They played a significant role in assisting people undergoing turbulent changes and many engaged in civic organizations out of benevolence; simultaneously, individuals and groups on both ends of this NGO chain profited. The effort to build civil society from scratch was based on the erroneous assumption that socialist societies were atomized or even in a state of anomie. This image excluded various institutions that were not considered "civic" in the Western context, but had functions similar to civil society under socialism, such as networks of families and friends, religious institutions, trade unions, as well as state-sponsored organizations like sports clubs, women's leagues, and professional unions (Kubik 2000; Buchowski 2001a:117–136). These groups mobilized people to activities that facilitated their lives both locally and nationally, counterbalanced the state's ubiquitous power, and opposed total penetration of public space by ideological politics. "Civil society" shifts its place in various polities according to circumstances. Anthropological studies on emerging forms of civil society in the postsocialist world support this conclusion by showing that these forms depend on historical experiences of collective actions, but also on the particular social situation in a given community at a certain moment and often in relation to international agents and agencies (Hann and Dunn 1996; especially Sampson 1996b).

Property Relations

Property is one of the most debated topics in Central European postsocialist studies, and was particularly popular in the 1990s, when anthropologists were influenced by the socialist period to favor research in rural issues. The sheer quantity of studies on the radical consequences of systemic change in property relations impresses; each country has its experts in this field: Romania (Verdery 2003), Bulgaria (Creed 1998), Slovakia (Danglová 2003; Torsello 2003), and Russia (Humphrey 1998). This phenomenon has also been put in a comparative perspective (e.g. Leonard and Kaneff 2002; Hann et al. 2003). Anthropologists insist that decollectivization and privatization of land in the postsocialist world cannot be reduced to economic processes, since "property is about social relations. These include both relations among persons and the power relations in which people act" (Verdery 1998:180). Therefore, ownership changes imply enormous social and cultural transformations, and anthropologists continue to study the way that the material order, or in this case land, correlates to people's identities, values, and the social order.

Perhaps the least obvious case can best illustrate this point. In Poland, the revolution in agriculture was not as radical as elsewhere, since agriculture was not collectivized. However, my fieldwork in Dziekanowice, Poland, where private and state properties coexisted, reveals connections between material and social transformations. Private property, the "naturalness" of which neoliberals propagate, and anthropologists so rightly criticize, is nevertheless perceived exactly as "natural" by most ordinary people. This ownership system has started to shape social relations in a new way. Unlike in the socialist past, property, or economic capital, now gauges individuals' social capital. This conversion of economic into symbolic value is eagerly accepted by those who own land. The landless oppose such a cultural order because it demotes them to a lower status within the community. The privatization of socialist property also means that the state partially abandoned its liability toward those who worked on it; privatization of land means also privatization of "social security." Former state farm workers are commonly considered by others and themselves to be the wretched of the earth of postsocialism. Now they have to work for rural entrepreneurs and this has caused changes in social structure, relationships and identity. By retreating from the property system, the state also privatized social affairs in the sense that personalities are constructed on the basis of direct, non-state-mediated relations to other community members. Subjective individual and group identities have been redefined alongside changes in "objective" property relations based on the hegemonic idea of private ownership (Buchowski 2009). Like other postsocialist processes, these changes are often riddled with emotions and worries about losing one's economic and social status (cf. Svašek 2006).

However, rural development can also generate positive emotions and consequences. For example, foreign investment in agribusiness does not necessarily involve a "doomsday scenario" (Kürti 2009:153). The community of Lajosmizse in Hungary has undergone every typical agricultural transformation, that is, the collapse of collectivized farms, reprivatization, and a change in ownership of companies. Swiss investment in this community, already known for its rabbit production, was carried out "with care and attention rather than exploitation and destruction" (Kürti 2009:180) and has changed the community's internal social relations. The rabbit-processing company has given jobs to many people and suppliers, has proven to be environmentally sensitive, and has introduced new farming techniques that have made the whole regional industry successful and able to compete on international markets. This case proves the above-mentioned more optimistic view on postsocialist transformation held by insiders.

Vanishing and Emerging Classes

For neoliberals, the restructuring of class composition has become an important part of transformation. Due to the modernization of the agriculture sector and European Union policies, the reprivatization of land should not, according to policy-makers, ultimately lead to the ruralization of society, but to an emergence of rural entrepreneurs. Perceived by communists as an "awkward" class that impedes progress, peasants have again become an obsolete social group, this time for capitalist reformers. In their eyes, the reconstruction of industry should diminish the importance of the working class that was put on a pedestal by communist parties, and in many countries actually became a leading anticommunist force. David Kideckel concludes that today "workers are beset by multidimensional onslaught" which leads to and makes visible labor's "decline in postsocialism and Western influence on that decline" (2008:31). In the new system, the middle class were expected take the lead, and building it became an urgent and largely ideological task.

Focusing on the creation of a "middle class," considered so vital for modern capitalist society by neoliberal reformers, will reveal not only the dogmatic nature of class system reconstruction, but also the fragility of "class" as a label. For instance, if we combine Edmund Mokrzycki's (1996:193–194) and Steven Sampson's (1996a:99–101) accounts, the list of candidates for a "new middle class" was quite long: private entrepreneurs and craftsmen owning small ventures under communism, former communist managers who skillfully privatized state assets into their hands, former wage-workers, people active in the "second economy," as well as former state employees with technical skills and cultural capital that can be converted into economic capital, and members of "traditional liberal" professionals. To Mokrzycki, the last two groups form a "declassed intelligentsia," an already qualified "knowledge class" indispensable to a modern Western-type society. Do all these groups constitute a social category we can call class?

According to the Marxist criterion of property relations, entrepreneurs constitute a class, since they own the means of production. Various studies in the postsocialist regions show that they employ a labor force, which makes them producers of capital (cf. Schröder and Vonderau 2008). However, in making social distinctions one should also consider social and symbolic capital. From this perspective, entrepreneurs comprise a diversified collection of people who have roots in various social milieus that span the working class, peasantry, intelligentsia, and craftsmen, and whose education ranges from the elementary to the university level. Some do well financially, while others' membership in this class is persistently in flux as they struggle to maintain their economic well-being.

If culture, understood as negotiated "reality," helps us to define a class, then we can say that a renegotiation of cultural meanings and new patterns of social relations take place and can potentially lead to the emergence of the new postsocialist middle class (Buchowski 2001b). Entrepreneurs partly internalized their new identities, but inherited culture still creates distinctions within this group, which is united by its location in relation to the means of production and by belonging to the "knowledge class." Consumption, often understood as a unifying factor, cannot forge a sociologically meaningful category of class based on distribution of wealth, since it can be practiced by even more diversified societal groups. Until now, the middle class in postsocialist societies has been neither grounded in the subjectivity of those who might identify with it, nor in the "objective conditions" of social life – economic, social, and cultural – implied by the notion of class.

This discussion on class formation or dissolution allows insights into the role of culture during periods of rapid change. Slobodan Naumović's case-study of a Serbian technocrat who turned to private entrepreneurship shed light on the complexities of and relations between class and culture. People can skillfully use the cultural resources at their disposal, such as network of family and friends, experience during communism that gave them knowledge about the way business actually functions, and acquired economic education on free market principles. However, such findings should not lead to "cultural determinism," in which culture becomes a shaping factor of human relations and practices. To the contrary, this research shows that actions undertaken by individuals in postsocialist contexts are coping strategies that occur within the structural framework of post-Balkan-Wars Serbia, which Naumović describes as characterized by conspicuous corruption, politicking, lack of state protection, inadequate legal frames, and lack of capital and credits. Moreover, this case supports Eric Wolf's (1999) view that culture should be treated as rather a "resource for" than "source of" economic and other activities. Thereby "the functioning of 'socio-economic culture(s)' is properly contextualized, linked to actual periods, processes, and persons, then it has to be seen as neither the only, nor the principal factor that can explain observable behaviour, particularly in rapidly changing political, economic, institutional, and legal settings" (Naumović 2006:119). Culture matters as long as it works together with social events, structural or institutional frameworks, and with actors' conceptualizations of events. In postsocialism – as in any other system – people should be not seen as ossified individuals, but rather as active agents who live in certain historical circumstances that determine their behaviors and who simultaneously co-shape the context in which they live.

Transformations of Labor and Personhood

Martha Lampland's research on the commodification of labor in Hungary demonstrated that several processes associated with capitalism also developed under socialism. It implied "the conflation of labor's objectification in particular acts of production with it[s] more general status as the source and arbiter of value" (1995:11). Such analogies between the structure and functioning of capitalist and socialist societies enabled anthropologists to take further steps in undermining ethnocentric notions.

However, it is true that labor relations were redefined in socialist countries. As already mentioned, in postsocialist Dziekanowice, existing social relations prevented rural workers from working for farmers for a long time after the end of socialism. This was against their dignity because it violated their understanding of independence and equality. At the grass-roots level the state had been an anonymous employer and therefore deemed superior to a private one. In Hungary, according to Lampland, the state figured as a personalized subject in contrast to the depersonalized "hidden hand of a free market" of today's capitalism. This was also the case in socialist Poland, but more at the political level, where industrial workers directly protested against the "personalized" Party state. However, now, the free market remains incomprehensible and mysterious for rural proletarians in both Poland and Hungary, while an employer, a farmer or rural entrepreneur, is a visible person, coming often from the same community. In the past, managers of state farms merely acted for the socialist state and were regarded as similar to other workers that it hired. Now the "invisible market" is not that invisible, since it is embodied in a tangible employer, owner, and manager – all in one. For workers it is hard to appreciate the capitalist model of production relations, incurring further commodification of labor and unfavorable reclassification of social relations.

These issues also arise for farmers, who have always gauged a person's value through "work." For farmers, work "is a material property of human actors, bearing physical, nearly tangible qualities. It is also "the touchstone, the foundation, of subjectivity and morality" (Lampland 1995:11). Therefore, labor has been the cornerstone of farmers' identity, prosperity, reputation, and merit, and constitutive of their personhood. As owners, they feel independent and oppose the appropriation of their labor. However, these connections between labor and personhood have been weakened by the free market relations penetrating economic relationships. The amount of work input no longer correlates to earnings; the moral capital of a diligent person does not translate into economic capital. Consequently, effort and labor do not determine consumption possibilities. The merit of labor as measure of a person collides with invisible market forces. For farmers this means the depreciation of the core of their identity, that is, hard work.

The privatization and marketization of the economy is equally intense in the industrial sector. Socialism was a system characterized by a shortage economy, and as having a shortage of labor, politicized consumption, with state dictatorship over needs, soft budget constraints for companies, and clientelism (Verdery 1996:19–38). It also produced certain kind of persons that in retrospect are described by anthropologists as "partible," or a composite of multiple relations, who are inextricably embedded in their social relations. Such persons "contain a generalized society within" and "are frequently constructed at the plural and composite site of the relationship that produced them" (Strathern 1988:13). (In)dividuals' identity is defined by their position in the network of social relations. *Známosti* in Czechoslovakia, *blat* in Russia, *protekció* in Hungary or *znajomości* in Poland (Wedel 1986) are conceptualized as connections to other people that smoothed everyday life and established persons as composites of social relations. In capitalism people are perceived as "individuals who are owners of their 'parts,' or qualities" (Dunn 2004:126). Of course, it should be argued that in the West individuals function also as "divisible," but popular discourse claims that everyone can be measured according to his or her intrinsic worth. In the post-Fordist system, employees on the shop floor are grouped according to their "aptitude," and work performance is measured with "scientific methods." Persons become detached from social settings and their classification becomes legitimized by supposedly "objective" gauges. But as Dunn shows in her ethnography of a food-producing plant bought by a multinational company in Poland, female workers resist such classification by referring to their social conception of the person. Birgit Müller arrived at a similar conclusion in her study of the East German transformation of labor. "Faced with the individualistic model of the market economy, which emphasized competition and responsibility, the employees tried to apply a 'We model' that provided them with authentication" (2007:228).

This finding leads to the issue of how power operates, since the control of labor is a part of a broader control of people. The individualization of persons weakens the power of collective actors, so it is not surprising that people defy such redefinition. Under socialism, power was evident both in the political domain and on the shop floor. Today, by shifting power from the political to the supposedly scientific and rational domain, "power comes from the creation of an accepted version of 'reality' rather than from exhortations, overt ideological formations, or brute force and is hence less visible and more difficult to challenge" (Dunn 2001:278). But this acquiescence is not so obvious and people oppose such containment in various ways, not only by outward protests and strikes, but also in daily practices.

Resistance

As we have seen, people are constantly classified by others. The elevation of workers and peasants under communism did not necessarily converge with the actual hegemonic cultural order. Capitalist reclassification deals with the unemployed and uneducated, too, who are made accountable for their own poor position and for obliterating reforms that otherwise would bring prosperity to all. Opinions like the one expressed by a leading Polish economist have become common: "It is not Polish capitalism that has been slowed down in its development, but rather the people who grew up in the lumpenproletariat milieu whose lack of standards stopped the process of evolution in the direction of capitalist normality!" (Winiecki 2001).

Social relations always create hierarchies in which some are considered to be more powerful. In the process of postsocialist transformations it has become a pattern that "victims of economic downturn," mainly former state and collectivized farm workers as well as industrial workers, "are held to blame for that same downturn" (Kideckel 2002:115) and their own misfortune. The strategy of blaming the victims has been successfully implemented. Such (de)classification of thereby declassed groups puts them in an inferior position. They are treated as remnants of the past, *Homo sovieticus*, immobilized and excluded from history. Johannes Fabian's (1983) idea of allochronism that places contemporaneous tribal societies in the times of yore finds its full implementation in Europe at the turn of the twenty-first century. Such immobilization of social actors denies them agency.

It is no wonder that these degraded groups oppose the system that is perceived by them as alien, as fitting of the "others" – be they local businessman, national politicians or international agents of capitalism. In their self-defense, new outcasts turn to similar rhetoric of blaming their "oppressors," hence reversing the flow of accusations. Postsocialist subalterns overtly reproach elites for the transformation's hardships. But such mobilized defiance – labor and hunger strikes, street demonstrations and road blockades – exposes them to further criticism, because by protesting they purportedly prove their inability to understand capitalism and lack of creativity through using certain symbols epitomizing collective solidarity. These actions and symbols are immediately described by those more powerful as outmoded postcommunist reactions, thereby enabling elites to classify resisting groups as backward, populist, and culturally inferior. A paradoxical conclusion follows: "struggle and resistance are themselves implicated in the reproduction of culturally based class differences" (Kearney 2004:309). By opposing the new social order subalterns actively participate in their subordination engendered by material relations of production and legitimized by hegemonic cultural order (Buchowski 2006). Unfortunately, the disenfranchised and poor who appear in most social scientists' works are presented as unable to adapt, backwards, dependant and deviant.

An anthropological shift can make this apparent resignation "a proof of cultural activity; a proof that many people in a fully tense way experience what happened after 1989 – live it in a way adequate to their culture" (Rakowski 2009:17). Rakowski's thorough monograph, in which he empathizes with his primarily poor research participants and presents their points of view, proves that such a perspective is both humane and innovative. His research also critiques academic studies of postsocialist "deprived groups" for relying on the 1960s notion of a "deviant" subculture of poverty that reproduces its own values (cf. Lewis 1959), and, despite its apparent compassion, is exclusionary, patronizing, and dehumanizing by denying agency.

Gender and Religion

Gender is inherently intertwined with power structures and social images analytically placed outside of it. Although under socialism gender equality was an official political tenet, this did not mean that this parity existed in the cultural order or practice. Gender relations have been especially well-analyzed in Romania, where Gail Kligman (1998) showed that women were treated by patriarchal communist leaders as constituting the reproductive means, if not vessels, of the nation-building project. Therefore, for example, abortion was illegal there. But this kind of nationalist-communist policy was universal. Despite churches' protests, in most countries abortion was permitted, but social benefits for pregnant women and mothers of infants were also relatively generous. The change of regime has reduced social benefits and in Poland, abortion rights have become strictly restricted. The end of socialism has caused multiple redefinitions of gender relations; there is no single path for the whole region. Discourses and politics regarding the reproductive realm especially influence women's professional careers, positions in their families and communities, engagement in political life, relations with men, and finally, their subjectivities (cf. Gal and Kligman 2000).

These issues of gender, women's emancipation, and feminism must be contextualized. Western feminist models do not apply universally, though they were initially and incorrectly applied to phenomena in postsocialist Europe. Anthropological case studies demonstrate that emancipation, in this context, often requires different actions than those assumed by Westerners. Anika Keinz (2008) shows that in Poland, women first have to dissociate their cause from the socialist past, which is almost universally denied as antinational, and reappropriate their struggle for emancipation in other spheres of public discourse, such as family. These developments are contingent upon many factors, such as international influences, local understandings of "normalcy" and women's understandings of possible courses of action. It turns out that many ideologies and clandestine, unconscious scripts inform notions of feminism and gender. In other words, postsocialist notions of feminism and gender are always particular to their local context.

Such particularity can assume various forms. Monika Baer (2003) studied a businesswomen's club and rightly connected it with the issue of class. What on the surface looks like women engaging in emancipatory activity proves to be more a class-exclusionary self-definition and distinction. However, actual emancipation can assume entirely unexpected forms that are markedly different from Western secular and liberal feminism. Agnieszka Kościańska (2009) published an ethnography of highly religious women, practitioners of a Brahma Kumaris cult. Through silence and retreat from social and sexual life with their life-partners, they gain personal emancipation. These practices encourage understandings of womanhood, agency, and feminism itself as having multiple forms that can vary according to context. Though "classical" feminism does not recognize such religiously motivated behavior as constituting emancipation, it is exactly emancipation that these women achieve through rejecting Western-type feminism, perceived by them to be aggressive. Such radical religiosity represents its own form of feminism through expressing dissatisfaction in private, rather than public, spaces. Religion, which for diverse reasons is so important in the lives of so many people in postsocialist Europe (for an overview see Hann et al. 2006), functions here in an entirely unexpected way.

Memory and Nation

Memory is a key issue in the postsocialist context. Postsocialist populations have been habitually described by many political commentators as nostalgic, as *Homo sovieticus* longing for a glorious and cozy bygone lifeworld; this approach is captured by the well-known German term *Ostalgie*. However, this view runs afoul of anthropologists' findings demonstrating that the past is made in the present.

Images of the past are constructed at several levels and by many actors. First, the construction of memory relates to how the new post-1989 political authorities settled accounts with their predecessors. According to Borneman (1997:9), by the mid-1990s one could observe (i) a radical approach with a rather weak insistence on retributive justice, that is, only some recognition of the victims and no persecution for the communist functionaries (Poland, Hungary, the Czech Republic, Slovakia, and Slovenia); (ii) a minimal change in the regime and virtually no retributive justice (Serbia, Croatia, Romania, Russia, and other Soviet Republics excluding the Baltic States); and (iii) significant regime change, compensation for the victims and persecution of the wrongdoers (Estonia, Latvia, Lithuania, Bulgaria, Albania, and Germany). Such official policies vary according to any one country's political relations and legal system, which has its roots in political philosophy.

Second, initial enthusiasm for change caused an erasure of the past in most Central European countries. Examples of such erasure include changes in street names, the removal of communist monuments, erection of new memorials, changes of national emblems, the exchange of banknotes and coins, the introduction of new state holidays, the reburial of previously denied heroes (remnants of whom were often brought home from abroad), and the rewriting of history in textbooks, documentary films, and public ceremonies. Through such actions, the politics of remembrance becomes sponsored by political authorities or various societal groups; it is in this contentious context that people create and evoke memories, while anthropologists try to grasp these changing meanings. People experienced communism, their acts were embedded in daily life, and now these encounters are objectified. This is a collective process, but various groups have different rationales for their actions and construct disparate meanings that can vary from the glorification of the past and the validation of one's youth or life course to total condemnation and rejection of communism. Overall, this is a tense process during which both past and present are inherently entwined (cf. Watson 1994; Haukanes et al. 2004; Kaneff 2004).

The politics of memory is directly related to the question of nation. Nationalism and minority issues have almost become hallmarks of postsocialist transition, due to the wars in former Yugoslavia and the cause of the Roma people. Nationalism studies comprise a regional discipline in itself. A discussion about the peculiarity of "Eastern" nationalism, an idea that reaches back at least to Hans Kohn's book (1944), and was to a certain extent upheld by Ernest Gellner (1983), has been undermined by contemporary studies (for instance, Brubaker 1998; Kuzio 2001), which agree with anthropologists' arguments that in both public discourses and many academic studies, national and ethnic identities are essentialized and postsocialist societies exoticized. More attention must be paid to the local contexts that made ethnic atrocities possible, especially in the Balkans (cf. Halpern and Kideckel 2000). Such essentializing practices ascribe people to one fixed, primordial ethno-national identity. However, identities do not exist "out there," somehow preceding collective practices or determining cultural configurations. Additionally, the significance of boundaries between communities is to a large extent negated by actual practices, through which national and ethnic identities are constantly produced and recreated. "Essentializers" ignore multiple forms of social life, the multivocality of statements, and the multicultural contexts or range of social settings in which people act. These phenomena are especially visible in the context of migration, another major research question that I cannot address due to space (but see Wallace and Stola 2001; Keough 2006). People manipulate their identities according to circumstances, interest or even transitory feelings. Many experts (e.g. Stewart 1997) have shown that Roma tend to be flexible in thus manipulating their identities, though they are at the same time subject to many discriminatory practices, and their position has actually deteriorated since socialist times.

In this context, where identities are fluid and intimately linked to the past and to the nation, "war ethnography" has become a hotly discussed topic. Croatian anthropologists tried to give an account of the violent events in which they became unavoidably involved. Their radical form of anthropology "at home" presented a "reaction to international lack of understanding of the war in Croatia" (Čapo-Žmegač 2002:104). They were even accused by some Westerners of practicing national propaganda (Greverus 1995). The point Croatian anthropologists tried to make in two important books (Feldman et al. 1993; Jambrešić Kirin and Povrzanović 1996) was that "*the lived experience of violence* is recognized . . . as a highly undesirable but almost inevitable 'essentializing' category which decisively defines identities in spatial/territorial terms" (Povrzanović 2000:154, emphasis in original). Sensitive to issues of shifting identities, anthropological representation, ethnographic authority, engaged anthropology, and autoethnography, they conveyed a message that gave voice to people who experienced violence. However, their own voice was immediately classified as disguised nationalism always already present in the Balkans (Bowman 1994), as if this phenomenon was miraculously inherent in territory and people, including anthropologists. Ines Prica ironically commented that these scholars' criticism recreated the "general, critical and deconstructive paradigm of *imagined national identity which, supported by pre-civilized forms of consciousness, turns into bloodshed* bears the traces of the same mythic consciousness it is so eager to proscribe" (Prica 1995:10; emphasis in original). In other words, Western scholars' attempts to unmask the hidden nationalism of Croatian scholars who gave an insider's view of the war turned out to be suffused with entrenched images about the chauvinist East, as represented by local anthropologists. It is as if the Western scholars said: "Whatever you do, you cannot escape your nature and destiny."

Conclusion

Prica's point brings us back to the issue of Central and Eastern European ethno-anthropologists' assumed preoccupation with national issues, and hierarchies of knowledge produced in centers and on peripheries. The "orientalization" of the postsocialist region hardens discourses so deeply that even those who try to deconstruct them, that is, local anthropologists, are accused of contributing to their hardening, simply because they are seen as Easterners themselves. It is high time to break with the sheer inequality of this model, or else anthropology will remain a mere part of wider relations of power between East and West. Therefore, in this chapter I have tried to merge these horizons of center and periphery by considering these perspectives with equal weight. I also hope that by showing several anthropological case studies it has become clear that the deeply entrenched exoticization of postsocialist Europe is not only ethnocentric, but also fabricated and misleading. Popular images about socialist habits and cultural patterns (often invented and stereotypical themselves) do not do justice to the potential of people to be social agents. Global transformations have caused dramatic changes at both individual and societal levels and have transformed identities and practices; these changes are practiced and lived by actual individuals in these postsocialist contexts, and as such, their voices must be heard, including those of postsocialist anthropologists. Toward this end, it is necessary to merge perspectives from the "East" and "West" in order to create a truly equal and innovative anthropology in Central and Eastern Europe.

NOTES

1 I would like to thank Jessica Robbins for her valuable comments and help in writing this text in comprehensible English. I wrote this paper as a senior fellow at Collegium Budapest – Institute for Advanced Study, where in spring 2010 I worked on the project *Anthropology of European Postsocialism: Modes of Invention and Representation.*

REFERENCES

Baer, Monika
2003 Women's Spaces: Class, Gender, and the Club. An Anthropological Study of the Transitional Process in Poland. Wrocław: Uniwersytet Wrocławski.
Bahro, Rudolf
1977 Zur Kritik des realexistierenden Sozializmus. Cologne: Bund-Verlag / Frankfurt am Main: Europäische Verlagsanstalt.
Bettelheim, Charles
1969 Appendix I. Theoretical comments. *In* Unequal Exchange. A Study of the Imperialism of Trade. Arghiri Emmanuel, ed. pp. 271–322. New York: Monthly Review Press.
Borneman, John
1997 Settling Accounts: Violence, Justice, and Accountability in Postsocialist Europe. Princeton, NJ: Princeton University Press.
Bowman, Glen
1994 Xenophobia, Phantasy, and the Nation: The Logic of Ethnic Violence in Former Yugoslavia. *In* The Anthropology of Europe: Identity and Boundaries in Conflict. Victoria A. Goddard, Josep R. Llobera, and Cris Shore, eds. pp. 143–171. Oxford: Berg.
Brandtstädter, Susanne
2007 Transitional Spaces: Postsocialism as a Cultural Process. Critique of Anthropology 27:131–145.
Brubaker, Rogers
1998 Myth and Misconceptions in the Study of Nationalism. *In* The State of the Nation. John S. Hall, ed. pp. 272–306. Cambridge: Cambridge University Press.
Buchowski, Michał
2001a Rethinking Transformation: An Anthropological Perspective on Post-Socialism. Poznań: Humaniora.

2001b Encountering Capitalism at a Grass-Root Level: A Case Study of Entrepreneurs in Western Poland. *In* Poland Beyond Communism: "Transition" in Critical Perspective. Michał Buchowski, Edouard Conte, and Carole Nagengast, eds. pp. 281–305. Fribourg: Fribourg University Press.

2006 The Spectre of Orientalism in Europe: From Exocitized Other to Stigmatized Brother. Anthropological Quarterly 79:463–482.

2009 Property Relations, Class, and Labour in Rural Poland. *In* Postsocialist Europe: Anthropological Perspectives from Home. László Kürti and Peter Skalník, eds. pp. 51–75. New York: Berghahn.

Burawoy, Michael, and Katherine Verdery, eds.

1999b Uncertain Transition: Ethnographies of Change in the Postsocialist World. Lanham, MD: Rowman and Littlefield.

Buyandelgeriyn, Manduhai

2008 Post-Post-Transition Theories: Walking on Multiple Paths. Annual Review of Anthropology 37:235–50.

Čapo-Žmegač, Jasna

2002 Petrified Models and (Dis)Continuities: Croatian Ethnology in the 1990s. *In* Die Wende als Wende? Orientirungen Europäischer Ethnologien nach 1989. Konrad Köstlin, Peter Niedermüller, and Herbert Nikitsch, eds. pp. 94–109. Europäische Ethnologie 23. Vienna: Verlag des Instituts für Europäische Ethnologie.

Chari, Sharad and Katherine Verdery

2009 Thinking Between the Posts: Postcolonialism, Postsocialism, and Ethnography after the Cold War. Comparative Studies in Society and History 51:6–34.

Chirot, Daniel, ed.

1989 The Origins of Backwardness in Eastern Europe: Economics and Politics from the Middle Ages until the Early Twentieth Century. Berkeley: University of California Press.

Conte, Edouard, and Christian Giordano

1999 Pathways of Lost Rurality: Reflections on Post-Socialism. *In* Es war einmal die Wende . . . Sozialer Umbruch der ländlichen Gesellschaften Mittel- und Südosteuropas. Edouard Conte and Christian Giordano eds. pp. 5–33. Berlin: Centre Marc Bloch.

Creed, Gerald

1998 Domesticating Revolution: From Socialist Reform to Ambivalent Transition in a Bulgarian Village. University Park: Pennsylvania State University Press.

Danglová, Olga

2003 Decollectivization and Survival Strategies in a Post-Socialist Co-operative Farm. Anthropological Journal on European Cultures 12:31–56.

Dunn, Elizabeth

2001 Carrots, Class, and Capitalism: Employee Management in a Post-Socialist Enterprise. *In* Poland Beyond Communism. "Transition" in Critical Perspective. Michał Buchowski, Eduard Conte, and Carole Nagengast, eds. pp. 259–279. Fribourg: University Press.

2004 Privatizing Poland: Baby Food, Big Business and the Remaking of Labor. Ithaca, NY: Cornell University Press.

Fabian, Johannes

1983 Time and the Other: How Anthropology Makes Its Object. New York: Columbia University Press.

Feldman, Lada Čale, Ines Prica, and Renata Sjenković, eds.

1993 Fear, Death, and Resistance: An Ethnography of War, Croatia 1991–1992. Zagreb: Institute of Ethnology and Folklore, Matrix Croatica, X-Press.

Gal, Susan, and Gail Kligman, eds.
2000 Reproducing Gender: Politics, Publics, and Everyday Life after Socialism. Princeton, NJ: Princeton University Press.
Gellner, Ernest
1983 Nations and Nationalism. Ithaca, NY: Cornell University Press.
Greverus, Ina-Maria
1995 Speak Up or Be Silent? On an Ethno-Anthropological Approach to War. Anthropological Journal on European Cultures 4(2):87–9.
Halpern, Joel M., and David Kideckel, eds.
2000 Neighbors at War: Anthropological Perspective on Yugoslav Ethnicity, Culture and History. University Park: Pennsylvania University Press.
Hann, Chris
1994 After Communism: Reflections on East European Anthropology and the Transition. Social Anthropology 2:229–249.
2002 Farewell to the Socialist "Other." *In* Postsocialism: Ideas, Ideologies and Practices in Eurasia. Chris Hann, ed. pp. 1–11. London: Routledge.
Hann, Chris, and the Civil Religion Group
2006 The Postsocialist Religious Question. Münster: LIT.
Hann, Chris, and Elizabeth Dunn, eds.
1996 Civil Society: Challenging Western Models. London: Routledge.
Hann, Chris, and the Property Relations Group
2003 The Postsocialist Agrarian Question: Property Relations and the Rural Condition. Münster: LIT.
Haukanes, Haldis, Deema Kaneff, and Frances Pine, eds.
2004 Memory, Politics and Religion. The Past Meets the Present in Europe. Münster: LIT.
Hörschelmann, Kathrin, and Alison Stenning
2008 Ethnographies of Postsocialist Change. Progress in Human Geography 32: 339–361.
Humphrey, Caroline
1998 Marx Went Away – But Karl Stayed Behind. (A revised edition of Karl Marx Collective. Economy, Society and Religion in a Siberian Collective Farm) Ann Arbor: University of Michigan Press.
2002 Does the Category of "Postsocialist" Still Make Sense? *In* Postsocialism: Ideals, Ideologies and Practices in Eurasia. Chris Hann, ed. pp. 12–15. London: Routledge.
Jambrešić Kirin, Reanta, and Maja Povrzanović, eds.
1996 War. Exile, Everyday Life: Cultural Perspectives. Zagreb: Institute of Ethnology and Folklore.
Kalb, Don
2002 Afterword: Globalism and Postsocialist Prospects. *In* Postsocialism: Ideas, Ideologies and Practices in Eurasia. Chris M. Hann, ed. pp. 317–334. London: Routledge.
Kaneff, Deema
2004 Who Owns the Past? The Politics of Time in a "Model" Bulgarian Village. New Directions in Anthropology 21. New York: Berghahn.
Kearney, Michael
2004 Changing Fields of Anthropology: From Local to Global. Lanham, MD: Rowman and Littlefield.
Keinz, Anika
2008 Polens Andere: Verhandlungen von Geschlecht und Sexualität in Polen nach 1989. Bielefeld: Transcript.

Keough, Leyla J.
2006 Globalizing "Postsocialism": Mobile Mothers and Neoliberalism on the Margins of Europe. Anthropological Quarterly 79:431–461.
Kideckel, David
2002 The Unmaking of an East-Central European Working Class. *In* Postsocialism: Ideals, Ideologies and Practices in Eurasia. Chris Hann, ed. pp. 115–132. London: Routledge.
2008 Getting By in Postsocialist Romania: Labor, the Body, and Working Class Culture. Bloomington: Indiana University Press.
Kligman, Gail
1998 The Politics of Duplicity: Controlling Reproduction in Ceausescu's Romania. Berkeley: University of California Press.
Kościańska, Agnieszka
2009 Potęga ciszy: Konwersja a rekonstrukcja porządku płci na przykładzie nowego ruchu religijnego Brahma Kumaris. Warsaw: Wydawnictwa Uniwersytetu Warszawskiego.
Kubik, Jan
2000 Between the State and Networks of "Cousins": The Rule of Civil Society and Noncivil Associations in the Democratization of Poland. *In* Civil Society Before Democracy. Nancy G. Bermeo and Philip G. Nord, eds. pp. 181–207. Lanham, MD: Rowman and Littlefield.
Kuper, Adam
1996 Anthropology and Anthropologists: The Modern British School (3rd revised and enlarged edition). London: Routledge.
Kürti, László
2009 Olivia's Story: Capitalism and Rabbit Farming in Hungary. *In* Postsocialist Europe: Anthropological Perspectives from Home. László Kürti and Peter Skalník, eds. pp. 151–187. Berghahn: New York.
Kürti, László and Peter Skalník
2009 Introduction: Postsocialist Europe and the Anthropological Perspective from Home. *In* Postsocialist Europe: Anthropological Perspectives from Home. László Kürti and Peter Skalník, eds. pp. 1–28. Berghahn: New York.
Kuzio, Taras
2001 "Nationalizing States" or Nation Building? A Critical Review of the Theoretical Literature and Empirical Evidence. Nations and Nationalism 7:137–154.
Lampland, Martha
1995 The Object of Labor: Commodification in Socialist Hungary. Chicago: University of Chicago Press.
2002 The Advantages of Being Collectivized: Cooperative Farm Managers in the Post-socialist Economy. *In* Postsocialism: Ideas, Ideologies and Practices in Eurasia. Chris M. Hann, ed. pp. 31–56. London: Routledge.
Leonard, Pamela, and Deema Kaneff, eds.
2002 Post-Socialist Peasant? Rural and Urban Constructions of Identity in Eastern Europe, East Asia and the Former Soviet Union. Basingstoke: Palgrave.
Lewis, Oscar
1959 Five Families; Mexican Case Studies in the Culture of Poverty. New York: Basic Books.
Mokrzycki, Edmund
1996 A New Middle Class? *In* Culture, Modernity and Revolution, Richard Kilminster and Ian Varcoe, eds. pp. 184–200. London: Routledge.

Müller, Birgit
2007 Disenchantment with Market Economics: East Germans and Western Capitalism. New York: Berghahn.
Naumović, Slobodan
2006 On the Heaviness of Feathers: Or What has Culture Got to do with the Failure to Establish an Organic Poultry Production Business in Contemporary Serbia? Етноантрополошки проблеми н.с. 1(1):103–124.
Povrzanović, Maja
2000 The Imposed and the Imagined as Encountered by Croatian War Ethnographers. Current Anthropology 41(2):151–162.
Prica, Ines
1995 Between Destruction and Deconstruction: The Preconditions of the Croatian Ethnography of War. Collegium Antropologicum 19:7–16.
Rakowski, Toamsz
2009 Łowcy, zbieracze, praktycy niemocy. Gdańsk: Słowa/obraz terytoria.
Sahlins, Marshall
1999 Two or Three Things that I Know about Culture. Journal of the Royal Anthropological Institute 5:399–421.
Sampson, Steven
1996a Turning Money into Culture: "Distinction" among Eastern Europe's Nouveaux Riches. *In* À la recherche des certitudes perdues . . . Birgit Müller, ed. pp. 92–113. Berlin: Centre Marc Bloch.
1996b Social Life of Projects: Importing Civil Society to Albania. *In* Civil Society: Challenging Western Models. Chris M. Hann and Elizabeth Dunn, eds. pp. 121–142. New York: Routledge.
Sárkány, Mihály
2002 Cultural and Social Anthropology in Central and Eastern Europe. *In* Three Social Science Disciplines in Central and Eastern Europe. Handbook on Economics, Political Science and Sociology (1989–2001). Max Kaase and Vera Sparschuh (with Agnieszka Wenninger), eds. pp. 558–566. Berlin–Budapest: Social Science Information Centre (IZ)/Collegium Budapest.
Schröder, Ingo W., and Asta Vonderau, eds.
2008 Changing Economies and Changing Identities in Eastern Europe. Münster: LIT.
Stark, David and László Bruszt
1998 Postsocialist Pathways: Transforming Politics and Property in East Central Europe. Cambridge: Cambridge University Press.
Stewart, Michael
1997 The Time of the Gypsies. Boulder, CO: Westview.
Stocking, George
1982 Afterword: A View from the Center. Ethnos 47:72–86.
Strathern, Marilyn
1988 The Gender of the Gift. Berkeley: University of California Press.
Svašek, Maruška, ed.
2006 Postsocialism: Politics and Emotions in Central and Eastern Europe. Oxford: Berghahn.
Todorova, Maria
1997 Imaging the Balkans. Oxford: Oxford University Press.
Torsello, D.
2003 Trust, Property and Social Change in a Southern Slovakian Village. Münster: LIT.

Turner, Victor W.
1967 The Forest of Symbols. Ithaca, NY: Cornell University Press.
Verdery, Katherine
1996 What Was Socialism, and What Comes Next? Princeton: Princeton University Press.
1998 Property and Power in Transylvania's Decollectivization. *In* Property Relations: Reinventing the Anthropological Tradition. Chris M. Hann, ed. pp. 160–180. Cambridge: Cambridge University Press.
2003 The Vanishing Hectare: Property and Value in Postsocialist Transylvania. Ithaca, NY: Cornell University Press.
Wallace, Claire, and Dariusz Stola, eds.
2001 Patterns of Migration in Central Europe. New York: Palgrave.
Watson, Ruby
1994 Memory, History and Opposition Under State Socialism. Santa Fe, NM: School of American Research Press.
Wedel, Janine
1986 The Private Poland. New York: Facts on File.
Winiecki, Jan
2001 Historia polskiego marginesu. Rzeczpospolita 303 (29 December).
Wolf, Eric
1999 Anthropology among the Powers. Social Anthropology 7:121–134.
Wolff, Larry
1994 Inventing Eastern Europe: The Map of Civilization on the Mind of the Enlightenment. Stanford, CA: Stanford University Press.

CHAPTER 6 Europe in Eurasia

Chris Hann

INTRODUCTION

It may seem odd to future historians of the anthropological sciences that the first centuries brought no consensus concerning the fundamental units of disciplinary inquiry. Should it be a universal humanity, or should it be the societies (some would prefer to say cultures) into which humans are grouped? We know that societies and cultures are fuzzy, unstable constructions, and yet the habit of generalizing about "the X" is so thoroughly engrained in anthropology that we often fail to notice the implications. Leach (1970[1954]) opted for a territorial framing rather than foregrounding collective identities, but he was the first to acknowledge that this step did not resolve all the problems. How should one define the boundaries of the territorial entity? Can one justify a study called "the anthropology of A" if the internal diversity to be found within territory A is greater than the diversity to be observed between A and neighboring territories B and C?

These problems are acute in the present instance. Where are the boundaries of this entity we call Europe, which is evidently more than just another society or culture? We habitually classify it as a continent, and often as a civilization, but what exactly do these terms mean for an anthropologist? The difficulties of geographical demarcation are most evident in the east, where the Urals hardly compare as a physical boundary to the Pyrennées, the Alps, or the Caucasus. They were nominated for the role of boundary marker only in the middle of the eighteenth century, when Russian intellectuals were determined to prove that the Czarist empire, or at any rate its capital and historic core, belonged to Europe rather than to Asia. South of the Urals there is no consensus at all about where to draw Europe's eastern boundary. The steppe zone of central Eurasia has been characterized over millennia by the continuous movement of peoples, technologies, and ideas. The same is true of

A Companion to the Anthropology of Europe, First Edition. Edited by Ullrich Kockel, Máiréad Nic Craith, and Jonas Frykman.

the Mediterranean and the "Middle East," where in recent years the absurdities of our pervasive symbolic geographies have become acute. Thus Israel can, at least for certain cultural purposes, be readily incorporated into Europe, while in many countries of the so-called European Union (EU) the eligibility of Turkey for membership is challenged on civilizational grounds. In some accounts, Eastern Christians (those of Moscow as well as those of Baghdad) are considered to belong to a separate world, with the Greeks an awkward exception. Europe tends to be thought of as the unique civilization created by the various strands of Western Christianity. An influential spokesman for this position is the late Samuel Huntington (1996), a political scientist who posited a "fault line" between Eastern and Western Christianity, distinct from the continental divide.

By contrast, many historians have pointed to entanglement and continuous osmosis across the membranes which temporarily divide societies and civilizations. The contributions of Eastern Christians, Jews, and Muslims to the formation of modern Europe have been amply documented and there is no need to summarize that story here. Instead, following the anthropologist Jack Goody and the archaeologist Gordon Childe, I shall argue that this history needs to be extended much further back – to the urban revolution of the late Bronze Age, the impact of which was not restricted to the Middle East but extended across South and East Asia. It is important to distinguish this level of *Realgeschichte* from pervasive representations of European identity and difference. When the latter are thoroughly internalized by a population, no one would deny that they can have very real effects. For anthropologists, as for many other scholars, tracing the origins, content, and dissemination of discourses and images of Europe is certainly a demanding and worthwhile activity. I shall touch on this sort of work in the first section. The danger that I see in all the attention that has been devoted to constructions and inventions of Europe is that one loses sight of material processes in wider frameworks, and paradoxically reinforces the boundaries and identities that one was initially inclined to deconstruct.

This chapter is intended as a scholarly contribution, but of course the question of Europe and European identity is topical and political. There are good reasons why European anthropologists should be aware of this context, since various strands of their discipline were profoundly shaped from the beginning by the politics of nation-states or empires (and in some cases both). Some of our predecessors did more than document local or regional customs; they contributed to the emergence and dissemination of a sense of national belonging that was new, or at any rate not yet widely shared by the putative members of the national community at the time. For several decades the cultural commissars of the EU have been seeking to emulate this feat, that is, to disseminate a sense of European identity where it remains weak or nonexistent (Shore 2000). They need all the help they can get, including that of anthropologists. Some of the latter have begun to examine the emergence of Europe "from below," as the result of local initiatives and intensified interaction between the citizens of different countries and regions (Johler 2010). Many, perhaps particularly those who work in academic departments called European Ethnology, sincerely experience this shift to the level of Europe as progressive, because it means transcendence of the delusions of the nation. But I shall argue that we should reject this role and distance ourselves from all invitations to naturalize and celebrate Europe. Instead of repeating the errors of our predecessors on a larger scale, we would do better to pay attention to imperialist power relations and *longue durée* similarities across Eurasia.

FABRICATIONS

Just as we have come to recognize the constructed character of national identities, we need to understand the contingencies that have led to the western peninsula of the Eurasian landmass being thought to form a separate continent. Many factors should lead us to see this classification as implausible. The variety of habitats and linguistic and societal diversity are just as great in India and Pakistan, yet we have learned to refer to this territory only as a "subcontinent." In terms not only of population but sociocultural, political, and commercial unification, China too would seem to have just as strong a case to be considered as a continent. So the question arises: When was Europe?

The history of Europe (and the name itself) is conventionally traced back to the Ancient Greeks, who laid stress on their difference from their Persian and Scythian neighbors in basically the same way that the Han of the "Middle Kingdom" asserted their difference from the barbarian nomads beyond the Great Wall. These various collectivities were already intimately linked by a kind of Bronze Age world-system involving the movement of goods, technologies, and ideas across the Eurasian landmass (Wilkinson et al. 2011). Revisionist accounts allow for the influence of both Asian and North African civilizations on these Greeks, and also for the fact that a good deal of Hellenic knowledge had to be reimported into Europe by Islamic empires after falling into temporary oblivion.

The central narratives of Europe were consolidated much later, following the expansion of Christianity. The assemblage uniting the fragmented peoples of Eurasia's western peninsula was known as *Christianitas*, not *Europa*. The primary "Other" at this time was not the Oriental but the Pagan. With the coming of the Reformation, North came to mean Protestant rather than heathen, and a kind of rotation took place: East–West became more salient than North–South in the mental maps of increasingly secularized elites (Wolff 1994). No one disputed that the Renaissance was primarily an Italian contribution, but the modern myth of Europe was disseminated during the centuries when economic, political, and military power shifted to the northwest. Europe was now associated with scientific and industrial revolutions, enlightenment and democratic government, colonization, and finally the global domination of the North Atlantic. Eastern Christianity was left in a highly ambiguous situation, especially in those extensive territories which had fallen into Turkish hands. In the age of enlightenment, some Frenchmen believed that the Ottoman Empire could become European. At any rate Turks were not perceived to be inherently less European than Orthodox Russians. British and Russians alike viewed the Ottoman Empire as "the sick man *of Europe*." Greece was heroically rescued from Ottoman domination in a war of independence in the early nineteenth century but, like the other small countries which emerged or reemerged in the age of nationalism, its relationship to the new centre of gravity in the west remained problematic. These tensions persisted throughout the era of Marxist-Leninist and Titoist socialism, and I shall return to them briefly below.

The power and wealth of northwestern Europe began to wane in the latter half of the twentieth century, in just the decades that its fragmented states embarked on processes of economic and political consolidation. Evidently these processes have helped call forth a new level of identity construction, to promote which governments invest generously in European Studies programs and disseminate the rhetoric of "European values." It is fascinating to observe the struggle to project these values as human rights, the secular religion of our embryonic world society, at the very moment when Europe and its offshoots in North America are relinquishing economic ascendancy. Intellectuals who think of themselves as liberal typically evade the question of Europe's boundaries. What matters, they say, is identification with an ideal and the acceptance of the norms and values that were pioneered in European modernization. They fail to notice that this reduction of Europe to a state of mind serves only to reinforce the myth of Europe as a continent, while China and India are merely countries that have grown to be rather large.

One might expect that critical social scientists would expose myths, and take pains to distinguish them from what really happened in history. This seldom happens. Many courses in European Studies barely distinguish between Europe and the European Union (especially following the enlargement process completed in 2007, which has brought several large ex-socialist states into the EU as full members). Sociologist Maurice Roche in his recent study goes some way to modifying older versions of the myth. For example, he is ready to incorporate barbarians into his history, since Celts and others played a major role in the spread of iron-making technologies (Roche 2010). For this author what matters is the "historical sociological imagination." The triumphal continental story has been internalized to become a "deep structure" of the Europeans. But there is little evidence for such claims about subjectivities, and plenty of evidence to show that contemporary Europeans have enormous difficulty in forging a common collective memory (see Macdonald, Chapter 14 in this volume). Roche's simultaneous attempt to portray Europe as forming an objective "civilizational complex" is hardly more satisfactory than that of Huntington (for whom the recent enlargement compromises the principles of Western civilization by admitting populations whose prime religious tradition is Orthodoxy).

The hegemonic narrative of Europe is worse than a selective representation of the past. It is a systematic distortion, based on ignorance of the histories and capacities of Asia, especially of China (Goody 2007). These fabrications provide a fascinating example of how the stories told by particular groups can spread and insidiously shape conceptions of the world, even of serious scholars who have taken or given numerous courses about the perils of prejudice, Eurocentrism and orientalism. The main features of the civilizational complex identified by Maurice Roche, including a transcendental faith, complex polities featuring considerable social stratification and high literacy rates, which all emerged from advanced forms of agriculture (based on the plough) and have structured kinship and domestic institutions in specific ways, are unevenly distributed within Europe and not restricted to this region. Indeed, none of these features originate here. It follows that we need to question our basic units, and recognize in our privileging of Europe the teleology that has dominated Western historiography in the centuries of Western domination. Anthropologists should join those historians able to look outside these blinkers in looking more carefully at how "the idea of Europe" has changed over time (Pagden 2002). But they should also be ready to move beyond this level of discourse, in collaboration with archaeology and the emerging "deep history." I shall now consider four fields in which large claims are put forward concerning the historical distinctiveness of Europe. In all four I find that similar features may be found in Asia, while internal variation is enormous in both so-called continents.

Religion

As already noted, religion is prominent in the mythical charter of the territory we now call Europe. In practice, however, Christian unity was continuously undermined by fission, even before the Great Schism between the Eastern and Western Churches of 1054. Orthodox Churches were decentralized, and more exposed to invasions from the steppes, such that the Roman Catholic Church in a state such as Poland came much later to be represented as a bulwark of civilization itself (the *Antemurale*). The balance of power between the Eastern and Western Churches generally favored the latter. This was demonstrated most clearly in the wake of the Counter-Reformation with the incorporation of large Eastern congregations into the universal Catholic Church (the Uniates, also known since the eighteenth century as Greek Catholics).

Meanwhile the Reformation changed the complexion of the north–south divide. The most influential scholar of the impact of Protestantism is Max Weber, who argued that European economic breakthrough was nourished by the "Protestant ethic," and especially Calvinism (1958). As a subtle exercise in cultural exploration, the theory has proved fertile; but it is not ultimately falsifiable, and can hardly be taken seriously as the definitive proof of European exceptionalism. We need to remind ourselves that Christianity is intimately linked historically to the Islamic and Jewish faiths. The Abrahamic religions in turn form a Middle East subset of the world religions, whose emergence in the "Axial Age" is to be explained in terms of the emergence of new forms of polity, the rise of a new class of literate religious specialists, and above all of a novel notion of transcendence (Arnason et al. 2005). The privileging of certain strands of Protestantism as the culmination of this long history has grossly distorted Western social theory by setting up a single ideal-type of "modernity." Emphasis on the sacred text and direct communication with God were as important for the Islamic *ulema* as they were for the puritans of northern Europe, and the Prophet of this faith was himself a merchant. That Europe did not need Luther and Calvin to discover economic calculation is abundantly demonstrated by the great medieval Catholic banking families in Italy, and by Orthodox and Jewish trading diasporas in the Byzantine empire and elsewhere. Is Roman Catholicism a barrier to economic growth in Poland and Lithuania today? Or Orthodoxy in Romania and Russia? Or Hinduism, Buddhism and Confucianism in various parts of Asia?

The spread of Christianity from its origins in the Middle East throughout western Eurasia is a fascinating historical process, but it does not differ in its essentials from the spread of Islam in Central and South Asia, North Africa, and (for many centuries) Europe, or from the spread of Hinduism and Buddhism. Many key features, such as the institutions of monasticism and pilgrimage, are to be found in all of these faiths.

In all of them, anthropologists have explored the complex syncretisms which followed the impact of a new world religion on earlier "magical," "folk," and "shamanic" practices. The world religions are a phenomenon of the *longue durée* in Eurasia; there are no grounds for privileging the European expansion of Christianity in this context.

POLITICS, GOVERNMENT, BUREAUCRACY

The word "democracy" is usually central to the Europeanist narratives. It is of Greek origin – but then so are "tyranny," "oligarchy," and numerous other terms less likely to appear in Europeanist discourses. Europe alone, it is sometimes claimed, pioneered forms of representative government, while Asia suffered under "Oriental Despotism," a phantom which distorted the late writings of Karl Marx on the "Asiatic mode of production," and which was given new life in the twentieth century with Karl Wittfogel's (1957) concept of the "hydraulic society." This located the ultimate source of modern totalitarianism in the need for concentrated power to control irrigation systems. In fact, new forms of state power, none of them resembling democracy or totalitarianism in the modern senses, were developed in many other ecological contexts. The attempts of contemporary scholars such as Jared Diamond (1997) to reduce sociopolitical evolution to geography and ecology are no less reductionist than those of predecessors such as Wittfogel.

Various forms of political participation, self-government and "rule of law" are found all over the world. Hierarchy, oligarchy, and imperialism are characteristic of the modern history of both eastern and western Eurasia. The Greek city states offered civic participation to elite males, but not to women, let alone to slaves. Tensions between the merchants who lived in such city states or other "ports of trade" and the landed gentry who lived outside them can be documented in much the same way in many parts of the Eurasian landmass. The European polities of the Middle Ages were fragmented in comparison with the Chinese empire, but power-holders drew on comparable ideologies of divine mandate. The feudalism which evolved in northwest Europe bore a closer resemblance to premodern Japan than to political structures in other parts of Europe at the time. Eric Wolf (1982) suggested the term "tributary mode of production" to escape from the Eurocentric specificities of feudalism. Sub-Saharan Africa also developed political hierarchies, but the degree of stratification and differentiated living standards were modest in comparison with the cleavages which opened up in the agrarian empires of Eurasia.

In more recent times, no one would deny that there were differences between the empires that carved up Poland at the end of the eighteenth century; but to allege that one of them, the Russian, belongs in a different category altogether because somehow contaminated by Asia, is to reproduce an old nationalist cliché of Polish historiography. The Ottoman Empire differed again, but hardly enough to justify diagnosis of a "continental" distinction. This Turkish dynasty was able to capture Constantinople and consolidate its presence over several centuries in what we nowadays call the Balkans thanks to techniques of social organization and military technology brought from Central and East Asia. The evocation of suffering under centuries of "Turkish yoke" is a poor foundation for studying the modern history of this region (though such images are regularly deployed in strengthening opposition to the cases of Turkey and Albania for EU membership). It is equally unhelpful to idealize the Ottoman Empire as an early variant of modern liberal multiculturalism; but, in their "negative tolerance" of religious difference, the Ottomans were closer to the "European values" of today than were their Christian contemporaries.

More interesting for anthropologists than the reductionist works of Wittfogel or Diamond are the attempts of Louis Dumont to oppose the holism of caste hierarchy in India to the fundamental egalitarianism of the modern West (1970[1966]); or Norbert Elias's depiction of the "civilizing process" as it unfolded from European court society (1994[1939]). But these too are ultimately shot through with a Western bias that does not stand up to scrutiny. The shabby confusion of centuries of orientalizing discourses is nowhere more evident than in discussion of bureaucracy. It is generally agreed that formal-rational authority is a feature of modern politics, and that impersonal bureaucracy is the institutional means by which it is realized. Again, Max Weber is the key figure in the sociological formulation of these ideal types. Yet in his insistence that *das Abendland* carried the torch of modernity, he was obliged to explain away the significance of much older traditions of competitive recruitment by examination in the vast bureaucracy of imperial China.

Economy

Weber's first academic specialization was in economics (*Nationalökonomie*) and, notwithstanding the importance of religious doctrines and the rise of bureaucracy, he recognized that the process he termed rationalization also depended critically on innovations in the economic domain, such as double-entry bookkeeping. Unfortunately he overlooked the extent to which this was already practiced in mercantile communities throughout Eurasia, and especially in China. This should not come as a surprise in view of the basic similarities of economic development from the late Bronze Age onwards. Craft and trade specializations were made possible by growing urban populations, which were sustained by more intensive forms of agriculture than those found in sub-Saharan Africa and matched only much later in the Americas. Plough agriculture was not invented in Europe, but spread there from the Middle East. Similar mechanisms of transfer ensured that innovations in other domains were diffused in the centuries which followed. For much of this history the technological advantage lay with East Asia.

But how then did Europe come to achieve its undisputed ascendancy in the nineteenth and twentieth centuries? Jack Goody rejects all attempts to ground an alleged "European miracle" in the intrinsic superiority of Western institutions as they had evolved in the *longue durée*. To answer this question, a *courte durée* analysis of contingencies is warranted. It was not so much the maritime expansion of northwest Europe from the sixteenth century onwards but rather the industrial revolution of the eighteenth, made possible above all by the fossil resources available in Great Britain, which led to the "Great Divergence" (Pomeranz 2000) and the subjection of China in the nineteenth century by military means to the status of quasi-colony. The recent reemergence of China as a major force in the world economy, rivaled in scale and dynamism only by India, shows a reversion to the ancient pattern of alternation between eastern and western Eurasia. From this perspective, the superiority won by (certain parts of) Europe as a result of the industrial revolution was only an ephemeral moment in the long-term swing of the pendulum between west and east. We need, therefore, to recognize a "Eurasian miracle," not a breakthrough which took place in Europe alone (Goody 1996, 2010).

Goody has also illustrated his arguments in original ways with respect to the consumption side of the economy, for instance, the social and ritual use of flowers is characteristic of Eurasia (1993), where rival *hautes cuisines* reflect greater social differentiation, contrasting with the more egalitarian cooking practices of sub-Saharan Africa (1982). In consumption, as in production, the similarities between various regions of Eurasia, broadly corresponding to the extent of agricultural intensification and political hierarchy, are more striking than east–west differences. At the same time, the internal diversity of both Europe and Asia is greater than the alleged intercontinental variation.

Kinship, Relatedness, the Person

So far I have argued that there is no evidence of a uniquely European miracle in any of the conventional macrolevel domains of social organization: religion, politics, economics. What about the microfoundations of social life, where the anthropologist is sometimes considered to be the primary scholarly specialist? Kinship terminology varies significantly within Europe, as it does within other macroregions of the landmass. It was thought by some in the nineteenth century that the "stem family" form of household organization might be distinctively European. It has taken a long time to recognize that it is also widespread in Asia, notably in Japan (Fauve-Chamoux and Ochiai 2009). For nearly half a century scholars have been debating a "European marriage pattern," involving late age of marriage and relatively high rates of celibacy (Hajnal 1965). The pattern is not found east of a line that stretches between St Petersburg and Trieste. Diehard believers in the uniqueness of Europe have no trouble with this, accustomed as they are to restrict Europe to the zone of Western Christianity. But variation within this western zone is more problematic. Alan Macfarlane put forward an ambitious theory which attributed England's leading role in the industrial revolution to a unique "individualism," which he traced back deep into the Middle Ages (1978). Undoubtedly there were distinctive features in the English case, though critics argued that they had more to do with the institutions of the common law than with household and community social organization. In later work Macfarlane noticed numerous similarities between England and Japan, which he eventually attributed to the common factor of "islandhood" (1997).

A more comprehensive analysis would start from the fact that farming societies across the entire landmass faced basically the same problem: how to transmit land and capital to the next generation in such a way as to match population to resources without allowing the fruits of one's own labor to be appropriated by strangers. Again, the perspective of Jack Goody is illuminating. In his account, the spread and intensification of agriculture is associated with the devolution of property to both sons and daughters, which has far-reaching consequences for what he terms the "domestic domain" (Goody 1976). In comparison with sub-Saharan Africa, Eurasia displays certain common features: "vertical" transfer of dowry rather than "horizontal" bridewealth payments, concubines rather than co-wives, and formal adoption rather than informal fostering. Even where women's share of the inheritance is significantly less than that of men, as in Islamic law, the endowment of females reflects the status preoccupations of societies which have become more differentiated and hierarchical thanks to their new productive systems (Goody 1990).

Of course, theories at this level cannot explain all the variation across the landmass in time as well as in space. Critics point to cases of bridewealth in many peripheral regions of the Eurasian landmass, and they ask why bridewealth payments should be resumed and massively expanded in recent decades in China. Nonetheless, Goody's general theory offers a better foundation than attempts to squeeze Chinese kinship into the terms refined in African tribal contexts (lineage analysis). Closer inspection of the Eurasian cases suggests that bridewealth remains most conspicuous in regions which have not experienced agricultural intensification. When the resources transferred at marriage are used to endow the new couple, in particular the bride, this is more appropriately viewed as "indirect dowry" and easily reconciled with Goody's proposition that vertical property transfers are characteristic of Eurasia in recent millennia.

The study of kinship has in recent years evolved into (or been partially replaced by) a more broadly construed interest in "relatedness" and in concepts of personhood. It has been suggested that European, or Euro-American, individualism differs from the "distributed" forms of personhood found elsewhere. For example, whereas Macfarlane (1978) thought that only the English were truly individualist, his Cambridge colleague Marilyn Strathern has contrasted the Euro-American notions with those of Melanesia (1988). Such contrasts continue old anthropological habits of alterity thinking ("the West versus the rest"). Closer inspection reveals the pitfalls of such simple dichotomies. Not all sections of Euro-American society are equally individualistic. Strathern's "dividuals" have parallels in other parts of Eurasia, for example in Hindu communities in India, whose self-conceptions turn out to be rather more complex than allowed for in the neat model of Louis Dumont (Marriott and Inden 1977). Notions of distributed personhood seem particularly prominent in Eastern Christian communities "on the margins" of Europe (Hann and Goltz 2010).

This is not to say that Hindu and Greek Orthodox villagers leave no space at all for persons to act as utility-maximizing individuals according to the "Euro-American" stereotype. The Greek case is especially telling because of its salience in Europeanist myth-making, as Michael Herzfeld has pointed out in numerous publications. Notions and practices of *eghoismo* among Cretan shepherds are rooted in a repudiation of the Hellenic heritage rather than its celebration (Herzfeld 2002). More generally, while the emergence and repeated enactment of such simplistic stereotypes (e.g. Russians as primordially communitarian) are interesting phenomena that deserve ethnographic attention, they should not be confused with social realities. Herzfeld issues a salutary warning that both the individual and the nation-state are the constructions of elites. The main job of the ethnographer should be to uncover the complexities which they conceal. Tropes of individualism turn up in various forms in different locations, but their consolidation as part of a unified Europeanist discourse is highly problematic. Thus the idea of a "European self" makes no sense for Herzfeld.

Behind such discourses, patterns of kinship, residence, and support-based relatedness continue to vary significantly within contemporary Europe (Heady 2010). If the number of persons who live alone is taken as an indication of individualism, this is much more pronounced in Scandinavia than in the Mediterranean countries, where unmarried children are far more likely to continue residing with their parents. Yet where the kin groups are weaker, support from the state is proportionately more significant; the Scandinavian welfare states are not the products of "individualist" societies. Such patterns, and the basic question of "who helps whom," need to be addressed in wider contexts of space and time. As India and China develop economically, the task of reconciling family and state provision of support will become increasingly similar to the challenges being faced in Europe. Neither in the past nor in the present do kinship ideas and residence practices provide grounds for constituting Europe, or pre-enlargement EU Europe, as a unified entity.

Postsocialist Eastern Europe

If Greece is one instructive setting in which to probe representations and realities of Europe, its neighbors in Eastern Europe which were subjected to some form of socialism until the 1990s provide another. The political boundaries did not coincide with Huntington's fault line. Setting aside the complexity of Tito's Yugoslavia, most states of this region could be assigned to the sphere of either Eastern or Western Christianity. As noted above, the idea that Poland is a bastion of Western civilization is an enduring trope of national self-representations. In Bulgaria, by contrast, long-standing affinities to Russia were strengthened in the era of the Soviet bloc. Generally, slogans celebrating a "return to Europe" had less resonance in the Balkan countries (except for certain regions formerly incorporated into Habsburg *Mitteleuropa*) than in Budapest, Prague, and Warsaw. Russia itself has experienced a resurgence of "Eurasianist" ideas – referring in this case to nationalist distortions of earlier philosophical attempts to transcend dualistic continental conceptions (Humphrey 2002).

These differences were largely invisible to Western observers, for whom east was east and the whole of ex-socialist Eastern Europe was now an interstitial zone. Some Westerners might even feel that secularized Bulgaria was more modern and European than highly religious Poland. The symbolic geography of Europe retained its fundamental east–west cleavage, and the new democracies of Eastern Europe were subjected to a novel variety of orientalism (Hann 1996). Some intellectuals in these countries bought into these stereotypes. When "shock therapy" resulted not in prosperity but in high unemployment, economic dislocation and even more blatant corruption than that recalled from the socialist decades, Polish sociologist Piotr Sztompka attributed all these shortcomings to the "civilizational incompetence" of his fellow citizens (see discussion in Buchowski 2001). Of course such diagnoses did not disturb the enduring perception that the real barbarians were the neighbors to the east.

Similar ambivalences can be found throughout *Mitteleuropa*, a quasimythical realm that corresponds roughly to the territories of the Austro-Hungarian empire, home of so much outstanding European cultural activity, from Brahms and Mahler to Kafka, Freud and Wittgenstein (see Kiliánová, Chapter 7 in this volume). But in what sense is this a *European* historical region? In a late–Cold War polemic, Milan Kundera (1984) insisted on a binary model and placed his Bohemian homeland firmly in the West. Should we perhaps draw more precise boundaries within *Mitteleuropa*? For some, the orientalizing discourses begin not in eastern Galicia, Bukovina or Transylvania, but at the tiny river Leitha, just to the east of Vienna. Indeed, the Magyars are historically a nomadic people originating in Central Asia. In the era of nationalism, their elites had renewed recourse to these Asian traditions in order to distinguish themselves from all of their neighbors. But for a thousand years these nomads from the steppe, after settling in the Carpathian basin, accepted Western Christianity and were integrated into the European state system. The dual mythology persists in the postsocialist era. On the one hand, most Hungarians could celebrate the end of the Iron Curtain at the Leitha, and "rejoin" Europe with enthusiasm. On the other, "Europe" could also be blamed for the disappointments and high social costs of the "transition." Nationalist *ressentiments* are directed not only against local Roma and the tiny surviving Jewish community but also against anonymous bureaucrats in Brussels. Right-wing politicians and intellectuals invoke the noble warrior heritage of the Magyars to justify their repudiation not only of socialism but also of the liberal social and economic policies which they associate with the EU. In conditions of economic depression such rhetoric has a widespread appeal (though in fact not even the most extreme nationalist parties have formally opposed EU membership). Meanwhile their liberal and socialist opponents write open letters to Paris thanking the French authorities for accepting Roma refugees, and bemoaning the fact their own state is incapable of matching up to "European" standards (Böröcz 2006).

From a long-term historical viewpoint, the trajectory of the Magyars from barbarian nomads to *mitteleuropäische Hochkultur* exemplifies the unity of Eurasia; but the story cannot be celebrated in this way because we remain imprisoned in the dualistic continental model. More generally, *Mitteleuropa* demonstrates the limitations of attempting to distinguish historical regions in a shallow timeframe. More fruitful contrasts and comparisons must be sought over the *longue durée*. Stefan Troebst (2009) has argued persuasively for identifying "historical meso-regions" as a foundation for comparative research within Europe, but he acknowledges the difficulties which arise in specifying the epochal links between a recent political coinage such as "postsocialist Eastern Europe" and Habsburg *Mitteleuropa*. It is no coincidence that the concept of the mesoregion (*Geschichtsregion*) has been most actively cultivated by specialists in the history of Eastern Europe, where the intercontinental divide was most suspect. But from the perspective of Jack Goody, the whole pseudocontinent of Europe deserves to be classified as a mesoregion, endowed with its "specific cluster of structural markers," within the macroregion of Eurasia.

Conclusion

It is easy to see where the impulse for an "anthropology of Europe" and "Europeanist anthropology" is coming from, and to welcome it. For the renewal of the discipline, it is important to transcend the old imperialist and nationalist frames of reference. Impetus is also provided by the staggering events of our age, including the speed with which so many former socialist states have been incorporated into the European Union. Within just a few decades, the EU has come to represent the peoples of western Eurasia more comprehensively than any precursor. But of course many observers balk at the claim "represent" and lay charges such as "democratic deficit." Interest and participation in the political process at the European level is weak. Today's citizens still identify much more with their own states, just as the subjects investigated by the early *Volkskundler* still identified more with their locality and region. Precisely because of that history, today's anthropologists should be wary of allowing themselves to be dragged into new consciousness-raising projects.

The alternative to such complicity, I suggest, is stringently to question this entity "Europe," into which so much scholarly and political energy is nowadays invested. To do so is not to devalue of the contributions made by different peoples in western Eurasia, especially in recent centuries. But the accomplishments of the Renaissance and the Enlightenment need to be situated in wider contexts. For this purpose it is helpful to adopt a naive epistemology that separates the effects of "real" processes from the effects of how people think and talk about these processes. In this chapter I have opposed a mythical history of Europe, exemplified by Max Weber's vision of *das Abendland*, to the *Realgeschichte* offered by Jack Goody, who has shown, following the archaeologist Gordon Childe (1964[1942]), that structural similarities between developments at the western and eastern ends of the Eurasian landmass are at least as interesting as the differences. Stratified societies with plough-based agriculture, highly differentiated consumption patterns, and the "diverging devolution" of a family estate as the prime form of property transmission, form a sharp contrast to the more egalitarian societies of sub-Saharan Africa, with their hoe-based economies and more inclusionary kinship systems. Within Eurasia one can observe complex processes of exchange and borrowing between east and west, with alternating leadership over the centuries. Sometimes diffusion seems to have played the key role (with or without the migration of the original carriers of the elements in question), while in other cases similar patterns seem to have emerged independently as a response to similar structural conditions. Peoples such as the Magyars embody the unity of the landmass, though dominant representations of their history tell a different story by insisting on a bifurcation.

Of course, these real historical processes did not proceed evenly and uniformly. Vast regions of northern Eurasia remained "structurally" more similar to remote and inhospitable parts of Africa until their colonization by the Russian and later Soviet empires; elsewhere on the landmass the imperial power was the Qing, the British or the French. Since the most influential traditions in European social anthropology focused mainly upon European colonies outside Eurasia, the affinities between these different forms of empire have yet to be adequately explored in the scholarly literature.

The purpose of this chapter is therefore *not* to substitute a reified notion of Europe as a civilization stretching back to time immemorial with an equally indefensible notion of Eurasian unity. Rather, the modest aim is to challenge pervasive contemporary assumptions concerning Europe by expanding the usual spatial and temporal horizons. These can of course be expanded still further since, according to present archaeological knowledge, there is no doubt that modern humans first appeared on the scene in southern Africa. As Troebst (2009) makes clear, historical regions come and go. But for the last 5000 years it makes a lot of sense to take Eurasia as the macroregion. The rise of its western extremity in the last 500 years should not be viewed teleologically; the elevation of Europe to the status of continent is a part of this distortion. The anthropologists who study how this is being promoted need to remain critical of the whole endeavor.

REFERENCES

Arnason, J., S. Eisenstadt, and B. Wittrok, eds.
2005 Axial Civilizations and World History. Leiden: Brill.

Böröcz, J.
2006 Goodness Is Elsewhere: The Rule of European Difference. Comparative Studies in Society and History 48(1):110–138.

Buchowski, M.
2001 Transformation: An Anthropological Perspective on Post-Socialism. Poznań: Wydawnictwo Humaniora.

Childe, V. G.
1964[1942] What Happened in History? Harmondsworth: Penguin.

Diamond, J.
1997 Guns, Germs, and Steel: A Short History of Everybody for the Last 13 000 Years. London: Vintage.

Dumont, L.
1970[1966] *Homo hierarchicus*: An Essay on the Caste System. Chicago: University of Chicago Press.

Elias, N.
1994[1939] The Civilizing Process. Oxford: Oxford University Press.

Fauve-Chamoux, A., and E. Ochiai, eds.
2009 The Stem Family in Eurasian Perspective: Revisiting House Societies, 17th–20th Centuries. Berne: Peter Lang.

Goody, J.
1976 Production and Reproduction: A Comparative Study of the Domestic Domain. Cambridge: Cambridge University Press.
1982 Cooking, Cuisine and Class: A Study in Comparative Sociology. Cambridge: Cambridge University Press.
1990 The Oriental, the Ancient and the Primitive: Systems of Marriage and the Family in the Pre-Industrial Societies of Eurasia. Cambridge: Cambridge University Press.
1993 The Culture of Flowers. Cambridge: Cambridge University Press.
1996 The East in the West. Cambridge: Cambridge University Press.
2007 The Theft of History. Cambridge: Cambridge University Press.
2010 The Eurasian Miracle. Cambridge: Polity.

Hajnal, J.
1965 European Marriage Patterns in Perspective. *In* Population in History; Essays in Historical Demography. D. V. Glass and D. E. C. Eversley, eds. pp. 101–143. London: Edward Arnold.

Hann, C.
1996 The Skeleton at the Feast: Contributions to East European Anthropology. Canterbury: CSAC.
Hann, C., and H. Goltz, eds.
2010 Eastern Christians in Anthropological Perspective. Berkeley: University of California Press.
Heady, P., ed.
2010 Family, Kinship and State in Contemporary Europe. Frankfurt am Main and New York: Campus.
Herzfeld, M. 2002 The European Self: Rethinking an Attitude. *In* The Idea of Europe: From Antiquity to the European Union. A. Pagden, ed. pp. 139–170. Cambridge: Cambridge University Press.
Humphrey, C.
2002 "Eurasia," Ideology and the Political Imagination in Provincial Russia. *In* Postsocialism. Ideals, Ideologies and Practices in Eurasia. C. M. Hann, ed. pp. 258–276. London: Routledge.
Huntington, S. P.
1996 The Clash of Civilizations and the Remaking of the World Order. New York: Simon & Schuster.
Johler, R., ed.
2010 Wo ist Europa? Dimensionen und Erfahrungen des neuen Europa. Tübingen: Institut für Empirische Kulturwissenschaft.
Kundera, M.
1984 The Tragedy of Central Europe. New York Review of Books 31(7):33–38.
Leach, E. R.
1970[1954] Political Systems of Highland Burma: A Study of Kachin Social Structure. London: Athlone Press.
Macfarlane, A.
1997 The Savage Wars of Peace: England, Japan and the Malthusian Trap. Oxford: Blackwell.
1978 The Origins of English Individualism. Oxford: Blackwell.
Marriott, M., and R. Inden
1977 Toward an Ethnosociology of South Asian Caste Systems. *In* The New Wind: Changing Identities in South Asia. K. David, ed. pp. 227–238. The Hague: Mouton.
Pagden, A., ed.
2002 The Idea of Europe: From Antiquity to the European Union. Cambridge: Cambridge University Press.
Pomeranz, K.
2000 The Great Divergence: China, Europe, and the Making of the Modern World Economy. Princeton: Princeton University Press.
Roche, M.
2010 Exploring the Sociology of Europe. London: Sage.
Shore, C.
2000 Building Europe: The Cultural Politics of European Integration. London: Routledge.
Strathern, M.
1988 The Gender of the Gift. Berkeley: University of California Press.
Troebst, S.
2009 Meso-Regionalizing Europe: History Versus Politics. *In* Domains and Divisions of European History. J. Arnason and N. Doyle, eds. pp. 78–93. Liverpool: Liverpool University Press.

Weber, M.
1958[1904–1905] The Protestant Ethic and the Spirit of Capitalism. New York: Charles Scribner's Sons.
Wilkinson, T. C., S. Sherratt, and J. Bennet, eds.
2011 Interweaving Worlds: Systemic Interactions in Eurasia, 7th to 1st Millennia BC. Oxford: Oxbow Books.
Wittfogel, K.
1957 Oriental Despotism: A Comparative Study of Total Power. New York: Vintage.
Wolf, E. R.
1982 Europe and the People without History. Berkeley: University of California Press.
Wolff, L.
1994 The Invention of Eastern Europe: The Map of Civilization and the Mind of Enlightenment. Stanford: Stanford University Press.

CHAPTER 7

Mitteleuropean Ethnology in Transition

Gabriela Kiliánová

My aim in this chapter is to give an account of twentieth-century developments and current changes in ethnology in the Central European region. By the term "ethnology" I understand (i) the discipline which in German-speaking countries was most frequently called *Volkskunde* (people-lore, folklore studies) until the 1970s or 1980s, and was designated *národopis* in Czech and Slovak, *narodopis* in Slovenian, *néprajz* in Hungarian and *ludoznawstwo* in Polish, and also (ii) the terms ethnography and folkloristics. *Národopis*, *néprajz*, and *ludoznawstvo* might equally be translated as "a description of the people" (Hann et al. 2005:6). Since the 1970s and 1980s this discipline has most frequently been named "European ethnology" in German-speaking countries, or it has received the double designation of European ethnology and cultural anthropology, while university and research centers have also used other names such as *Empirische Kulturwissenschaft* [empirical cultural studies], *Kulturgeschichte* [cultural history], *Regionalethnographie* [regional ethnography], among others (Bausinger 1978:1; Korff 1996). In the formerly socialist countries of East–Central Europe the renaming of the discipline as a rule came later, especially after the political changes of the 1990s, but the new name – ethnology, European ethnology, or ethnology and cultural anthropology – did not become established in all countries (Hann et al. 2005:4–6). Whether and to what extent the renaming of the discipline brought changes in scholarly inquiry, stimulated critical reflections, and opened new perspectives for research in Central European ethnology, is a question which I will address in the present study.

By the term "ethnology" I understand this to be the discipline which was established as an independent scientific discipline in Central Europe in the course of the nineteenth century and which gradually focused on researching the "folk" and its culture. The "folk" was most often understood to mean the given nation's peasants, whose culture was considered the foundation of the national culture.

A Companion to the Anthropology of Europe, First Edition. Edited by Ullrich Kockel, Máiréad Nic Craith, and Jonas Frykman.

The Central European region, which will be at the center of attention in this chapter, is normally defined as bounded on the west by the German-speaking countries and regions, Austria, Germany, and Switzerland. To the east, the countries most often listed as belonging to Central Europe are the Czech Republic, Slovakia, Poland, Hungary, and Slovenia. Depending on the author's scholarly purposes, the geographical compass may be extended to the west, east, or south of Europe. In this chapter, however, I shall be concerned above all with the area delineated by those countries which I have named above. Although I designate this area with a single name, it by no means represents a homogeneous region where one could describe a unified canon of the discipline of ethnology. The contrary is the case. During the last three to four decades ethnology in Central Europe (just as in other regions, e.g. Scandinavia or southeastern Europe) has been distinguished by broad thematic scope, varying methodological approaches and the use of diverse, sometimes frankly divergent theoretical models. For researchers, therefore, the question legitimately arises whether one can speak at all of a single science which may use a single name (Niedermüller 2002a:28–30). From the mid-1960s – in the west as well as the east of what was then a divided Central Europe – discussions were gradually leading to attempts to change the conception of central categories of the science, such as folk and folk culture in the new era of the modern industrial world (Noah and Krause 2005; Posern-Zieliński 2005; Sárkány 2005; Skalník 2005; Kaschuba 2006:78–96). However, Regina Bendix has astutely perceived that despite the shift toward a reflexive and deconstructive approach to (everyday) culture in the modern age, which became more or less mainstream in the German-speaking countries during the 1980s and 90s, the perpetuation of research in the spirit of traditional *Volkskunde* continued. A great many studies and scholarly monographs in the 1980s were still being devoted to documenting the "expressive culture of a folk, defined as predominately agricultural, albeit one that was confined historically and regionally" (Bendix 1997:159). This statement may be applied in large measure also to the East–Central European formerly socialist countries, where the traditional canon of *Volkskunde* lingered on even longer, often until the fundamental political changes of the 1990s. This state of affairs was bolstered considerably by restriction of opportunities for free scholarly discussion by the undemocratic regimes, imposition of ideology on the discipline, isolation, and limited access to international scientific discourse. However, again one must bear in mind that conditions in the individual socialist countries were various and changed in varied ways during the second half of the twentieth century. A political liberalization occurred in the countries of East–Central Europe during the 1960s, and this continued in Poland, Hungary, and Slovenia (which was then part of Yugoslavia) during the 1970s and 80s. Meanwhile Czechoslovakia, after the violent termination of the Prague Spring by the Soviet armies and their allies in August 1968, experienced the return of a dogmatic communist regime, which was called normalization (Podoba 2005; Posern-Zieliński 2005; Sárkány 2005; Skalník 2005).

In this chapter I will analyze key developments in ethnology in Central Europe in the historic context of the twentieth century. For the first half of the twentieth century I will concentrate on the prevailing shared disciplinary canon of *Volkskunde*. Furthermore, I will describe the convergent and divergent developments in ethnology in a divided Central Europe after World War II. In the concluding section I will focus on changes in the paradigm of ethnology, as well as new research perspectives, which emerged in the altered social, cultural, and ideological reality during the period of the second modernity and also after fundamental political changes in Central Europe.

Ethnology in Central Europe to the Mid-Twentieth Century: The Canon of "National Science"

The discipline of ethnology began in association with the development of topography, statistical history and geography, and research of the country and its people/folk during the eighteenth-century Enlightenment period. In the nineteenth century this discipline was conceived in both broader and narrower senses, but as a rule it was orientated toward the culture of the "folk," meaning the lowest social classes in the rural areas. The German tradition developed from the ideas of Wilhelm Heinrich Riehl, expounded in his lecture "*Volkskunde* as Science" in 1858, where he called for research of ethnological phenomena in their functional relationships "*durch ihre Beziehung auf den wunderbaren Organismus einer ganzen Volkspersönlichkeit* . . . [through their relationship to the wondrous organism of an entire folk personality]" (Riehl 1958:29). Riehl's goal was a complex study of the folk, but paradoxically the development of *Volkskunde* in German-speaking countries led to the analytical investigation of partial cultural phenomena rather than a synthetic study of culture as a whole. Ethnology concentrated especially on researching customs, songs, dances, fairytales, costumes, and so forth, while material culture, such as folk building construction, furniture, working tools, and utensils, remained in the background. The influences which favored researching spiritual culture came not only from ethnology's links to the humanities (linguistics, literary science, comparative religious studies, etc.) but equally from the political and ideological goals of the discipline. Ethnology was supposed to develop a national awareness inspired by aesthetically pleasing phenomena (songs, dances, costumes, and so forth), which were thought of as expressions of folk culture and at the same time national culture (Bausinger 1978:3–8).

However, *Volkskunde* was established institutionally as a discipline in the German-speaking countries only in the last two decades of the nineteenth century, when professional journals began publication, and scholarly associations and museums came into being. There was a similar development, roughly in the same time period, in the other countries of Central Europe. Bernd Jürgen Warneken has pointed out that the establishment of the discipline in Germany was influenced by models from abroad: from England, France, the Netherlands, and even the United States. The aim of the various folklore societies was to collect and preserve the phenomena of traditional culture, which were disappearing under the influence of modernization processes, in museums and archives. In Germany, when the establishment of the discipline of *Volkskunde* was in its beginnings, its researchers declared common goals with the discipline of *Völkerkunde* (the study of non-European peoples and their culture). Hence Adolf Strack, first president of the main professional association, the *Verein für Volkskunde*, not only called for the cultural phenomena of their own folk to be compared with relevant phenomena in other countries, but went on to emphasize that researching one's own people must necessarily be conceived in the context of researching all mankind (Warneken 1999). Nonetheless, the subsequent development of *Volkskunde* and *Völkerkunde* in Germany was notably divergent. Two scholarly disciplines emerged which had separate institutions and scientific communities. In this regard the German-speaking countries followed a distinct path in the twentieth century, compared with the countries of Western and Eastern Europe (Johler 2002).

During the nineteenth century, ethnology in Central Europe had been influenced by Johann Gottfried Herder's philosophy of history, which ascribed an important role in historical evolution to the folk or nation. Herder pointed out that the development of nations in history influences their distinctive character, "the spirit of the nation." His philosophy had a powerful influence not only on the development of the disciplines of national history and geography, including ethnology, but also on national movements in the Central European countries. The study of "folk culture" at the end of the nineteenth century did not only serve scholarly purposes. It also gave ideological justifications for the nation's existence and right to self-determination. Since the majority of nationalities in Central Europe lived in multinational states, the need for self-definition of one's own nation, and simultaneously its differentiation from others, could be all the more urgent. Ethnology's scientific findings were therefore used for constructing an image of "folk culture" as the authentic culture of one's own nation as distinct from the culture of another nation. In the late nineteenth century and at the beginning of the twentieth, ethnology was more and more becoming a discipline which concentrated on the "folk" – the peasants, as distinct from the inhabitants of the multinational, cosmopolitan urban centers, which were undergoing the process of the first modernization at the turn of the twentieth century. Hence ethnology also is considered a child of the first modernization. It is a discipline which includes in its fundamental scholarly apparatus concepts such as authenticity, originality, unity, and tradition. These concepts gave secure foundations to the modern human being, unsettled by a changing mode of life. Folk culture or folklore offered an ideal escape from modernity, and actually became a metaphor for what is not modern, hence fundamentally traditional (Bendix 1997:7).

Although the national tendency of ethnology gradually grew in force in Central Europe, it was not the sole orientation. Austrian ethnologists of the nineteenth and early twentieth centuries broke away from the mainstream, attempting to describe the diverse population of the entire monarchy and thus contribute to patriotism and unity in the state. "Ethnographies of the Austrian monarchy" emerged from the mid-nineteenth century, culminating in the 24-volume encyclopedia *Die österreichisch – ungarische Monarchie in Wort und Bild* [The Austro-Hungarian monarchy in words and pictures] (1886–1902), which was the ethnographers' final attempt to present the unity of the state in its diversity. The contributors to this monumental work included, along with the foremost Austrian ethnographers such as Raimund Friedrich Kaindl, prominent researchers from the individual parts of the monarchy. Several of them, including Lubomír Niederle (Czech territories), Pál Hunfalvy (Hungary), Pavol Socháň (Slovakia), and Gregor Krek (Slovenia) became founders of "national" ethnology in their countries (Schmidt 1951; Fikfak and Johler 2008).

Political relations in Central Europe changed fundamentally after World War I. While in the west there was a united Germany, in the east, by contrast, following the dissolution of the Habsburg Empire, new states were formed on the principle of national self-determination. However, the newly formed "national" states often represented multiethnic territories, where the state-forming nation acquired political power and the populations of other nationalities became minorities, with restricted access to political power and economic and other resources. For example, in the post-1918 Czechoslovak Republic there were German, Hungarian, and other minorities; within the borders of the newly formed Hungarian Republic the lesser nationalities included Germans, Slovaks, and others. Ethnology as an ideological national discipline suffered no loss of importance in the new political situation. On the contrary, to a considerable degree it reinforced collective identity among the state-forming nations on the one hand and the newly emerged minorities on the other.

The academic situation in the Czech lands and Moravia offers a good illustration of the orientation of ethnology during the period of national processes from the mid-nineteenth century. After the breakup of the Habsburg monarchy, two scholarly disciplines functioned in the new Czechoslovak Republic, separated institutionally and in personnel: Czech *národopis* and German *Volkskunde*. Their divergent development had begun in the mid-nineteenth century, and was in large measure influenced by national conflicts. The Czech ethnologists Čeněk Zíbert (1864–1932), Lubor Niederle (1865–1944), and others, focused on researching the folk culture of the Czechs, and more broadly the Slavs, at the turn of the twentieth century. They were active in the Czech universities, in the Czech National Museum, and in Czech professional associations. After the emergence of the new state, Czech institutions understandably gained in political and economic strength. On the other hand, at the turn of the twentieth century the German ethnologists August Sauer (1855–1926), later Gustav Jungbauer (1886–1942), and others working in the Czech lands and Moravia, established research which was focused on the German population, and continued on these lines after the birth of Czechoslovakia. German researchers in the interwar period developed the method of so-called *Sprachinselvolkskunde* [ethnological research of language islands] and *Grenzlandvolkskunde* [ethnological research of border areas], but they continued to investigate only one group of an ethnically defined population (Lozoviuk 2008:297–314).

The Czech ethnologists proceeded in similar fashion. To the extent that they engaged in comparative study, they focused particularly on the interrelationships of the Slavic cultures. Works devoted to the comparative study of folk prose by Jiří Polívka (1858–1933), who collaborated closely with German researchers, represent an exception in Czech ethnology (Lozoviuk 2008:297–317). We could trace parallels of similarly separated "national" ethnologies, for instance among Slovak and Hungarian researchers at the turn of the twentieth century, and after 1918 in other countries.

Despite changes in the politico-geographic divisions of Europe and the advance of the Slavic nations, *Volkskunde* sustained its position as a scholarly tendency which in large measure influenced scholarly discourse in the region, frequently providing the basic literature of reference and offering sources of inspiration. Ethnology in the Central European countries was linked by a shared scholarly paradigm: researching the culture of one's own nation.

The ideological abuse of *Volkskunde* reached its most tragic extent from the 1930s and during World War II, while the National Socialists were in government in the German Reich (Bendix 1997:160–167). During that period some German ethnologists developed basic concepts of the discipline – for example, folk, folk character, folk soul – in the spirit of National Socialism, and promoted scholarly discourse in accordance with state doctrine. Bendix pointed to the fact that the basic principles of National Socialist ideology – "faith in the leader, the surrender of the individual to the community, a belief in the master race and a corresponding obsession with racial purity, and defense of *Blut und Boden* [blood and earth]" – could find resonance and support in the ethnological theories of this period. For example, there were discussions on the relationship of the creative individual to the community, expressed, for instance, in the opinions of Hans Naumann (1922) on the "communal folk spirit lacking individuality." Likewise, in ethnological research there was a "preoccupation with cleansing folk materials from the debris of the ages, coupled with latent assumption of the superiority of Indo-Germanic origins." The development of ethnology toward social-psychological and evolutionary models brought with it the use of concepts such as race and tribe, while at the same time scholars began to explain cultural differences on the basis of racial arguments. Scholarly opinions based on the search for "purity" of the folklore material, taking the principle of race as the basis of the folk, were current in ethnology. From the 1930s these took on political connotations under the National Socialist government, whether scholars were aware of that or not. It follows that with their scholarly terminology ethnologists could support, and some of them did openly support, Nazi ideology. What was at issue especially was a "cleansing of Germanic race and restoration of the spiritual unity and purity of folk." This idea led in the final analysis in political practice not only to the ostracization of other ethnic and racial groups but even to the physical liquidation of the "Others" and to one of the greatest catastrophes in the history of humanity (Bendix 1997:160–167).

Deviation from the canon of "National Science" before World War II

From the beginning of the twentieth century, ethnology in Central Europe was predominantly a discipline explicitly focused on researching one's own folk and one's own country. Nevertheless, tendencies appeared during the interwar period which opened up interesting possibilities of new methodological approaches.

In the mid-1930s the Prague Linguistic Circle was established in Czechoslovakia, focusing on the structural study of language. Its representatives, including the Russian linguist Roman O. Jakobson (1896–1982) and the Russian ethnologist Pyotr Grigoryevich Bogatyriov (1893–1971), both of whom lived in Czechoslovakia at that time, the Czech literary scientist Jan Mukařovský (1891–1975), and others, gradually created a new method which they implemented not only in linguistics but also in other human and social sciences. Bogatyriov developed the functional-structural method as part of a broader interdisciplinary perspective for ethnology. He called for investigation of the whole structure of a society's culture, because in this way it would be possible to reveal its origin and social developmental processes. Transformations and changes in culture and society were explained in terms of relations between structures and functions (Bogatyriov 1935). Czechoslovak structuralism gradually gained a response in the international scientific community from the 1930s onward. After World War II Claude Lévi-Strauss also made use of its findings (Schiwy 1969; Toman 1995). However, political relations at the end of the 1930s and the outbreak of war put a halt to this promising scholarly tendency. It is one of the paradoxes of development that structuralism attained its greatest fame and popularity in Western Europe and the United States after World War II, while in Eastern Europe it became an unappreciated and politically persecuted scholarly tendency, along with British functionalism (Jasiewicz 2005; Kiliánová 2005; Skalník 2005).

In certain countries of East–Central Europe, particularly Hungary, a tendency developed in the 1930s which focused on the social conditions of the peasants and was not so much concerned with the "national characteristics and magnificent culture of the past" (Hann et al. 2005:8). This tendency continued to find adherents, especially among sociologists, while also leaving certain traces on the work of ethnologists and helping toward changes in the discipline's orientation after World War II.

One of the most important social anthropologists of the twentieth century was a Central European, the Pole Bronisław Małinowski (1884–1942), who defined long-term fieldwork and participant observation as the basis of anthropological method and developed functionalism in social anthropology. Małinowski's works were used by researchers in Poland and the other Central European countries. For example, the Slovak ethnologist Andrej Melicherčík (1917–1966) gave relatively extensive consideration to Małinowski's functionalism in his book *Teória národopisu* [Theory of ethnography] (1945). Melicherčík was inspired by functionalism and functional structuralism when propounding his theoretical categories and methodology of *národopis*, and his book is one of the fundamental theoretical works which appeared in Czechoslovakia after World War II.

Ethnologists in Central Europe forged links with the above-mentioned tendencies or ideas when there was renewed discussion of the main research goals, methods, and ideas of ethnology, following the political liberalization of the 1960s.

Ethnology in a Divided Central Europe: Convergences and Divergences

After World War II the division of Europe into Western democratic and Eastern socialist (communist) states produced two political and ideological blocs, whose border, known as the Iron Curtain, ran through the countries of Central Europe. The region's division into a Western and an Eastern part seriously affected the maintenance of scholarly contacts among ethnologists, and produced a divergent scholarly development.

Ethnology in the democratic states of Central Europe

Volkskunde in the German-speaking countries faced the difficult task of discussing anew the object of a scholarly discipline whose basic concepts and names were associated with national ideology. Gradually three paths appeared toward a change of the discipline's research orientation and goals. One of these possibilities was opened up by the efforts to establish comparative studies of cultural phenomena in the area of Europe. At an international conference of ethnologists in Arnhem (Holland) in 1955 a new name was proposed for a discipline with that orientation – *Ethnologia Europaea*. The name was connected with ideas of Scandinavian researchers prior to World War II and also with the similar term "European ethnology" used by Sigurd Erixon in 1938 (Bringeus 1983:229). European ethnology, while being expected to concern itself with the culture of the population of its own country, was supposed to study cultural phenomena comparatively with regard to the entire European continent as a historic and cultural space. These ideas were the starting-point for, for example, the project of a European ethnographic atlas, which was intended to bring an overall view to cultural phenomena in European countries. However, it was not possible to realize this ambitiously conceived project (Rooijakkers and Meurkens 2000); only partial all-European studies were completed (e.g. Zender 1980). Instead of an overall view of the European space, the project more or less ended in parallel studies: researchers in their own countries studied diverse cultural phenomena, which they published in the national versions of ethnographic atlases (Roth 1995:168). The postulated attempts at a thoroughgoing employment of comparative method in the study of individual cultural phenomena accordingly remained an aspiration rather than the accepted practice of researchers. Later discussions in European ethnology shifted the standpoint toward comparison of "cultural relations and cultural currents within and to Europe, as well as the mutual dependence and interactions between groups and nations" (Roth 1995:165), and spoke of the diversity of the regions of Europe and their cultures.

From the 1950s a second opportunity to transform *Volkskunde* was indicated, for instance by Hans Moser and Karl-Sigismund Kramer, founders of the historical school in ethnology, later also known as the Munich School (Kaschuba 2006:82–83). They maintained that cultural phenomena should be described exactly in time, dated precisely, and localized. Historically orientated research in ethnology focused on regional or local forms of selected phenomena of folk culture, for example in the eighteenth and nineteenth centuries. Ethnologists at the same time made particular use of the study of archive sources and came close to historiography in their methods. Case studies emerged on everyday life and work in specific villages, on the historical changes of everyday life in a single region, and on the historical transformation of some given phenomenon (Kramer 1967; Moser 1985).

This tendency contributed to the fact that later, especially at the end of the 1960s and the beginning of the 1970s, the general social science concept of "everydayness" came to the center of attention for ethnology (Jeggle 1978). As Niedermüller has shown, use of this concept opened up new opportunities for ethnology to forge interdisciplinary cooperation, especially with sociology and social and cultural history. The concept of everydayness directed researchers' attention to the action and behavior of ordinary people at a concrete historical time in a concrete place. However, "everydayness" could also be conceived as a symbolic and cultural space in which all the activities of human beings ran their course, where people gained social experience and from this derived their life strategies. Culture, as a Central idea of ethnology, was subsequently defined as everyday practice. According to Niedermüller, ethnology with these bearings was devoted to the everyday history of ordinary people, and its place was between social history and the social sciences. One can agree with the author that this orientation had a striking influence on ethnology in several European countries (Niedermüller 2002a:36–38).

However, the findings of the historical school in ethnology had other theoretical consequences. The historical study of concrete cultural phenomena revealed how ethnology in the nineteenth and at the beginning of the twentieth century had described folk culture, but at the same time constructed it on the basis of miscellaneous data and thus "constructed traditions." Such "folk traditions" were afterwards spread among broad layers of the population – that is to say, among the "folk" (Moser 1954).

Soon afterwards Herrmann Bausinger's groundbreaking book appeared, *Volkskultur in der technischen Welt* (1961) [*Folk Culture in a World of Technology* 1990]. In unison with the historical school, Bausinger contended that cultural phenomena should be studied in a concrete time and in concrete forms. But his demands went further still. He wanted ethnology to study the *contemporary* cultural manifestations of ordinary people (Bausinger 1961:54ff.). The shift of research perspective from the past to the present, and the investigation of current forms of everyday culture in modern society, amounted to a fundamental change of scientific paradigm. Bausinger and his pupils, who were grouped in the so-called Tübingen School, thus opened up a third option through which a new, postwar orientation of ethnology might come into being. This change not only involved new opportunities for interdisciplinary cooperation with the social sciences but also prepared the conditions for the "anthropological turn" in ethnology in subsequent decades. However, before giving an account of this tendency I will concisely describe developments in East–Central Europe after World War II.

Ethnology in the socialist states of Central Europe

When communist regimes came to power in East–Central Europe in the late 1940s, a new paradigm was introduced – Marxist social theory, based on historical materialism. For the most part this was a new and unknown theory for ethnologists. In general, they had not been among those left-oriented intellectuals who visited the Soviet Union during the interwar period, or read the works of Marx, Engels, and Lenin. Certainly there were exceptions, for example the Czech researcher Bedřich Václavek (1897–1943, died in the Auschwitz concentration camp), theoretician of art, historian and writer, who devoted himself among other things to researching folk oral traditions. His work on folk songs and narratives, which appeared posthumously (Václavek 1963), became a fundamental work for ethnologists, though only after the retreat of dogmatic Marxism-Leninism in the 1960s. Another example is the Slovenian ethnologist Vinko Möderndorfer (1894–1958), who became acquainted with Marxism in the interwar period and focused on the economic and social basis of the phenomena under study. However, Slovenian researchers after World War II did not explicitly develop his work (Fikfak 2008:33ff.; Slavec-Gradišnik 2008:238ff.). Similarly, Polish ethnologists of the 1950s did not associate themselves with the research works of Ludwik Krzywicki, based on Marxism, which had appeared before World War II (Jasiewicz 2005:167).

After the assumption of power by communist regimes ethnologists reacted relatively quickly to the new political relations. In 1949, for example, Gyula Ortutay, Professor of Folklore Studies and Minister for Education and Religion of the Hungarian Republic, gave a programmatic lecture to the Hungarian Ethnographic Society, in which he criticized the approach of Hungarian ethnologists hitherto. According to him, they had paid little attention to social stratification and historic changes in rural society. Ortutay demanded that ethnologists should apply historicism and the dialectical method and should concentrate on the socialist transformation of rural society and the culture of the working class (Sárkány 2005:87–89). Very similar declarations were made by scholars in Czechoslovakia at the first and second statewide conferences of ethnologists held in Prague in 1949 and 1952 respectively (Skalník 2005:58ff.). But neither in Hungary nor in Czechoslovakia were these programmatic declarations followed by a professional discussion on fundamentals among ethnologists. The powerful political pressure promoting Marxism-Leninism as the only, "correct" approach caused most researchers simply to use various quotations in their own writings from Lenin, Stalin (mainly his works on the nation and nationalities), Marx and Engels. Researchers in the 1950s did not much concern themselves with the theoretical application of Marxism. During that period ethnologists mainly carried on with the intensive collection of phenomena of the vanishing traditional folk culture. Researchers continued the historic-genetic approaches, which they gradually modified in favor of a more thoroughgoing historical approach. This meant that they focused on a more exact determination in time and space of the phenomena under study. After World War II ethnology was considered a historical discipline in the majority of socialist countries (Kuti 2005; Podoba 2005).

Studies of social and cultural changes among workers in industrialized areas proceeded only hesitantly from the 1950s onward. While research was begun among the peasants and in the collective farms, the political and social contexts in which the collectivization of agriculture was effected were often *de facto* impossible to describe in print, due to their "unsuitable" content, and these research works remained unfinished (Skalník 2005:62ff.).

After the political relaxation of the 1960s, ethnologists in East–Central Europe often associated themselves with currents of ideas that had prevailed in their own countries before World War II. There was the stimulus of functional structuralism in Czechoslovakia and Hungary, and the collaboration between ethnography, sociology, and social anthropology in Poland. These impulses culminated in a more extensive study of current social changes in the rural areas and gradually also in the urban milieu.

On the other hand, the more liberal conditions of the 1960s enabled ethnologists in East–Central Europe to renew their hitherto "frozen" contacts with colleagues in Western Europe, acquire scholarly literature and follow professional discussions. In folklore studies there was a relatively large response to the works of Hermann Bausinger and the Tübingen School.

Ethnologists also began studying the works of Claude Lévi-Strauss, Edmund Leach, Victor Turner, and other anthropologists, thereby opening the way toward an "anthropological turn" in ethnology in the socialist countries (Godina 2002:6–12). These scholarly influences directed attention toward contemporary cultural phenomena, demanded detailed ethnographic documentation, and in the course of the 1960s stimulated new discussion (as they did also in the western part of Central Europe) on what the object of research was in ethnology, and what methods needed to be used (Kiliánová 2005; Sárkány 2005; Skalník 2005).

As regards a distinctive creative contribution to Marxism, one can mention, for example, Ferenc Tökei in Hungary, who from the early 1960s was attempting to bring the concept of an Asiatic mode of production into harmony with the Marxist conception of history (Sárkány 2005:98–99). This concept was also important for ethnology in the former German Democratic Republic (Noah and Krause 2005:35–36). However, the development of theory and methodology on Marxist-Leninist principles was something of a rarity in the East–Central European countries. Researchers were more positively inclined toward the reception of works by Soviet authors. From the 1970s, for example, there was Yulian V. Bromley's theory of *ethnos.* His book *Etnos I etnografiya* [Ethnos and ethnography] (1973), which appeared in several translations – Hungarian (Budapest 1976), German (Berlin 1977), and Slovak (Bratislava 1980), among others – was liberally cited, but less often creatively applied.

A striking case of how the discipline developed in the changed political conditions after World War II is furnished by ethnology in the former German Democratic Republic (GDR). In the early 1950s, the Institute of German *Volkskunde* and the Institute of *Völkerkunde* were merged into the single Department of Ethnography. Shortly after the war, the German Academy of Sciences was formed (later, from 1972 to 1991, known as the Academy of Sciences of the GDR), which on the one hand claimed continuity with the German learned societies, but on the other hand was organized according to the Soviet model as a group of scientific-research institutes. In 1949 the Academy acquired an Institute of *Volkskunde*, headed by Wolfgang Steinitz from the early 1950s. Steinitz was not an ethnologist focused on research in Germany, but rather a specialist in Finno-Ugrian languages. As a communist and a Jew he had managed to emigrate in 1934 from Germany to the Soviet Union, where he survived World War II. Thanks to Steinitz, in the early 1950s the prominent Soviet ethnologist Sergey Aleksandrovich Tokarev came to lecture in the GDR, where he emphasized the need to investigate contemporary social and cultural changes in both countryside and towns. His point of departure was the concept of the "way of life," whose state and transformations in the concrete social milieu must be the goal of ethnological research. Thanks to the good contacts between German and Soviet researchers, the postwar transmission of Soviet scholarship to the GDR was rapid and effective (Noah and Krause 2005).

The fusion of *Volkskunde* and *Völkerkunde* in the GDR proceeded slowly, and a certain division into two wings existed throughout the entire period of the GDR's existence. Despite this, a unified *Ethnographie* was bonded by the common concept of the "way of life" [*Lebensweise*], which was elaborated both by specialists in non-European ethnology (Guhr 1976; Noah and Krause 2005:40–46), as well as scholars focused on research in Germany (Mohrmann 2005). *Ethnographie* was defined as a discipline which studied culture and "way of life." "*Lebensweise* put the emphasis on social relations [. . .]; 'social man' was studied in his affiliation with groups of all kinds, including social class, status, or professional group, family, tribe, gens, community, territory, locality, town, village, religion, and ethnos" (Noah and Krause

2005:41). Culture was conceived both as precondition and result of social activity. At the same time, there was a broad understanding of culture as the material and spiritual forms of human existence, which it was necessary to trace in their historical evolution down to the present (Kaschuba 2006:88). In the GDR the concept "way of life" was applied especially in research of the working class, but the majority of ethnologists on the *Volkskunde* wing continued to devote themselves to the history of the various phenomena of protoindustrial culture in rural areas, and to regional historical studies (Mohrmann 2005:202–203). *Ethnographie* as a discipline seeking to merge *Volkskunde* and *Völkerkunde* in the GDR disappeared after the unification of Germany. The Department of Ethnography at Humboldt University was changed to The Institute of European Ethnology, where research was directed above all toward investigations in Europe, with non-European studies relegated entirely to the background. The Academy of Sciences of the GDR ceased to exist and with it also the Institute of *Volkskunde*. In the new federal lands of the unified Germany the academic community reverted to the older model of *Volkskunde* and *Völkerkunde* as separate disciplines, and the combined model created in the GDR disappeared entirely from the academic agenda in Germany (Johler 2002:155–156; Noah and Krause 2005:25–27).

The "Anthropological Turn" in Ethnology – an Attempt to Transform the Discipline

Hitherto I have emphasized the distinction between ethnology as a science focused on researching European countries on the one hand, and social and cultural anthropology on the other hand, which was devoted especially to non-European countries. However, roughly in the 1950s, social and cultural anthropology began extending its field of interest to the European lands. The "discovery of Europe" by anthropologists began in the peripheral southern and southeastern area of the continent and also in remote, less industrialized parts of Western Europe. As a rule, anthropologists at first investigated smaller settlements and actually transferred the classic anthropological community studies to the European continent, using their original theoretical and methodological apparatus. What this amounted to was anthropology *in* Europe, not an anthropology *of* Europe (Goddard et al. 1994; Vermeulen and Roldán 1995; Niedermüller 2002a:46–48). With gradual political relaxation, West European anthropologists began research in some East European socialist countries, and from the 1970s these territories were slowly integrated into an anthropology of Europe (Hann 1994, 1995). Also associated with the anthropology of Europe tendency were those later anthropologists and ethnologists who concentrated on researching European integration as a unique historical, social, economic, political, ideological, and cultural process. For example, they investigated the construction of European identity and its symbols; further targets of research were the European institutions and the ambivalent nature of integration processes in the various parts of coalescent Europe, to mention just a few examples from a broad thematic range (Wilson and Smith 1993; Abélès 1996; Buchowski 1998; Bellier and Wilson 2000; Shore 2000; Fikfak and Vivod 2009).

Another research tendency whose methodological apparatus had an influence on discussions in ethnology in Central Europe was anthropology at home (Messerschmidt 1981; Jackson 1987). Researchers strove to acquire the most precise knowledge of the concrete form of cultural and social phenomena and processes, mainly of a global or society-wide character in a concrete place and at a concrete time. The presupposition for research was that studying phenomena in one's own country was not by any means easier than studying the culture of some other country. Even while researching *at home* the anthropologist does not know, or does not know sufficiently, which attitudes and opinions are held by the community, institutions, groups or individuals being studied, or what the nature of their behavior is. The research field of anthropology at home, for example in the United States, overlapped with the social-scientific research of large cities and the emerging urban anthropology (Niedermüller 2002a:51–54). However, although researchers traced macrosocial processes, as a rule they remained on the microsocial level as regards their methods of acquiring data. That is to say, anthropology at home above all used qualitative methods of fieldwork based on observation and interview, with the help of which the researchers described people's behavior, activity, and opinions.

The various movements in cultural and social anthropology mentioned here lent their inspiration to ethnology in Central Europe, but in differing degrees. Wolfang Kaschuba considers that in the transformation of ethnology in Germany the influences of social and cultural anthropology were to be seen principally in urban studies from the 1970s. In other research areas ethnology in Germany drew rather upon inspiration from British cultural studies, history of folk and everyday culture, and history of mentalities, as represented in the works of the historians Edward P. Thomson, Fernand Braudel, Carlo Ginzburg, and others (Kaschuba 2006:103–106). Discussions on the use of anthropology at home were reopened during the 1990s, when cultural anthropologists researched German unification and the transformation processes in the former GDR (Greverus 1999).

Following the political liberalization of the late 1960s, there was a transmission of influences from social and cultural anthropology in the East–Central European countries, where in most cases lectures in social and cultural anthropology gradually became part of the ethnologist's professional formation (Godina 2002:3–6). While such influences continued in Poland, Hungary, and Slovenia during subsequent decades, in Czechoslovakia from the 1970s onward the turn toward social and cultural anthropology was in large measure limited by political pressure. Ladislav Holý and Miroslav Stuchlík, who initiated the study of anthropology during the 1960s in Prague (where it was then called *cizokrajná etnografie* [ethnography of foreign lands]), emigrated during the 1970s and developed careers in Great Britain as social anthropologists (Kandert 2002). However, a certain turning toward research of contemporary cultural phenomena, not only in the rural but also in the urban milieu, had already occurred and continued further.

Open discussion of the relationship of ethnology to social and cultural anthropology gradually emerged in Poland, for example, during the 1980s, while in most of the other East–Central European countries this happened mainly after 1989 (Godina 2002:6–12). However, the relationship of ethnology to anthropology remains an unresolved problem, as an animated recent discussion in the Czech Republic showed

(Nešpor and Jakoubek 2004). The fact is, in postsocialist countries after 1989 discussions on ethnology and social/cultural anthropology were linked with attempts to create institutional conditions for the development of social and cultural anthropology as an independent discipline, which would have its own chairs in universities as well as independent research institutes, separate from ethnology. Hence, discussions of the mutual relations of the two disciplines could be connected with the struggle for position in the academic world and access to financial resources.

New chairs of social anthropology have emerged in Slovakia at the University of Comenius in Bratislava, while in the Czech Republic social anthropology forms an independent department under the Chair of Anthropological and Historical Sciences at the Philosophical Faculty of the Western Czech University at Pilsen. In other postsocialist countries, for example Slovenia or Poland, there tends rather to be joint chairs of ethnology and anthropology. One must bear in mind also that in most of the postsocialist countries of Central Europe the discipline has been renamed, with the emergence of chairs of European ethnology or ethnology and cultural anthropology.

The influence of social and cultural anthropology on ethnology in the postsocialist countries of Central Europe after 1989 is plainly legible. It is expressed, for example, in current research of the economic, social and cultural transformation in the postsocialist period, or of the integration processes after accession to the European Union (Buchowski 2001; Hann and Sárkány 2003; Pine and Podoba 2007). To the extent that ethnologists take part in this research, they have frequent recourse to works of cultural and social anthropology, hoping to find theoretical and methodological inspiration and support. Apart from the new opportunities of access to anthropological literature, they are motivated also by the fact that the theory of social change has not been elaborated much in ethnological literature (Niedermüller 2002b).

Conclusion

Contemporary ethnology in Central Europe as a rule finds itself on the frontiers between the historical and social disciplines. Niedermüller, for example, defines ethnology (using the term European ethnology) as a discipline which is aimed at researching complex late modern societies, with preference given to one's own societies. Although research is focused on the present, this is seen as an "extended present," that is, phenomena are generally investigated in the historical dimension also. According to Niedermüller, European ethnology investigates the cultural constructions of late modern societies, concerning itself with the functions and transformations of cultural concepts and their influences on the sociocultural logic of local (and global) worlds. Thematically, ethnology in Central Europe addresses the most diverse manifestations of the majority society as well as the subcultures of various groups, which are defined locally, ethnically, generationally, socially, and so forth. An important part of research is devoted to the transformation processes in the formerly socialist countries. Ethnologists continue to investigate various expressions of the traditional culture of ordinary people, whether in the preceding historical periods (hence by historical methods) or currently, as expressions of cultural heritage. The contemporary ethnologies in Central Europe remain polycentric disciplines with a broad diffusion of themes. While ethnologists are inspired by a variety of methodological approaches from related scholarly disciplines, the orientation toward social and cultural anthropology and the social sciences remains relatively strong.

REFERENCES

Abélès, Marc

1996 En attente d'Europe. Paris: Hachette.

Bausinger, Hermann

1961 Volkskultur in der technischen Welt. Stuttgart: W. Kohlhammer.

1978 Volkskunde in Wandel. *In* Grundzüge der Volkskunde. Grundzüge 34. Hermann Bausinger, Utz Jeggle, Gottfried Korff, and Martin Scharfe, eds. pp. 1–15. Darmstadt: Wissenschaftliche Buchgesellschaft.

1990 Folk Culture in a World of Technology. Elke Dettmer trans. Bloomington: Indiana University Press.

Bellier, Irène and Thomas M. Wilson

2000 An Anthropology of the European Union: Building, Imagining and Experiencing the New Europe. Oxford: Berg.

Bendix, Regina

1997 In Search of Authenticity: The Formation of Folklore Studies. Madison: University of Wisconsin Press.

Bogatyriov, Pyotr Grigoryevich

1935 Funkčno-štrukturálna metóda a iné metódy etnografie a folkloristiky. Slovenské pohl'ady 51:550–558.

Bringeus, Nils-Arvid

1983 The Predecessors of "Ethnologia Europaea." Ethnologia Europaea 13:228–233.

Bromley, Yulian V.

1973 Etnos i etnografiya. Moscow: Nauka.

Buchowski, Michał

1998 Divided Europe: The Social Case of the Present Perfect Tense. *In* The Task of Ethnology, Cultural Anthropology in Unifying Europe. Aleksander Posern-Zieliński, ed. pp. 7–26. Poznań: Wydawnictwo Drawa.

2001 Rethinking Transformation: An Anthropological Perspective on Post-socialism. Poznań: Humaniora.

Erixon, Sigurd

1937–1938 Regional European Ethnology. Folkliv 1–2:89–108, 263–294.

Fikfak, Jurij

2008 Med delom in celoto: Nekatera vprašanja etnološkega raziskovanja in reprezentacje. Traditiones 38:27–43.

Fikfak, Jurij, and Reinhard Johler, eds.

2008 Ethnographie in Serie. Zu Produktion und Rezeption der "österreichisch-ungarischen Monarchie in Wort und Bild." Veröffentlichungen des Instituts für Europäische Ethnologie der Universität Wien. Vienna: Verlag des Instituts für Europäische Ethnologie.

Fikfak, Jurij, and Maria Vivod, eds.

2009 Europe. Imagination and Practices. Ljubljana: Založba ZRC, Inštitut za slovensko narodopisje SAZU. (The issue was published in 2010).

Goddard, Victoria A., Chris Shore, and Joseph Llobera, eds.
1994 The Anthropology of Europe: Identity and Boundaries in Conflict. Oxford: Berg.
Godina, Vesna
2002 From Ethnology to Anthropology and Back Again: Negotiating the Boundaries of Ethnology and Anthropology in Postsocialist European Countries. *In* The Struggles for Sociocultural Anthropology in Central and Eastern Europe. Peter Skalník, ed. pp. 1–15. Prague Studies in Sociocultural Anthropology 2. Prague: Set Out.
Greverus, Ina-Maria
1999 The Politics of Anthropology at Home. *In* The Politics of Anthropology at Home II. Theme issue. Anthropological Journal on European Cultures 8:7–26. (The issue was published in 2000.)
Guhr, Günter
1976 Über die Komplexität von Kultur und Lebensweise. Acta Ethnographica Academiae Scientiarum Hungaricae 25:1–2, 119–137.
Hann, Chris
1994 After Communism. Reflections on East European Anthropology and the Transition. Social Anthropology 2:229–49.
1995 The Skeleton at the Feast. Contributions to East European Anthropology. CSAC Monographs 9. Canterbury: University of Kent.
Hann, Chris, and Mihály Sárkány
2003 The Great Transformation in Rural Hungary: Property, Life Strategies, and Living Standards. *In* The Postsocialist Agrarian Question. Chris Hann, ed. pp. 117–142. Münster: LIT.
Hann, Chris, Mihály Sárkány, and Peter Skalník
2005 Introduction. *In* Studying People in the People's Democracies: Socialist-Era Anthropology in East–Central Europe. Halle Studies in the Anthropology of Eurasia 8. Chris Hann, Mihály Sárkány, and Peter Skalník, eds. pp. 1–20. Münster: LIT.
Jackson, Anthony, ed.
1987 Anthropology at Home. London: Tavistock.
Jasiewicz, Zbigniew
2005 The Adaptation of Soviet Models in Polish Anthropology before 1956. *In* Studying People in the People's Democracies. Socialist-Era Anthropology in East–Central Europe. Halle Studies in the Anthropology of Eurasia 8. Chris Hann, Mihály Sárkány, and Peter Skalník, eds. pp. 159–169. Münster: LIT.
Jeggle, Utz
1978 Alltag. *In* Grundzüge der Volkskunde. Grundzüge 34. Hermann Bausinger, Utz Jeggle, Gottfried Korff, and Martin Scharfe, eds. pp. 81–126. Darmstadt: Wissenschaftliche Buchgesellschaft.
Johler, Reinhard
2002 Wieviel Europa braucht die Europäische Ethnologie? Die Volkskunde in Europa und die "Wende." *In* Die Wende als Wende? Orientierungen Europäischen Ethnologien nach 1989. Veröffentlichungen des Instituts für Europäische Ethnologie der Universität Wien 23. Konrad Köstlin, Peter Niedermüller, and Herbert Nikitsch, eds. pp. 150–165. Vienna: Verlag des Instituts für Europäische Ethnologie.
Kandert, Josef
2002 The "Czech School" in Social Anthropology. *In* The Struggles for Sociocultural Anthropology in Central and Eastern Europe. Prague Studies in Sociocultural Anthropology 2. Peter Skalník, ed. pp. 43–48. Prague: Set Out.
Kaschuba, Wolfgang
2006 Einführung in die Europäische Ethnologie. 3rd edition. Munich: C. H. Beck.

Kiliánová, Gabriela

2005 Continuity and Discontinuity in an Intellectual Tradition under Socialism: The "Folkloristic School" in Bratislava. *In* Studying People in the People's Democracies. Socialist Era Anthropology in East–Central Europe. Halle Studies in the Anthropology of Eurasia 8. Chris Hann, Mihály Sárkány, and Peter Skalník, eds. pp. 257– 271. Münster: LIT.

Korff, Gottfried

1996 Namenwechsel als Paradigmawechsel? *In* Fünfzig Jahre danach. Zur Nachgeschichte des Nationalsozialismus. Sigrid Weigel and Birgit Erdle, eds. pp. 403–434, Zürich: VDG Hochschulverlag.

Kramer, Karl-Sigismund

1967 Volksleben im Hochstift Bamberg und im Fürstentum Coburg (1500–1800): Eine Volkskunde auf Grund archivarischer Quellen. Beiträge zur Volksforschung, 15. Veröffentlichungen der Gesellschaft für fränkische Geschichte, Series 9, 24. Würzburg: Schöningh.

Kuti, Klára

2005 Historicity in Hungarian Anthropology. *In* Studying People in the People's Democracies. Socialist Era Anthropology in East–Central Europe. Chris Hann, Mihály Sárkány, and Peter Skalník, eds. pp. 273–284. Halle Studies in the Anthropology of Eurasia 8, Münster: LIT.

Lozoviuk, Peter

2008 Interethnik im Wissenschaftsprozess: Deutschsprachige Volkskunde in Böhmen und ihre gesellschaftliche Auswirkungen. Schriften zur sächsischen Geschichte und Volkskunde, 26. Berlin – Göttingen: Leipziger Universitätsverlag.

Melicherčík, Andrej

1945 Teória národopisu. Liptovský Svätý Mikuláš: Tranoscius.

Messerschmidt, Donald A., ed.

1981 Anthropologists at Home in North America. Methods and Issues in the Study of One's Own Society. Cambridge: Cambridge University Press.

Mohrmann, Ute

2005 Volkskunde in the German Democratic Republic on the Eve of Its Dissolution. *In* Studying People in the People's Democracies. Socialist Era Anthropology in East–Central Europe. Chris Hann, Mihály Sárkány, and Peter Skalník, eds. pp. 195–209. Halle Studies in the Anthropology of Eurasia 8, Münster: LIT.

Moser, Hans

1954 Gedanken zur heutigen Volkskunde. Bayerisches Jahrbuch für Volkskunde: 208–234.

1985 Volksbräuche im geschichtlichen Wandel: Ergebnisse aus fünfzig Jahren volkskundlicher Quellenforschung. Forschungshefte 10, Herausgegeben vom Bayerischen Nationalmuseum. Munich: Deutscher Kunstverlag.

Naumann, Hans

1922 Grundzüge der deutschen Volkskunde. Leipzig: Quelle & Meyer.

Nešpor, Zdeňek R., and Marek Jakoubek

2004 Co je a co není kultúrni/sociálni antropologie? Námět k diskusi. Český lid 91: 53–80.

Niedermüller, Peter

2002a Europäische Ethnologie: Deutungen, Optionen, Alternativen. *In* Die Wende als Wende? Orientierungen Europäischen Ethnologien nach 1989. Konrad Köstlin, Peter Niedermüller, and Herbert Nikitsch, eds. pp. 27–62. Veröffentlichungen des Instituts für Europäische Ethnologie der Universität Wien, 23. Vienna: Verlag des Instituts für Europäische Ethnologie.

2002b Sozialer Wandel und kulturelle Repräsentation. Skizzen zu ethnologischer Transformationsforschung. Schweizerisches Archiv für Volkskunde 98:271–285.

Noah, Karoline, and Martina Krause

2005 Ethnographie as a Unified Anthropological Science in the German Democratic Republic. *In* Studying People in the People's Democracies. Socialist Era Anthropology in East–Central Europe. Chris Hann, Mihály Sárkány, and Peter Skalník, eds. pp. 25–53. Halle Studies in the Anthropology of Eurasia 8. Münster: LIT.

Die Österreichisch-ungarische Monarchie in Wort und Bild

1886–1902 Vienna: Kaiserlich-königliche Hof- und Staatsdruckerei.

Pine, Frances, and Juraj Podoba, eds.

2007 Changing Social Practices and Strategies. Case Studies from Central and Eastern Europe and Mongolia. Bratislava: Institute of Ethnology of the Slovak Academy of Sciences.

Podoba, Juraj

2005 On the Periphery of a Periphery: Slovak Anthropology behind the Ideological Veil. *In* Studying People in the People's Democracies. Socialist-Era Anthropology in East–Central Europe. Halle Studies in the Anthropology of Eurasia, 8. Chris Hann, Mihály Sárkány, and Peter Skalník, eds. pp. 245–255. Münster: LIT.

Posern-Zieliński, Aleksander

2005 Polish Anthropology under Socialism: Intellectual Traditions, the Limits of Freedom, and New Departures. *In* Studying People in the People's Democracies. Socialist-Era Anthropology in East–Central Europe. Halle Studies in the Anthropology of Eurasia, 8. Chris Hann, Mihály Sárkány, and Peter Skalník, eds. pp. 109–128. Münster: LIT.

Riehl, Wilhelm

1958 Volkskunde als Wissenschaft. *In* Volkskunde. Ein Handbuch zur Geschichte ihrer Probleme. Gerhard Lutz ed. pp. 23–37. Berlin: Erich Schmidt.

Rooijakkers, Gerard, and Peter Meurkens

2000 Struggling with the European Atlas: Voskuil's Portrait of European Ethnology. Ethnologia Europaea 30:75–95.

Roth, Klaus

1995 Europäische Ethnologie und Interkulturelle Kommunikation. Schweizerisches Archiv für Volkskunde 91:163–181.

Sárkány, Mihály

2005 Hungarian Anthropology in the Socialist Era: Theories, Methodologies, and Undercurrents. *In* Studying People in the People's Democracies. Socialist-Era Anthropology in East–Central Europe. Halle Studies in the Anthropology of Eurasia, 8. Chris Hann, Mihály Sárkány, and Peter Skalník, eds. pp. 87–108. Münster: LIT.

Schiwy, Günter

1969 Der französische Strukturalismus: Mode. Methode. Ideologie. Hamburg: Rowohlt.

Schmidt, Leopold

1951 Geschichte der österreichischen Volkskunde. Buchreihe der Österreichischen Zeitschrift für Volkskunde N.S. 2. Vienna: Österreichischer Bundesverlag.

Shore, Chris

2000 Building Europe: The Cultural Politics of European Integration. London: Routledge.

Skalník, Peter

2005 Czechoslovakia: From Národopis to Ethnographie and Back. *In* Studying People in the People's Democracies. Socialist-Era Anthropology in East–Central Europe. Halle Studies in the Anthropology of Eurasia, 8. Chris Hann, Mihály Sárkány, and Peter Skalník, eds. pp. 55–86. Münster: LIT.

Slavec-Gradišnik, Ingrid
2008 Pogledi in podobe: K vprašanjem o produkcii znanja. Traditiones 38:217–250.
Toman, Jindřich
1995 The Magic of Common Language: Jakobson, Mathesius, Trubetzkoy and the Prague Linguistic Circle. Cambridge, MA: MIT Press.
Václavek, Bedřich
1963 O lidové písni a slovësnosti. Prague: Československý spisovatel.
Vermeulen, Han F., and Arturo Alvarez Roldán
1995 Fieldwork and Footnotes. Studies in the History of European Anthropology. London: Routledge.
Warneken, Bernd Jürgen
1999 "Völkisch nicht beschränkte Volkskunde." Eine Erinnerung an die Gründungsphase des Faches vor 100 Jahren. Zeitschrift für Volkskunde 95:169–196.
Wilson, Thomas M., and M. Estellie Smith, eds.
1993 Cultural Change in the New Europe. Perspectives on the European Community. Boulder, CO: Westview.
Zender, Matthias, ed.
1980 Die Termine des Jahresfeuer in Europa. Erläuterungen zur Verbreitungskarte. Göttingen: Otto Schwarz.

PART II European Integration

CHAPTER 8

Anthropological Studies of European Identity Construction

Lisanne Wilken

The integration processes in Europe are creating the largest legally and economically integrated political system in recent times. Starting as an economic cooperation between six countries in the mid-1950s, today the European Union (EU) has 27 member states and a population of almost 500 million people. Since its inception in 1957, and through several political reforms, the member states of the EU have negotiated their way toward the abolition of internal borders, the creation of a single market with free movement of money, goods, and people, and the implementation of a common currency.

The processes of integration have raised several questions regarding culture and identity. It has, for instance, been debated whether popular identification with the EU and its institutions is necessary for integration, or whether a European identity can be engineered "from above" through cultural policies; it has also been asked whether European identities will eventually evolve "from below."

Anthropologists are well-positioned to contribute to discussions about identity in relation to European integration. Anthropology has a long history of contributing to social science research in identity construction and identity politics. For a long time anthropologists primarily studied identity construction at the subnational level, but since the 1980s – with the historic turn in anthropology, and the emerging interest in identity politics and the nationalization of states – anthropologists in Europe have also contributed to our understanding of identity construction at the supralocal level. Perhaps more importantly, anthropology has a unique perspective on identity construction: anthropologists often strive to understand the social world from the perspective of the people they study. In the case of EU studies, this translates into an interest in the ways that various actors engage in, make sense of, and position themselves in relation to the integration processes. Furthermore, anthropology has a distinct methodology – participant observation – which leads to a different kind of

A Companion to the Anthropology of Europe, First Edition. Edited by Ullrich Kockel, Máiréad Nic Craith, and Jonas Frykman.

analysis than those produced with the more conventional methods of neighboring disciplines (European Commission 2008:14). In this way anthropology can make genuine contributions to our understanding of European integration.

In this chapter I will discuss three very different anthropological approaches to the discussion of identity construction in the European Union. The first approach focuses on the attempts to "engineer" a European identity through cultural policies: since the early 1980s EU institutions have adopted various symbols and launched several campaigns in order to "boost people's awareness of a European identity" (European Commission 1988). These institutional attempts to construct a European identity have been the subject of several anthropological analyses.

The second approach considers identity construction among officials in EU institutions. Since the early 1990s several anthropologists have done fieldwork in EU institutions, where, among other things, they have explored whether the officials who work together to make integration happen are themselves becoming EUropeans.

These two approaches focus on identity construction "from above." The third approach I want to examine discusses the possible construction of European identities "from below." Rather than focusing on cultural policies, this research suggests that the unification processes in Europe provide a new frame for identity construction locally and across Europe. It explores how people and organizations increasingly define themselves in relation or opposition to the European Union and demonstrates how this creates identities that may or may not be in compliance with the official cultural policies, but which are nevertheless European.

I will start with a brief discussion of how European integration became relevant to anthropology, and then I will turn to the discussions of the possible construction(s) of Europeans.

Anthropology and the European Union

Anthropology is a latecomer to the interdisciplinary field of EU studies: the first anthropological studies of EU-related events were published approximately 30 years after the Treaty of Rome came into force in 1957 (see Wilken 1999). Looking back, this is not surprising. As stressed in several critical reviews of anthropological research in postwar Europe, anthropology was for a long time oddly out of sync with the macropolitical and macroeconomic developments taking place on the continent. During a time when societies were being rebuilt after a devastating war, when several international organizations were founded in order to secure peace, prosperity, communication, and cooperation, and when a divided Europe was coming to terms with a new world order, Europeanist anthropology was by and large mimicking regional anthropologies elsewhere. By focusing on small-scale local communities and attempting to identify the cultural rules that regulate local life, anthropology created an image of a "tribalized continent" (Boissevain 1975), where local communities appeared to be only remotely connected to or affected by the forces of states, nations, and markets (see, e.g., Macdonald 1993).

In the 1970s this focus on local communities was increasingly being criticized from within anthropology itself. The critique was linked to the emerging discomfort with the "classical concept of culture" which tended to equate "cultures" with local communities and to define them as static, closed, and bounded entities (Eriksen 1996:73). In Europeanist anthropology this discomfort was related to the growing awareness that anthropology might be missing the exact aspects that are most European about Europe, such as supralocal identity and culture (the "nation"), specific ways of organizing the public domain (the "state"), specific ways of sharing and discussing information (the "media"), specific ways of organizing socialization (the "education system") and particular ways of organizing production and consumption (the "economy") (Macdonald 1993:6). As a consequence, anthropologists increasingly turned their attention to the study of nations, both as the cultural foundation of the political community of states and as the cultural foundation of the "stateless nations" of minorities.

The anthropological interest in nations was to a large extent inspired by the simultaneous historic interest in the nationalization of European states and the *construction* of nation-states in Europe during the eighteenth and nineteenth centuries. Benedict Anderson's book (1983) about the development of imagined political communities in the form of nation-states has inspired many anthropological analyses of culture in Europe since the 1980s, and Eric Hobsbawm's (1983) notion of invented traditions has often been employed to explain how cultural traditions, that were presented as having defined a given nation or people "forever," were in fact often fairly recent inventions. It was within this analytical framework, which focused on identity politics that an anthropological interest in European integration emerged.

When discussing why anthropologists have been so slow to develop an interest in the European Union, it is relevant to recall that up until the mid-1980s the EU (at that time the European Economic Community) was still fairly small, and only a few of the original member states (France and Italy) were objects of anthropological research in any significant way. Also, the community's image as an economic club for the richer countries of northwestern Europe with a growing legitimacy problem did not fit the traditional anthropological research agenda. The southern enlargements of the 1980s that admitted the former dictatorships of Greece, Portugal, and Spain made the community more relevant to anthropology, as it brought in more Mediterranean countries.

Furthermore, at this time the EU was changing. Preparations for the Inner Market, with the free movement of people, money, and goods, necessitated harmonization of legislations and practices in the member states. This harmonization was accompanied by a number of cultural policies aimed at boosting popular identification with the community and its institutions. This development of cultural policies was, as Cris Shore has pointed out, practically an invitation to anthropology to get involved. While anthropologists may previously have felt estranged from the EU due to the focus on macrolevel economics, politics, and law, the "cultural turn" in the integration processes of the 1980s made European integration relevant for anthropology, both theoretically and empirically (Shore 2000).

In the following sections I will introduce the development of cultural policies in the European Union and discuss some of the analytical approaches to the attempt to construct a European identity "from above."

EU Cultural Policies

The EU's cultural policies were officially introduced with the Maastricht Treaty in 1993. In this treaty it is stated *inter alia* that the EU "shall contribute to the flowering of the cultures of the Member States while respecting their national and regional diversity and at the same time bring their common cultural heritage to the fore." However, political discussions about the necessity of a cultural dimension to the integration processes started much earlier. According to Maryon McDonald, it was in the late 1960s that politicians and officials within EU institutions began to stress the need to create a cultural foundation for the integration processes. At this time it was realized that the legitimacy which the European Community had held in the 1950s as a supranational organization to create peace in Europe was disappearing as new generations grew up in the western part of a divided Europe in relative prosperity and with a new set of hopes, fears, and limitations. In order to move the integration processes forward it was considered necessary to create feelings of communality among the participating countries (McDonald 2006:220). The first step in this direction was the adoption in 1973 of a "Declaration on the European Identity" in which the fundamental values of the European cooperation were defined. According to this declaration the member states are defined by shared political values such as democracy, rule of law, market economy, social justice, and respect for human rights.

During the 1980s, cultural policies were increasingly being discussed as a political necessity in order to create the Single European Market and the Economic and Monetary Union (McDonald 2000:57). Official reports from both the European Parliament and the European Commission argued that it was necessary to strengthen the solidarity between the people of the member states and to enhance their knowledge of European culture (Shore 1993). Heads of states and governments approved the introduction of common symbols and cultural policy measures in order to boost popular awareness of the EU and facilitate integration. Over the years the EU got a passport, a driver's license, a flag, an anthem, a motto, a memorial day, and a common currency. Events and rituals were invented to celebrate the community's existence, like European Years, European Decades, and European Cities of Culture; and programs regarding arts, architecture, music, film, student exchange, and minority languages were launched in order to preserve and promote what was perceived as the cultures of the member states and to secure the interaction between them.

In the 1990s the EU elaborated on its foundational values; the Amsterdam Treaty (1999) included an antidiscrimination paragraph, and official documents and declarations increasingly stressed that the European Union was build on values such as tolerance, multiculturalism, antiracism, anti-antisemitism, anti-islamophobia, gender equality, and respect for minorities.

Anthropological analyses of the EU's cultural politics differ in their approaches and in the questions they ask. Some focus on the political purpose of the EU's cultural politics and discuss whether their aim is to create a European *demos* for an emergent European superstate. Others focus on the discursive construction of European culture and identity in the various policies that have been created over the past 20 years. And others again analyze their interpretation and practical implementation in the member states. Below I will discuss some of the most prominent approaches to the EU's cultural politics.

Creating "*Homo europaeus*"?

British anthropologist Cris Shore, who is one of the first and, without rival, the most productive scholar of the EU's cultural politics, has suggested that the introduction of cultural politics can be understood as an attempt to artificially create a European people. Shore has argued that European integration is an elite project to create some sort of European state (Shore 2001:55). Initially it was expected that popular identification with this emerging superstate would automatically develop as "spillover" from economic and legal integration. However, during the 1980s it became clear that, "despite making impressive legal, economic and institutional advances toward a united Europe, EU elites [had] failed to create a 'European people'" (Shore 2001:55). Instead they had created "an embryonic state without a nation" (Shore 2001:57). According to Shore this is why EU institutions launched a series of cultural policies: in order to create Europeans (Shore 1995:217).

Cris Shore defines EU cultural politics as "the various cultural strategies, discourses, and political technologies that function to make certain ideas about Europe authoritative while alternative ideas are rendered marginal and muted" (2001:54). With reference to this definition he has analyzed a wide range of campaigns, reports, documents, and speeches in order to understand how officials in EU institutions perceive Europe. Shore's analyses are grounded in a discursive and cognitive approach to culture. He sees the culture political initiatives as reflections of the way elites perceive European culture, and many of his analyses focus on linguistic categories, systems of classifications, discourses, metaphors, and symbols, which as he has argued may help us understand how political actors in Brussels and Strasbourg understand "Europe" and "the Europeans" (e.g. Shore 1993, 1995, 1996, 1997, 2000, 2001).

Shore relates the EU's cultural politics to discussions about what political scientists refer to as the EU's "democratic deficit" (Shore 2001, 2006; see also Abélès 2004). Discussions of the democratic deficit refer both to the political discussions about whether the institutions of a union of democracies need to be democratic, and to the normative discussions about whether the EU can be democratic without a *demos* (e.g. Habermas 2001). According to Shore, the democratic deficit is in fact a "cultural deficit": political regimes, especially democracies, customarily seek legitimacy in the cultural domain and thus presuppose shared cultural values between rulers and ruled (2001:56). In the case of the European Union, Shore claims that there are no shared values and no *demos* to be ruled democratically (Shore 2006:714).

In his early work Shore appears to be open to the possibility that the EU's cultural politics may eventually promote a sense of common identity in Europe. As he points out (Shore 1993:790–791), anthropological theories often stress that the political reality is symbolically constructed and that it is through symbols that people come to know about the structures that unite and divide them. Symbols do not simply enable individuals to interpret the political reality, they largely create it. Therefore, Shore argues, "it is reasonable to assume that with a steady consolidation and expansion of the European tier of authority the more recently created European political reality will herald a gradual but steady undermining of authority of existing nation states." At the same time Shore maintains that the culture political initiatives are based on a conceptual naïveté which resembles the concept of identification in Evans-Prichard's structural-functionalism (Shore 1993:790–791). Later he claims that the EU's cultural policies were unlikely to ever be embraced by people in Europe. Comparing the cultural construction of the EU to that of nation-states, Shore claims that:

> the nation-state may well have been arbitrarily constructed, but its existence – and social meaning – is anything but arbitrary today. The factors that give it substance and legitimacy are historical and social, and embedded in the fabric of everyday culture. Because of its history, and because its institutions have been adapted and reformed by successive generations, it has succeeded (where the EU has signally failed) in getting closer to its citizens and winning their consent to be governed. That process took many decades to achieve. (Shore 2004:40)

Nationalizing Europe?

Shore's approach to the EU's cultural policies may help us understand how EU officials perceive European culture and culture's role in the forging of identities. But they tell us very little about the practical effects – if any – of the EU's cultural policies. In order to assess what they mean outside the institutions we need to analyze in detail how EU cultural policies are communicated to people in the member states and how they are interpreted and implemented locally.

If we assume that the attempts to construct a cultural foundation for the integration processes in Europe are comparable to the creation of a cultural foundation for nation-states (e.g. Shore 1993, 1996), it becomes obvious that the EU lacks the institutions that have been most instrumental in forging national identities, especially schools and media (e.g. Anderson 1983). Aside from a handful of elite schools related to EU institutions (Shore and Baratieri 2006) and a couple of failed attempts to create European media (Neveu 2002; Llobera 2003), the EU suffers from a communication and enculturation deficit which has consequences for the institution's abilities to communicate with citizens and to install a sense of belonging to the union. As has been pointed out in several studies, people in the member states get most of their information about the EU from national media, which means that the information they get varies and almost always has a national angle (Peter and de Vreese 2004).

Over the years, EU institutions have attempted to create various platforms for direct communication with people. They have, for instance, published numerous information pamphlets about the rights and opportunities of citizens in the member states: materials that are available in all official languages and sometimes in some of the minority languages, and made available from public libraries and EU information offices in the member states. But this way of communicating is not very efficient, as it requires that people seek out the information themselves.

In recent years the most important platform for institutional attempts to communicate with its citizens and the wider world has been the Internet. Central to the EU's Web presence is the Europa site (europa.eu) which makes information available to citizens and other actors and which attempts to engage people in various forms of interactions. The Europa site features among other things a "kids' corner" with interactive games, a "teachers' corner" with educational resources, as well as debate forums, blogs, a shop, and a media center. The European Commission has also established an EU channel on YouTube (EUTube), where infomercials about EU politics are made available and where one can find videos where the president and vice-presidents of the European Commission address "the public." But like the pamphlets, the Internet is not a very efficient tool for communication. The availability and demographic use of Internet in Europe varies widely, and people still have to actively seek to be informed by the EU – which the majority does not necessarily do. Looking at the EU channel on YouTube, one can note that at the time of writing it has fewer than 11 000 subscribers and that most of the available videos have fewer than 5000 views. Rather than relating the EU's information politics to that of nation-states, it is almost tempting to recall the late Pierre Clastres' (1977) theory of the institution of power in primitive societies, in which he claimed that it is the duty of the chief in primitive societies to speak, but that "the words of the chief are not spoken in order to be listened to . . . nobody pays attention to the discourse of the chief." According to Clastres this made sure that the institution of power would (and could) not be assumed by an individual.

Grasping the EU's cultural politics

Not all of the culture-related initiatives discussed in EU institutions reach the European public. However some have been implemented in the member states. Studying those may help us understand what EU cultural politics can accomplish.

In a recent article, ethnologist Johan Fornäs (2009) addressed this issue with regard to EU symbols. In order to understand how the symbols work Fornäs has suggested that it may be helpful to distinguish between two different types of symbol. The first type includes symbols that have a purely discursive or symbolic application – the flag, the anthem, Europe Day, and the motto, for instance. These symbols signify the EU in an abstract way and are not (yet) embedded in people's everyday life. The other type of symbol has a double function, as both a symbolic expression of identity and a material tool of integration; this type of symbol includes the passport, which is a personal document of belonging that literally distinguishes "us" from "them" – for instance when "we" stand in other lines than "them" in EU airports. It also includes the euro, which was introduced in 2002 and which is currently used by 300 million people in 15 member states in their daily economic transactions. Drawing on Michael Billig's theory of banal nationalism, in which he included money among the "unwaved flags" that construct our perceptions of who we are (Billig 1995:41), Fornäs has identified the euro as a symbol of EU identity which is simultaneously a practical tool in the making of everyday life and a medium which enlightens us as to what EUrope is (Fornäs 2009:126). Fornäs has for instance argued that the design of the euro notes and coins creates a narrative about unity and diversity, which is reinforced by the way that money is circulated. The fact that nationally distinct euros can be used in any and all of the countries in Euroland represents a form of intercultural interaction beyond economics (Fornäs 2009:137).

Similarly, in her analysis of the European City of Culture program, Monica Sassatelli (2002, 2008) has analyzed the actual making of Cities of Culture in Europe rather than the policy decisions to make them. The promotion of European Cities of Culture was initiated in the mid-1980s as one of the EU's cultural policies. According to the EU Web site, European Cities of Culture is the brainchild of the late Greek Minister of Culture, Melina Mercouri, who allegedly argued that, "culture, art and creativity are no less important [to European integration] than technology, commerce and economics."

Each year a European City of Culture is elected as a way "to highlight the richness and diversity of European cultures and the features they share, and promote greater mutual acquaintance between European Union citizens" (Sassatelli 2002:441). While the European City of Culture was thus invented by EU institutions, it is in the implementation by officials and artists in the cities in question that notions of European culture are being created. The European Council selects the cities and supports them with a small sum of money, but each city is free to determine its own cultural program (Sassatelli 2002:436). In practice this means that representatives of local communities co-construct the notion of the European culture which is promoted with this initiative. This suggests that the outcomes of EU cultural politics cannot be reduced to the intentions of the policies.

The EU's "Others"

Anthropologists who have studied the official attempts to create a common European identity have paid particular attention to the simultaneous co-construction of one or more "Others." As Shore (2006) has pointed out, the discussion of Others in relation to the EU – and the politics of defining them – is complicated. The EU itself may be defined as a union of Others; practically all member states are or have been the significant Other to one or more of the other member states. Furthermore the EU's borders are not final. Therefore it is difficult to point to those on the other side of the borders as EU's Others, since they, too, may become part of the EU one day.

In the 1960s and 1970s EUropean identity was officially defined in terms of common political values such as democracy, human rights, market economy, and so on. In relation to these values the significant Others were the totalitarian regimes south and east of the European Community. In the 1980s the community opened for a renegotiation of its southern and eastern borders. The admission in the first half of the 1980s of Greece, Portugal, and Spain moved the EU's southern borders to the Mediterranean, which made it increasingly relevant to discuss exactly how far south the EU would eventually stretch. The rejection of Morocco's membership application in 1986 on the grounds that Morocco is not a European country indicated that it is in fact possible to draw a boundary between Europe and non-Europe (Eder 2006). The most pressing question was then whether this boundary would include or exclude Turkey.

The changes in Eastern Europe in the 1980s also made it relevant to consider the possible "homecoming" of Eastern European countries. During this period community discourse increasingly defined the EU culturally in opposition to the United States. The EU and the United States were still "the West" in opposition to "the

East," but at the same time Americanization was presented as the most immediate threat to European culture (Shore 1993).

In the 1990s the EU faced two enormous political challenges. Internally, there was a growth in neonationalism, antisemitism, and islamophobia (Holmes 2000; McDonald 2006); externally, the EU was preparing southeastern enlargements. These challenges fed into a new identity discourse which focused on the necessity to overcome the past. A European past of war, conflict, division, repression, and discrimination exemplified with references to colonialism, racism, warfare, holocaust, communism, totalitarianism, and xenophobia was juxtaposed on an EUropean present, which was defined with reference to values such as peace, tolerance, multiculturalism, antiracism, anti-antisemitism, anti-islamophobia, and respect for minorities. This positioned "Europe of the past" and in particular "Europe of the nation-state" as the EU's most significant Other.

These official attempts to define the EU's Other do not necessarily reflect commonly accepted Others. Some scholars have pointed out that the most popularly accepted Others in the EU at the moment are Muslims and Islam (e.g. Klausen 2005; Meinhof and Triandafyllidou 2006). What they do reflect are the official attempts to give the EU an identity.

Officials into Europeans?

When discussing if the integration processes in Europe will lead to the creation of a common European identity or perhaps even to the creation of EUropeans, one group has been singled out as particularly interesting: the EU officials who work together to make integration happen. Questions regarding their identities have fuelled a small interdisciplinary research field which has developed since the early 1990s. What marks the literature in this field "is the dominance of the anthropological approach" (Cini 2001). In this section I will look at some of the contributions to this field. I will start with a brief discussion of the anthropological interest in Eurocrats and some of the methodological challenges that this interest entail. I will then introduce studies of identity construction in the European Commission, and finally I will discuss the possible emergence of transnational European identities.

Studying Eurocrats

Anthropological interest in EU institutions developed in the early 1990s when a number of anthropologists did fieldwork inside EU institutions. One study was undertaken by a French–British team consisting of three anthropologists: Marc Abélès, Irène Bellier, and Maryon McDonald, who had been invited by the then President of the EU Commission Jacques Delors to explore "the existence or not of a specific Commission culture, plus the weight of the different languages and national cultural traditions and their impact on working relationships and how a European identity might emerge in such a context" (Cini 2001:4). This team also did fieldwork in the European Parliament.

Another study was carried out by Cris Shore who had worked as a *stagiare* in the European Parliament in the mid-1980s (Shore 2004:27) and who later did fieldwork in the Commission. Shore's work has primarily focused on EU cultural policies (see above) but he has also contributed to the analysis of identification and cooperation in various institutions (e.g. Shore 1995, 2000).

Other anthropologists have also contributed to our understanding of identity construction in EU institutions: for example Danish anthropologist Signe Ejersbo (1993) and American anthropologist Stacia Zabusky (1995, 2000), who have both studied the processes of cooperation and identification among scientists in EU-related organizations, and Swedish anthropologist Renita Thedvall (2006, 2007), who has studied Eurocrats in motion between national and European political institutions.

Anthropologists doing fieldwork in EU institutions face a number of challenges. These are especially related to methodology. By now there is a solid tradition in anthropology for "studying up" (Nader 1972) and for having elites and bureaucrats as informants (e.g. Herzfeld 1992; Shore and Nugent 2002). It is also generally accepted that the anthropological research methods which were originally developed for data collection in small-scale societies, do in fact produce valuable insights when applied to larger-scale societies. Still, in the context of EU institutions, where many of the informants have a background in the social sciences, and therefore specific expectations of social research, both the methods and the results they produce are often questioned by informants, who may find the research design "fuzzy" and the results "unrepresentative" or even "anecdotal" (Ejersbo 1993; Zabusky 1995; Shore 2000:11). Anthropologists doing fieldwork in EU institutions thus often find themselves involved in "a struggle" concerning the production and interpretation of data (Bourdieu 1990:21–22). This struggle is embedded in the relationship which already exists between anthropology and other social sciences, and it creates a situation where the informants are not simply co-constructing data but competing for their interpretation.

Making Europeans

A majority of the research on identity construction among EU officials has focused on the Commission. One argument for this is that the Commission is "an unusual social entity" staffed with people from different countries who have sworn allegiance to the EU and its interests over and above their national governments (McDonald 1996:52; Bellier 1997:92). Another argument is that it is officials in the Commission who design the cultural policies, and who maintain that the creation of an EU identity is imperative (Shore 1995, 2000).

The Commission is often perceived as having a moral obligation to be both the promoter and the exemplar of European unity. According to Marc Abélès (2004) this perception frames the way that officials talk about themselves in relation to culture and identity. Officials in the Commission often state that they are above stereotypes, that they don't think in terms of national differences and that there is an *esprit européen* and a European identity in the Commission. Similarly Cris Shore has argued that there is a self-perception among officials of having moved past the Europe of the nation-states and of being the vanguard in an evolution toward a unified Europe (Shore 1995:225).

At the same time, however, officials also stress that cultural diversity is fundamental to the integration processes in Europe and that cultural differences should be recognized and respected. This sometimes leads to a distinctive way of classifying differences: there are "benign" cultural differences that are part of "Europe's rich cultural heritage," and then there are "negative" differences which are often attributed to people's personalities (Abélès 2004:15).

Despite this official rhetoric of unity and (benign) diversity, officials in the Commission make distinctions regarding culture and identity all the time. At the most basic level they distinguish between the EUropean bureaucracy and national bureaucracies (Abélès 2004:16). Here the distinction regards those who are working for EUrope and those who (still) work for their own national interests. Within the EU bureaucracy, officials tend to identify with specific Directorates-General and institutions. Both Shore and McDonald have shown that officials identify with various units in the organizational structure, for example: "we in the Commission," "we in the court," or "we in the translation section," and so on (Shore 1995:224; McDonald 2000:53).

Another distinction which more clearly refers to perceived cultural differences is the one which is made between the North and the South (and with the latest enlargements also between the East and the West). The distinction between North and South refers to a widely held mutual classification where the North considers itself modern in opposition to the backward South and the South considers itself civilized in opposition to the barbarian North (Eder 2006:262). "North" and "South" do not refer to a simple geographical division in Europe. Rather they are metaphors referring to moral and political distinctions (McDonald 2000:115; Abélès 2004:18–19).

The distinction between North and South became relevant after the first enlargement in 1973. This enlargement is often described as particularly traumatic, because it marked a transition from "a single Europe" working together to create peace after World War II, to a diverse Europe where the member states had different perceptions of Europe and different expectations of the cooperation (McDonald 2000:65–70). The transition is most clearly marked by the shift in the de facto working language from French to English, but it involved a wide range of "surprises and irritations relating to the different ways of doing anything from writing memos to managing meetings" (McDonald 1996:52). This disruption of the "culture of compromise" (Abélès and Bellier 1996) which has evolved in the Commission is repeated with every new enlargement and constructs new distinctions between "us" and "them."

Despite the intention of "being above it," nationality does play a significant role in the way that people make sense of interactions in the Commission. Irene Bellier explains this with reference to the national organization of the political scene in EU institutions: there are signs of nations everywhere, so it is difficult to escape this particular way of classifying differences (Bellier 1997:93). Maryon McDonald explains it with reference to a language trap: cultural differences in Europe are structured by a language where "nations and nationalities provide the conceptual boundaries by which difference is most easily constructed and recognized" (McDonald 2000:113). Like most Europeans, officials in the Commission habitually classify differences in terms of nationality, and therefore such differences are experienced as being very real and confirmed in everyday interaction (McDonald 2000:113; Abélès 2004). One way of attempting to escape the trap of national identification is to refer to regional identities. Bellier has argued that officials in the Commission sometimes identify as Catalan or Scottish instead of Spanish or British (Bellier 1997).

Identity construction in trans- (or post-?)national Europe

While the early work on identity construction among officials in EU institutions primarily focused on identification within the institutions, recent work has focused more on the increasing overlap between national and European institutions and discussed the possible emergence of a transnational (or perhaps postnational) political space as a new frame for identification (e.g. Shore 2006; Thedvall 2006, 2007).

Shore has argued that cooperation at the European level has led to the emergence of a transnational space which expands into the realm of the national through webs of networking between a growing number of transnational agents; European politicians and officials are linked to transnational lobby organizations, to journalists working in the European sphere, to international networks of professionals, and so on. According to Shore, these transnational networks are forming an intimate institutional microcosm which is governed by its own informal rules and norms and has its roots in the "insular and detached cultural space in the Brussels environment" (Shore 2006:715). He maintains that there still is a clear and important division between the national political spaces and a transnational European political space where people of many different nationalities socialize and cooperate in networks that are increasingly detached from the European nation-states (Shore 2000:715). Shore compares EU officials to expatriates and colonial officials who are characterized by having high salaries, professional autonomy, and being excluded from the societies within which they live, which promotes a sense of internal solidarity and distinction (Shore 2002:7, 2006). In this respect EU officials are portrayed as just another tribe or culture in a world of cultures.

In another study, Renita Thedvall (2006, 2007) has focused on the blurring of boundaries between the political spaces of the EU institutions and that of member states. Thedvall has followed Swedish bureaucrats as they move between the political institutions in Sweden and the European institutions in order to negotiate politics which will have implications not just in Sweden but in the entire European Union. She has paid particular attention to the ways that these "EU Nomads" as she calls them (2007) shift in and out of identity categories. Characteristic for "EU Nomads" is that they have to represent national and European interests simultaneously: the governments who employ them expect them to represent national interests in political negotiations "in Europe," but in the negotiations they still have to compromise in order to create results that all the different member states can live with. In this process the contours of "the national" and "the European" is constantly being negotiated. The blurring of boundaries in Thedvall's analyses refer both to the blurring of the national and the European political decision-making processes, and to the blurring of the national and the European as identity categories. It is not entirely clear whether these EU Nomads are European or national, or when they are European and when they are national. According to Thedvall (2007) this blurring is leading to some sort of postnational political space as a framework for identity construction.

Bringing in the People

So far I have focused on anthropological contributions to our understanding of European identity construction from above. In the following sections I will briefly consider contributions to our understanding of the construction of European identities from below.

Since the late 1980s, several anthropologists have studied how EU integration affects life in the member states and how membership of the EU (or not!) increasingly frames identity construction in various localities in Europe. Many of these studies have focused on people and places with ambiguous relationships to Europe and the EU, like Herzfeld's (1987, 1997) studies of Greece and Mitchell's (2002) study of Malta. Over the past couple of years there have also been studies that explore how some people – one way or another – increasingly identify themselves as Europeans.

Becoming Europeans

People belonging to the category of autochthonous minorities were among the first to be systematically studied by anthropologists with reference to construction of European identities "from below" (e.g. Jaffe 1993; Wilken 2001, 2008; Nic Craith 2005; Adrey 2009). The context for these studies has been the proactive approach that many of the movements and political parties representing autochthonous minorities took to the integration processes in the 1970s and their involvement in European politics since the 1980s.

Autochthonous minorities include "kin-state minorities" that found themselves stranded on the wrong side of national borders after centuries of war between powerholders in Europe; linguistic minorities that have kept languages alive despite nation-states' attempts to wipe them out; and "micronations" that have nations but not states. To them – or at least to some of their political representatives (Wilken 2008) – European unification has presented an opportunity to reframe questions of culture and identity. In a Europe of nation-states, autochthonous minorities have been perceived either as victims of nationalization who struggle to survive against all odds or as traitors who forsake their "own culture" for that of the majority. In a European Union stressing unity in diversity as the cultural ideal for cooperation and integration, autochthonous minorities have the opportunity to become co-creators of a new political reality. They can reconstruct themselves as "Welsh Europeans" or "Catalan Europeans" and gain cultural recognition within a broader European context.

Representatives for autochthonous minorities have participated actively in various forms of European cooperation. They have set up EUrope-wide institutions (for instance the European Bureau for Lesser Used Languages) that function as NGOs in relation to European and worldwide institutions. They have even created a Europe-wide political party (the European Free Alliance) which represents autochthonous minorities in the European Parliament. Active minority participation in European cooperation has changed the perspective on minority culture and languages in a number of ways; representatives of autochthonous minorities increasingly embrace bilingualism rather than fight for minority monolingualism; more minority languages have become officially recognized as part of the "European cultural mosaic"; some minority languages have even obtained the status of co-official languages in EU institutions.

There are significant differences between various groups of autochthonous minorities and their commitment to European integration. But as a category they are represented as the prototype of a new kind of multilingual and multicultural European which fits well into the cultural vision of "unity in diversity" (Wilken 2001).

Competing visions

Anthropologists have also expressed interest in the Europeanization of radical nationalism in Europe. In the 1980s and 1990s political movements and parties were formed across Europe with the intention to protect national or regional cultures against perceived threats from immigrants, elites, and Eurocrats in Brussels (Holmes 2000; McDonald 2006). In recent years radical nationalist parties have emerged in Eastern Europe as well. According to political scientist Christina Liang (2007:295) there are currently more than 100 radical nationalist parties in Europe.

The growth in radical nationalism has been the subject of a number of anthropological studies in relation to European integration (e.g. Holmes 2000, 2008; McDonald 2006). While official EU discourse increasingly stresses tolerance, intercultural dialogue, respect for diversity, and nondiscrimination as core values of the integration processes, radical nationalists usually stress intercultural incompatibilities between native and "foreign" cultures and advocate assimilation or even expulsion of people from "foreign cultures." Radical nationalism is therefore often defined as diametrical opposition to the EU (McDonald 2006).

However, as pointed out by Holmes (2000, 2008) among others, most radical nationalist parties do express a belief in a common foundation for the various national cultures of Europe. In radical nationalist discourse, European nations are often referred to as a "family of cultures" that share a common heritage and have roots in Greek and Roman civilization and in Christianity. European nations are therefore presented as having similar moral values and social norms. The idea of a common foundation for European cultures is often used to differentiate between those who do and those who don't belong in Europe.

Radical parties do not have the same ideas about what Europe is or where it begins and ends, but practically all of them agree that Islam is not European, which means that Turkey is excluded from Europe. Some subscribe to Samuel Huntington's idea of an essential difference between the West and the Orthodox East, which exclude most of Eastern Europe and Russia from "the real Europe." Some define certain philosophical and political ideas, for instance communism and socialism, as non-European, and some define globalization as external to Europe.

Radical nationalist parties often come across as EU-rejectionists but their rejection is usually directed more at the "elitist, corrupt bureaucrats in Brussels" than at Europe or European cooperation as such (McDonald 2006). In fact most of these parties belong to one or more transnational European networks, like for instance the European National Front or EuroNat. They also join forces in the European Parliament, where they usually are members of the same political groups (McDonald 2006;

Holmes 2008). In 2007 radical nationalist parties even formed their own group in the European Parliament. It only existed for a few months and demonstrated grave incompatibilities between radical parties in Europe; nevertheless radical nationalists operate with reference to an imagined community of European cultures and contribute to the practical and discursive construction of Europe.

Unlikely Europeans

Since the mid-1990s sociologists and political scientists have discussed how European integration affects immigrants and their descendants living in the member states. On the one hand these discussions have concerned EU politics that affect immigrants in Europe – EU citizenship, racism, immigration laws, and so on (Soysal 2002). On the other hand they have concerned the engagement of immigrant representatives in European politics through participation in transnational European NGOs or representation in the European Parliament (Favell 2003). Some years ago political scientist Riva Kastoryano (1997) coined the term "non-European Europeans" in an attempt to conceptualize the ambiguous position of these immigrants as simultaneously included in and excluded from EUrope.

Recently, anthropologists have also begun to discuss immigrants with reference to a broader European framework. Christina Moutsou (2006) has, for instance, studied the relevance of the EU in relation to identity-construction among Turkish and Greek immigrants in Brussels. This identity-construction is on the one hand framed by the specific Brussels context, and on the other hand by the relationship that Turkey and Greece have with the EU, and that the immigrant communities have with EU institutions.

In another study Máiréad Nic Craith (2009) has explored how intellectuals of immigrant background – primarily from Eastern Europe, Turkey, and Maghreb – make sense of their lives in Europe and as Europeans. Starting from an analysis of autobiographies and memoirs she has analyzed how these intellectuals "talk about and interpret their experience of Europe, what emotions the notion of Europe arouses and how they portrait their experience of liminality" (Nic Craith 2009:198).

Nic Craith defines these intellectuals as "liminal" because they live between cultures without being rooted in any particular culture or place. Most are able to speak several languages fluently, and all have families, histories, and social relationships in several geographical locations (Nic Craith 2009:202). In this way they may be defined in opposition to the stereotypical European national, who have one mother-tongue, one nationality, and one set of roots. In many ways these immigrant intellectuals are constructing the same kind of multilingual, multicultural European identity as the one constructed by various groups of autochthonous minorities, but they generally feel that their approach to European identity is unappreciated by nationals and the EU bureaucracy alike.

Conclusion

Anthropology is a rather late addition to the interdisciplinary field of EU studies; it is only within the past 20 years that anthropologists have contributed to our understanding of European integration. Anthropological interest in the EU was among other things inspired by "the cultural turn" in the integration processes during the 1980s, which made discussions about culture and identity relevant. In this chapter I have discussed three different anthropological approaches to questions regarding culture and identity in relation to EU integration.

The first approach focuses on EU cultural policies and the attempts to create popular identification with the EU and its institutions "from above." This approach was introduced in the early 1990s and is primarily identified with Cris Shore. Shore has contributed to a critical discussion of EU cultural politics in relation to the alleged democratic deficit. His analyses focus on the ways that culture is perceived by officials in EU institutions and the ways that it is used to forge a European identity. In recent years there has been some discussion of how to approach the practical aspects of cultural policies through analyses of their incorporation in everyday life; this is a research area where there is great potential for further development.

The second approach discusses identity construction among the officials in EU institutions. Since the early 1990s, several anthropologists have done fieldwork in EU institutions and contributed to the interdisciplinary discussions of identity construction among EU officials. These studies focused initially on identity construction in relation to the intercultural interactions in the EU's institutions. Analyses in recent years have focused more on identity construction in relation to the blurring of boundaries between national and European political spaces. This has led to discussions of the possible creation of a transnational or postnational political space in Europe as a new framework for identity construction.

The third approach I discussed focuses instead on the possible construction of European identities "from below." Such analyses discuss how the integration processes in Europe have occasioned a recontextualization of identity construction among various groups of Europeans. Anthropological analyses have, for instance, shown how representatives of autochthonous minorities have engaged in various forms of political cooperation in Europe and how they have used this cooperation to reposition themselves in relation to European nation-states and to reframe their identities in a European context. Anthropologists have also discussed how radical nationalists who often define themselves in opposition to the EU are at the same time defining themselves as part of an imagined European family of cultures which creates a different kind of European identity. During the last couple of years there have also been a few studies which analyze how various groups of immigrants – the proverbial Others to culture in Europe – define themselves in relation to the integration processes and sometimes even create European identities.

The three approaches discussed illustrate how anthropology so far has contributed to our understanding of European integration, and in particular to our understanding of the implications for identity construction in Europe.

REFERENCES

Abélès, Marc

2004 Identities and Borders: An Anthropological Approach to EU institutions. Twenty-First Century Papers: On-Line Working Papers from the Center for 21st Century

Studies. Milwaukee: University of Wisconsin. Electronic document. http://www4.uwm.edu/c21/pdfs/workingpapers/abeles.pdf (accessed November 5, 2011).

Abélès, Marc, and Irène Bellier

1996 La Commission Européenne: du compromis culturel à la culture politique du compromise. Revue Française de Science Politique 46(3):431–455

Adrey, Jean-Bernard

2009 Discourse and Struggle in Minority Language Policy Formation: Corsican Language Policy in the EU Context of Governance. Basingstoke: Palgrave Macmillan.

Anderson, Benedict

1983 Imagined Communities: Reflections on the Origin and Spread of Nationalism. London: Verso.

Bellier, Irène

1997 The Commission as an Actor: An Anthropologist's View. *In* Participation and Policy Making in the European Union. H. Wallace and A. R. Young, eds. Oxford: Oxford University Press.

Billig, Michael

1995 Banal Nationalism. London: Sage.

Boissevain, Jeremy

1975 Introduction: Towards an Anthropology of Europe. *In* Beyond the Community: Social Processes in Europe. J. Boissevain and J. Friedl, eds. pp. 9–17. The Hague: Department of Educational Science of the Netherlands.

Bourdieu, Pierre

1990 In Other Words: Essays towards a Reflexive Sociology. Cambridge: Polity.

Cini, Michelle

2001 Reforming the European Commission: An Organisational Culture Perspective. Queen's Papers on Europeanisation, No. 11. Belfast: Queen's University.

Clastres, Pierre

1977 Society Against the State: Essays in Political Anthropology. New York: Urizen Books.

Eder, Klaus

2006 Europe's Borders: The Narrative Construction of the Boundaries of Europe. European Journal of Social Theory 9(2):255–271.

Ejersbo, Signe

1993 Visionerne fra Babel: om sprog og nationalitet i euro-europæisk kontekst. Institut for Kultursociologi, Københavns Universitet.

Eriksen, Thomas Hylland

1996 Opplysning og romantikk: Nittitallets håndtering av kulturbegrepet. Norsk antropologisk tidskrift 2:73–8.

European Commission

1988 A People's Europe: Communication from the Commission to the European Parliament. COM (88) 331/final. Luxembourg: Bulletin of the EC, Supplement No. 2.

1998 What? Me? A Racist? Luxembourg: Office for Official Publications of the European Communities.

2008 Anthropological Perspectives in a Changing Europe: Bringing People In. Electronic document. ftp://ftp.cordis.europa.eu/pub/fp7/ssh/docs/ssh_seminar_anthropological_perspective_en.pdf (accessed November 5, 2011).

Favell, Adrian

2003 Games Without Frontiers? Questioning the Transnational Social Power of Migrants in Europe. European Journal of Sociology 44:397–427.

Fornäs, Johan
2009 Meanings of Money: The Euro as a Sign of Value and of Cultural Identity. *In* We Europeans? Media, Representations, Identities. William Uricchio, ed. pp. 123–140. Oxford: Intellect.
Habermas, Jürgen
2001 Why Europe Needs a Constitution. New Left Review 11:5–26.
Herzfeld, Michael
1987 Anthropology Through a Looking Glass: Critical Ethnography in the Margins of Europe. Cambridge: Cambridge University Press.
1992 The Social Production of Indifference: Exploring the Symbolic Roots of Western Bureaucracy. Chicago: University of Chicago Press.
1997 Cultural Intimacy: Social Poetics in the Nation-State. London: Routledge.
Hobsbawm, Eric
1983 Introduction: Inventing Traditions. *In* The Invention of Tradition. E. Hobsbawm and T. Ranger, eds. pp. 1–14. Cambridge: Cambridge University Press.
Holmes, Douglas
2000 Surrogate Discourses of Power: The European Union and the Problem of Society. *In* An Anthropology of the European Union: Building, Imagining and Experiencing the New Europe. I. Bellier and T. M. Wilson, eds. pp. 93–115. Oxford: Berg.
2008 Experimental identities (after Maastricht). *In* European Identity. J. T. Checkel and P. J. Katzenstein, eds. pp. 52–80. Cambridge: Cambridge University Press.
Jaffe, Alexandra
1993 Corsican Identity and a Europe of Peoples and Regions. *In* Cultural Change and the New Europe: Perspectives on the European Community. T. Wilson and E. Smith, eds. pp. 61–80. Boulder, CO: Westview.
Kastoryano, Riva
1997 Participation transnationale et citoyenette: Les immigrés dans l'Union europeéne. Culture et Conflit 59–75.
Klausen, Jytte
2005 The Islamic Challenge: Politics and Religion in Western Europe. Oxford: Oxford University Press.
Liang, Christina Schori
2007 Europe for the Europeans: The Foreign and Security Policy of the Populist, Radical Right. *In* Europe for the Europeans: The Foreign and Security Policy of the Populist, Radical Right. Christina Liang, ed. pp. 1–32. Aldershot: Ashgate.
Llobera, Joseph
2003 The Concept of Europe as an Idée-forcé. Critique of Anthropology 23(2): 155–175.
Macdonald, Sharon
1993 Identity Complexes in Western Europe: Social Anthropological Perspectives. *In* Inside European Identities: Ethnography in Western Europe. S. Macdonald, ed., pp. 1–26. Oxford: Berg.
McDonald, Maryon
1996 Unity in Diversity: Some Tensions in the Construction of Europe. Social Anthropology 4(1):47–60.
2000 Accountability, Anthropology and the European Commission. *In* Audit Cultures: Anthropological Studies in Accountability, Ethics and the Academy. M. Strathern, ed. pp. 106–132. London: Routledge.
2006 New Nationalisms in the EU: Occupying the Available Space. *In* Neo-nationalism in Europe and Beyond: Perspectives from Social Anthropology. A. Gingrich and M. Banks, eds. pp. 218–236. Oxford: Berghahn.

Meinhof, Ulrike, and Anna Triandafyllidou
2006 Transcultural Europe: Cultural Policy in a Changing Europe. Basingstoke: Palgrave Macmillan.
Mitchell, Jon P.
2002 Ambivalent Europeans: Ritual, Memory and the Public Sphere in Malta. London: Routledge.
Moutsou, Christina
2006 Merging European Boundaries: A Stroll in Brussels. *In* Crossing European Boundaries: Beyond Conventional Geographical Categories. New Directions in Anthropology 24. J. Stacul, C. Moutsou, and H. Kopnina, eds. pp. 120–136. Oxford: Berghahn.
Nader, Laura
1972 Up the Anthropologist: Perspectives Gained from Studying Up. *In* Reinventing Anthropology. D. H. Hymes, ed. pp. 284–311. New York: Pantheon.
Neveu, Erik
2002 Europe as an Unimaginable Community? The Failure of the French News Magazine *L'European* (March–July 1998). Journal of Contemporary European Studies 10(2):283–300.
Nic Craith, Máiréad
2005 Europe and the Politics of Language. Basingstoke: Palgrave Macmillan.
2009 Writing Europe: A Dialogue of "Liminal" Europeans. Social Anthropology 17(2):198–208.
Peter, Jochen, and Claus H. de Vreese
2004 In Search of Europe: A Cross-National Comparative Study of the European Union in National Television News. Harvard International Journal of Press/Politics 9(4):3–24.
Sassatelli, Monica
2002 Imagined Europe: The Shaping of a European Cultural Identity through EU Cultural Policy. European Journal of Social Theory 5(4):435–451.
2008 European Cultural Space in the European Cities of Culture. European Societies 10(2):225–245.
Shore, Cris
1993 Inventing the "People's Europe": Critical Approaches to European Community "Cultural Policy." Man 28:779–800.
1995 Usurpers or Pioneers? European Commission Bureaucrats and the Question of European Consciousness. *In* Questions of Consciousness. A. Cohen and N. Rapport, eds. pp. 217–326. London: Routledge.
1996 Imagining the New Europe: Identity and Heritage in European Community Discourse. *In* Cultural Identity and Archaeology: The Construction of European Communities. P. Graves-Brown, S. Jones, and C. Gamble, eds. pp. 96–115. London: Routledge.
1997 Metaphors of Europe: Integration and the Politics of Language. *In* Anthropology and Cultural Studies. S. Nugent and C. Shore, eds. pp. 126–159. London: Pluto.
2000 Building Europe: The Cultural Politics of European Integration. London: Routledge.
2001 Inventing *Homo europeaus.* The Cultural Politics of European Integration. *In* Europe: Cultural Construction and Reality. P. Niedermüller and B. Stoklund, eds. pp. 53–66. Copenhagen: Museum Tusculanum.
2004 Whither European Citizenship? Eros and Civilization Revisited. European Journal of Social Theory 7(2):27–44.
2006 Government without Statehood? Anthropological Perspectives on Governance and Sovereignty in the European Union. European Law Journal 12(6):709–724.

Shore, Cris, and Daniela Baratieri
2006 Crossing Boundaries through Education: European Schools and the Supersession of Nationalism. *In* Crossing European Boundaries: Beyond Conventional Geographical Categories. J. Stacul, C. Moutsou, and H. Kopnina, eds. pp. 23–40. Oxford: Berghahn.
Shore, Cris, and Stephen Nugent, eds.
2002 Elite Cultures: Anthropological Perspectives. London: Routledge.
Soysal, Yasemin
2002 Citizenship and Identity: Living in Diasporas in Postwar Europe. *In* The Postnational Self: Belonging and Identity. U. Hedetoft and M. Hjort, eds. pp. 137–151. Minneapolis: University of Minnesota Press.
Thedvall, Renita
2006 Eurocrats at Work. Stockholm Studies in Social Anthropology, 58. Stockholm: Almund and Wiksell.
2007 The EU's Nomads: National Eurocrats in European Policy Making. *In* Observing Government Elites: Up Close and Personal. R. Rhodes, P. 't Hart, and M. Noordegraaf, eds. pp. 160–179. Basingstoke: Palgrave Macmillan.
Wilken, Lisanne
1999 Antropologien og den Europæiske Union. Tidsskriftet Antropologi 39:219–232.
2001 Enhed I Mangfoldighed? Eurovisioner og Minoriteter. Aarhus: Århus Universitetsforlag.
2008 The Development of Minority Rights in Europe. *In* The Tension between Group Rights and Human Rights: A Multidisciplinary Approach. K. De Feyter and G. Pavlakos, eds. pp. 89–104. Oxford: Hart.
Zabusky, Stacia
1995 Launching Europe: An Ethnography of European Cooperation in Space Science. Princeton: Princeton University Press.
2000 Boundaries at Work: Discourses and Practices of Belonging in the European Space Agency. *In* An Anthropology of the European Union. I. Bellier and T. Wilson, eds. pp. 179–200. Oxford: Berg.

CHAPTER 9

Memory, Citizenship, and Consumer Culture in Postsocialist Europe

Ksenija Vidmar Horvat

This chapter addresses the questions of the European project and European identity after the last two European Union (EU) enlargements in 2005 and 2007. While the analysis embraces a broader question of the construction of the cultural image of Europe after the end of the Cold War, it places this inquiry in the specific contexts of postsocialist Central and Eastern Europe. The central issue which it raises is how to envision the Europe of the post–Cold War, post-Western, and postnational era (Habermas 2001; Delanty and Rumford 2005; Delanty 2007; Outhwaite 2008; Rizman 2008) and where, in this cultural, political, and social reconfiguration, to locate the postsocialist experience.

By postsocialist experience, I refer to a complex terrain of postsocialist "emotions" (Svašek 2006), including memory (together with nostalgia and trauma; Hann 2002; Forrester et al. 2004; Todorova and Gille 2010) as well as the reconstitution and redefinition of collective national identities which have taken place in the region after the collapse of the two socialist "empires" of the Soviet Union and Yugoslavia. My central argument is that the postsocialist experience should not be investigated as a separate social phenomenon, confined to area studies (or regional studies) but that postsocialist studies constitute a core of European studies; that postsocialism, to embark on a psychoanalytic concept, plays the role of the symptom of the new Europe, and, furthermore, that only by fully understanding the collective perceptions of Europe in postsocialist countries, will Europe be able to understand the implications of its own Eurocentrism and, hopefully, begin a (fully overdue) process of its dismantling. This does not mean that the critical redrawing of the attention to postsocialist Europe demands a reversal of the relationship between the roles of the "center" and "periphery" between the "West" and the "East." On the contrary, in my understand-

A Companion to the Anthropology of Europe, First Edition. Edited by Ullrich Kockel, Máiréad Nic Craith, and Jonas Frykman.

ing, the term "new Europe" should be divorced from the hegemonic geopolitical description for the new EU member states from former-socialist Europe, and should connote a significantly altered social, cultural, and political geography of the continent. This reshaping has as much to do with the fall of the Berlin Wall and European unification (i.e. with "domestic" EU politics) as it does with larger processes of transnationalization, globalization, and cosmopolitanization of European society.

In the limited scope of this chapter, the questions outlined above are approached through a narrow segment of investigation on how "we" consume Europe. Although the term "consumption" here is clearly used figuratively (avoiding the charge of being anthropophagic), it is also meant to be understood literally. That is, we ask how, through the formation of the single European market, "Europe" and "European identity" are being presented to its citizens. More specifically, the chapter asks how, through practices of consumption of goods with the label "made in the EU," cultural and political imaginaries of the new Europe are being formed, processed, and "digested" in the public. Therefore, whereas a main concern of social theory of Europeanization today has been how (and if) European identity *is yet to be produced* (Smith 1992; Shore 2000, 2006) the theoretical concern of this chapter is rather how European identity *has already been consumed*. In addition, it will be argued that in postsocialist Central and Eastern Europe, the encountering of Europe through consumption by and large has been framed by memories of the past, postwar divisions, and borders in the region. To put it in concrete terms, in postsocialist EU member states, memories of the borders and past border imaginaries play a central role in the negotiation of European identity and belonging in the new Europe. In light of the above argument, the negotiation of belonging, borne on past traumas and memories of exclusion, bears consequences for the current EU politics of identity and citizenship; as well as, and this will be stressed at the end of this writing, its ethics of transnational solidarity and global cooperation.

TRANSITION (TO) PREJUDICE

The incentive to study postsocialist culture(s) of consumption stems from my own autobiographical ethnography and the behaviors reported to me by my friends and relatives, namely of the practice of reading the labels of products in order to determine their place of origin. In the age of globalization of "geographies of consumption" (Jackson and Thrift 1996) and increased consumer consciousness regarding fair trade and global ecology, the reading of declaration notes would present no particular reason to study this practice in a culturally contained context of postsocialist Europe – were it not the case that in this region, the inquiries about the "origin" carry a specific cultural connotation. Namely, the efforts put into discovering the place of the production of the commodities (in the era of the obfuscation of travel between global markets and capital an oxymoron of a sort) are coupled with a (in my case a personally embarrassing) inquisition to make sure they were *not* made in "Eastern Europe." As mentioned, this is not an isolated case of personal consumer racism: others have confessed to me engaging in same practice whereas the theme of the "hidden agenda" as far as the shared European market is concerned, has been part of the public discourse in Slovenia since the country's joining of the EU.

When a consumer coming from postsocialist Slovenia resists purchasing goods "made in Eastern Europe" (the most frequent and stigmatized seem to be products coming from Romania and Hungary), it is time to raise the question of social significance and the political meaning of this resistance. In particular, one needs to ask what lies below the silent refusal to buy "Eastern." How is this practice of cultural selection meaningful when it is placed within the specific cultural, political, and ideological contexts of a former socialist state? How at all to decipher the cultural stigma attached to "Eastern Europe" in an age of European history that is supposedly moving into a post-Western phase (Delanty 2007; Outhwaite 2008); and when categories of "Western" and "Eastern" no longer can be used as stable markers of difference?

Here it is proposed that what we have at hand is a case of the reversal of the Veblen's notion of conspicuous consumption, reconstituted as an inconspicuous practice which nonetheless serves a similar function: to claim a certain cultural belonging, identity, sameness. In his *Theory of the Leisure Class* (1994[1889]), Veblen writes about vicarious consumption, shared across classes, which derives its pattern of imitation from the "leisure class scheme of life," and of which accumulation of wealth in commodities stands as a visible marker and the norm of reputability. In Veblen's observation of US society at the turn of the nineteenth century, the source of fascination lay in Western Europe and the cultural styles of its aristocracies. While today's cultural imitations of nobility and taste may have shifted in meaning, Western Europe continues to figure as an important point of reference around which cultural hierarchies of identity and belonging are being ordered in the contemporary "new Europe." In postsocialist cultural imaginaries, European identity continues to be projected as Western(ized), although modes of emulations of this imaginary identity construct today are perhaps less provocatively displayed. It may even be argued that they are manifested in a concealed way, through negation of the "Easterner" in ourselves. The "West," in this projection, of course, is a vanishing reference: it is a construct and a fabrication that is desired as much in Western as in Eastern Europe. Moreover, it is also a memory construct which yields power precisely from invoking idealized nostalgic projections of the world on the other side of the Iron Curtain. Yet, arguably, it is mostly this selective and polished image of the "West" as it once was that is shaping the ways in which the new East is being formed – both in the old and the new Europe.

The fictive character of the "West" notwithstanding, in former socialist Central and Eastern Europe it operates as a potent source for fueling processes of redefinition of collective identity after the "revolutions of 1989." However, contrary to the perception that what we have here is a case of an unfortunate, politically misguided mimicry of the (mature and developed) West by the (adolescent) East (in light of the crisis of the West this is an interpretation which is indeed encouraged, governed, and desired by the West, see Žižek 1993; Borcila 2004; Vidmar Horvat 2011), we want to argue that the dramaturgy of identification and difference, idealization and rejection, embroiled in consumer trivia, is politically costumed, and moreover, has to do with the post-1989 rewriting of history. In the concrete case of Slovenia, what we are witnessing here is not only a clear case of prejudice, but a transitional prejudice: a prejudice the articulation of which coincides with the reconstitution of collective cultural identity in the movement between two social orders, and whereby the cultural legitimacy of the latter is borne on the delegitimization of the former. "Europe,"

I will argue, appears constitutional in this process of restructuring and realignment of identity: in particular, it provides fictional material to the reimagining of national history away from its Yugoslav past.

In order to understand the ideological constellation of this prejudice, and its connection to the Europeanization of national identity, it is necessary to place it in relation to the kind of memories that it triggers. That is, in social theory, prejudices are conceptualized as "microideologies of the life-world" which shape the image of the other (Šabec 2007). It is important to underline that the construction of this image changes in time and place. Invoking Pickering's referential study (2001), Šabec argues that every critical social study of stereotypes and prejudices has to be based on "historical facts which are of vital importance for the understanding how prejudices and stereotypes acquired their symbolic meanings and values in the collective memory and consciousness of a (national) community, and how, in a complex interdependence between continuity and change, they were being passed on, reproduced and modified through time" (Šabec 2007:98). This means that prejudices have their own history and a dynamic form which, while taking cultural notes about the other, also adapts its scripture to the changing social circumstances, if (functionally) necessary. Yet the anatomy of the prejudice against the other is also a testimony of the self: by inscribing a difference and distance from the other, the prejudice speaks of (the desire) of one's own cultural location. Therefore, prejudices are always shot through with cultural fantasies of the self: they are as much systems of real differentiations as are collective fictions, powdered by maintaining, in Freudian terms, the narcissism of small differences.

Taking into account the above argument, in the remainder of this chapter, we therefore first provide a brief theoretical account of the study of memory in relation to Europe; we go on to outline the anatomy of the transitional prejudice in Slovenia through the spectacles of the cultural dialogue between the memories of the (socialist) past and the (postsocialist) present. We then draw a brief comparison with postsocialist experience in other parts of the Central and Eastern European region to, finally, problematize the current politics of identity, belonging, and citizenship in the larger contexts of the EU.

The Europeanization of Memory

In social theory, European identity has been conceptualized in ambiguous terms of both impossibility and possibility, as fiction as well as cognitive social reality (Shore 2000; Stråth 2002; Balibar 2004; Delanty and Rumford 2005). On the one side of the spectrum of theorization, authors like Anthony Smith and Cris Shore have questioned the feasibility of generating a European identity in a sense that will be meaningful to the peoples of Europe. In Smith's view, such a project has a weak potency of mobilizing people's identifications, in particular due to fact that, in contrast to national collectivity, a supranational community lacks a shared cultural fiber, as embroiled in memories or a sense of continuity between generations (Smith 1992). Cris Shore, too, has shared the view that, as a politically manufactured project, European identity can hardly yield a new, supranational state of belonging (Shore 2000, 2006). In contrast to both, Gerard Delanty claims that Europe does have a cultural existence. The problem with the view that argues to the contrary, Delanty writes in his critique of Shore, is that it is "based on a limited view of cultural identity as a community of fate and thus it is easy to prove that it does not exist beyond national contexts" (Delanty 2005:409). In fact, Delanty goes on to argue, "Europeanization has now reached [this] critical threshold of constituting itself through the articulation of a cultural model" (Delanty 2005:410; see also Delanty and Rumford 2005). Moreover, it is even possible to say that this model is carried by the development of a new ethics of commemoration. In Delanty's words, in today's Europe, "an ethics of memory has become a major site of public discourse on the nature of peoplehood" (Delanty 2005:410).

As can be derived from the arguments above, memory figures as an important and decisive moment of the success of the politics of European identity. However, in social theory and political discourse alike, European identity and memory are still often conceived and/or refuted predominantly in terms of the (im)possibility of reiterating the modern elite project and transcending it on supranational European levels; popular experiences and everyday life remain largely invisible in their potency to create "banal" (Billig 1995) modes of supranational claims. In this regard, it is intriguing that, given its mass dimensions of a daily practice, consumerism is a neglected site of public and theoretical discussion on integration and Europeanization. In cultural theory, consumerism and practices of shopping have long been recognized as carrying complex social, political, and cultural dimensions, ranging from emotional dynamisms of everyday private and family life to complex individual and group identity formations; anthropological accounts of "protest shopping," as discussed by commentators such as Mary Douglas, are especially relevant to our argument here as they provide an ample argument against the notion of "mindless consumerism" and can also be used to argue for an understanding of the political meaning of "people's tastes and preferences" (Miller et al. 1998:23).

In a similar vein, a research of mass consumerism in postsocialist Europe may, when it comes to investigating the relationship between memory and European identity, prove a sociologically and anthropologically relevant endeavor. This is particularly so if we consider most recent interest in the studies of consumerism in socialism and the popular memories of both (Crowley 2000; Švab 2002; Vidmar Horvat 2003; Luthar 2006). Cultural theory has classified memory into different categories of public remembrance of which popular memory carries an important value of both reinforcement and contestation of hegemonic visions of the past (Foucault 1989; Halbwachs 1992; Spigel 1995). Lynn Spigel underlines the difference between the official and the popular memory: "Popular memory is a form of storytelling through which people make sense of their own lives and culture [...] Whereas official history typically masks its own storytelling mechanism, popular memory acknowledges its subjective and selective status" (Spigel 1995:21). In the contexts of the pressing issue of the "democratic deficit" in the EU, the tensions between the official and the popular remembering of Europe therefore should be of prime interest to the political elites and provide a sound ground to fine-tune the European project to the imagination of people in different European settings.

For postsocialist Slovenia, remembering socialist "dictatorship over the needs" (Luthar 2006) has been a particularly potent site on which the image of the postsocialist citizen has been crafted: socialism, in this regard, appears as a Freudian child in the postsocialist adult, whose cultural, political, and ideological biography has been shaped by (censored) memories of consumerism in socialism. To understand how this projection has been tied in with the processes of the Europeanization of Slovenian national identity, it is necessary first to deconstruct the ruling myth of consumer culture in socialism.

Consumerism Between the East and the West

Consumerism (or the lack thereof) figured as an important part of collective identity formation in socialism. Contrary to the popular beliefs of the younger generations both in the East and the West, "Cinderella did go to the market," to rephrase the title of one of the publications demonstrating the recent rich feminist scholarly interest in the former socialist Europe (Einhorn 1993). Moreover, she went there dressed in different national and contentious cultural ways. With respect to socialist Yugoslavia, consumerism was indeed a hidden story behind its political economy and official state ideology. A different scholarly interest, which is beyond the purview of this chapter, might in fact uncover the scope and the importance of the antagonistic interlacing of the promises of consumer society and political structures in the enduring power of the socialist state and its hegemonic operation. It should be noted that, in this sense, the cultural histories of consumerism in Slovenia and Yugoslavia are quite unique with respect to the socialist countries forming the Eastern bloc, first and foremost because of Tito's breakup with Stalin, which set the country on the path of nonalignment, and second, and related to the former, because the independence from the Soviet area of influence gained the country political sympathies from the West and brought the society not only geographically but also culturally closer to the capitalist "enemy" (Vidmar Horvat 2007). To illustrate the point with only one example, which has been deemed prestigious until now, the Yugoslavian public television was a member of the Western Eurovision and held only the status of a member observer in the Eastern European association of TV stations Intervision. This enabled Yugoslavian TV stations to distribute Western TV shows (like *Peyton Place* and *Little House on the Prairie* of my youth) to their national audiences, while already in 1960, Ljubljana TV broadcast championships in ski-jumping in the world-famous Planica for its Western European partners.

Geographical position was equally crucial to the Yugoslavian "brand of socialism." In addition to the country's turn to more liberal social and economic policies in the 1960s,[1] the proximity of the border with the West contributed to the spread of consumer mentality and brought the Western consumer lifestyle closer to the people than was the case on the other side of the Iron Curtain. Tourist shopping became a national pastime practiced in various legal and illegal forms (Švab 2002; Vidmar Horvat 2003; Luthar 2006). Although the local and federal governments occasionally intervened and tried to restrict the scope of consumerism which travel abroad brought with it, it was also quietly endorsed by state powers. Domestic consumerism enhanced the official narrative of the prosperity of socialist society as a whole; the tourist shopping softened critical popular observations of the differences in the standard of people living on the opposite sides of the border. Therefore, whereas the Stalin style promises of "future bounty . . . in return for suppression of the appetite to consume in the present" (Crowley 2000:27), especially in the early postwar years, can be seen as shared across the socialist hemisphere, in Tito's Yugoslavia consumerism was gradually imbued with contradictory political and ideological functions. On the one hand, the official political discourse of the early postwar era used the narratives of the "rotten capitalist West" as an ideological means of countering the effects of the socialist state economy which created thrift and imposed restrictions on people's spending. On the other hand, it was the same "rotten West" that gave material evidence and credence to the dream of the prosperous society in the making by the socialist state.

However, as already mentioned, with the onset of liberalism in Slovenia, starting in the mid-1960s and embodied in the Slovenian political dissident Stane Kavčič, consumerism took on a new force in shaping the cultural landscape of the country. It was this wave of consumerism that intensified the consciousness of the origin of consumer goods and their quality. Foreign, mainly Italian, washing powders, for instance, were deemed better quality and cheaper (not to mention their mass availability) than the Yugoslavian ones. In contrast, some Western goods produced by Yugoslav food factories were considered tastier than the original. The Swiss chocolate "Milka" produced in a Slovenian food factory, for instance, still figures in my own and my friends' memory as the best there was, better than the one purchased in either neighboring Italy or Austria. In postsocialism, when grocery stores are again filled with imports, this time also with Milka from Eastern Europe, I and my chocolate-loving friends are unanimous that now "Gorenjka," a local Slovenian brand of chocolate, surpasses in taste both the import product available in Slovenia and the original Milka across the borders in Italy and Austria. Textiles, to continue with examples, were imbued with a similarly imprecise value. I vividly remember my mother's smirking at the poor quality of the clothes bought at the famous Italian Ponte Rosso market in Trieste: "You will wash this only once and it will not be the same any more," she used to warn me (a prophecy, which more often than not came true). When it came down to discussing garments, for my mother and her women friends, cultural superiority was clearly on the side of Slovenia.

These vignettes attest to the slippery cultural signification of commodities in socialism, which exchanged political meanings with cultural values more indeterminately than it is now popularly remembered. Not all commodities produced by the socialist state economy were considered bad in taste, nor were they embraced or disqualified because of their socialist origin; by the same token, not all Western products gained prime attention and endorsement. The perception of the socialist East in constant thrift and open-handedly welcoming any kind (and quality) of consumer goods is of a post-1989 origin, when images of the "Easterner," fascinated with the Western consumer abundance, began to circulate in the West (Crowley 2000:17). The socialist state, Katherine Verdery writes, forced Eastern Europeans to "build their social identities specifically *through consuming* . . . To acquire objects became a way of constituting your selfhood against a regime you despised" (Crowley 2000:14; emphasis in original). However, we also need to clarify this view in the sense that socialist culture produced citizens who were both loyal and disloyal to the state – in both cases not necessarily because of political beliefs but because they acted as pragmatic consumers indulging in the vices of spending and consumption beyond immediate ideological considerations of their "political correctness."

The Postsocialist Consumer Ethic and Border Imaginaries

With the move to a market economy and political democracy, post-1991 Slovenia experienced a massive "transition" toward the culture of consumerism and spending. The turn is best exemplified with the rapid growth of advertising as reflected in the increase in the number of advertising agencies: from a single company dominating the advertising space since 1973 to more than one hundred large agencies and small studios that came onto the scene in 1991 (Vidmar Horvat 2003). The spread of advertising agencies has been accompanied by a completely new quantitative and qualitative cultural landscape of imagery, borrowing from both local and global media production. In the early years of transition, political and cultural reconstitution and redefinition of the Slovenian collective identity drew from the culture of consumerism and, as argued elsewhere (Vidmar Horvat 2003), used new public displays of the iconography of consumerism, particularly openly sexualized ones, to claim Slovenian cosmopolitan character and Westernness. The country's accession to EU membership prior to and after 2004 unleashed a fresh installment of popular political narratives of Europeanness of Slovenian national and cultural identity. This sentiment flourished again with the joining of the Schengen area in December 2007.

As expected, this latter historical event became a stage for invoking memories of past borders and zones of divides. The collapse of the borders was the occasion not only for a celebration of the end of administrative obstacles; the by-now-invisible divide gained in power as the clashing narratives about the meaning of the past emerged. In an intriguing way, the moment – meant as symbolic confirmation of "our" shared European identity and belonging – was consumed in public, predominantly through antagonistic remembering of socialism. Among the diverse public recollections of socialism, a shared theme emerged to the surface, one which concerned memories of illegal trafficking (the popular "*šverc*" in the broad Yugoslavian use of the term) of petty consumables. In this section, we analyze three authors who, in contributions to one of the two leading Slovenian dailies, *Dnevnik*, invoked the past figure of the *švercer* as a means of comparison between "back then" and "today."

In "Od šverca na Šentilju do Tuševih paštet" [From "Šverc" at the Šentilj border to Tuš Pasta][2] (2007), Crnkovič protests against the fact that the collapse of the borders in Slovenia triggered an especially strong avalanche of reminiscences of the past prohibitive barriers to consumerism as if, of all peoples, the Slovenes were the most firmly placed behind the Iron Curtain. He then substantiates his doubts over the collective memory with the observation that nostalgia for past times is more alive here than elsewhere. Crnkovič goes on to argue that in socialist Yugoslavia, we were allowed to travel freely which, in his view, was the smartest of the inventions by which Tito maintained his regime and covered up the actual lack of freedom in the country. However, the author sees the freedom of the cross-border shopping movement also as a byproduct of fostering "primitive consumerism" among the masses. Crnkovič argues that today's consumerist frenzy, which involves both sellers and buyers of cheaper goods, originates from those times of illusory freedom. He says that he felt sick back then when watching the "švercerji" at the Šentilj, and he feels just the same today when he watches television ads promoting pasta or other goods at bargain basement prices (Crnkovič 2007:9).

When making consumer choices, Veblen wrote over a hundred years ago, the leisure class makes sure that, in its selection (according to his observation, most notably the selection of intoxicating beverages and narcotics, Veblen 1899 [1994]:44), it maintains distinctions by which the alleged cultural superiority of the upper class can be catered to. At the beginning of the twenty-first century, our superior place on the consumer scale of reputation is not secured mainly by certain designer outfits and pretty men's shoes, which, if one is to believe Crnkovič, are still chronically lacking in Slovenia; our position is perpetuated by *the absence of participation* in mass consumerism as such. While such an attitude may be assigned to the new urban elites across the globe, in its postsocialist variant, the contempt for mass shopping and mass tastes is burdened with socialist repression: as can be deduced from the author's writing, the conspicuously distasteful manners of the masses are dragging us collectively back to the lowbrow, styleless culture of the past.

In this projection, the whole nation is assigned to the inferior status of "Easterners," whose patterns of consumerism distance us irreversibly from the cultured collective (Western) European subject. The ending of the article is telling in this regard. Crnkovič concludes his lament with a "border anecdote" from JFK airport in New York where, although by now carrying a Slovenian passport, to his disbelief, he was still placed together in a room with "Africans in costumes." Crnkovič relates how, tired of being harassed, he stepped forward to the customs officer and explained to him that he was from Europe and was not used to this kind of long wait; this apparently worked as he was instantly let go. Crnkovič confesses to not having been totally honest, but instead of admitting that this was precisely the kind of treatment that the socialist state trained us for collectively, he turns to invoking the image of Europe as shot through with borders and divisions. Waiting for hours in long lines was the experience mainly of socialist citizens, not the whole of Europe. In this narrative segment, Crnkovič's memory browses through the past in a selective manner which enables the author to rewrite national history. In its selective commemorative mode, it also speaks of the desire to be let in, to be recognized as part of Europe – that is, the other Europe, the cultivated, noble, and reputable Europe.

To be let in may be described as a shared trauma, replete with individual stories of denial and exclusion. Traces of this can be found in Ervin Hladnik Milharčič's (2007a) "Začasna" [Temporary]. As he recalls, socialism was in many ways an educational project, teaching you how not to get what you want. At best, it allowed you the choice between one icon of popular culture and another (he cites Bob Dylan and Jefferson Airplane), but never the possession of both. In contrast, in the "multiple-choice society" across the border, the temptation got too hard to bear. Faced with a choice of Lou Reed and the Velvet Underground, the Grateful Dead and the Doors, and only going home with one Jefferson Airplane record made it difficult for a normal person to accept this socialist system as the new world order (Hladnik Milharčič 2007a).

In "Zbogom, Rdeča hiša" [Farewell, the red house] (Hladnik Milharčič 2007b:16), he provides a different memory. He shares with the reader a first-person testimony of how, for the first time after the collapse of the borders, he took his children to experience the new freedom of driving from Slovenia to Italy without even having to slow down.

He explains to his young passengers that they are about to have a wonderful experience: for the first time they were about to cross the border without being stopped. As he drives his children toward the great experience, Hladnik Milharčič revives memories of the border crossing of his childhood. He, too, invokes the practice of *šverc*. How should he explain to his children, he wonders, that the Red House is where, at the age of three, he was found to have a package of cigarettes in his coat pocket, smuggled across the border by his mother to buy a toy pistol for the boy on the other side? A border, the author concludes, is rather an intimate thing, a delicate object of private memories which soon one will not be able to pass down to the younger generation without causing a conflict.

Indeed, the border in this media narrative already is an object of cross-generation tension. Hladnik Milharčič confesses his irritation as he recounts his experience, of the voice from the back of the car that asks him what a border is. He can accept that the children don't know who Tito was but the border, which for him holds a kind of spiritual bond with the ancestors, is something they need to understand. In this reminiscent piece, the author thus struggles with himself as he is revisiting the past. In contrast to Crnkovič, who urges in public to forget socialism, Hladnik Milharčič's feelings for the past oscillate between anger and nostalgia, denial and regret, liberation and loss – including the loss for the family biographies whose albums will soon for ever be stripped of pleasurable testimonies of cross-generational collaboration in defeating the socialist state.

Those were great times, writes Simon Tecco in "Do You Still Remember, Comrades, We Were All 'Švercarji'" (Tecco 2007). Tecco, a Chilean journalist who immigrated to Yugoslavia in the 1970s, recalls how the 1970s and 1980s, which he experienced in Yugoslavia, were a period of daring, ingenious resourcefulness when a stubborn yet capriciously minded people, just as nowadays, would not have a blind trust in their leaders, and preferred to cross the border in search of solutions to social issues that the regime sought to suppress. To be a *švercer* one needed to be courageous, determined, and smart. Setting up ways to persuade the customs officer that the book which you carried in your luggage, despite its suspicious appearance, was not foreign propaganda, Tecco explains, created a live laboratory of civic trickery. *Šverc* formed bonds of solidarity (I myself remember the sadness with which I observed people at the borders who were caught smuggling goods from Italy or Austria), sometimes even, unexpectedly, with the customs officers, the servants of the repressive state. Tecco narrates his memory of smuggling a guitar across the border for a friend and being caught by the customs officer. Inside the interrogation room, however, the officer enthusiastically engaged Tecco, who knew nothing about playing the guitar, in conversation about the instrument. As a sign of solidarity among musicians, he finally let him continue to travel to Slovenia – with the guitar on board.

Claiming European Identity in Postsocialism

As can be deduced from the discussion above, the three stories, each told from a different angle and subject location, meet in the figure of the *švercer*, the emblematic embodiment of the consumer in socialism. While the three accounts differ in the meaning ascribed to the figure – from distancing contempt to protesting distance and, finally, to political identification – a perplexing question arises from reading these publicly articulated memories, namely, how to account for the desire to situate the figure of the socialist consumer in present-day perspective? To put it differently, in what way do the conflicting narratives embroiled in the *švercer* from the past resonate with the clashing discourses in the present? In what way does the image of the socialist consumer overlap with the identity of the consumer in postsocialism?

So far, it has been argued that, in its political meaning, consumerism was an important terrain on which socialist citizenship was semiautonomously created, negotiated, and contested. The argument can be expanded to state that, in the present, individual and collective memories of the past not only manifest themselves in the way commodities are meaningfully consumed; acts of consumption struggle against these memories to claim new forms of collective identities and citizenship. That this is an emerging "structure of feeling" shared *across* former socialist Europe can be illustrated with two additional cases.

The first story relates to the award-winning 2004 film, *Český sen* [The Czech dream]. In the film, which was directed by two young Czech students (Vít Klusák and Filip Remunda) as their final film school project, a team of alleged marketing specialists set up an advertising hoax operation in which they announce the opening of a new hypermarket. For their project they manage to get the help of advertising and PR agencies, which launch a massive street campaign involving large billboards on highways and street pamphlets distributed in Prague. Basing their plot on the negative campaign slogans "Don't come" and "Don't spend," the filmmakers nonetheless succeed in attracting more than three thousand shoppers for the grand opening. Gathering in front of a huge wall, supposedly concealing the shopping heaven, they fill the atmosphere with expectation and excitement until the very last moment when the two directors, performing the role of the "managers," cut the ribbon. The wall is pulled down to show the heaven to be merely an empty space (of dreams).

Pulling a practical joke worthy of Freudian interpretation, the film conveys the message of the stupefying effects of consumerism supported by the deceiving strategies of the advertising and PR industries. Operating in the politically entrenched contexts of post–Cold War Central and Eastern Europe, however, the joke becomes a site of traumatic encounter with the subject in postsocialism. For me, a viewer in postsocialist Slovenia, the film, together with the shots of people facing the disappointment with either anger or vague smiles, is hard to watch. I find it neither funny nor critical but rather deeply disturbing, for it plays (in a questionable ethical framework, in my view) with people's desires. Moreover, it imprints these desires with the "shadow of Easternness" as if this kind of frantic consumerism and collective irrationality are endemic to the former Eastern bloc and could not be triggered anywhere else, especially not in the consuming West. In a way, the film is a painful discursive gesture of mockery by which the cultural turn toward claiming European identity, based on the notion of consumerist abundance, has been carried out. It is also a cultural document of the act of self-colonization of the collective subject, furnished with exactly the cartoonish images that the West has constructed for the (former) East.

Postsocialist studies describe the processes of self-colonization of Eastern Europe with reference to postcolonial theory (Forrester et al. 2004). In postcolonial theory, the mechanism of internalization of and identification with the image projected on to the colonized by the colonizer has been explained with the notion of "epidermalization of the inferiority." "Black skin white masks," to recount Frantz Fanon, may take on different shapes and can be, despite the obvious and concrete historical context from which Fanon speaks, transferred to the contemporary European situation in the countries who have moved from the era of ideological repression of the socialist State to the era of the "epistemic violence" (Bhabha 2008:xxv) of post-Western Europe. To substantiate this claim, let us consider the scandal surrounding the 2007 Eurovision Song Contest.

To briefly recount the story: the winning song at the 2007 Contest in Helsinki was "Molitva" ("The Prayer"), performed by the Serbian singer Marija Šerifović. Soon after the contest in which, according to the journal *Dnevnik*, the "Eastern bloc" swept the board, a scandal erupted when the winning song was accused of being plagiarized: it was alleged to be a version of a previously recorded Albanian song entitled "Ndarja." In addition, the Maltese representatives at the contest claimed that the telephone voting was carried out incorrectly, with Eastern European states performing "bloc voting," mutually rewarding each other's contestants, while they also attempted to entice the Maltese team to join in the scheme. Because 14 out of the first 16 songs came from Eastern European countries, a protest was also issued from Germany: Why should Western European states continue to contribute most of the finances to the EBU? (*Dnevnik* 2007a). When Šerifović's song was confirmed as the winner after an investigation by the EBU (*Dnevnik* 2007b), a proposal emerged to have two separate contests, one for Eastern and one for Western countries. Finally, in November 2007, Austria announced that it would not compete in the 2008 contest, which was to be held in Belgrade, as it felt the contest had become nothing short of a "political kitchen."

Eventually, a month later, the European Committee began an inquiry into whether the winning singer, being a supporter of the Serbian radical party candidate Tomislav Nikolić in the presidential campaign, was worthy of carrying the title of "ambassador of intercultural dialogue" given to her on the occasion of the launch of the "European Year of Intercultural Dialogue."

In his 2006 article "Visions of Europe," Göran Bolin defines the Eurovision Song Contest as a media site in the construction of national identity. In one part of his discussion, Bolin focuses specifically on the cultural technologies used by former communist countries re-aligning themselves. As can safely be inferred from the affair and the consequent public reaction, the pop media spectacle to be consumed by the imagined community of EU citizens has grown to the point of also carrying the power of symbolically structuring the cultural terrain of new Europeans and their claims of belonging in the enlarged EU. Reflecting on the Eurosong scandal, in an article "More and Less Valued," a Slovenian commentator wrote that if the EU wants to serve the whole of Europe, then surely the idea of two Eurosongs should be stopped at the very beginning (*Vovk* 2007). This comment invokes the fear of reviving an older vision of "two Europes," the superior Western and the inferior Eastern one, while in fact, without considering alternative arrangements that may indeed be more practical or fair, the Eurosong incident mobilized the perception of the incommensurability of Western and Eastern European identities. The notable success of the Eastern European countries, as interpreted by the West, was employed to reproduce the cultural boundary splitting Europe into two halves. Instead of being viewed as merely the latest in a long line of voting confidence tricks associated with the Eurovision Song Contest (the most frequent one of my youth was the "Scandinavian" vote cartel), the alleged deceit was labeled with cultural and political meanings of the fraudulent "East."

The conflict surpasses the issue of the popular contest and its voting ethics. Several institutional and daily experiences attest to the public perception that there are indeed "two Europes" that come to life through "two markets," operating within the boundaries of the EU. Research in Slovenia shows that 62.5% of people agree with the sentiment that for foreign markets, multinational corporations use ingredients of a lower quality than those used for their own markets. Consequently, if given a choice between the same product from a domestic and foreign brand producer, 93% would lay their trust in the domestic product. While this last figure may speak of a certain naïveté invested in the national "captains of production," read together with the previous one, it conveys an important message about the value put on consumer equality and democratic treatment of consumers' desires. Moreover, according to the Consumer Association of Slovenia, while products obviously differ with their markets, there is no concrete evidence that products sold in Eastern European countries are of poorer quality (*Nika* 2007). Yet, the suspicion has grown to become a matter of common knowledge: as the title of a supplement to a Slovenian daily suggests, in the consumer markets in Slovenia one finds second-class goods at first-class prices (*Ona* 2007).

A journalist writes of her consumer experience, as a housewife, of a "dangerous discrimination":

> It is about the quality of goods from the Western European market. I am not sure whether you have noticed or not, but some products of the same brand on our shelves are of a lower quality than those you can buy in any of the Western European countries. For instance, the washing powder bought in Austria or Italy will have a slightly different packaging and you will find instructions written in Western European languages whereas with ours, the instructions will be in Slovenian, Croatian, Serbian, Czech, Polish or some other "Eastern" language; and the washed laundry will be less white than if you bought the powder across the border. (*Vovk* 2007:2, translation K. Vidmar Horvat)

I began this chapter with the question of my own petty obsession with reading the product labels and their place of origin. The points of departure were a puzzling confession to myself that, unconsciously, my consumer ethics make cultural distinctions between the "made in the West" and "made in the East" of EU labels; and the observation that, despite the awareness of globalization of economy, consumers in postsocialist Slovenia in general tend to associate the uneven distribution of goods on the EU markets as the marker of their status as second-class consumers and, in effect, second-class EU citizens. When I read the lines above, I again struggle with memories of my own consumer racism. However, while both my own and the reporter's testimonies of perceptions of quality of goods are equally troubling (for their lack of scientific evidence, to say the least!), they convey the message that the sentiment passes into a collective frustration and, as such, should be studied in its impact on how Europe is being imagined.

European Citizenship and Consumer Belonging

We have argued that in the context of European integration and the Europeanization of shared cultural space, consumerism presents a neglected side of how notions of shared citizenship, belonging, and loyalty are being articulated. Because, in postsocialist Europe, memories of consumption in socialism (often unconsciously) govern the construction of the meaning of consumerism in postsocialism, while these memories frequently bring back traumatic experiences and recollections of denials of consumer desires, it is necessary to incorporate popular cultural pools of remembering in theoretical and political accounts when considering the project of the Europeanization of identity. This is even more the case when consumption is perceived as a tool of stratification, of the ordering of citizens into "first" and "second" class of belonging, based on the past imaginaries of cultural inferiority of the East, and historical superiority of the West.

To understand the relationship between consumerism and European identity in postsocialist cultures, it is necessary to account for the memories of the socialist past, which circulate, in omnipresent though repressed forms, in the collective consciousness in the present. Campbell writes that the goal of the search for pleasure is not to have, but to desire to have (Campbell 1987:132); in the case of postsocialist Europe, this is not entirely the case. To actually have validates the desire and retrospectively allows for the reclaiming of decency denied by socialist state intrusion into privacy through measures of restriction. In this regard, encountering the products which, with their origin of production, connote Easternness could be read as a resistance to socialist consumerism, its imposed rule of conduct, which made us all *švercerji* and robbed us of daily acts of choice. As they get articulated in daily practices of consumption, these memories are not only sites of unification but also points of division and conflict – particularly in former socialist countries which, through the ways the West remembers them, struggle to exit the vicious circle of defrosting and refreezing (Borcila 2004) in the symbolic image of the cultural "other."

At the same time, memories also play a role in what we called a (complicit) "self-recolonization" of the "East." The colonial condition, Bhabha recounts Fanon's assertion, operates "through image and fantasy – those orders that figure transgressively on the borders of history and the unconscious" (Bhabha 2008:xxvi). In Slovenia, since gaining independence in 1991, consumerism has figured as a powerful terrain of this fantasy work whereby the "West" has denoted the superior and the

"East" the inferior culture. To nurture this distinction as a means of collective renegotiation of national identity as fully (Western) European, acts of forgetting have been needed. On the one hand, socialist Europe has been re-membered, recomposed into a historical zone of desubjectified masses, unable to reflect or locate the limits to their oppression by the State (Borcila 2004). The erasure of the memory of alternative spaces of self-articulation in which the socialist citizen practiced acts of resistance and emancipation is perpetuated by the overproduction of the images of the indulgence in a mindless consumerism in postsocialism. The overproduction serves both the "West" and the "East" of the post-1989 new Europe: it is used as epidermal evidence for this deeply historically traumatized structure of collective mind. In this stroke of censoring mental histories and cultures of Europe, there is not much room for memories which speak of a different past.

On the other hand, the amnesia operates through the isolation of the socialist world from world history. This is especially symptomatic in post-Yugoslav Slovenia, which is reluctant to be reminded of its role in the nonaligned movement: the image of the "Africans in wardrobes" seems to be an especially traumatic one. The same subject to whom the socialist citizen once was connected by ties of transnational solidarity and political alternative to global capitalism, becomes relocated to the position of the eternal "other": the memory of Yugoslav politics of cosmopolitanism is suppressed in servile affirmation of nationalist hegemony of (Western) Eurocentrism.

However, in the era of an emerging cosmopolitan, postnational constellation, the need to undermine the power of colonial violence is ever more present. Translated into our case of the European politics of memory, this means pushing public culture toward pluralization of memory, to open its narratives in diverse in contradictory directions. In this regard, the transition prejudice, with which we began this chapter, may be reconceptualized away from a traumatized toward a critical ground on which processes of deconstruction and reconstruction of memory are taking place. This can also be proposed as a shared ground for the democratization of European identity. In fact, it may turn out that in the realignment of past with the present, the memory of socialist consumerism carries a trans-European political value.

That is, in an era of global consumerism, and global exploitation of human and natural resources, the question of how the same subversive practices which once arose from the culture of thrift can be reactivated to tame the culture of abundance and greed may soon prove to be quite a relevant one.

NOTES

An earlier version of this chapter entitled "Consuming European Identity: The Inconspicuous Side of Consumerism in the EU," appeared in the *International Journal of Cultural Studies*, 2010, 13(1):25–41.

1 The late 1950s and 1960s were also the years of intense socialist modernization across the Eastern bloc. In this regard, one should not forget the famous "kitchen debate" between Nikita Khrushchev and Richard Nixon in Moscow in 1959. To prove superiority, the two front men of the Cold War did not turn to listing advances in military industry of their respective countries; they "quarreled" about household appliances. In 1978 Vaclav Havel

nicely circumscribed the lesson: "Our system is most frequently characterized as a dictatorship or, more precisely, the dictatorship of a bureaucracy over a society [...] What we have here is simply another form of consumer and industrial society . . . [T]he post-totalitarian system has been built on foundations laid by the historical encounter between dictatorship and the consumer society" (in Crowley 2000:25).

2 Tuš is one of the three chain grocery stores holding a monopoly in Slovenia.

REFERENCES

Balibar, É.

2004 We, the People of Europe? Reflections on Transnational Citizenship, Princeton: Princeton University Press.

Bhabha, Homi K.

2008 Foreword to the 2008 edition. *In* Black Skin White Masks. Frantz Fanon, C. L. Markmann, trans. pp. xxi–xxxvii. London: Pluto.

Billig, Michael

1995 Banal Nationalism. London: Sage.

Bolin, Göran

2006 Visions of Europe: Cultural Technologies of Nation-States. International Journal of Cultural Studies 9(2):189–206.

Borcila, Andaluna

2004 How I Found Eastern Europe: Televisual Geography, Travel Sites, and Museum Installations. *In* Over the Wall/After the Fall: Post-Communist Cultures through an East–West Gaze. Sibelan Forrester, Magdalena J. Zaborowska, and Elena Gapova, eds. pp. 42–66. Bloomington and Indianapolis: Indiana University Press.

Campbell, Colin

1987 Romantična etika in duh sodobnega porabništva. Ljubljana: SH.

Crnkovič, Marko

2007 Od šverca na Šentilju do Tuševih paštet. Dnevnik, December 29:9.

Crowley, David

2000 Warsaw's Shops, Stalinism and the Thaw. *In* Style in Socialism. Modernity and Material Culture in Post-War Eastern Europe. David Crowley and Susan E. Reid, eds. pp. 25–47. Oxford: Berg.

Delanty, Gerard, and Chris Rumford

2005 Rethinking Europe: Social Theory and the Implications of Europeanization. London: Routledge.

Delanty, Gerard

2007 Peripheries and Borders in a Post-Western Europe. Eurozine. Electronic document. http://www.eurozine.org/articles/article_2007-12-20-delanty.html (accessed November 5, 2011).

Dnevnik

2007a Evrosong: Je Marija Šerifović osvojila Evropo s plagiatom? Dnevnik, May 16:18.

2007b EBU Claims There Was No Deal with the Votes in Eurovision 2007. Dnevnik, August 14:27.

Einhorn, Barbara

1993 Cinderella Goes to Market: Citizenship, Gender, and Women's Movements in East Central Europe. London: Verso.

Forrester, Sibelan, Magdalena J. Zaborowska, and Elena Gapova, eds.

2004 Over the Wall/After the Fall: Post-Communist Cultures through an East–West Gaze. Bloomington and Indianapolis: Indiana University Press.

Foucault, Michel
1989 Foucault Live. New York: Semiotexte.
Habermas, Jürgen
2001 Postnational Constellation. Cambridge: Polity.
Hann, Chris, ed.
2002 Postsocialism: Ideals, Ideologies and Practices in Eurasia. London: Routledge.
Halbwachs, Maurice
1992 On Collective Memory. Chicago: University of Chicago Press.
Hladnik Milharčič, Ervin
2007a Začasna. Dnevnik, December 20.
2007b Zbogom, Rdeča hiša. Dnevnik, December 27:16.
Jackson, Peter, and Nigel Thrift
1996 Geographies of Consumption. *In* Acknowledging Consumption: A Review of New Studies. Daniel Miller, ed. pp. 204–237. London: Routledge.
Luthar, Breda
2006 Remembering Socialism. On Desire, Consumption and Surveillance. Journal of Consumer Culture 6(2): 229–259.
Miller, Daniel, Peter Jackson, Nigel Thrift, Beverley Holbrook, and Michael Rowlands
1998 Shopping, Place and Identity. London: Routledge.
Nika
2007 For the Slovenes Is Less Good Equally Good? Nika, March 14.
Ona
2007 Second-Class Goods, First-Class Price. Ona, February 13.
Outhwaite, William
2008 European Society. Cambridge: Polity.
Pickering, Michael
2001 Stereotyping: The Politics of Representation. New York: Palgrave.
Rizman, Rudi
2008 Negotiating Identity in the Age of Globalization. *In* The Future of Intercultural Dialogue in Europe: Views From the In-Between. Ksenija Vidmar Horvat, ed. pp. 33–45. Ljubljana: Faculty of Arts.
Šabec, Ksenija
2007 Kolektivni spomini in stereotipne podobe Italijanov v slovenski kolektivni zavesti: primer slovenske tržaške književnosti. Družboslovne razprave 23(55): 95–113.
Shore, Cris
2000 Building Europe: The Cultural Politics of European Integration. London: Routledge.
2006 "In uno plures"? EU Cultural Policy and the Governance of Europe. Cultural Analysis 5:7–26.
Smith, Anthony D.
1992 National Identity and the Idea of European Union. International Affairs 68:55–76.
Spigel, Lynn
1995 From the Dark Ages to the Golden Age: Women's Memories and Television Reruns. Screen 36(1): 16–34.
Stråth, Bo
2002 A European Identity: To the Historical Limits of a Concept. European Journal of Social Theory 5:387–401.
Švab, Alenka
2002 Consuming Western Image of Well-Being: Shopping Tourism in Socialist Slovenia. Cultural Studies 16(1):63–79.

Svašek, Maruška, ed.

2006 Postsocialism: Politics and Emotions in Central and Eastern Europe. Oxford: Berghahn.

Tecco, Simon

2007 Še pomnite tovariši, vsi smo bili "švercarji." Dnevnik, December 29:31.

Todorova, Maria, and Szusza Gille, eds.

2010 Post-Communist Nostalgia. Oxford: Berghahn.

Veblen, Thorstein

1994[1889] The Theory of the Leisure Class. New York: Dover.

Vidmar Horvat, Ksenija

2003 Žensko telo, globalno potrošništvo in slovenska tranzicija: sociološki fotoesej. Teorija in praksa 40(5):839–859.

2007 The Globalization of Gender: Ally McBeal in Postsocialist Slovenia. *In* Feminist Television Criticism. 2nd edition. Charlotte Brunsdon and Lynn Spigel, eds. pp. 288–301. Maidenhead: Open University Press.

2011 The Predicament of Intercultural Dialogue: Reconsidering the Politics of Culture and Identity in the EU. Cultural Sociology 1749975511401280, doi:10.1177/1749975511401280

Vovk, Maja

2007 More and Less Valued. Dobro jutro, August 25:2.

Žižek, Slavoj

1993 Caught in Another's Dream in Bosnia. *In* Why Bosnia? Writings on the Balkan War. Rabia Ali and Lawrence Lifschutz, eds. pp. 233–240. Stony Creek: Pamphleteer's Press.

CHAPTER 10

The Europe of Regions and Borderlands

Thomas M. Wilson

A "Europe of the Regions" has been a rallying cry for many versions of a changing European Union for decades, yet its dimensions remain unclear despite the longevity of the concept and the expansion of the EU to 27 member states. What is clear, however, is that in the inevitable gamesmanship of winners and losers in the twin processes of European integration and Europeanization, some regions in and across the borders of the EU's member states have successfully used EU development money and other forms of intervention to change their political, economic, social, and cultural conditions. These border regions have in fact been the focus and locus of many European Commissions and national and subnational governmental schemes to right economic imbalances within and between member states.

The goals of these schemes are many. In terms of the overall European project, economic and political imbalances between regions within and across national boundaries might make difficult the achievement of an ever-closer union and the continuing support for EU widening and/or deepening by European citizens in less-favored regions. National and subnational programs of regional development have often been part of regionalization policies that have a great deal to do with the changing nature of nation-states in Europe. And regional social movements and identity politics also call for recognition of and actions related to their historical and contemporary cultures and identities. All of these policies, programs, and practices have one thing in common: they give definition to territorial entities, called "regions," which have yielded various forms of regional government, governance, economies, societies, and cultures. Even if a Europe of the Regions does not in fact exist in any institutional sense, and may never exist given the trajectory of the European project today, regional Europe is alive and flourishing in the cores and peripheries of every country on the continent.

Since the 1970s, anthropologists have been at the forefront of the comparative study of regions in Europe, including the analysis of the related processes of

A Companion to the Anthropology of Europe, First Edition. Edited by Ullrich Kockel, Máiréad Nic Craith, and Jonas Frykman.

regionalism and regionalization, but these approaches in research and writing have waxed and waned according to the tides of academic scholarship. So too has anthropological interest in nations and states in Europe. But one area of increasing importance in ethnographic and ethnological scholarship in Europe, namely the anthropology of borders and frontiers, has consistently brought together scholars of European integration, nationalism, and the changing territorial and political economic dimensions of the state, all within critiques of globalization, mobility, enclosures, and hybridity. This is not surprising due to the changing nature of anthropology worldwide as well as the evolving scholarly interests in various theories of identity, territory, and power.[1] But the anthropology of borders and frontiers in Europe has also involved increased attention to the interplay of regions, nations, states, and the European Union (EU), as integral aspects of local, national, and European life. In this last sense, scholarly interest in borders and borderlands in Europe has been driven by interest in and the relevant programs of the European integration project. This confluence of region and borderland in EU study is clearly represented in a hypothesis suggested by the sociologist Martin Kohli (2000) a decade ago. According to Kohli, for a supranational European identity to succeed, it would have to be based on alternative identities to national ones. Moreover, to Kohli, European borderlands might provide excellent venues for the study of multiple, hybrid, creolized, alternative identity formations – experimental sites, perhaps, for the formation of new forms of Europeanness. In this view, and it is one that is shared in a great deal of social science on borderlands and border people in Europe and beyond, it is suggested that because borderland people have had more occasion and more of a need to adapt to other peoples and identities, they will be the most interested and amenable to adapting to the affective dimensions of the European project, and perhaps first or best able to adopt a European identity on an order to rival that of national identity. And while this hypothesis remains provocative but relatively untested, it indicates the resonance of border peoples and regions in wider interests in European integration and Europeanization.

The anthropology of borders and frontiers has kept pace with the rise of regions and regionalism in Europe over the last two decades, and has a great deal to offer the comparative study of regions, nations, states, and the EU. However, the overall anthropology of the European Union has not been particularly direct in its approaches to the impact of European integration in border and other regions. Overall, while anthropologists have mirrored the multilevel approaches by the EU to European integration, by and large they have concentrated their efforts on capital cities and in the halls of decision-making in Brussels. Recently, however, anthropologists and other ethnographers have increasingly examined the ways in which regions have redefined themselves, in terms of governance and government, economic infrastructure and relations, social institutions, and cultural and other identities. This confluence of transformed regions within a transforming Europe is particularly clear in border regions, many of which have used their long-standing ties to their regional counterparts across the old state borderlines to reconstruct themselves as cross-border and transnational spaces of new European governance and identity. This chapter will review the major trends in border regional life in Europe as one way to explicate how a Europe of the regions may be rhetorical but alive nonetheless in the political and economic movements in a Europe of borderlands.

The Europe of the Regions

The ideas and meanings connected to the notion of regions are many, and are sometimes contradictory, sometimes complementary. It is also true that there are as many meanings of the term in the social sciences, including in anthropology, as there have been and are in past and contemporary European countries (Keating 1998:11).[2] It is clear that region as a term refers to contextual and constructed space, but that space can be delimited or defined functionally in so many ways that are political, territorial, economic, administrative, social, and cultural. For example, in Europe today regions are organized in terms of political jurisdiction, administrative competence, economic zones, historical traditions, social structures, and majority and minority cultures and identities, and are not necessarily constrained by international borders. While all regions are territorial entities, the definition, traditions, practices, and meanings attached to that territory can differ greatly across time and space, and among the peoples who identify (many who identify with) that territory. Regions are clearly geographical spaces, but these spaces "can be conceptualized at several different spatial scales, from the local to the supranational" (Keating 2004). Although there is a Basque region in Spain, which approximates but does not coincide with an autonomous province, there is also the larger transnational Basque region that includes people and territory in France (Douglass 1998). Historic Catalonia not only encompasses areas of present-day Spain and France, but also helped to create the limits of both countries, upsetting the standard notion that regions were and are peripheral (Sahlins 1989). Euro-regions are situated wholly within some European countries, but stretch to include areas in two or more countries elsewhere in Europe, some of which are not entirely within the EU. Some regions have historical antecedents, but their contemporary dimensions are different, sometimes due to administrative and political history, such as historic Brittany and its postrevolutionary division and present-day compartmentalization within the departments of France (Nicolas 2006). Regions in Europe today are historical in scope, but very much a contemporary development shaped by European integration and the internal and external forces that are transforming the nature of both capitalism and of the nation-state in Europe.

After years in which regionalism in Europe was primarily about state-based spatial planning and policies, it was given a boost in the 1960s and 1970s due to the changing nature of the European Economic Community and its expansion to nine members in 1974. But regionalism stalled a bit due to economic crisis in the 1970s, to be revived and enlarged as a concept and practice in the 1980s and 1990s, when it was given a new impetus by economic restructuring, state reforms, globalization, and especially by European integration (Keating 1998:16), which fostered a renewed European Regional Policy (Hooghe and Keating 1994). The Delors presidency of the European Commission rededicated the EU's interest in regions as a means to both right economic development imbalances within states and across the general membership, and to build an affective dimension among European citizens by seeking to instill confidence and trust in European intentions and institutions (Bellier and Wilson 2000). But the impact of European integration on regions and regionalism goes beyond the initiatives started under the Delors regime.

It puts into question the monopoly of the nation-state as a container for social, economic, and political processes and opens the prospects for new forms of autonomy. It threatens to marginalize some regions, unable to compete in the single market, while offering benefits to others. Where functions formally devolved to regions are Europeanized this can represent a double loss of control, to Europe but also to the state, since it is the states who are represented in the Council of Ministers, the main decision-making body of the European Union (Keating 2004:xiv).

Due to these forces of European integration and Europeanization, in which there is a reordering of territory and identity in the lives of Europeans (Borneman and Fowler 1997), regionalism is often a movement that originates from below, in localities where both new and old traditions, ideas, and practices are given particular territorial and geographical emphases at levels of social, political, economic, and cultural integration below the level of the state, and in some cases above that of the state. But regionalism is also a statist movement, a top-down initiative of government, where the subservient, devolved, and autonomous functions of the region may change according to the transformations in the nature of the state (Loughlin 2000). Regardless of its origins, all countries in Europe today have clearly demarcated political and administrative regions, all of which have their attendant social and cultural dimensions that offer frames of membership and affect that are at the heart of the anthropological enterprise.

A regional approach in social and cultural anthropology has had just as many fits and starts as has any notion of a Europe of the Regions. The beginnings of an anthropology of regions in postwar Europe followed a course largely parallel to the developing nature of regions as political and economic entities within European states. At first, anthropologists were slow to see regions as geographical spaces that transcended the limits of the state, although they were quick to outline the nature of nations and nationalism that could not be contained within a state framework. In fact, the anthropologists who first turned to regional analysis were those who had begun to recognize that local peasant communities were only part-communities, and were entwined in social, political, and economic networks that tied them to many people and institutions beyond the village community.[3] These anthropologists began to theorize the causes, extent and effects of community relations with agents and structures of the nation and state.[4] This growing body of work in ethnography in Europe sought to document how local communities were important participants in much wider relations of power, exploitation, domination, and subversion, tied in various ways to changing forces of capitalism and national and international political economy.

It is not surprising that anthropologists interested in delineating the nature of political and economic processes beyond the village and neighborhood should begin to theorize the nature of space, place, and territory, particularly as they relate to ethnic and national cultures that are subservient to elites elsewhere in their respective countries. As John Cole summarized in his 1977 assessment of the state of the anthropology of Europe, the interrogation by anthropologists of the variety of forces in which localities found themselves as both agents and pawns led them to see the region as a unit of analysis (1977:365). Many of these regional anthropologists did research in relatively peripheral areas of nation-states, but ones with historical and continuing cultural identities as regions, such as Sicily (Schneider and Schneider 1976), Catalonia (Hansen 1977), and Trentino (Cole and Wolf 1974). The thread that ran through most of this regional anthropology in the 1960s and 1970s, and which has continued to some extent to the present, was that a region was not just an expression of geographical and cultural proximity, nor was it the conglomeration of various communities with long-standing residence in some national backwater. On the contrary, and borrowing from the work of Schneider et al. (1972), he saw that the region as "a unit of political ecology, where local resources and people are organized by an elite which is interposed between community and nation – and which may even bypass the nation in its relations with the world system" (Cole 1977:365). With license to substitute some terms for those which were more salient in the 1970s, Cole and his contemporaries, and many anthropologists who have done regional research since (see, e.g., Grillo 1980; McDonald 1990; Kockel 1991; Cole 1997; Stacul 2003), have sought to see the ways in which institutions of power external to localities frame if not direct aspects of local life. Much theorizing today in fact is about how localities bypass the nation and state in their relations with the global, and within these analyses there is a great deal of ink spilled investigating the neoliberal aspects of such relations, and although the study of elites has been hard to find recently, the study of those who have and wield power – some of whom are corporate and political leaders – has been the mainstay of our profession of late.

While the impact of the region as a new form and unit of analysis, which began with bursts of ethnographic research activity in Western and in Southern Europe in particular,[5] has been long-standing, for much of the 1990s and since then it has declined as a strategy and motif in writing anthropology, due in large part to the reflexive turn in ethnography. To a great degree anthropological reflexivity and the ethnographic critique of the mid-1980s have led to an anthropological domain in which bounded space and culture have been theorized out of existence. But as we have seen, regions themselves have grown in importance and have proliferated in Europe, and more Europeans than ever live and work every day within a social, economic, cultural and/or political framework known as the region. Anthropologists today have increasingly returned to the evaluation of region precisely because our hosts and respondents see regions as important if not vital to many of the things they hold dear. And no matter how much evidence there is to the contrary in contemporary anthropological teaching, research, and publishing, anthropology is still more about what others do, say, and believe than it is about what anthropologists do, say, and believe about them (and I assert this with a full appreciation of our interpretive roles within a highly humanistic social science). Said differently, if anthropologists can stop theorizing about themselves so much they might just accept the notion that regions, nations, and states, in Europe at least, are still the primary political and economic structures within which everyday lives are framed, and as such must be an abiding concern of anthropologists.

This is of course not to deny that regions are themselves highly contested ideas and institutions. This is palpably so in the symbolic arena that is European integration. A Europe of the Regions, which survives as rhetoric more than realized politics, government, and society, is unlikely to survive much longer in European policy circles (but I am quick to remind myself and the reader to never say never in the dynamic world of an ever-closer and ever-distant union of the EU!). Thus in terms of anthropological interests the subject and object that is the region might perhaps be better approached by social scientists and policy-makers as regional Europe. In the analysis of regional Europe, anthropologists and other scholars can approach the myriad issues of people and their regions and identifications with their regions from the bottom up, from the top down, and from the inside out and outside in. This ability to see regions within their horizontal and vertical integration and disintegration, within hierarchies and within autonomous frames, and with their many forms of resonance and dissonance within countries but across a continental landscape of like and unlike regions, would also allow a degree of liberty from the many forms of rhetoric regarding the Europe of the Regions (which in the past also involved calls for a Europe of the Peoples, a Europe of Nations, and a Europe of States).

Anthropological attention to regional Europe encompasses regions in Europe, however defined, but also includes regional policies and practices that originate in the national states of the EU, which in the vast majority of cases entail shared competencies among the three levels of governance, that is, region, nation(state), and Europe (the EU). In a regional-Europe approach, policies of regionalism and regionalization, among others, and the programs and practices of government and politics, would be necessary components of any and all analyses of regional spaces, functions, institutions, and identities. In my view this confluence of anthropological approaches to regions in Europe has been best represented in the growing anthropology of borders, frontiers, and borderlands.

A Europe of Borderlands

Martin Kohli, in his presidential address to the European Sociological Association meetings in Amsterdam in 1999, presented an overview of European identity which was published as "Battlegrounds of European Identity" (2000). His essay considers a number of interesting hypotheses, but two are particularly relevant to this article. As mentioned above, Kohli suggests that European identity must be based on something other than the national, and European borderlands are one of the few principal arenas within which a European identity might take root. Of course he does not conclude that borderlands are the only sites of such hybrid or postnational identity formation. There are certainly such processes of identity reformulation in places and among many groups other than those of borderlands: the social science of migrants everywhere in Europe clearly shows us a host of locations where new identifications and identities are taking shape, as they are as well in transnational institutions like corporations, NGOs, and supranational bodies, for example. Furthermore, Kohli's hypotheses put forward a notion that borderland people have more occasion and need to adapt to other peoples and identities, an assertion that the sizeable literatures on globalization, deterritorialization, and postnational identities dispute. These assertions about borderland people seem to be predicated on a notion that national identities are the basic or principal identity to which all other political identities should take a back seat. However, Kohli has offered us an enticing idea, that European integration and Europeanization might have its greatest impact in borderlands.

But which borderlands I wonder would be most receptive to such changes, in a Europe that has more borderlands, of nations, states, and regions, than ever before in its history? And given this exponential increase in borders, and despite the rhetoric of a borderless Europe, who in Europe does not live near a border? Who are the Europeans who are not borderland people?

These hypotheses need to be tested and evaluated in European borderlands, which are increasing in both numbers and types. The European Union enlargement process may indeed make some international borders into something new and different, that is, internal and external borders of the EU. These borderlands will be sites of changing local, national, and European identity, as well as fertile areas in which to study the interplay of these identities. But how do the construction of new borders and the reconstruction of the old relate to the processes of Europeanization, and the overall impetus of European integration?[6] The answers to these questions have been sought by many anthropologists who over recent years have turned to European borderlands to investigate the changing nature of territory, polity, and identity in European societies and cultures. At the same time anthropologists who do research on borders, boundaries, and frontiers have from their end become increasingly interested in what the EU and other forms of political and economic integration and disintegration have been accomplishing across Europe.

The convergence of interest in borders and the policies and programs associated with European integration and Europeanization is hardly surprising. The EU represents what is perhaps the greatest experiment in postnational and supranational polity building in the world today, and the greatest reconfiguration in political space since the days of the British Empire when empire- and nation-building were on the agenda. And scholars from all persuasions are interested in the future of the nation and state. After all, a principal thrust of scholarly globalization rhetoric has queried the ability of the contemporary nation-state to fully provide for the safety of its people, territory, and capital, for it is widely asserted that the state no longer is the guarantor of its own sovereignty, security, and economic well-being. Not surprisingly, borders, the physical and symbolic manifestation of the state at the territorial limits of its power, have figured prominently in both the study of geopolitical borders and in the examination of the metaphorical boundaries of identity in a globalized world (Heyman 1994). As if the external pressures of nation-states to share sovereignty, to adopt neoliberal agendas that support capitalism but hardly keep it in check, and to provide security from terrorism and unwanted labor but ensure greater freedoms of movement and mobility were not enough, countries in modern Europe are also under pressure from within, and not least from regionalist sources. Regions seek devolution, autonomy or independence, and ethnic, national, religious, and political minorities of all sorts want a better say in the affairs of the nation. This popular rhetorical bent in globalization studies aside, there are perhaps just as many anthropologists, based on their ethnographic research on nation, state, territory, and borders in Europe and elsewhere, who have disputed the notions of a weakened state. They, in turn, have favored a model of a contemporary state which has transformed itself in form and function, but not declined in its overall power to frame and intrude in the lives of its citizens and residents (Wilson and Donnan 1998a, 2005; Donnan and Wilson 1999).

The turn to border studies in the anthropology of Europe since the 1970s was not just a reaction to the changing terrain of political territory and identity represented in the new regionalisms that have been discussed above. This new emphasis on borders has in fact been growing worldwide across the field of anthropology, due no doubt to the scholarly turn to reflexivity, identity, and globalization, but also due to real-time and fast-moving changes to the business and politics of global capitalism and its neoliberal responses. However, it should also be remembered that ethnographic studies of borders and boundaries have a long history in anthropological research, if not a very deep record in terms of studying regions, nations, and states. Before the 1990s most anthropological studies of boundaries were those done of ethnic groups. The modern anthropological study of nations, nationalism, and political ecology in borderlands dates to the groundbreaking study done by Cole and Wolf (1974) in Northern Italy. Since then, and particularly since the Common Market expanded to nine countries from its original six, anthropologists have steadfastly researched the cultural dimensions to European integration, and have done so with particular attention to cities and regions.[7] Moreover, all research done on borders and frontiers in Europe by anthropologists is part of the global attention to similar matters, as may be seen in recent anthropological collections (see, e.g., Wilson and Donnan 1998b, 2005; Haller and Donnan 2000; Heyman and Cunningham 2004; Horstmann and Wadley 2006).

Anthropologists who have done research on the history, politics, economics, societies, and cultures of borderlands and border regions in Europe have not simply followed the leads of scholars elsewhere. In fact, ethnographic analyses of European borderlands have begun to lead the movement toward new theorizing of borders and border cultures more generally in anthropology, displacing somewhat the formerly hegemonic models derived from research in the US–Mexico border regions. This has occurred precisely because of the many forces already discussed above that may be found only or best in Europe, where multiple nations and states, with multiple national and state cultures, and multiple and overlapping definitions of majority and minority citizenship, identity, government, and power, may be found on a continental level, all within a frame of a truly supranationalist and growing EU. The comparative study of borders worldwide has been imbued with its own Europeanism due to the groundswell of interest by scholars of and in Europe on issues of mobility, migration, racism, nationalism, illicit trade, smuggling, and all of the social and cultural aspects of new nations, new borders, new policies, new citizenships, and new forms of government and governance across a continent.

In what constitutes the most effective influence on anthropology worldwide since the heady days of Wolf and the original students of regional analysis in the 1970s, these groundbreaking anthropologists have provided the inspiration for anthropological analyses that reach beyond the limits of Europe. No longer is the anthropology of Europe confined to models developed elsewhere, or to internal debate that does not seem to reach wider audiences. Thus, we have work such as Ballinger (2002) on history, memory, nationalism, and regionalism in Italy/Istria, Borneman (1992, 1998) on urban regions, social integration, and borders in Berlin and Germany, Berdahl (1999) on postsocialism, memory, and the state in Germany, Bray (2004) on government and nationalism in the Basque lands, Cole (1997) and Cole and

Booth (2007) on racism and the everyday lives of immigrants in Sicily, Driessen (1992) on empire and identity where Spanish Europe meets North Africa, Green (2005) on identity and power in various borderlands of the Greek peoples and state, Kurti (2001) on Hungarian national borders that extend into a neighboring state's region, Pelkmans (2006) on religion and nationalism in the Caucasus, Schneider and Schneider (2003) on regional Sicily and the rise and demise of social movements, and Stacul (2005) on Trentino in northern Italy and the role of the region within the changing dimensions of European integration and northern Italian political movements. Research and writing based on border and regional Europe that have had an impact beyond Europe are much more numerous than the few examples, restricted to research that has led to book-length analyses, given here. If the many new journals in anthropology were examined for essays on the comparative anthropology of borders and frontiers in Europe, then a fuller picture of the depth and breadth of an anthropology of regional Europe might be found.

However, given this turn to theorizing place, space, borders, identity, and power in anthropology in Europe and beyond, it is still somewhat disconcerting to recognize that relatively few anthropologists, including those researching in Europe, have focused on public policy in regions and borderlands. With few exceptions, in fact, the regions of Europe are overlooked in an effort to theorize borders. More surprising perhaps, given the growing number of European anthropologists, ethnographers, and ethnologists who are investigating the dimensions of European integration in the everyday lives of Europeans, border regions have just as often been overlooked (a notable exception has been the work on regions and development in Europe by Kockel 1991, 2002). Policy at a regional and national level has largely been treated relatively unproblematically by anthropologists, who perhaps due to disciplinary training or bias see it as beyond their interest or expertise, as a factor external to the region and to the analysis. The reasons for this also go beyond disciplinary strengths – where political scientists study policy and anthropologists study culture – for in the social sciences in general there has been a move to theorize culture and identity as they relate to interpersonal power rather than in regard to their relationship to state structures and political programs. These theoretical interests in interpersonal power often consider governmentality before governance, and governance before government. Nonetheless anthropologists of border regions have a great deal to contribute to the comparative study of how policy and culture intersect in the new social orders of an integrating Europe. This might be achieved, for example, in the investigation of how policies about culture are designed, implemented, and received across international borders and in border regions (Anderson et al. 2001, 2003a, 2003b). Another important area of investigation is on European development and peace and reconciliation policies, most of which are filtered through national governments but with a few emanating directly from the European Commission and their impact on transnational cooperation across borders and in border regions (Wilson 2000). But the many directions in which such research might go are of secondary importance to the fact that Europe is a changing landscape of regions, nations, and states. Each and all of these entities put a great deal of effort into defining, maintaining, and understanding their borders and the roles they play in social, cultural, political, and economic lives. Anthropologists must be charged with doing no less.

CONCLUSION

Border regions in Europe are beset by the same contradictions to be found in all regions in Europe. Michael Keating's (1998:16) analysis of the contradictory logics of economic restructuring offers a wonderful insight into what is a more far-reaching tension in the complementary logics of political, social, and cultural restructuring within a globalizing and transnationalizing Europe. To Keating, economic development in regions is part of a logic of transnational capital flows where certain borders need to be made permeable to allow freedom of movement that is vital to economic restructuring. At the same time, however, there is a contradiction between this borderless rationality of neoliberal capitalism and that of locally based regional communities who are dependent on this inward investment and expertise. A borderless world of capital finance and trade is needed, but communities of practice and reception in regions also need borders to be maintained in order to retain for themselves the material benefits that can be achieved through the economic definition of the region. And we are all aware of the dominance of this model of region: every major airport in Europe extols the virtues of investing in a particular region associated with that airport or that state, where the enticing conditions of tax incentives, infrastructural networks, educated (and presumably inexpensive) labor, and quality of life all converge to make that region a prime candidate for inward capital investment. As a result of the changes which the nation-state has experienced in Europe, whether these be changes that force a retreat of the state or just new strategies of state sovereignty, control, and security, regions are forced into competition with capital cities and other regions in order to attract people, capital, services, and policy support (Le Galès 1998). In essence globalization has made regions into economic actors which may be seen to compete with their own nation-states for critical resources, and are supported in this by their states and the EU overall.

Such contradictory logics may also apply to political, social, and cultural aspects of regional Europe. Anthropologists, who have traditionally but as we have seen above certainly not exclusively been interested in the social and cultural dimensions of place and space in Europe, are faced with similar processes to the economic in their analyses of the cultures of regions in Europe, whether these regions are border ones or core urban regions that are also gaining renewed prominence in anthropological and sociological studies in Europe today. Whereas many anthropologists theorize cultural flows, hybridity, globalization, and multiculturalism, in ways that suggest there is a borderless world where the old definitions of community and cultural boundary hold little to no analytical validity, they are confronted daily by the persistent logic of everyday life in Europe, including in regional Europe, where people, in groups, acting across a range of social and political institutions, seek to maintain the borders of place, space, and culture. An overriding notion of these regions is that they represent a new political level of integration in Europe, one that rests uneasily but squarely between those who seek to make the EU into some sort of federal system of states, and those who want to keep it a relatively looser association of sovereign states in what has been termed the intergovernmental form of European integration. Thus some regions take particular shape and importance from their roles as subnational governments. But all regions in Europe are key players in the new European forms of multilevel governance (Hooghe and Marks 2001), where governance may be seen as "a process of co-ordination of public and private actors, social groups, and institutions in order to attain clear aims, which are debated and defined collectively, in uncertain and fragmented environments" (Le Galès 1998:243).

The governmental and governance functions of regions in Europe are the result of both top-down and bottom-up forces, where national movements for autonomy, development, devolution, and recognition of all sorts meet headlong with Eurocrats and nongovernmental institutions who see regions as ways to defuse past nationalisms, to right economic, political, and social imbalances within and across states, and to raise the quality of life for all Europeans, particularly those in peripheral regions. Nevertheless, to some elites in Europe, and to many elites in the governments so important to these new levels of governance, the region must take on a formal political role in order to play a significant part in the lives of its people. As the NGO Assembly of European Regions declared in 1996, in their bid to play an important role in the evolution of the EU by injecting a common regional voice into EU lobbying, the region is a territorial body of public law, recognized in the national constitution of their relevant countries, established at the level immediately below the State and endowed with political self-government (AER 1996:Article 1).[8] This adherence to law, policy, government, and governance was reaffirmed by the AER in 2010 when it presented its own study on the state of regionalism in Europe (AER 2010), but in that study they also reaffirm that the political economy of regions must also be viewed with an eye to the various paths to regionalism in each European country, many of which involve important social and cultural factors that define regions. Their assessment is that despite some past hindrances regions will continue to provide the foundation for future European integration. As Danuta Hübner (2010), Chairwoman of the European Parliament Committee on Regional Development, concluded in her Foreword in the 2010 AER report, regional policy in the EU is there to help economic and social structures in regions to deal with internal EU market and currency restrictions, but also to meet and adapt to forces of global competition. In her view regions are still among the best areas for economic development planning in Europe and she calls for the region to be the focus of efforts to achieve sustainable competitiveness in response to the economic challenges of globalization and the EU's single market. For her, "[i]nvesting in regions and cities means progress for Europe" (Hübner 2010:9). Leaving aside any consideration of what constitutes progress, sentiments such as these clearly underpin regional policy as well as other policies that have an impact on regions, and are the veritable stuff of the political ecology approach that was championed first by anthropologists in Europe in the 1960s and 1970s.

The AER and EU committees on regions obviously have vested interests in maintaining regions as important levels of government in Europe, but their assertions and conclusions are clear reflections of major transformations in European society since the 1960s. Their notions of the importance of regions are also supported by the breadth of their membership in terms of the sheer number of self-identified regions that now exist in governmental and administrative form across the continent. Moreover, there is an abiding and growing evidence in all European countries that regions are in varying ways important and powerful institutions and frames of reference to many if not most people in Europe, and that regions, in all manner of political, economic, social, and cultural ways are here to stay. But what of the anthropological gaze on the everyday in Europe and how it relates to this startling transformation in the political and economic landscape in Europe? What future lies ahead for anthropological attention to the political ecology of regional Europe? Here, too, Eurocrats may speak for many of our friends and respondents in Europe when they conclude, as does Hübner in the aforementioned 2010 document, that there is a great deal going on in regions today that merits attention and, here I hasten to add, study. With reference to why regions continue to be in need of investment, Hübner outlines what might constitute the building blocks of an anthropological revival of regional political ecology, or at the least she offers a research agenda to any anthropologist truly interested in the quality of everyday life of most if not all Europeans:

> There are new expectations of consumers. There are new markets emerging. Jobs are created in new sectors. Society is aging with all the consequences for public finance, labor market policy, migration policy, and new demands. Moving toward lowcarbon economy implies huge structural transformation. All changes will have dramatic impacts on our society, on social fabric, on social capital. There is a risk that cohesion, this magic glue Europe has always been so proud of, will suffer. (Hübner 2010:9)

Whether the magic glue suffers or not in the future is a matter for empirical research, as is whether new forms of European identity and identification will take root first or best in European borderlands. So too must we continue to ask whether Europe will be a continent of regional identities and a political space where "the nation is dead, long live the region" (Hans Mommsen as quoted in Applegate 1999). Or perhaps we should query whether the political ecology of Europe today is about "the state is dead, long live the state," wherein European integration strengthens the role of the state in local and regional affairs (Smith 1998). And if the continent is as much involved with regional frames of reference as perhaps it is with nations and states, regional borders may become as important as past national ones. Simply put, as the regions of Europe have proliferated so too have its borders and frontiers, and the roles they all play in the lives of Europeans will continue to call to anthropologists. In the shifts that have taken place in the logics of territoriality, governance and governmentality across the continent (Lagendijk et al. 2009), both the people of Europe and their social science interlocutors must search for a relevant area within which to operate:

> The transformation of the international system has set all the actors – political forces and bureaucratic machineries, economic operators, and private networks, citizens and identity groups – off in frantic pursuit of a relevant area for action. Everywhere in the world dynamic forces are at work, tracing out new borders within the states, cutting across existing multinational wholes and creating new areas of exchange, if not of solidarity. New competing forms of regionalization are coming up, sometimes intentionally, sometimes accidentally, sometimes real, sometimes imaginary. (Smouts 1998:33)

In considering the regions of Europe as new levels of government and governance, as forces in the transformation of the nation and state, and as new imagined communities, this chapter has offered the thriving anthropology of borders and frontiers in Europe as evidence of one useful way for anthropologists to attempt to recognize and understand the complexities of political ecology in regional Europe.

NOTES

1 For a historical and contemporary review of the anthropology of borders and frontiers, see Donnan and Wilson (1999).

2 For excellent reviews of the difficulties related to the usage and definition of "region" in Europe, see Keating (1998, 2004).

3 The scholars who sought to go beyond the limits of village community studies were aware that most past classic studies of village communities in Europe included data on village ties to the nation, such as in Arensberg (1937) and Arensberg and Kimball (1968), but they sought to examine the nature of these ties in order to construct a more dynamic and fluid model of the wider social processes in which local communities were immersed; for good examples of this turn in anthropological research in Europe, see Boissevain (1975) and Boissevain and Friedl (1975). See also Grillo (1980) for the first and still one of the best explications of how anthropologists should view the differences between nation and state.

4 These early studies of the community–nation ties took various paths, such as the investigation of local communities" roles in the construction of national culture and its related notions of civilization (Silverman 1975), the exploration of imperial and other historical causes for multiple national cultures in one area of a country (Wolf 1962), and various forms of patron–client relations that connected individuals and groups across the expanse of regions and nations (Blok 1974). Much of this research was inspired by the work of Eric Wolf, whose groundbreaking analysis (1966) of social relations that existed in between the more formal structures of society, polity and economy offered a model on how anthropologists might ethnographically approach the difficult task of doing participant observation research in more than one locality and across multiple institutions. It is also worth noting that a great deal of this research on community and nation-state adopted the language of centre, periphery and core (in a manner similar to those scholars who were at the time theorizing dependency, the development of underdevelopment, and world-systems), and formed the basis, along with the blossoming anthropology of Central and South America, of a Marxian or Marxist anthropology that came to be known in the United States as the political economy approach in anthropology (Roseberry 1988). While most of this research and publishing was about rural communities, anthropologists in the 1960s and 1970s also viewed neighborhoods and cities from the same perspective (see, e.g., Kenny 1962; Kenny and Kertzer 1963). My own doctoral research was on a regional agricultural elite in Ireland (Wilson 1988). For an update of the state of Europeanist anthropology since Cole's (1977) agenda-setting article, see Ulin (1991).

5 This research, done in villages but from a regionalist perspective, quickly spread across Europeanist anthropology, as may be seen in the late 1960s and early 1970s in a number of special issues on regional and political economy approaches which were published in anthropology journals, such as that edited by Freeman (1973).

6 The anthropology of European integration has in many ways been asking these questions for a generation, as it has sought to understand how Europeans have participated in and been affected by initiatives to build, imagine, and experience the many new Europes that are represented in European integration. For a variety of approaches in the anthropology of European integration and Europeanization, which is growing at least as fast as an anthropology of borders in Europe, and perhaps even faster, see Wilson (1998), Bellier

and Wilson (2000), and Shore (2000). Borneman and Fowler (1997) theorize that Europeanization is a process and a spirit which must be kept analytically distinct from EU integration, although many of the forces which drive it emanate from EU institutions and policies. In fact, they suggest that there are five practices of Europeanization in everyday life which can easily be seen to escape the bounds of the EU's many projects, at least in part. These practices, namely those involving language, money, tourism, sex, and sport, are also clearly of interest to ethnographers, both in Europe and more globally, and all have been investigated as aspects of what travels across and what stay in borderlands (Donnan and Wilson 1999).

7 The first book in anglophone anthropology to examine European integration was Wilson and Smith (1993), but other anthropological studies followed quickly, impelled by the rapidly growing importance of "Europe" in the lives of the people of 9, now 27, member states. For examples of ethnographic approaches to European integration, see Giordano (1987), McDonald (1996), Bellier and Wilson (2000), and Shore (2000).

8 According to its Web site, the Assembly of European Regions (AER) is the largest independent network of regional authorities in Europe, with a membership of 270 regions drawn from 33 countries along with 16 interregional organizations. It was established in 1985 as a forum for interregional cooperation and as a lobbyist for regional interests on the European stage. It counts as some of its successes the creation of key advisory bodies to the Council of Europe (Congress of Local and Regional Authorities) and the European Commission (Committee of the Regions). See http://www.aer.eu/about-aer/vocation/an-introduction-to-the-leading-network-of-regions-in-europe.html (accessed November 5, 2011).

REFERENCES

AER (Assembly of European Regions)

1996 Declaration on Regionalism in Europe. Strasbourg: Assembly of European Regions.

2010 The State of Regionalism in Europe: An AER Report. Strasbourg: Assembly of European Regions.

Anderson, James, Liam O'Dowd, and Thomas M. Wilson

2003a Culture Co-operation and Borders. *In* Culture and Cooperation in Europe's Borderlands. James Anderson, Liam O'Dowd and Thomas M. Wilson, eds. pp. 13–29. Amsterdam and New York: Rodopi.

2003b Culture and Cooperation in Europe's Borderlands. James Anderson, Liam O'Dowd and Thomas M. Wilson, eds. Amsterdam and New York: Rodopi.

Anderson, James, Liam O'Dowd, and Thomas M. Wilson, eds.

2001 Cross-Border Co-operation. Theme Issue. Administration: Journal of the Institute of Public Administration of Ireland 49(2).

Applegate, Celia

1999 A Europe of Regions: Reflections on the Historiography of Sub-National Places in Modern Times. The American Historical Review 104(4):1157–1182.

Arensberg, Conrad M.

1937 The Irish Countryman. Cambridge, MA: Macmillan.

Arensberg, Conrad M., and Solon T. Kimball

1968 [1948] Family and Community in Ireland. 2nd edition. Cambridge, MA: Harvard University Press.

Ballinger, Pamela
2002 History in Exile: Memory and Identity at the Borders of the Balkans. Princeton: Princeton University Press.
Bellier, Irène, and Thomas M. Wilson
2000 Building, Imagining, and Experiencing Europe: Institutions and Identities in the European Union. *In* An Anthropology of the European Union: Building, Imagining and Experiencing the New Europe. Irene Bellier and Thomas M. Wilson, eds. pp. 1–30. Oxford: Berg.
Berdahl, Daphne
1999 Where the World Ended: Re-unification and Identity in the German Borderland. Berkeley: University of California Press.
Blok, Anton.
1974 The Mafia of a Sicilian Village, 1860–1960. Oxford: Blackwell.
Boissevain, Jeremy
1975 Introduction: Towards a Social Anthropology of Europe. *In* Beyond the Community: Social Process in Europe. Jeremy Boissevain and John Friedl, eds. pp. 9–17. The Hague: Department of Educational Science of the Netherlands.
Boissevain, John, and John Friedl, eds.
1975 Beyond the Community: Social Process in Europe. The Hague: Department of Educational Science of the Netherlands.
Borneman, John
1992 Belonging in the Two Berlins. Cambridge: Cambridge University Press.
1998 Grenzregime (Border Regime): The Wall and Its Aftermath. *In* Border Identities. Thomas M. Wilson and Hastings Donnan, eds. pp. 162–190. Cambridge: Cambridge University Press.
Borneman, John, and Nick Fowler
1997 Europeanization. Annual Review of Anthropology 26:487–514.
Bray, Zoe
2004 Living Boundaries: Frontier and Identity in the Basque Country. Brussels: PIE Peter Lang.
Cole, Jeffrey E.
1997 The New Racism in Europe: A Sicilian Ethnography. Cambridge: Cambridge University Press.
Cole, Jeffrey E., and Sally S. Booth
2007 Dirty Work: Immigrants in Domestic Service, Agriculture, and Prostitution in Sicily. Lanham, MD: Lexington.
Cole, John W.
1977 Anthropology Comes Part-Way Home: Community Studies in Europe. Annual Review of Anthropology 6:349–378.
Cole, John W., and Eric. R. Wolf
1974 The Hidden Frontier: Ecology and Ethnicity in an Alpine Valley. New York: Academic Press.
Donnan, Hastings, and Thomas M. Wilson
1999 Borders: Frontiers of Identity, Nation and State. Oxford: Berg.
Douglass, William
1998 A Western Perspective on an Eastern Interpretation of Where North Meets South: Pyrenean Borderland Cultures. *In* Border Identities. Thomas M. Wilson and Hastings Donnan, eds. pp. 62–95. Cambridge: Cambridge University Press.
Driessen, Henk
1992 On the Spanish–Moroccan Frontier. Oxford: Berg.

Freeman, Susan Tax
1973 Introduction to Studies in Rural European Social Organization. American Anthropologist 75:743–750.
Giordano, Christian
1987 The "Wine War" between France and Italy: Ethno-Anthropological Aspects of the European Community. Sociologia Ruralis 27:56–66.
Grillo, R. D.
1980 Introduction. *In* "Nation" and "State" in Europe: Anthropological Perspectives. R. D. Grillo, ed. pp. 1–30. London: Academic Press.
Green, Sarah
2005 Notes from the Balkans: Locating Marginality and Ambiguity on the Greek–Albanian Border. Princeton: Princeton University Press.
Haller, D., and H. Donnan, eds.
2000 Borders and Borderlands: An Anthropological Perspective. *In* Theme issue. Ethnologia Europea 30(2):126.
Hansen, Edward C.
1977 Rural Catalonia under the Franco Regime: The Fate of Regional Culture since the Spanish Civil War. Cambridge: Cambridge University Press.
Heyman, Josiah
1994 The Mexico–United States Border in Anthropology: A Critique and Reformulation. Journal of Political Ecology 1:43–65.
Heyman, Josiah, and Hilary Cunningham, eds.
2004 Movement on the Margins: Mobilities and Enclosures at Borders. *In* Theme issue. Identities: Global Studies in Culture and Power 11(3):303–327.
Hooghe, Liesbet, and Michael Keating
1994 The Politics of European Union Regional Policy. Journal of European Public Policy 1(3):367–393.
Hooghe, Liesbet, and Gary Marks
2001 Multi-level Governance and European Integration. Lanham, MD: Rowman and Littlefield.
Horstmann, Alexander, and Reed L. Wadley, eds.
2006 Centering the Margin: Agency and Narrative in Southeast Asian Borderlands. Oxford: Berghahn.
Hübner, Danuta
2010 Foreword. The State of Regionalism in Europe: An AER Report. Strasbourg: Assembly of European Regions.
Keating, Michael
1998 Is There a Regional Level of Government in Europe? Regions in Europe. London: Routledge.
2004 Regions and Regionalism in Europe. Michael Keating, ed. Cheltenham: Edward Elgar.
2006 Europe, the State and the Nation. *In* European Integration and the Nationalities Question. John McGarry and Michael Keating, eds. pp. 23–34. London: Routledge.
Kenny, Michael
1962 A Spanish Tapestry: Town and Country in Castile. Bloomington: Indiana University Press.
Kenny, Michael, and David I. Kertzer, eds.
1963 Urban Life in Mediterranean Europe: Anthropological Perspectives. Urbana: University of Illinois Press.

Kockel, Ullrich

1991 Regions, Borders, and European Integration. Liverpool: Institute of Irish Studies, University of Liverpool.

2002 Regional Culture and Economic Development: Explorations in European Ethnology. Aldershot: Ashgate.

Kohli, Martin

2000 The Battlegrounds of European Identity. European Societies 2(2):113–137.

Kurti, Laszlo

2001 The Remote Borderland. Albany: State University of New York Press.

Lagendijk, Arnoud, Bas Arts, and Henk van Houtum

2009 Shifts in Governmentality, Territoriality and Governance: An Introduction. *In* The Disoriented State: Shifts in Governmentality, Territoriality and Governance. Bas Arts, Arnoud Lagendijk, and Henk van Houtum, eds. pp. 3–10. New York: Springer.

Le Galès, Patrick

1998 Conclusion – Government and Governance of Regions: Structural Weaknesses and New Mobilisations. *In* Regions in Europe. Patrick Le Galès and Christian Lequesne, eds. pp. 239–267. London: Routledge.

Le Galès, Patrick, and Christian Lequesne

1998 Introduction. *In* Regions in Europe. Patrick Le Galès and Christian Lequesne, eds. pp. 1–10. London: Routledge.

Loughlin, John.

2000 Regional Autonomy and State Paradigm Shifts in Western Europe. Regional and Federal Studies 10(2):10–34.

McDonald, Maryon

1990 We Are Not French: Language, Culture, and Identity in Brittany. London: Routledge.

1996 "Unity in Diversity": Some Tensions in the Construction of Europe. Social Anthropology 4:47–60.

Nicolas, Michel

2006 Breton Identity Highlighted by European Integration. *In* European Integration and the Nationalities Question. John McGarry and Michael Keating, eds. pp. 290–307. London: Routledge.

Pelkmans, Mathijs

2006 Defending the Border: Identity, Religion, and Modernity in the Republic of Georgia. Ithaca, NY: Cornell University Press.

Roseberry, William

1988 Political Economy. Annual Review of Anthropology 17:161–85.

Sahlins, Peter

1989 Boundaries: The Making of France and Spain in the Pyrenees. Berkeley: University of California Press.

Schneider, Jane C., and Peter T. Schneider

1976 Culture and Political Economy in Western Sicily. New York: Academic Press.

2003 Reversible Destiny. Mafia, Antimafia, and the Struggle for Palermo. Berkeley: University of California Press.

Schneider, Jane, Peter Schneider, and Edward Hansen

1972 Modernization and Development: The Role of Regional Elites and Noncorporate Groups in the European Mediterranean. Comparative Studies in Society and History 14(3):328–350.

Shore, Cris

2000 Building Europe: The Cultural Politics of European Integration. London: Routledge.

Silverman, Sydel
1975 Three Bells of Civilization: The Life of an Italian Hill Town. New York: Columbia University Press.
Smith, Andy
1998 The Sub-Regional Level: Key Battleground for Structural Funds? *In* Regions in Europe. Patrick Le Galès and Christian Lequesne, eds. pp. 50–66. London: Routledge.
Smouts, Marie-Claude
1998 The Region as the New Imagined Community? *In* Regions in Europe. Patrick Le Galès and Christian Lequesne, eds. pp. 22–28. London: Routledge.
Stacul, Jaro
2003 The Bounded Field: Localism and Local Identity in an Italian Alpine Valley. Oxford: Berghahn.
2005 Claiming a "European Ethos" at the Margins of the Italian Nation-State. *In* Crossing European Boundaries. Jaro Stacul, Christina Moutsou, and Helen Kopnina, eds. pp. 210–228. Oxford: Berghahn.
Ulin, Robert C.
1991 The Current Tide in American Europeanist Anthropology. Anthropology Today 7(6):8–12.
Wilson, Thomas M.
1988 Culture and Class among The "Large" Farmers of Eastern Ireland. American Ethnologist 15(4):680–695.
1998 An Anthropology of the European Union, From Above and Below. *In* Europe in the Anthropological Imagination. Susan Parman, ed. pp. 148–156. Upper Saddle River, NJ: Prentice-Hall.
2000 The Obstacles to European Union Regional Policy in the Northern Ireland Borderlands. Human Organization 59(1):1–10.
Wilson, Thomas M., and Hastings Donnan
1998a Nation, State and Identity at International Borders. *In* Border Identities: Nation and State at International Frontiers. Thomas M. Wilson and Hastings Donnan, eds. pp. 1–30. Cambridge: Cambridge University Press.
Wilson, Thomas M., and Hastings Donnan, eds.
1998b Border Identities: Nation and State at International Frontiers. Cambridge: Cambridge University Press.
2005 Culture and Power at the Edges of the State: National Support and Subversion in European Border Regions. Münster: LIT.
Wilson, Thomas M., and M. Estelle Smith, eds.
1993 Cultural Change and the New Europe: Perspectives on the European Community. Boulder, CO: Westview Press
Wolf, Eric R.
1962 Cultural Dissonance in the Italian Alps. Comparative Studies in Society and History 5(1):1–14.
1966 Kinship, Friendship and Patron–Client Relations in Complex Societies. *In* The Social Anthropology of Complex Societies. Michael Banton, ed. pp. 1–22. London: Tavistock.

CHAPTER 11 Citizenship(s) in European Contexts

Catherine Neveu and Elena Filippova

> To speak of imperfect citizenship . . . is not only suggesting that citizenship is a defective, rectifiable, improvable institution; it is more suggesting that citizenship is rather a practice and a process than a stable shape. It is always "in the making."
>
> (Balibar 2001)

"Citizenship" has, in the last decade or two, become an important topic for a growing number of anthropologists. Whether analyzed through public policies or mobilizations, used as an analytical tool, studied in governmental or vernacular discourses, or through governmental practices and projects, anthropology's contribution to the study of citizenship has opened valuable insights in a field more commonly occupied by political scientists, philosophers, or sociologists.

This chapter does not aim to propose a precise overview of the now-abundant and diverse anthropological literature on citizenship; rather it will first concentrate – starting from the authors' research and locations (cf. Gupta and Ferguson 1997) in France and Russia – on the need to better distinguish between different meanings of citizenship, and in particular its diverse connections with issues of (national) identities. The discussion will then be enlarged to the many other fields of research anthropological approaches to citizenship processes can explore. Our approach thus starts from empirically located data, so as to open up some often-obscured dimensions of citizenship studies, and point to general issues for anthropologists.

Such a comparative approach does not, however, aim at merely detailing the differences in the various types of citizenship. Obviously, insofar as it is a social and political construct (Leca 1991), as it is "manufactured" (Bénéï 2005), citizenship takes different shapes and forms according to the historical, political, or cultural formation of any given society. Merely collecting and registering such diversity would indeed be of little interest if it was not analyzed as reflecting disputes between distinct, opposite, and even antagonistic meanings attributed to the very notion of citizenship.

A Companion to the Anthropology of Europe, First Edition. Edited by Ullrich Kockel, Máiréad Nic Craith, and Jonas Frykman.

By discussing changing representations of, and discourses about, citizenship in a diversity of contexts and approaches, this chapter will thus aim to underpin the ways that specific meanings attributed to citizenship constitute integral elements of distinct political projects.[1] It will also take a step toward underlining the need to better "locate" anthropologists themselves when they conduct research on such issues, and stress the essentially contested meanings of citizenship.

Citizenship in the Anthropology of Europe

When examining bibliographical resources using the keywords "citizenship" and "anthropology," and trying to locate research done in and/or about Europe,[2] one is first struck by the paucity of references as compared with research dealing with both North and South America, or other parts of the world.[3] The second striking point, apart from this relative scarcity, is a very clear predominance of research dealing with citizenship in relation to nationalism and/or national identity issues. This is not surprising if, following Bénéï, one considers "loyalty to the national community" as fundamental among the duties of citizens and how "this places citizenship, nationality, and nationalism on extremely intimate terms to the extent that studies of European nationalism have long assumed a close (even if variable) overlap of these categories" (Bénéï 2005:13). Nic Craith also supports this analysis when she considers, following Rex, that "The concept of citizenship 'is intimately related to the question of belonging to a nation'" (Nic Craith 2004:289). One could then wonder, and it will be one of the aims of this chapter, if such views are not at least partly due to the fact that "the relationship between nationality and citizenship is a blurred one. A quasi-equation between citizenship (belonging in a political sense, the entitlement to civic, political, and social rights and duties) and nationality (belonging to a national historic community) has existed in many languages and institutions of modern states. In English-speaking countries, the two are often seen as synonymous" (Bénéï 2005:13). Indeed, when reading English-language literature, a reader whose first language is French is often troubled by such a frequent blurring, not absent even from Bénéï's own book's title that reads (emphasis added): "Manufacturing *Citizenship*. Education and *Nationalism* in Europe, South Asia and China." What remains to be discussed is whether such a blurring is "always-already" constitutive of citizenship processes, or if it results from specifically crystallized "bundlings" between these, the concept of citizenship and issues of national identity.

Obvious reasons for both this commonly found blurring (with its consequences for the analysis), especially in the English language, and the relative weight of research concerned with nationalism can be found in historical and political processes in Europe; thus the concomitant growth of "modern citizenship" and of the modern state form, together with processes of "nationalization" of citizenship rights (Balibar 2001), have certainly strongly contributed to such a blurring of two types of membership: to a political community and to a national one.

But it seems necessary to linger somewhat longer on the language issue: if it comes as no surprise, especially for anthropologists, that words do not translate easily from one language to another (or even within the same language and/or society, from one period to another; see Williams 1988), we are confronted here with particularly complex sets of connections and blurring. If one considers "nationality," one notices that not only is it often used in English as being synonymous with citizenship; it also refers to two different meanings: on the one hand, the legal status of an individual as the (potential) bearer of a passport, and, on the other, belonging to a cultural and historical community. The fact that these two meanings are so often subsumed into the same word, "nationality," makes it even more difficult to analyze the political processes at stake. It could thus be useful to clarify what we are trying to grasp by better distinguishing three different processes and their – sometimes close – connections: *citizenship* as political membership, activity, and relations; *nationality* as the legal link between a state and an individual, what Lochak (1988) suggests to call "*étaticité*" – "staticity"; and, following Anderson, *nationness* (". . . nationality, or, as one might prefer to put it in view of that word's multiple significations, nationness" (Anderson 1983:12)) as a feeling of belonging to a historical cultural community.[4]

In Russian, the terms *nacional'nost'* (usually translated as nationality/*nationalité*) and *grazhdanstvo* (citizenship/*citoyenneté*) have very different meanings. The first, very close to the above-mentioned nationness, means "ethnic belonging," while the second refers to membership in a political community. Until 1997, on the Soviet internal passport (officially named "Soviet Citizen's Passport") there was a special entry "*nacional'nost'*" that provided information on the holder's ethnicity (e.g. Russian, Tatar, Yakut, etc., but also Jew, which had been considered an ethnic rather than religious identification). Nowadays, in Russia and in some of the New Independent States, the *nacional'nost'* entry is excluded from passport and personal data files, a change that manifests, to some extent, a "privatization of ethnicity." It is maintained in Kirghizstan, Tajikistan, Kazakhstan, and can be entered in Belarus if the passport bearer so chooses. Thus for instance in Kazakhstan, one can distinguish between (ethnic) Kazakhs and Kazakhstanis, citizens of Kazakhstan. According to Gitelman, "In the decade after the fall of the USSR, the successor states divided themselves into those seeking to construct themselves as 'civic' states – where the nexus that ties citizens to each other and to the state is political and not based on race, ethnicity, religion, or culture – and those that prefer to be 'ethnic' states, based on one nation and serving it primarily" (Gitelman 2001:215). Meanwhile, individuals are still questioned about their "nationality" during population censuses; therefore the "nationality" entry in the so-called "foreign passport" used by Russian citizens for traveling abroad, as well as in visa application forms, can provoke misunderstandings. Some people of non-Russian cultural background would rather respond by declaring their ethnicity instead of writing in "Russian." These semantic differences between the terms *nacional'nost'* and *grazhdanstvo* cause endless confusion on an everyday level. Abroad, holders of Russian passports are considered Russian regardless of their ethnic background, whereas in Russia the French, the British, and sometimes even US citizens, are perceived as an *ethnos*. This sometimes leads to anecdotic arguments used by ethnoseparatist movements according to which "If the French can have their own state, why cannot the Tatars have one?," or to the widespread interpretation of the 2005 unrests in the French suburbs by many Russian journalists and even social scientists as "Arabs and Blacks fighting against the French for the right to cultural identity and special status," rather than a struggle of citizens *de jure* to achieve equality of rights *de facto*.

Other examples could be given in many other languages and/or contexts; but they would all point to the need to fully take into account both the specific history of the terms in different contexts, and the constitutive diversity of the social, cultural, and political narratives and imaginations connected to them. In other words, "As a phenomenon that exists vis-à-vis dynamic social relations and political struggle, citizenship can only be adequately understood through an interpretive engagement with the specific contexts of social struggle – as messy and convoluted as they are – in which it is *practically* brought into being" (Beyers 2008).

"Unbundling" Citizenship and Nationness

In France's French, where both the notions of "nationality" and "citizenship" are commonly used, the distinction between the two is not always a clear-cut one, especially in certain state's ordinary practices.[5] Thus in their analysis of naturalization ceremonies, Fassin and Mazouz quote a *préfet* addressing new nationals; after having stressed how their acquisition of "the quality of French *citizen*" is an event in their life, he evokes "the valuable character of French *nationality*" and stresses that "French people have a demanding conception of *citizenship*" defined as "a way of thinking, a way of debating, a way of acting, in brief rules of the game that are common to all of us" (2007:741, emphasis added). Indeed, "*nationalité*" and "*citoyenneté*" are closely intertwined in dominant representations in France, as well as in legal terms, since full citizenship, that is, including the right to vote in local, regional, general, and presidential elections is only granted to nationals. The 1992 Maastricht Treaty creating a citizenship of the EU has nevertheless extended this right to EU nationals living in France, but only for local and European elections. Lochak's analysis of this specific configuration is inspiring, especially because it insists on the need to locate it within a specific history: "*in the French tradition*, which on that issue has largely faded on other countries, only the national is a citizen . . . *There is* thus *a necessary link between nationality and citizenship*, the origins of which and implications thereof, both need to be reconstituted" (Lochak 1988:81, emphasis added). This necessary link finds its origins in the French Revolution. It is then:

> that the word "citizen" gains a radically new meaning: the citizen is no longer simply the inhabitant, but is the member of the nation – a new concept that designates the collective entity formed by all the citizens and sole depositary of sovereignty within the state. The word citizen thus from this point on condenses in itself two distinct but inseparable conceptual meanings: it designates the national of the country and the bearer of civic rights as one and the same person; French citizenship is French nationality in so far as the later confers the prerogatives attached to the quality of citizen. (Lochak 1988:81)

Lochak, meanwhile, underlines reservations to be made; indeed, it took a long time (a century and a half) for the "national = citizen" equation to be fully translated in facts or even the law; and during the French Revolution, "The 'fatherland' to be defended was indeed about fidelity to principles rather than to a territory limited by borders; it was, very simply, the country where one was a citizen" (Lochak 1988:82).

The shift has thus been from a "universalist conception of the nation to one that is both territorial and 'nationalist', the later being understood *with the meaning this term is endowed with today*" (82, emphasis added).

Echoes of such a "double coding of the nation," "the nation of compatriots" and "the nation of citizens" (Habermas 1998:123) can be found coming back to the Soviet and Russian contexts. There, the "nation" is not a political entity, but rather just one of the many possible forms of ethnic communities. During the Soviet era there was never an issue about the "Soviet Nation," but about the "Soviet People," officially defined as "a new historical community," composed of many "nations" (*načii*), peoples (*narody*), and "nationalities" (*narodnosty*). The concept of a "Soviet People" did not allow for an individual identification: no one could choose to declare oneself as "Soviet" in response to the nationality question.[6] Continuing this tradition, today's Constitution of the Russian Federation stipulates in its preamble: "We, the multinational people of Russia . . ."

Some intellectuals and politicians recently made an attempt at introducing a concept of "Rossian nation" (*Rossiyskaja nacija*) into the social discourse, alongside more traditional terms such as "peoples of Russia" (*narody Rossii*, ethnic groups living in the Russian Federation) or "people of Russia" (*Rossiyskij narod*, citizens of the Russian Federation regardless their ethnic belonging). This new "Rossian nation" is defined as a civic, political entity whose membership does not rely on cultural or language traits; an individual could identify himself or herself as a *Rossiyanin* whether or not he or she has an ethnic Russian background. However, close similarity between the Russian-language adjectives indicating belonging to the Russian ethnos or to the Rossian nation (*russkij* versus *rossijskyj*) makes it almost impossible to express this distinction in a foreign language and therefore makes it more difficult for people who are ethnically non-Russian to identify themselves as "Rossiyanin." To avoid such confusion, some propose to introduce into international documents the new English spelling of the country's name, *Rossian* Federation. This semantic shift would, according to its proponents, allow consideration of the Russian Federation as a legitimate nation-state and not as a "multinational empire" doomed to decay:

> The most important innovation in political symbolism could be a national idea of Rossia [a precise transliteration of the name of the country in the Latin alphabet] as a national state of "Rossians" [*rossiyane* is a widely used word, different from the word *russkie* defining ethnic Russians] as citizens of the state. The idea of a "Rossian" nation is not loaded with ethnic meaning as the "Russian" (*russkaya*) nation is. Similar definitions exist for British, Indian, Spanish, American, Chinese, Canadian, Malaysian and many other multiethnic nations. (Tishkov 1995)

Tishkov (1995) argues that, historically

> the two words "Russian" and "Rossian" [*russkaya* and *rossiiskaya*] were used most often as synonyms and did not carry strong ethnic or cultural connotations. This was motivated by the very fact that in the Russian Empire ethnic boundaries were loose and ethnic group identities, including ethnic Russians, were non-exclusive and carried a multiplied character. These identities were overpowered by other forms of loyalties based on religion, regional characteristic, dynastic and clan affiliations, landlord fidelities, etc.

He acknowledges, however, that "to a certain extent the orthographic 'mixture' has reflected a dominant status of Russian language and culture" (Tishkov 1995).[7]

But these attempts to introduce the concept of "Rossian nation" are viewed with concern by Russian nationalists as well as by national ethnic minority elites, who perceive them as a threat to their positions. This resistance has brought forth further definitions of the Russian Federation as a "multi-peoples nation" (instead of the currently accepted "multinational people"), or even as a "nation of nations."

All these elements (and many others, see for instance the very stimulating analysis of the Greek context in Tzanelli 2006) point to the central argument introduced above, that issues of citizenship, in their troubled connections with issues of national identities or nationness, can only be grasped and made sense of "through an interpretive engagement with the specific contexts of social struggle . . . in which [they are] *practically* brought into being" (Beyers 2008).

To make such an argument does not imply that connections between citizenship and nationness are made *in practice* (by governments, political groups or social movements); but *contrary* to a very widely held view, including in the social sciences, there is no *necessary* relation between the two, unless one converts a historically contingent version of such "bundling" into an inescapable and essential one. Returning to the French context can usefully support this point, and stress the need to consider identification issues in terms of power relations. Indeed it is not "cultures" in themselves that are at stake, but reciprocal identification processes inasmuch as they are sociopolitical relations.

Following Lochak, one can indeed consider how *citoyenneté* in France went through not only a process of nationalization but also a process of naturalization; the 1993 reform of the Nationality Act provided an enlightening example of this when it required nationals *jus soli*, and only them, to explicitly express their will to be French. Such a willingness was deemed natural for nationals *jus sanguini*, and thus autochthonous French were considered as "more French" than those who were seen as having "merely" their residence in France. Such a move could be characterized as the activation of an "autochthony myth" similar to the one analyzed by Loraux in ancient Athens, where the *poiétoi* citizen (adopted or naturalized), if he was apparently a member of the city, "was not always perceived as such, since his patronym still designates his father as of foreign origin" (Loraux 1989:13; for a more detailed analysis see Neveu 1994). More than 15 years after the reform of the Nationality Act, Fassin refers to the same kind of process when he states that:

> It became clear inequalities had to be analyzed not simply in terms of traditional categories of social class, profession, or even nationality, but also from the point of view of origin, real or presumed, as identified through skin color or foreign sounding names. . . . Discrimination is directed not so much against foreigners as against people seen as illegitimate members of French society, whatever their nationality (the majority of them are French and born in France). (Fassin 2006:18)[8]

In such processes, it is not cultures that are at stake, but what Lorcerie describes as "national primordialism" (Lorcerie 2007:327), a set of identification processes that naturalizes membership to both the national community and those described as ethnic ones, and expresses struggles around the right to legitimately belong to French society; the tensions thus induced "between Republican principles and a non-avowed primordialism is a major mode of conflictuality in French society" (Lorcerie 2007:303).

European Citizenship, Citizenship of/in Europe

If contextualization is obviously required when discussing citizenship processes, so as to locate them (Gupta and Ferguson 1997), the same goes for the theoretical discussions and empirical analysis they give birth to. We already pointed to the complex language issue connected to the many meanings, imaginations, and stakes associated with words like citizenship, *citoyenneté*, or *grazhdanstvo*; and some of their most powerful crystallizations, as has just been seen through the issue of its connections with nationness, have consequences for research. Thus, in the French context, the scarcity of anthropological research on citizenship processes results partly from the specific site this notion came to occupy in representations, the often strongly normative character of the notion contributing to its construction as an "improper" object for anthropologists (see Neveu 2009). In Russian research, citizenship issues are mainly discussed by jurists, particularly within the framework of human rights discourse. Sociologists and philosophers show little concern for them; as for anthropologists (in Russia they are called "ethnologists"), they do not consider them as related to their domain of expertise, which is strongly oriented toward issues of ethnic groups. From the very beginning, Russian ethnography was strongly influenced by German *Volk* studies and, more generally, following Herder, by German romantic philosophy. The Soviet "theory of ethnos" considered ethnicity as a people's essence and granted ethnogenesis a crucial role in human history (Blum and Filippova 2006). Adopting Austrian Marxist and East European social democrats' political and academic language, Soviet scholars defined nations as ethnonations or as a "highest type of *ethnos*." The "socialist nations" had been proclaimed by and purposefully constructed in the Soviet Union on a basis of existing or invented cultural differences, through a system of official registration of ethnic affiliation ("nationality" on a principle of *jus sanguini*) and through the territorialization of ethnicity according to a principle of ethnic federalism (Tishkov 1995). Faithful to one of anthropology's central asset, we thus plea for "enstrangement" and distancing from "methodological nationalism" (Wimmer and Glick-Schiller 2003), and for being more reflexively engaged when analyzing citizenship processes.

We discussed in the first part of this chapter some of the sources, of and problems raised, in anthropological approaches to citizenship, by discussions that tend to adopt an acritical view of connections between *citoyenneté* and issues of nationness. In order to both further this discussion and open up less-explored avenues for anthropological approaches to citizenship, we now want to discuss a particularly relevant and significant type of citizenship: EU citizenship. Indeed, the creation by the Maastricht Treaty in 1992 of a status of EU citizen provides an illuminating example of both the deeply embedded difficulty in envisioning a citizenship differently connected to national dimensions and the many other dimensions of citizenship processes anthropologists can explore, at the EU as well as at national or local levels.

The creation of a citizenship of the European Union has fostered many debates, including among social scientists, about its feasibility, desirability, or originality. While most of these discussions remained theoretical ones, they are worth briefly noting here since they underline some of the conundrums of the debates on citizenship issues (see Neveu 2000).

In line with the aforementioned tendency to equate citizenship and nationality, and to consider the first as essentially connected to the second, many analysts have either declared EU citizenship to be doomed to failure, or have celebrated it as a radical breakthrough in the history of citizenship. In both cases, "national citizenship" was the yardstick, and at stake was the very possibility of disconnecting citizenship and nationness. Thus, according to some proponents of what was described as a "postnational" citizenship,[9] EU citizenship constituted a unique opportunity to replace a historically contingent model of citizenship (the "Westphalian" one, linking nationness, citizenship, and territory) with one in which identity and politics would at last be separated (Tassin 1994), that is, to consider the European building process as a unique experiment in "*Gesellschaft* building" (Meehan 1996). Such a move would have been all the more necessary, given that the settlement and practices of third-state nationals, enjoying social, economic, and sometimes political rights and formulating new claims, have displaced more traditional conceptions of the "limits of citizenship" (Soysal 1994). Conversely, other analysts considered that in creating an EU citizenship the "ethnic realities of any concrete society but above all the necessity to integrate these ethnic realities in the concrete political organization, even the one calling on the principle of citizenship" (Schnapper 1997:219) had been underestimated. According to that line of argument, EU citizenship would remain an empty formal status as long as there was no homogenous European identity, shared by all EU citizens, to support it.

However, as Elizabeth Meehan stressed: "Too often the arguments about European integration and citizenship are put in terms of the feasibility or desirability of a transformation of national citizenship as we have known it on a grander scale – as though it would be the same but in a new state, a superstate called Europe" (1996:121). Indeed, one of the main obstacles to a living EU citizenship was, according to its critics, that the EU presents none of the characteristics of nation-states (or that attempts at endowing it with them have been a failure):

> Despite the predominance of English, the EU lacks a common *lingua franca*, and has no uniform system of education or mass media. There have been some attempts to develop a set of EU symbols such as the EC anthem, emblem and flag, and harmonised EU passports and car number plates, but these have failed to inspire individual citizens. There have also been EC-funded initiatives that have had little overall impact such as the European City of Culture, the European Woman of the Year Award and the Jean Monnet awards for universities. (Nic Craith 2004:295)

One of us has argued elsewhere (Neveu 2000) for the need for empirical research that would indeed aim at grasping the extent to which EU programs and Europe-wide social mobilizations contribute to foster a sense of common membership, by precisely observing actual processes or attempts that contribute in the emergence of feelings of commonality amongst Europeans (see Shore and Wright 1997); if that implies close observation of already ongoing European practices of citizenship and practices of European citizenship.[10] It remains to be discussed if, and why, this sense of membership should be (or is actually) thought of in terms of cultural homogenization rather than as a shared and contested political space (see Sassatelli 2009 for an excellent, and empirically based, discussion of European culture and identity). Indeed, as Meehan argues: "When based on a need for homogeneity, this way of understanding or explaining the argumentation about Europe conceals an implicit assumption that successful politics are communitarian" (Meehan 1996:121).

Citizens as Political Subjects

It seems to us this is a set of issues anthropologists are potentially particularly well-equipped to document empirically. But there are other fundamental dimensions of citizenship processes to be explored than their connections with nationness, and to which we now want to turn. First, because nationness is not the only way through which the "community of citizens" can be thought of. Second, because the rights and recognition a diversity of political subjects claim for or are granted are not limited to cultural rights, but include a much wider range of resources, both symbolic and material, such as housing, social benefits, voting rights, or education, to name just a few.

This implies at least two moves anthropologists should be familiar with: to enlarge and diversify empirical research to the many sites where citizenship is "manufactured," and not reduce it to "[t]he coldly constitutional view of citizenship as only entailing a rational, contractual relationship ideally premised on rights and duties . . . [that] has led to an overemphasizing of the study of explicitly political sites of the manufacturing of citizenship such as electoral and other institutionalized processes" (Bénéï 2005:4–5); and to include in the analysis the noncitizens excluded from dominant definitions – individuals who struggle against them and thus formulate new discourses and practices of citizenship, and their different forms of political action that, although a constitutive part of the process of citizenship-building, are frequently ignored in its analysis. This is stressed, among others, by Sassen, who argues (Sassen 2005:84) that "[c]itizenship results in part from the practices of the excluded," and Balibar, who states that "[t]he practical confrontation with different modes of exclusion . . . always constitutes the founding moment of citizenship, and consequently its periodical litmus test" (Balibar 2001:125). Such a change of focus thus takes into account and connects the statutory dimensions of citizenship with its other, more "horizontal" dimensions, that is, with practices and representations of political subjectivation that are not the sole production of the state.[11]

As mentioned at the beginning of this chapter, citizenship processes seem not to have attracted much attention among anthropologists of Europe (although European anthropologists study them elsewhere; see for instance Jacob and Le Meur 2010); we would like now to both discuss issues that could usefully be analyzed from an anthropological point of view and consider anthropological research that, while not explicitly referring to these issues, offers interesting contributions to their exploration.

The development of an "anthropology of policy" is one of the many channels through which citizenship processes can be analyzed. As Shore and Wright argue in the introduction to their edited volume: "policy language and discourse . . . provides a key to analysing the architecture of modern power relations," and to understanding "the ways in which new political subjects of power are constituted by, and through, policies" (Shore and Wright 1997:12). Since citizenship is indeed about political subjectivation, studying how public policies, whether they are concerned with health, housing, policing, or education tend, avowedly or implicitly, to create or support the emergence of different types of subjects provides useful sites for analysis.[12] Hyatt's analysis in that same volume provides an interesting example of such "technology of citizenship-methods for constituting active and participatory citizens" (Cruikshank quoted in Hyatt 1997:224), aimed at deeply transforming council tenants' subjectivity and position in relation to (local) government, metamorphosing them "from subjects once dependant on the expert guidance of others into autonomous beings already possessed of their own expertise" (Hyatt 1997:224). Analyzing both policy documents produced about the transfer of estate management to tenants, and interviews with those tenants that agreed, at least at the beginning, to become estate managers, Hyatt shows how "the 'self-managing tenant' has, therefore, become one of the heroes of the New Right ideology, the poor citizen who is self-reliant rather than dependent, self-governing rather than governed, empowered rather than powerless" (Hyatt 1997:232); and also how the changes entailed by this transfer were met with ambivalence by the women involved in the scheme, who finally "decided not to become 'self-managing tenants' when they realized that being practitioners of policy also involved policing" (Shore and Wright 1997:33).

Such research, and other work, points to two fundamental issues for anthropological approaches to citizenship; first how public policies can contribute to the formulation and circulation of new "norms" about what it means to be a "good citizen" (or a bad one), about the relative responsibilities of governments and citizens, or on the legitimate grounds on which to base "communities of citizens." Forms of classification and categorization are a particularly fruitful field of study; because analyzing the words used (citizens, residents, tax-payers, consumers, but also *immigrés*, aliens…), the varied meanings they are endowed with (Williams 1988) and their effects, provide clues through which to grasp the political projects at play (Alvarez et al. 1998). In Roubaix, in the North of France Neveu thus analyzed the different publics implied by the term "inhabitants," used by both local authorities and neighborhood activists: while in the late 1960s, used in the singular and with a capital "I" ("Inhabitant"), it was the equivalent in the housing struggles of "the working class," it became a way to mobilize social forces at the neighborhood level to better urban management in the mid-1970s; later in the 1980s, it was a term used to refer to the poor, the participation of whom public policies had to enhance, before referring in the early 2000s to those bearers of an "expert knowledge" gained in the daily routine use of the neighborhood (Neveu n.d.). Not only have the changing (and cumulative) meanings of this apparently shared word marked a change from social movements' claims to public policies' requirement for "participation;" the transformation also shows a passage from collective mobilizations to a call to individuals, from a confrontational logic between social movements and government to one of cooperation and exchange between the two. In each of these meanings the word "inhabitants" has been endowed with different and even opposed conceptions of both citizens and their relations to (local) government. The picture is even more revealing when such categories are analyzed in relation to others; it is then also the specific competences each "public" is deemed to possess, or required to demonstrate, and the levels at which they are supposed to be deployed, that can be grasped and made sense of (Neveu n.d.).

Taking classifications and words, along with their uses and effects, seriously, as one of the ways through which attempts are made to create new types of (political) subjects, or reactivate previous ones, can thus constitute a privileged point of entry. Valli et al. (2002) explored the logics at work among social workers in Swiss unemployment and welfare agencies, and how categorizations of "good" or "deserving" unemployed people are built in the interactions between these agents and agencies' users. But such "manufacturing processes" can indeed also be observed through the analysis of practices and spatial arrangements; studying the *mise en scène* of spaces in public welfare offices in Geneva, insightful researchers stress how:

> analyzing materially and symbolically architectural arrangements, observing how limits are, implicitly or explicitly, expressed, as well as sometimes their very transgressions, mapping authorized, assigned or forbidden passage ways, listing objects but also discourses about them, allow for a specific vision to be built on those places and things that organize the relations between social workers and their [publics]. (Ossipow et al. 2006)

Analyzing policy (as discourses, practices, and places) from an anthropological perspective is very relevant indeed; but we should be concerned not to consider that policy necessarily produces the types of subjects it intends to, nor that these policies are monolithic and univocal (Sassatelli 2009). In a recent study of the publics of public services in Britain, Clarke et al. (2007) investigated how and why people were or were not using terms like "patients," "users," "members of the public," "consumers," or "citizens" to define themselves. Not only did they notice that very few of them did so by endorsing the role the British government was fostering, which was that of "consumer," but they also stressed the reflexivity people could deploy in discussing the different positions available for them: "they are *dialogic* subjects. They understand the dominant discourse and understand how they are spoken for within it. But they draw on a variety of 'residual and emergent' discursive resources to distance themselves from it, from the identifications it offers them and from the model of the future that it offers" (Clarke et al. 2007:154). So, if it is important to try and understand how policies aim at "shaping" citizens, it is as important to analyze how the latter react to such attempts (resisting, complying with, appropriating, or subverting them). This also means trying not to evaluate the changing forms and shapes of citizenship according to a pure, abstract standard, but to fully take into account vernacular experiences of them. "Reforms" in Eastern European countries after the end of the Soviet period, and processes of democracy-building under the auspices of international institutions and NGOs (Gossiaux and Petric 2007), are often presented as the long-awaited progress toward Western ideals of democracy and civil society;

but the way local populations experience such "progress" can indeed be at odds with this kind of simplistic assessment. Studying citizenship regimes in Siberia, David Anderson stresses how "the employees of the state farm Khantaiskii were as often clients of the state as they were autonomously acting citizens. However, these 'clients' insist that they never felt as constrained, marginalised and impoverished in the days of their 'passive citizenship' as during the début of reforms" (Anderson 1996:114).

This points to the second fundamental issue for anthropological approaches to citizenship: if states are important producers of it, they are not the only ones, and anthropologists have an important task at hand in exploring a diversity of sites where citizenship is produced, contested, and debated.

In the French context, the "Vincennes Malians" episode is revealing of such processes. It is not possible here to describe at length the successive events that marked the unfolding of it (see Daum 2006); suffice to say that it began in May 1992, when 130 families of mostly West African origins decided to camp in front of Vincennes Castle (near Paris), thus confronting to the lack of public housing, the high price of privately owned houses, and the discriminatory practices of many public housing authorities. This occupation of a well-known and visible public space aimed to publicize their housing needs and claimed their right to decent housing. Indeed, these families were calling upon the state to comply with its own laws, like those introduced in May 1990 according to which "a right to housing constitutes a duty of solidarity for the whole of the nation." If only benefitting a few families, this occupation, and many other struggles on housing issues, have largely contributed to exposing the harsh living conditions of many people in France: "Far from being an exotic demonstration or a residual one of anachronistic behaviors, African families in Vincennes or elsewhere raise a public interest issue and allow for the official set language to be exposed as such. . . . Indeed the issue of a right to housing has here been dealt with in a citizenly manner, i.e. in active solidarity claiming for equality in access to housing" (Daum 2006:213).

Such practices are common, where people organize collectively to claim a right, to assert their "right to have rights," thus redefining who is to be counted as citizens and contributing to the public debate about equality and what life in society should be. If they are often formulated in reaction to public policies, anthropologists can also contribute to the highlighting of more "discrete" practices, through which, for instance, the sharing of actual *topos* is negotiated daily (Massey 2004), or where a subject's positions are reflexively transformed in personal as well as public spheres (for a US example, see Coll 2010).

The postcolonial character of most European societies is a powerful incentive here to try and grasp how citizenship is transformed by practices of circulation and multiple belongings. The practices and claims of "transnational" populations and of ethnicized/racialized minorities are indeed powerfully questioning the supposed natural order of things according to which citizenship, state, and territory (and eventually nationness) should neatly correspond; or more precisely they remind us of the contextual and historically contingent nature of such a "bundling": "citizenship in the twenty-first century, and even before, is not immobile, solidified by universalistic philosophical principles – whether liberal or socialist – but a changing, dialogic and inventive concept, able to adapt itself to world events, i.e. to a negotiated political order"

(Werbner 2007:323). Wemyss's exposure of "the invisible Empire" at work in London's East End is a particularly relevant approach here, that also underlines the need to adopt a less homogenizing view of "communities": "In both past and present, the processes of categorizing South Asian people into racialized 'types', racialized categories of workers, or religiously defined 'communities' have contributed to the circumscription of their citizenship rights and increased their vulnerability to the political ambitions of groups and individuals within and outside these 'communities' whose interests are to exaggerate difference at the expense of commonality" (Wemyss 2009:179).

Conclusion

While the anthropology of citizenship processes is still an underexplored field in European contexts, it can benefit from much of the research conducted throughout the world, as well as within other disciplinary fields, that has already introduced valuable insights to both the empirical study and the conceptual discussion of citizenship. Werbner underlined in 1998 why citizenship was a particularly "good to think" topic for anthropologists, because of its strong connections with issues of difference and identity, inclusion, and exclusion (Werbner 1998). Anthropology's contribution can of course be furthered in the analysis of the complex links built through time between nationness and citizenship, as a status; but it requires one to denaturalize such connections and problematize them more deeply, and to include in this picture the many other ways that "communities of citizens" are envisioned both by governments and (non)citizens themselves.

Anthropologists can also contribute to a critical reappraisal of the often assumed "cultural blindness" of citizenship, not by once again essentializing cultures, but by considering, following Rosaldo, how "cultural citizenship" is enacted in struggles and mobilizations: "Cultural citizenship refers to the right to be different (in terms of race, ethnicity, or native language) with respect to the norms of the dominant national community, without compromising one's right to belong, in the sense of participating in the nation-state's democratic processes" (Rosaldo 1994:57).

Indeed, most discussions on citizenship are today "conducted in what is virtually an empirical void" (Lister et al. 2005:114). Empirically exploring policies as well as social movements' efforts at shaping citizens' resistance to, compliance with and avoidance of these governmental as well as vernacular discourses of citizenship, and their interactions, can indeed provide fruitful insights on Europe's and European contemporary political and social transformations.

The task at hand for citizenship debates within anthropology is to develop an "anthropology of the present" whose task is to

> unsettle and dislodge the certainties and orthodoxies that govern the present . . . it involves detaching and repositioning oneself sufficiently far enough from the norms and categories of thought that give security and meaning to the moral universe of one's society in order to interrogate the supposed natural or axiomatic "order of things" . . . As has often been pointed out in anthropological studies of language, native speakers are usually quite unconscious of the metaphors and rules that make up what D'Andrade

(1984) has called the "cultural meaning systems," or the normative cognitive structures that shape their reality. (Shore and Wright 1997:17)

NOTES

1 C. Neveu's work on citizenship processes benefits from an ongoing collaboration with J. Clarke, K. Coll, and E. Dagnino, begun in 2007 during an IPAS funded by Fondation MSH and Columbia University.

2 For an interesting problematization of the very notion of "Europe" in anthropological research, see Herzfeld (2008).

3 It should be noted here, as will be seen below, that some research confronts issues very close to those of citizenship under another heading; see for instance Hann and Dunn (1996), or Shore and Wright (1997).

4 Crowley suggests that "the lexical work" is relatively simple in French since *citoyenneté* would refer to a "political status, source of specific internal rights and obligations defined towards counterparts as well as the collectivity," while *nationalité* would refer to a "juridical link, source of obligations (i.e. serving in the army), privileges (the monopoly on certain types of jobs), as well as of rights that can be opposed to other juridical entities (such a diplomatic protection)"; while the "identity-building" dimension would be most of the times referred to through terms like national identity. He carries on stating that "in English the situation is much more complex, thus reflecting the complexity of categories themselves and of underlying social representations. The political status is called citizenship. The word citizenship is simultaneously used, with a different meaning, in a juridical context" (Crowley 1995:57). As will be seen later, considering citizenship only as a status is rather problematic.

5 We'll come back later on the need to fully consider such ordinary and routine state's practices and representations, so as to grasp citizenship issues not solely from the point of view of the state's own prose (Lopez Caballero 2010).

6 That was possible in former Yugoslavia, where "Yugoslav" was a legal answer alongside "Serb," "Croat," or "Macedonian."

7 However, the close similarity between the Russian-language adjectives indicating belonging to the Russian ethnos or to the Rossian nation (*russkij* vs *rossijskyj*) makes it almost impossible to express this distinction in a foreign language and therefore makes it more difficult for ethnically non-Russians to identify themselves as "Rossiyanin." To avoid such confusion, Valery Tishkov proposed, in vain, to introduce in international documents the new English spelling of the country's name, *Rossian* Federation.

8 As Helly usefully reminds us: "Identity and culture shouldn't be confused; the former is an interpretation of a socio-political relation, of which the meaning assigned to cultural differences is only a symbolic expression" (Helly 2000).

9 The "postnational" character of EU citizenship can indeed be questioned since only member-states' nationals are EU citizens; the inclusion of third states' residents in EU citizenship eligibility could have make a difference.

10 "Such a distinction is essential in that understanding European citizenship implies . . . to observe and analyze both how European citizens act *qua* European citizens (i.e. individuals endowed with specific legal rights by the Maastricht Treaty), and how Europeans act as citizens at the European level and/or by articulating different levels of citizenship practices (i.e. local, regional, national and European levels)" (Neveu 2000:129).

11 As Balibar stresses: "I don't think one can fully follow lawyers and political scientists who define *as of principle* citizenship as a status (like nationality). Because what makes for the continuity in history between different modes of citizenship institution . . . is precisely

the fact that the notion of the citizen . . . expresses a collective capacity to 'constitute the state' or the public sphere. In other words it expresses a social link in which the rights and freedoms recognised to individuals, and the obligations that are their counterparts, as *limited* as they may be, do not emanate from a transcendent power but solely from the 'convention' of citizens" (Balibar 2001:251–52).

12 Such research is already well developed in the global South, or emerging countries; see for instance Ong (1999), or Grey Postero (2007).

REFERENCES

Alvarez, Sonia, Evelina Dagnino, and Arturo Escobar, eds.
1998 Cultures of Politics/Politics of Cultures: Revisioning Latin American Social Movements. Boulder, CO: Westview Press.

Anderson, Benedict
1983 Imagined Communities: Reflections on the Origin and Spread of Nationalism. London: Verso.

Anderson, David
1996 Bringing Civil Society to an Uncivilised Place: Citizenship Regimes in Russia's Arctic Frontier. *In* Civil Society: Challenging Western Models. C. Hann and E. Dunn, eds. pp. 99–120. London: Routledge.

Balibar, Etienne
2001 Nous, citoyens d'Europe? Les frontières, l'Etat, le peuple. Paris: La Découverte.

Bénéï, Véronique, ed.
2005 Manufacturing Citizenship: Education and Nationalism in Europe, South Asia and China. London: Routledge.

Beyers, Christiaan
2008 The Cultural Politics of "Community" and Citizenship in the District Six Museum, Cape Town. Anthropologica 50(2):359–373.

Blum, Alain, and Elena Filippova
2006 Territorialisation de l'ethnicité, ethnicisation du territoire: Le cas du système politique soviétique et russe. Espace géographique 4:317–327.

Clarke, John, Janet Newman, Nick Smith, Elizabeth Vidler, and Louise Westmarland
2007 Creating Citizen-Consumers: Changing Publics and Changing Public Services. Thousand Oaks, CA: Sage.

Coll, Kathleen
2010 Remaking Citizenship: Latina Immigrants and New American Politics. Stanford: Stanford University Press.

Crowley, John
1995 Etat, identité nationale et ethnicité au Royaume-Uni. Anthropologie et Sociétés 19(3):53–69.

D'Andrade, Roy
1984 Cultural Meaning Systems. *In* Culture Theory: Essays on Mind, Self, and Emotion. R. Shweder and R. LeVine, eds. pp. 88–119. Cambridge: Cambridge University Press.

Daum, Christophe
2006 Le citoyen et l'étranger. L'Homme et la Société 160/161:199–219.

Fassin, Didier
2006 Nommer, interpréter: Le sens commun de la question raciale. *In* De la question sociale à la question raciale? Représenter la société française. D. Fassin and E. Fassin, eds. pp. 17–36. Paris: La Découverte.

Fassin, Didier, and Sarah Mazouz
2007 Qu'est-ce que devenir français? La naturalisation comme rite d'institution républicain. Revue Française de Sociologie 48:723–750.
Gitelman, Zvi Y.
2001 A Century of Ambivalence: The Jews of Russia and the Soviet Union 1881 to the Present. Bloomington: Indiana University Press.
Gossiaux, Jean-François, and Boris Petric
2007 La construction de la démocratie sous l'égide des organisations internationales: Le cas du Kirghizstan. *In* Cultures et pratiques participatives: Perspectives comparatives. C. Neveu, ed. pp. 193–212. Paris: L'Harmattan,
Grey Postero, Nancy
2007 Now We Are Citizens: Indigenous Politics in Postmulticultural Bolivia. Stanford: Stanford University Press.
Gupta, Akhil, and James Ferguson
1997 Anthropological Locations: Boundaries and Grounds of a Field Science. Berkeley: University of California Press.
Habermas, Jürgen
1998 The Inclusion of the Other: Studies in Political Theory. C. Cronin and P. De Greiff, eds. Cambridge, MA: MIT Press.
Hann, Chris, and Elizabeth Dunn
1996 Civil Society: Challenging Western Models. London: Routledge.
Helly, Denise
2000 Pourquoi lier citoyenneté, multiculturalisme et mondialisation? *In* Citoyenneté, multiculturalisme et mondialisation. M. Elbaz and D. Helly, eds. pp. 223–256. Québec–Paris: Presses de l'université Laval–L'Harmattan.
Herzfeld, Michael
2008 Ouvrir les frontières de l'Europe: La géographie bureaucratique d'une discipline. Ethnologie Française 38:597–604.
Hyatt, Susan
1997 Poverty in a "Post-Welfare" Landscape: Tenant Management Policies, Self-Governance and the Democratization of Knowledge in Great Britain. *In* Anthropology of Policy: Critical Perspectives on Governance and Power. C. Shore and S. Wright, eds. pp. 217–238. London: Routledge–EASA.
Jacob, Jean-Pierre, and Pierre-Yves Le Meur, eds.
2010 Politique de la terre et de l'appartenance: Droits fonciers et citoyenneté locale dans les sociétés du Sud. Paris: Karthala.
Leca, Jean
1991 Individualisme et citoyenneté. *In* Sur l'individualisme: Théories et méthodes. P. Birnbaum and J. Leca, eds. pp. 159-209. Paris: Presses de la Fondation nationale des sciences politiques.
Lister, Ruth, Noel Smith, Sue Middleton, and Lynne Cox
2005 Young People Talking About Citizenship in Britain. *In* Inclusive Citizenship: Meanings and Expressions. N. Kabeer, ed. pp. 114–131. London: Zed Press.
Lochak, Danièle
1988 Etranger et citoyen au regard du droit. *In* La citoyenneté. C. Wihtol de Wenden, ed. pp. 74–85. Paris: Edilig-Fondation Diderot.
Lopez Caballero, Paula
2010 Le nationalisme ordinaire, un régime de vérité pragmatique? Anthropologie des symboles nationaux au Mexique. Raisons politiques 37:79–88.

Loraux, Nicole
1989 Les méandres de l'hellénitude. EspacesTemps 42:17–22.
Lorcerie, Françoise
2007 Le primordialisme français, ses voies, ses fièvres. *In* La situation post-coloniale: Les Postcolonial Studies dans le débat français. M. C. Smouts, ed. pp. 298–343. Paris: Presses de Sciences Po.
Massey, Doreen
2004 Geographies of Responsibility. Geografiska Annaler 86 B(1):5–18.
Meehan, Elizabeth
1996 European Integration and Citizens' Rights: A Comparative Perspective. Publius 26(4):99–121.
Neveu, Catherine
1994 Of a Natural Belonging to a Political Nation-State: A French Case. Paper for the International Symposium 117: Transnationalism, Nation-state Building and Culture. Mijas, Spain: Wenner–Gren Foundation for Anthropological Research.
2000 European Citizenship, Citizens of Europe and European citizens. *In* An Anthropology of the European Union: Building, Imagining and Experiencing the New Europe. I. Bellier and T. Wilson, eds. pp. 119–136. Oxford: Berg.
2009 Comment faire l'anthropologie d'un objet "trop lourd"? Approche anthropologique de la citoyenneté en France. Anthropologie et Sociétés 33(2):25–42.
n.d. Habitants, citoyens: interroger les catégories. *In* Généalogies de la démocratie participative. M-H. Bacqué and Y. Sintomer, eds. Paris: La Découverte, à paraître.
Nic Craith, Máiréad
2004 Culture and Citizenship in Europe: Questions for Anthropologists. Social Anthropology 12(3):289–300.
Ong, Aihwa
1999 Clash of Civilizations or Asian Liberalism? An Anthropology of the State and Citizenship. *In* Anthropological Theory Today. H. L. Moore, ed. pp. 48–72. Cambridge: Polity.
Ossipow, Laurence, Isabelle Csupor, and Alexandre Lambelet
2006 Lieux et objets d'assistance: mises en scène dans cinq Centres d'action sociale et de santé (CASS). Ethnographiques.org 9. Electronic document. http://www.ethnographiques.org/2006/IMG/pdf/ArOssipow.pdf (accessed December 18, 2011).
Rosaldo, Renato
1994 Cultural Citizenship in San Jose, California. PoLAR 17(2):57–64.
Sassatelli, Monica
2009 Becoming Europeans: Cultural Identity and Cultural Policies. Basingstoke: Palgrave Macmillan.
Sassen, Saskia
2005 The Repositioning of Citizenship and Alienage: Emergent Subjects and Spaces for Politics. Globalizations 2(1):79–94.
Schnapper, Dominique
1997 The European Debate on Citizenship. Daedalus 126(3):199–222.
Shore, Cris, and Susan Wright
1997 Anthropology of Policy: Critical Perspectives on Governance and Power. London: Routledge–EASA.
Soysal, Yasemin
1994 Limits of Citizenship: Migrants and Postnational Membership in Europe. Chicago: University of Chicago Press.

Tassin, Etienne

1994 Identités nationales et citoyenneté politique. Esprit January:97–111.

Tishkov, Valery

1995 What is Russia? Prospects for Nation-Building. Security Dialogue 26(1):41–54.

Tzanelli, Rodanthi

2006 "Not MY Flag!" Citizenship and Nationhood in the Margins of Europe (Greece, October 2000/2003). Ethnic and Racial Studies 29(1):27–49.

Valli, Marcelo, Hélène Martin, and Ellen Hertz

2002 Le "feeling" des agents de l'Etat-Providence: Analyse des logiques sous-jacentes aux régimes de l'assurance chômage et de l'aide sociale. Ethnologie Française 37:221–231.

Wemyss, Georgie

2009 The Invisible Empire: White Discourse, Tolerance and Belonging. Farnham: Ashgate.

Werbner, Pnina

1998 Exoticising Citizenship: Anthropology and the New Citizenship Debate. Canberra Anthropology 21(2):1–27.

2007 Translocalité de la culture chez les Indo-Pakistanais. Ethnologie Française 37:323–334.

Williams, Raymond

1988 Keywords: A Vocabulary of Culture and Society. London: Fontana.

Wimmer, Andreas, and Nina Glick-Schiller

2003 Methodological Nationalism: The Social Sciences, and the Study of Migration. An Essay in Historical Epistemology. International Migration Review 37(3):576–610.

CHAPTER 12

Local Practices of European Identity on the New Eastern Borders of the EU

Justyna Straczuk

> In 1876 Bismarck dismissed Europe, as Metternich had once dismissed Italy, as "a geographical notion." Seventy years later Jean Monnet, "the Father of Europe," saw the force of Bismarck's disdain. "Europe has never existed," he admitted; "one has genuinely to create Europe."
>
> (Davies 1996)

Disseminating the idea of a European cultural community is one of the most important tasks of EU policy. Built on a specific cultural content, identification with Europe – as it is conceived by EU technocrats – should encourage people to create real bonds and a sense of being a member of the community. Such identity, fulfilled with symbolic essence, has a special goal to achieve: it should legitimize the activity of a political institution. The more we talk about European identity and European culture, the more real they become. As a result, activities which are often described as searching for or researching European consciousness are, as a matter of fact, the acts of its creation, the building of its certain vision. The constant focusing on the Europeanization of EU citizens' identity brings a European identity slowly into being (Diez 2004). We are thus witnessing the process of building a European myth which aims at reconfiguring people's imagination in accordance with political considerations. "Identity formation" and "culture building" have become explicit political objectives in the campaign to promote what EU officials call *l'idée européene* or the European Idea. However, this raises the fundamental question, what exactly are "European culture" and "European consciousness" and how might these be nurtured and diffused (Shore 2000:26)?

As the process of Europeanization accelerates, the mechanisms of its construction are becoming more visible. This is why, perhaps, the problem of European identity is still perceived more as an institutional creation than as real people's experience. According to empirical studies (e.g. Mach and Niedźwiedzki 2002; Armbruster et al.

A Companion to the Anthropology of Europe, First Edition. Edited by Ullrich Kockel, Máiréad Nic Craith, and Jonas Frykman.

2003), Europeanness and European identity, in their subjective dimension, are still not general and obvious categories of identification for the EU citizens – not in Western Europe, and even less so in Eastern Europe. "Despite four decades of institutional attempts to build Europe at the level of popular consciousness the 'peoples of Europe' have simply not embraced the 'European idea' in the way it was hoped for or, indeed, predicted by neofunctionalist models of integration" (Shore 2000:19). The problem probably lies not only in the novelty character of such identity, but in the fact that a European consciousness, understood as a sense of identity with a political and economical supranational organization, stands to a considerable degree in opposition to national identity, not least because it is created in its likeness and image, by using similar symbolism: an anthem, a flag, currency, maps, censuses (Anderson 1985). "Unlike belonging to the nation, which has a specific cultural content, identification with Europe is an empty sign," argue Borneman and Fowler (1997:492), stating that European identity, in order to be effective, should adopt quite different forms, concerning categories of exchange, difference, and value, rather than religion, folk, or national defense.

The other reason for the EU policy's relative failure could be that the sense of Europeanness often appears not in the context of the EU institutions and not in forms desired by the European Commission officials – constantly present, fully conscious, and verbalized, capable of producing definite identifications – but in such forms as are expressed in local idioms, not always directly, often nondiscursively, and dormant but still having important symbolic value (Macdonald 2004). It is still somehow assumed that membership of the European Union is not tantamount to being European. What it means to be European is actually as enigmatic and unstable as the mere notion of Europe. As Maryon McDonald (1996:49) argues, we can "see 'Europe' traveling through different conceptual systems, finding new meanings, becoming a different reality . . . The geographical boundaries expand and contract, the salient conceptual relations change, the moral frontiers and content shift considerably, and 'Europe' is invented and reinvented accordingly." Europe thus has never been a uniform whole, as it is often presented in the EU rhetoric. Under the pretext of supporting regional, cultural, and national difference endorsed by their most promoted idea of "unity in diversity," EU policy-makers, who strive to create a coherent narrative of their agency, reinforce and favor everything that is (supposed to be) common: common European heritage, common European culture, common European values.

Nevertheless, Europe – cut along and across by different geopolitical, social, and symbolic boundaries – has always been internally diversified and divided. And these are those numerous definite and virtual divisions that have a more or less serious impact on the mode of conceiving, imagining, and presenting Europe. Probably the most salient of these symbolic boundaries which forms different images of Europe is the long-lasting split between "the civilized West" and "the barbarian East." Its "influence is so strong that some commentators can talk disparagingly of a 'White Europe' in the West and a 'Black Europe' in the East. The division of Europe into two opposing halves, therefore, is not entirely fanciful" (Davies 1996:27).

Because of this enduring division, the process of EU enlargement poses a serious challenge for the promoted vision of a common and unified Europe. European identity, as it has been presented in EU policy so far, has been built on that very East–West opposition. Eastern Europe used to be one of (Western) Europe's "others," necessary for feeding its identity. Along with the geographical area extension of the EU, the problem of redefinition and self-definition of the new Europe's identity appeared. It turned out that the dichotomy breaking up Europe into the "better West" and the "worse East" is still vivid in the rhetoric of the new members "returning to" or "accessing" Europe. Eastern European countries are still treated as "younger Europe" which has yet to reach full European maturity in order to fit the cultural image of the West. Such an evolutionary perspective only revives the old divisions: integration is going to be fulfilled not through unification or mutual adaptation of two equal wholes, but through submitting one of them to the other. In her article on Europe's eastern expansion, Merje Kuus (2004:473) describes the process in terms of *postcoloniality*, and argues that "enlargement is underpinned by a broadly Orientalist discourse that assumes an essential difference between Europe and Eastern Europe, and frames difference from Western Europe as a distance from, and a lack of, Europeanness. Enlargement reconfigures the specific borders of Europe but not the underlying dichotomy of Europe and Eastern Europe."

The East–West framework, though overwhelming, is nevertheless unstable geographically. Bakic-Hayden (1995), describing a phenomenon he calls "nesting orientalism," states that the discourse of Europe and the East is not only characteristic for the Western countries in their attitude to Central and Eastern Europe, but may be attributed in different circumstances to different locations. It is also used by the accession countries to orientalize their eastern neighbors, in order to shift the borders of Eastness further and thus locate themselves in the "proper" Europe. Therefore, not strictly defined, "East" is an indispensable oppositional "other," which builds up European identity regardless of the geographical situation.

The new geopolitical eastern border of the EU, sealed and closed, will thus create a new constellation of Europe's identity based on a new definition of the East, which could be put into opposition to the enlarged union. It may reinforce the process of orientalizing Russia and the other neighboring countries which have not accessed the community, not only by the old countries of Western Europe but also by the accession countries searching for their new European identity. The former European geopolitical border between West and East, symbolized in the image of an Iron Curtain, is now moving eastward, gradually overlapping with the older boundary of salient significance for the image of "Europe": the religious boundary between the Western and Eastern Church, which has been dividing Europe for well over a millennium and is regarded by many scholars as the most durable cultural boundary of the whole continent (Kłoczowski 1982:12). This religious boundary, often treated as the border of civilizations – Roman and Byzantine – and strongly etched in social concepts (Huntington 1996), may now become more pronounced, and this would intensify the political and cultural exclusion of "the world on the other side."

"Anthropological studies of borders often highlight an extremely problematic area for any new Europe" state Bellier and Wilson (2000:140), pointing to the most recognized anthropological claims regarding the role of symbolic boundaries in the creation of group identity (Barth 1969) and the heightening of people's awareness of and sensitivity to their community (Cohen 1985). How local, regional, national, and supranational identities are discursively shaped may be best analyzed at community borders where one may observe everyday practices of exclusion and inclusion. Are the new EU geopolitical borders going to form the symbolic boundaries of the European community? Do they demonstrate sufficient symbolical effectiveness in separating the imagined Europe from non-Europe?

Let us consider these questions from a grass-roots perspective of people living in the borderland and experiencing the border in their everyday life. In what follows, I will analyze some empirical data collected during short ethnographic fieldwork carried out in 2008 (Kurczewska and Bojar 2010) in Bielsk Podlaski – a small borderland town inhabited by Catholic and Orthodox believers, situated 50 km from the Polish–Belarusian political border, which is now also the new eastern border of the EU. The fieldwork was conducted only three years after Poland had acceded to the European Union. We asked inhabitants who were in the main representatives of local elites – cultural activist, teachers, journalists, and local politicians – about their perception of the new European border and about their demand for EU programs addressing the management of local cultural resources. We were eager to learn to what extent the new geopolitical border had corresponded to or contradicted former boundaries, in physical as well as in symbolic terms. Has the EU border spurred processes of othering the Eastern neighbors and changed the ways of self-identity construction? Has it modified former images of Europe? What new contents and social meaning has the new border brought into the local community's everyday existence, and how is this reflected in the consciousness and practices of local elites who are especially likely to create and propagate the "European idea" in their local community?

"We Do Not Have To Be Enlightened," or "There Has Already Been a Union Here"

Bielsk Podlaski is a specific place which fits perfectly the EU rhetoric about cultural diversity and dialogue, mutual tolerance, difference, and so on. The local activists who animate the cultural life of the town are fully conscious of this fact. There are plenty of references to some elements of the EU's "cultural diversity" policy in their statements. When we asked about the most characteristic feature of the region which would distinguish it from the rest of the country, the standard and almost automatic answer pointed simply to "cultural diversity." This had become a kind of catchphrase of this region, appearing constantly both in public discourse and in everyday speech. The term "cultural diversity" as used here has many meanings. It denotes linguistic diversity, that is, local dialects, called simply "local speech," classified by some as Belarusian and by others as Ukrainian, and used in parallel with standard Polish in different social functions. "Cultural diversity" means also different national identities acknowledged by Bielsk residents: Polish, Belarusian, or Ukrainian, or an individual constellation of all of them. However, the most important meaning of diversity, as it seems to be, concerns the religious sphere, that is, the division into Catholic and Orthodox believers, though there are also some other denominations here of minor significance. "Cultural diversity" is described by our interlocutors only in superlatives. It is presented as the region's greatest treasure, making the inhabitants especially inclined to be open, tolerant, and spiritual, attached to tradition, and having a strong and unshakeable self-identity.

> What first comes to my mind, it is so-called "cultural diversity." These regions are inhabited by people of different nationalities: Polish, Belarusian, Ukrainian, and others. And this diversity, taking care of tradition . . . this is such an important part of our life. And I think that people who have lived here for generations cohabit and cooperate with each other really very well, and this is of great value, this cultural diversity is our value. And this is something that singles us out from other regions. [O 1][1]

> We are the relic of the Commonwealth of Diverse Nations [a reference to the Polish–Lithuanian Union between the fifteenth and eighteenth centuries]. Podlasie [the name of the region] in itself is our treasure and our chief asset. We are the most authentic region of Poland in terms of retaining this real relic, but in a good sense, because it is still alive, vibrant, and quality. [A 3]

Such statements perfectly correspond with EU recommendations of "best practice" to be followed in multicultural settings. Are, then, the local animators of culture influenced by the EU doctrine propagated in different projects on regional and cultural policy? Do they follow in any way the EU directives, and have these directives changed the character of cultural activity relevant to Bielsk residents? In our research, we did not find much evidence for this. The local activists are not eager to enroll on EU programs. They complain about the extended bureaucracy and many difficulties with accounting for expenses. If they embark on any programs at all, they treat them rather instrumentally, as a possible source of money and not as a reservoir of ideas.

There is also another cause of reluctance in adopting ideas promoted by EU programs. Our interlocutors definitely differentiate being a European from being a member of the EU – categories that are often treated as synonymous in EU documents. The European Union is rather equated in this region with Western Europe, and its suggestions about "becoming European" are perceived as a bit intrusive and preachy, since, as all of the interlocutors insisted, they have always lived in Europe and been European.

> It annoys me, this expression that we are "accessing Europe." Personally, I think I have been taught, ages ago in grammar school, that I had been in Europe. [T 3]

> I am currently in Europe and I never ponder whether I will be in Europe when I go to Białystok, to Warsaw or to Berlin. I think I am in Europe, I am and I have always been, not only geographically. [T 1]

One cannot discern any provincial complex in these statements, since the citizens of Bielsk have a firm conviction of their Europeanness, stemming from strong local patriotism, and a feeling of strong emotional ties with the town, which they regard as a place of great cultural value. The strong local identity of elites in Bielsk correlates with their strong European identity. Almost all of the interviewed persons define themselves as Europeans, referring at the same time to their other identities: regional, ethnic, or national. This is especially characteristic for this borderland, which has an open character and where different types of identities do not exclude but rather mutually support each other.

> I consider myself a citizen of Bielsk. I consider myself Polish and European. This does not exclude each other. No, the opposite. The one contains the other. [O 1]

The local elites of Bielsk also claim that strong local identity, emotional attachment to Bielsk is one of the basic criteria of their Europeanness. Their work for Bielsk is simultaneously their work for Europe. There is no need for leaving the local reality to feel settled in Europe. Europe is here and now. The concepts of locality and Europeanness are overlapping. Being a European means being a good citizen of Bielsk.

> I do not have to say what I do in my everyday work I do for Europe. It is sufficient when I say I do it for myself, for my family, for my friends, for my acquaintances. For this place where I am, that's enough. [T 1]

The inhabitants of Bielsk are also sure that their region and their town are a very important part of Europe's heritage. The Europeanness of Bielsk does not have to be confirmed. When asked about specific examples of monuments on a European scale, they without hesitation point to numerous sacred objects, Catholic and Orthodox churches, which are the most tangible signs of cultural diversity in Bielsk.

> This culture [is] connected to the church, this one and the other one, that have been here, and this is, I think, undoubtedly a part of European heritage and we cannot forget about it. And what is more, we have to remember that this town has always been multicultural, multireligious, and we talk about Poles, Belarusians, but let us remember also about Jews, who had played a crucial role here. [T 1]

> Surely Supraśl, the [Orthodox] monastery in Supraśl is such a pearl of Podlasie. This was the cultural center of this region in the seventeenth and eighteenth centuries, where there was the biggest library in the Grand Duchy of Lithuania, where there were priceless manuscripts, and deeds were created. This was a center of Orthodox spirituality, the seat of an archbishop and bishops. And certainly the sacred [Orthodox] mountain of Grabarka, this is something exceptional on Polish and on European scale. . . . Towns, this is Bielsk and Drohiczyn, rather because of their history than present time, but Bielsk as a town of two cultures that are living together and competing together – this is like a bridge. In general, Podlasie is a local region which is unique in all Europe. [A 3]

The uniqueness of the European heritage of Bielsk lies in its frontier character, connecting the traditions of Eastern and Western Christianity, the peaceful coexistence of the two great denominations. The ideas of a diversity policy promoted by the EU are nothing new here, since they have been practiced in everyday life in an obvious way, without any need of institutional support. And it is often underlined that it is not the inhabitants of Bielsk, but the citizens of the other EU states who could learn "best practice" here.

> We are boasting about what is good and beautiful in ourselves, what we have here and I think that we can learn something from Europe, this is important, but that we can also teach Europe – that is, I think perhaps even more important. That we can share with what we have [that is] good in ourselves. [T 2]

> There is a place for everybody in Europe and in our Commonwealth of Many Nations in Podlasie we are, just we are, the real Europeans, because there are many cultures here. Such a fashionable word "cultural diversity" – it exists here and it has always been here and we do not have to create anything or revive anything. It just exists and there are not any problems with it. [T 2]

Just before Poland's accession to the EU a significant exhibition entitled "There has already been a Union here," organized by an association called "We are Searching for Poland" from Białystok was presented in the Regional Museum at Bielsk. The main idea of this exhibition was to emphasize the fact that Podlasie has its own, centuries-old traditions of cultural diversity and tolerance, rooted in the times of the Polish–Lithuanian Union, which could be regarded as a prototype of the European Union:

> And if somebody claims that Poland accesses the European Union, let us remember that this is only a rerun, that we – Poles, Belarusians, Ukrainians, Lithuanians – already formed a stable and affluent Eastern European Union centuries ago. We have to cultivate the memory of it not only in museums and archive photos, but also in vibrant educational effort, not only in the name of Polish culture, but also the European one. This treasure of ours, when wisely protected, is our liferaft which will rescue us from the invasion of European and in many aspects unified mass culture. . . . It is important in the face of inevitable transformations not to lose our native asset which, just in the European Union, may blossom as never before. (Wiśniewski 2004)

We may see an ambivalence toward the EU: an expression of full accordance with the EU's multicultural policy, but also a certain anxiety and feeling of risk connected to unification. The European Union is perceived both as an opportunity and, at the same time, a threat to the region's culture. The mere word "union" carries negative connotations here. This is best seen in the statements of some interlocutors who, talking about the European Union, refer at the same time to another union that influenced the history of this region to a great extent: the religious Union of Brest, created in 1596, which turned the local Orthodox believers into "Greek Catholics" and placed them under the Pope of Rome.

As it appears from our conversations, it is not so much the local world that should benefit from European integration, but Western Europe which should learn the local practices of intercultural dialogue, and the tried and trusted ways of managing cultural diversity. This shifting of perspectives – who is going to be the coach and who is going to be coached in European norms and standards – could be explained in terms of a "peripheral complex," which prompts disadvantaged groups to bring about a reversal of the "normally" perceived order of things and, in this way, to render their stigma as a positive value. It is rather obvious that the process of othering Eastness is being felt more strongly here than in central Poland because many of our interlocutors are Orthodox believers, and they feel excluded in a state where Roman Catholicism is a dominating religion.

> There was a local guidebook called "An Exotic Poland" or something like that. Many people were indignant about it: why, living here, am I exotic? I am not exotic. I am from the minority, someone else is from the majority. It depends on the point of view. [A 2]

The feeling of marginality thus permeates local thinking about Europe – or rather, about the European Union. It is more visible in eager attempts to situate the local world in the very heart of the imagined Europe. As Herzfeld (1996:130) suggested, political marginality and the idea of historical centrality are often bound tightly together.

"Entering Schengen Has Been a Catastrophe for This Region," or "Where Are the Borders of Europe?"

The Polish political border with Belarus and Ukraine, which has now become the new eastern border of the EU, plays a crucial role in local residents' perception of the EU and Europe as such. Bielsk Podlaski is situated 50 km from the border, but that border was always important in the town's social life. When we asked about its significance for the inhabitants of Bielsk, before Schengen rules were implemented,[2] people first of all pointed to its economic values – free exchange of commodities, development of border trade, local markets, and small enterprise, giving local people additional possibilities to earn a living. The "import" of wives for the local bachelors who could not find willing candidates from their vicinity is also considered a significant gain brought by the border:

> Country girls from Belarus are eager to come here and they marry here and this is such a demographic injection, for this a somewhat deserted land. [A 1]

Although the present eastern border of the EU overlaps with the eastern political border of Poland, it is quite differently perceived and valued, especially after it was closed and limitations on crossing it were introduced. The Polish–Belarusian (formerly the Polish–Soviet) border had, for the 60 years of its existence, an important sociocultural meaning. In spite of all the obstacles and difficulties connected with crossing the border, it triggered a constant motion – the targets of which were not only economic advantages, but also social and cultural exchanges, both in private life and in institutional cooperation. And this was an exchange between equal partners: the state border separated two equal political structures.

The present EU border modifies the former meanings of the Polish eastern border. Indeed, the political strength and the unavoidable objectivity of its existence stand in opposition to its previous symbolic value. The new geopolitical border of the EU brings again a sense of obligation and limitation, which had been reduced during the previous 60 years of the border's functioning. The closing and strengthening of the present border limits to a great extent the previous possibilities of using it as a resource for making profit, and thus its arbitrariness becomes more perceptible. The sudden change is perceived by local people, first of all, in terms of economy: local companies dealing with international trade collapse; there are many fewer traders from abroad at the local market; crossing the border is more difficult and expensive. However, there are also further consequences mentioned: social activists complain about serious limitations of international contacts and cooperation in the domain of culture and education, especially in the partnership with Belarus, which has been very intense in the past.

> We have now the pitiful results of Poland accessing Schengen, because I can only see negative effects of it, me and people living here in the East, who do not have any business in the West. [A 3]

The EU border in its symbolic dimension stands in contradiction with itself, because as it is intended to draw a line of division between Europe and non-Europe, it becomes a border of two incommensurable worlds. However, the political borders of the EU fail evidently to meet the concept of Europe, as it is defined by our interlocutors. European integration means, in this case, a division of Europe into two parts, cutting one of them off from a crucial part of European cultural heritage.

> This is the main division, and the border arises from it, this new eastern wall, that is Schengen, as it is called. There, behind this wall, is a world which defends traditional values, their own. This is as it was thousands of years ago when Chinese emperors build a wall to prevent another nation getting to the land of a great culture. [A 3]

> Europeans are divided by this border with Belarus and Ukraine, because this part of Europe is still not . . . We have still those states Belarus, Russia, which are still not in the structures of EU, although they are in Europe. [J 2]

The former border had encouraged cultural differentiation between the inhabitants of both sides, as expressed by their declarations of identity: Belarusians and Ukrainians living in Poland claimed to be different to Belarusians and Ukrainians from the other side of the border, and called themselves "Polish Belarusians" or "Polish Ukrainians." This was done to differentiate themselves from, but also align themselves with, the people living beyond the border. The EU border does not encourage such identifications. It politically excludes people who are "just the same as we are"; who are Europeans just the same. Thus the border does not fulfill its crucial function: it does not make the people living beyond it other and alien. This is why the European Union cannot represent the locally imagined Europe; it is rather perceived as a political institution dividing Europeans into ones who are "better," who are in the EU structures, and ones who are "worse," who have been excluded. Therefore, it is regarded as needless, arbitrarily imposed, separating.

> For example Ukrainians. They are Europeans as Poles are. I meet them very often, I go away. And especially now I know how aggrieved they are, how they are treated when crossing borders . . . Not as people, especially by Polish customs officers. [T 2]

> We would like if this European border did not exist, to move the border a bit further. These people, it would be fine if Belarusians, Ukrainians also were associated with Europe. Life would be easier for them, they have such great heritage and we could take advantage and work together, cooperate. [A 2]

The opening of Poland's western borders into the EU does not compensate for the loss. It is eastern, not western, Europe, which is closest to this local world; the eastern side is where many people have their business and interests. Bielsk residents find themselves in a liminal position – being both Western and Eastern, having a mission to connect the two worlds, and a task which seems to compensate all the inconveniences of living on peripheries. Instead of marginalizing them, their borderland situation is perceived as making them more likely to be at the very center of Europe.

> I have only one dream: that Europe would open to the East, that this Europe would not be divided, because it is still divided, and I don't speak about the Asian steppe, because I don't need them at all, but I speak about Belarus and Ukraine, because as long as they won't be unified, those different cultures of the West and the East . . . But we are in the middle of all that. [T 1]

When asked about the boundaries of their imagined Europe, our interlocutors did not refer to the political borders, but drew wider circles which testified to the Central European situation of Bielsk. The common understanding is of a Europe that includes both the West and the East. Such a concept of Europe, despite its geopolitical borders, has primarily cultural connotations.

> [*Where would you delimit the borders of Europe?*] I would delimit such geographical borders. I would certainly not cut here along the Belarusian or Russian border – quite the opposite. As they run geographically . . . for me Europe associates with geographical borders, so there is Russia, Belarus, Ukraine, and some others there. . . . I would like, I support Ukraine's efforts to access the EU. It would be also good if Belarus accessed it and Russia also. There should be one great community, we should not divide. [O 1]

> [*Where, do you think, do the borders of Europe run?*] On the Ionian Sea from the east, and Kamchatka, and from the west up to Alaska. America and Africa are not Europe. This is Australia, New Zealand, even Antarctica . . . So this is the most genuine Greek Europe, because everything that is European comes from Greece and from Egypt also. . . . But Europe has commenced even earlier, from Mesopotamia. [A 3]

Conclusion

The enhancement of control and restriction of the eastern border of the European Union has separated the inhabitants of Bielsk from an important part of their world, from the second half of their Europe. It has thus become anti-European as it cuts Europe into two halves – instead of integrating, it separates East and West. From the point of view of the inhabitants of Bielsk – who claim their region as being the meeting point of two great civilizations, Latin and Byzantine – their town appears to be at the very center of Europe, not on its periphery. They have no doubts that the borderland of Catholicism and Orthodoxy, the symbiosis between Latin and Byzantine tradition, is the most precious heritage they have to bequeath to a unified Europe. Strong regional identity, emotional attachment to the place of their living, rich regional traditions, and memories of the past make the locality full of cultural content, giving a sense of being in the center of everything that is important. This is the reason why the demand here for external ideologies coming from Brussels is rather faint.

Perhaps the new eastern border of the EU, a very strong symbolic sign of a divided Europe, makes the inhabitants of Bielsk perceive the vision propagated by EU technocrats of a unified Europe as a mere political stratagem, and makes them especially conscious of its illusoriness. Despite having a strong European identity, the inhabitants of Bielsk do not eagerly call themselves citizens of the European Union. Their negative attitude toward the shape of European integration as proposed is reinforced by the disproportionate significance of the EU borders – their openness to the West where most people do not have any interests, and their closure to the East where their removal would be most desired. Thus it is the open world of the West, which appears to be alien – not one's own – and not the world of the East, separated by the border, which is much closer because of its similar culture, mentality, and language, and therefore ease of communication.

The closed political border contradicts the idea of an open borderland phenomenon (Kłoskowska 1996); this is an everyday experience of Bielsk inhabitants. The negation of practices most valued locally creates a distance to arbitrarily imposed borders, which are not there to be negotiated but to definitely separate. The EU, by establishing impassable borders to the East, orientalizing and excluding the closest neighbors, people who are "the same as we are," has made itself appear to be an intrusive institution, because it does not correspond with the local images about the shape of Europe and about the people living on the other side of the border. As Anthony Cohen once argued (1985:98), "community exists in the minds of its members . . . and . . . the reality of its boundaries similarly lies in the mind, in the meanings which people attach to them, not in their structural forms." It seems therefore that the sense of European cultural community promoted by the EU will not be legitimized here for a long time, since the borders which mark the edge of the political system lack their symbolic meaning.

NOTES

1 All the interviews were carried out by researchers Mirosław Bieniecki, Piotr Binder, and Mikołaj Pawlak in Bielsk Podlaski in winter 2008. The anonymous interviewees were the representatives of local cultural activists [A], teachers [T], journalists [J], politicians [P], and officials [O].

2 "Schengen" refers to an agreement concerning border controls within the EU and between the EU and third countries. Signatory states commit to minimizing controls at borders with other signatories while maintaining highly restrictive controls of their borders with nonsignatories.

REFERENCES

Anderson, Benedict R.
1983 Imagined Communities: Reflections on the Origin and Spread of Nationalism. London: Verso.

Armbruster, Heidi, Craig Rollo, and Ulrike H. Meinhoff
2003 Imagining Europe: Everyday Narratives in European Border Communities. Journal of Ethnic and Migration Studies 29(5):885–899.

Bakic-Hayden, Milica
1995 Nesting Orientalism: The Case of Former Yugoslavia. Slavic Review 54(4): 917–931.
Barth, Fredric, ed.
1969 Ethnic Groups and Boundaries: The Social Organisation of Culture Difference. Oslo: Universitetforlaget.
Bellier, Irene, and Thomas M. Wilson
2000 An Anthropology of the European Union: Building, Imagining and Experiencing New Europe. Oxford: Berg.
Borneman, John, and Nick Fowler
1997 Europeanization. American Review of Anthropology 26:487–514.
Cohen, Anthony P.
1985 The Symbolic Construction of Community. London: Tavistock.
Davies, Norman
1996 Europe: A History. Oxford: Oxford University Press.
Diez, Thomas
2004 Europe's Others and the Return of Geopolitics. Cambridge Review of International Affairs 17(2):319–335.
Goddard, Victoria A., Josep R. Llobera, and Cris Shore, eds.
1997 The Anthropology of Europe: Identities and Boundaries in Conflict. Oxford: Berg.
Hertzfeld, Michael
1996 Cultural Intimacy: Social Politics in the Nation State. London: Routledge.
Huntington, Samuel P.
1996 The Clash of Civilizations and the Remaking of World Order. New York: Simon & Schuster.
Kłoczowski, Jerzy
1998 Młodsza Europa: Europa Środkowo-Wschodnia w kręgu cywilizacji chrześcijańskiej średniowiecza. Warsaw: Państwowy Instytut Wydawniczy.
Kłoskowska, Antonina
1996 Kultury Narodowe u Korzeni. Warsaw: Wydawnictwo Naukowe PWN.
Kohli, Martin
2000 The Battlegrounds of European Identity. European Societies 2(2):113–137.
Kurczewska, Joanna, and Hanna Bojar, eds.
2009 Wyciskanie Brukselki? O Europeizacji Społeczności Lokalnych na Pograniczu. Warsaw: Wydawnictwo IFiS PAN.
Kuus, Merje
2004 Europe's Eastern Expansion and the Reinscription of Otherness in East–Central Europe. Progress in Human Geography 28(4):472–489.
Macdonald, Sharon. J.
2000 Historical Consciousness "From Below": Anthropological Reflections. *In* Approaches to European Historical Consciousness: Reflections and Provocations. Sharon. J. Macdonald, ed. pp. 86–102. Hamburg: Körber-Stiftung.
Mach, Zdzisław, and Dariusz Niedźwiedzki, eds.
2002 Polska lokalna wobec Unii Europejskiej. Kraków: Universitas.
McDonald, Maryon
1996 "Unity in diversity": Some Tensions in the Construction of Europe. Social Anthropology 4(1):47–60.
Pagden, Anthony, ed.
2002 The Idea of Europe: From Antiquity to the European Union. Cambridge: Cambridge University Press.

Said, Edward W.
1994 Orientalism. New York: Vintage Books.
Shore, Cris
2000 Building Europe: The Cultural Politics of European Integration. London: Routledge.
Wilson, Thomas M., and Hastings Donnan, eds.
1998 Border Identities: Nation and State at International Frontiers. Cambridge: Cambridge University Press.
2006 Culture and Power at the Edges of the State: National Support and Subversion in European Border Regions. Reihe: European Studies in Culture and Policy.
Wiśniewski, Tomasz
2004 Unia Już tu Była. Electronic document. http://www.szukamypolski.com/wystawy/unia/ (accessed November 5, 2011).

CHAPTER 13 European Politics, Policies, and Institutions

Marion Demossier

> Given the chance, would European Union voters ban minarets on mosques, copying the recent popular vote in Switzerland? Invite citizens to draft new EU legislation, and would they demand new rights for the disabled, cleaner rivers and more aid for the developing world? Or are Europeans in a sour, recession-struck mood: would they seek tighter curbs on immigration, protectionist tariffs on Chinese imports, or new hurdles to EU enlargement (bye-bye, Turkey)?

So asked the author Charlemagne in an article entitled "Allons, citoyens de l'Europe" (2010), which warned the public of the consequences of adopting the "citizen's initiative" stipulated in Article 11, Paragraph 4 of the Lisbon Treaty. That document commits the EU to an experiment in direct democracy: it will be possible to launch the first European Citizens' Initiatives from April 1, 2012. One million EU citizens from a significant number of countries will be given the opportunity to propose new draft laws. This development offers an excellent example of how Europe, its institutions, and peoples, can provide a fascinating field for anthropological investigation, revealing the many contradictory processes of transformation and redefinition that are taking place.

In an article published by *Social Anthropology*, the journal of the European Association of Social Anthropologists (EASA), Andre Gingrich (2006:161) reminded us of how these contested processes of "redefining" and "building" or "constructing" Europe are profoundly shaped by the broader global context. The last decade brought renewed urgency to the issue with the two successive cycles of EU enlargement, that of 2004 (the addition of Cyprus, Czech Republic, Estonia, Hungary, Latvia, Lithuania, Malta, Poland, Slovakia, and Slovenia), and of 2007 (the addition of Romania and Bulgaria), punctuated by the constitutional crisis following the referenda in Ireland, France, and the Netherlands. International crises such as the Iraq war, the supposed threat of global warming, the banking failure of 2008 and the subsequent

A Companion to the Anthropology of Europe, First Edition. Edited by Ullrich Kockel, Máiréad Nic Craith, and Jonas Frykman.

recession, leading to a crisis of the eurozone, have forced Europe to try to redefine itself internally and externally. Yet most of these attempts have been unsuccessful and have created more tensions and doubts about the future of what Jean Monnet described as "the laboratory of Europe."

From six member states, the EU has expanded to 27, and is still envisaging further expansion, creating new challenges in terms of the governance and the management of a rich and varied diversity of cultures. The process of European integration has oscillated between the protection of national interests by a multileveled system of governance and a new supranational state looking for recognition as a legitimate political actor. In this process, culture as a central category of discussion of European integration has come to the fore. The institutional and political landscape created by this "*object politique non identifié*" (citing Jacques Delors) requires, according to most commentators, the creation of a civic space to accompany its development and guarantee its democratic foundations. Without a *demos*, there will not be Europe, or Europe will remain associated with those tasks that the nation cannot or does not wish to deal with. As Kürti (2008:27) has argued, "transnational bodies, such as the EU, can decide on many things and there are growing possibilities and opportunities to leave the former domestic domains and enter into the more open and larger EU arena." This is certainly true for the recently acceding countries. Yet despite its rapid development and its growing presence in the public sphere, European integration remains for the majority of its citizens a technobureaucratic policy-making process that is treated with suspicion on account of a supposed lack of political legitimacy. Some commentators such as the historian, Eli Barnavi, have described Europe as frigid, incapable of inspiring. A "negative imaginary" dominates the public sphere: very few articles are devoted to the positive aspects of the EU, a phenomenon Gingrich (2006:162) claims is partly explained by the inherent difficulties involved in trying to conceptualize a political object which defies even the best efforts of political and social scientists.

In the burgeoning field of studies addressing issues of Europeanization and integration at a time of transition, social anthropologists from different national traditions have been to the fore in investigating themes pertaining to issues of culture, politics, and identity. What is particularly innovative about their approach is that it aims to address the links between political processes and culture in the widest sense of the term. Most of the research conducted in this field seeks to examine whether or not Europe could become a meaningful and emotional political object by analyzing the representations and practices associated with the development of European integration and the various groups at the core of the process. Scholars have either studied the EU from inside focusing on European institutions and the making of Europe as a tapestry of cultures, or they have engaged with the process of Europeanization defined by Borneman and Fowler (1997:48) as "an accelerated process and a set of effects that are redefining forms of identification with territory and people." In both areas, they have generally adopted a critical stance adding layers of complexity to the analysis, trying to unpack the cultural dimension of any political process and giving more critical depth to the study of EU policy-making.

In their contribution to the wider debates about the concept of governance, policy-making, and institutional culture, anthropologists differ radically from other social scientists in their approach to definitions of politics, identity, and culture. The volume compiled and published in 2000 by Irène Bellier and Thomas Wilson, entitled *An Anthropology of the EU: Building, Imagining and Experiencing the New Europe*, provides a striking example of what anthropology can bring to the study of European integration. Presenting a series of microstudies based on the ethnographic analysis of a wide variety of political sites with the global/local articulation of issues and their effects, the editors defined the discipline's contribution to the field of European integration as the science of man and a cultural critique of politics. According to Bellier and Wilson (2000:2), the volume "seeks to delineate the ways in which culture acts to distinguish or to obscure EU institutions, policies, leaders, ideologies, and values in the daily lives of people on the peripheries and localities of the EU as well as those at the centres of EU decision-making." Unveiling the complexity of these political, economic, and cultural transformations, anthropologists "have thus far proved the European project to be a dynamic site of meaning making over which larger questions of sovereignty and identity are conveyed" (Firat 2009:5). Tensions between micro- and macrolevels, or local and global scales, constitute the bulk of the work undertaken.

The recent eastern enlargement of the EU and the possible entry of Turkey, Croatia, and Macedonia provide new challenges to the anthropological approach toward European integration. Because of the collapse of the Soviet Union and the new "confusing geopolitical conglomeration" (Kürti 2008:25) resulting from the addition of Central and Eastern Europe, European policies and institutions are facing another challenge which will add further complexity to the European project, but also will provide anthropologists with a wider range of issues to tackle, be it in terms of constituting a common worldwide research agenda (Ribiero and Escobar 2006) or in confronting different and/or similar intellectual traditions. Most of the current work being undertaken by anthropologists remains confined to the microlevel and largely defined by ethnographic methods failing to engage with wider concerns. Trying to establish a European agenda and network for example around the anthropology of farming communities has revealed to be a challenge as most of the research remains disparate, fragmented, and lacking a cohesive framework.

This chapter aims to review some of the main areas of debate relating to European integration, policies, and institutions by mapping out the scholarly literature produced by anthropologists from different national traditions and by bridging the scholarly divide between East and West (Kürti 2008). As a result, it will consider the impact on European integration and democratization through the effects of policymaking and governance. The study of European integration could be characterized as an ongoing and healthy research area with a growing number of postgraduate students attached to it, and with an increasing number of postgraduate Politics programs integrating the anthropological approach to Europe as a compulsory module. This interest in anthropology is reflected in the development of interdisciplinary methodologies based upon fieldwork and interviews that have been used in a number of political and international relations research projects. However, this chapter aims to concentrate primarily upon the anthropological dimension and where appropriate its engagement with other disciplines. Increasingly anthropologists have adopted innovative research methods when dealing with European integration, including multi-sited ethnography, illustrated by, for example, the work of Douglas Holmes (2000) who has used heuristic means of questioning the intricacies of the local and global. The recent field of anthropology of policy has also contributed to the redefinition of some of the issues attached to European integration, notably through the work of Cris Shore and Susan Wright (1997) and, more recently, Cris Shore's contribution *Building Europe* (2000). New and original themes have also emerged in postcommunist countries, where scholars have examined the transformation of the anthropological landscape following the Bologna Agreement and their integration into a market economy, a different mode of governance, and Europe. As a result, anthropological studies on European integration have proliferated, but they still remain very fragmented.

Questioning the EU and European Integration

Most social anthropologists would agree that the construction of the EU represents one of the most exciting and profound developments in European politics and society of the twentieth century (Shore 2000:xi). Qualified either as a "normative power," a "supra-national entity," a "postnational government," or a "transnational hybrid power," the EU has challenged our understanding of traditional politics. From its inception during the 1950s, with the creation of the European Coal and Steel community, based on an economic integration between Germany, France, Italy, the Netherlands, Belgium, and Luxembourg, it has been transformed into a nearly fully fledged hybrid state. As a result, it has captured the interest of a generation of anthropologists careful to leave behind the nation-state and the postcolonial cultures attached to it. Its very nature and the "bizarre" principles on which it has established its premises challenge the notions of democracy and governance. Because of its "exotic" characteristics and its hybrid post-Westphalian configuration, the EU crystallizes another kind of exoticism and thus constitutes for social anthropologists an exciting puzzle (Demossier 2007). The pervasive effects of European integration on, for example, everyday European life has obliged the discipline to review its concepts, tools, and methods, in an attempt to adapt to the challenge of multilocale fieldwork, policy-focused culture, and multilevel governance which all provide serious obstacles to any anthropological study.

In any study of the EU and European integration, a lot of ground has already been mapped out by other disciplines (political sciences, international relations, sociology, and policy-based research), especially in relation to macroprocesses of governance or discourse analysis. However, the anthropology of Europe remains quite isolated and marginalized when examining European issues, compared to the fields of international relations or political sciences. There is however a need for an interdisciplinary dialogue when dealing with notions of culture and identity through their politicization. It is equally true that anthropological contributions to EU analysis, which are often neglected, ought to provide a more complex microperspective of issues of identity and culture than the ones traditionally deployed in the study of the political sciences or international relations.

The idea of questioning the nature of the EU and the process of European integration first appeared on the anthropologists' intellectual radar in the late 1980s at the time of the fall of the Berlin Wall. On November 9, 1989, the Berlin Wall was pulled down and the border between East and West Germany was opened for the first time in 28 years, leading to the reunification of Germany in October 1990. These momentous events presented an immense challenge for the EU, and for anthropologists they marked the dawn of a new era. The end of the Cold War transformed the geopolitical status of Europe. Leaving behind the study of French local politics, the French anthropologist, Marc Abélès (1993), for example, began to study transnational politics as practiced in the European Parliament. As he explained matters: "From 1989 to 1992, I did field research on the European Parliament. I think this was the first ever anthropological study of the EU, which at that time was still known as the European Community" (Shore and Abélès 2004:10). A Franco-British team composed of Marc Abélès and his colleagues, Irène Bellier and the British social anthropologist, Maryon McDonald, was offered the opportunity by the Delors cabinet and commission officials to conduct fieldwork inside the European Commission. The start of their mission coincided with the signing of the Maastricht Treaty and the creation of the single market, both of which were key political changes necessitating further public legitimacy and democratic support. As pointed out by political scientists such as Michelle Cini, the focus on European Commission culture(s) was, to a large extent, a byproduct of the blossoming of research on the EC, and more specifically on its supranational nature, over the course of the 1990s.

In the course of their research, the Franco-British team questioned the nature of Europe as a new multicultural political object, and while their respective publications went in different directions, they nevertheless all contributed to a better understanding of the EU as an institution. Key concepts such as "virtual Europe," "unity in diversity," and "organizational and managerial cultures" demonstrated the ongoing, dynamic flux of cultures attached to decision-making processes. Policy was defined as negotiated between different sets of actors transforming the political machine into a forward-looking entity creating new social categories which affected the relationship between institutions and the EU's population (Bellier and Wilson 2000:15). They also underlined some of the values at the core of the project of European integration, questioning the absence of a common direction taken by the EU or the formation of a European elite of civil servants who could be characterized as truly European. For Abélès (2004:1), the anthropological approach to EU institutions, which could be defined by an endless quest and a lack of reflexivity, sheds some light onto the evasive and contradictory nature of European integration. The nature of the project is itself doubtful because in wanting to link "virtual Europe" to a sense of belonging and collective identification, elites have never fully questioned the sense of purpose of their trajectory: "Building Europe is a metaphor of construction in which the end-product is in dispute, with the smaller feats of engineering required to get there also being contested because of a lack of agreement about the reasons, methods, and functions of the building itself" (Bellier and Wilson 2000:17).

The same sense of confusion about the precise purpose of various cultural phases designed to encourage a sense of collective European belonging was revealed by the authors of the Franco-British research team, and has been repeated in more recent publications. During the 1990s, Cris Shore, for example, conducted the bulk of his fieldwork in the European Commission (EC), but his position was less compromised in the sense that his research had not been commissioned by it and was not subject to the same political constraints. The area of cultural policy, especially in relation to the communication of a European identity, formed the core of his research. He argued that the European Commission's cultural characteristics were a reflection of the rules, norms, and the "system of political bargaining and networking" that pervaded the organization (Shore 2000:173), and that they bore the "stamp of the ideas and practices that prevailed at the time of its creation" (2000:177). Highly critical, Shore denies the success of the European Commission in creating a European identity capable, by the application of political symbols and traditional tools through the ingenious use of EC-funded "cultural actions," of underpinning future integration. The European Commission's various cultural initiatives bore, for him, a striking resemblance to the strategies and techniques used by national elites in the formation of European nation-states during the nineteenth century (Shore and Abélès 2004:10). Europeanness, as a cultural process, occupied most of his attention, but his overall analysis remained critical of the European Commission and its culture, which according to him was deemed to "create conditions that are ideal for encouraging practices of fraud, nepotism, and corruption" (Shore 2000:176).

Since the publication of Bellier and Wilson's volume on the EU, the study of European politics, policies, and institutions has expanded beyond its traditional "Western" frontiers to question some of the categories and constructions of the dominant anthropological intellectual landscape, especially with the transformations of Central and Eastern European anthropology following the collapse of the Soviet Union in 1989. Laszlo Kürti (2008:25), former president of EASA, has strongly criticized the ways in which western traditions of European integration have largely ignored the research produced by colleagues in Central and Eastern Europe. Questioning the effects of the enlargement on Eastern European anthropology, Kürti (2008:29) denounces what he sees as "a rather unbalanced, uneven, and unstable European integration process, both in the political–economic and the cultural–educational fields." Referring to the work of the political scientist, Jan Zielonka (2007), he discusses the extent to which joining the EU has changed the nature of democracy in the new member states, and concludes that enlargement and EU membership are far from rallying the masses. As he describes matters: "Citizens view the results of the massive economic, judicial and political transformation as a necessary headache causing high rates of unemployment, insecurity, crime, double-digit inflation, and a relatively observable second-class status in Europe" (2008:27). Moreover, if "both state and local governments have been enlarged, becoming more and not less bureaucratic in that process" (2008:27), the effects of European integration might appear to be of variable and unequal benefit and might tend to further marginalize new member states (Zielonka 2007:173). If anthropologists studying postcommunist societies in Eastern Europe have turned from analyses of the cultural practices of groups on the margins of modernizing state projects to accounts of how communities are shaped by systemic changes in the political economy of states (Wolfe 2000), the European Union has not yet become their prime object of research.

Cultures and Power in EU Institutions

What seems to bridge the East and the West in terms of scholarly debates about the process of European integration is the central role of policies, "norms," or "standards" implemented from above by the EU on to its member states through the cultural, educational, or other spheres regardless of their diverse economic or political situations. The use of a specific bureaucratic and managerial vocabulary such as "transition," "normalization," or "standardization" hides, in fact, a process of implementation of a set of practices that are seen as major improvements of the national political scenery, a kind of bureaucratic Western imperialism which, far from recognizing its shortcomings, pretends to a universalistic mission of Europeanizing the vast populace. This new European bureaucratic model has recently emerged in France, and several research institutions such as the ANR (L'Agence nationale de la recherche – National Agency for Research) have adopted English alongside French, as well as some of the practices of the EU managerial culture. Yet they often coexist with deep-rooted national practices of institutional culture such as that of "*fléchage*" (a post already given to somebody despite the call for applicants), which are still widely accepted.

"Europe" and its laws are increasingly encroaching on the daily lives of European people from Portugal to Poland, but as Maryon McDonald (2005:3) has argued, the European Union is policy centered, and self-defining "policy-makers" make up its elite officials. The EU and its policies thus offer anthropologists a remarkable field for the study of institutions and power, interpretation and meaning, ideology, rhetoric, and discourse, the politics of culture, ethnicity, and identity, and interactions between the global and the local (Shore and Wright 1997). Wedel and Feldman (2005:1) underlined the anthropologist's contribution to the study of governance and policy-making. Anthropology offers a distinctive approach because it constructs its object of study in a particular dynamic, contested, and fluid way: it uses a multi-faceted methodology based on an array of methods such as ethnography, the "extended case method," and discourse analysis. Finally, it theorizes policy processes using power relations and interactions of parties. The ability to match microperspectives derived from intense fieldwork with holistic macroperspectives derived from inductive reasoning and comparativism (Gingrich and Fox 2002) defines the anthropological perspective. Yet several obstacles remain because of the nature of the institutions involved in the making of Europe which necessitate full participant observation. As Verlot (2001:351) has argued: "It is only by participating and knowing the consequences of this kind of work that one is able to begin to understand the full complexity of institutions and escape the trap of coming to see them as bodies characterised by unity and common function."

By being commissioned to study the culture of the EC, the Franco-British team appeared to have been able to examine the culture of the European Commission in depth. Yet if my analysis of their various publications is correct, their approach was not characterized by long-term participant observation of everyday practices in the European Commission, but by a multi-sited ethnography of some of the sites. In their study, the three researchers were asked to investigate "the existence or not of a specific Commission culture, plus the weight of the different languages and national cultural traditions and their impact on working relationships, and how a European identity might emerge in such a context." As the authors believed that ideas and action are enmeshed, they showed that culture was inseparable from politics and other aspects of organizational life, a plethora of competing cultures constructed on the basis of nationality and language, but also at times built around departmental identities tied closely to specific policy areas or functions performed (Abélès et al. 1993). Their main contribution to the analysis of institutional culture and policy-making is to give credit to the complex range of choices facing politicians, be it in terms of their dealings with the multicultural nature of their daily encounters or the growing importance of managerial training. This working culture has shifted from the agent of "the construction of Europe" to a managerial type of culture encapsulated by one of Maryon McDonald's respondents who said of the younger generations of staff: "we had a European ideal and now they have to go to management courses to learn motivation" (McDonald 1996). Interestingly enough, the idea of a European training school created on the same basis as the French *Grandes Écoles* was suggested by anthropologists such as Irène Bellier, and has now been given form.

These aspirations may have been particularly strong in what one official called "the heroic age when building Europe was the business of a few enthusiasts," but this is no longer the case. Problems of communication, misunderstanding of cultural traditions, pluralism, and opacity are widely prevalent amongst these bureaucrats who tried to aim at a "common good" defined by Abélès as a "floating signifier" (2000), which oscillates between what is best for Europe and what is dictated by their national affiliation. Abélès quoted Claude Lévi-Strauss using this concept of "floating signifier" to designate notions that are both essential and vague, allowing for their evocation alone to be of great significance. It is a marking function and it attests to the power of acknowledgement attributed to this concept. Bargaining and negotiating have become central to the governance of the EU.

Shore, on the other hand, adopted a more distanced methodology, combining a wide array of techniques such as interviews, attendance at a daily round of EU activities for six months, conversations, meetings, and exchanges as well as the use of statistical data, survey research, historical archives, textual analysis, and biographies (2000:7–8). Some commentators have criticized his claim to have identified evidence of a homogenous "nation-building" bureaucracy, which seems far from the realities of Brussels and which he depicts as a united and homogeneous group of EU elites seemingly defined by frauds and corruption. Marc Verlot, anthropologist by background but actively involved in EU affairs, argues against the view that policy-makers and EU civil servants can be analyzed as a united and coherent group of individuals "benders of the truth and, at worst, potential participants in corruption" (Verlot 2001:350) embodying the system that they represent. Advocating the understanding of social relations by paying more attention to the human agency within institutions and behind policies, Verlot provides the anthropologist with a more useful theoretical perspective. Verlot underlines the nature of the contradictory tasks facing these elites, the angst and fear of making a wrong decision, the accountability associated with it, the complex nature of the individuals composing the group of policy-makers, and their human condition. He argues persuasively that "policy is (wo)man made, a subjective process as much as a product, made through daily negotiation" (2001:347).

Recent works conducted on policy-making in the EU have indeed underlined the complexity and nonunified characteristics of the world of policy-makers which cannot be reduced to a top-down process or to an elitist decision. Most policy-making areas have to adapt to the pressures of globalization, and have increasingly become multileveled and multidimensional in nature, requiring us to take into account not only the civil servant's work of transcribing a complex situation into a legal document, but also national and regional or group views represented by lobbyists or NGOs. New paradigms of governance have thus been conceptualized by European integration specialists to illustrate this growing complexity. The example of agricultural policy, one of the oldest areas of policy-making in the EU, and one which has been significantly affected by the pressures of enlargement, has been exemplified by the work of Isabelle Garzon (2007) an insider in the European Commission. She demonstrated how, since the Uruguay Round Agreement, complex agricultural policy reforms have necessitated a different approach from European policy-makers, suggesting that the macro- dimension to policy-making cannot be ignored by anthropologists. Fieldwork conducted in 2009 in French wine regions illustrates the growing salience of globalization and Europeanization in professional discourses. For some EU members Europe has undeniably become a relevant category of representation as well as an "imagined, but contested community."

Another striking illustration of the complex and contextualized nature of EU policy changes is provided by the growing importance of the bottom-up level of governance, such as lobbyists. Several examples could be given of bottom-up social and professional movements which have developed and have entered the global arena. The Slow Food movement as well as the iconic figure of José Bové incarnate the antiglobal stance which characterizes some European societies. The development of local products and foodstuffs accompanied by the revitalization of rural festivals has struck a chord with urban dwellers in quest of their roots. A few miles from Millau, the cradle of the French antiglobalization movement, wine producers from Languedoc–Roussillon have, however, a different story to tell about modernity, fighting what they see as the EU's "traditional and backward" definition of wine-making. A recent project conducted between 2005 and 2008 by INRA (Institut national de la recherche agronomique – Institute of Agronomic Research) and an interdisciplinary team composed of biologists, sensorial analysts, economists, and sociologists, funded by the ANR, examined the possibility of producing wines with lower alcohol content, advocating a rupture with traditional *terroir* products. Appointed as an anthropologist to lead the consumption team, I was struck by the modern, liberal, and pro-European stance of the local wine professionals who embraced globalization, competition, and the free market. The project was an example of a bottom-up attempt to engage with Europe, and I was able to witness the power of the wine lobby which negotiated directly with the EC with the aim of provoking a change in the legal definition of wine production. This offers an illustration of the complex and multilevel context when engaging with Europe as a political and administrative force.

Adopting a macro- and policy-oriented perspective, social anthropologists in Central and Eastern Europe provide a fresh and more critical stance toward issues of EU policy-making. Focusing on different national case studies, they argue that EU policies might lead to a Europe traveling at different speeds (Zielonka 2007; Ekiert

2008) and threaten democracy. According to Kürti (2008:28), the hegemony of EU policies risks the further marginalization of new member states, with the sole exception of Poland (the largest of them), which might lead to serious political, economic, and foreign policy conflicts in the future. Tensions between national discourses and new forms of identification also prove to be crucial. As a result, a growing number of scholars from Central and Eastern Europe have started to examine the constitution of this new bureaucratic culture, questioning for example how the first generation of Slovene civil servants within the EU construct Europeanness through their move to Brussels and their negotiation with categories of the "East" and "West" (Bajuk Sencar 2008) or how in Macedonia accession to the EU has impacted on religious and ethnic boundaries in a village composed of Muslims and Orthodox Christians (Marcin Lubaś 2008). The impact of EU construction and of its political effects on everyday life still remains embryonic in terms of anthropological analysis, and the fragmentation of the research landscape, with very few interdisciplinary dialogues, remains a major obstacle for the development of the discipline. Yet the process of Europeanization creates further differentiation and complexity in the cultural arena, which makes the role of anthropology more vital than ever in the political sphere.

Policies in Places, Experiencing Europe

With 27 member countries and a population of nearly half a billion, the EU covers a large part of the European continent. On the Europa Web site (europa.eu), a recently added category named "Take Part" illustrates the growing consciousness of its need to gain popular legitimacy and to ensure further consolidation in the public sphere. As a result of the failure of the constitutional treaty to be directly ratified by the Netherlands and France, the EU sought to develop alternative ways of involving Europeans in its decision-making processes. That the EU is obliged to ask its citizens to "Have your say on European policies," reveals very clearly the ongoing crisis of legitimacy that it faces. Shore and other anthropologists have discussed the invention and use of statistics in creating categories of social perception. In his book *Building Europe*, Shore (2000) argues that since 1990, new Eurobarometer and Eurostat statistics have become powerful instruments for creating knowable, quantifiable and hence more tangible and governable "European populations" and "European space"; they are also powerful molders of consciousness that furnish the metaclassifications within which identities and subjectivities are formed. There has not been, to my knowledge, any serious anthropological study of these new instruments, and especially of how they were constituted or are currently reassessed. Yet they offer a valuable indicator of how the EU is constructing Europe through categorizations, but also how Europe is perceived, and they are systematically cited without being questioned by social scientists, which clearly has implications for any discussion of policy-making.

If we examine public attitudes toward policy-making in detail, it is interesting to note that the EU is felt to play an important role especially in relation to global issues where the nation-state is not expected to be the sole actor. A majority of Europeans believe that the EU plays a positive role in 9 of the 15 policy areas included in the survey. In fact, an outright majority feel that the EU plays a positive role in research and environmental protection (51% each) in their country. Close to half of Europeans deliver a positive assessment with regard to the EU's role in the fight against climate change (48%) and more than four out of ten Europeans believe that the EU plays a positive role in their country's security (44%), the role of their country in the world (42%), and consumer safety (42%). More than a third of Europeans think that the EU plays a positive role in their country in terms of the energy supply (39%), fighting crime (38%), and the economic situation (36%). In two other areas, Europeans are more divided about the role of the Union: agriculture, where a third of Europeans feel that the EU plays a positive role but where, equally, a third think that the EU's role is negative (33% each); and the healthcare system, where four out of ten Europeans believe that the EU's role is neither positive nor negative (40%).[1]

If these statistics provide evidence of a growing recognition of the role of the EU in global affairs, they do not shed much light on how issues are perceived and experienced at either national or local level. Zabusky (2000:179) has suggested that "when it comes to standardizing and centralizing European policy on a variety of issues, people seem to hold tighter to their local identities." Anthropological studies of policy-making, at the local level of city or province, including policy arenas of agriculture and fisheries, and the cultural and regional policies of European integration, have attested to the fact that policy-makers act within a cultural interpretative framework that is visible to an ethnographic eye which enables the ethnographer to document the process rather than simply the product of policy-making (for example Firat 2009:6). They have also demonstrated with conviction that the project of a united Europe very often creates a stark contrast between what occurs under the labels of professionalism and policy within the EU's institutions, and what relates to issues of citizenship, national identity, and feelings of belonging among European individuals, in their localized contexts (Bellier and Wilson 2000:15). The ethnography of Burgundian wine-growing communities that I have conducted over the last 20 years offers one example of how issues continue to be framed in local/global terms rather than national and/or European and that the sense of belonging in this part of the world is still based on having "three graves in the cemetery" (Demossier 1999, 2010).

Interactions between local/regional identities and the cultural resources provided by the EU is an area where anthropologists have demonstrated convincingly that culture can play a formative role in creating new imaginings of the locality. Indeed, discourses on local culture have often been constructed around counterreactions to intense processes of globalization, and local cultures are presented as the provider of new resources for social and economic growth. In his analysis of construction of heritage in the *Pays Cathare*, or the Ulster-Scots heritage, Ullrich Kockel (2007:85–101) examined processes where culture and identity are utilized under the banner of "heritage" for tourist development. Most cultural traditions can be seen as vibrant and organic forces challenging the fixation of cultural heritage, and the EU may find itself in a difficult position as identities will not simply respond to political processes. Kockel argues that the expanding EU will therefore find it increasingly difficult to engineer a coherent European identity perceived as based on a common past, and this will be even more difficult when European heritage is viewed as fluid, undefined, and ambiguous in its expression. The Morvan, which was the political fief of the French president, François Mitterrand, is a helpful example of the complex interaction between national and local attempts to fashion identities. In 1990, Mitterrand decided to create two museums using EU funding designed to record the history of two local examples of migrations – those of the *nourrices* (wetnurses) to Paris and the *galvachers* (male cattle drivers) from this notoriously poor region. I was appointed by the local *maire* to research the *galvache*, as part of an EU-funded project. In the course of my fieldwork, I rapidly ran into opposition from local historians, folklorists, and political actors who were all determined that the *galvache* be established as a male equivalent to the well attested history of the *nourrices*. When I presented my conclusion stating that there were no historical or ethnographic evidence of a male migration of the same extent, and that this was purely a folkloric and local invention, the local community reacted vehemently and ignored my findings. Moreover, a few years later, after the election of a new *maire*, who was in fact one the local folklorists, they tampered with the content of the local museum established on the basis of my research to suit their local definition of the Morvan as a new emblematic region. This project funded by the EU became framed in national and local terms to serve specific political interests.

Another example of the tensions between different cultural forms is provided by the growing economic importance attributed to food and foodstuffs in the EU and the ways in which access to the various labels of geographical origin has a direct impact on regions and the identities attached to them. In 1992 the EU enacted a regulatory framework which certified and authenticated products with a specific place of origin – *terroir* – and this subsumed and incorporated national legislation. The regulations create International Property Rights which cover a rising proportion of world trade in foodstuffs, and have created major tensions within the World Trade Organization (Pratt 2007:290). Numerous ethnographic studies (Faure 1999; Grasseni 2003) have been devoted to analyzing the social and economic transformations following the recognition of products and the economic systems put in place as a result. Presented as traditional local products, they are not survivals as such, and they are frequently the result of sustained commercial activity, state regulatory systems and international trade agreements (Pratt 2007:291). Yet without their recognition, they would have not survived in the market economy. Their legal status has facilitated the establishment of a wider network of experts and the organization of a consortium of producers working closely with chambers of commerce and the tourist industry. They have also contributed to the local economic revitalization of specific areas which otherwise would be qualified as in decline. Yet my own research on *terroir* in Burgundy reveals to what extent the discourse on *terroir* has also been socially constructed by a wide range of interested actors and how many producers have been marginalized in the process (Demossier 2010).

Multiculturalism and cultural policy provide another significant area of preoccupation for policy-makers and anthropologists. In a recent publication entitled *The Multiculturalism Blacklash: European Discourses, Policies and Practices* (2010), Steven Vertovec and Susanne Wessendorf argue that politicians and public intellectuals have increasingly criticized a perceived shift toward "too much diversity." Yet at the same time, policy-makers in Europe are increasingly framing cultural policies in terms of national security, a trend that is tied to the neo-right's success in establishing immigration as a subject of mainstream political debate (Feldman 2005:2). Although in its constitutional charter, Europe, as a multicultural society, advocates and guarantees the protection of minorities and emphasizes the establishment of the conditions for preserving cultural diversity, discourse on European identity remains one of essentialism, ethnocentrism, racism, and exclusion, just like the national identities on which it is modeled (Grillo 2007:78). These contradictions are at the core of any discussion of European identity, and its future development encapsulates many of the potential conflicts between a top-down model of European legislation and the desire to build Europe from the bottom up by taking into account the aspirations of its citizens.

Anthropological studies conducted in different nation-states have examined the issue of exclusion and inclusion by focusing on the language of policies or on how migrants have adapted to some of the challenges posed by the nation-state in terms of integration. They have tended to adopt a critical stance toward the politics of immigration and integration, but they have also endorsed the necessary imperative of adopting a broader perspective on these questions. The work of Didier Fassin, for example, on the "Biopolitics of Otherness" (2001), illustrates this point and raises important issues concerning the status and treatment of the multicultural question in Europe. In France, as in most Western European countries, the question of illegal immigration has become a critical public policy issue. The creation of the Schengen space represented an attempt to bring a policy solution to issues of mobility and work at the European level – but one whose limits are clearly revealed by the continuing influx of immigrants from the Balkans to the Italian coast and from Africa to Spanish beaches. Examining how biopolitics affects the definition of otherness in France, Fassin argues that its legal basis is established on one major foundation, the recognition of the body as the ultimate site of political recognition, but in reality it takes two parallel paths. On the one hand, the suffering body manifests itself as the ultimate (but not unique) resource, supplanting all other social justifications for immigrants to be granted legal status and residing in a basic right to keep oneself alive as long as possible. This is a minimalist vision, but one which tends toward a universal horizon. The racialized body, on the other hand, extends from the foreigner to the national and introduces internal frontiers founded on physical difference. This is a discriminatory concept, which creates hierarchies among people.

Another illustration of the shifts of representations operating in the postcolonial context in Europe could be given by the example of the museum sector in France (Demossier 2008). While some of the national museums devoted to the study of "Other" have closed their doors, new museums have been launched: for instance, the Quai Branly or the Cité nationale de l'histoire de l'immigration (CNHI). While it could be argued that these new museums have emerged against the background of Europeanization and globalization, the exhibitions themselves continue to be framed in national terms. Several Anglo-Saxon commentators have raised the various tensions and contradictions in the nature of such projects, but they have found themselves largely ignored by these institutions. Outside Paris, similar projects conducted at local level and well implanted in local and social terms have achieved greater success and have also bridged some of the gaps between different types of visitors, enabling a more successful kind of integration exemplified by the exhibitions held in Lyon during 2008 and 2009.

From Policies to Politics and Societies: Fears in the Imaginings of Europe

As discussed previously, policies play a major role in the shaping of Europe, and as such contribute to the ways in which local populations experience and imagine the EU. Bellier and Wilson (2000:17) have argued that institutional discourses have a direct impact on the construction of European identity, inside and outside institutional boundaries. The deterritorialization of political practices and policies means that the European discourse and vision – even if incoherent and heterogeneous – penetrates other levels of society and therefore shapes some of the ways of imagining Europe. In return, individuals, groups, political parties, or nations engage with the European sphere in an effort to impose their vision or protect their interests. The politicization of culture has come to play a major role in several of the national debates, as has been the case in Norway or more recently in France, demonstrating the limits of the use of culture in the political arena.

At a national level, the issues of multiculturalism and immigration have become an increasingly significant and contested part of the political agenda. In France, for example, President Sarkozy has launched a major debate on national identity, resulting in, amongst other things, a proposal to outlaw the burqa in public buildings. Several anthropologists have commented on the increasing upsurge of "cultural anxiety" (Grillo 2003) exploited by political parties of both the mainstream and the fringe together with a "backlash against difference" (Grillo 2002:15) and a reassertion of core values. France, to some extent, crystallizes these cultural anxieties, and the election of Sarkozy in 2007 was seen by some commentators as the triumph of both the right and extreme right. Yet, paradoxically, the president immediately appointed left-wing ministers, illustrating the new kind of ideological shift in political beliefs defined by Douglas Holmes (2000) as "integralism." In a fascinating study of the European Union, Holmes (2000) demonstrated convincingly the links between what he perceived as "fast-capitalism" and what he called "integralism," a term he applied to those political movements or parties in Europe that are capable of integrating heterogeneous elements that appear to be neither "left nor right," "integralism" being defined as a sensibility under which he subsumes all kinds of chauvinistic, territorially based essentialism that, in its most benign form, enables people to maintain their ethnic identity and solidarity within the context of an increasingly pluralistic society. For Holmes, "integralism" plays a key role in shaping mainstream political discourse on Europe and exclusionary policy practices.

The rejection of the EU constitution by French and Dutch voters in spring 2005 could be seen as a landmark in the project of further European integration, although in reality for many the vote was seen as an opportunity to pass judgment on the national government. However, one might ask if Europe has really something to do with this rejection, as most voters had little or no knowledge of Europe and its projects. The political climate was described as tense and questions were raised both about the development of Europe without the blessing of Europeans and the impact of a growing multicultural context. Yet most political leaders decided in the second round of "democratic consultation" to use their national parliaments to ratify the revised constitutional treaty. Among the various anxieties raised by the European public during the consultative process, issues of immigration and integration were seen of primary concern. A rhetoric of belonging seems to have taken more salience in various parts of the European continent. Across political parties and national debates, the definition of "others" has penetrated the political sphere. According to Gingrich (2006:197), the position most of these right-wing political parties and movements take toward multicultural topics in general, and the issue of immigration and integration in particular, can be identified as a major similarity among them. Specific essentialized forms of identity have always served as important mobilizing factors in the success of these groups and parties.

What seems to be undeniable is that so far Europeanization has provoked a powerful discourse of negativity which represents an obstacle for further political integration. Anthropologists have contributed to the critical assessment of Europe as a political object, by engaging more forcefully with some of the key issues set up by the European Union. Irène Bellier (2008:605–616) noted recently the relative absence of social anthropologists in the European Research Area, which she sees as a world to be built. By engaging with other disciplines such as political sciences and international relations, and by fighting nationally defined disciplinary boundaries and adopting a constructive approach to the establishment of a collective research agenda, anthropologists of Europe and its institutions can become more visible and can be heard.

Conclusion

As discussed in this chapter, policy-making has been a focus of many anthropological studies of European integration and Europeanization, but work remains to be done in terms of consolidating the discipline's position in the field of European Studies. The "Anthropology of Europe" needs to establish itself as a recognized research landscape through the establishment of an ambitious research program, through a dialogue with other social sciences, especially politics and international relations, and the development of a postgraduate community. This could be achieved through various strategies, but the visibility of the discipline needs to be emphasized through more collaboration and discussion of anthropology's distinctive contribution. The European research agenda should also take account of new EU members, and new methodological or intellectual issues ought to be discussed in a constructive fashion, as was the case with publications dealing with multiculturalism or belonging (Modood and Werbner 1997; Gingrich and Banks 2006).

According to Michael Herzfeld (2008), anthropology has long served as the basis of a critique of Western supremacism, which makes it politically unpopular in many circles. For him, it is nevertheless important as the source of grassroots-level insights into concealed dimensions of cultural politics, including the contents of various countries' zones of cultural intimacy, the dynamics of racism within "civil society," and especially because it serves as the most substantive critique of Eurocentrism (the uncritical assumption of Western, and especially European, superiority). For all these reasons, anthropology is a source of critique; it is also, from the perspective of some of the more rigid state structures, subversive – but this is what renders it important, since (unlike some other social sciences) it is not commonly implicated in large-scale policy-making. By combining ethnographic and empirical research with a cultural perspective, anthropologists are in a unique position to offer a critical interpretation of the process of European integration and to illustrate the impact of culture in any process of political change. Both international relations and the political sciences have witnessed a cultural turn in recent years, and perhaps it is time for anthropologists to engage further with these disciplines and contribute to the wider debates surrounding the European question and the issue of culture.

A growing number of academics have started to question the social constructions and categorizations attached to the concept of Europe. By the same token, national ethnographies are reevaluated within a more European or global context which sees both debates about teaching and research at national level. The volume published by Peter Skalník in 2007 entitled *Anthropology: Teaching and Research* reflects this trend in Central and Eastern Europe. As pointed out by Bellier and Wilson (2000:1–27), Europe is as much a construction as it is a reality, which makes the anthropological discipline the perfect match for an understanding of social and cultural processes. The study of European integration is dominated by the growing role of political sciences, which has frequently borrowed some of anthropology's qualitative methodological tools. Time is ripe to engage with other disciplines and bring our cultural expertise back to the center of the debate on the EU and on the relationship between culture and politics.

NOTES

1 The above statistics are gathered from the Eurobarometer survey of 2009 and can be found at http://www.europarl.europa.eu/pdf/eurobarometre/EB70/5603ElectionsEuropeennes_finalEN.pdf (accessed November 5, 2011).

REFERENCES

Abélès, Marc

1993 Political Anthropology of a Transnational Institution: The European Parliament. French Politics and Society 11(1):1–19.

2000 Virtual Europe. *In* An Anthropology of the European Union: Building, Imagining and Experiencing the New Europe. Irène Bellier and Thomas M. Wilson, eds. pp. 31–52. Oxford: Berg.

2004 Debating the European Union: An Interview with Cris Shore and Marc Abélès. Anthropology Today 20(2):10–15.

Bellier, Irène, and Thomas M. Wilson, eds.

2000 An Anthropology of the European Union: Building, Imagining and Experiencing the New Europe. Oxford: Berg.

Bellier, Irène
2008 L'anthropologie dans l'Espace européen de la recherche: Un monde à construire. *In* L'Europe et ses ethnologies. Theme Issue. Ethnologie française 4:605–616.
Borneman, John, and Nick Fowler
1997 Europeanization. Annual Review of Anthropology 26:487–514.
Charlemagne
2010 Allons, citoyens de l'Europe. Economist January 14. Electronic document. http://www.economist.com/node/15269065 (accessed December 29, 2011).
Demossier, Marion
1999 Hommes et vins: Une anthropologie du vignoble bourguignon. Dijon: Éditions universitaires de Dijon.
2007 The European Puzzle: The Construction of European Identities at a Time of Transition. Oxford: Berghahn.
2010 Wine Drinking Culture in France: A National Myth or a Modern Passion? Cardiff: University of Wales Press.
Ekiert, Grzegorz
2008 Dilemmas of Europeanization: Eastern and Central Europe after the Enlargement. Acta Slavica Iaponica 25:1–28.
Fassin, Didier
2001 The Biopolitics of Otherness: Undocumented Foreigners and Racial Discrimination in French Public Debate. Anthropology Today 17(1):3–7.
Faure, Muriel
1999 Un produit agricole "affiné" en objet culturel. Terrain 33:81–92.
Feldman, Gregory
2005 Essential Crises: A Performative Approach to Migrants, Minorities and the European Nation State. Anthropological Quarterly 78(1):213–246.
Firat, Bilge
2009 Negotiating Europe/Avrupa: Prelude for an Anthropological Approach to Turkish Europeanization and the Cultures of EU Lobbying in Brussels. European Journal of Turkish Studies 9:1–17.
Garzon, Isabelle
2007 Reforming the Common Agricultural Policy: History of a Paradigm Change. London: Palgrave Macmillan.
Gingrich, Andre
2006 Introduction: Re-defining Europe: Perspectives From Socio-Cultural Anthropology. Social Anthropology 14(2):161–162.
Gingrich, Andre, and Marcus Banks, eds.
2006 Neo-nationalism in Europe. Oxford: Berghahn.
Gingrich, Andre, and Richard G. Fox, eds.
2002 Anthropology by Comparison. London: Routledge.
Grasseni, Christina
2003 Packaging Skills: Calibrating Cheese to the Global Market. *In* Commodifying Everything. Susan Strasser, ed. pp. 259–288. London: Routledge.
Grillo, Ralph
2002 Towards a Multicultural Europe. Slovak Foreign Policy Affairs 3(2):12–22.
2003 Cultural Essentialism and Cultural Anxiety. Anthropological Theory 3(2):157–173.
2007 European Identity in a Transnational Era. *In* The European Puzzle: The Political Structuring of Cultural Identities at a Time of Transition. Marion Demossier, ed. pp. 67–82. Oxford: Berghahn.

Herzfeld, Michael
2008 Cultural Intimacy and the Reconfiguration of Nationalism in 21st-Century Europe: "Bringing People In." Paper presented at the Seminar Anthropological Perspectives in a Changing Europe. Florence, October 23–24.
Holmes, Douglas R
2000 Integral Europe: Fast-capitalism, Multiculturalism, Neofascism. Princeton: Princeton University Press.
Kockel, Ullrich
2007 Heritage versus Tradition: Cultural Resources for a New Europe. *In* The European Puzzle: The Political Structuring of Cultural Identities at a Time of Transition. Marion Demossier, ed. pp. 85–101. Oxford: Berghahn.
Kürti, Lászlo
2008 East and West: The Scholarly Divide in Anthropology. Anthropological Notebooks 14(3):25–38.
Lúbas, Marcin
2008 Culture Across Cultures: Social Boundaries and Mutuality in a Western Macedonian Village. Paper presented at the European Association of Social Anthropologists, Ljubljana, August 26–30.
McDonald, Maryon
1996 "Unity in Diversity." Some Tensions in the Construction of Europe. Social Anthropology 4(1):47–60.
2005 EU Policy and Destiny: A Challenge For Anthropology. Anthropology Today 21(1):3–4.
Modood, Tariq, and Pnina Jane Werbner, eds.
1997 The Politics of Multiculturalism in the New Europe. London: Macmillan.
Pero, Davide
2008 Doing Ethnography and Getting Involved: Reflections From Researching Immigration, Exclusion and Resistance. Paper presented at the European Association of Social Anthropologists, Ljubljana, August 26–30.
Pratt, Jeff
2007 Food Values: The Local and the Authentic. Critique of Anthropology 27(3): 285–300.
Ribiero, Gustavo Links, and Arturo Escobar, eds.
2006 World Anthropologies: Disciplinary Transformations within Systems of Power. Wenner–Gren International Symposium Series.
Sencar, Bajuk
2008 Shifts in European Identity within the Institutions of the European Union. Paper presented at the European Association of Social Anthropologists Conference, Llubljana, August 26–30.
Shore, Cris
2000 Building Europe: The Cultural Politics of European Integration. London: Routledge.
2004 Debating the European Union: An Interview with Cris Shore and Marc Abélès. Anthropology Today 20(2):10–15.
Shore, Cris, and Susan Wright, eds.
1997 Anthropology of Policy: Critical Perspectives on Governance and Power. London: Routledge.
Skalník, Peter, ed.
2005 Studies in Sociocultural Anthropology, vol. 3. Anthropology: Teaching and Research. Prague: SetOut.

Verlot, Marc
2001 Are Politicians Human? Problems and Challenges of Institutional Anthropology. Social Anthropology 9(3):345–353.
Vertovec, Steven, and Suzanne Wessendorf
2010 The Multiculturalism Backlash: European Discourses, Policies and Practices. London: Routledge.
Wedel, Janine R., and Gregory Feldman
2005 Why an Anthropology of Public Policy. *In* Theme issue. Anthropology Today 21(1):1–2.
Wilson, Thomas M.
1998 An Anthropology of the European Union, from Above and Below. *In* Europe in the Anthropological Imagination. Susan Parman, ed. pp. 148–156. Upper Saddle River: Prentice Hall.
Wolfe, Thomas.C.
2000 Cultures and Communities in the Anthropology of Eastern Europe and the Former Soviet Union. Annual Review of Anthropology 29:195–216.
Zabusky, Stacia E.
2000 Boundaries at Work: Discourses and Practices of Belonging in the European Space Agency. *In* An Anthropology of the European Union: Building, Imagining and Experiencing the New Europe. Irène Bellier and Thomas M. Wilson, eds. pp. 179–200. Oxford: Berg.
1995 Launching Europe: An Ethnography of European Cooperation in Space Science. Princeton: Princeton University Press.
Zielonka, Jan
2007 Europe as Empire: The Nature of the Enlarged European Union. Oxford: Oxford University Press.

PART III European Heritages

CHAPTER 14

Presencing Europe's Pasts

Sharon Macdonald

How people variously experience, construct, perform, contest, and understand the past has become the focus of intense interest and extensive ethnographic research in the anthropology of Europe. It is discussed under numerous labels, such as social memory, historical consciousness, commemorative practice, and cultural heritage; and it is bound up with a massive expansion of interest in these and related topics elsewhere in the academy and in popular culture. The field is vast, and this chapter does not attempt a survey. Instead, through selected examples – many of which come from the fieldwork areas in which I have worked myself – it seeks to highlight what I take to be significant developments, themes, debates, and approaches.

The history of interest in questions about the past is not uniform across the anthropology of Europe. In most continental European countries, history has always been a central and in some respects taken-for-granted aspect of the discipline, with historical methods, including oral history, frequently employed. In British social anthropology, by contrast, those trying to establish an "anthropology of Europe" in the mid-1970s and 1980s frequently identified history as a matter that had been little addressed in earlier studies conducted in Europe and in British social anthropology more generally. The call to pay more attention to history was also a function of the self-evidence of social change and the *presence* of the past, not least in the form of historical documents, in Europe (Silverman and Gulliver 1992:3). Despite these different backgrounds and some continuing variations of emphasis and approach, anthropologies across Europe have seen an increased problematizing of questions of the past and its relationship with the present. Rather than regarding the past primarily as a prelude to the present or as a set of ethnographic worlds to be studied in their own right, the major emphasis of more recent studies is on more constructivist, subjective and present-oriented, approaches to history: that is, on matters such as how pasts are selectively recalled and used within the present, and how they are

A Companion to the Anthropology of Europe, First Edition. Edited by Ullrich Kockel, Máiréad Nic Craith, and Jonas Frykman.

performed and lived. Through in-depth ethnographic case studies, the anthropology of Europe has provided numerous and often nuanced examples of the ways in which people in different parts of Europe may, for instance, construe particular histories for themselves, choose to commemorate certain events and ignore others or express relationships between past, present, and future in their daily lives. Such concern with the past has, indeed, become a major focus in the contemporary anthropology of Europe.

While important strands of this work have sought to explore how national histories make themselves felt within localities, many studies have highlighted divergences between local and official histories, and between everyday concerns and practices and those at state or national level. This revelation of alternative historical narratives and experiences to those usually recorded in archival records has been a key contribution that the anthropology of Europe has made to understanding both the history of particular nations and of Europe overall. It is important to note that this has not just been a matter of exposing a variety of historical *content* held across Europe. Rather, ethnographic work has also often shown the diversity of ways in which people may grasp and articulate the past, and the multiple *forms* which historicizing may take. As part of this, the anthropology of Europe has contributed not only empirical data about people's constructions of the past, it has also offered methodological and theoretical insight, raising questions about what kinds of "sources" we use in anthropological work and how. The fact that anthropologists working in Europe often experience what we might call "analytic double-take," that is, they find that they are using the same concepts (e.g. tradition, modernity, heritage, nostalgia) as the people they are studying, has sometimes been deemed a challenge to research. But it has also proved a productive lever for raising questions about concepts and models that might otherwise be taken for granted. In what follows, I focus on some of these in order to describe and discuss what I see as some of the most significant contributions of anthropological work on Europe to questions about a field that I term *past presencing*.

Past Presencing

Past presencing is concerned with the ways in which people variously draw on, experience, negotiate, reconstruct, and perform the past in their ongoing lives. It is a more specific focus than the anthropology of history, a broad field that sometimes includes historical ethnography. It distinguishes the more recent development noted above – exploring how the past is experienced and performed in the present – from both historical ethnography and the provision of historical narrative in anthropological work or the work of historians themselves. As Silverman and Gulliver note, a "linking of the past with the present seems to be distinctly anthropological" (1992:35).

It also avoids the problematic distinction between "history" and "memory" that has infused many academic and popular accounts. In some of these, history stands as the established and verified past relative to memory's individual and relatively fallible accounts. In others, in an interesting twist, history is the canonical and thus relatively untrustworthy other to memory's subjective veracity. Of course, any attempt to refine a field can make consideration of such questions part of its subject matter, and this has been the case especially in more recent work in the anthropology of history and that of memory and in memory studies more generally. "Memory," like "history," however, is an equally and perhaps even more enormous field, including matters such as cognitive capacities to remember day-to-day tasks, as well as topics such as commemoration and reminiscence work. It also raises further methodological problems, such as the tendency to conceptualize social or cultural memory on models of individual memory, and thus sometimes to naturalize the kinds of processes involved. In addition, it does not lead readily to consideration of the way in which the past may establish particular frameworks or contexts for action – for example, through material effects – beyond issues of remembering and forgetting (at least as these are usually conceived). For these reasons, and also because the frequently rehearsed debates about various possible terminologies – social memory, cultural memory, remembrance, and so on – seem to me less productive than the questions that I can raise through a focus on "past presencing," I prefer the latter, more specific, demarcation of the field. I should note that, nevertheless, a good deal of what I will discuss might also be considered under the labels of anthropology of "memory" or "history," and that these terms feature frequently in what is to follow.

Other alternatives, such as focusing on cultural heritage or commemoration, are valid but overly constrict the field, preventing potentially fertile cross-cutting analysis of what are surely linked phenomena. Another possible alternative label, which I have used elsewhere – as have others, especially in Germany and Scandinavia – and that I use in part of what is to follow is that of "historical consciousness." One advantage of "historical consciousness" over history and memory is that it more readily draws attention to questions of the frameworks through which the past is conceptualized and presented. However, it seems to restrict its focus to matters about which participants are consciously aware and to privilege the cognitive rather than also taking into account the more experiential, embodied, and felt aspects of relating to the past – areas which are increasingly being emphasized in ethnographic work. Past presencing, by contrast, is intended to draw attention to the multiple ways in which the past may be (and be made to be) present – as well as represented – whether articulated verbally or experienced and performed in other ways.

I should note here that while there is an inherent presentism in the field that I have demarcated, insofar as it is concerned with mobilizations of the past at particular moments, these may themselves be moments in the past; and, indeed, any recorded moment is already past. As such, "the present" is an analytical standpoint for conducting research and not privileged as inherently more worthwhile to study than "the past" itself. It is simply a different field from that of history. It should also be noted that "past presencing" does not necessarily rule out consideration of matters such as how the present and future are conceived, for these – and questions of temporality more widely – are almost invariably bound up in the presencing of the past.

In what follows, I look at various dimensions of past presencing that have been highlighted by ethnographic work in Europe. Although these are presented separately here, one feature of ethnographic work is that it is usually fairly complex, with attention to a wide array of practices and experience even within single studies. What this also means is that while there are some trends that can be identified in terms of general emphases of interest, the overall picture is one of the establishment of a *range* of areas of focus and of approaches which may exist side-by-side, sometimes even in the same account. This multiplicity – and the play and tensions between the various dimensions – is part of the strength and liveliness of this field.

Making Histories, Traditions, and Europes

The 1980s saw new levels of exploration of the relationship between the past and the present in anthropology and various other disciplines. In particular, interest burgeoned in the way in which histories could be constructed or traditions invented (Hobsbawm and Ranger 1983). A major focus was on histories and genealogies created by nation-states – especially European – as part of their self-legitimation. The interest was also fueled by a growing identity politics, in which minorities of various kinds sought to challenge aspects of nation-state hegemony and at the same time asserted their own cultural and historical distinctiveness.

Attention to the calculated construction of historical accounts and tradition invention was not without precedent in European anthropology. In Germany, for example, the way that the National Socialists had devised histories and genealogies, and created traditions and monuments – and the role that German *Volkskunde* (folklore) had played in this – meant that there was certainly awareness of how the past could be manipulated to political ends. But while this contributed to some revision of disciplinary perspective, not least in prompting some institutes to rename themselves as either *Europäische Ethnologie* (European Ethnology) or *Empirische Kulturwissenschaft* (Empirical Cultural Studies), it did not foreground the construction of the past as a general topic for anthropological researchers. This was in part a function of the fact that the main emphasis in anthropological work in Europe before the 1980s was on looking at what were perceived as more persistent and minority folkways, distinct from the nation-state and regarded as part of authentic ways of life, rather than studied in relation to questions of calculation or political maneuvering.

This did not mean that traditions were always perceived as fixed and unchanging; though the tendency was to see them, if not as stable, as adaptively responding to change. Hermann Bausinger's *Folklore in a World of Technology* (1990), originally published in German in 1961, drew attention to the making of traditions in modern societies, arguing that ethnologists should give consideration to matters such as how modern technologies became the subject matter of new lore; and arguing that it was as legitimate to study what he called "second-hand traditions" – those adopted and usually altered by people who did not originally produce them – as "first-hand" ones. Eugenia Shanklin's ethnographic study of sheep farmers in southwest Donegal – a part of the world in which it was commonly assumed that traditions were dying out – likewise pointed out that rather than disappearing, "traditions" were changing "in order to fit present circumstances" (1985:xiii) and that this was probably the usual rather than exceptional state of affairs. Although Shanklin's work partly fits the pre-1980s emphasis on tradition-making as adaptive, she also makes a significant move that is characteristic of the turn that begins in the 1980s. This is to treat "tradition" not as a given or as something that she, as the anthropological analyst, is straightforwardly able to identify, but as a discursive construct. As such, her work charts how the term is deployed and what gets to be *counted* as "tradition." In an innovative chapter, she presents the voices of five different farmers, showing how "tradition" could be variously opposed to "modernity," sometimes being viewed as worth preserving and at other times as something to be transcended in order to develop.

Discourses of this type amongst those studied, together with self-evident change, were also part of what prompted attention to questions about what was "traditional," what kinds of "past" persisted into the present or what aspects of the present came to be inscribed as part of a longer, more enduring temporality. The development of cultural tourism and the marketing of tradition and heritage – and a set of wider developments that got dubbed with names such as "heritage epidemic" and "memory boom" – also brought to the fore questions about "tradition" as a resource for selling places and the consequences for localities of the marketing of the past, as I discuss further below. This came together with a wider reflexive critique of anthropological disciplines, questioning their own search for tradition and "authenticity," and the ways in which this might play into certain perceptions of Europe (Herzfeld 1982, 1987; Bendix 1997).

While Hobsbawm's original formulation of "invented traditions" defined these primarily on the grounds of their rapid establishment ("a matter of a few years perhaps," 1983:1), often coupled with drawing up longer histories for themselves, it fueled a distinction between invented and noninvented traditions, in which the latter were assumed to be outside political process and somehow more authentic. "Traditional societies," Hobsbawm speculated, would have much less invented tradition owing to their greater social and political stability. As Eric Wolf's *Europe and the People without History* (1982) had shown, however, many non-European cultures were falsely depicted as traditional and unchanging – as somehow outside history – and this was part of a constitutive role that they were made to play in the imagining of Europe. The same was also true, as various anthropologists came to argue, of many parts of Europe itself, especially those favored as field sites by anthropologists: depicted as outside or untainted by wider global and national historical and political processes, they were construed as repositories of authentic traditionality.

One way in which ethnographers of Europe sought to tackle this was by emphasizing how supposedly marginal areas were *part of* wider historical and political processes: the ethnographic present, in other words, was situated *in* history instead of sealed off from it. For example, researchers in the Hebrides showed how an apparently traditional practice such as crofting (a form of landholding in which people have small amounts of land in order to be able to undertake small-scale farming) was not the ancient way of life that some romanticized accounts presented it as being but a product of nineteenth-century capitalist development which served to bind local populations into unfavorable labor relations that maximized profits for landlords (e.g. Parman 1990; Macdonald 1997a). This did not mean that this way of life had not taken on other meanings since, but ethnographers saw part of their task as to look beyond the immediate to try to see where different ideas about traditionality and related notions, such as community, might have come from and what this might also show about the present. My own experience of this kind of work was that reading historical materials – and especially primary sources – helped me to better understand some of the selections (and silences) involved in official or better-known accounts of Scottish Highland history, and thus meant that I was aware of what was *not* recalled or that I was alerted to understated or coded forms of expression that I might not have noticed otherwise. For example, in everyday speech there were sometimes subtle allusions to people whose families had gained from the redistributions of land following the nineteenth-century land wars that I would have been less likely to notice if I had kept in mind only the popular accounts of local togetherness and community, and not the more complex situation that the primary sources revealed (1997). This did not mean that my aim was to dismiss popular or romanticized accounts: on the contrary, I also attempted to explore how they were variously mobilized and put to work – for example to distinguish different kinds of people or moral positions – in everyday life.

Anthropological work of this kind, then, took on board the notion of histories and traditions as created but instead of viewing this as just a feature of *some* histories and traditions, it regarded history-making – and present-making – as more ramifying ongoing processes with continuing implications. In doing so, it also showed that making histories was not the preserve of political elites – though, getting to hear other kinds of accounts, which were typically relatively inaudible both in the historical record and in the present, posed a greater methodological challenge. This was, however, one which anthropologists were well-placed to tackle, with their attention to those who were beyond the political mainstream and with their methodologies for attending to orally recounted memories or expressions embedded in everyday life.

Other Histories and Historical Consciousnesses

By exploring local memories and other ways of telling the past in everyday life, and also by exploring lesser-used archival sources, anthropologists of Europe were able to reveal what a volume edited by Kirsten Hastrup referred to as "other histories," that is, accounts that differ from more mainstream or official ones, thus "demonstrating the inherent plurality of history in Europe . . . [and] breaking down modern European history's alleged uniqueness and unity" (1992:1). In some cases, this constituted major challenges to official accounts, prompting wider revisionism or even political outrage. In others, it exposed not just differing memories of the past but also alternative ways of conceptualizing the nature of history and temporality.

Work of this kind came from many parts of Europe. One particularly productive location, however, was Greece, ethnographers of which contributed some especially rich studies that drew attention to questions of history-making and historical consciousness; and for that reason I choose in this section to present Greek examples as illustrations of some of the significant directions in past presencing in the anthropology of Europe. That Greece was the location for such significant work was in some ways not surprising, as Michael Herzfeld argued, in that it had occupied an ambivalent position of being, on the one hand, the historical "ancestor" of Europe and thus in a sense the most "European" of Europe's countries, and, on the other, of being relatively marginal within the newer European economy and polity (1987). In addition, the complex history of the Ottoman Empire, World War II occupation and

Civil War; of strong nationalism on the one hand and, on the other, strong regional and island identities, ethnic minorities, and several and shifting borders with other countries, all contributed to Greece as an especially fertile ground for exploring questions of relations between past and present, and what was "remembered," why, and how.

One theme in past-presencing research in Greece, as indeed elsewhere, was the construction of national histories and the ways in which these intersected with local or regional accounts of the past, these sometimes differing and at other times being mutually reinforcing. Inevitably, this raised questions about nationalist historical narratives, as in Anastasia Karakasidou's *Fields of Wheat, Hills of Blood: Passages to Greek Macedonia 1870–1990* (1997). Although Karakasidou began with a model – rooted in her own upbringing and education in Greece – of "local Greeks" and "refugees" who had arrived later from elsewhere, her historical and ethnographic research showed that rather than there being a "pure Greek" historical trajectory back to the ancient kingdom of Macedon, Slavic speakers had continually been present, and in greater numbers than usually acknowledged. They had, however, been written out of the official national historical record and had also often come to conceal their Slavic identities in everyday life. Thus her work showed revision of histories at national, regional, and even personal levels. Conducted at a time when the question of Macedonia was becoming even more politically contested – namely, in the aftermath of the breakup of Yugoslavia and the establishment of an area north of Greece as the Former Yugoslav Republic of Macedonia, an independent, Slavic, country – her work was widely seen as unpatriotic. Not only did this show the significance with which history was imbued, it also highlighted some of the particular challenges that might be faced by anthropologists working on such questions in their own countries. The fact that some of the most notable works on Greek past presencing came from anthropologists based elsewhere – or those, like Karakasidou, who were partly educated and lived abroad – was surely not coincidental.

One of the most difficult aspects of her research for Karakasidou to deal with was the fact that the model of which she was critical was widely shared by the people with whom she worked. Alternative, or "other histories," were relatively muted not only in the historical record but also in daily life. Other researchers of Greece too found that there was often indirection in addressing certain perspectives or pasts. Michael Herzfeld has shown how (in this case, of Rethemnos, Crete) because "criticism of the national ideal is unthinkable, the alternative must suffice. They fight against the bureaucrats" (1991:xiv). In fieldwork in central Greece, Anna Collard was puzzled to discover that villagers would make "constant comment" (1989:95) about a late eighteenth- to early nineteenth-century "Ottoman period" as though they had directly lived through it, while mostly ignoring the more recent traumatic period of German occupation in the early 1940s. On the one hand, reference to the Ottoman period – "celebrated as a time of freedom fighters (and brigands), of national resistance, of patriotism and heroic deeds" (1989:96) – fostered links "with a national culture of patriotism, Greek heroism, and ideas about a united Greek nation." Equally, however, it allowed an indirect way of talking about "a less officially acceptable past" and "the 'forbidden' topic of self-government during the occupation period" (1989:97). As well as showing how selective "social memory" (as Collard called these mobilizations of the past in daily life) could be used to morally evaluate the present, Collard's work also showed interesting "other historical consciousnesses," to adapt Hastrup's term. For the Greek villagers not only made their own particular selections from the historical record, they also flouted usual temporalities, for example in their collapsing of certain distant time periods together or talking about a period before they were born as though they had directly experienced it.

Other work, too, showed not just other histories but other historical consciousnesses. Michael Herzfeld's extensive Greek ethnography often addressed such questions. In *A Place in History* (1991), for example, he explored how the people of Rethemnos, in their fight to resist bureaucratic controls on what alterations they were allowed to make to their homes, attempt to "reclaim their lives from a detemporalized past and a desocialized present, and to develop other kinds of historical consciousness" (1991:9–10) than that of the "monumental conception of history" – or "monumental time" – produced by the modern bureaucratic nation-state. These other historical consciousnesses are rooted instead in what he calls "social time." As Herzfeld explains:

> Between social and monumental time lies a discursive chasm, separating the popular from official understandings of history. Social time is the grist of everyday experience. It is above all the kind of time in which events cannot be predicted but in which every effort can be made to influence them. It is the time that gives events their reality, because it encounters each as one of a kind. Monumental time, by contrast, is reductive and generic. It encounters events as realizations of some supreme destiny, and it reduces social experience to collective predictability. Its main focus is on the past – a past constituted by categories and stereotypes. (1991:10)

By exploring the contests over restoration and conservation of property in Rethemnos, Herzfeld was able, then, not only to illustrate the fact that people chose different historical periods to preserve or obliterate but also how these selections were thoroughly embedded in ongoing social relations and specific ways of conceptualizing time and the nature of history. Importantly, this shaped not only the town's present but also its future – creating a physical heritage that would endure into the future and, in the process, making certain other histories less visible in the future townscape (see also Herzfeld 2009).

This attention to physical and embodied dimensions of the past or memory is a further major theme of research on past presencing, as I discuss further below. It expands upon the more discursively focused aspects of historical consciousness, highlighting that the ways in which the past is apprehended and mobilized are not necessarily only linguistic. This is well illustrated in the final example that I want to discuss in this section: David Sutton's *Memories Cast in Stone: The Relevance of the Past in Everyday Life* (1998). A detailed ethnography of the island of Kalymnos, it addresses the question: "How does the past matter in the present?" Taking "historical consciousness as its subject" (1998:9), Sutton explains that a good deal of his book *is* concerned with the discursive, especially as it occurs in everyday life – in conversations, comments, and asides as well as lengthier historical narratives. To this end, he provides a rich account of different modes of talking about history – for example, as something relatively autonomous or as providing analogical patterns for the present.

But this is not all there is to it. Historical consciousness, he writes, "comes in many forms other than articulated written or oral histories" (1998:10) – and these do not necessarily "say" the same thing: "discursive, narrated historical consciousness is sometimes supplemented by, sometimes contradicted by, ritual and kinship practices" as well as by other embodied practices. For example, he describes a ritualized throwing of dynamite (as dangerous as it sounds) at Easter, which "subtly bring[s] to mind different periods of the island's past" – ones which "often remain unarticulated in everyday conversation because direct articulation would explicitly question the relationship between Kalymnos and the local and national authorities" (Sutton 1998).

This need for indirection, so often found in anthropological work on Greece but also elsewhere in Europe (e.g. Skultans 1998; Jerman 2006), is in part due to the fact that those involved "see the past as alive and active in the present" (Sutton 1998:203). Such a past, Sutton suggests, "has the potential to be dangerous to the present." This he regards as rather different from "cut off history" (a notion he adapts from Collingwood 1939) – that is, pasts that are "commodified for tourist consumption, museumified, made an object of nostalgia" (1998). At the time that he was writing, such pasts seemed to be becoming increasingly prevalent in Europe (and indeed elsewhere) and, as the following section discusses, have themselves been the subject of considerable attention from anthropologists – not all of whom found them as "cut off" from the present as others expected.

Commodification, Heritage, and Nostalgia

The increase in pasts that were variously performed in heritage sites and museums – a development that was sometimes dubbed "the heritage industry" (Hewison 1987) – was regarded by some researchers not only as an alternative to the more everyday histories with which anthropologists such as Sutton were concerned, but as deeply worrying. Davydd J. Greenwood, in an article originally published in 1977, expressed particularly starkly what he saw as the dangers involved. On the basis of study of the town of Fuenterrabia in Northern Spain as it became a tourist-magnet from the late 1960s, Greenwood charts how an annual ritual commemoration of a siege of 1638 – a commemoration of a historical event in which local people forgot their differences and all worked to resist and triumph over outsiders – was turned from a meaningful celebration of local togetherness into a tourist spectacle. Due to the number of tourists wanting to view the ritual, the municipal council decided in 1969 to charge for entry to the town to see it and also required the local population to perform it twice in order to maximize viewing opportunities. This, Greenwood argues, is a "commodification of culture" in which paying confers rights, and local meanings are subsumed to these economic interests. Local people, he reports, became reluctant to participate. More widely, he suggests, we are seeing a growth of such commodification, a process which "robs people of the very meanings by which they organize their lives" (1989:179).

Although in a postscript to his earlier article, Greenwood drew back from some of the most generalizing aspects of his analysis, he retained his concern – a concern which found numerous echoes in many areas of public discourse and academia as well as anthropology. One text that expressed this especially well, and that became widely cited, was *The Heritage Industry* (1987), by cultural critic Robert Hewison. The new emphasis on the past that was sweeping Britain, as most of the rest of Europe, was, he argued, basically about selling the past because of a loss of real manufacturing industry and with nothing much else to flog. What was being sold in the numerous heritage sites springing up around the country was a rose-tinted nostalgic vision of the past, in which people knew their place and could feel a sense of both local and national significance and pride. There was certainly insight in this lively analysis; and there has recently been a call by some anthropologists elsewhere in Europe to return to the hard-hitting questions about the commodification of heritage and politicized constructions of history that were forcefully raised by Hewison and others (Frank 2007). But the original arguments – unlike those of Greenwood – were largely made without attention to how these developments were being viewed on the ground; the people who lived in heritage locations or visited them being largely cast as dupes, sedated into nostalgic, romanticized views of the past by calculating heritage industry entrepreneurs. In other words, the arguments were largely made without the kinds of perspectives that anthropologists – on the basis of firsthand fieldwork – could bring to bear.

Prompted by what was going on in their fieldwork locations as well as the wider debates, anthropologists in the 1990s began to provide more of these on-the-ground perspectives – and thus to provide a more informed as well as nuanced picture of the kinds of relationships to the past involved in the booming of heritage and tradition. Jeanette Edwards, for example, working in a former mill town in the north of England, argued that local people's concerns with preserving their industrial past were not about an externally imposed romantic nostalgia for that period but more a way of themselves – variously and in particular contexts – making claims of belonging through knowledge of local history (1998). Some forms of preserving or restoring the past, such as in the local museum, would be enthusiastically supported by some locals, she showed, while other plans, such as to erect "Victorian railings" in the town centre, would be soundly rejected. What was involved was not some blanket nostalgia for the past or a wish to return to it but a select discourse embedded in ongoing social relations. My own work on the Isle of Skye likewise highlighted a range of different kinds of past presencing, whose variability, I argued, "depends upon the politics, social relations and technologies in which they are enmeshed" (1997:31).

What I encountered in the field also directly challenged some of the ideas about heritage as "safe" or sanitized history, and as "cut off" from the present. A new heritage centre that at first glance seemed to neatly fit some of the suspicions about a dangerous commodification of history turned out to tell a rather different story (Macdonald 1997b). Although it *was* intended as a commercial venture, for which tourists and others would have to pay, this was not all that it was. Set up by young Gaelic-speaking entrepreneurs, the exhibition that they created sought, they said, to tell a different, more radical, "people's" history from the one that they saw being performed in other heritage locations on the island – especially the castles of the landowning clan chiefs, a false history that they referred to as "myth." The exhibition presented a historical narrative in which Gaelic language and culture managed to persist against the odds, readily absorbing external cultural influences as it did so.

This account also supported one of their main – very conscious – intentions: to oppose the distinction so often made between "commerce" and "authenticity." By being entrepreneurial and marketing aspects of their history, they were not selling it off or selling it short, but helping to support the local economy and raise awareness – for local people as well as tourists – of a more radical popular history which could shore up contemporary local identity.

More conventional performances of heritage or tradition too could be used to manifest local identities or make negative moral evaluations of dimensions of modernity. Referring again to my own work on Skye, a museum of folk life established by an islander was neither a straightforward product of "the heritage industry" nor a reaction to modernity in the way that Pierre Nora had so famously argued of what he called *lieux de memoire* (usually translated as "sites" or "realms" of memory) in a series of volumes first published in French between 1984 and 1992. Instead, the museum was both intended as a moral commentary on what its maker regarded as negative aspects of modernity – including commentary on commodification processes themselves – and, at the same time, it was a sensuous evocation of a valued past through material objects – "old things" (Macdonald 2002a).

Anthropological studies such as these also problematized cultural critics' use of terms such as "authenticity" and "nostalgia." Because such terms were deployed by those being studied, they called out for analysis as part of the cultural field. What this usually showed was how they might be contested and used to make evaluative judgments; and also how their meaning or referents might change. Attending to this could often provide a powerful lens on to subtle changes underway. One of the most interesting examples of this was nostalgia for aspects of the socialist past in some postsocialist countries.

Daphne Berdahl's account of this in Germany – where it went under the name *Ostalgie* ("nostalgia for the East") – is one of the most insightful of these. What she argues, essentially, is that there have been different phases of *Ostalgie*, none of which has as its object or objective "recovery of a lost past" (2010:55). The first arose in the early 1990s, after an initial rejection of all things Eastern, and was, she argues, about those from the former German Democratic Republic asserting "identity as East Germans" (2010:43). This was mostly a fairly low-key minority movement, instances including middle-aged women wearing the work-smocks that they had discarded in the immediate aftermath of the *Wende* (transition). By the mid-1990s, however, a "nostalgia industry" seemed to have developed, with increased production and consumption of East German products, such as particular brands of beer or detergent (Berdahl 2010), and also special East German ("Ossi") discos and television shows. It was commonly reported in the press as a rather retrograde romanticization of the socialist past engineered by capitalist entrepreneurs. What Berdahl argued, however, on the basis of her long-term, in-depth acquaintance with East Germany (see also Berdahl 1999), was that it allowed them to share and express their knowledge of the former East, "of a period of time that differentiates Ossis" (2010:44). In addition, the focus on consumer products, she suggested, "reveal[ed] a certain mourning for production" (1999), expressive of a sense of real loss. The new millennium saw the continuation of some of these themes, especially that of shared knowledge, but also "a playful appropriation and ironic parody of Ostalgie [in which]

East German things became 'camp' rather than objects of nostalgic longing or counter-memory" (2010:121–2).

Both postsocialist transition and the wider heritage industry, in different ways, then, made clear that dealing with "the past" was neither a once-and-for-all process nor uniform. "Transition" did not entail a straightforward before and after – although it was often thought of as such, as in the idea of it as a "turn" or "new beginning" – but was a longer-term, ongoing process in which the past was continually reconfigured in the changing present. So, too, heritage developments were not simply introduced as a monolithic form and related to in a single enduring way. In both, different approaches and phases could be detected; though these were often quite subtle matters, not easily deduced just by paying attention to the heritage products that were produced. At the same time, however, products – or, more specifically, *material things* – did seem to have considerable significance to both, and to how past presencing was performed more generally.

Material, Embodied, and Affective Pasts

The fact that objects and other material forms – such as heritage sites – have been the focus of so much commemorative activity, or other modes of memory work, in Europe raises questions about the power and role of the material in relation to mediating past, present, and future. It also opens up methodological possibilities of approaching past presencing through a focus on things or embodied events and the experience of them.

While a good deal of the anthropological research already discussed includes some consideration of the material, embodied, and felt – be it in ritual, heritage sites and museum objects, commodities, or townscapes – the main emphasis of that work has been on the discursive and the various ways in which the past is constructed. More thoroughgoing attention to the physical – as I will collectively dub this area – tends to argue that, rather than focusing so heavily on spoken and other representational dimensions of life, research needs to take more account of experience that is not necessarily mediated in this way. Paul Connerton, for example, argues that it is through *performance* of various kinds – he singles out commemorative ceremonies and bodily practices as especially significant – that collectives, such as societies, "remember" (1989). Performance is the instantiation of "habit-memory" (1989:35), a means of keeping "the past . . . in mind by a habitual memory sedimented in the body" (1989:102). Drawing variously upon phenomenology, older anthropological work such as that of Mauss or Hertz, actor–network theory or object-biography approaches among others, more physically oriented research seeks to explore the ways in which, say, objects may evoke particular memories or feelings, or how the past may be materially embodied and capable of working beyond representation. While adjectival versions of all of the terms of the subheading above – material, bodily, affective – have been coupled with the notion of "turns" in anthropology (and other disciplines), we have already noted how the idea of a "turn" can obscure continuities and re-turns, as well as variations. In particular, a good deal of work, especially in relation to discussion of the past, tends to be undertaken in conjunction with attention to the discursive rather than in its exclusion. Nevertheless, the more ramifying and nuanced focus on the physical has produced some significant insights about the nature of past presencing and of the workings of the stuff – the *materia* – of the past in the present.

Nadia Seremetakis has provided some relatively early and compelling discussion (1991, 1994a). In an essay that begins with a sensuous description of her own recollections of a particular kind of peach – known as the Breast of Aphrodite – she explores sensory memories and what she calls "the historical unconscious" (1994b). As she explains:

> The senses are . . . implicated in historical interpretation as witnesses or record-keepers of material experience. There is an autonomous circuit between inner and outer sensory states and fields, that constitutes an independent sphere of perceptual change and reciprocity. (1994b:6)

Memory, she suggests, might be understood as:

> a distinct meta-sense [which] transports, bridges and crosses all the other senses. Yet memory is internal to each sense, and the senses are as divisible and indivisible from each other as each memory is separable and intertwined with others. (1994a:9)

This does not mean that the senses are outside culture – or history. On the contrary, she emphasizes how these are thoroughly mutually implicated. The peach that she remembers has all but disappeared, a consequence of European "economic and social transformations" (1994a:3) – it has become history, in the sense of no longer extant. Her memory is, thus, nostalgic; but as she explains, this kind of nostalgia is not a romantic "freezing" of the past but "evokes the transformative impact of the past as unreconciled historical experience" (1994a:4). A starting point of an object, and the embodied and sensory experiences of it, thus leads into questions of remembrance, both personal but also, inevitably, entangled in wider sociocultural histories. Seremetakis's approach, then, is partly methodological: beginning with a powerful embodied memory and using this as a journey into a specific cultural history, one in which the senses themselves are historicized. It is, however, also a manifesto for recognizing the centrality of the sensory, embodied, and material in how we apprehend history and historicity. Rephrasing one of her questions (which her essay surely answers in the affirmative) as a statement, her argument is that "memory [is] stored in specific everyday items that form the historicity of a culture, items that create and sustain our relationship to the historical as a sensory dimension" (1994a:3).

Seremetakis's emphasis on "everyday items" and experiences is characteristic of much work undertaken in more recent years. It is also worth noting that past presencing research has increasingly been undertaken under the rubric of "memory" – sometimes referred to as "social," sometimes by variations (with different inflections and implications) such as "cultural" or "collective." While this may in part be simply terminological, and influenced by the fact that there is considerable discussion of "memory" across many disciplines and popular culture, it may also reflect another tendency that we see in recent research, namely, to attend closely to individual testimonies and experiences. An example is Cathrine Degnen's research in the former mining and steelworking town of Dodworth in the north of England (2005), in which she reports the significance of what she calls "three-dimensional memory" for the older people whose lives she investigates. This is not concerned for the most part with more publicly visible types of commemoration, centered on monuments or official memorial practices, but on "nearly mundane ways of remembering the past" (2005:730), especially recollections of changes in the townscape and its social use, such as who lived in which houses.

Place is a frequent theme in research on the physical, in both of the types of "place memory" identified by Connerton (2009); namely, the *locus*, a lived taken-for-granted emplacement, as in Degnen's account, and the *memorial* – more active and conscious designation of some places as significant for remembrance. In practice, these "types" often blend into one another or become transformed over time, as, for example, when everyday knowledge and memory become recorded into official memorials and heritage, as Jane Nadel-Klein describes of the fisherfolk of Ferryden, Scotland (2003). The focus on memories of place is not only refracted through accounts of temporal change, however. It is also seen in a flourishing of work on migration, displacement, border crossing, and diaspora (e.g. Hecht 2001; see also Byron, Chapter 4, and Wilson, Chapter 10, in this volume). In these, the role of particular technologies of past presencing – and especially forms of remembrance via material objects – often come to the fore. A comment by one of Helena Jerman's Russian émigré interlocutors in Finland, as they sat together looking at photographs and talking about recollections of movement between places, nicely expresses the capacity of memory, and its technologies, to transport between places: "memory moves" (Jerman 2006:135).

Capacities of different kinds of technologies, materializations or objects to convey memories, or allow access to distant pasts and places, or to generate particular kinds of responses, have been the focus of some recent work. Food – with its direct sensory force and evocative capacities – has generated a good deal of discussion (e.g. Sutton 2001; see also Welz, Chapter 21 in this volume). In a different vein, Paul Basu's study of "roots tourism" to the Scottish Highlands (2007), from places such as Australia and Canada as well as spatially nearer locations, includes consideration of materializations of place and memory, such as in a heritage centre, but also the role of the Internet – especially Web sites dedicated to helping people to trace their ancestors and find past-based connections to locations from which they are now displaced. Daniel Miller, whose work has been very important in foregrounding the significance of material culture, takes a London street and explores the meanings of "things" – which range widely from furnishings to clothing to Internet images – for their various inhabitants (2008). By doing so, he paints a vivid portrait of the multiple memories and capacities with which they are invested. In my own research on Nuremberg, Germany, I sought to explore the question of the significance of particular kinds of forms that endured from the past, especially buildings or architecture (2006, 2009). I focused on the remains of the former Nazi Party Rally Grounds, with their large monumental buildings and spaces, familiar to many from black-and-white film footage. Their relative – but by no means absolute – intransigence to change was one of my concerns here; and, as such, part of my interest was in how material forms can influence beyond the intentions or hopes of some of those struggling to variously forget or otherwise cope with them.

In addition, I wanted to explore remembrance of particular kinds of pasts – in this case, a horrific or "difficult" past – in order to expand and make more differentiated accounts of past presencing. Other recent work has also sought to investigate the capacities of particular kinds of objects, places, and histories and affective responses to them. Elisabeth Hallam and Jenny Hockey (2001), for example, have provided a broad review of ways in which death and remembrance are materialized in European cultures. At a more specific ethnographic level, Yael Navaro-Yashin's research on Turkish-Cypriots' experience of living in houses which before the war and partition of the island belonged to Greek-Cypriots, "officially construed as 'the enemy'" (2009:3), details a particularly intimate uncomfortable presence of the past. These homes – and the things belonging to previous householders with which they are often filled – generate a particular kind of feeling, a "state of mental depression, deep and unrecoverable sadness, and dis-ease," called "*maraz*" in the local dialect and glossed by Navaro-Yashin as melancholia (2009:4). Here, we have physical things – objects and spaces which somehow carry something of the loss experienced by their former owners – coming to occupy their new owners' bodies through powerful and disconcerting affect.

Other studies, too, have described the embodied consequences of memories. Allen Feldman (1991) and Neil Jarman (1997), for example, variously depict the embodiment of Northern Ireland's divided past, in violent acts, political parades, and graffiti. Vieda Skultans explores expressions of recollections of trauma and loss through particular illnesses, especially that of neurasthenia or "nerve damage" in post-Soviet Latvia (1998). Tomasz Rakowski, likewise, finds that discourses of past and present in a postindustrialist, postsocialist Polish village centre on discussions of illnesses (again, especially "derangements of the nervous system") and the possibilities of obtaining – or not obtaining – a pension (2006). What is involved is not only illness as a metaphor, though it is very much used as a way of talking about the sickness of the state and remembrance of healthier times. Beyond this, however, bodies physically incorporate or embody the sense of incapacitating social change. As he puts it: "bodily experience . . . has become the very field of remembering" (2006:43), "The body is a kind of groundwork and creative tool – it is a vast field for the social memory of the last years' transformation as well as for the memory of life itself, the life of these people" (2006:45).

As noted above, some of this work on the material, embodied, and affective has generated new methodologies. Rather than beginning with communities of people, some of it has sought to begin with spaces which people normally encounter on a more transient basis, such as the Rally Grounds that I investigated; and it has also sought to undertake "multitemporal" research, moving between time frames in order to explore the "multidirectional" relationships between past and present (Macdonald 2002b). Andrew Irving's innovative research includes HIV/AIDS sufferers, recording their memories (especially of deaths of friends) as they walk the streets of London, a technique through which he produces new visual and oral records of place as well as memories (2006). In Bucharest, Alyssa Grossman likewise conducted "walking" research, which she describes through the term "chorography," and recorded through the medium of film as well as written account (2010). She also set up a "memory meal" to which she invited acquaintances to bring foods that reminded them of the socialist era – a technique that created an ephemeral encounter in which recollections of the past, and the taste of the past, were exchanged and evaluated. More widely, the use of objects to elicit memories has been used in both academic practice and in contexts such as museums or old peoples' homes (e.g. Arigho 2008; Edwards 2010) – in this way, not only reflecting on questions of the past and memory but also contributing to their production and visibility.

CONCLUSION

A discussion such as this is inevitably partial, in both senses of the term. By couching my account under the term "past presencing" I have sought to cut across some of the usual demarcations of focus, such as that into heritage and commodification on the one hand, and memory and embodiment on the other. By doing so, I hope to have illustrated how all of these are in one way or another concerned with the representation and experience of the past in the present. In this way, my intention is not to suggest a progressive momentum through the areas that I have discussed but to point out the importance of the various questions that they each address and the richness of research that has been carried out. What I have managed to include here is but the tip of an iceberg – or of some of a multitude of icebergs, those of many of Europe's anthropologies and regions having been sadly neglected, or left submerged, through lack of space here.

This is not to say that there have not been some important developments in past presencing research. Recognizing the significance of reflexivity of anthropological (and other) work, of the everyday, of the embodied, and the affective have all added to our understanding of the workings of the present upon the past and – equally important – the past upon the present. But perhaps it is in combination of some of these areas that we will see some of the most significant work in the future. For example, researching the affective consequences of particular heritage formations and the playback of these into heritage-making – perhaps through decisions about how to display the past in public – would cut across these areas in a productive way. So too might investigation into how different historical consciousnesses might produce different experiences, as well as interpretations, of a certain period or remembered place. Or research that moves more explicitly between intimate and domestic mnemonic practices and those of institutional or more official public history. The possibilities are multiple.

Some of these are seen in part in various ongoing areas of research. Interest in the politics of the past continues to flourish but what we see increasingly is that this extends beyond debates about the local and the national to also address the role of the global, Europe or of international policy-making, such as UNESCO heritage developments (see, for example, contributions to Hemme et al. 2007). Topics such as "tradition" are reenergized in relation to these questions, which often raise in a new form dilemmas of local voice and authenticity (see, for example, the discussion of food heritage in Cyprus by Welz (2007) and Chapter 21 in this volume). The inclusion of so-called "intangible heritage" in UNESCO policies also provides further grist for the still relatively undeveloped concern with the differential capacities of different mnemonic forms and media; as well as prompting the need for more anthropological research into the making and implications of legal practice, such as copyright, and the instantiation and remolding of policies in specific lived contexts. The transnationalization of the past and heritage also raise questions about what Levy and Sznaider (2002) have called "cosmopolitan memory" – memories (e.g. of the Holocaust) that are not "contained" by the nation but are of events commemorated beyond the borders of the nations in which they occurred. Anthropological research has only begun to address some dimensions of this (e.g. Daugbjerg 2009; Macdonald 2009); and, certainly, more needs to be done. Without the detailed engaged accounts that anthropologists are able to produce of both the production of the past for the public and its consumption there is a danger that generalizations about how transnational – as well as local and national – histories are produced and operate will colonize policy expectations of the workings of the past in the present.

It is on this note – about the applications and potential implications of anthropological research on past presencing – that I would like to conclude. I have recently argued for the need in the anthropology of Europe in general for more of what I have termed "synthetic work to try to piece together the findings from individual studies" (2008:62). It is clear, I think, from the discussion above that there is scope to bring together ethnographers' rich research findings to bring out some of the wider insights into commonalities and differences in ways of making and experiencing the past in Europe. To do so will not only help to make clear the contribution of anthropology to understanding the nature of memory, heritage, and related areas in Europe but can potentially also contribute productively to the public policy-making, representations and understandings.

REFERENCES

Arigho, Bernie
2008 Getting a Handle on the Past: The Use of Objects in Reminiscence Work. *In* Touch in Museums. H. J. Chatterjee, ed. pp. 205–212. Oxford: Berg.
Bausinger, Hermann
1990 Folk Culture in a World of Technology. E. Detmer, trans. Bloomington: Indiana University Press.
Bendix, Regina
1997 In Search of Authenticity: The Formation of Folklore Studies. Madison: University of Wisconsin Press.
Berdahl, Daphne
1999 Where the World Ended: Re-Unification and Identity in the German Borderland. Berkeley: University of California Press.
2010 On the Social Life of Postsocialism: Memory, Consumption, Germany. Bloomington: Indiana University Press.
Collard, Anna
1989 Investigating "Social Memory" in a Greek Context. *In* History and Ethnicity. E. Tonkin, M. McDonald, and M. Chapman, eds. pp. 89–103. London: Routledge.
Collingwood, R. G.
1939 An Autobiography. Oxford: Oxford University Press.

Connerton, Paul
1989 How Societies Remember. Cambridge: Cambridge University Press.
2009 How Modernity Forgets. Cambridge: Cambridge University Press.
Daugbjerg, Mads
2009 Pacifying War Heritage. International Journal of Heritage Studies 15(5): 431–446.
Degnen, Cathrine
2005 Relationality, Place and Absence: A Three-Dimensional Perspective on Social Memory. Sociological Review 53(4):729–744.
Edwards, Elizabeth
2010 Photographs and History: Emotion and Materiality. *In* Museum Materialities: Objects, Engagements, Interpretations. S. Dudley, ed. pp. 21–38. London: Routledge.
Edwards, Jeanette
1998 The Need for a Bit of History: Place and Past in English Identity. *In* Locality and Belonging. N. Lovell, ed. pp. 147–167. London: Routledge.
Feldman, Allen
1991 Formations of Violence: The Narrative of the Body and Political Terror in Northern Ireland. Chicago: Chicago University Press.
Frank, Sybille
2007 Grenzwerte – Zur Formation der Heritage Industry am Berliner Checkpoint Charlie. *In* Prädikat Heritage: Wertschöpfungen aus kulturellen Ressourcen. D. Hemme, M. Tauschek and R. Bendix, eds. pp. 297–322. Münster: LIT.
Greenwood, Davydd J.
1989 Culture by the Pound: An Anthropological Perspective on Tourism as Cultural Commoditization. *In* Hosts and Guests: The Anthropology of Tourism. 2nd edition. V. L. Smith, ed. pp. 171–185. Philadelphia: University of Pennsylvania Press.
Grossman, Alyssa
2010 Chorographies of Memory: Everyday Practices of Remembrance Work in Post-Socialist EU-Accession-Era Bucharest. PhD dissertation, University of Manchester.
Hallam, Elizabeth, and Jenny Hockey
2001 Death, Memory, and Material Culture. New York: Berg.
Hastrup, Kirsten
1992 Introduction. *In* Other Histories. K. Hastrup, ed. pp. 1–13. London: Routledge.
Hecht, Anat
2001 Home Sweet Home: Tangible Memories of an Uprooted Childhood. *In* Home Possessions. D. Miller, ed. pp. 123–45. Oxford: Berg.
Herzfeld, Michael
1982 Ours Once More: Folklore, Ideology, and the Making of Modern Greece. Austin: University of Texas Press.
1987 Anthropology Through the Looking-Glass: Critical Ethnography in the Margins of Europe. Cambridge: Cambridge University Press.
1991 A Place in History: Social and Monumental Time in a Cretan Town. Princeton, NJ: Princeton University Press.
2009 Evicted from Eternity: The Restructuring of Modern Rome. Chicago: Chicago University Press.
Hewison, Robert
1987 The Heritage Industry. London: Methuen.
Hobsbawm, Eric
1983 Introduction: Inventing Traditions. *In* The Invention of Tradition. E. Hobsbawm and T. Ranger, eds. pp. 1–14. Cambridge: Cambridge University Press.

Hobsbawm, Eric, and Terence Ranger, eds.
1983 The Invention of Tradition. Cambridge: Cambridge University Press.
Irving, Andrew
2006 The Skin of the City. Anthropological Yearbook of European Cultures 15:9–36.
Jarman, Neil
1997 Material Conflicts: Parades and Visual Displays in Northern Ireland. Oxford: Berg.
Jerman, Helena
2006 Memory Crossing Borders: A Transition in Space and Time among Second and Third Generation Russians in Finland. Anthropological Yearbook of European Cultures 15:117–141.
Karakasidou, Anastasia N.
1997 Fields of Wheat, Hills of Blood: Passages to Greek Nationhood in Greek Macedonia, 1870–1990. Chicago: Chicago University Press.
Levy, Daniel, and Natan Sznaider
2002 Memory Unbound: The Holocaust and the Formation of Cosmopolitan Memory. European Journal of Social Theory 5(1):87–106.
Macdonald, Sharon
1997a Reimagining Culture: Histories, Identities and the Gaelic Renaissance. Oxford: Berg.
1997b A People's Story? Heritage, Identity and Authenticity. *In* Touring Cultures: Transformations of Travel and Theory. C. Rojek and J. Urry, eds. pp. 155–175. London: Routledge.
2002a On Old Things: The Fetishization of Past Everyday Life. *In* British Subjects: An Anthropology of Britain. N. Rapport, ed. pp. 89–106. Oxford: Berg.
2002b Trafficking in History: Multitemporal Practices. Anthropological Journal of European Cultures 11:93–116.
2006 Words in Stone? Agency and Identity in a Nazi Landscape. Journal of Material Culture 11(1/2):105–126.
2008 Museum Europe: Negotiating Heritage. Anthropological Journal of European Cultures 17:47–65.
2009 Difficult Heritage: Negotiating the Nazi Past in Nuremberg and Beyond. London: Routledge.
Miller, Daniel
2008 The Comfort of Things. Cambridge: Polity.
Nadel-Klein, Jane
2003 Fishing for Heritage: Modernity and Loss along the Scottish Coast. Oxford: Berg.
Navaro-Yashin, Yael
2009 Affective Spaces, Melancholic Objects: Ruination and the Production of Anthropological Knowledge. Journal of the Royal Anthropological Institute 15(1):1–18.
Nora, Pierre
1984–1992 Les Lieux de mémoire (7 vols.). Paris: Gallimard.
Parman, Susan
1990 Scottish Crofters: A Historical Ethnography of a Celtic Village. New York: Holt, Rinehart and Winston.
Ralowski, Tomasz
2006 Body and Fate: The Pension as a Practice of Social Remembering. Anthropological Yearbook of European Cultures 15:37–48.
Seremetakis, C. Nadia
1991 The Last Word: Women, Death and Divination in Inner Mani. Chicago: Chicago University Press.

Seremetakis, C. Nadia, ed.
1994a The Senses Still: Perception and Memory as Material Culture in Modernity. Chicago: University of Chicago Press.
1994b The Memory of the Senses. Part I: Marks of the Transitory. *In* The Senses Still: Perception and Memory as Material Culture in Modernity. C. N. Seremetakis, ed. pp. 1–18. Chicago: University of Chicago Press.
Shanklin, Eugenia
1985 Donegal's Changing Traditions: An Ethnographic Study. New York: Gordon and Breach.
Silverman, Marilyn, and P. H. Gulliver
1992 Historical Anthropology and the Ethnographic Tradition: A Personal, Historical, and Intellectual Account. *In* Approaching the Past: Historical Anthropology through Irish Case Studies. M. Silverman and P. H. Gulliver, eds. pp. 3–72. New York: Columbia University Press.
Skultans, Vieda
1998 The Testimony of Lives: Narrative and Memory in Post-Soviet Latvia. London: Routledge.
Sutton, David E.
1998 Memories Cast in Stone: The Relevance of the Past in Everyday Life. London: Routledge.
2001 Remembrance of Repasts: An Anthropology of Food and Memory. Oxford: Berg.
Welz, Gisela
2007 Europäische Produkte: Nahrungskulturelles Erbe und EU-Politik. Am Beispiel der Republik Zypern. *In* Prädikat Heritage: Wertschöpfungen aus kulturellen Ressourcen. D. Hemme, M. Tauschek, and R. Bendix, eds. pp. 323–336. Münster: LIT.
Wolf, Eric
1992 Europe and the People without History. Berkeley: University of California Press.

CHAPTER 15

An Anthropology of War and Recovery: Lived War Experiences

Maja Povrzanović Frykman

Wars have been instrumental in shaping political and economic development in Europe for centuries. Indeed, twentieth-century conflicts in Europe, including the two World Wars, involved unprecedented civilian deaths. At the very end of the century, it seemed that wars in Europe belonged to history. However, the conflicts which occurred in former Yugoslav countries proved such a belief to be incorrect. Moreover, these conflicts involved the targeting of civilians in the most blatant ways.

The lives of civilians in wartime Europe have been documented largely by historians (see, e.g., Atkin 2008), but also researched by scholars from other disciplines that deal with the concept of memory and modes of commemoration. The 1991–1995 wars in the former Yugoslavia were the first examples to be thoroughly dealt with by anthropologists and ethnologists as the conflict was actually ongoing.

Innumerable books and articles have been published on Yugoslavia, on the reasons for its dissolution, on the wars in the nineties, and on their outcomes. These have been written by journalists, political analysts, and scholars from different disciplinary backgrounds. They often reflect their authors' perceptions of the events either as civil war or as foreign military aggression, and tend to reduce the wars to their ethnic dimensions. An extensive and meticulous review of this literature is offered in the introduction to the book *The New Bosnian Mosaic* (Bougarel et al. 2007:1–35). Focusing on Bosnia-Herzegovina, the editors explain that, while the wars were going on, the issue of defining the war was so central that many crucial issues remained neglected, such as the role of economic incentives for warfare (see, e.g., Bojičić and Kaldor 1999; Andreas 2004), the full complexity of political and military developments on the ground (see, e.g., Bjelaković and Strazzari 1999; Bax 2000a), the specific local histories of interethnic relations, and the relativity of the perceived opposition between urban and rural people (see, e.g., Bougarel 1999; Allcock 2002).

Bougarel et al. (2007:11) point out that the majority of more recent literature is written by legal scholars and political scientists, and thus remains dominated by the approach "from above" producing "top-down" analyses and relying heavily on

A Companion to the Anthropology of Europe, First Edition. Edited by Ullrich Kockel, Máiréad Nic Craith, and Jonas Frykman.

international organizations' official reports. The approach "from above" ignores lived war experiences and postwar uncertainties, or tends to reduce them to data from opinion polls and NGO leaders (Bougarel et al. 2007:34).

The work conducted by anthropologists and ethnologists, pursuing understandings "from below" and shedding light on "bottom-up" perspectives, is considerable. However, the impact of their work on the overall understanding of those wars is difficult to estimate. Although several academic publications (see, e.g., Donia and Fine 1994; Malcolm 1994) and, notably, anthropological studies based on research done before war (Bax 1995; Bringa 1995) refuted the thesis on "ancient ethnic hatreds" (Kaplan 1993), some of us who did fieldwork in conflict and postconflict Croatia and Bosnia-Herzegovina still feel an urge to convince different audiences that the wars were not "ethnic" to start with, and that the eruptions of violence were not merely an outburst of primitive passions.

Taking into account the entire body of anthropological work regarding the post-Yugoslav wars (even without referring to Kosovo 1999) would hardly be possible in a single essay. This chapter, therefore, attempts to explain how the view that those wars were the result of "ancient ethnic hatreds" is repudiated by fieldwork-based findings on civilians' experiences, attitudes, and agency in war and postwar contexts in both Croatia and Bosnia-Herzegovina. Notwithstanding the importance of other titles concerning the post-Yugoslav wars, only ethnographic fieldwork among civilians rendered refined knowledge of daily life, processes of identification, and patterns of action. Such knowledge often remains overlooked, especially in the shadows of the many analyses of political discourses, documents, institutions, and the role of the media. However, such ethnographic work is central to any understanding of the effects of military violence on people and the difficulties they meet in the processes of individual and societal recovery. These methods urge a rethinking of identity theories by exploring patterns of identification in the context of humiliation, fear, limited choices, and affiliations imposed by military violence. The knowledge about lived war experiences is, therefore, also central to solving social problems after the war.

In turn, fieldwork concerning postwar contexts produces locality-sensitive knowledge of current problems and their potential solutions (see, e.g., Bougarel et al. 2007). Such research also encourages a reconsideration of relations between citizens and institutions on various levels. Insisting on a "bottom-up" perspective, it contributes to an understanding of constructions of identity, place, and home as dynamic social processes. Finally, it sheds light on the local effects of international politics and policies that are meant to enable but sometimes disable processes of recovery in the aftermath of war.

Methodologically, this chapter is thus confined to ethnographic fieldwork concerning civilians' experiences. Whilst ethnographic research cannot entirely replace research based on other methods, it cannot be regarded as merely a "storytelling" complement to that research either. Instead, ethnography provides the core knowledge necessary for understanding what war does to people and what ordinary people may do in extraordinary, violent circumstances.

The thematic thread of this chapter – contesting the "ethnic hatred" explanation – is chosen due to the fact that it connects most fieldwork-based anthropological texts on both Croatia and Bosnia-Herzegovina. Fieldworkers *see* that "ethnic hatred" is often a simplistic explanation, and sometimes not valid at all. As the political implications of the ethnic paradigm have been far reaching, anthropologists, who *understand* its locally specific relevance before, during, and after the wars from the perspective of the very people involved, have continually challenged this paradigm. They do not deny the existence of a continuum between nationalist and antinationalist stances and practices, but prioritize shedding light on nonnationalist positions articulated in everyday life, as these are fully assessable only through fieldwork.

Theoretically, this chapter is about turning ethnicity into a matter of empirical research, not using it as a lens whenever thinking about Yugoslavia and post-Yugoslav issues. The wars induced ethnonational categories as pervasive and rigid (see, e.g., Sorabji 1995; Halpern and Kideckel 2000); they became more closely related to religious markers and institutions (see, e.g., Bringa 2002; Maček 2009). However, at the same time they remained relative and challenged (see, e.g., Kolind 2008), which allowed for some forms of interethnic cooperation. The anthropologists who did fieldwork among the civilians assess the importance of ethnoreligious background and ethnonational identity (Maček 2009:124) as intermingled with place of residence, age, gender, education, profession, and urban versus rural belonging. They explain how people (from both "minority" and "majority" groups) avoided, resisted, or adopted the political position of "their" group's decisions, often imposed on them by politics and intense violence that was beyond their control.

There is no "neat," singular, simple, or generally valid explanation of the post-Yugoslav wars, of 1991 to 1995. The anthropology of war and recovery offers explanations that are contextualized, and pay appropriate attention to the ambiguities and contradictions of identity-formation processes and agency situated in unstable, confusing, and threatening circumstances. The fieldwork-based studies discussed in this chapter relate to the seminal anthropological studies of violence, social suffering, and recovery (Das et al. 2001) and to those studies that privilege lived experience in their attempt to understand violence and its impacts (see, e.g., Daniel 1996; Nordstrom 2004; Finnström 2008). They do not focus on cultural mediations of violence and its place in collective memory, on instrumental uses of violence in struggles over resources and power, on violence as offering benefits of material gain and social recognition, or on violent imaginaries (narrative, performative, or visually displayed) of conflicts that leave no room for ambiguity about "sides" in a conflict (Schmidt and Schröder 2001:8–15).

The editors of *Anthropology of Violence and Conflict* favor an operational approach that "links violence to general properties of human nature and rationality and to general concepts of social adaptation to material conditions" as it looks for "parameters transcending cultural specificity and the boundedness of violent events in time, space and society" (Schmidt and Schröder 2001:17). They see as most common the cognitive approach that portrays violence as culturally constructed, as a representation of cultural values (Schmidt and Schröder 2001:17). They criticize the experiential approach for its tendency to "neglect cultural generality in favour of pure fragmented subjectivity," which leads to "a randomizing view" of violent events, supposedly useless for anthropological comparison (Schmidt and Schröder 2001:18).

Most of the anthropological texts on the 1991–1995 wars in Croatia and Bosnia-Herzegovina discussed in this chapter focus on lived war experiences. Indeed, they offer an empirical critique of structurally inspired anthropological analyses of war and war-related violence (Kolind 2006). It posits that identity is built on difference, and that violence is employed to recreate difference when it becomes too small. Yet, even if violence were to create unambiguous identities, these identities are a consequence, and not an explanation of war (Kolind 2006:448). Further, claiming that violence creates unambiguous identities "only accounts for a part of the process relevant for understanding the relationship between violence and identification" (Kolind 2006:448). The fact that there is polarization between "us and them" does not say anything about how particular people or particular groups of people react to it. The literature presented below shows that some people resisted exclusive antagonistic ethnic identifications.

What Happened, and Why?

As established after World War II, Yugoslavia comprised six republics (Slovenia, Croatia, Bosnia-Herzegovina, Serbia, Montenegro, and Macedonia), along with two autonomous provinces (Vojvodina and Kosovo, both within the Republic of Serbia). A period of destabilization started following the death of Yugoslav president Tito in 1980. It culminated in violent conflicts that involved the Yugoslav People's Army, paramilitary groups, newly formed national armies, and millions of victimized civilians (see Bringa 2002:206–216; *The Scholars' Initiative* 2006; Povrzanović Frykman 2008:163–171).

Indeed, it was the plight of civilians – killed, orphaned, maimed, raped, tortured, displaced, and exiled – that made the post-Yugoslav wars front-page news. It caused incredulous shocks, international political negotiations, massive humanitarian actions, and protracted court proceedings at the International Criminal Tribunal for the former Yugoslavia in The Hague.

Generally speaking, international readiness for humanitarian help and moral indignation over organized violence that was raging only "two hours from London" (Craigie 1995), was coupled with overtly deficient insights into its political origins. Scholarly analyses that focus on ethnic mobilization in relation to state security stress the need of understanding the nature of the communal identities and the history of their antagonisms within a geopolitical context (Sekulić 1997; Fenton 2010:161–164). They point to the role of international actors and their perception of the importance of the creation and the dissolution of Yugoslavia, the interaction of geostrategical considerations and internal elite strategies, and the production of legitimacy as the result of geostrategical success or failure (Sekulić 1997:177). Yugoslav legitimacy depended on its "buffer" position between East and West and on antifascism rather than communism – the ideology accepted by a small minority of population (Sekulić 1997:174). Pro-Western sentiments in Slovenia and Croatia were clashing with a Serbian imperialism that replaced Yugoslavism and included defending the "imperiled" Serbs in Croatia, Bosnia-Herzegovina, and Kosovo (Fenton 2010:162–163). In short, "people came to *choose* to act and were *forced* to act" (Fenton 2010:164, emphasis added) in terms of ethnic categories, under a particular set of conditions. The inability of the Yugoslav socialist system to resolve the economic, political, and social crisis in the 1980s resulted in intense political infighting, ethnonationalist movements and eventually armed conflicts.

Yet, the wars in Croatia and Bosnia-Herzegovina appeared to many international observers as messy and hard to grasp: they were so close to the geographical center of Europe, yet so distant in terms of the cultural geography of (post)socialist Others. Unlike the case of World War II, it was not easy to discern the good "side" from the bad one. And when it was attempted, a "balanced approach" was put forward, by showing that people of a certain ethnicity who were victimized in one village appeared as perpetrators in another. The "balanced" talk about victims becoming perpetrators, and *vice versa*, is a logical outcome of defining people in ethnic terms, and seeing them as representatives of "their" groups. Guilt by association makes sense if "ethnic groups" ("sides") and not individuals are concerned – that is, if explanations are attempted on the scale of political maps and units of governance and not on the scale of concrete locations of death and destruction. Such explanations rest on the routinely used phrases "the war in Yugoslavia" and "the war in the Balkans," that dismiss the important fact that only parts of "the region" have been exposed to warfare. Ethnographic research points not only to the generalizing nature of such phrases, but also to the limitations of such explanations when applied to an entire country. For instance, "the war in Croatia" meant heavy destruction and war crimes in some parts of the country, while in other areas it was something only to be seen on TV (Čale Feldman et al. 1993). In different parts of Bosnia, the war was radically different from one location to the other; it could have had different intensity and outcomes even between neighboring villages.

For a number of reasons, the nationalist character of much of the 1990s politics in post-Yugoslav countries has trapped their entire populations in an image of fierce nationalism. In the public discourse dominating international media and politics, the adjective *Yugoslav* was coupled with the use of the notions of *Balkans*, *fratricide*, *ethnic hatred*, and *ethnic cleansing*. This discourse exoticized the wars and contributed to blurring the lines between perpetrators and victims. It became easy to treat all sides in the conflict as equally guilty and not get involved in ways that would prevent more casualties (Bringa 2002:203).

The phrases "centuries-old hatred" and "they cannot live together" first appeared in a speech by the Serb nationalist leader Karadžić a few weeks before the barricades were set up in Sarajevo, when a Serb-controlled area was separated from the rest of the city in spring 1992. Phrases such as these became a staple of Karadžić's public speech repertoire, picked up by many representatives of the Western media and international mediators. As suggested by the Norwegian anthropologist Tone Bringa:

> The implication behind the "centuries-old hatred" mantra was that the war could not be stopped but had to run its natural cause, or, as E.U. mediator Lord Owen suggested, that "the warring fractions would have to fight it out." . . . By implication, the international community could only try to alleviate some of the suffering by making sure that food and medicines were delivered to the survivors. (Bringa 2002:202)

In response to the exoticizing depictions of the post-Yugoslav wars as expressions of "ancient" Balkan hatred, many social scientists have argued that they involved competing nationalisms centered upon very modern technologies of power and knowledge (Jansen 2005a). One of them involved the mapping of nationality on to territory. While the "maps of ethnic distribution" in Yugoslavia delineated the deeds of "ethnic cleansing," critical observers use these maps with the opposite aim: "their vivid splinter of colours evoke the complexity of the prewar situation, and the contrast with the much 'neater' postwar maps testifies to the bloody processes by which territories were homogenized nationally" (Jansen 2005a:47). The British-based anthropologist Stef Jansen (2005b) thus argues that the uncontextualized use of those prewar maps and the image of the mosaic of the "ethnic" territories they convey entail dangers of misrepresentation. The "maps of ethnic distribution" suggest the fixedness and importance of ethnic categories that might have had little bearing for people's own self-perceptions and their peacetime life in "mixed" territories. In most instances, ethnicity was not a defining feature that pervaded people's daily interactions in Yugoslavia. The reorganization of life around ethnonational divisions was a process that many found deeply disturbing (Maček 2009:124).

Indeed, "ethnic cleansing" was primarily about "the 'destruction of alternatives' and the elimination of people who represented those alternatives by virtue of identifying or being identified with another ethnic or political community" (Bringa 2002:213). The very personalized violence that is a hallmark of "ethnic cleansing" proved that a majority of people did not want the new social order that was being imposed on them. "The level of fear and violence needed to engage people (or rather to disengage people – that is, to silence their opposition) is an indicator of the weak power of ethnic sentiment as a mobilizing factor" (Bringa 2002:218; see also Sorabji 1995). The Swedish anthropologist Ivana Maček (2009) provided abundant ethnographic proof for the claim that people who had not identified strongly with their ethnoreligious background found that it became more salient over the course of war as they searched for people whom they could trust. This shift was not merely a matter of the political exploitation of ethnonational identities, but was produced and reinforced by the war itself (Maček 2009:124).

This claim has been reinforced by the political scientist V. P. Gagnon Jr (2004), whose analysis of the political and economic background of the post-Yugoslav wars shows that the image of ethnic groups in conflict must be seen as "part of a selective, ideological construct in which 'ethnic groups' are portrayed as actors by nationalist politicians and historians" (Gagnon 2004:32). The real importance of these tensions was that they contributed to the maintenance of inter-group boundaries and fostered a distrust that enabled politicians to mobilize "their" group against others. Drawing on archive, media, and statistical material, Gagnon corroborated the conclusion made on the basis of ethnographic research quoted above, that

> (T)he key in politics is to make certain identities more relevant than others, and others irrelevant to politics. . . . This doesn't necessarily require changing people's self-perceived identifications. Rather, it means forcing them in particular contexts to act – or not act – within the narrow range of one "identity" defined in a very specific and particular way. (Gagnon 2004:26–27)

The sense of security provided by a feeling of belonging to a group, not important in the stable circumstances of peacetime, becomes crucial when group belonging is experienced as difference between life and death: therein lies its immense political potential (Maček, 2009:124).

Writing as Acting: The Quandaries of Partiality

In Srebrenica almost 7000 Bosniak (Muslim) men were slaughtered in the week in which the town was taken by Serb forces in July 1995, notwithstanding the fact that it was one of the six UN-protected safe areas in wartime Bosnia (Research and Documentation Center Sarajevo 2008). In Sarajevo, UNPROFOR's (United Nations Protection Forces) transporters helped people to cross those streets exposed to sniper fire, but did not help to stop the siege that lasted for 1395 days, and was the longest in modern history (Kapić et al. 2006). The Open Society Fund sent 2 million dollars worth of pumpkin, carrot, tomato, lettuce, and corn seeds (Kapić et al. 2006). Looking at the seeds grow and enjoying the fruits might have filled people with hope, confirming the existence of a framework of meaning that was not affected by war-violence – a framework of natural cycles, of *life* itself (see Povrzanović Frykman 2002, on ecological order versus war disorder). However, at the same time, this was also a message about the nonexistence of the will to deal with the root causes of the situation (Povrzanović Frykman 2008:184–185). As observed by Maček (2009), inaction could be tolerated, since the terror that informed the Sarajevans' lives made them essentially different from the Westerners. After years of isolation, Sarajevo was turned into a *symbol* of terror.

This elucidates the context of scholarly attempts to document and explain what was going on in wars in Croatia and Bosnia-Herzegovina, from 1991 to 1995. For domestic scholars, a number of issues implied in any ethnographic research – such as access and partiality, being native and going native – became especially pertinent, as the subject matter at hand was people's suffering on one's own doorstep, and the quest for scientific detachment in an emergent anthropology at home appeared as dubiously immoral.

Croatian war ethnographers have been criticized for profiling their research in "a thematically restrictive way" that was lacking balance, and for producing a "controversial," "militant ethnography of 'fears and tears' " in which they oscillated "between the roles of victim and author" (Naumović 2002:11). In their turn, painstakingly aware of their own emotional involvement, and struggling with the instances of being reduced to their national belonging, they could not consider the critique based on the lack of research on the "other side" – which was a virtual impossibility for them in the early 1990s. They could not help being hypersensitive to choices of terms that at that time seemed to reflect the stances of othering and balancing of guilt explained above (see Halpern and Kideckel 2000:5–7; Povrzanović 2000).

Instead of dissecting their country's leaders' national(ist) discourse, Croatian ethnographers elucidated the role of weapons as the "missing link" between discourse and dying. They were interested in the ways people thought and acted beyond the monovocal national narrative (see the contributions to Bennett 1995a, and to Jambrešić Kirin and Povrzanović 1996). They found that lived war experiences were not expressed in narrative frames of "suffering nation." People's personal narratives about war revealed a multiplicity, diversity and complexity of experience that challenged the uniqueness of the national narrative (Jambrešić 1995; Jambrešić Kirin 1996a, 1996b). The use and interpretations of national symbols were also taken up, in relation to visual representations and political mobilization (Senjković 1995a, 1995b, 1996). So were the instances of political humor meant to "teach humility" to the authoritarian Croatian president (Čale Feldman 1995a).

Ethnographic methods, used along with the oral history method of recording individual perceptions of local and national history, helped in formulating narrative cognitions pertaining to a new area of studies in Croatia. Importantly, writing about war became a process of rethinking some of the fundamental issues in anthropology, such as insider versus outsider dilemmas (Bennett 1995b; Čale Feldman 1995b; Povrzanović 2000) and the predicaments of anthropological research on, and representations of, suffering. The self-reflexive discussions of the epistemological position "between destruction and deconstruction" (Prica 1995a, 1995b) added a dimension to the issues concerning regimes of truth and textual representations examined in the book *Writing Culture* (Clifford and Marcus 1986). Surrounded by "uncomfortable and semantically shaken, nearly reversible" oppositions of individual conscience and collective cause, Croatian war ethnographers "reached for autocathartic devices, treating their own lives as texts that ought to be written against mainstream interpretations, whether they are coming from outside or from inside the jeopardized country" (Čale Feldman 1995b:85). They "tried to find their courage in playing the postmodern game. . . . they 'acted out,' as psychoanalysts would say, in an impossible situation, and saved their intellectual consciences" (Čale Feldman 1995b:87).

Daily Life in War

Grounded in civilians' experiences, strategies of coping, humiliation, resistance, belonging, and choice appeared as central concepts. Writing about air-raid alarms and shelters, about food, water, and hygiene, about neighbors, friends, and helping strategies, about fear, obstinacy, and courage, Croatian war ethnographies presented examples of everyday interactions and communications either radically reduced or newly introduced due to siege and shelling. They outlined a wartime politics of identity based on strategies of survival, but also showed that everyday routines, political rituals, and music are an efficient means of coping with war-provoked deprivation and anxiety in everyday realms (Čale Feldman et al. 1993; Pettan 1998).

My research on Dubrovnik under siege – Dubrovnik is a town on Croatia's Adriatic coast with some 60 000 inhabitants – shows that the tendency to situate one's own identity in spatial terms was significantly intensified as a result of people's lived encounters with deprivation and violence. People become aware of the importance of their physical position within, and physical dependency on, the surrounding landscape and urban structure. Many talked in detail of their bodily experiences of the material world in situations of extreme restrictions imposed by siege. In such a context, the exclamation "this is my town!" did not express nationalism, but the fact that nonmediated experiences of the place were put to the fore (Povrzanović 1997; Povrzanović Frykman 2002).

The first civilian killed in Dubrovnik by a piece of mortar shell hitting him in his apartment was a Serb. The knowledge of his ethnic affiliation cannot contribute to the explanation of what happened to him and why. It is the *where* and *when* that are important – the attachment to one's *own place* and the moment in which the haphazard violence turns a home into a site of death. The explanation, then, cannot be based on ethnicity, but on the fact that this man decided to stay behind in *his town*.

In opposition to the new definition of their town as a military territory to be threatened, shelled, and set on fire, people's efforts to circumvent the imposed victim-identity were many. Baking a birthday cake in improvised conditions? Insisting on the evening walk in Dubrovnik? Organizing a concert? People were often successful in keeping – in minimized form – the established forms of urban community and culture. The war-related narratives I collected among the people of Dubrovnik outline a wartime politics of identity, based on strategies of survival in the context of siege, military attacks, injury, death, and destruction. They show that everyday routines were an efficient means of coping with war-provoked deprivation and anxiety. Swimming in the sea (in order to wash oneself) despite the potential exposure to snipers, or going to the café, to drink coffee made out of mineral water (as the water supplies were cut off), were not instances of irrational behavior, but experimental-experiential, culturally specific "trials" of what aspects of "normality" were possible in a town changed by violence.

Belonging to Europe

In that context, the conviction that Dubrovnik – a town on UNESCO's World Heritage list – and its inhabitants "belong to Europe," was of special importance. This has been taken for granted not only because of the town's geographical location, but also because the people living there had inherited, lived with, and taken care of some of the most distinguished objects of European architectural cultural heritage. In the political discourse on Croatia's right to independence, Dubrovnik featured as a prominent piece of national soil. In the discourse of cultural heritage, it was the most significant proof of Croatia's belonging to Europe. For the people in the besieged town, Dubrovnik was the site of "resistance" consisting of perseverance and preservation of a minimal *normality*. When the shells were destroying the town, the buildings otherwise viewed as cultural heritage to be proud of served to protect endangered bodies. When the circulation of goods was stopped because of the siege, the palm trees – a tourism symbol *par excellence* – were chopped down and used for heating. When all the taps were dry in the town, the surrounding sea was not something to be appreciated for its beauty, but for saving people from humiliating stench and infection.

Local people perceived the historical center of Dubrovnik as "protected" by the importance of cultural heritage. They firmly believed that *Europe* would not let it be damaged. Ironically, however, the UNESCO flags denoting the precious heritage eventually served as demarcations of the most valuable objects to be damaged. After heavy bombing substantially damaged the historical center on December 6, 1991, people suddenly realized – "everyone was crying in the streets, men, women, elderly, kids" – that the historic city walls guaranteed no protection from a common war destiny (Povrzanović 1997:158). The illusion that their place could be excluded from war because of the value of its cultural heritage was lost. They understood that symbols could not stop the war, that culture could not overpower weapons – neither in the form of heritage nor as a perceived "belonging to Europe" (Povrzanović Frykman 2002).

This lesson was far more bitterly learned by the people who stayed behind in Sarajevo under siege. While concerned whether they were still "normal" in terms of norms and habits of their prewar selves (Maček 2009), they could refer to Europe as an idiom for a lost normality of a cosmopolitan Sarajevo. Evocations of internationally recognizable references, such as the Olympic Rings – now made out of barbed wire – were reminders of the fact that Sarajevo used to be a part of "Europe and the world" at the time when the Winter Olympic Games were held there in 1984 (Maček 2009:59). However, these international symbols remained unanswered cries for recognition of belonging that should have implied an obligation to help on those who shared the message.

Lived Experiences and Identifications

When people are shot at or expelled from their homes because of their ethnicity, it goes without saying that ethnicity gains in importance, both as an imposed and "reactively" chosen – aspect of identity. Yet, ethnicity might also cease to matter when the shared lived experience of violence forms the basis of a feeling of belonging to a place. Despite the war-induced relevance of belonging to one of the three major ethnic groups in Sarajevo, a "fourth nation" was recognized, consisting of people who experienced and valued the multiethnic life in Bosnia, identified themselves as *Sarajevans*, and did not allow ethnic animosity to take over their personal social relations. Those were predominantly the people who stayed behind in Sarajevo under siege.

Work by Ivana Maček (2009) stands out as the most systematic in-depth effort to illuminate the civilian's experiences of the war from within: she conducted fieldwork in Sarajevo while the town was under siege. She collected narratives on the experiences of civilians struggling to continue their everyday life in the midst of violent threat and destruction and offered first-hand observations of the processes she dubbed *negotiation of normality*. They implied fascinating instances of creativity in the struggle against hunger, thirst, dirt, and cold, black humor in relation to United Nation's forces, stories of disgrace and embarrassment, and efforts to keep one's urbanity and intellectual life in spite of the danger of getting killed by a sniper whenever stepping into the street.

Maček presents contradictory moral stances that Sarajevans adopted in the context of "imitation of normal life." When social norms taken for granted in peace could not be met due to violence, people oscillated between "civilian," "soldier," and "deserter" mode of perceiving and making sense of the war. The *civilian mode* foregrounds the shock of the outbreak of war and the belief that it is not possible that "safe" social norms could collapse. The *soldier mode* refers to the recognition of the reality of war and of the logic of "sides" people have to take; a moral rationale for fighting is provided, and the destruction and killing gain sense. The *deserter mode* comes out of the abandonment of the neat divisions between citizens, armies, friends, and foes that mark the other two modes, and expresses profound skepticism toward any ideals that justify violence: everyone is individually responsible for one's actions. These three modes of feeling and thinking are highly contextual; they have been employed simultaneously, or people shifted back and forth between them in their efforts to make sense of what was happening (Maček 2009:5).

Importantly, Maček also showed how importance of religion was reinforced by the constant threat of death, but also by the fact that, except for UNHCR, religious organizations were the primary source of subsistence goods. Hunger forced those Sarajevans who were not religious before the war to recognize "their" religion: "Thus, religion entered the everyday life of most Sarajevans in an organized and institutionalized way" (Maček 2009:85). They followed the traditional lines connecting ethnic and religious backgrounds – Croats being perceived as Catholics, Serbs as Orthodox and Bosniaks as Muslim, regardless of their actual religious (in)activity.

> Almost every detail of everyday life was subject to constant evaluation and reevaluation, the most intensely charged and deeply disputed domain was that of ethnonational identification. Sarajevans had to reconcile their own lived experiences as members of ethnocultural groups in a multicultural city with the mutually exclusive, even hostile construction of ethnonational identity that political leaders formulated and the war increasingly forced upon them. (Maček 2009:9–10)

Yet, ethnic identifications are not relevant in the discussion of fears, adaptation strategies, and daily practices of numerous individuals. For instance, a ten-year-old boy from Sarajevo stated: "If I'll have three children, I shall call them Electricity, Water and Gas!" (Maček 2009:62). It was not his ethnicity making him fully aware of the vital importance of those basic resources, but his war experience in the town under siege. He could have been a Muslim, a Croat, or one of the Serbs who stayed in Sarajevo and risked their lives in the attacks by the Serbian military forces (which they did not perceive as "protecting their interests"; cf. Povrzanović Frykman 2008). Ethnic identification is not relevant if the focus is on the humiliation suffered by kneeling in the street in order to try to save the broken eggs in Dubrovnik under siege (Povrzanović Frykman 2008).

A lasting contribution has been made by Tone Bringa and the crew that produced the documentary *We Are All Neighbours* (Bringa 1993; see also Caplan 2002). Bringa revisited the villagers she had made friends with during her research on Bosnian Muslims in the 1980s (Bringa 1995). She was given the opportunity of filming the process of local ethnic consolidation while military violence was engulfing the Croatian–Muslim village and finally victimizing its Muslim inhabitants. The "before" and "after" perspective, documented in the period of only a few weeks, gives a unique insight from within: hearing the detonations only a couple of kilometers away, people still chose to believe that the war would not hit their village and insisted on the strength (and "normality") of long-lasting friendships between neighbors regardless of their ethnic and religious backgrounds. Yet, fear was the reason for them to succumb to "ethnic" thinking. Subsequent exposure to targeted violence eventually proved them right. The film also witnesses how difficult it is for anyone emotionally involved to keep the "balanced" view and resist ascribing guilt by association to all members of an ethnic group, regardless of their individual deeds.

The Dutch anthropologist Mart Bax, writing against "a national or central leader perspective that seems to dominate in most of Western analyses of Balkan society" (Bax 2000b:332), showed that a study from below is crucial to an understanding of the dynamics and the developmental logics of the processes named "ethnic cleansing." In the case of the Marian pilgrimage center of Međugorje in Herzegovina, the history of economic competition between rival family clans was central to local events in the context of the 1990s war. Bax described in detail the cruelty of targeted destruction and killing between the clans. Yet, that violence can be explained neither in terms of manipulations from above, nor in terms of interethnic antagonisms. It occurred within an ethnic group; it was nonethnic in origin, but ethnicized in the course of its development. "What might seem random and unpredictable on a higher societal level demonstrates a large extent of regularity and explainability on local level" (Bax 2000b:333).

The British-based anthropologist Stef Jansen did not find an English-language publisher interested in publishing his dissertation on a pronounced instance of anti-nationalism among intellectuals in the midst of the post-Yugoslav wars: a pro-peace network established between Zagreb and Belgrade. With the prevalence of the "ethnic hatred" explanation of post-Yugoslav wars noted above, it is perhaps not surprising that his work was seen as a "misfit." It was however, welcomed by a Belgrade publisher and translated into Serbian (Jansen, 2005b).

Ethnographies of Postwar Developments

But what do identity options look like after the wars, after they have been narrowed down by the experiences of fear, prosecution, and brutal violence as well as by lasting losses and material hardship? Atrocities, destruction, and the war-born importance of ethnic affiliations are facts. So is the high unemployment rate in the postwar period. Which alternatives, then, appear as viable, to the people living in, or returning to, places that have been enmeshed in war?

Stef Jansen criticizes the *discourse of sedentarism* prevalent in refugee studies and policies, that naturalizes the link between people and places, and is "all the more problematic when combined with an exoticist approach to non-Western Others, somehow locating them closer to nature" (Jansen, 2007:16). Embodied attachment to place should not be taken for granted but analyzed as a possible dimension of homemaking. "Home" yearned for in exile is never identical to the place exiles return to: places are changed because of war, and people are changed for having lived elsewhere. Defying the logics of refugee-return policies, they do not necessarily wish to, or want to, return to their "proper" homes. Investigating minority returnees in two different ethnic majority contexts in Bosnia-Herzegovina, Jansen found that people were more preoccupied with finding a "cool ground" – a safe place in which they could reestablish their lives, than with the return itself. The return to the original home was only wished for if it could offer such "cool ground" (Jansen 2007:16). He therefore calls for an investigation of "the conditions in which certain (re)makings of 'home' come to be seen as more feasible than others," and of "the importance of place in 'home' through an emphasis on personhood and transformative social relations" (Jansen 2007:17).

Basing her book on long-term ethnographic fieldwork in the Croatian town of Knin and its rural hinterland, Carolin Leutloff-Grandits (2006) offered a detailed picture of the postwar dynamics of local intergroup relations that were shaped by property interests. While she observed the expected cleavage between local and newcomer population, she also documented the less expected – indeed, impossible, if ethnic hatred had been a cause of war! – cross-ethnic respect for property rights, and cooperation that opened up pathways to reconciliation between native Croats and Serbs.

Danish anthropologist Torsten Kolind (2008) conducted fieldwork in the small town of Stolac in Bosnia-Herzegovina, to which Bosniaks (Muslims) returned after having been expelled by the Croats. In collecting and investigating their narratives on the war and postwar situation, he found that war-related violence and the postwar ethnic policy discriminating against Bosniaks had penetrated everyday life. Yet, he also found that people create and mold other, *nonethnic categories* that can be used for moral evaluation (such as, for instance, "decent people" as opposed to "politicians," or "our Croats" as opposed to the attackers but also to the displaced people who settled in the town from rural areas). People continuously blur ethnic categories, both as part of a more deliberate ideology of antinationalism and coexistence, as well as the logic of sharing the place of everyday life, in which meetings occur on bases other than the ideological. Kolind's research also showed that the experience of living in a certain place featured as a prominent ground of identification that helped avoid political juxtapositions along ethnic lines. People have to live with ambiguities and contradictions; they sometimes adopt and sometimes defy the dominant public discourses on war. They try different narrative strategies to incorporate these contradictions into a new, postwar reality.

This can be related to Jasna Čapo Žmegač's (2007) analysis of the processes of identification among the Croats native to the Srijem region in Vojvodina, northern Serbia, who, due to the dissolution of Yugoslavia, resettled in northeastern Croatia. Although the context was one of "coethnic migration," indigenous people and newcomers perceived one another as strangers. The fact that they were all Croats in an independent Croatia was not relevant for the local constructions of difference. While the local population did not see the Croats from Srijem as "true" Croats because they had been living in Serbia, they felt culturally superior. Their narrations of difference in relation to the local population insisted on cultural otherness and impossibility of social contacts. However, their everyday life, as observed by the researcher in the course of her long-term fieldwork, defied narration inasmuch as it brought about contacts that led to gradual integration.

On the local level, ethnic affiliations may not appear as the primary basis for collective identifications in postwar contexts. A "classical" example concerns the difficulties in reestablishing prewar realms of community between people who stayed behind in war zones and those who returned from refuge after the war. The difficulties in understanding each other's experiences and recognizing the choices of leaving and staying behind as equally moral, have been witnessed not only among people of the same ethnicity, but even among family members.

Those who stayed in Sarajevo, met by the Danish anthropologist Anders H. Stefansson (2004a, 2004b), claimed the moral high ground and accused the returners of fleeing and getting rich in the West. They, in turn, employed the strategy of "invisibility": if possible, they avoided talking about their refugee life in the West. Competing discourses of suffering in war and in exile created powerful cultural stereotypes that could, but did not necessarily hamper relations between those who stayed and returners. The gaps between them were not absolute or impossible to bridge.

Tone Bringa's second film (Bringa and Loizos 2001) on the villagers whose wartime victimization was documented in the film from 1993 mentioned above, documents their return to their partially repaired homes six years after their war plight. In the first film, some claimed that they would never ever come back; in the second film, they are filled with energy and plans for the future rebuilding of their homes, for which they carefully collected furniture and other property during the years of displacement. Even if war events made ethnicity and the related religious identifications far more important than before, some Muslims and Croats cherish good neighborly relations, finding a common ground not only in the memories of former life in the village but also in the fact that, albeit on different "sides," they all experienced the loss of home and life as refugees.

Finally, the book *The New Bosnian Mosaic* (Bougarel et al. 2007) focuses on matters "beyond ethnicity," "beyond ancient hatreds," and "beyond protectorate" in postwar Bosnia-Herzegovina. Ethnonational identification is still very much a contested issue. The contributors to the volume analyze the ways in which a number of war-related categories are used by nationalist parties. In the context of meager resources, houses, jobs, and other benefits are distributed in relation to wartime roles. Different ethnonational groups have often diametrically opposing versions of the same event. However, there are no uniform and uncontested interpretations of the war that would differentiate "sides" in a clear-cut way.

Importantly, this book offers critical assessments of the presence and role of "the international community" in postwar Bosnia-Herzegovina, encompassing both international workers and local staff employed in various international organizations. Due to their "elite" salaries, and the fact they do not depend on the same banking system, security, healthcare, or transportation as the local population, they live in a parallel world. These workers remain out of touch with local realities, while being frustrated with the locals' perceived shortcomings that hamper the process of establishing the "civil society" these international workers are paid to promote.

Anthropologists' Contributions to Recovery and Understanding

A collection of Stef Jansen's articles on postwar developments in Croatia and Bosnia-Herzegovina, including those quoted above, has been translated into Croatian (Jansen, n.d.). Tone Bringa's (1995) book on ethnic and religious identities as lived in a Muslim–Croat village in Bosnia in the 1980s and Ivana Maček's (2009) book on Sarajevo under siege in the 1990s have been translated into Bosnian (Bringa 2009; Maček n.d.).

Their work is seen as a valuable contribution to the postwar recovery, welcomed by domestic intellectuals who hope that this will influence wider audiences. Not "going native," but relying on their own extensive field insights, the anthropologists ground their research priorities in the issues recognized as important by the very people they meet in the field. Their work particularly contributes to the knowledge claimed to be central for the anthropological study of violence, and also to a fuller cultural analysis in general – the knowledge of the "struggles over memory and history, the importance of culturally specific narratives for the expression of grievances, and the local constructions of 'choice,' 'competition,' and 'opportunism' (Warren 2001:3 of the Web edition).

It also sheds light on the uses of gender(ed) positions. In examining the workings of public and "everyday" discourses in a Muslim-majority area of Bosnia-Herzegovina, in a community straddling the imagined boundaries of East and West, American anthropologist Elissa Helms (2008) showed a range of competing (re)configurations of East–West and related dichotomies. Importantly, they are reconfigured through notions of gender. While some of these (re)articulations seem to challenge dominant orientalist and Balkanist frameworks, Helms argues that they ultimately reproduce notions of opposing East and West civilizations. She shows that women have become more visible symbols of Balkan backwardness while orientalist depictions have moved from emphasizing erotic sexuality to a focus on heavily veiled and controlled women, symbolizing the political threat of the East/Islam.

In postwar Bosnia, women raped, displaced, and bereaved during the war have become the symbol of ethnic victimization and innocence, especially among Bosniaks (Helms 2007:237). Politically active women are caught in a contradiction. They want to retain the moral purity ascribed to women who conform to their roles as passive victims and keepers of the home and family, yet they also seek to be taken seriously as political *actors* (Helms 2007:240). Helms explored the discursive strategies they use to gain support and justify their involvement in the male-associated sphere of the political, and the importance of the support by the "international community," of a broad-based, multiethnic group of women NGO activists and politicians from a range of political parties, who formed a non-nationalist movement of women calling for increased participation in politics and attention to a variety of "women's issues" (Helms 2007:236).

The ethnographic writing on post-Yugoslav civilians' war experiences feeds into the general knowledge that contests the ideas about "violent instincts" and irrational hatred as causes of war (see Bower 2000; Nordstrom and Quinones Giraldo 2002). Theories concerning home, hope, and mobility may be another important outcome of research on postwar social processes (see, e.g., Long and Oxfeld 2004; Markowitz and Stefansson 2004; Jansen and Löfving 2008).

Furthermore, this research questions a set of explanations for the popular support of nationalism that, from a constructivist perspective, tends to attribute explanatory power to political propaganda and media manipulation, and seeks causes for ordinary people's adherence to nationalism in collective structural factors. The political (and ethical) drawback of such explanations is that "through their disregard for individual agency, they preclude questions of responsibility to an uncomfortable extent and further marginalize existing alternative narratives of past and present as well as dissident routes of action, which have been silenced in recent times" (Jansen 2006:436). Stef Jansen (2006) focused on the agency of the Croatian returnees formerly expelled from their homes in Croatia. His observations of contextual interpretations and strategic moves in the course of daily life deconstruct the perception of internal (nationalist) homogeneity. He found that individual coping strategies in a context of relative powerlessness entail *strategic essentializing* in relation to dominant nationalist discourses.

The British anthropologist Cornelia Sorabji is also sensitive to individual choices and paths of action. Writing about how memories are managed in postwar Sarajevo (Sorabji 2006), she proposes a focus on the *individual as active manager of one's own memories* – again, reachable only through fieldwork, not through analysis of official or media texts. She opposes the idea that people's memories of traumatic events will continue to importantly affect social fabrics.

> At the far end of this general approach to questions of memory are the "ancient ethnic hatred"-style studies which imply that everyone who experiences war is lastingly, psychologically deformed and that the deformity can be xeroxed down the generations by the simple means of repeating stories of suffering to one's children. This is what seems to be implied . . . by the depiction of Bosnia a land "deeply divided and steeped for generations in tales of heroism and imbued with a quasi-religious ethos of revenge . . . " This vision makes it hard to understand why anything ever changes at all and why children do not always and everywhere repeat their parents' animosities and wars. (Sorabji 2006:2)

Sorabji shows that there have been gradual changes to common interpretations of the meanings, motivations, and portents of violence among the people who stayed in Sarajevo throughout the war: from urban–rural opposition in the early days of war, via ideas about innate or semi-innate aggression of Serbs both during the peak and at the end of war, to later interpretations that position Serbs, and even their wartime president, as mere dupes and instruments of global powers (Sorabji 2006:13). She accounts for a hesitation – shared by many – toward the Serbs' return to the city. In purely moral terms, Sorabji's collocutors who had stayed behind in Sarajevo believe that every person should be judged individually, but since they lack specific knowledge about the war conduct of many returned Serbs, they would rather avoid meeting these returners, as even thinking about the Serbs who left raised painful memory-management issues (Sorabji 2006:14). The challenge posed by returning Serbs is thus not in any fixed interpretation of Serbs as a group, but in "the simple unpleasantness of the memory management process itself" (Sorabji 2006:14). As it is most often not possible to make an individual judgment of who may be guilty for what, only those Serbs who remained in the town during the war are met in unproblematic ways.

Ethnographic insights by Sorabji and other anthropologists researching identities, memories, and moral claims in postwar Bosnia-Herzgovina (Bougarel et al. 2007) underscore the need for understandings "from below" and the recognition of micro-local conditions of recovery. By looking at political processes through the notions of masculinity and femininity, ideas about the relationship between politics and society, understandings of public and private realms, and categories of morality and victimhood, they illuminate some of the otherwise hidden ways in which power and identities are being contested and shaped in the postwar period. "Ethno-national classifications and nationalism may intersect with these elements but they are not the only stakes upon which political debates turn. This contrasts sharply with what is implied by most depictions of Bosnia since the break-up of Yugoslavia" (Helms 2007:273).

Looking Ahead, Grasping Contradictions

Postwar Bosnia-Herzegovina is being shaped by a number of state and statelike effects. Foreign donors and local NGOs deliver public services and distribute social benefits in a new interplay of "national" and "international," "governmental" and "nongovernmental," "political," and "humanitarian" (Bougarel et al. 2008:33). Fieldwork is thus a basis for an anthropology of "state-building" that draws on the anthropology of "transition," the anthropology of state, and the anthropology of violence and recovery. At the same time, ethnographic insights inform the upcoming analyses of postsocialist processes in the countries that, in the last two decades, were singled out as examples of ethnic conflict, nationalism, and "failed states." Known for being exemplary in the way they combine knowing and caring for the people they write about and their academic rigor (including fluency in local languages) the anthropologists engaging with postwar issues will hopefully become an increasingly important source of knowledge for aid donors and policy-makers as well as for critical reflections from within the societies they write about.

The group of (mostly young) scholars consisting of anthropologists and ethnologists both from Western and post-Yugoslav countries are currently interrogating the usefulness of postsocialist analytic frames (Gilbert et al. 2008). Finding post-Yugoslav societies to be an excellent place to test the concepts of European and Western modernity, they focus on the multiplicity of imaginaries and practices in post-Yugoslav countries that are overshadowed, but not exhausted, by the recent history of war and violence. They explore the feasibility of hope – people's temporal orientations, expectations, and engagements with possible future – as the central notion in an analysis of social transformation.

The scholars engaged in research in post-Yugoslav contexts have a stake in the processes of societal recovery. On the one hand, the need is paramount for fieldwork-based knowledge that reveals multiple possibilities of perceiving self and others beyond nationalist politicians' designs. On the other hand, it is crucial not to downplay the reality of traumas, the emotions they may entail, and the pervasiveness of competing moral categories and claims coming out of war experiences. In that sense, "balanced" insights are a necessary basis for any purposeful action toward betterment and the assessment of best locality-sensitive practices. They have to take into consideration a cluster of elements that defy explanations in terms of clear-cut group identifications and ethnic antagonisms. War experiences are an integral part of social fabrics already fragmented in many ways. It is therefore important to "comprehend people's understandings of the contradictory tensions, and the heterogeneous personal and collective interests in their lives" (Warren 2001:3 of the Web edition).

Anthropological research on war and recovery in post-Yugoslav countries contributes to the general knowledge coming out of anthropological studies of violence (Warren 2001), namely that politics cross-cuts ethnic, religious, and linguistic difference and complicates the picture of hybrid identifications and coexisting groups formed on diverse grounds. Ethnicity is just one among many such grounds. This, however, does not lessen the fact made clear by the ethnographers quoted above, that people in postwar contexts move back and forth between ethnonational homogenization and building social solidarity along other lines. In the context of war-traumas and precarious resources, potential uses of ethnicity as the foundation of fear and separation should not be underestimated.

ACKNOWLEDGMENTS

My sincere thanks to Stef Jansen, Orvar Löfgren, Ivana Maček, and the editors of this volume, who all offered helpful comments on earlier versions of this text.

REFERENCES

Allcock, John B.

2002 Rural–Urban Differences and the Break-Up of Yugoslavia. Balkanologie 6(1–2):101–134.

Andreas, Peter

2004 The Clandestine Political Economy of War and Peace in Bosnia. International Studies Quarterly 48:29–51.

Atkin, Nicholas, ed.

2008 Daily Lives of Civilians in Wartime Twentieth-Century Europe. Westport, CT: Greenwood Press.

Bax, Mart

1995 Medjugorje: Religion, Politics and Violence in Rural Bosnia. Amsterdam: VU Uitgeverij.

2000a Warlords, Priests and the Politics of Ethnic Cleansing: A Case Study from Rural Bosnia-Herzegovina. Ethnic and Racial Studies 23(1):16–36.

2000b Planned Policy or Primitive Balkanism? A Local Contribution to the Ethnography of the War in Bosnia-Herzegovina. Ethnos 65(3):317–340.

Bennett, Brian C., ed.

1995a Socio-Cultural Analyses of the Political and Economic Democratization Processes in East/Central Europe. Theme Issue. Collegium Antropologicum 19(1):7–119.

1995b Directions for Croatian Anthropology: Reflexive Anthropology. Theme Issue. Collegium Antropologicum 19(1):257–263.

Bjelaković, Nebojša, and Francesco Strazzari

1999 The Sack of Mostar 1992–1994: The Politico-Military Connection. European Security 8(2):73–102.

Bojičić, Vesna, and Mary Kaldor

1999 The Abnormal Economy of Bosnia-Herzegovina. *In* Scramble for the Balkans: Nationalism, Globalism and the Political Economy of Reconstruction. Carl-Ulrik Schierup, ed. pp. 92–118. Basingstoke: Macmillan.

Bougarel, Xavier

1999 Yugoslav Wars: The "Revenge of the Countryside" between Sociological Reality and Nationalist Myth. East European Quarterly 33(2):157–175.

Bougarel, Xavier, Elissa Helms, and Ger Duijzings, eds.

2007 New Bosnian Mosaic: Identities, Memories and Moral Claims in a Post-War Society. Aldershot: Ashgate.

Bower, Bruce

2000 Inside Violent Worlds: Political Conflict and Terror Look Different Up Close and Local. Science News 158:88–90.

Bringa, Tone

1993 We Are All Neighbours. Documentary film. Director: Debbie Christie. Disappearing Worlds series. Manchester: Granada Television.

1995 Being Muslim the Bosnian Way: Identity and Community in a Central Bosnian Village. Princeton: Princeton University Press.

2002 Adverted Gaze: Genocide in Bosnia-Herzegovina, 1992–1995. *In* Annihilating Difference: The Anthropology of Genocide. Alexander Laban Hinton, ed. pp. 194–225. Berkeley: University of California Press.

2009 Biti Musliman na bosanski način: Identitet i zajednica u jednom srednjobosanskom selu. Sarajevo: Šahinpašić.

Bringa, Tone, and Peter Loizos

2001 Returning Home: Revival of a Bosnian Village. Documentary film. Sarajevo: Saga Video.

Čale Feldman, Lada

1995a The Image of the Leader: Being a President, Displaying a Cultural Performance. Collegium Antropologicum 19(1):41–52.

1995b "Intellectual Concerns and Scholarly Priorities": A Voice of an Ethnographer. Narodna umjetnost. Croatian Journal of Ethnology and Folklore Research 32(1):79–90.

Čale Feldman, Lada, Ines Prica, and Reana Senjković, eds.

1993 Fear, Death and Resistance. An Ethnography of War: Croatia 1991–1992. Zagreb: Institute of Ethnology and Folklore Research, Matrix Croatica, X-Press.

Caplan, Pat

2002 "We Are All Neighbours": Review. *In* The Best of Anthropology Today. Jonathan Benthall, ed. pp. 179–183. New York: Routledge.

Čapo Žmegač, Jasna

2007 Strangers Either Way: The Lives of Croatian Refugees in Their New Home. Oxford: Berghahn.

Clifford, James, and George E. Marcus

1986 Writing Culture: The Poetics and Politics of Ethnography. Berkeley: University of California Press.

Craigie, Jill

1995 Two Hours from London. TV – Single documentary film, broadcast on BBC 2 in 1995.

Daniel, E. Valentine

1996 Charred Lullabies: Chapters in an Anthropology of Violence. Princeton: Princeton University Press.

Das, Veena, Arthur Kleinman, Margaret Lock, Mamphela Ramphele, and Pamela Reynolds, eds.

2001 Remaking a World: Violence, Social Suffering and Recovery. Berkeley: University of California Press.

Donia, Robert J., and John V. A. Fine
1994 Bosnia and Hercegovina: A Tradition Betrayed. London: Hurst.
Fenton, Steve
2010 Ethnicity. Cambridge: Polity.
Finnström, Sverker
2008 Living with Bad Surroundings: War, History and Everyday Moments in Northern Uganda. Durham, NC: Duke University Press.
Gagnon, Valère Philip, Jr
2004 The Myth of Ethnic War: Serbia and Croatia in the 1990s. Ithaca: Cornell University Press.
Gilbert, Andrew, Jessica Greenberg, Elissa Helms, and Stef Jansen
2008 Reconsidering Postsocialism from the Margins of Europe: Hope, Time and Normalcy in Post-Yugoslav Societies. Anthropology News 49(8):10–11.
Halpern, Joel M., and David A. Kideckel
2000 Introduction: The End of Yugoslavia Observed. *In* Neighbors at War: Anthropological Perspectives on Yugoslav Ethnicity, Culture, and History. Joel M. Halpern and David A. Kideckel, eds. pp. 3–18. University Park: Pennsylvania State University Press.
Helms, Elissa
2007 "Politics is a Whore": Women, Morality and Victimhood in Post-War Bosnia-Herzegovina. *In* The New Bosnian Mosaic. Xavier Bougarel, Elissa Helms, and Ger Duijzings, eds. pp. 235–253. Aldershot: Ashgate.
2008 East and West Kiss: Gender, Orientalism, and Balkanism in Muslim-Majority Bosnia-Herzegovina. Slavic Review 67(1):88–119.
Jambrešić, Renata
1995 Testimonial Discourse between National Narrative and Ethnography as Socio-Cultural Analysis. Collegium Antropologicum 19(1):17–27.
Jambrešić Kirin, Renata
1996a Narrating War and Exile Experiences. *In* War, Exile, Everyday Life: Cultural Perspectives. Renata Jambrešić Kirin and Maja Povrzanović, eds. pp. 63–82. Zagreb: Institute of Ethnology and Folklore Research.
1996b On Gender-Affected War Narratives. Narodna umjetnost. Croatian Journal of Ethnology and Folklore Research 33(1):25–40.
Jambrešić Kirin, Renata, and Maja Povrzanović, eds.
1996 War, Exile, Everyday Life: Cultural Perspectives. Zagreb: Institute of Ethnology and Folklore Research.
Jansen, Stef
2005a National Numbers in Context: Maps and Stats in representations of the Post-Yugoslav Wars. Identities: Global Studies in Culture and Power 12:45–68.
2005b Antinacionalizam: Etnografija otpora u Zagrebu i Beogradu. Belgrade: XX Vek.
2006 The (Dis)Comfort of Comformism: Post-War Nationalism and Coping with Powerlessness in Croatian Villages. *In* Warfare and Society: Archaeological and Social Anthropological Perspectives. Tom Otto, Henrik Thrane, and Helle Vandkilde, eds. pp. 433–446. Aarhus: Aarhus University Press.
2007 Troubled Locations: Return, the Life Course, and Transformation of "Home" in Bosnia-Herzegovina. Focaal. European Journal of Anthropology 49:15–30.
n.d. Razlog za dom: antropologija post-jugoslavenskih prostora. Zagreb: Institut za etnologiju i folkloristiku.
Jansen, Stef, and Saffan Löfving, eds.
2008 Struggles for Home: Violence, Hope and Movement of People. Oxford: Berghahn.

Kapić, Suada, Ozren Pavlović, and Nihad Kreševljaković
2006 Sarajevo Survival Map. Sarajevo: Fama International.
Kaplan, Robert D.
1993 Balkan Ghosts: A Journey Through History. New York: St Martin's Press.
Kolind, Torsten
2006 Violence and Identification in a Bosnian Town: An Empirical Critique of Structural Theory of Violence. *In* Warfare and Society: Archaeological and Social Anthropological Perspectives. Tom Otto, Henrik Thrane, and Helle Vandkilde, eds. pp. 447–468. Aarhus: Aarhus University Press.
2008 Post-war Identification: Everyday Muslim Counterdiscourse in Bosnia Herzegovina. Aarhus: Aarhus University Press.
Leutloff-Grandits, Carolin
2006 Claiming Ownership in Postwar Croatia: The Dynamics of Property Relations and Ethnic Conflict in the Knin Region. Münster: LIT.
Long, Lynellyn D., and Ellen Oxfeld, eds.
2004 Coming Home: Refugees, Migrants, and Those Who Stayed Behind. Philadelphia: University of Pennsylvania Press.
Maček, Ivana
2009 Sarajevo Under Siege: Anthropology in Wartime. Philadelphia: University of Pennsylvania Press.
n.d. Rat iznutra: Svakodnevni život u Sarajevu tokom opsade. Sarajevo: Dani.
Malcolm, Noel
1994 Bosnia: A Short History. Basingstoke: Macmillan.
Markowitz, Fran, and Anders H. Stefansson, eds.
2004 Homecomings: Unsettling Paths of Return. Lanham, MD: Lexington Books.
Naumović, Slobodan
2002 The Ethnology of Transformation as Transformed Ethnology: The Serbian Case. Ethnologia Balkanica 6:7–37.
Nordstrom, Carolyn
2004 Shadows of War: Violence, Power, and International Profiteering in the Twenty-First Century. Berkeley: University of California Press.
Nordstrom, Carolyn, and Adriana Quinones Giraldo
2002 Four Ways to Tell a Story on Violence. Reviews in Anthropology 31:1–19.
Pettan, Svanibor, ed.
1998 Music, Politics, and War: Views from Croatia. Zagreb: Institute of Ethnology and Folklore Research.
Povrzanović, Maja
1997 Identities in War: Embodiments of Violence and Places of Belonging. Ethnologia Europaea 27:153–162.
2000 The Imposed and the Imagined as Encountered by Croatian War Ethnographers. Current Anthropology 41(2):151–162.
Povrzanović Frykman, Maja
2002 Violence and the Re-discovery of Place. Ethnologia Europaea 32(2):69–88.
2008 Staying Behind: Civilians in the Post-Yugoslav Wars 1991–95. *In* Daily Lives of Civilians in Wartime Twentieth-Century Europe. Nicholas Atkin, ed. pp. 163–193. Westport, CT: Greenwood Press.
Prica, Ines
1995a Between Destruction and Deconstruction: The Preconditions of the Croatian Ethnography of War. Collegium Antropologicum 19(1):7–16.

1995b "To Be Here – To Publish There." On the Position of a Small European Ethnology. Narodna umjetnost. Croatian Journal of Ethnology and Folklore Research 32(1):7–23.

Research and Documentation Center Sarajevo

2008 Rezultati istraživanja "Ljudski gubici '91–'95." Electronic document. http://www.idc.org.ba/index.php?option=com_content&view=section&id=35&Itemid=126&lang=bs (accessed October 30, 2011).

Schmidt, Bettina E., and Ingo W. Schröder

2001 Introduction: Violent Imaginaries and Violent Practices. *In* Anthropology of Violence and Conflict. Bettina E. Schmidt and Ingo W. Schröder, eds. pp. 1–24. London and New York: Routledge.

The Scholars' Initiative: Confronting the Yugoslav Controversies

2006 Project Director Professor Charles Ingrao, Purdue University. Electronic document. http://www.cla.purdue.edu/history/facstaff/ingrao/si/prospectus.pdf (accessed October 23, 2011).

Sekulić, Duško

1997 The Creation and Dissolution of the Multinational State: The Case of Yugoslavia. Nations and Nationalism 3(2):165–180.

Senjković, Reana

1995a The Use, Interpretation and Symbolization of the National. Ethnologia Europaea 25(1):69–80.

1995b Ideologies and Iconographies: Croatia in the Second Half of the 20th century. Collegium Antropologicum 19(1):53–63.

1996 Image of Warrior. Narodna umjetnost. Croatian Journal of Ethnology and Folklore Research 33(1):41-57.

Sorabji, Cornelia

1995 A Very Modern War: Terror and Territory in Bosnia-Herzegovina. *In* War: A Cruel Necessity? The Bases of Institutional Violence. Robert A. Hinde and Helen Watson, eds. pp. 80–95. London: Tauris.

2006 Managing Memories in Post-War Sarajevo: Individuals, Bad Memories, and New Wars. Journal of Royal Anthropological Institute (N.S.) 12:1–18.

Stefansson, Anders H.

2004a Refuge Returns to Sarajevo and Their Challenge to Contemporary Narratives of Mobility. *In* Coming Home: Refugees, Migrants, and Those Who Stayed Behind. Lynellyn D. Long and Ellen Oxfeld, eds. pp. 170–186. Philadelphia: University of Pennsylvania Press.

2004b The Home(s) of Homecomings. *In* Homecomings: Unsettling Paths of Return. Fran Markowitz and Anders H. Stefansson, eds. pp. 54–75. Lanham, MD: Lexington Books.

Warren, Key B.

2001 Violence in Anthropology. *In* International Encyclopedia of the Social and Behavioral Sciences. pp. 16202–16206. Science Direct, at http://www.sciencedirect.com/science/referenceworks/9780080430768 (accessed November 4, 2011). doi:10.1016/BO-08-043076-7/00974-8

CHAPTER 16

European Religious Fragmentation and the Rise of Civil Religion

Peter Jan Margry

In 2008 Dutch mass media got wind of a new religious group that had established itself in the small village of Hoeven. Under the ominous name of the Order of Transformers,[1] the members practice a form of fundamentalism based on Christianity which focuses on the purity of the original (apocryphal) scriptures as well as physical naturism. Living in a strict community, members must experience the influence their choices have on their daily lives and learn how to banish the associated "weak links and destructive routines" from their personal lives in order to achieve a state of harmony. This community is an example of the splintering of modern religious life, and also of the way in which new religious movements try to bring balance into the growing subjectivation of religion in modern Western society, in part by a collective "renewal" based on a Christian heritage. With their autonomous operation and the eclectic way in which they have put together their belief system, these "transformers" are in that respect children of their time.

This chapter concentrates on religion and belief systems in modern Europe. It is not intended to be a general overview, but instead focuses on a number of specific religious phenomena from the recent past. Furthermore, it will show how we can relate these changes to the history of Europe and the way in which new developments, both on an individual and collective level, are inspired by the (Christian) past.

A Christian Europe?

During the last decade, belief systems in contemporary Europe showed a strong intrinsic and extrinsic dynamism. Notwithstanding its long and broad historical basis, Christianity, which was once the dominant religion of Europe, has for decades now been rapidly losing ground to a general subjectivation of religion, and this has caused a fragmentation of faith, resulting in various spiritual forms and new religious

A Companion to the Anthropology of Europe, First Edition. Edited by Ullrich Kockel, Máiréad Nic Craith, and Jonas Frykman.

movements such as the charismatic movement, Pentecostalism, neopaganism, Scientology, esotericism, pluriform New Age, and so on (e.g. Hanegraaff 1996; Coleman 2000; Partridge 2004; Heelas and Woodhead 2005). In a diachronic perspective, this development is not a completely new phenomenon; there has been a tension between the dominant Christian religion (i.e. Orthodoxy, Protestantism, Roman Catholicism) on the one hand, and on the other hand undercurrents of heterodoxy or nonconforming religious movements and the individual's search for other "truths," as expressed in paganism, syncretism, Gnosticism, superstition, Satanism, freemasonry, rationalism, modernism, and so on. However, these movements and sectarian cults remained relatively small and did not constitute a serious threat to Christianity as a whole. Within Europe, Christianity has thus been the main religious expression, without any serious competition. It was the dominant culture without being universal or uniform.[2]

Religion is embedded in a sequence, and is being constantly renewed and reinvented in all of its manifestations in opposition to preceding systems and movements. In this way, Christianity and new and alternative religious movements stemming both from outside and from within Christianity itself have continually influenced one another. It was, however, not until the twentieth century that Christian Europe became confronted with a major change in its social and religious paradigms. For centuries, European unity had been without serious competition, despite the division caused by the Great Schism of 1054, which created a separation between the West and Orthodoxy (in Eastern Europe, Greece, and Russia) and the division of Western Christianity itself in the sixteenth century, that developed further along the somewhat looser Protestant lines of the Reformation and via the hierarchic and centralistic Roman Catholic Church. These two schisms are still geographically represented in a "southern" Catholicism, "northwestern" Protestantism, and "eastern" Orthodoxy, divisions whose lines more or less concur with the Roman, German, and Slavic language territories. This seemingly simple division of the continent into three parts should not obfuscate our idea of the cultural and religious complexity of what we call "Europe," mostly unified but consisting of an exceptional variety of ethnicities, communities, and networks.

Although intrinsically divided, the strong staying power of Christendom was only sporadically threatened by the single competitive neighboring monotheistic religion of Islam.[3] Judaism always maintained some level of cultural influence, but remained quantitatively small, existing in minority communities within the Christian realm. Having underscored the dominance of Christianity in a historical perspective, it is relevant to note here that it remains unclear how Christian the past actually was at the level of everyday culture, and the extent to which it remained "pagan," affected by superstitious practices of popular or lived religion, remains unclear too (Delumeau 1971; Milis 1998). So, roughly speaking, Christianity represents two different realities: that of the formal Churches and that of the vernacular, the collective, and individual practice of everyday life (cf. Primiano 1995; Ammermann 2007).

The basis of the shift toward personal religiosity as it is expressed nowadays can be traced back to the Enlightenment; and even the critical and self-reflexive religious movements of the Reformation at the start of the early modern period could in a way be seen as precursors of the radical Enlightenment. This rationalistic movement rejected the existence of God and praised the freedom of the autonomous self. Philosopher Baruch Spinoza introduced a humanistic approach, with which, based on human reasoning, the religion was deconstructed and perceived as a cultural invention (Israel 2001:218–229). The nineteenth century, subsequently, had its own secular prophets, of whom Friedrich Nietzsche may have been the bluntest when he described Christianity and/or religion as a drug or a curse, and as one great lie maintained in order to control the people. Nietzsche's shocking atheist theorizing (for example in *Die fröhliche Wissenschaft* from 1882) was possible thanks to the enlightened mindset and the reordering of Europe after the French Revolution, which led to the creation of nation-states and new societal ideologies such as capitalism and communism, which arose and challenged the hegemony of Christianity.

From a historic point of view, it is interesting to note that within modern Europe Catholicism managed to regain for one more time some of its direct political influence. This was during the run-up to the collapse of the Iron Curtain and, in combination with the people's movement, with its leading role in the downfall of communism in Poland in 1989; similarly, in Croatia and Lithuania, Catholicism and nationalism were connected, playing a role in the breakup of Yugoslavia and the Soviet Union (Borowik 2002; Knippenberg 2005).

For many people in Europe, World War II provided the ultimate confrontation with themselves and with the existential values and uncertainties of life. From a theological viewpoint, this human catastrophe would later even raise questions about the very existence or meaning of God in the light of the possibility of "Auschwitz" (Morgan 2001a, 2001b). The total desperation of Europe following World War II revived processes of change which would shake the European belief systems to their core. And it was around the middle of the twentieth century that an overall shift in the European religious paradigm took place. The rise of the welfare state in Western Europe in particular went hand in hand with a decrease in the fundamental need for the existing church communities along which people's daily lives were structured. The "long 1960s" represented a "revolutionary" new age in which a religious revolution also took place, triggered by sociocultural and internal ecclesiastical renewals and an emerging ecumenical movement. The subsequent erosion of traditional church structures opened the way to voluntary and eclectically created forms of religion mainly situated and organized in and from the private domain. This was a momentous shift from universal to more strongly individually defined "systems" of beliefs and ways of giving meaning to life. This process of driving back the existing dominant Churches from the public domain and its collective religious practice can be seen as a form of pseudosecularization as it created space for new and different forms of religion and spirituality and Church renewals.

Renewal and Revival

The "long 1960s," however, can be described as a second Enlightenment, within which the individual was better able to make his or her own religious choices, separate from tradition and without institutional norms and guidance. The simultaneous massive opening up of the world by travel, tourism, and media made the acquaintance with a wide range of non-Western rituals and religious views possible. The message of self-development from those days opened the way for what is today known as religious shopping, or do-it-yourself or patchwork religion. Reenchanted Europe also experienced a renewed interest in its pre-Christian, pagan spiritualities. Although the term spirituality (derived from the Latin *spiritus* = spirit) is embedded in older classical and Christian uses, since the mid-twentieth century it has also become a generic term for the wide range of Western and neopagan spiritualities and new religious movements as well as Eastern religions and spiritualities and all their related practices. Although some qualify spirituality at a lower level as, for example, being "undemanding," "ad hoc," or "uninstitutionalized," and therefore not a "real" religion (Taylor 2002:113), from my perspective this is not the case. The emergence of spirituality in combination with the repositioning of some of the major religions refuted the secularization theory which had been the leading religion research paradigm for decades (cf. Berger 2002).

In general, the new movements no longer represent lifetime moral frameworks, but epitomize open spiritual communities, which are often chosen by people – "spiritual seekers" – in a sequential or eclectic way, each one being related to a specific phase of life with its corresponding existential problems, interests, and preferences. As long as the existential self of the "common Westerner" is not threatened or disorientated, nowadays a limited or low-level demand for religion or spirituality is implied. This religious pragmatism turns to religion when it is necessary; religion has become an optional extra. Thus when unhappiness, loneliness, problems, and untreatable diseases or mental illnesses impinge upon daily life, people's perceptions change and they tend to feel some kind of religious need.

For the Catholic Church, the outcome of the Second Vatican Council (1962–1965) proved to be a factor in the undermining of its own position. The Council's aim of modernizing the Church was the ultimate cultural expression of the period of change in which it took place. One effect of the renewal of the Church in combination with what was seen as an increasing "moral decay" of society was the creation of smaller countermovements of Christian-related traditionalism and scattered fundamentalism in Europe. Although comparatively small, the influence of these groups of activists is relatively strong. They are organized in autonomous alternative groupings or informal prayer groups, often related to visionaries and contested apparitional devotions through which they avow that Jesus or Mary personally proclaim the universal truth directly to mankind (to them) instead of via what they call the "false church of Rome" with its subjectified interpretations. These circles of individualistic devotees are also an expression of the fragmentation of religion in Europe. Despite their small size they have gained a relatively large influence through their high degree of digitalization and their use of Web services, and by creating what I have called the network of divergent Marian devotion (Margry 2004; Apolito 2005). This network has its origins in Europe but nowadays represents a global fabric of Catholic-inspired traditionalism, which has produced an alternative grassroots and contestative devotional circuit of traditionalist clerical leaders, visionaries, and devotees. These groups move in the grey areas on the outskirts of the Church. For example, the cult of Our Lady of Medjugorje, which for decades was formally banned and denounced in Bosnia and Herzegovina, has become so powerful that it seems on the verge of mainstream acceptance. In reaction to such disintegrating forces, nowadays the weakened Catholic Church opts for pragmatic politics and tries to normalize and reintegrate important heretical devotions. Church officials then start to acknowledge that the visionary shrine might indeed produce indirect benefits for the church, such as conversions and priestly vocations, and that these should be now interpreted as proof of its authenticity (Margry 2009).

The undermined position of the Church as a moral and ethical paradigm caused religious people to shift from the Church to new religious movements which could offer religious absolutism and inerrancy. In response to this, the Catholic Church started to battle religious fragmentation and encouraged the incorporation of deviancy, heresy, or cognate religious domains. The Marian cult of Medjugorje has already been mentioned, but also excommunicated movements like the Lefebvrists (Society of St. Pius X) have been invited to return to the "mother church." Renewal and convergences are also visible in Protestantism, where Protestants are searching within Catholic traditions for their roots and for renewing inspiration in rituality and sensorial experiences. The evangelical/Protestant section of European Christianity also shows an important renewal movement, which is induced by the success of African and American evangelicalism and Pentecostalism and by charismatic Protestantism (Jenkins 2007). Inspired by new movements brought to Europe through immigration, new and flourishing local communities have come into being. These movements attach much importance to collective ritual and the performance of the individual body and the use of the senses. One very popular – as individually connected to issues of life and illness – instrumental ritual element within these new movements is the practice of prayer or faith healing. This ritual makes it possible for an individual to emerge from the group, to present themselves, and it brings him or her into contact with the religious specialist.

With their appropriation and convergence policies, the churches are trying to halt the erosion of institutional religion. Although they have had a certain amount of success in this, they have also had to give way to the invasive appearance and broad popularity of alternative spiritualities in the West.

Religious Fragmentation as a Paradigm

It is central to the argument of this chapter that the fragmentation of religion means that an insight into the current state of religion in Europe can only be obtained through ethnological and anthropological research methods and a focus on everyday life and the local (cf. Knott 2005). Since religion is more a matter of context than system, I will now go deeper into the cultural contexts of religious fragmentation and the rise of civil religion.

The developments here described are not autonomous, but part of a much wider process of reevaluating, repositioning, and redefining religion and the sacred in people's lives. The fragmentation of the territory of the traditional church was initiated and stimulated by a process of declining churchgoing or secularization followed by repeated cycles of secularization and desecularization or sacralization. During this period the churches lost their monopoly on the definition of the sacred and of transcendental symbolism, but in this case globalization did not result in cultural homogenization or monolithization. Together with a growing individualization[4] and subjectivation in Western society, the loss of the monopoly broke through cultural barriers and generated a proliferation and mingling of languages, ethnicities, religions, and religious movements. Thus cosmopolitan–religious forms of cultural globalization, coupled with individual processes of laying claim to local or regional rituals and symbolic practices, created increased opportunities for a personalized religious praxis. As far back as the early 1960s, the German sociologist Thomas Luckmann noted the discrepancy between the subjective autonomy of the individual and the objective autonomy of the primary (ecclesiastical) institutions in the public domain. He asked himself to what extent the modern sacred "cosmos" legitimized or was a cause of the fact that the individual was retreating into the realm of the private and personal, and so increasingly sanctifying his own subjective autonomy (Luckmann 1967, 1990).

Seen in this way, the breaking open of the former traditions of authority and the opportunity to exercise freedom of choice led to a far-reaching fragmentation and pluralization of the religious domain and to the erosion of tradition within religion ("detraditionalization"). Another German sociologist, Klaus Eder, then coined the concept of a "post-secular society." He identified the paradox of the rise of religion in what is seemingly a secular society. This has also been recognized by a former protagonist of the secularization theory, Harvey Cox, who depicted the theory as "the myth of the twentieth century."

In any case, secularization and the withdrawal of the traditional Church from the public domain has created more space for smaller movements of Christian fundamentalism, cults, forms of open spirituality and New Age, as well as the need – in times of crisis – to experience a sort of religious communion in rituals and new forms of religion, in addition to the seemingly endless individual choices available.

Nevertheless some countries, whilst being highly unchurched or secularized, still show paradoxically high figures for Church adherence, although these figures may be distorted as people tend not to go to the effort of resigning their church membership. In some of these countries, the rejection of a personal God gave way to a generally noncommittal or nonengaged idea that is expressed in the fact that, when asked, many are prone to answer that there *might* indeed be *something*. The God idea becomes overruled by an indefinite belief in a transcendent power. This religion of "somethingism," may become, or is already in some northwestern European countries, the biggest group of "believers" (Hamberg 2003:48–49). This attitude, which stems from rationalism, is closely bound up with a continuing uncertainty regarding the existence of a God ("probabilism").

This "somethingism" is not always translated into an actual religious practice but it exists in people's minds as a reasoned potentiality. More often it finds its way into a broad variety of expressions of New Age spiritualities. In her fascinating research into modern Scottish shamanic practices, Burgess found that those involved made a specific choice for spiritual growth and service and to undergo this transformative process because of all the changes in the world and in their lives. These new shamans are not so much seeking traditions as "spirit" and "guidance" to help them be able to function better in a global society (Burgess 2008:175–176). Generally speaking, European religious heritage forms a fertile ground from which all manner of religious reifications based on heritage and indigenous traditions have flourished: neopaganism, Avalon, Wicca, Atlantis/UFOs/ druidism, Grail spirituality, Celticism, Satanism, Cabalism, and so on.

"Institutional religions are currently faltering in their ability to help people move through their transformational change in meaningful ways," states Burgess. The power structures of the religious institutions which ruled over people are being replaced by a personal and identity-related interpretation; the holistic concept of a general consciousness or interrelatedness with all life. New religions can offer support and guidance to spiritual consciousness, without doctrines and the instruments of power as wielded by the churches (Burgess 2008:195–197). In "liquid modernity," spirituality and religion, like notions of the sacred, are themselves being transformed and the participants feel a certain sense of engagement as co-creator of emerging global spiritualities.

An important element in the whole array of modern religious forms and movements is the aspect of gender. New religious movements have a much larger role for female interpretation, one that challenges the patriarchal paradigm of religion in general. Within major (fundamentalist) global forms of worship also, the role of women has greatly increased. For example, the controversial cult of the Lady of All Nations in Amsterdam explicitly wants to reinforce the public female element. Researchers asked: What draws women to religion? Their initial conclusion was that women tend to look within rather than outside for answers regarding the meaning of life. New spiritualities also draw more upon personal experience and intuitive knowing, which is understood as a more feminine aspect. Moreover, men undergo a different process of detraditionalization to women. Posttraditional women, who experience burdens and anxieties in relation to negotiating daily life, tend to focus more on spirituality than on the Church (Aune et al. 2007:222–223). It emerges that they have an important need for direct opportunities to experience the sacred in their daily lives. This also explains the enormous popularity of home altars among women. It turns out that feminism exercises some influence on religion: full-time workers are less involved in religiosity.

THE EXISTENTIAL IN RELIGION

In discussing European religious fragmentation, a new perspective can help us understand modern people's behavior in the religious domain: the concept of the existential. Here the concept is operationalized with the notion of the problem of human existence – *la condition humaine* – a prompting factor in relation to contemporary religiosity. Religiosity should be researched in its very locus: as it is lived and experienced by individuals in everyday life. This means that, within the sociocultural setting of a religion, I see the personal experience and reflections of an individual on his or her human condition as a primary motive for their religious choices and behavior. This approach also emphasizes the influence of the human psyche on such processes, instead of addressing a mere social experience of the surrounding world. Implemented in the religious domain, this perspective assumes that religiosity in Europe is strongly induced by giving personal meaning to one's existence and that people's reactions to threats and anxieties relate directly to their own existence. These meanings are induced by the personal choices the self has to make. This approach is based on what Kierkegaard wrote on human anxieties, as a troubled mental state being "the pivot upon which everything turns." Kierkegaard stated that through anxiety the self becomes truly aware of the finite and the infinite of human existence (Kierkegaard 1980:41–46). This theoretical framework also brings the American theologian Paul Tillich in view, who, also inspired by Kierkegaard, described the self as "being grasped by an ultimate concern," namely, an ultimate concern about the meaning of one's life and the meaning of "being" as such (MacKenzie Brown 1965).

In the past, the control of anxieties and concerns regarding the ultimate have become socially embedded in cultural and moral communities that have developed into institutional churches, such as the Christian churches in Europe. In this way the churches created a collectively organized safety net for their followers and met their implicit desire for security, a desire which the French historian Jean Delumeau conceived as the major motive in human existence. This is what I term mankind's way of "dealing with doom." How do people behave with the prospect of fate and destiny, how do they react when actually confronted with "doom" and in what way is this related to personal religiosity?

Late modernity turned things upside down again as in the welfare states, health and security became professionally organized by the state and its secular institutions. Fate and doom seemed to be increasingly distant from daily life, and the churches lost their dominant "life-saving" position. This referential framework of the existential explains how it was possible for the religious identity crisis of the 1950s to the 1980s to become so widespread and to give rise to such a "spiritual revolution."

Nowadays, Europeans have the freedom and opportunity to make an endless variety of choices from religions and spiritualities to fulfill their spiritual needs. This freedom of choice is an existential element for the self. So the central question in this regard can be formulated as follows: how does the cultural–existential human being create and determine his or her religiosity? And, what is the significance or consequence of that position, on an individual level and for society as a whole?

In answering these questions I do not want to fall back on the overused "shell" concepts of popular spirituality (Heelas and Woodhead 2005; Knoblauch 2009), but instead I prefer to keep to the term religion (and, *a fortiori*, religiosity), by which I understand all notions and ideas that human beings have regarding their experience of the sacred or the supernatural in order to give meaning to life and to gain access to transformative powers that may influence their existential condition (cf. Margry 2008:17). I use religion as a generic term that refers to what the self experiences as transcendental.

Religion in today's Europe is strongly induced by experience, sense, and feeling, by emotions and sentiments, and by threats to, or insecurities about, one's existence. These perceptions give way to new cultural expressions in symbols, texts, ritual, practices, and can even become a "system" when these become corporate, organized, and institutionalized. As the personal aspect prevails in the context addressed here, it therefore contests the Durkheimian interpretation of religion as "an eminently collective thing," and I therefore regard religion as an eminently individual thing.

The relation of religion to the existential can also be clarified by discussing religious differences within Western culture. One difference between Europe and the United States that is often raised compares "secular" and "unchurched" Western Europe to the "religious" United States. This distinction has recently been addressed again by Peter Berger (Berger et al. 2008; cf. Davie 2002), but is still not explained in a satisfactory manner. As I see it, a partial solution can be found in the dissimilar ways both modernities deal with human existence. In the United States with its "proverbial" ultimate personal freedom and "frontier mentality," people basically rely only on themselves without the backing of strong governmental safety nets. As a country of immigrants it is a survival society, potentially more dangerous. A cultural expression of that mentality is clearly illustrated in the issue of weapon possession and the fundamental right to defend oneself. This mentality also explains, for example, why there was a fundamental problem in realizing a universal healthcare system there. The restraint of government prompts the need for alternative moral, religious communities by which the individual feels shielded. This need is expressed in the strong foothold of traditional religions in the United States and the great variety of sects, cults, and new religious movements (NRMs). As the old continent by contrast turned into a highly organized and intensely regulated union of welfare states, governments had largely taken over the existential responsibilities from its individual citizens. Life is more or less secure, economically and medically speaking, and is only threatened at times of trouble, when the trusted security measures ultimately fail. So where political-ideological individualism is the strongest, institutional religion flourishes, and where social–cultural individualism is dominant, institutional religion fades.

The influence of prosperity and the market economy has led investigators to regard these religious changes as the result of a process similar to economic choice – Peter Berger terms it "religious preference" – or rather perhaps as "pluralist competition," which according to Stark might also be explained on the basis of the Rational Choice Theory (Berger et al. 2008). Could this be in part the reason why Europe is an exception in the modern world, as Davie (2000) suggests? Can we indeed speak of "Eurosecularity," to use Berger's term? Whatever the case may be, religion has a different position in politics and society as a result. In Europe the Enlightenment tradition, in both its radical and more moderate forms, has certainly had its effects, and religion has to a large extent been reduced to the private domain. Or as Davie puts it: "believing without belonging" to a religious institution. As I see it, one can perceive a way of believing which is at the same time extremely pluriform and individual, in which institutional–ecclesiastical bonds have largely disappeared or have been reduced to shared perceptions on values of a mere cultural–historical nature. By revitalizing, operationalizing, and transforming Europe's "Christian" heritage it proves possible to establish and affirm a collective European identity, based on Christian roots and values, which I will discuss in more detail below.

The rise of a global culture war of religions and the appearance of partly related new forms of violence in Europe – terrorism and "senseless violence" – during the last two decades, has introduced new general insecurities into life. This social disturbance increased a need for norms and values for today's society and made people reevaluate their faded Christian traditions. Within Europe's secularist culture it even prompted a revival of creationist–evolutionist debates and the idea – suggested as a sort of compromise – of the world as the result of "intelligent design." On the other side of the spectrum of religious life, scientists try to explain, or better still to reduce, religion to a mere functionality of the brain. For example, by stimulating the temporal lobes of the brain in a laboratory setting, neuropsychologist Michael Persinger succeeded in evoking visions, and religious and quasi-mystical experiences (Persinger 1987). In this way he tried to find the biological basis of the "God experience." Nicholas Wade reasoned in line with a connection of genome and religion and stated that the binding and motivating forces of religion have been giving evolutionary benefits (Wade 2009). From a Darwinist perspective, militant atheist and "cultural Christian" Richard Dawkins provoked the discussion by trying to eliminate the idea of the existence of God at all with his polemic book *The God Delusion* (Dawkins 2006). The debate continues with the question of the functionality or necessity of religion in the world or for the personal self. Charles Taylor, for example, argues that there is a need for spirituality because man is not purely an explainable object. Where certain expressions of religion disappear, other expressions inevitably take their place. This indicates the necessary function of religion, even a "secularized" variant such as civil religion.

Civil Religion in Europe

The American scholar of religion José Casanova once wondered about the necessity of a civil religion based on Enlightenment principles in relation to the normative integration of modern differentiated societies (i.e. the EU). He reflected on this issue in relation to the discussion about the preamble of the new European constitution and its mention of the "spiritual and moral heritage" of the continent and the inability of Europe to openly recognize Christianity as a constitutive component of European identity. He explained it in terms of politicians' general desire for secular neutrality, notwithstanding the strong link of religion to the Enlightenment. He argued the need for a reflexive recognition of a Christian encoding within the EU (Casanova 2006:37; cf. Hervieu-Léger 2000). In reply to his query, I point to a renewed instrumentalization of a geographically encoded form of Christianity, specifically expressed in the pilgrims' ways of Europe, which I understand as an expression of a trans-European form of civil religion (cf. Margry 2011).

A clear example of an active use of the Christian–European heritage is the successful revitalization of the transnational network of European pilgrim routes, including the addition of new, invented routes. Started as an elitist cultural project, this revitalization expanded to become a pan-European grassroots movement of European citizens who, by utilizing their Christian heritage, have found a means to heal and reaffirm themselves and implicitly search for community again. This performative form of heritage creation not only helps to reaffirm Europe in its Christian essence and combat contemporary moral decay, it also forms a counterpoise to a "threatened" Europe in its cultural clash with Islam. Against the background of an apparent cultural identity crisis of the EU, which consists of a wide variety of states with different cultural backgrounds, Europe's need for an appealing, overarching idea or politicoreligious value system has dynamized the continent's Christian heritage.

Many Europeans who "belong" to the traditional churches, but do not really believe anymore, have created new religious networks. One of these consists of a rapidly increasing number of spiritual trails all over the continent. It is made highly performative through its pilgrims, while capitalizing on the new religious and spiritual demands created by the process of "unchurchization," as secularization in the sense of abandoning the established Church. It generates a trans-European form of revaluation by which Christian heritage is more and more disconnected from its ecclesiastical roots and is more operationalized as an overarching value and a symbol system for European society.[5]

John Coleman (1970:69–70) defined civil religion as the religious symbol system which relates the citizen's role and society's place in space, time, and history to the conditions of ultimate existence and meaning. In dissimilar, secularized Europe (compared to the United States) I would like to shift the civil religion focus from state-organized rituals to ritual practices from the grassroots of society and to apply it on a transnational scale. Moreover, I would also like to stress the role of modern processes of mediatization and show that ritual and symbolic language reach their full potential and may transcend into civil religion when mediatized throughout society.

In recent decades the aforementioned pilgrim routes have become a universal spiritual logistical system. Generally speaking, the unsuspected combination of rationality, spirituality, and mysticism can be found in contemporary foot-pilgrimages all over Europe. For individualized modernity, these pilgrimages can be seen as an inquiry and a quest of the self for values and meanings in life, as well as for the understanding of life and its hereafter. The pilgrims tend not to be Catholic devotees but they come from all strata of society and different denominations and perform the pilgrimage as a metaphor of human life. For many walkers the pilgrimage has become an individual rite of passage, or "a pilgrimage to one's self" as Eberhart once called it. Trekking the pilgrim trails has become an inwardly orientated activity for questioning oneself or giving meaning to oneself in relation to the world.

A completely new genre of travel books and diaries written by pilgrims to Santiago de Compostela and from other trails yields ample evidence for this quest, explaining how going on pilgrimage is about "how to travel outward to the edges of the world while simultaneously journeying to the depths of your soul." The ultimate goal of such pilgrimages is no longer to be found in the sacred destination of the Church, but in the individual activity of *making* the pilgrimage, the actual walking itself. The real art is to perform this basic activity in the proper, sublime way, so that as a combined physical-sensory activity, when connected with the human capacity for reflection, it will create sufficient satisfaction and a sense that deeper thoughts or spiritual experiences will flow from it. The pilgrims not only find inspiration from the past, but their wanderings also help them to cope with any insecurities, doubts, and life problems they might have. Apart from the very individual experience provided by this kind of pilgrim trek, the network signifies a general public reconfirmation of Christian roots and values for modern Europe. It forms an implicit response to the demand for shared and historically inspired (i.e. Christian-inspired) European values and meanings in times of uncertainty and crisis. The pilgrim ways have thus become a transnational instrument that creates connections for a new heritage-based overarching imagined spiritual "community" throughout the whole of Europe.

The bringing in of historical, cultural, and heritage elements, however, introduced new elements to pilgrimaging. Pilgrims feel that they are traveling back in time and back to the wanderings of the early missionaries, who by their *peregrinatio* gave shape to the spiritual "grand tour" of the early Middle Ages. It was by their wanderings that Christian thought was broadly dynamized for the first time and spread across Europe as a culture and religion. And today that is happening anew. Heritage and Christian history are again being mobilized, and new forms of religiosity are arising from this. With their cultural religious memory, individuals become part of an implicit community that links past, present, and future members and actively produces new forms of heritage. This is what Hervieu-Léger describes as the "chain of memory and tradition" that facilitates the handing over of culture (Hervieu-Léger 2000). She reconsiders the revival and political strength of varying religious traditions around the world and explains the endurance of religion in modernity as rooted in traditions that should connect members of a cultural system in past, present, and future. Whereas in the case of Europe, connections were interrupted, the pilgrimage network proved to be able to reestablish and acquire new meanings and functions.

The idea and the importance of a spiritual network were endorsed at an early stage by such institutions as the Council of Europe and later the European Union. The potential of such a value-creating network, which, moreover, was transnational in character, dovetailed perfectly with Europe's political ambitions. In 1987, the Council proclaimed the Route of Santiago de Compostela as the first European Cultural itinerary: "a testimony to the power of the Christian faith among people of all social classes and from all over Europe," according to UNESCO. It represented the canonization of the rediscovered Christian pilgrimage as an instrument of trans-European cohesive force. This was actually an institutional appropriation of a highly individually performed, intangible culture. To that end, similar routes were sought, found, and, moreover, created *ex nihilo* all over Europe. In relation to Paul Connerton's view, it is clear that the images of the past pilgrimage and the recollected knowledge about it are conveyed and sustained by the modern ritual performance of the new pilgrims. So the construction of a mythical network of trans-European pilgrim ways reflects how Europe is imagined as a thoroughly Christian subcontinent, and how Christian heritage is being reinvented. This spiritual-logistic network forms, in interaction between the grassroots and Europe's institutions, one of the implicit answers to European confusion about religion and spirituality in general, and it symbolically and practically repositions Christianity in a civil-religious way as a unifying historical factor.

Following a period of undervaluation of its own field of popular religiosity, the Catholic Church initiated a defense strategy of reappropriation of this successful public performative form of religiosity and giving meaning to life. Originally the walking journeys were a necessary evil; nowadays the Church is repositioning them as a "tradition" or pilgrimage heritage and sees them as a missionary tool. The effects are reflected on an institutional level as, under the auspices of the Bishops' Conferences in Europe, an international pilgrimage to Santiago de Compostela was held to mark the expansion of the EU. Pope John Paul II used this occasion to once again underline how the "soul of Europe rests on Christian values."[6] Moreover, according to him, Christianization had led to the unification of Europe which then, in 2004, was ultimately sealed on an economic and political level within the context of the EU. And indeed, the EU endorsed this with a policy on intercultural exchange and dialogue in order to minimize differences within the EU and encourage European identity and citizenship. The paradox in the practice is, however, that at the same time as the pilgrims routes were being employed from the top down, and being turned into a European trademark, a new narrative was being created that caught the popular imagination, and an informal bottom-up Europeanization was taking place, which transcends the nation-state and nationalism. The whole network of pilgrims' ways functions as a portmanteau construct in which contemporary pan-European needs for new forms of religiosity and spirituality can be generated. This pilgrimaging prompts Europeans to maintain Europe's vocation to its teleological history and moral order.

Silent Marches

New expressions of civil religion in Europe are increasingly seen on a national level (cf. Hvithamar et al. 2009). In the Low Countries, for example, the collective public manifestation *stille tocht*, or silent march, has become a general and widely accepted ritual in crisis situations since the1990s (Post et al. 2003:79–186). Hundreds of such marches have since been organized. In order to show how civil religion comes into being at a grassroots level, I will elaborate on this example.

The silent march ritual, which takes place specifically in times of social turbulence, has acquired a place as a prototype in national observance and memorialization practice and has, based on a proven ritual tradition, the power to enhance societal cohesion and reduce societal tension. For example, on October 22, 2002, in the Dutch city of Venlo, a 22-year-old man, René Steegmans, saw two teenagers on a motor scooter narrowly miss an elderly woman. He shouted to them to show more respect for the elders. With this, both teenagers turned on him and began to beat and kick him so severely that he died of his injuries shortly after. In order to discharge some of the tension in the atmosphere of crisis, and to promote cohesion in the divided Dutch and Moroccan communities in the city, three days later a silent march was held in which 17000 people took part, out of a total population of 90000 residents.

The march ritual is first and foremost a grassroots collective expression of grief and mourning over what has happened to a person, family, or group, usually ending at the site of the trauma, where a temporary memorial (notes, pictures, candles, stuffed animals, etc.) is often created as well. As a rule, these well-attended mourning marches are also an expression of widely shared feeling of moral indignation, addressed to the (Dutch) government or society as a whole. The silent march delivers a more or less implicit protest against such phenomena as senseless violence and dangerous conditions (particularly involving traffic and transportation) and the traumas which these cause. Silent marches, therefore, are also a performative practice of individuals battling existential anxieties and dealing with personal fate.

The development and the rise of the silent march in its present form can be explained in the first place by the feelings of disharmony between our ideals and the harsh reality of the world as we know it. The hypostatization of individual freedom has lead to a less social way of living and subsequently a disintegration of community, and senseless violence is perceived as one of the consequences of this. The second reason is people's strongly decreased acceptance of premature, illogical, or irrational ("senseless") death in modern society. The idea has taken root that, in the contemporary, technological, closely regulated world, with the marvels of modern science and medicine, death can be banished to a considerable extent. When people are then still confronted by a premature death without rhyme or reason, the grief is all the greater and the process of dealing with that grief all the more difficult. The more so because where once traditional religion and ritual were the proper instruments to deal with such situations, people now often lack these. And then, of course, relatives today also feel the need to inform the world at large of the "injustice" – no longer an act of God – that has taken place. The reason for this behavior is twofold: on the one hand it helps the person affected to cope with the trauma, and on the other it involves the outside world in a general healing process for the shock that was aroused by the disaster.

Participants in a silent march express the feeling of being united in a national alliance against irrationality and subsequently personal existential anxieties, and the lack of norms in society. They regard the feelings involved in this as being symbolically represented in the march. By participating in a performative march they wish to draw attention to these problems at a national level, and appeal both to the authorities and to society itself (and potential perpetrators within it) to help prevent new cases and reinstate central values in and for society. This new public ritual whereby individuals could be mobilized for general societal anxieties came as somewhat of a surprise to Dutch society. As this development is contrary to the tendency for individualization seen in today's society it has remained in the focus of the media.

It is, however, important to realize that this media focus is fundamental to the meaning and impact of the phenomenon of the silent marches. Apart from the effects of a silent march at a local level, the cohesive and appeasing power of the civil religion it generates is only realized by the coverage given in the media, and in particular the national media. The experience of transcendence in a silent march at a national level is in fact totally dependent on intermediality. Without the presence of the media and their widespread broadcasting and publishing, the marches could not be observed so closely by so many people and would consequently not gain their attributed meanings. Even after so many have taken place, new silent marches still receive devoted coverage in the media. Although their functionality after more than a decade of marches has been disputed, they continue to fulfill a meaningful role in restoring the delicate emotional and existential balances in society.

Despite the fact that as a rule they are responses to local events by locally organized groups, both spokespersons and commentators insist that, in their perception, these marches represent feelings that are found elsewhere too, nationally and throughout society. They serve to exorcize the "evil," to control and redress individual existential anxieties, and make a public, national appeal for the maintenance of norms and values in contemporary society. In the search for the characteristic Dutch norms and values, and *a fortiori* for a new Dutch identity and better society, reference is often made to the Christian roots of the nation. This is particularly the case for marches following incidents of senseless violence, when quite often there is explicit reference to the "Ten Commandments" and the fading away of Christian practice in individualized modernity, and which, it is suggested, must again be imposed as a moral guide for society.

Participants in the marches usually admit that the march helps to control emotionality at a personal and local level, while commentators in the media state that the aroused collective indignation to a certain extent also soothes and conciliates the affected (national) community. The mediatized active participation of people in the street makes thus a strong appeal to the national community. This reassurance thus creates a temporary overarching unity in society, which may be called civil religion.

The Sacred Self

The subjectivation of religion requires a connection to religious immanence in the world and especially within the human self. New religious movements endorse this view and stress the importance of looking into oneself to find peace, realize inner balance, and create and experience religiosity in private, in the home environment. In relation to this way of dealing with meaning and spirituality, the wave of idolizing and memorializing celebrities as well as common citizens that has spread across the Western world has become, in its current magnitude, a unique phenomenon (Doss 2010). Memorialization is no longer limited to traditional monuments authorized by governments and society, but involves grassroots, individualized memorialization, such as the roadside monuments and improvised and temporary memorials and rituals after a traumatic death (Margry and Sánchez-Carretero 2011). This practice is also connected with the presentistic and much wider way of memorializing through which individuals themselves seek to make their mark and erect their own "monument," not only postmortem, but, preferably, premortem. In our mediatized society, every individual wants to count, and not have his or her existence pass unnoticed. As may be seen from the proliferation of Web sites, wikis, blogs, Facebook pages and postings on YouTube, this kind of self sacralization or memorialization is overwhelmingly present today, particularly in its digital form. Everyone is seeking their five minutes of fame on TV, and if that is too long coming, then, as YouTube says in its logo, "broadcast yourself." These are not only new possibilities of communication, but, as messages are addressed to a general audience, these presentations of the self refer on the one hand to a wish for fame while on the other to a basic existential anxiety regarding meaninglessness of life and mortality. In this case, oblivion is also at stake: being noticed and self-presentation is relevant for the now, and not after death. Seen at their widest, these expressions can however also be conceived as ways of assigning meaning, and even as religiosity. In any case, people seek to validate their existence and find meaning in it. However superficial this sometimes may appear, the creation of a digital or virtual personality with the aid of media can construct an apparently timeless monument for someone, giving them the significance they seek.

A comparison with the present-day cult of idolatry cannot be ignored. The concept of idolatry has its roots in the worship of idols – false gods or images – and traditionally held a somewhat negative connotation. These days the "idolatrous" has been iconized via global TV formats such as the program *Pop Idols.* An interesting analogy with religion can be seen in the successor to *Idols*, the television music talent show *X-Factor*. The title of this program refers to the indefinable "something" – a mixture of talent and charisma – that makes for star quality, although it must be said that this "X-factor" is often lacking in the candidates and is mainly a product of the media. These heroes and stars only exist by virtue of mass media extolment. Specific groups find meaning in this, and in the same way as we can detect an X-factor, it is in different cases also possible to identify an R-factor, in which the R refers to a religious dimension. This connects two expressions of today's implicit religion: the "somethingisms" of idols and of the religion-less spiritual seekers.

These examples show clearly that a strict demarcation between secular and sacred is not possible, although a nonreflected "symbiosis" does not make any sense either. A confusing use of secular and religious is parallel to the concepts of the modern idol and the ecclesiastical saint idol. As both elements are often to be found in both, it is often difficult to discern the religious fact among idols and heroes. The exercising of virtue has been assessed by Frijhoff (1998) as essential for sainthood and it would therefore be incorrect to accord the status of saint to popular celebrities. For this reason he prefers to use the term "idol" for such cases, as this term does not have any connotation of virtue. The problem remains that in this way people continue to associate the word "saint" with Christianity, as it is the Christian virtues that lead to saintliness, whilst virtues and qualities are filled in and attributed per group or person. As I see it, the modern generic (i.e. not specifically ecclesiastical) image of an idol is made up of four characteristics, which are equally valid for the "consumer" and the "saint" version.

The idol is subjected to (i) mediality, which leads to glorification, illusion, and fame. He or she is familiar with (ii) humanity, with its characteristics of meaningfulness, mercy, virtue, and even heroism. There is a measure of (iii) sacrality, in which the sacred (godly) is presented. And finally, idols have (iv) finality or functionality: they are an example, a role model, or in a wider sense they are a helper in times of need – ranging from giving meaning to life and providing spiritual nourishment to giving physical healing.

Do modern humans then prefer idols and heroes to ecclesiastical saints? Seen in relation to the changes within the domain of religion and church, the answer seems simple: people call upon the traditional saints less frequently in this day and age, as they no longer appear relevant to modern society and do not appeal to the experiential worlds and imagination of younger generations. Living a relatively worry-free existence in European welfare states, most people attach more relevance in their daily lives to celebrity idols, because of their primary consumer-led aspects of pleasure and identification, being a more relevant role model. In simplified terms one could say that the more carefree the existence, the greater the role of these new idols, and the more difficult life becomes the more attention is paid to religion. If the "perceived threat to life" increases, in other words, in times of emergency, a role reversal can take place and the "secular" idol can be appointed a different task, that of giving meaning to life and being a savior in time of need.

At the beginning of this chapter I referred to the coming into being of a new religious movement in the Netherlands. Although these "Transformers" are, indeed, demonstrably, and not only by their name, children of their time, society at large remains suspicious about such alternative communities searching for new truths. In the media they are rapidly disqualified as sects or cults, especially when, as in the case of this group, a seventeen-year-old girl proved to be one of the spiritual role models. The Internet shows how the general public subsequently developed a very negative attitude toward the group and its ideas and rejected such deviancies from traditional, Christian-inspired, norms and values. The threats to the Transformers enhanced the togetherness of the community and reinforced their individual beliefs.

Conclusion

For a long time Christianity was the dominant cultural and religious factor in Europe. However, the faltering of community-creating qualities of the institutionalized Church, the arrival of religions from outside the continent, and a broad emergence of new spiritualities have undermined its position during recent decades, while the spiritual and moral leadership of the Church has been further damaged by various scandals. Along with the strong humanistic and Enlightenment tradition, this drove European society into a phase of religious reconfiguration, a process that continues to this day. This is a renewal stimulated by foreign developments and an internal repositioning, which tries to adjust the Church to the massive influx of individually orientated alternative forms of religiosity and alternative groupings.

The meaning of formal religion has turned strongly in favor of a more optional way of believing or, to be more accurate, of experiencing spirituality. The democratic welfare states of Europe have given the individual the freedom to make his or her own choices in this. Apart from the social structures within which religion is often expressed, it is clear that religion is primarily an individual, existential affair. The "R-option" is nowadays individually exercised, particularly when people are confronted with existential problems, and then a wide choice range of religious forms is available to all. Is there a relationship between the fragmentation of (traditional) religion, this range of new forms of religiosity and the rising importance of (supra) national, more "secular" religions, like civil religion? I think there is. The need for alternative overarching meaningful value systems has brought, for example, a reevaluation of European Christian value heritage, as performatively exercised in a trans-European pilgrim's network or through trauma-related marches.

NOTES

1 In Dutch: Orde der Transformanten, see: www.ordedertransformanten.nl (accessed November 5, 2011).

2 For a modern overview of the situation see the *Cambridge History of Christianity* (2005–2009).

3 The major threats were the conquest of Spain by the Moors in the eighth century, the fall of Constantinople in 1453, the conquest of Bosnia in 1463, and the sieges of Vienna in 1529 and 1683.

4 Here taken to mean a process of deinstitutionalism with regard to the established churches and the denominational-social "pillars" or sectors; besides a process of individualization regarding the dominant views and values held in society.
5 In 1967 Robert Bellah unfolded his renowned model of a transcendent civil religion as a universal belief system within American society (cf. Bellah and Hammond 1980). Although often presented as a mainly American topic, he stated that "all politically organized societies have some sort of civil religion."
6 Jean-Paul Willaime (1996) suggested that this pope's visits to European institutions in themselves were part of a process of developing a civil religion for Europe by conserving the European soul.

REFERENCES

Ammerman, Nancy T., ed.
2007 Everyday Religion: Observing Modern Religious Lives. Oxford: Oxford University Press.
Apolito, Paolo
2005 The Internet and the Madonna: Religious Visionary Experience on the Web. Chicago: University of Chicago Press.
Aune, Kristin, Sonya Sharma, and Giselle Vincett, eds.
2007 Women and Religion in the West: Challenging Secularization. Aldershot: Ashgate.
Bellah, Robert, and Phillip Hammond
1980 Varieties of Civil Religion. San Francisco: Harper & Row.
Berger, Peter L.
2002 Secularisation and De-Secularisation. *In* Religions in the Modern World: Traditions and Transformation. Linda Woodhead et al., eds. pp. 291–298. London: Routledge.
Berger, Peter L., Grace Davie, and Effie Fokas
2008 Religious America, Secular Europe? A Theme and Variations. Aldershot: Ashgate.
Borowik, Irena
2002 The Roman Catholic Church in the Process of Democratic Transformation: The Case of Poland. Social Compass 2(49):239–252.
Burgess, Mary Catherine
2008 A New Paradigm of Spirituality and Religion: Contemporary Shamanic Practice in Scotland. London: Continuum.
Byrnes, Timothy A., and Peter J. Katzenstein, eds.
2006 Religion in an Expanding Europe. Cambridge: Cambridge University Press.
Cambridge History of Christianity
2005–2009 9 vols. Cambridge: Cambridge University Press.
Casanova, José
2006 Religion, European Secular Identities and European Integration. *In* Religion in an Expanding Europe. Timothy A. Byrnes and Peter J. Katzenstein, eds. pp. 65–92. Cambridge: Cambridge University Press.
Coleman, John
1970 Civil Religion. Sociological Analysis 31(2):67–77.
Coleman, Simon
2000 The Globalisation of Charismatic Christianity: Spreading the Gospel of Prosperity. Cambridge: Cambridge University Press.

Davie, Grace
2000 Religion in Modern Europe: A Memory Mutates. Oxford: Oxford University Press.
Davie, Grace
2002 Europe: The Exceptional Case: Parameters of Faith in the Modern World. London: Darton, Longman and Todd.
Dawkins, Richard
2006 The God Delusion. London: Bantam.
Delumeau, Jean
1977 Catholicism between Luther and Voltaire: A New View of the Counter-Reformation. London: Burns and Oates.
Doss, Erika
2010 Memorial Mania: Public Feeling in America. Chicago: University of Chicago Press.
Frijhoff, Willem
1998 Heiligen, idolen, iconen. Nijmegen: SUN.
Hamberg, Eva M.
2003 Christendom in Decline: The Swedish Case. *In* The Decline of Christendom in Western Europe, 1750–2000. Hugh McLeod and Werner Ustorf, eds. pp. 47–62. Cambridge: Cambridge University Press.
Hanegraaff, Wouter J.
1996 New Age Religion and Western Culture: Esotericism in the Mirror of Secular Thought. Leiden: Brill.
Heelas, Paul, and Linda Woodhead
2005 The Spiritual Revolution: Why Religion is Giving Way to Spirituality. Oxford: Blackwell.
Hervieu-Léger, Danièle
2000 Religion as a Chain of Memory. Cambridge: Polity.
Hvithamar, Annika, Margit Warburg, and Brian Arly Jacobsen, eds.
2009 Holy Nations and Global Identities, Civil Religion, Nationalism, and Globalisation. Leiden: Brill.
Israel, Jonathan I.
2001 Radical Enlightenment: Philosophy and the Making of Modernity, 1650–1750. Oxford: Oxford University Press.
Jenkins, Philip
2007 God's Continent: Christianity, Islam and Europe's Religious Crisis. Oxford: Oxford University Press.
Kierkegaard, Søren
1980 The Concept of Anxiety: A Simple Psychologically Orienting Deliberation on the Dogmatic Issue of Hereditary Sin. Princeton: Princeton University Press.
Knippenberg, Hans
2005 The Changing Religious Landscape of Europe. Amsterdam: Het Spinhuis.
Knoblauch, Hubert
2009 Populäre Religion: Auf dem Weg in eine spirituelle Gesellschaft. Frankfurt am Main: Campus.
Knott, Kim
2005 The Location of Religion: A Spatial Analysis. London: Equinox.
Luckmann, Thomas
1967 Invisible Religion: The Problem of Religion in Modern Society. New York: Macmillan.
1990 Shrinking Transcendence, Expanding Religion? Sociological Analysis 51(2): 127–138. doi: 10.2307/3710810

MacKenzie Brown, Donald
1965 Ultimate Concern: Tillich in Dialogue. New York: Harper Colophon.
Margry, Peter Jan
2004 Global Network of Divergent Marian Devotion. *In* Encyclopedia of New Religions: New Religious Movements, Sects and Alternative Spiritualities. Christopher Partridge, ed. pp. 98–102. Oxford: Lion.
2009 Marian Interventions in the Wars of Ideology: The Elastic Politics of the Roman Catholic Church on Modern Apparitions. History and Anthropology 3(20):245–265.
2011 Civil Religion in Europe: Silent Marches, Pilgrim Treks and Processes of Mediatization. Ethnologia Europaea 41(2):5–23.
Margry, Peter Jan, ed.
2008 Shrines and Pilgrimage in the Modern World: New Itineraries into the Sacred. Amsterdam: Amsterdam University Press.
Margry, Peter Jan, and Cristina Sánchez-Carretero, eds.
2011 Grassroots Memorials: The Politics of Memorializing Traumatic Death. New York: Berghahn.
Milis, Ludo J. R., ed.
1998 The Pagan Middle Ages. Woodbridge: Boydell.
Morgan, Michael L.
2001a Beyond Auschwitz: Post-Holocaust Jewish Thought in America. Oxford: Oxford University Press.
Morgan, Michael L., ed.
2001b A Holocaust Reader: Responses to the Nazi Extermination. Oxford: Oxford University Press.
Partridge, Christopher, ed.
2004 Encyclopedia of New Religions: New Religious Movements, Sects and Alternative Spiritualities. Oxford: Lion.
Persinger, Michael A.
1987 Neuropsychological Bases of God Beliefs. New York: Praeger.
Post, Paul, R. L. Grimes, A. Nugteren, P. Pettersson, and H. Zondag
2003 Disaster Ritual: Explorations of an Emerging Ritual Repertoire. Leuven: Peeters.
Primiano, Leonard N.
1995 Vernacular Religion and the Search for Method in Religious Folklife. Western Folklore 54(1):37–56.
Taylor, Charles
2002 Varieties of Religion Today: William James Revisited. Cambridge, MA: Harvard University Press.
Wade, Nicolas
2009 The Faith Instinct: How Religion Evolved and Why It Endures. New York: Penguin.
Willaime, Jean-Paul
1996 Les religions et l'unification européenne. *In* Identités religieuses en Europe. Grace Davies and Danièle Hervieu-Léger, eds. pp. 291–314. Paris: La Découverte.

CHAPTER 17

Studying Muslims of Europe

Gabriele Marranci

Today, around 5.5% of Europe's population has some sort of Muslim background (Nielsen et al. 2009) and increasingly the terms "Islam" and "Muslims" appear in the paper and electronic pages of mainstream European newspapers as well as blogs and Internet forums; albeit rarely in a positive fashion. It would not be an exaggeration to say that many aspects of Muslim life are becoming a major concern of the European public as well as of politicians. Minarets, dress codes, theological terminology, religious practices: no single area of Muslim life and Islamic beliefs has been left unscrutinized, debated, defended, attacked, or denigrated. From the "*Affaire du Foulard*" (Bowen 2007); to the cartoon controversies (with a recent new appearance in the Facebook "Draw Mohammed Day"); to the banning of minarets in Switzerland, and the niqab[1] and burqa[2] in Belgium and France; the opposition to the construction of new mosques (Cesari 2005); and the fear of young Muslims radicalizing in national prisons, Europe seems to have found its new "other" to fetishize (Bhabha 1994). Although antecedent to 9/11, as the Honeyford affair in 1984 (Halstead 1988) and the Rushdie affair in 1989 (Asad 1990; Modood 1990; Halliday 1995) show, this increased attention to the Muslim population of Europe has reached its apex during the "war on terror" and the few, well-publicized, cases of terrorism that affected London, Madrid, and Glasgow. Consequently, these events and their chronicles have affected the study of Muslims in Europe, and in a certain sense, as we shall see, not in a positive way.

In this chapter I wish to offer a critical discussion of how anthropologists may study Muslims in Europe and the challenges we, as anthropologists, may face in such a process. I have no intention of providing a full review of the critical study of the anthropology of Muslims in Europe, since the available space does not allow such an endeavor. Furthermore, as Varisco has rightly observed, tracing the specific studies conducted, for instance in a Christian or, as in this case Islamic, context, would appear absurd since "It is easy to create unity out of diversity but seldom does it serve an analytic purpose" (2005:135–136).

A Companion to the Anthropology of Europe, First Edition. Edited by Ullrich Kockel, Máiréad Nic Craith, and Jonas Frykman.

DEFINING MUSLIMS

The first challenge we face, in a study of Muslims in Europe, is one which is often left unaddressed: how do we define Muslims in Europe? Nadia Jeldtof (2009) has rightly observed the problematic beyond what might seem to be an innocent and easy task of classification:

> When we [...] categorise (and thereby identify) Muslims in Europe, this expresses a categorisation of "Muslims" who can be distinguished from other social groups by virtue of their "Muslimness." This categorisation reflects a use of the contested categories – Muslims are not simply and only "Muslims." Some, but not all, of the members of the minority group of Muslims will fit into the scholarly understanding and categorisation of what it means to be Muslim. However, not all Muslims think of themselves as distinctly Muslim but rather in ethnic, national or cultural terms or in a mixture of, for example, ethnic and religious terms, while others do wholly self-identify as Muslims and actively articulate their Muslim identity as separate from their ethnic/national identity. (2009:12)

Let me observe another aspect: terms such as Muslims in Europe, European Muslims, and European Islam are all utilized for communication and share the power of classifying. They mark and create differences which make differences. Bateson noticed that a "difference which makes a difference is an idea" (2000:242). In other words, "Muslims in Europe" or "European Muslims" are not descriptions of a "real" group of people, a state of material reality, but rather such conceptualizations exist as ideas which can be shared, passed from person to person or group to group, as mental representations. These keywords may be compared to maps attempting to represent a territory; yet as Alfred Korzybski loved to remind us, "the map is not the territory" (1948:58). Therefore, we, as anthropologists, need to ask at which level are we speaking when using the above keywords: are we discussing the map, the territory, or conflating the two – and committing a mistake of logical type – by believing that the map is the territory, where the idea is the material fact?

This fallacy is typical of much political discourse, and politicians often end up, by virtue of politics, reinforcing a general perception that what is real and important is the map, particularly when culturally defined. Unfortunately, I have to admit that, during the past 40 years, my own discipline of social anthropology has followed the same trend, especially in the case of the study of Muslim minorities. The reason for this may be found in the omission of two important material aspects: the individual and the way individuals make sense of themselves and their environment through emotions and feelings (see Marranci 2008). Mine is certainly not a new criticism, albeit new when applied to the study of Muslims in Europe. Indeed, some other anthropologists, among them Rapport, have highlighted such a failing in social scientific studies. Rapport has noticed:

> [a] social-scientific tendency to regard the individual actor as put upon rather than "putting on." I find much here in the critique of displacement which accords with social-scientific analysis of individual behaviour in social-cultural milieux per se: "because"

> motives are widely inferred while "in order to" motives barely figure. Questions such as how individuals deal with life, how they make meaning in the midst of everyday life and change, suffering and good fortune, become questions largely of social determination. (2003:52)

By contrast, Rapport has suggested the centrality of individuality as far as social action is concerned, since "it is the individual – in individual energy, creativity, will – that the force of the social and cultural lies" (2003:6; see also 1997:2 and Hornborg 2003:98). This viewpoint is extremely relevant to an anthropological study of Muslim minorities, which are too often seen as a monolithic entity.

There is need, therefore, to pay more attention to the individual and understand society not as a mysterious, self-achieving, self-controlled mechanism, but rather as consisting of the dynamics of individuals, which means to recognize the cybernetic (i.e. communicational) property of what we call society. In the case of Muslims living in Europe this last point is extremely relevant. Muslims can be seen as *in* or *of* Europe (AlSayyad and Castells 2002; Marranci 2004). In the former case, Muslims are understood as "strangers," even in the case of new generations born and educated in European societies, rather than as a natural, integral part of Europe (Asad 1997; Allievi and Nielsen 2003). Bryan Turner has rightly observed:

> In Latin, a stranger/guest is called *hostis* and *hospes* (Benveniste, 1973). While *hospes* is the root of "hospitality," *hostis* is an "enemy." Both "guest" and "enemy" derive from "stranger," and the idea of "favourable stranger" evolved eventually into "guest," but "hostile stranger" became the enemy. (2007:289)

Muslims living in Europe after 9/11 have been increasingly perceived as enemies within, and Islam as a dangerous alien entity (Werbner 2005), and increasingly a call for an "integration" of Muslims is made by European politicians (Pauly 2004; Abbas 2005; Brighton 2007). Yet if my research, including a five-year study on current and former Muslim prisoners in the UK as well as research on "Muslim" gangs in London and the Leeds area (Marranci 2009) has taught me anything, it is that, in reality, Muslims of various ethnic origins and backgrounds are actually integrating, but not within an Andersonian (1991) abstract dimension of national community. Instead, the integration occurs within the local, and even the microlocal, dimension of everyday life. In my book (Marranci 2009), I have provided a detailed description of the socioeconomic realities with which many Muslims live in the United Kingdom, and it is not difficult to conclude that instead of being able to integrate into safe and prosperous neighborhoods, Muslims in many parts of Europe are often situated within highly underprivileged environments that are affected by both social dysfunction and crime. It is perhaps then to be expected that, when compared proportionally to the wider population, the instances and typology of crimes are very similar between non-Muslim Whites and Muslims. Difficult urban spaces have an impact upon the crime level in the general population. Muslims tend, however, to be more vulnerable because of the rejection that they often receive from mainstream society, mainly because of their ethnic and/or religious identities.

Anthropology of Muslims *of* Europe or *in* Europe?

As a postgraduate student of anthropology with a strong interest in Muslims in Europe, I became aware very quickly that anthropologists have normally considered it to be less attractive to study Islam than to study "primitive" religions. The reason is that many of them had perceived Islam as lacking interesting cultural and symbolic features, such as complex symbolic rituals or ceremonies. In other words, Islam, with its iconoclastic traditions, abstract conception of God, and focus on orthodoxy, appeared extremely plain. If an anthropologist met Muslims, it was primarily in the context of villages. There, anthropologists studied saints (Sufis), complex kinships, lineages, and agricultural and pastoral economics. Indeed, as Gilsenan has recalled, Islam remained a difficult element to incorporate within anthropological analysis: "There was effectively no model in monographic or theory terms to indicate what should be done, let alone how, not in what ways such disparate secondary materials might be incorporated into something that would be taken to be recognizably "anthropological" (1990:226). Between the end of the 1960s and the end of the 1980s, ethnographic studies of Muslims observed mainly Middle Eastern and North African populations.

During the 1980s some young anthropologists increasingly started to pay attention to new fields of research, such as Muslim immigrants, second-generation Muslims, Muslim transnational networks, virtual ummahs, and the integration/assimilation of Western Muslim communities. Yet their research remained marginalized within mainstream European (but also American) anthropology (Marranci 2008). The work of these anthropologists (Haddad and Qurqmazi 2000) found refuge in more interdisciplinary fields such as migration studies, gender studies, education studies, and global studies. Nonetheless, no differently from the "exotic" anthropology of Islam (see Geertz 1960, 1968; Gellner 1981), European studies of Muslims eventually ended up offering a culturalist viewpoint in which Islam becomes the ultimate shaper of Muslims' lives (Hunter 2000), despite the different identities, traditions, contexts, realities, and subjectivities. In these cases, authors (cf. Shadid and van Koningsveld 1992; Nauck 1994, among others) have suggested that Muslims, despite their differences in ethnicity, nationality, and status, should be understood mainly as Muslims. Another issue with this approach is that the emphasis, as I have discussed above, is on the "community," the collectivity seen as "ummah," instead of being on the individuals as they interact with society as Muslims of various backgrounds (Buijs 1998, 2000). Indeed, as I will discuss later, one of the most evident characteristics of Islam in Europe is its heterogeneity; a reality which still remains understudied within the field of anthropology.

While the study of Middle Eastern and Southeast Asian Muslim populations have, since the end of the 1960s, started to develop a paradigm, seeing the development of departments and institutes, the study of Muslims living in Europe, even in the 2000s, has been marked by a constant lack of rational planning, paradigm, and structure. It would not be too wrong to suggest that the little we have today of a European anthropology of Muslims is the result of fragmented studies on those topics made popular by the mass media and the political discourse concerning Muslim integration and more recent issues, such as religious–political extremism. The fact that the study of Muslim communities living in Europe developed around national characteristics greatly helped the fragmentation of the field and the lack of a real attempt to understand the phenomenon in a "European" comparative perspective. Yet this was a natural consequence of various European states' colonization of specific Muslim countries, which later resulted in Muslim migrations to Europe from the former colonies. It is thus not surprising, then, that in the United Kingdom the research has concentrated on South Asians (see, e.g., Werbner 1996 and 2002; Ali 2000; Eade and Garbin 2002), in France on Northern African Muslims (see, e.g., Brulard 1997; de Wenden 1998), in Germany on the Turkish community (see, e.g., Horrocks and Kolinsky 1996; Schiffauer 1999; Argun 2003), and so on (Goehlert et al. 2006). The debate is also linked to the "political" aspects of each country so that, for instance, in France the debate is often in the defense of French *laïcité* from Islamic identities, and the consequent strategy of assimilating, in particular, children of Muslim origin, while in Germany the debate focuses more on issues surrounding the level of education within the Turkish community, and in the United Kingdom women in Islam appeared, until recently, to be the most popular topic (Haddad and Qurmazi 2000).

In other words, we may observe, as Abu-Lughod (1989) did in the case of anthropological studies of Muslims in the Middle East, that during these years certain recurrent "zones of theorizing" have formed. Among these "zones" are included themes such as integration (de Wenden 1998; Modood 1998; Bartels 2000; Werbner 2000; Bowen 2004; Freedman 2004; Schmidt 2004), Westernization (Brulard 1997; Eade 2000; Timmerman 2000), gender (Basit 1997; Benn and Jawad 2003), veil (Auslander 2000; Brown 2001; Saas 2001; Beller 2004; Carle 2004), second generations (Dwyer 1999; Archer 2001), extremism (Abbas 2005; Wiktorowicz 2005), and, by far the most prominent today, terrorism (Mohammed 1996; Shaw 2002; Jones and Smith 2005). This has clearly affected the research field. Yet it is not difficult to trace the process by which, for instance, Pakistanis in the United Kingdom, Algerians in France, Moroccans in Italy, or Turkish immigrants in Germany became simply "Muslims." With the unplanned settlement of guest workers, and the development of a second generation, Islam became visible as part of the identity of these new communities. Consequently, if earlier studies focused mainly on ethnicity and nationality, now an overwhelming majority of them featured the word "Muslim" in their titles. New studies, therefore, would focus on "young Muslims," "Muslim communities," "Muslim girls," "Muslim women," "Muslim teachers," "Muslim extremists," and so forth.

Furthermore, the awareness that the, now redefined, Muslim immigration was a permanent feature of Western societies redirected the social scientific research mainly to address the difficulties that Muslim immigrants had to face in maintaining their Muslim identity and community in the new environment. Very few anthropological studies, compared, for instance, to the case of Muslims in the United States (Leonard 2003), have discussed the positive and successful contribution of Muslims of Europe, both as individuals and organizations, to the social, economic and – even less – political well-being of their European countries. Here again, we may notice, at the academic level, the differences between understanding Muslims as in Europe or of Europe, especially when the common political question of loyalty produces a faulty essentialism: Islam risks being – and often is – reduced to the same category of a national or ethnic identity.

This is the reason why it is important to form, through a renewed academic debate, a paradigm for an anthropology of Muslims of Europe in which, at the center, is not just Islam, seen as an all-shaping cultural symbolic determinism, but rather Muslims as humans involved in different social actions and interactions. My emphasis, expressed also elsewhere (Marranci 2008), on an anthropology which reconsiders the "human being" as not only a "cultural animal" but also an "animal who makes culture" through his or her relationship with the surrounding environment, mediated through emotions, feelings, and, in the first instance, neurons, is, in the case of the study of Muslims of Europe, even stronger. The main risk of continuing to "regard the individual [Muslim] actor as put upon rather than 'putting on'" (Rapport, 2003:52) is not just a flawed social (un)science but, more perniciously, risks reinforcing the trends of dehumanization that are so common in research focusing on Muslims today, seen mainly as "followers of Islam" instead of followers of their desires, imaginations, identities, and passions. Furthermore, as I have explained in my work (Marranci 2008), the idea that identities are "real" essences based on cultural processes has brought some authors, as we have seen, to represent, or at least to describe, the identities of Western-born Muslims in terms of a risky and questionable (at least at the level of loyalty to the "West" and its "Democracy") in-between.

Notwithstanding the relevance that difference and differentiation, as well as boundary-making processes, have in social interaction, I have argued that they may not be prominent in the formation of personal identity. Rather, I have argued that while the self and the autobiographical self are real (Damasio 1999), identity is a machinery of personal imagination allowing vital coherence between the individual and his or her environment. Hence, emotions and feelings are central to the development of personal identities more than cultural constructs. In other words, I am suggesting that it would be flawed to read the expression "I am Muslim" as solely meaning "I follow Islam as a religion," "I was born Muslim," or "Islam teaches me how to be." Rather, it is my contention (Marranci 2008) that the statement "I am Muslim" should be understood, anthropologically, as meaning "I feel to be Muslim." I have suggested that it is by focusing on that "feel to be" more than the symbolic "Muslim" that we can understand how Muslim identity, in particular among Western-born Muslims, is expressed, formed, and developed beyond the imposed stereotypes which, after more than 60 years of Muslims contributing to postwar Europe, and four generations of Muslims born in Europe, we still discuss. From this perspective, the question of whether a "Euro-Islam" is forming or if "Euro-Islam" is "real" Islam or not (AlSayyad and Castells 2002) becomes an intellectual discussion distant, for the great majority of European Muslims, from the concerns of everyday life.

Rethinking the Anthropological Study of Muslims as "*of* Europe"

In the previous sections we have discussed both how essentialist and monolithic definitions of "Muslim" and the fragmented and often overly culturalist understanding of European Muslim communities has remained mostly unchanged, and rarely challenged, in the last 60 years. The questions, as we have seen, normally focused on Muslims as "aliens," difficult to integrate and assimilate, or, more recently, resistant to the "Western" way of life. A very quick database search, not only of the very few anthropological studies, but of social scientific in general, will show that, for instance, out of 2500[3] academic works mentioning "Muslims in Europe" less than a hundred pay attention to positive aspects of the communities or the contribution they have made to the development of Europe and its individual nations. It is also interesting how the phrase "Muslims of Europe" is mentioned only in 158 items, and none of them are anthropological studies. Hence, we may wish to ask: "What does it mean to research and study Muslims as *of* rather than *in* Europe?" I have asked this very question during all my years of research. I will try to share here, briefly, what I consider some of the main characteristics of such paradigmatic shift.

First let me start from an aspect that has affected how Muslims in Europe are studied: religious extremisms. Since 2001, more than 100 books and 5600 articles have been published on Islamic fundamentalism. Broadening the research to agnate labels – such as Islamism (about 200 books and 243 articles), political Islam (345 books and 4670 articles) and Islamic extremism (only 16 books and 1610 articles) – we can appreciate the amount of scholarly publication pressed into the past few years. The reasons behind such an abundance are multiple. Two military campaigns (in Afghanistan and Iraq) under the banner of "the war on terror," as well as terrorist attacks in different parts of Europe have further increased the number of publications, both academic and popular, to an unprecedented level. Said (1978, 1981) and Said and Viswanathan (2001) may have even suggested that Western writers and publishers exploited the morbid Western orientalistic curiosity about the violent oriental man combining the divine with the political, and the political with holy violence. Yet it is interesting how in many of these books and journal articles, the majority of peaceful, law-abiding Muslims remain an invisible presence. Their opinions, their ideas, their contributions and efforts toward ensuring the security of their European nations, as well as their effort to "moderate" those Muslims who seem to take the path of radicalism, remain practically unstudied, in particular by anthropologists, who in reality would be in an advantageous position, because of their methodology, to discuss it.

Another example of the need to shift from studying Muslims in Europe to studying Muslims of Europe is the overly studied "veil" within the topic of "Muslim women" (Auslander 2000; Brown 2001; Saas 2001; Beller 2004; Carle 2004). Recently, as I was mentioning above, European countries have moved from the debate over the headscarf to a more aggressive debate concerning the ban of both burqas and niqabs (Moors 2009; Shirazi and Smeeta 2010). Thousands of academic works, between articles, chapters, and books, have focused on veiling often as an antagonistic element (Brown 2001) toward the alleged "secular" identity of Europe, or as an explicit marker of "Islamic identity" of second-generation Muslims and converts. Nonetheless, during my research and fieldwork I became very aware that Muslim women wearing niqabs and burqas are statistically a tiny proportion, and those who wear a headscarf do not represent the majority of Muslim women in Europe. Indeed, a considerable number of Muslim women adopt Western styles and some wear even miniskirts, or, as I observed in London, a mix of both ethnically traditional dress and Western styles. There are Muslim women who have adapted their Islamic dress code to European subcultures such as goth culture; and others who have developed their own individual style of Islamic dress. Despite the variety, eclecticism, and hybridization so typical of young Europeans, Muslims included, few studies have provided an anthropological analysis of it. Indeed, if one attempts to find a single study of Muslim women living in Europe and adopting, despite still identifying as a Muslim, Western-style clothes, including miniskirts, the search will remain, up to today, frustrated. The reason for such a serious lack of study is that the anthropology of European Muslims still makes sense epistemologically of the new generations though the paradigm developed to study migrants.

The epistemological fossilization which has affected the field is even more evident when we move to other examples. Therefore, when we observe those studies which discuss Muslims in Europe and politics, we can easily notice that in the great majority of the cases, the focus is on the "rejection" of secularism and democracy (Jackson 2009; Joppke 2009; Connor 2010). Yet it is only a tiny minority of Muslims in Europe who reject democracy, while a substantial number of them, instead, partake in it (Gould 2009). Again, we can only notice the lack of research and academic work which studies such politically engaged Muslims. In each country, the number of Muslims sitting in national parliaments and having responsibility within governments is gradually increasing, and Muslims are also involved in non-Muslim NGOs, associations, and organizations, such as charities (Body-Gendrot 2010). The change in epistemological paradigm (from studying Muslims in Europe to studying Muslims of Europe) in this case would be marked by anthropological research paying attention to that silent majority who engage and contribute, in this case through social actions and political involvement, to European nations and to the European community. Indeed, my personal research has highlighted how Muslims in European countries tend to support the EU as a political entity.

Finally, among the many available, there is another aspect of studying Muslims of Europe which needs to be addressed: what Richard C. Martin has defined as the "hidden bodies in Islam," or in other words, secular Muslim identities. Martin has indeed observed:

> [A] very large percentage of the world Muslim population do not adhere strictly, if much at all, to the fundamental beliefs and practices of their religion. That is, while retaining some form of Muslim, if not Islamic, identity, they lead secular lives and think through most of life's problems and challenges by means of secular world views, though they may not necessarily renounce their faith or think ill of family and friends who are religious. The significance of secularism among Muslims goes largely unexamined in most works on Islam and Muslim societies. (Martin 2010:131)

Instead, within the widespread, and ever-spreading, "Culture Talk" (Mamdani 2004) affecting the representation of Muslims both in the West and in Muslim-majority countries, Islam is understood as a blueprint, so that Muslims are reduced to embodied traditions (Bruce 2000). In the debate about Islam and secularism, which is mirrored in the discussion of the compatibility of "Islam" with "democracy," "Culture Talk" has allowed Western politicians, commentators, and intellectuals to divide the world between "modern" and "premodern." The increasingly predominant view that "real" Muslims, because of Islam, cannot accept, adapt, or assimilate within democratic systems and consequently they may represent a danger and threat to them, seems to confirm what Mamdani has highlighted as one of the main characteristics of "Culture Talk": the idea that Muslims "made" culture at beginning of history, but in the contemporary world they are only able to conform to culture

> According to some, our [Muslim] culture seems to have no history, no politics, and no debates, so that all Muslims are just plain bad. According to others, there is a history, a politics, even debates, and there are good Muslims and bad Muslims. In both versions, history seems to have petrified into a lifeless custom of an antique people who inhabit antique lands. Or could it be that culture here stands for habit, for some kind of instinctive activity with rules that are inscribed in early founding texts, usually religious, and mummified in early artefacts? (2004:18)

Those Muslims who, although defining their identities as Muslim, have embraced a "secular" approach to their understanding of Islam remain understudied exactly because of the dynamic that Mamdani has highlighted. It is also relevant, in this case, as I have noticed during my research, that when some Muslims define themselves as "secular," they adopt a similar differentiation between "secular" and "secularism." Asad has noticed that "the secular is neither singular in origin nor stable in its historical identity" (2003:25), and should not be thought of as

> the space in which real human life gradually emancipates itself from the controlling power of "religion" and thus achieves the latter's relocation. It is this assumption that allows us to think of religion as "infecting" the secular domain or as replicating within it the structure of theological concepts. The concept of the secular today is part of a doctrine called secularism. Secularism doesn't simply insist that religious practice and belief be confined to a space where they cannot threaten political stability or the liberties of the "free-thinking" citizens. Secularism builds on a particular conception of the world ("natural" and "social") and of the problems generated by that world. (Asad 2003: 181)

Indeed, during my research as an anthropologist, I have found some Muslims who have argued against secularism and secularization, but inevitably, while observing their daily lives, they had to socially interact and adapt to the surrounding environment.

As Oliver Roy (2007:43–48) has noticed, today within Europe different solutions exist that go from a total reformation of Islam to a passive accommodation of the social norms within an Islamic framework. However, we should be careful not to end in generalizations that then become models of "Culture Talk," within which Muslims can be labeled "good" and "bad" according to the necessity of a given political ideology. Indeed, it is my contention that an anthropology of Muslims of Europe needs to rediscover the "human" aspect of social interaction.

Conclusion

While, for instance, Middle East Studies, Islamic Studies, and the anthropology of Muslims in Southeast Asia have developed through debates within the fields, the study of Muslims living in Europe remains still a very fragmented area of studies. The reasons are historical and linked to the shift of interest from ethnic studies in the 1960s to a focus on Muslims as mainly followers of Islam during the 1990s. In the chapter, I have highlighted some of the issues which have affected the, often scarce, anthropological study of European Muslims. It is very clear that Muslims are seen, debated, and discussed as in Europe, despite the length of time that these communities have established themselves at both local and European level. Certainly 9/11 has increased the feeling of facing an "enemy within." Yet terrorism is not new to Europe, and young Europeans, of various backgrounds, have been involved in such actions for decades in the Old Continent (Jongman 1992). Even in this case, the very small number of European Muslims who have been involved in terrorist actions are normally not presented as a product of their own European societies.

In this chapter, I have tried to invite a reconsideration of the way in which we can develop an anthropology of Muslims of Europe that overcomes much of the issues affecting the previous studies. One of the main important aspects of such a process is to move from seeing Muslims in Europe as mainly an expression of their own religion and material culture. Hence, this means to develop new research which tries to understand Muslims as human beings moving in multiple contexts and discourses, one of which, of course, is Islam and the Muslim community. We need, in other words, today more than ever, a paradigm through which we can effectively study Muslims as human beings rather than living symbols of a religion. Taking this approach, as I have advocated in the present chapter, means also paying more attention to the "individual," the agent of action and interaction. Too often the study of Muslims living in Europe has suffered from an over-focus on the "community" or on the power that the "community" and community rules have on the individual. There also exists a lack of acknowledgment of the power of will and agency, as rightly Rapport has argued for within anthropology in general, and so we will need, if we aim toward a serious approach to the study of Muslims of Europe, to rediscover and study "the universality of the individual as the fount of agency, consciousness, interpretation, and creativity in social and cultural life" (Rapport 1997:6).

NOTES

1 Niqab is a cloth covering the mouth adopted by a very small minority of Muslim women in Europe both for national, cultural, ethnic and religious reasons.
2 Burqa is a traditional Afghan Muslim dress covering the entire body, which in reality is extremely rare among the European Muslim population.
3 Google Scholar was employed for this example.

REFERENCES

Abbas, T.
2007 Muslim Minorities in Britain: Integration, Multiculturalism and Radicalism in the Post-7/7 Period. Journal of Intercultural Studies 28(3):287–300.

Abbas, T., ed.
2005 Muslim Britain: Communities under Pressure. London: Zed Press.
Abu-Lughod, L.
1989 Zones of Theory in the Anthropology of the Arab World. Annual Review of Anthropology 8:267–306.
Ali, J.
2000 Changing Identity Constructions among Bangladeshi Muslims in Britain. Birmingham: Centre for the Study of Islam and Christian–Muslim Relations.
Allievi, S., and J. S. Nielsen, eds.
2003 Muslim Networks and Transnational Communities in and across Europe. Leiden: Brill.
AlSayyad, N., and M. Castells, eds.
2002 Muslim Europe or Euro-Islam: Politics, Culture, and Citizenship in the Age of Globalization. Lanham, MD: Lexington.
Anderson, B.
1991 Imagined Communities: Reflections on the Origins and Spread of Nationalism. London: Verso.
Archer, L.
2001 Muslim Brothers, Black Lads, Traditional Asians: British Muslim Young Men's Constructions of Race, Religion and Masculinity. Feminism and Psychology 11(1):79–105.
Argun, B. E.
2003 Turkey in Germany: The Transnational Sphere of Deutschkei. New York: Routledge.
Asad, T.
1990 Ethnography, Literature, and Politics: Some Readings and Uses of Salman Rushdie's The Satanic Verses. Cultural Anthropology 5(3):239–269.
1997 Europe against Islam: Islam in Europe. Muslim World 87(2):183–195.
2003 Formations of the Secular: Christianity, Islam, Modernity. Stanford, CA: Stanford University Press.
Auslander, L.
2000 Bavarian Crucifixes and French Headscarves: Religious Signs and the Postmodern European State. Cultural Dynamics 12(3):283–309.
Bartels, E.
2000 Dutch Islam: Young People, Learning and Integration. Current Sociology 48(4):59–73.
Basit, T. N.
1997 I Want More Freedom, But Not Too Much: British Muslim Girls and the Dynamism of Family Values. Gender and Education 9(4):425–439.
Bateson, G.
2000 Steps to an Ecology of Mind. Chicago: Chicago University Press.
Beller, E. T.
2004 The Headscarf Affair: The Conseil d'État on the Role of Religion and Culture in French Society. Texas International Law Journal 39(4):581–623.
Benn, T., and H. Jawad, eds.
2003 Muslim Women in the United Kingdom and Beyond: Experiences and Images. Leiden: Brill.
Benveniste, E.
1973 Indo-European Language and Society. Coral Gables, FL: University of Miami Press.
Bhabha, H.
1994 The Location of Culture. London and New York: Routledge.

Body-Gendrot, S.
2010 European Policies of Social Control Post-9/11. Social Research 77(1):181–204.
Bowen, J. R.
2007 Why the French Do Not Like Headscarves. Princeton: Princeton University Press.
2004 Does French Islam Have Borders? Dilemmas of Domestication in a Global Religious Field. American Anthropologist 106(1):43–55.
Brighton, S.
2007 British Muslims, Multiculturalism and UK Foreign Policy: Integration and Cohesion In and Beyond the State. International Affairs 83(1):1–17.
Brown, M. D.
2001 Multiple Meanings of the Hijab in Contemporary France. *In* Dressed to Impress: Looking the Part. William J. F. Keenan, ed. pp 105–121. Oxford: Berg.
Bruce, S.
2000 Fundamentalism. Cambridge: Polity.
Brulard, I.
1997 Laïcité and Islam. *In* Aspects of Contemporary France. Sheila Perry, ed. pp. 175–190. London: Routledge.
Buijs, F. J.
1998 Een Moskee in de Wijk. De Vestiging van de Kocatepemoskee in Rotterdam-Zuid. Amsterdam: Het Spinhuis.
2000 Multiculturele samenleving en democratie. Migrantenstudies 16(3):131–147.
Carle, R.
2004 Hijab and the Limits of French Secular Republicanism. Society 41(6):63–68.
Cesari, J.
2005 Mosque Conflicts in European Cities: Introduction. Journal of Ethnic and Migration Studies 31(6):1015–1024.
Connor, P.
2010 Contexts of Immigrant Receptivity and Immigrant Religious Outcomes: The Case of Muslims in Western Europe. Ethnic and Racial Studies 33(3):376–403.
Damasio, A. R.
1999 The Feeling of What Happens: Body, Emotion and the Making of Consciousness, London: Vintage.
de Wenden, C. W.
1998 How Can One Be Muslim?: The French Debate on Allegiance, Intrusion and Transnationalism. International Review of Sociology 8(2):275–88.
Dwyer, C.
1999 Contradictions of Community: Questions of Identity for Young British Muslim Women. Environment and Planning 31(1):53–68.
Eade, J., and D. Garbin
2002 Changing Narratives of Violence, Struggle and Resistance: Bangladeshis and the Competition for Resources in the Global City. Oxford Development Studies 30(2):137–149.
Freedman, J.
2004 Secularism as a Barrier to Integration? The French Dilemma. International Migration 42(3):5–27.
Geertz, C.
1960 Religion of Java. Chicago: Chicago University Press.
1968 Islam Observed. New Haven: Yale University Press.
Gellner, E.
1981 Muslim Society. Cambridge: Cambridge University Press.

Gilsenan, M.
1990 Very Like a Camel: The Appearance of an Anthropologist's Middle East. *In* Localizing Strategies: Regional Traditions of Ethnographic Writing. R. Fardon, ed. pp. 222–239. Edinburgh: Scottish Academic Press.
Goehlert, R., J. Russell, K. Homo, and J. Glogowski, eds.
2006 Muslims in Contemporary Europe: A Guide to Selected Resources in English. Bloomington: Indiana University Press.
Gould, A.
2009 Muslim Elites and Ideologies in Portugal and Spain. West European Politics 32(1):55–76.
Haddad, Y. Y., and I. Qurqmazi
2000 Muslims in the West: A Select Bibliography. Islam and Christian–Muslim Relations 11(1):5–49.
Halliday, F.
1995 Islam is in Danger: Authority, Rushdie and the Struggle for the Migrant Soul. *In* The Next Threat: Western Perceptions of Islam. J. Hippler and A. Lueg, eds. pp. 71–81. London: Pluto.
Halstead, M.
1988 Education, Justice and Cultural Diversity: An Examination of the Honeyford Affair 1984–85. Brighton: Falmer.
Hornborg, A.
2003 From Animal Masters to Ecosystem Services: Exchange, Personhood, and Human Ecology. *In* Imagining Nature: Practices of Cosmology and Identity. A. Roepstorff, N. Bubandt, and K. Kull, eds. pp. 97–116. Aarhus: Aarhus University Press.
Horrocks, D., and E. Kolinsky, eds.
1996 Turkish Culture in German Society Today. Providence, RI: Berghahn.
Hunter, S. T., ed.
2002 Islam in Europe: The New Social, Cultural and Political Landscape. New York: Praeger.
Jackson, P. I.
2009 Measuring Muslim Integration in Europe. Democracy and Security 5(3): 223–248.
Jeldtof, N.
2009 On Defining Muslims. *In* Yearbook of Muslims in Europe. J. S. Nielsen, S. Akgönül, B. Maréchal, and C. Moe, eds. pp. 9–14. Leiden: Brill.
Jones, D. M., and M. L. R. Smith
2005 Greetings from the Cybercaliphate: Some Notes on Homeland Insecurity. International Affairs 81(5):925–950.
Jongman, A. J.
1992 Trends in International and Domestic Terrorism in Western Europe, 1968–1988. Terrorism and Political Violence 4(4):6–76.
Joppke C.
2009 Limits of Integration Policy: Britain and Her Muslims. Journal of Ethnic and Migration Studies 35(3):453–472.
Korzybski, Alfred
1948 Science and Sanity: An Introduction to Non-Aristotelian Systems and General Semantics. Lakeville CT: The International Non-Aristotelian Publishing Co.
Leonard, K. I.
2003 Muslims in the United States: The State of Research. New York: Russell Sage Foundation.

Mamdani, M.
2004 Good Muslim, Bad Muslim. New York: Pantheon.
Marranci, G.
2004 Multiculturalism, Islam, and the Clash of Civilization Theory: Rethinking Islamophobia. Culture and Religion 5(1):107–119.
2008 The Anthropology of Islam. Oxford: Berg.
2009 Faith, Ideology and Fear: Muslim Identities Within and Beyond Prisons. London: Continuum.
Martin, R. C.
2010 Hidden Bodies in Islam: Secular Muslim Identities in Modern (and Premodern) Societies. *In* Muslim Societies and the Challenge of Secularization: An Interdisciplinary Approach. G. Marranci, ed. 131–148. Dordrecht: Springer.
Modood, T.
1990 The British Asian Muslims and the Rushdie affair. The Political Quarterly 62(2):143–60.
1998 Multiculturalism, Secularism and the State. Critical Review of International Social and Political Philosophy (CRISPP) 1(3):79–97.
Mohammed, J.
1996 The Home Office Strategy for Islam and Muslims in Britain: A Discussion Paper. London: Muslim Parliament of Great Britain.
Moors, A.
2009 The Dutch and the Face-Veil: The Politics of Discomfort. Social Anthropology 17(4):393–408.
Nauck, B.
1994 Les transformations des familles d'immigrés turcs en Allemagne. *In* Musulmans en Europe. B. Lewis and D. Schnapper, eds. pp. 165–180. Poitiers: Actes Sud.
Nielsen, J. S., S. Akgönül, B. Maréchal, and C. Moe, eds.
2009 Yearbook of Muslims in Europe. Leiden: Brill.
Pauly, R. J.
2004 Islam in Europe: Integration or Marginalization? Aldershot: Ashgate.
Rapport, N.
1997 Transcendent Individual: Towards a Literary and Liberal Anthropology. London: Routledge.
2003 I Am Dynamite: An Alternative Anthropology of Power. London and New York: Routledge.
Roy, O.
2007 Secularism Confronts Islam. New York: Columbia University Press.
Saas, C.
2001 Muslim Headscarf and Secularism in France. European Journal of Migration and Law 3(3/4):453–456.
Said, E. W.
1978 Orientalism. New York: Pantheon.
1981 Covering Islam: How the Media and the Experts Determine How We See the Rest of the World. New York: Pantheon.
Said, E. W., and G. Viswanathan
2001 Power, Politics, and Culture: Interviews with Edward W. Said. New York: Pantheon.
Schiffauer, W.
1999 Islamism in the Diaspora: The Fascination of Political Islam among Second Generation German Turks. Oxford: Oxford University Press.

Schmidt, G.
2004 Islamic Identity Formation among Young Muslims: The Case of Denmark, Sweden and the United States. Journal of Muslim Minority Affairs 24(1):31–45.
Shadid, W. A. R., and P. S. van Koningsveld
1992 De Mythe van het Islamitische Gevaar. Hindernissen bij Integratie. Kampen: Kok.
Shaw, A.
2002 Why Might Young British Muslims Support the Taliban? Anthropology Today 18(1):5–8.
Shirazi, F., and M. Smeeta
2010 Young Muslim Women on the Face Veil (Niqab). International Journal of Cultural Studies 13(1):3–62.
Timmerman, C.
2000 The Revival of Tradition, Consequences of Modesty: The Case of Young Turkish Women in Belgium. Folk: Journal of the Danish Ethnographical Society 42:83–100.
Turner, B.
2007 The Enclave Society: Towards a Sociology of Immobility. European Journal of Social Theory 10(2):287–303.
Varisco, M. D.
2005 Islam Obscured: The Rhetoric of Anthropological Representation. Basingstoke: Palgrave Macmillan.
Werbner, P.
1996 Fun Spaces: On Identity and Social Empowerment among British Pakistanis. Theory, Culture and Society 13(4):53–79.
2000 Divided Loyalties, Empowered Citizenship? Muslims in Britain. Citizenship Studies 4(3):307–24.
2002 Imagined Diasporas among Manchester Muslims: The Public Performance of Pakistani Transnational Identity Politics. Oxford: James Currey.
2005 Islamophobia: Incitement to Religious Hatred – Legislating for a New Fear? Anthropology Today 21(1):5–9.
Wiktorowicz, Q.
2005 Radical Islam Rising: Muslim Extremism in the West. Lanham, MD: Rowman and Littlefield.

CHAPTER 18

Roma and Sinti: The "Other" within Europe

Sabrina Kopf

Since the enlargement of the European Union in the years 2004 and 2007, Roma and Sinti have come to represent the largest ethnic minority within the EU, with an estimated population of 10–12 million people. The terms "Roma" and "Sinti" denote a rather heterogeneous ethnic group; one that is marked by the existence of several subgroups, such as Sinti (Manouche), Traveler, Lovari, Kalderash, Calé, Romungre, or Beash (Kovats 2001:113). Although a number of Romani groups emphasize their cultural autonomy, linguistic, historic, and regional differences, there are some distinctive similarities, of which their persistent discrimination, structural inequality, and their collective exclusion from the majority societies in Europe, are the most evident ones. Roma and Sinti still live at the margins of society, while their social advancement is hampered by the complex interplay of various factors. This has been especially true in Eastern Europe, which is home to an estimated 6–8 million Roma – the largest concentration on the continent.

The Roma in Eastern Europe belong to the poorest section of the population, due to high unemployment, poor education, and institutionalized discrimination. The segregation of Roma and Sinti and the disregard of their social situation in the educational system have led to a disproportionally high number of illiterates and school dropouts. Restricted access to public services and health care, housing in substandard accommodation, and isolation in often illegally built settlements characterized by inadequate infrastructure, have contributed to this increased segregation. Moreover, the living conditions of Romani groups worsened considerably after the breakdown of the socialist regimes in Eastern Europe because the subsequent political transformation and the transition to liberal market economies have increased the socioeconomic pressure on them. Describing the situation of Romani groups in Hungary, Stewart (1997:232) declares that ethnic hatred and race-motivated attacks against Roma and their settlements have become a serious problem in postsocialist countries.

A Companion to the Anthropology of Europe, First Edition. Edited by Ullrich Kockel, Máiréad Nic Craith, and Jonas Frykman.

However, structural discrimination and marginalization of Roma and Sinti are not specific to the new European Union member states in Eastern Europe but constitute a pan-European issue. The Council of Europe and the European Commission, therefore, stress their joint responsibility to promote the social inclusion of Romani groups in the member states. Although Roma, Sinti, (and Travelers) have been recognized by the Council of Europe Parliamentary Assembly in 1993 (Recommendation 1203[1993]) as a "true European minority," which is said to accord them a special place among other minorities due to their dispersal throughout Europe, related policy issues have gained salience on the European agenda only since the accession of Eastern European countries. Besides providing a legal framework to prohibit discrimination on ethnic grounds and to foster equal treatment irrespective of ethnic origin, the European Union supports the inclusion of Roma and Sinti by providing various funding mechanisms. Within the European Social Fund (ESF) and the European Regional Development Fund (ERDF) – the EU's major funding programs – a wide range of national, transnational, and locally based activities are being financed to improve the living conditions of Romani groups. Within these, investments in the education of Roma and Sinti and their integration into the labor market are defined as specific target areas. Furthermore, the European Union has been taking action to combat poverty and exclusion of Romani groups by establishing a section for Roma-related issues within the European Commission that is responsible for the coordination of various programs and actions targeted at the minority.

Indeed, the provision of considerable financial resources for the implementation of activities in the member states can be regarded as evidence of the EU's efforts to integrate Roma and Sinti into the respective majority societies. But one may ask why, although the member countries have utilized the various European funding programs to promote the social inclusion of Roma and Sinti since the late 1990s, their situation is perceived as not having changed at all in the past number of years? If the funding mechanisms have been used by public authorities, NGOs, and social partners in the member countries, what implications did they have at the local level? In this chapter, I draw on fieldwork conducted in Eastern Slovakia and discuss two Roma projects that were funded by the ESF and implemented in the Roma community of Vel'ká Ida.

EU Projects for Roma in Slovakia

The village of Vel'ká Ida is situated near the Hungarian border in rural Eastern Slovakia. It has 3139 inhabitants, of whom 32% belong to the Roma minority. Living segregated from the Slovak majority on the outskirts of the village, Roma inhabit two settlements, which lack access to the supply of water, electricity, and sewerage. The vast majority of the 569 people in Vel'ká Ida who were listed as unemployed according to the 2001 census were unofficially identified as belonging to the Roma community. Due to high unemployment among Roma in Vel'ká Ida, the local community was chosen as a target group for two EU-financed projects, which were implemented by the Agency for Support of Regional Development Košice (ARR Košice) between 2005 and 2008. The projects were titled "Maxim" and "Ružena," and aimed at increasing the employability of Roma by providing basic education, various short-term training, and vocational counseling. While Maxim focused on the activation of Roma men through training and networking with potential employers, Ružena targeted the many disadvantages that Roma women have been facing when entering the labor market. Improving numeracy and literacy as well as basic education were defined as the main areas for activity, because Roma women were said to lack any formal education or training necessary to enter the labor market. This has been primarily due to the high numbers of school dropouts among Roma girls, and a societal position which obliges women to stay at home and take care of the household and children. When I first heard of Maxim and Ružena some months prior to my arrival in Slovakia, the projects seemed feasible, if not very promising; I soon realized just how problematic their implementation was.

It was early afternoon and I had been sitting behind the elementary school of Vel'ká Ida for some hours, watching 10 Roma women – participants of the Ružena project – while they were weeding the grass on the sports ground. During summer, the participants were able to earn some money by doing so called "activation work" on the grounds of the elementary school before their courses in reading and writing started again in autumn. Being exhausted from their hard and monotonous work, they took a short break and sat down next to me. Talking about their lives in Vel'ká Ida and their dream of going and working abroad, the women also revealed to me their disappointment and dissatisfaction with the project and its coordinators. Since that day was the payment date, and five of them had not received any money the month before, the women were waiting for the local project staff to arrive with their salary. Not knowing why some of the women left empty-handed, Anna, one of the participants whose sister was among those five women, told me that this incident had aroused nervousness and jealousy among all the participants. Furthermore, the women had thought that they would be trained in how to apply successfully for a job and were thus very disappointed that Ružena merely comprised the learning of reading and writing skills. Since most of the women had learnt how to read and write in elementary school, they agreed that Ružena was only helpful for those who did not have any education at all. Kristina, a middle-aged mother of five grown-up children and the most talkative in the group, expressed her frustration with the project, explaining that "I have visited elementary school, it is not helping me. Why should I go to school? Because I'd rather go working and I have school already behind me." Furthermore, the belief that participation in the project would not help them to find any employment afterward was widespread among the participants, and was put forward as the reason for the low motivation and the high dropout rates. Instead, Kristina stressed that "what motivated me to go to class was not any promise of a job later but it was the fact that there will be activation work. If there is no money I don't go there."

Indeed, a quite different outlook on the projects had been presented to me by Gejza Legen, senior project manager of Maxim and Ružena, just a few days before. Sitting in the office of ARR Košice, he confessed his disappointment about the performance of the projects with a rather unexpected frankness, telling me that they were "not really a success." He identified as the main problems difficulties in mobilizing participants for the various activities, and the necessity of constantly searching for further interested persons due to the high dropout rates during the projects. Searching for the reasons for the projects' weak performance, he admitted that "the internal management was rather weak . . . and the focus of the projects was a little bit too ambitious, too vague and too big." Nevertheless, he blamed the Roma for being responsible for all the problems that had occurred so far. Stressing their lack of commitment and their unreliability as the actual stumbling blocks, he believed that "it's generally the attitude, not only the weak commitment" of the Roma, which had caused problems during the implementation. Matej and Pavel, two community workers in Vel'ká Ida who had also worked with the Roma community during the Maxim project, shared his point of view and noted that the demand of the various kinds of training offered in Maxim was low on behalf of the Roma because "they just didn't want to work."

What is evident from these short episodes from my fieldwork is that the Maxim and Ružena projects were a disappointment to the project staff and Roma alike, although diverging perceptions and experience prevailed within both groups. Therefore, being much more than a random glimpse on two Roma projects, these episodes are valuable resources that shed some light on the apparently unaltered situation of Roma in Slovakia. With a population estimated at somewhere between 90 000 and 480 000, Roma form the second-largest minority group in the Slovak Republic. Yet although the willingness of the political authorities to promote their social inclusion has increased during the 1990s, and several EU-financed projects have been implemented since the accession to the European Union in 2004, Roma still form the weakest section of the population in terms of socioeconomic status and political power. Moreover, an examination of Maxim and Ružena revealed that the participants were confronted with various negative ascriptions by the project staff; these described Roma primarily as a social-problem group, said to be characterized by an unchangeable culture. Following Csepeli and Simon, who remark that "Roma are the most rejected of all minority groups" (2004:133), I argue that the negative ascriptions toward Romani groups are based on an historic image of the "Gypsy." Before describing how this negative image of the "Gypsy" was reproduced within Maxim and Ružena, I will highlight the development of this pejorative image of the "Gypsy" by illustrating its distinguishing marks as well as science's contribution to the codification of the negative attitude toward Roma and Sinti.

The Historic Construction of the "Gypsy"

The negative image of the "Gypsy" emerged after the first groups of Roma and Sinti arrived in Europe during the fifteenth century. Regarding its outstanding timeliness, Maciejwski (1996:12) points out that the creation of this image has to be seen as the result of various events and processes that were fundamental to the development of contemporary Europe. Likewise, Hancock argues that the image of the "Gypsy" "was stimulated by a combination of the responses to industrialization, colonialism and emerging nineteenth-century ideas of racial hierarchy" (2002:65). The first encounters between Roma and Sinti and the domestic population were dominated by religious beliefs, because the first Romani groups presented themselves as Christians on pilgrimage. Although Roma and Sinti were received well at first (Reemtsma 1996:34), the majority's attitude changed quickly and the arrivals were soon viewed as heathens and spies for the Muslims. The Catholic Church played an essential role in creating and reproducing negative ascriptions toward Roma and Sinti by associating their black skins with darkness and evil. Before the end of the fifteenth century, Roma and Sinti were said to be in league with the devil (Wippermann 1997:71). Kenrick and Puxon remark that "the conviction that blackness denotes inferiority and evil was already well-rooted in the Western mind. The nearly black skins of many Gypsies marked them out to be victims of this prejudice" (1972:19).

The emergence of the "Gypsy image" was also closely linked to the beginning of academic "Gypsy studies" – "*Zigeunerkunde*" – during the eighteenth and nineteenth centuries in Europe, which were guided by a popular image of Roma and Sinti as bandits, thieves, sorcerers, and messengers from an exotic world (Willems 1996:97). Early "Gypsy studies" were marked by the conviction of the "Gypsy's" immutability, "oriental" ancestry, and foreignness. The research of anthropologists and "Gypsy folklorists," such as Heinrich Grellmann, Christian C. Rüdiger, and August F. Pott, focused on the supposed ethnic "inferiority," criminal addiction, and laziness of Roma and Sinti and, thus, had a momentous impact on nation-states' approach to Romani groups.

Furthermore, the creation of the "Gypsy image" was influenced by various political transformations, which had far-reaching consequences on the perception of "strangers." During the emergence of nation-states in Europe, Roma and Sinti were instrumentalized as the image of "the stranger" par excellence by the political elites in order to effectuate homogenization of the population and its identification with the national territory (Hund 1996:25; Maciejwski 1996:17). Due to their unfamiliar appearance and mode of living, Roma and Sinti formed a welcome object for projection. Exploiting the popular image of Roma and Sinti as thieves, beggars, and beguilers who move from town to town, they were defined as the categorical "Other" and regarded as a threat to the community of citizens. The exclusion and persecution of Roma and Sinti as outlaws were thus also based on the denunciation of the "Gypsy-like lifestyle" and used as a necessary disciplinary action. Most of all, the instrumentalization of Roma and Sinti was reflected by a specific "Gypsy" policy and several anti-"Gypsy" laws, which were enacted throughout Europe between the fifteenth and nineteenth centuries, providing the legal basis for their expulsion and persecution (Reemtsma 1996:40; Vuolasranta 2006:20). These laws emphasized a supposed "criminality" as the essential character trait of the "Gypsy." Maciejwski (1996:18) points out that as a result, Roma and Sinti were treated increasingly as a security problem and subject for action by the police during the nineteenth and early twentieth centuries.

The negative "Gypsy image" was continuously reproduced and extended by a racist component during the early twentieth century. From the 1930s onward, the research of anthropologists, biologists, medics and scientists served the racial policy of Nazi Germany. Like Jews, Roma and Sinti were viewed as being "racially inferior" and, thus, were classified "unworthy of life." Robert Ritter, head of the Racial Hygiene and Population Biology Research Unit in Berlin, was one of the most popular proponents of the Nazi racial doctrine. Together with his assistants he collected data on

Romani groups to find a connection between Roma genetics and their supposed criminal nature as well as to make further recommendations for racial policy. Ritter's work was based on the presumption that "Gypsies" were a "primitive" people, incapable of adapting to normal civilized life (Wippermann 1997:80; Willems 2001:26). In this vein, the racial and biological evaluation of Roma and Sinti by Ritter and other racial scientists laid the ground for, and legitimized, the extermination of approximately 1.5 million Roma and Sinti in Nazi Germany and occupied Europe between 1939 and 1945 (Latham 1995:2; Gingrich 2005:121ff.).

From the 1970s until the present day, folklorists have continued to study the culture, history, and way of life of Romani groups by glorifying and searching for the "true Gypsy." Again, the historic "Gypsy image" was reproduced within "tsiganology" by emphasizing the cultural foreignness and alleged unwillingness of "Gypsies" to integrate themselves into the majority societies.

However, the stereotypical image of the "Gypsy" is also the dominating element in today's public and political discourse on Roma and Sinti, in which they are presented as the counterpart to a rational, modern, and enlightened world. In fact, Heuß (1996:120) argues that the continuing instrumentalization of Roma and Sinti by nation-states is characterized by their definition as a "social-problem group" denying them ethnic or historic autonomy while legitimizing policies of assimilation. Indeed, Liégeois and Gheorghe agree that "according to the definition imposed upon them and the image by which they are characterised, Roma/Gypsies are thought to have no linguistic, cultural or ethnic roots. They are instead a 'social problem' requiring 'rehabilitation' and 'reintegration'" (1995:12f). As a result, policies toward Roma and Sinti are limited to combating unemployment, lack of education, inadequate housing, and health problems instead of targeting ethnic discrimination and segregation.

Between Paternalism and Marginalization

Disclosing several barriers and shortcomings, an evaluation of the Maxim and Ružena projects speaks volumes about the structural problems within EU-financed activities as well as today's stereotyping of Roma and Sinti. Looking at the performance of the projects, problems in mobilizing participants for the various activities as well as high numbers of dropouts were the most evident results. Instead of achieving improvements for the Roma community, the projects have instead shattered the expectations of Roma and reproduced negative stereotypes and existing mechanisms of marginalization. The structure and composition of the European Social Fund exerted a decisive influence on the projects' performance, since EU funding mechanisms determine the guidelines for the development and implementation of activities. For example, the exclusive focus on short-term activities – and specifically on the integration of Roma and Sinti into the labor market, viewed as the most important precondition for social inclusion within the ESF framework – prohibited the implementation of an integrative and sustainable approach, which is necessary when working with marginalized and deprived communities. As Jeff Graham, project staff of a Slovak NGO working with Roma, stressed, "complex problems cannot be addressed by short term, piece by piece projects." He went on to explain that "sometimes [such projects] can do more harm than good because they raise expectations, start achieving some success and then they end."

As with experienced Roma NGOs, representatives of the Roma communities and Slovak academics emphasized the need for a holistic approach to improve the living conditions of Roma. As Dáša Frivalská, representative of the regional office of the Slovak Government Plenipotentiary for Roma Communities in Košice, noted, "employment alone doesn't solve the problem – there must be a complex solution including housing, education, acceptance in society and then afterwards we can put them into employment."

But major weaknesses were also to be found within the local project management. Financial problems and bureaucracy were a challenge for the project staff during the implementation of Maxim and Ružena. Various members of the project staff complained about work overload due to administrative demands and constant requests for information by European institutions and the Slovak National Managing Authority. For Silvia Hricková, project manager of Maxim and Ružena, the never-ending paperwork made it difficult to focus on the actual activities for Roma because "a lot of money was put into the bureaucracy and the papers for administration, but the meaning of the project has disappeared in these papers." Furthermore, the failure to conduct an analysis of the target group's needs and of the local realities as well as the marginalization of Roma and experienced NGOs during the design, implementation, and evaluation of the projects had hindered the development of a sense of ownership of the implemented activities in the community. Instead, Maxim and Ružena were designed without paying attention to the target group's specific situation, and were implemented in a top-down approach. Gejza Legen explained the agency's approach in the following way: "We already knew that there is high unemployment and thought it would benefit the Roma to work. But the problem is that we decided what they [the Roma] want to do and what kind of education they want to undertake in the project."

When talking to the participants in the projects, it became quite clear that the paternalistic approach of the project staff members, their indifference toward the ethnic group's needs, and the lack of communication between both groups caused considerable distrust among the Roma in Vel'ká Ida. Anna and her sister Renata expressed their skepticism about the benefit of EU-financed projects for Roma and explained why few women in Vel'ká Ida wanted to participate in Ružena: "A lot of things were promised but not kept. This is why the women stopped going there. . . . There's a lot of money from the EU and if we saw at least one promise fulfilled, the women would stay in the project." Being aware of EU subsidies for Roma but having never seen any employee from ARR Košice in Vel'ká Ida, they assumed that a lot of money must have gone into the pockets of corrupt officials or members of the project staff.

Besides structural shortcomings inherent in EU funding programs and local project management, paternalism and discriminating ascriptions toward Roma and Sinti by project staff were the main reasons for excluding the target group from participating actively in the design and implementation of Maxim and Ružena, and thus for the projects' weak performance.

The Reproduction of the "Gypsy Image" in Slovakia and EU-Financed Projects

The classification of Roma as a "social-problem group" and the reproduction of the "Gypsy image" characterize contemporary public discourse in Slovakia. Since the breakdown of the socialist regime in 1989, the public attitude toward Roma in Slovakia has worsened dramatically. Roma are not only confronted with social marginalization, that is, exclusion from the labor market, public services, and political participation, as well as segregation in isolated settlements, but they also have to face discrimination and racial hatred. Kristina, who lives with her family in the Roma settlement of Vel'ká Ida, referred to her life in Slovakia in the following way: "There is high inequality and I feel that it will never improve to the better in this area. No matter where we go, for example to the doctor or the social welfare office, we are humiliated everywhere."

The negative attitude toward Roma in Slovakia is based on various stereotypes, which imply very often contradictory ascriptions and highlight the allegedly ignorant, lazy, carefree, greedy, or criminal "nature" of Roma. Talking about the precarious living conditions of Roma in Slovakia, Pavel reflected on the reasons for their weak socioeconomic position: "They are not willing to rise to another level. They are not even wanting or willing to come to this level." Furthermore, the perception that Roma are not able or willing to adapt to general social standards and norms is commonly stressed to legitimize their social exclusion and discrimination. Indeed, Vašečka points out that disregard of Roma in Slovakia is constant among all classes of people regardless of age, sex, education, nationality, political inclinations, or size of the municipality (2007:14). Arne Mann, professor of cultural anthropology at the Komenskeho University in Bratislava, remarks in this regard that the negative attitude toward Roma represents the biggest barrier to integration as "the majority society is unable to accept them and welcome them to society." Facing different stereotypes, discrimination, and social exclusion in their daily life, Roma do not understand the reasons for the disregard of their ethnic group. Ladislav and Roby, two inhabitants of the Roma settlement in Vel'ká Ida, told me: "We absolutely don't know why they are disrespecting us; because we are black and the *Gadje* [non-Roma] don't like Blacks and that's just it. In the village there is absolutely no reason to be disliked." Consequently, the negative image is being incorporated by Roma and increases their frustration and lethargy.

However, the pronounced negative attitude toward Roma also found its way into the projects Maxim and Ružena, and represented a crucial barrier to the successful implementation of activities. On the one hand, Roma were perceived by the project staff as a "social-problem group" whose members were said to ignore prevalent social norms and values, while on the other hand specific cultural traits were ascribed to them and held responsible for the lack of integration into mainstream society. Their alleged unreliability as well as their "backward" and carefree lifestyle were seen as the main problems during the implementation of the projects. When talking about the weak performance of Maxim and Ružena and the reasons for the low commitment of Roma, Gejza Legen explained to me that they were too indifferent or not able to realize the necessity and importance of education. "They don't take responsibility over their life and fate and their future. They don't appreciate the education and the investment to their self development. . . . Living for today – you know – and not for the future." Moreover, the alleged lethargy, laziness and unreliability of Roma in Vel'ká Ida were regarded as proof of their common image as a "social-problem group" and the reasons for their weak socioeconomic position.

Indeed, Roma were said to have no motivation to work but, rather, were characterized as happy to live exclusively at the expense of the state and tax payer. Tomaš Demko, employee at the municipality of Vel'ká Ida and technical assistant in Maxim, remarked that "they live from what the social [welfare] system will give them. There are some of them who want to be like White people. They want to achieve more, but that's probably 5% of them." Both Matej and Pavel shared his opinion and stressed that Roma "have no motivation to work; they stopped to take it seriously. They get social money, money for the children, housing money and medical care. So, they have no need to work, but we are working and don't get any money." Instead of contributing to society, Pavel asserted: "Roma people only suck from our breast or the state's," and thought that this was the reason why Roma were disliked in Slovakia. "It's not racism that people hate Roma, I think they hate this attitude," explained Gejza Legen. Indeed, due to the low education of many Roma, their segregation and lack of qualifications for the labor market, they are highly dependent on social benefits and this has contributed to their image as a "social-problem group."

Due to a lack of official statistics, estimates of unemployment and education among Roma vary wildly. While Cöster and Pfister (2005:12) rate unemployment and illiteracy among Roma at 90–100% in the deprived rural parts of Eastern Slovakia, results of the 1991 census draw a quite different picture. The census states that 76.68% of the Roma population in Slovakia attended elementary school (Vašečka 2007:23), but it fails to document that many Roma are leaving school uneducated and semi-illiterate because of low school-attendance rates and their placement in "special" schools for physically and mentally disabled children. The "mentality" of Roma was especially held responsible for their poor education and high unemployment rates. Both Matej and Pavel felt that, despite job opportunities, Roma mentality was one of not liking to work. Simultaneously, by stressing the lack of education and the indifference among Roma, the project staff managed to justify the paternalistic approach within the projects. "Why didn't we ask them? If we asked them, they would not do anything, for sure," explained Tomaš Demko.

The belief that Roma are caught in traditions that keep them from "developing" themselves and from adapting to a modern world has added to the stereotypical image of Roma as being lazy, carefree, and indifferent. Silvia Hricková pointed out that "sometimes Roma are stuck in old traditions, which push them back, and we cannot force them to change when they don't want to." The threat of a specific "Roma culture," which is characterized by poverty, violence, alcoholism, drug abuse, and lethargy, and the image of a so called "culture of poverty" that is closely linked to the Roma community, are widespread in Slovakia today. The Roma's supposed nomadic lifestyle, their lack of a written culture, and their life within extended families were seen as central elements of the "Roma culture" and were described as barriers to their successful integration. Explaining the difficulties in teaching Roma, Gejza Legen stated: "There is a cultural reason lying behind the education. It means that education was never valued among the Roma in the past because they were travelling." Regarding the high birthrate of Roma, many respondents feared that in 15 to 20 years Vel'ká Ida would be "overpopulated" by Roma who could neither read nor write. Therefore, Tomaš Demko, Matej and Pavel emphasized the need to reduce the birthrate among Roma, and supported special boarding schools for Roma children far away from their families. Otherwise, they were sure that Roma children would become like their parents and "will start to take drugs and drink alcohol."

Reflecting on the problems that arose during the implementation of the projects, Matej and Pavel were convinced that the voluntary segregation of Roma from mainstream society was another central barrier to their successful inclusion. "Roma people always distanced themselves even though we tried to put them together with us. But they would rather live on their own and care about their stuff and that's perhaps what's specific about them." But instead of blaming a fictional "Roma culture," Vašečka argues that the exclusively negative elements, which coined the ethnic group's image in Slovak mainstream society, have to be seen as the results of assimilation, marginalization, and interventions into the social life of Roma communities. "Is there something like a Roma culture, which is causing problems? No, I don't think so. I strongly believe that this is caused by two hundred years of assimilation, loss of tradition, agony, alienation."

CONCLUSION

The precarious living conditions of Roma and Sinti in Europe have forced the European Union to set measures to promote their social inclusion. Although European institutions and member states have recognized their joint responsibility, claiming in their official rhetoric to use "all the instruments and policies for which they have the respective competence" (European Commission n.d.) to combat the poverty and segregation of Romani groups, little improvement has been achieved by the activities financed by the EU in Slovakia. In discussing two local Roma projects, I have tried to demonstrate that EU-financed projects have not achieved their goal of improving the living conditions of Roma but rather failed to live up to the expectations of the project staff and Roma alike, despite generous financial and human resources.

Trying to identify the causes for the projects' weak performance, it seems clear that the European Social Fund has proved to be a quite unsuitable source of funding for implementing activities for Roma. Besides some technical and structural problems during the design and implementation of the projects, the continuing reproduction of culturalizing and discriminating ascriptions, as well as the pronounced paternalistic approach toward Roma, proved to be insurmountable barriers. Decisively, the negative attitude toward Roma that prevails in Slovakia today was also to be found among the members of the project staff, who adhered to a fictional image of a specific "Roma culture" and a classification of Roma as "social-problem group." Roma were, thus, conceived as lethargic, workshy, and nomadic strangers, who were hindering all attempts of integration by holding on to their "backward" way of living. I argued that the qualities ascribed to Roma are closely tied to a historic "Gypsy image"; one that developed in Europe between the fifteenth and nineteenth centuries and was reproduced continuously to enforce political and economic interests.

Unfortunately, the "Gypsy image" still permeates current political and public debates in Slovakia and has even found its way into activities directed at Roma. The reduction of Roma to passive beneficiaries of help in the EU's activities denies them the right and possibility to be recognized as active and equal partners. The analysis of the projects in Vel'ká Ida revealed that not all funding programs are equally suited to improve the situation of Roma and Sinti. Due to the numerous barriers with which Roma and Sinti are confronted in their daily life, a holistic approach is needed; one that takes into account their needs as well as the local realities. Instead of remaining victims of the perpetuation of the stereotype of the poor, indifferent "Gypsy," Roma and Sinti must be given the possibility to determine their future themselves, by being involved in the design and implementation of the activities directed toward them. What has become evident from two decades in which the EU and its member states have attempted to fight discrimination and the social exclusion of Roma and Sinti, is that it will probably take some more decades to make some progress, and that one-sided, short-term activities can do more harm than good. Therefore, awareness-raising campaigns in the member states as well as with NGOs and community centers situated in Roma settlements, and the offering of a variety of demand-orientated services, might be a first important step in the right direction.

REFERENCES

Cöster, Anna Caroline, and Monika Pfister

2005 Die Situation der Roma nach der EU-Osterweiterung am Beispiel der Slowakischen Republik. *In* Die Situation der Roma und Sinti nach der EU-Osterweiterung. Max Matter, ed. pp. 113–126. Otto Benecke Stiftung e.V. Beiträge der Akademie für Migration und Integration, 9. Göttingen: V & R Unipress.

Council of Europe Parliamentary Assembly

1993 Recommendation 1203 (1993) on Gypsies in Europe. Electronic document. http://assembly.coe.int/Main.asp?link=/Documents/AdoptedText/ta93/EREC1203.htm (accessed November 5, 2011).

Csepeli, György, and Dávid Simon

2004 Construction of Roma Identity in Eastern and Central Europe: Perception and Self-Identification. Journal of Ethnic and Migration Studies 30(1):130–150.

European Commission Employment, Social Affairs and Equal Opportunities

n.d. The European Union and Roma. Electronic document. http://ec.europa.eu/social/main.jsp?catId=518&langId=en (accessed November 5, 2011).

Gingrich, Andre

2005 German Anthropology during the Nazi Period: Complex Scenarios of Collaboration, Persecution, and Competition. *In* One Discipline, Four Ways: British, German, French, and American Anthropology. Fredrik Barth, Andre Gingrich, Robert Parkin, and Sydel Silverman. pp. 111–136. Chicago: University of Chicago Press.

Hancock, Ian

2002 We Are the Romani People: Ame sam e Rromane džene. Hatfield: University of Hertfordshire Press.

Heuß, Herbert

1996 Die Migration von Roma aus Osteuropa im 19. und 20. Jahrhundert: Historische Anlässe und staatliche Reaktion – Überlegungen zum Funktionswandel des Zigeuner-

Ressentiments. *In* Die gesellschaftliche Konstruktion des Zigeuners: Zur Genese eines Vorurteils. Jacqueline Giere, ed. pp. 109–131. Wissenschaftliche Reihe des Fritz-Bauer-Instituts, 2. Frankfurt am Main: Campus.

Hund, Wulf D., ed.

1996 Zigeuner: Geschichte und Struktur einer rassistischen Konstruktion. Duisburg: Duisburger Institut für Sprach-und Sozialforschung.

Kenrick, Donald, and Grattan Puxon

1972 The Destiny of Europe's Gypsies. The Columbus Centre Series. London: Heinemann.

Kovats, Martin

2001 The Emergence of European Roma Policy. *In* Between Past and Future: The Roma of Central and Eastern Europe. Will Guy, ed. pp. 93–116. Hatfield: University of Hertfordshire Press.

Latham, Judith

1995 First US Conference on Gypsies in the Holocaust. Current Affairs Bulletin No. 3-23928. Washington: Voice of America.

Liégeois, Jean-Pierre, and Nicolae Gheorghe

1995 Roma/Gypsies: A European Minority. Minority Rights Group [MRG] International Report, 95(4). London: MRG.

Maciejwski, Franz

1996 Elemente des Antiziganismus. *In* Die gesellschaftliche Konstruktion des Zigeuners: Zur Genese eines Vorurteils. Jacqueline Giere, ed. pp. 9–27. Wissenschaftliche Reihe des Fritz-Bauer-Instituts, 2. Frankfurt am Main: Campus.

Reemtsma, Katrin

1996 Sinti und Roma: Geschichte, Kultur, Gegenwart. Beck'sche Reihe, 1155. Munich: Beck.

Stewart, Michael

1997 The Time of the Gypsies: Studies in Ethnographic Imagination. Boulder, CO: Westview.

Vašečka, Michal

2007 Study on the Social and Labor Market Integration of Ethnic Minorities. Final Report on Slovakia. Bratislava: Centre for Research on Ethnicity and Culture.

Vuolasranta, Miranda

2006 Roma und Sinti – Europäische Identitäten: Antiziganismus muss erkannt und bekämpft werden. *In* Europäische Roma – Roma in Europa. Reetta Toivanen and Michi Knecht, eds. pp. 20–24. Berliner Blätter, Ethnographische und ethnologische Beiträge 39/2006. Münster: LIT.

Willems, Wim

1996 Außenbilder von Sinti und Roma in der frühen Zigeunerforschung. *In* Die gesellschaftliche Konstruktion des Zigeuners: Zur Genese eines Vorurteils. Jacqueline Giere, ed. pp. 87–108.Wissenschaftliche Reihe des Fritz-Bauer-Instituts, 2. Frankfurt am Main: Campus.

2001 Ethnicity as a Death-Trap: The History of Gypsy Studies. *In* Gypsies and Other Itinerant Groups: A Socio-Historical Approach. Leo Lucassen, with Wim Willems and Annemarie Cottaar, eds. pp. 17–34. Basingstoke: Palgrave.

Wippermann, Wolfgang

1997 "Wie die Zigeuner" – "wie die Juden." *In* NS-Vergangenheit, Antisemitismus und Nationalismus in Deutschland. Christoph Butterwegge, ed. pp. 69–84. Beiträge zur politischen Kultur der Bundesrepublik und zur politischen Bildung. Baden-Baden: Nomos.

CHAPTER 19

Landscape, Landscape History, and Landscape Theory

Norbert Fischer

On the Genesis of the Modern European Concept of Landscape

In various scientific disciplines, the term "landscape" is currently discussed controversially, newly conceptualized, and theoretically illuminated. New schools of landscape research have emerged, which have a broad variety of theories, concepts, and themes. The spectrum ranges from the classical concept of landscape in modern times to the particularized landscape view of postmodern approaches.

The understanding of landscape in Europe is fundamentally characterized by the different perspectives of natural and cultural sciences. From a scientific perspective, landscape arises from – and is altered by – the specific physical interactions between nature and man, that is, human work on nature. Historically, this was first reflected in different variants of agricultural economic activity, and later by the consequences of industrialization. From the perspective of cultural sciences, however, the concept of landscape is dominated by a subjective-aestheticized perception of selected areas that are perceived as in themselves homogeneous and mostly shaped by nature: landscape as a "beautiful countryside." The art historian Karin Wendt (2009) argued that we use the term landscape when we examine something with an interest in its particular formation, design, or organization and, in doing so, describe it at the same time from a distance; to see landscapes means, first of all, to get an idea of something.

Landscape thus represents both a substantive material heritage and a rich source of ideas and perceptions (Krzywinski 2009:9, 16–18). Landscapes have a specific meaning for particular social groups in their respective environments. This meaning is usually both culturally and socioeconomically founded. It changes and evolves in the course of historical change.

A Companion to the Anthropology of Europe, First Edition. Edited by Ullrich Kockel, Máiréad Nic Craith, and Jonas Frykman.

The concept of landscape was already known in the Middle Ages, when it referred to a defined space. At the beginning of the modern era in Europe, in conjunction with an aestheticization of nature, the term became symbolically charged. For the philosopher Joachim Ritter, the origin of the modern concept of landscape lies in the socially specific view of nature, which has developed in the face of the increasing alienation of human work from nature. In his seminal text on the understanding of landscape in modern Europe, he suggested that landscape is nature, which is aesthetically present in the gaze of a sentient and feeling viewer; that the fields outside the town, the river as "border," "trade route," and "challenge for bridge builders," the mountains and the steppes of the shepherds and caravans (or oil prospectors) are not, as such, "landscape." They become so only when human beings turn to them without practical purpose but rather in free appreciative contemplation, in order to be themselves in nature – nature changes its countenance as we enter it (Ritter 1963:18).

Landscape became at once both nature and art. It represented the view of a world perceived as harmonious. The catalyst of the aesthetic perception of nature was landscape painting, which unfolded in Europe since the transition from medieval to modern times, especially since the sixteenth and seventeenth centuries. It mediated and projected landscape through perspective into space (Büttner 2006:73ff; Schramm 2008). The production of landscape appeared both as an artistic and creative achievement as well as – by imitating it – a new "practice of seeing." Subsequently, the perception of landscape as "beautiful countryside" led to numerous highly charged paintings, especially in the era of Romanticism (Dinnebier 2004).

This Eurocentric perspective on landscape has been critically reflected in research on several occasions. William T. Mitchell, for example, pointed out that already in antiquity, Greek and Roman painters developed landscape perspectives (Mitchell 2002:5–34). Rainer Guldin (2010) showed the richness of the centuries-old tradition of Chinese landscape painting. From another point of view, the art historian Martin Warnke criticized Joachim Ritter's more modern compensatory-contemplative understanding of landscape. In contrast to this, Warnke (1992) unfolded the social-critical concept of the "political landscape."

In the modern-European landscape discourse at least, the art historical perspective also influenced the practice of gardening. Gardens and parks were modeled as semi-natural landscapes since the early modern period, for example, the English landscape garden at Dessau-Wörlitz in Germany (see Figure 19.1). Another example, the landscape park at Stourhead, Wiltshire in England (created between 1741 and 1780) was based on models from landscape painting. These and other landscape parks are thought to have had a compensatory role as points of refuge in a period when – under the dictum of the Enlightenment – rational structures increasingly dominated everyday life. From a scientific point of view, the concept of landscape was used since the eighteenth century for scientific systematization. The descriptions only became particularly scientific when we began more precisely, and by achieving general conventions, to define and differentiate landscapes, thus typifying and classifying them (Küster 2005:54–57).

However, "landscape" as an independent term was only gradually incorporated into the modern dictionaries and encyclopedias, which represented the knowledge held in their respective eras. In the Central European, German-speaking countries,

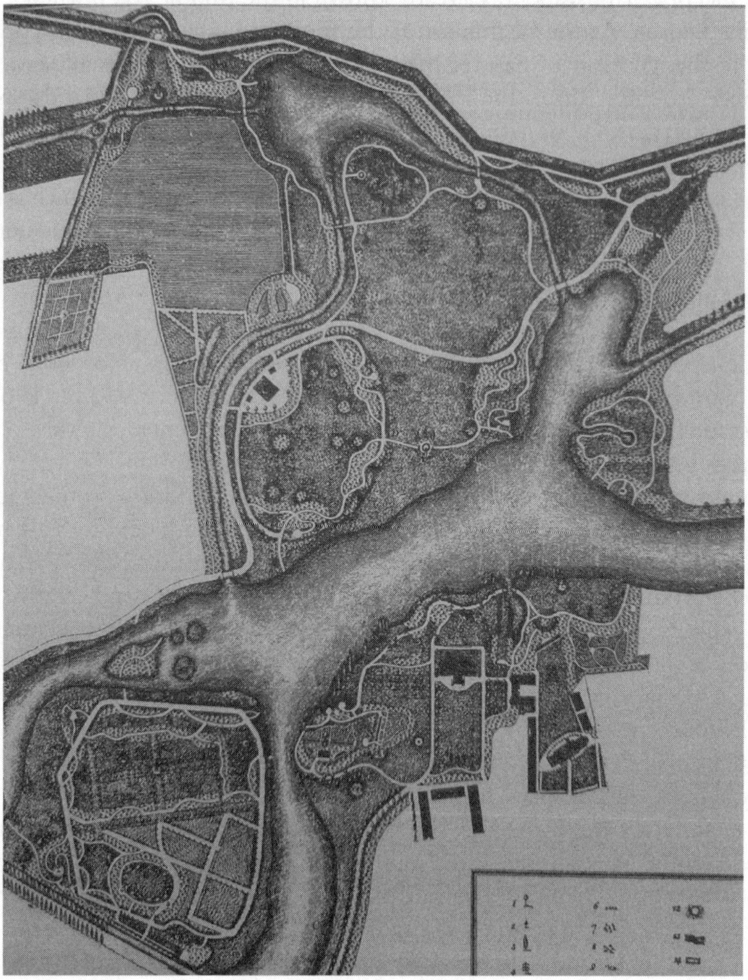

Figure 19.1 English landscape garden Dessau-Wörlitz (eighteenth century). (Reproduced from Marie Luise Gothein, *Geschichte der Gartenkunst*, vol. 2, Jena, Germany, 1926, p. 393.)

for example, the term didn't appear as a separate keyword either in Zedler's *Universal-Lexicon* of 1737 or the first *Brockhaus Enzyklopädie* of 1809. The subsequent history of German dictionaries and encyclopedias in the nineteenth century shows the increasing expansion of the term. On the one hand, the stock of knowledge, which the concept of landscape represents, increased; on the other hand, landscape gained importance as a separate keyword over the previously dominant compounds and submissions. This can be illustrated by the Grimm brothers' German dictionary, *Deutsches Wörterbuch* (released from 1854) where "landscape" appeared first of all as a "land complex, connected stretch of land." This is further specified thus: "area, land complex in relation to location and natural qualities" and "landscape as a socially cohesive entirety, area." And, "particularly in newer sources with regard to the impression that such an area makes on the eye . . . the artistic visual presentation of such an area" (Grimm and Grimm 12:131–133, translation author's own). *Meyers*

Figure 19.2 English landscape garden at Wilhelmshöhe, Kassel. Photograph © Norbert Fischer. (Reproduced courtesy of the author.)

Großes Konversations-Lexikon of 1905 definitively documented the multidimensionality of the concept of landscape that had emerged in the bourgeois era. On several pages, different meanings of "landscape," including compounds, are described (Meyers Großes Konversations-Lexikon 1905:121–125).

The holistic nature of "landscape" remained dominant throughout the bourgeois era. At the same time, during the nineteenth century, landscape – in the sense of "rural area" – became the antithesis of the urban environment. This became increasingly apparent and important as industrialization and urbanization progressed. The classic view of landscape, shaped by painting, influenced this insofar as it formed a basis for the romantic gaze of the citizen on an area they experienced as an unadulterated rural idyll (see Figure 19.2).

In the course of the twentieth century, the classic-bourgeois understanding of landscape was increasingly dissolved and particularized. The reasons for this change in the landscape concept lie in the developments of the industrial and post-industrial age. Rolf Peter Sieferle described the consequences of industrial modernity as "total landscape": in this total landscape, an older, spatial, and reliable pattern of differentiation is replaced by a new, unique, and volatile one (Sieferle 1998:164). The boundaries between city and country were becoming increasingly unrecognizable; the rural-urban antithesis lost its meaning. Suburban intermediate zones in metropolitan areas were no longer seen as *terra incognita* in terms of "landscape." The current landscape discourses emerging from this transition are outlined below.

Landscape in Current Research Discourse

The history of the landscape concept and its meanings also forms the basis of those research approaches that have unfolded in the humanities and cultural studies in recent years (N. Fischer 2008a). The theoretical discourse is currently dominated by the disagreement between the classical concept of landscape on the one hand and the new, particularized concept of landscape on the other hand. The gradual replacement, or at least modification, of the classical landscape concept with its standardization of the aesthetic manifests itself in very different disciplines. In the humanities – not least in European ethnology/cultural anthropology – the production and projection character is stressed (L. Fischer 2004; N. Fischer et al. 2007). In history, the changing concept of landscape is interpreted as representing social, economic, and political structures – for example, the growing mastery of nature as an expression of growing national self-confidence and political power aspirations (Blackbourn 2006). For historians of technology and environmental historians, landscape appears as civilized-technicized space, the transformation of which allows the tracing of, *inter alia*, infrastructural systems (Zeller 2007). In new cultural geography, after that discipline's "cultural turn," the new landscape school, with its understanding of landscape as a text to be interpreted, has pointed the way toward a dynamic understanding of landscape beyond a purely scientific and systematic description (McDowell 1994). For the development of approaches in urban, regional, and landscape planning, the transformation of the boundaries between town and country has been crucial, as has the inclusion of the supposedly "ugly." This is documented by new terms such as "landscape urbanism" (Waldheim 2006) and "landscapes abused" (ILA 2007).

Nevertheless, the classical European understanding of landscape has not lost its meaning. At present, it can mainly be found in the concept of "cultural landscape," which, since the late twentieth century, has acquired great importance not least in the political discussion. "Cultural landscape" refers to a landscape that is the result of human influence and that continues to exist in a certain form because of the ongoing human influence; moreover, the cultural landscape can be well explained by its antithesis – untouched, unspoilt nature; the realization of this duality is the basis for understanding and appreciating both concepts (Krzywinski 2009:13, 16). According to this definition, however, any area at least in Central Europe appears as a cultural landscape because there are hardly any areas untouched by humans (Küster 1995) – even designated nature reserves and national parks are subjected to human influence precisely through their protection. Often the concept of cultural landscape also implies an assumption of the agrarian cultivation of nature. Therefore, the term "cultural landscapes" in a Europe context is frequently used with reference to preindustrial agricultural landscapes. To put it another way, urbanization and industrialization are often seen as disruptive of traditional cultural landscapes (Dannebeck et al. 2009:51).

Nevertheless, the concept of cultural landscapes with its vision of conservation and protection has retained social and political importance. Among other things, it influenced the definitions of the European Landscape Convention of 2000. This document says in Chapter 1, Article 1: "'Landscape' means an area, as perceived by people, whose character is the result of the action and interaction of natural and/or human factors." Then the idea of protection is emphasized: "'Landscape protection' means actions to conserve and maintain the significant or characteristic features of a landscape, justified by its heritage value derived from its natural configuration and/or from human activity" (European Landscape Convention 2000).

This contrasts with the new, particularistic concept of landscape, which rejects both an ontologically framed concept of cultural landscape and the classical notion of self-contained, homogeneous spaces. A pioneer of a new landscape understanding is the US-American landscape researcher John Brinckerhoff Jackson. When establishing the field of cultural landscape studies, he incorporated the temporary, particular, and "ugly" into the concept of landscape. With his "vernacular landscapes," Brinckerhoff Jackson has opened up the landscape concept to the spatial particularity of modern and postmodern worlds (Brinckerhoff Jackson 1984).

Thus the current landscape discourses are no longer – at least not exclusively – dealing with questions of normative aesthetics, but also, for example, with places like industrial sites, traffic routes, and car parks (Hasse 2007). The objects of the new landscape discourses are not least those "intermediate cities" that have evolved in the context of gradually dissolving rural–urban polarities (Sieverts 1997). Various conceptualizations like "urban landscape" or "regional urban landscape" document the new landscape of urban and rural penetration (Boczek 2007; see Figure 19.3).

The particularistic understanding of landscape is evident not least in the concept of "micro-landscapes." We see the contemporary expression of landscape as an agglomeration of spaces, which we may call micro-landscapes; those micro-landscapes have only very little in common with a traditional concept of "landscape" and its "beauty" (Franzen and Krebs 2006:12). Rather, the concept of micro-landscapes relates particular "in-between terrains" to each other. In the background, there are the changes within postmodern society: altered practices and patterns of movement lead to new concepts of landscape. Human actors are no longer a contemplative audience – as they were in the landscape parks of the bourgeois era – but mobile, transitory players moving from place to place.

Even if the theoretical-conceptual reorientation is still in progress, we may summarize that this new, open understanding of landscape liberates the concept of landscape from an understanding of space as harmonious and idealized and deconstructs its centuries-old, aesthetically motivated "identity." Instead, newer theoretical concepts of landscape pick up on the patchwork-like particularization and dynamics of spaces.

A problem with the current discourse is the fraying of the landscape concept, which leads to difficulties not least in interdisciplinary debates. The literary scholar Ludwig Fischer criticized the seemingly limitless availability of the new, open landscape concept that wants to include all elements and ensembles of perceived environment. Moreover, a lack of differentiation from other categories of space and spatial awareness – such as, from the perspective of the new phenomenology, the concept of "environment" – can be noted with regret. Despite all the new approaches, it seems premature to entirely say goodbye to the classic old European concept of landscape. These traditions continue to have an effect because landscape shows itself – often in miniature – as an aesthetically founded endowment with meaning in the urbanized space, too (L. Fischer 2011).

Figure 19.3 Suburban area around Glinde, near Hamburg. (Reproduced with permission of Kreisarchiv Stormarn Sign. No. T 10-2328.)

Conceptualizations and Case Studies

This brings us to research topics and conceptualizations. The Swiss sociologist Angelus Eisinger calls for a greater use of the potentials of a dynamic landscape perspective. The focus of attention should lie – in addition to the manifestations of the new landscape – not least on the actors and networks, the interests and needs that produce and reproduce landscape. Eisinger demands that we engage with the fabric of socioeconomic and topographical, cultural, and mental aspects of the landscape; landscape can then be viewed as the framework in which society is characterized in the space (Eisinger 2007:71; see Figure 19.4).

The objects of research tend to be typical European landscapes, like the Alps (Boscani Leoni and Mathieu 2005) or the North Sea coast (L. Fischer 1997) in their "real" and "imagined" appearance. This also applies to classical landscape elements, such as the forest (Calhoon and Schultz 1996; Lehmann 1999). Other perspectives of cultural landscape research can be demonstrated by the example of the North Sea coast. In terms of cultural landscape, the following discussion deals with those sea dykes that seal off the inland areas from the sea with its tides and the danger of flooding. "North Sea coastal landscape" is here understood not as a description of idealized nature, but as an analysis of the sometimes very rapid change due to economic

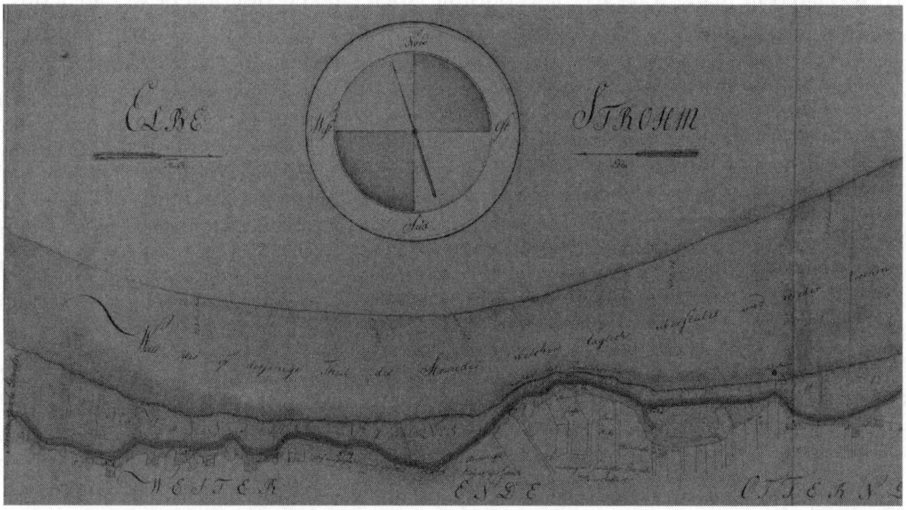

Figure 19.4 Between land and sea: historical dyke lines near the mouth of the River Elbe (around 1800). (Reproduced with permission of Niedersächsisches Staatsarchiv Stade KA neu 11369.)

and sociocultural settings. It is interaction – between nature on the one hand and economy, culture, and society on the other hand – that ultimately shapes the landscape at the North Sea coast. This can be seen by looking at the dyke as one of the most important elements of North Sea coastal landscape. What is a dyke and what is it used for? At first glance the answer seems to be simple: the dyke on the Northern Sea coast is a fixed earthen wall. It protects land from tides and storm surges. In an originally open, amphibious space, the dyke presents itself at first as a technical barrier against the water. On closer examination, however, the dyke forms – apart from its hydraulic function – a highly complex topographical boundary. Its symbolism represents spatial, cultural, and social patterns of order in the coastal societies at the North Sea. Historically, as today, water rarely came directly behind the dyke. An extensive strip of land lay beyond it: the salt marshes, which were regularly flooded by storm tides. In this way, the dyke once again showed itself to be a structuring element of the landscape: not only separating land and sea, but dividing different types of landscape. The dyke separates the cultivated inland from the inferior, marginalized land beyond the dyke; it separates "civilization" from "wilderness," the "wild" and "chaotic" outer dyke area, often influenced only by the forces of nature. At the same time the dyke represents aspects of spatial, cultural, and social patterns of order in coastal societies. Storm tides and currents have repeatedly forced people on the coast to set dyke lines back further inland, which therefore meant a spatial displacement of the boundary between land and sea. Since the end of twentieth century, ecological considerations have led to the parts of the once cultivated inner dyke area being turned anew into a "wilderness." Generally speaking, the dyke appears as a highly meaningful element of spatial segmentation of the coastal landscape – a segmentation that is related in many ways to the economic, societal, and political power structures. Both old and new dykes are visible to this day. Nowadays, dykes form an important part of the cultural landscape heritage at the North Sea coast (N. Fischer 2008b).

However, interest is increasingly turning toward those transformed spaces between town and country that appear not least as urbanized areas in metropolitan regions. These can no longer be fully captured by the classical concept of landscape. Thus, the classical idea of closed spatial entities with their identity-generating effect had to be dissolved in favor of a concept that is fulfilling the logic of the new spatial patchwork of small landscapes. The sociologist Rolf Peter Sieferle describes this new, patchwork landscape as "syncretism" with an "enormous plurality" of forms of expression and temporary artifacts (Sieferle 1998:165).

Therefore, what presents itself as "new landscapes" in an urbanized environment is the result of social processes in recent decades, notably the increasing particularization of everyday lifeworlds (work, living, shopping, culture, leisure, and recreation). The functional restructuring of the space in postmodernity has created the platform for those particularized worlds that are repeatedly recombined with each other in the everyday life of the mobile society. Through this, a kind of "sculpted landscape" evolved, which can be read as a map of new lifeworlds: living in urbanized areas of settlement, working, and shopping in trading estates, leisure and recreation in the countryside. Transport routes form the hinges between these partial worlds that are continuously rearranged in everyday life. This can be analyzed at the European level, for example, with regard to the way spatial planning has driven the development of metropolitan regions (N. Fischer 2009).

However, the classical landscape ideas are by no means forgotten in this context. On the contrary, they provide a reservoir for landscape architectural practice, when landscape and nature reserves are designated as river landscapes and wetlands and are restored to a "natural" state, and habitats are mapped. The very idea of landscape and nature conservation is grounded in the classical notion of closed and pristine landscapes, free from interference. In urbanized areas, these have a compensatory function and appear as island-like spaces – located in the postsuburban lifeworlds between transport axes and urbanized developments. This also applies to natural fallow and "wilderness."

Another important theme of current research is the relationship between "actual" and "imaginary" landscapes (Backhaus and Murungi 2009): how the classic understanding of landscape remains effective in a miniaturized form in the modeled imaginations of indoor environments (e.g. themed indoor waterparks). The longing for landscape is temporarily satisfied in these indoor imaginations; they represent discrete stations in the rapid succession of transitory micro-landscapes. These indoor imaginations, like the creation of landscaped gardens in the heart of cities during an earlier period, nevertheless show that the classical landscape ideal still retains relevance particularly in urban contexts. From a perspective of cultural research, and in the context of an open landscape concept, this opens up varied themes and approaches for investigation, especially the tracing of the links between indoor environments and urbanized lifestyles, but also an analysis of traditions of landscape symbolism.

Nature, thus, aestheticized as landscape in an entirely classical sense, was assigned a particular role in the context of processes of spatial differentiation. Landscape and nature reserves became polar opposites to economic-industrial compression and urban environs increasingly suffering environmental problems. In these compensatory spaces, a "modeled nature" developed as a result of urbanization – a nature that, even in its seemingly pristine form, the nature reserve – still reveals its planning functionality.

Finally, there is a concept that incorporates the collective knowledge associated with the idea of landscape from a cultural-scientific perspective: the concept of "landscape of memory." In the more recent studies, this draws on Pierre Nora's concept of *Lieux de mémoire* (Nora 1984), Simon Schama's path-breaking study *Landscape and Memory* (Schama 1995), and Aleida Assmann's work on memory and space (Assmann 1999). If one adds more recent approaches of landscape theory, these sites of memory can be regarded as elements of micro-landscapes, where landscape is understood as an open, hybrid space forever being reshaped through significant components.

That concept can be exemplified by the maritime memory landscape. In the coastal landscape of the European seas, regionally specific experiences of death are reflected in numerous artifacts from different historical periods: tombstones, individual monuments, but also larger memorials (see Figure 19.5). These are cultural symbols that, together, can be seen as a distinctly maritime "memory landscape." This maritime memory landscape is based on the historical experience of shipwrecks, storm surges, and inundations and the generally threatening unpredictability of water in an area that has been marked by extreme natural conditions. As the experiences of death and grief were passed on, reflected, and materialized in memorials, they gained historical importance and this ultimately made them perceptible as a memory landscape. How this memory was sedimented in the coastal landscape depended on the changing ways in which the experience of the threatening sea was being dealt with, which in turn was fed by different social needs. Under these conditions, the coastal landscape has been repeatedly reconfigured through the interaction of culture, mentality, and society. Taken together, the individual stages have produced a maritime memory landscape, the historical layers of which are anchored as a palimpsest in public space (N. Fischer 2007).

Conclusion

From a perspective of cultural research, landscape is not only found materially, but develops through a web of meaning in certain societies, cultures, and historical periods. In this process, physis and metaphysis are mutually contingent. Landscape can therefore only be understood relationally, not as predetermined factum, if one wants to grasp its specific internal logic in its historical evolution and in its potential for cultural research. Denis Cosgrove described landscape as a fertile category for research because it is both culturally and naturally conditioned (Cosgrove 2004:68).

Overall, it is clear that the history of humanity is inscribed with regard to landscape, its perception, and its transformation. Landscape can thus be described as "sedimented history" (Wormbs 1978:8). In the multi-causal interactions between landscape development, landscape perception, and landscape design we can trace the actions of the actors. Therefore, landscape is a promising key to the analysis of culture

Figure 19.5 Maritime memory landscape: *Madonna der Meere* at Hamburg harbor. Photograph © Norbert Fischer. (Reproduced courtesy of the author.)

and society. What is needed is a dynamic understanding of the category "landscape," and a sharpening of its definition and analysis. In particular, the term must be differentiated from related concepts, such as space, region, and environment.

Then, in the context of an interdisciplinary perspective and in view of the interactions between "natural" and "artificial" environment, between new representation, imagination, and social actors, this category offers diverse new fields of research.

REFERENCES

Assmann, Aleida

1999 Erinnerungsräume: Formen und Wandlungen des kulturellen Gedächtnisses. Munich: C. H. Beck.

Backhaus, Gary, and John Murungi, eds.

2009 Symbolic Landscapes. Berlin: Springer.

Blackbourn, David
2006 The Conquest of Nature: Water, Landscape and the Making of Modern Germany. London: Pimlico.
Boczek, Barbara
2007 Transformation urbaner Landschaft: Ansätze zur Gestaltung in der Rhein-Main-Region. Wuppertal: Müller and Busmann.
Boscani Leoni, Simona, and Jon Mathieu, eds.
2005 Die Alpen! Zur europäischen Wahrnehmungsgeschichte seit der Renaissance. Bern: Lang.
Brinckerhoff Jackson, John
1984 Discovering the Vernacular Landscape. New Haven: Yale University Press.
Büttner, Nils
2006 Geschichte der Landschaftsmalerei. Munich: Hirmer.
Calhoon, Kenneth S., and Karla L. Schultz, eds.
1996 The Idea of the Forest: German and American Perspectives on the Culture and Politics of Trees. New York: Peter Lang.
Cosgrove, Denis
2004 Landscape and Landschaft. Bulletin of the German Historical Institute 35:57–71.
Dannebeck, Sandra, Ansgar Hoppe, Hansjörg Küster, and Davy McCracken
2009 Einflussfaktoren auf Kulturlandschaften: ein Überblick. *In* Europäische Kulturlandschaften. Knut Krzywinski, Michael O'Connell, and Hansjörg Küster, eds. pp. 57–64. Bremen: Aschenbeck Media.
Dinnebier, Antonia
2004 Der Blick auf die schöne Landschaft – Naturaneignung und Schöpfungsakt? *In* Projektionsfläche Natur: Zum Zusammenhang von Naturbildern und gesellschaftlichen Verhältnissen. Ludwig Fischer, ed. pp. 61–76. Hamburg: Hamburg University Press.
Eisinger, Angelus
2007 Für den Landschaftsgebrauch. *In* Landscapes Abused – Missbrauchte Landschaften. Pamphlet 8. Ed. ILA and ETH Zürich. pp. 69–71. Zürich: gta-Verlag.
European Landscape Convention
2000 Electronic document. http://conventions.coe.int/Treaty/en/Treaties/Html/176.htm (accessed November 5, 2011).
Fischer, Ludwig, ed.
1997 Kulturlandschaft Nordseemarschen. Bredstedt: Nordfriisk Institut.
2004 Projektionsfläche Natur: Zum Zusammenhang von Naturbildern und gesellschaftlichen Verhältnissen. Hamburg: Hamburg University Press.
Fischer, Ludwig
2011 Landschaft – überall und nirgends? *In* Landschaft quer denken: Theorien – Bilder – Formationen. Stefanie Krebs and Manfred Seifert, eds. Leipzig: Leipziger Universitätsverlag.
Fischer, Norbert
2007 Gedächtnislandschaft Nordseeküste. *In* Inszenierungen der Küste. Norbert Fischer, Susan Müller-Wusterwitz, and Brigitta Schmidt-Lauber, eds. pp. 150–183. Berlin: Reimer.
2008a Landschaft als kulturwissenschaftliche Kategorie. Zeitschrift für Volkskunde 104:19–39.
2008b The Dike as an Important Element of North Sea Coastal Landscape. *In* Cultural Heritage and Landscapes in Europe. Landschaften: Kulturelles Erbe in Europa. Proceedings of the International Conference, Bochum June 8–10, 2007. Christoph Bartels and Claudia Küpper-Eichas, eds. pp. 393–400. Bochum: Deutsches Bergbau-Museum.

2009 Vom Hamburger Umland zur Metropolregion: Landschaftswandel zwischen Stadt und Land. Tà katoptrizómena: Das Magazin für Kunst, Kultur, Theologie, Ästhetik 62. Electronic document. http://www.theomag.de/62/kw64.htm (accessed November 5, 2011).

Fischer, Norbert, Susan Müller-Wusterwitz, and Brigitta Schmidt-Lauber, eds.
2007 Inszenierungen der Küste. Berlin: Reimer.

Franzen, Brigitte, and Stefanie Krebs, eds.
2006 Mikrolandschaften. Landscape Culture on the Move. Münster: Westfälisches Landesmuseum für Kunst und Kulturgeschichte.

Grimm, Jacob, and Wilhelm Grimm, eds.
2004 Deutsches Wörterbuch. Electronic edition. CD-ROM. Frankfurt am Main: Zweitausendeins.

Hasse, Jürgen
2007 Übersehene Räume: zur Kulturgeschichte und Heterotopologie des Parkhauses. Bielefeld: Transcript.

Institute for the History and Theory of Architecture (ILA)
2007 Landscapes Abused – Missbrauchte Landschaften. Pamphlet 8. Ed. ILA and ETH Zürich. Zürich: gta-Verlag.

Krzywinski, Knut
2009 Ihre einzige Gemeinsamkeit ist ihre Vielfalt: Die Bedeutung europäischer Kulturlandschaften. *In* Europäische Kulturlandschaften. Michael O'Connell and Hansjörg Küster, eds. pp. 9–21. Bremen: Aschebeck Media.

Küster, Hansjörg
1995 Geschichte der Landschaft in Mitteleuropa: Von der Eiszeit bis zur Gegenwart. Munich: C. H. Beck.
2005 Die Auffassung der Landschaft in den Naturwissenschaften. *In* La Cultura del Paesaggio: Le sue origini, la situazione attuale e le prospettive future. Rita Colantonio Venturelli and Kai Tobias, eds. pp. 53–65. Florence: Olschki.

Lehmann, Albrecht
1999 Von Menschen und Bäumen: Die Deutschen und ihr Wald. Reinbek: Rowohlt.

McDowell, Linda
1994 The Transformation of Cultural Geography. *In* Human Geography: Society, Space and Social Science. D. Gregory, D. Martin, and G. Smith, eds. pp. 146–173. London: Palgrave Macmillan.

Meyers Großes Konversations-Lexikon
1905 6th edition, vol. 12. Leipzig and Vienna: Bibliographisches Institut.

Mitchell, William J. T., ed.
2002 Landscape and Power. Chicago: University of Chicago Press.

Nora, Pierre, ed.
1984 Les lieux de mémoire. Paris: Gallimard.

Ritter, Joachim
1963 Landschaft: Zur Funktion des Ästhetischen in der modernen Gesellschaft. Münster: Aschendorff.

Schama, Simon
1995 Landscape and Memory. New York: Knopf.

Schramm, Manuel
2008 Die Entstehung der modernen Landschaftswahrnehmung (1580–1730). Historische Zeitschrift 287(1):37–59.

Sieferle, Rolf Peter
1998 Die totale Landschaft. *In* Neue Landschaften. Kursbuch 131. pp 155–169. Berlin: Rowohlt.

Sieverts, Thomas
1997 Zwischenstadt – zwischen Ort und Welt, Raum und Zeit, Stadt und Land. Braunschweig and Wiesbaden: Vieweg.
Waldheim, Charles, ed.
2006 The Landscape Urbanism Reader. New York: Princeton Architectural Press.
Warnke, Martin
1992 Politische Landschaft: zur Kunstgeschichte der Natur. Munich: Hanser.
Wendt, Karin
2009 Worin wir leben – Landschaften. Tà katoptrizómena: Das Magazin für Kunst, Kultur, Theologie, Ästhetik 62. Electronic document. http://www.theomag.de/62/kw64.htm (accessed November 5, 2011).
Wormbs, Brigitte
1978 Über den Umgang mit Natur: Landschaft zwischen Illusion und Ideal. 2nd revised edition. Frankfurt am Main: Roter Stern.
Zeller, Thomas
2007 Driving Germany: The Landscape of the German Autobahn, 1930–1970. New York: Berghahn.

PART IV Cultural Practice

CHAPTER 20

European Tourism

Orvar Löfgren

Armchair Travelers and Tourist Pioneers

The book from 1936 has an airplane circling the European continent on the cover. It is one of many collectors' albums, where children were supposed to paste new images arriving with every box of cereal or coffee mother brought home. The theme is European traveling, an activity that was still wishful thinking for most Europeans. Books like this became a daydreaming tool for imagining exotic and distant corners of the continent.

The presentation of Europe in 1936 hovers between picturesque nostalgia and high-tech modern, with peasants in folk costumes as well as modern industrial plants. Every country is represented by colorful sceneries that reflect ideas about what constitutes a beautiful view or an interesting sight. But there is also a division of labor that mirrors a long tradition in the production of European touristscapes.

Amsterdam is "the Venice of the North," the Café de la Paix in Paris is "the corner of Europe," and there is "merry old England." Some countries are depicted mainly as tourist destinations: Italy is all ruins and monuments; Spain is bullfights and the graceful dancers of Andalusia. Others like the Soviet Union are represented by oil wells and steel mills.

In the introduction to the album children are reminded to keep collecting all the color photos, because sooner or later the European countries – and even their borders – may look very different, and at that time it is great to have an album like this to be reminded of "the good old days of 1936," as the editor puts it.

What did Europe look like in those good old days? A journalist skiing between villages in northernmost Sweden reported in 1936 on the mental map of the locals:

> What's beyond the known local territories, doesn't seem like a real world, it is just one grey mist. One has heard of names, Boden, Stockholm, America. They are all located in the outskirts of the world or rather outside the world. Palestine has its own reality,

---

A Companion to the Anthropology of Europe, First Edition. Edited by Ullrich Kockel, Máiréad Nic Craith, and Jonas Frykman.

> probably close to Stockholm and America, if it isn't mixed up with the heavenly land of Kanaan. (Borelius 1936:156)

In some ways the landscapes of Bible still seemed more real and closer than many other distant places in the mindscapes of the locals, he points out. Leisure travel was still a luxury for the few, but 1936 was also the year of the first big Swedish leisure exhibition held in the town of Ystad. Here, modern ideas about mass tourism and "the democratization of leisure" were aired, as in many other European settings, but within very different ideological frameworks. The sun-loving and outdoor-oriented tourist was seen as an icon of a new modernity, and legislation about statutory paid holidays was under way in many European settings, backed by labor unions and left-wing parties. In the media there were worried debates all over Europe: Could ordinary people really handle the freedom of holiday life? In the summer of 1936 the new left government of the *Front Populaire* in France passed a legislation for two weeks paid holiday and in August 600000 French workers traveled on their first vacation by train thanks to a 40% reduction in fares on the national railways (Furlough 1998).

Across the Baltic from the Ystad exhibition another gigantic mass tourism project was taking shape on the peninsula of Rügen: Prora, the biggest resort in the world, planned to accommodate 20000 guests at a time in simple but modern hotel rooms, all with a guaranteed sea view. Add to this cinemas, cafés, and long beaches with a marina. The foundation stone was laid in 1936 by Adolf Hitler: the resort was part of the Nazi Party's scheme for developing and monitoring German mass tourism. KdF-Seebad Rügen, to give Prora its formal name, was part of the *Kraft durch Freude* [Strength Through Joy] movement started in 1933, aiming at creating a classless and dependable *Volksgemeinschaft* [people's community] of tourists, *Wandervögeln* [hikers], hobbyists, and holidaymakers (Zadnicek 1995). *Kraft durch Freude* (KdF) organized around 7 million package tours, from the Mediterranean to the Norwegian fjords, with Gestapo agents mingling with the pleasure-seekers to observe and report on "antisocial behavior." Hitler had his inspiration partly from Italy, where fascist programs for modern leisure to create a healthy workforce developed early (see, for example, de Grazia 1992).

In 1936 another kind of resort empire was started, as Billy Butlin opened his first British holiday camp in Skegness (where it is still open) and thus developed a prototype for "the all-inclusive summer resort" that would become an immensely successful form of mass tourism (see Ward and Hardy 1986) and later on take new forms like the French chain Club Med.

A few years later the outbreak of World War II put an end to transnational tourism, as well as many dreams of vacationing. When the war was over, boundaries had indeed been radically redrawn. The Iron Curtain reorganized travel and tourism. No longer did Germans flock to the fashionable beach resorts on the Baltic, and Hitler's grandiose but half-finished resort project was taken over by the Red Army in the new DDR. The Iron Curtain blocked access to a number of classic tourist destinations for Westerners, while a new state-organized tourist economy was slowly developed within the Soviet empire in the 1960s and 1970s. Workers from some socialist states visited the beaches of Romania and Bulgaria as well as Tito's Yugoslavia. After the fall of the wall in 1989 the tourist map of Europe was again radically redrawn. Prague emerged as a new favorite European tourist city, while, after the Yugoslavian wars, Western tourists flocked to the Croatian coast – later on marketed with the slogan "the Mediterranean as it used to be." Western Europeans acquired holiday bungalows in places like Bulgaria, and Germans returned to the old German territories in Poland to buy summer houses (Mai 2007).

In 1936 tourists were not a topic in European ethnology or anthropology, rather a disturbing element in fieldwork, threatening the authenticity of traditional cultures. It was not until the 1960s that tourism research was developed as a highly interdisciplinary field explored by sociologists, cultural geographers, social historians, and many more disciplines. The integration of this field has been hampered by traditional and stubborn European language barriers. The strong Anglo-Saxon tradition has had little contact with, for example, the rich vein of research published in German and French, and so in the following survey I have included some examples of such studies.

But what about the anthropological and ethnological contributions? They are often characterized by an ethnographic interest in the tourist experience rather than in the structure and organization of the tourist industry. After World War II, anthropologists, mainly from the United States, and later the United Kingdom, had started doing community studies in remote rural settings in southern Europe. When tourists became an increasing presence in some of these communities a research tradition looking at the interaction between locals and tourists started to develop (see, e.g., Smith 1989; Boissevain 1996). In this tradition the focus was on identity and "othering." In European ethnology, tourism entered the field of research along two main lines. First, ethnologists became interested in the ways in which folk culture and the national heritage was framed, packaged, and marketed in contemporary tourism and national self-understanding: this was research into tourist iconographies, texts, and symbols. A classic example is studies of how Tyrol and other regions were developed as touristscapes (Pöttler 1992). Second, there emerged an interest in studying tourism as a historical process, looking at the making of institutions from the travel guide and souvenir-collecting to the sightseeing trip or the wilderness hike.

In this latter perspective the focus has been on the constant making and remaking of tourist experiences – learning to be a tourist. The historical perspective has been used as a way of problematizing the present. When scholars have looked at the 1930s it is precisely because the interwar years provide such a rich ground for analyzing new and conflicting trends in European tourism development. Here it is possible to see how a new mobility and leisure time evolves in different political contexts. Some of these trends are still here, others have disappeared. Back in 1936 tourism could be the new cult of suntan (Fussell 1980) or wilderness camping, a new hedonism mixing ideas of the fit body and the open mind. Tourism was also seen as a tool for nation-building with slogans like "Know your country" or "Walk yourself English." Nostalgia for a national past was mixed with ideas of a modern future (Baranowski and Furlough 2001). Another tension was to do with the emancipatory potentials of the new leisure activities (Frykman 1993) as opposed to the attempts to use them as a disciplining project.

In the following I will use this formative perspective, looking at how travel is institutionalized, sights are judged, routines at the beach or in the summer cottage are made and unmade. Of special interest here are of course the ways in which tourism has Europeanized Europe, but also how the making of new ways of seeing and experiencing the world has been exported as European models of tourism to other parts of the world.

Going Abroad

"What is a tourist?" asked the Swedish writer Carl Jonas Love Almqvist in 1846, writing of a trip to Paris. "Tourist" was still a newfangled French term spreading through Europe, but touring Europe for leisure started out as an aristocratic tradition that became institutionalized already during the seventeenth and eighteenth centuries as a suitable experience for young noblemen. "The Grand Tour" became a standardized route for education, made possible by certain kinds of travel infrastructures, like networks of fellow-noblemen who would supply beds, food, and sophisticated conversation in the elite *lingua franca* of Latin or French. The classical Grand Tour was a limited itinerary, focusing on the antiquities of Italy, and did not include Greece or Spain; the former was politically volatile, still under Ottoman rule and, like Spain, lacked an accessible transport infrastructure. Only adventurers ventured into these dark corners of Europe.

It was through the institutionalization of the Grand Tour that many of the modern practices of tourism were tried out: the proper ways of approaching a cultural heritage, admiring a ruin, or daydreaming about the past, as well as the development of fixed tourist routes and a hospitality industry (see, for example, Black 1992; Buzard 1993).

Take Florence, for example, maybe the best example of a tourist hotspot that has survived for centuries. In 1697 a young Swedish nobleman writes in his diary about his arrival in Florence, impressed by the buildings as well as the beautiful women. Three centuries later the railway station of that same city was occupied by crowds of "inter-railers," doing a modernized version of the Grand Tour. In the early 2000s most of the European inter-railers were gone. The new generations of backpackers gathered in more distant and exotic locations, but American college students still explored Florence in their American version of "the Grand European Tour," creating their own mental maps and experiencescapes of Europe (Gmelch 2010).

The traditions of the Grand Tour are still alive in European tourism, not only as well-trodden paths through a landscape of sights and monuments, but also as a frame of mind and an education of the senses. A flood of handbooks as tools of instruction were published in the eighteenth and, above all, the nineteenth centuries.

In a sense the Swedish travel guide *How to Travel in Europe*, published more than 60 years ago (Stromberg 1951), still carries on that tradition. It is one of many in the flood of new travel literature that emerged after World War II. At last Europe was open for leisure travel again! But for whom? The author of the handbook tells the reader how to prepare for a journey out into Europe, and although one is recommended to travel light the packing list is extensive: from a miniature iron and a silk robe for walking to the bathroom in the hotel corridor to an extensive medicine chest. Reading the long list of medicines and remedies (always bring extra toilet paper, it is a scarce commodity abroad), the reader might have second thoughts about daring to leave home. This anxiety is not lessened by the detailed chapter on customs problems and border passages, where the author starts by stating "thoughts about the customs make travelers terrified" and then produces an impressive list of customs duties and currency regulations in Europe. "How many gramophone records or how much coffee is one allowed to bring across the border? Don't forget that art works are taxed according to the weight of the frame." To be a tourist in Europe is to be exposed to complicated regulations, a lot of paperwork and the whims of local officials. We are light-years away from the informal world of the Lonely Planet travel guides.

At the same time it is obvious that a guide like this addresses a tiny traveling elite. It was not until new forms of travel emerged that the social base of European tourism was broadened. It was the development of the package tour that made it possible for people without language skills, travel know-how, or plenty of money to risk a trip abroad. Busloads of Germans descended on the Italian coasts, while Scandinavians took the bus to look at the tulips in Holland or the sin in Montmartre. But it was two other means of transport that drastically changed traveling for leisure: the family car and the charter flight.

In the 1950s and 1960s motor tourism expanded. The car fostered new modes of perception and sensuality in travel, but also remodeled family life. The family could be squeezed into its own private, moving space, filled with all the props offered by the new leisure industry – everything from portable radios and camping equipment to leisurewear and leisure food. Campsites emerged everywhere in new, and what were often seen as far too uncontrolled, forms. The reaction of the traditional tourist business to the postwar expansion and the increasingly mobile tourism was mixed. Some felt that it threatened the traditional, established tourist pattern, with fixed weeks in boarding houses, rituals of shared meals, and well-worn paths for daily walks.

Now more and more adventurous drivers ventured across borders – Germans driving into Italy, Brits into France, Scandinavians into Germany. The institution of the summer motor holiday was documented in photo albums and collections of souvenirs, with memories of the exciting ritual start of leaving home with a loaded car, breakdowns in the middle of nowhere, and interesting contacts with fellow campers (see, for example, Pagenstecher 2009). Europeans learned about Europe in new ways. An infrastructure of gas stations, roadside cafeterias, motorist handbooks, road maps, and camping grounds emerged.

Sun, Sand, Sea, and Sin

The new mass tourism was, however, more dependent upon the arrival of cheap charter flights, mainly going from the North toward the Mediterranean. The longing for the South was a strong northern European tradition, especially among the British, who, as early as the nineteenth century, talked of a state of mind called "Mediterranean madness": a craving for sunlight, easy living, and a chance to explore new sides of yourself (Pemble 1987). For later tourist generations the longing for the South was often described in terms of the four "S's"– sun, sand, sea, and sin, and the place where these elements came together was the beach.

The making of the modern beach as a European playground has a special history, turning parts of Europe that earlier were seen as barren, ugly, or unproductive into favorite destinations. There is a strong body of French research analyzing this development, starting out with the tourist discovery of the coast (Corbin 1994). Later on scholars like Kaufmann (1995) and Urbain (2003) explored the modern beach as a cultural laboratory where people try out new aspects of themselves, but also learn to follow the many unwritten rules of how to behave, handling their bodies, their curiosity, and their relations with fellow sun-lovers in this tightly packed arena.

An expanding air-travel industry, and the innovations of jet flights and computer-based booking systems, helped to organize this craving, but also the fact that World War II had left an infrastructure of military airfields even on remote coasts and islands. It was the module of the week that made the package easy to administer and also created the rhythm of Mediterranean holidays of one or two weeks (see Löfgren 1999; Pons et al. 2009).

In the early 1960s Britons, Germans, Dutch, and Scandinavians made Spain the main charter destination, with Majorca and the huge resort development of the Costa del Sol on the mainland at the top of the popularity charts. The number of tourists skyrocketed, from 6 million in 1960 to 30 million in 1975. Seafront property was still relatively cheap and the cost of living low. The Franco dictatorship encouraged the development of large resort areas, which would make it easier to monitor and control tourist influences on or contacts with local people. Majorca became the prototype of the new package tour. Words like *playa*, *bodega*, *paella*, and *mañana* entered the *lingua franca* of tourism.

As the numbers of Mediterranean holidaymakers expanded greatly during the 1970s and 1980s, new territories had to be discovered and colonized, such as the Canary Islands, far out in the Atlantic. Here you could find a new important resource: a warm winter sun. Mediterranean tourism also moved east: Greece became a popular destination. As the Greek islands became more crowded and expensive, Turkey emerged as an alternative, and countries like Tunisia, Morocco, Egypt, and Israel started to market themselves as alternative destinations for winter sun.

Slowly the Mediterranean tourist map expanded into the old Eastern bloc. In the 1960s Yugoslavia, Romania, and Bulgaria started to emulate the successful West European tourist industry, a development sometimes hampered by the classic five-year-plan tradition. In Bulgaria, for example, the tourist ministry developed the main Black Sea resorts Golden Sands and Sunny Beach, which started to attract West Europeans in the 1960s, mainly because of the low prices. A large proportion of the visitors came from East European countries; for them the Black Sea represented the only chance of a southern holiday. They had to make do with the poorer accommodation, while the Westerners with their sought-after foreign currency got the best alternatives, but complained of the Eastern service culture: extensive menus but only two main dishes available, and slow and rude service, as the underpaid and resentful staff felt they had no reason to work their heart out to please these wealthy Westerners (Pearlman 1989).

We can thus follow how the tourist map of the Mediterranean has constantly changed over the last 30 years for economic, political, and cultural reasons. Behind the redrawing of the destination map also lies constant wear and tear. As small coastal communities are turned into popular destinations, overcrowding and pollution may emerge as a side-effect. They may be hit by what has been called "the Torremolinos effect," turning into tourist slums, where the only attraction is low prices, or "Happy Hour Holidays" as some locals call it.

The new mass tourism also revitalized an old critique of *Turistus vulgaris.* The old middle-class travelers often defined the new world of the package tour as shallow and vulgar. The new tourists chose security before adventure and could not tell the inauthentic from the authentic.

This critique missed the point that the new package tour travelers had other priorities than the classic sightseers. A week in the Mediterranean had first of all to be available at affordable prices, and this meant mass travel. Second it had to deliver certain basic elements: sun, sea, sand, and preferably also some local color. It had to supply freedom from regulated work and supervision, and freedom to do what you want: for example, nothing. The sense of liberation was very marked for the pioneers in this new mass exodus to the South. The hedonistic principle was central: "We are going to have fun!" The freedom was felt already in the airport lounge. You had checked in your baggage and left your worries behind you, and the first tax-free drink on the plane often became the magic *rite de passage.*

The whole construction of the New South was also based upon the needs of not-so-travel-savvy tourists who wanted to go abroad. It was precisely the certainty and the predictability that made the package tour a mass phenomenon. It opened up international travel for the vast majority of working-class families for whom a trip abroad had previously been a utopia.

City Breaks

The package tour can also be seen as a process of learning. Slowly, new groups and generations of Europeans developed travel skills and learned to handle life abroad; little by little they felt able to try more adventurous and individual forms of travel.

Charter flights created special paths of mobility, linking northern European cities to a constantly widening range of destinations in an ever-expanding Mediterranean area. With the advent of budget flights, especially during the 1990s, the European travel map changed again. No longer was there a dominant pattern of North going South, but a much more criss-crossing network of budget travel.

One good example of this is the development of the City Break industry in the 1990s. Just as with the development of the package tour, there were infrastructural conditions. Hotel chains built for business travels had problems filling their rooms during weekends, the deregulation of air travel created budget airlines that searched for inexpensive airports and slashed prices, and people learned to use the Web for planning travel to a wealth of new destinations. "The safety freak goes on an adventure charter to Samoa, while the real adventurer goes to Dresden" as a journalist put it back in 2004.

What should a perfect city break include so that a city can be consumed in 48 hours? Perhaps a program that includes a romantic candlelit dinner, an evening at the opera or a night club, a Saturday morning of shopping in a historic center with good pedestrian precincts, and a Sunday visit to an art museum? This is a cityscape originally geared toward the important market segment of middle-class and middle-aged couples. All over Europe, city planners were imagining how to present a cultural infrastructure that fits in with tourists like this. The Bilbao effect meant that new museums of modern art were being built or expanded in city centers all over the world. Local gastronomy became important, as well as innovative designer hotels. An event-grid was placed over the cities, selecting certain sights, situations, and experiences, avoiding others. There are a number of studies of the tourist consumption of cities as eventscapes that illustrate how a European matrix of perfect "citiness" has influenced not only travelers, but city planners, brand-makers, and local politicians, who learned to see their city through the tourist mode of consumption (see Willim 2005; Marling and Zerlang 2007). Concepts like "event" or "adventure," like many other buzzwords in what was called the new "Experience Economy," often have a short lifespan. They are exposed to a lot of cultural wear and tear, but above all they illustrate that experiences cannot be preprogrammed, but shaped by the ways in which the tourist creates her or his setting (see, for example, the discussions in Löfgren 2005 and O'Dell 2007).

The budget flight from Glasgow to Rome carries middle-aged couples still recreating the sightseeing of the Grand Tour, but also young women heading for the Prada outlet outside the city and a few days of power shopping, or male buddies off to see a Serie A soccer match. Travelers create their different eventscapes and experiences in unpredictable ways. In an ethnography of a week of shopping in London, Erik Ottosson (2008) follows a young woman and describes how she creates her own mental map and everyday routines, turning London into her own shopping town – selecting sights, streets, and activities, walking next to tourists who in their turn are busy producing their own personal versions of the city.

In these changing patterns, new European links are created and the tourist flow is no longer dominated by journeys from North to South. Italians flock to Scandinavia, Poles to London, Germans to Hungary . . .

Double Homes

Affordable travel has also helped to create a growing and increasingly diversified leisure landscape of double homes, linking Europe in new ways (Bendix and Löfgren 2007). In tourism research the term "second home" can refer to a summer cottage in the woods, a restored farmhouse in Tuscany or an *apartemento* on the Costa del Sol.

European elites developed a pattern of multiple homes far back in history. In order to escape the heat, the urban congestion, or health hazards, they built summer retreats for thousands of years, from Roman rural villas to renaissance summer palaces. In the late nineteenth century a tradition of establishing summer cottages on a somewhat broader social scale emerged, although the label of "summer cottage" may turn out to have a much wider range of forms, from fancy villas to a shed in an allotment garden – the latter an urban institution developed in Germany toward the end of the nineteenth century, and then spreading over Europe. A distribution map would show the highest proportion of summer cottages in northern Europe and above all in Scandinavia. There is also a strong cottage tradition in eastern Europe, as for example in the Russian *dacha* – a term which denotes anything from a small shack with a kitchen garden to exclusive mansions built for the former *nomenclatura*.

The upper middle class of professionals, academics, and managers came to dominate the new cottage cultures of the early twentieth century. These new settlements were shaped in the "back-to-nature" tradition, with an emphasis on privacy and a family-centered holiday life, away from the holiday crowds. They could often nostalgically celebrate a peasant-culture heritage, seen for example in the aesthetics of the buildings and in the styles of interior decoration.

Yet another seasonal second home lineage is linked to mountainous areas and sports. The "discovery of the Alps" in the late eighteenth century encouraged the development of guest housing and, eventually, grand hotels for the elites in mountainous regions. Later on, families enjoying summer hikes and winter skiing point to the draw of these quite different landscapes as well as to the rising importance of winter sports in engendering the wish for a second home.

A new development took form in the 1960s. It has a quite different geography as this type results from the search for winter sun. New settlements "in the sun" followed in the wake of mass tourist travel to new, year-round tourist destinations. Sun, warmth, easy living, and cheap property constitute the requisite bundle of attractions, especially for senior citizens. New settlements developed along the Spanish coasts and in regions like Provence and Tuscany (see, e.g., Seidl 2009).

A special version of the double home is being created by the mobility of labor migrants and refugees. People maintain ties with the old country in different ways. Building a house back home is perhaps the most prominent project for economically motivated migrants. Returning to the village or town they have left holds an emotional as much as a material appeal; the dwelling is first intended as a base for holiday visits but holds the promise of moving back completely when sufficient funds have been earned or one is ready to retire. Such dream houses stand waiting for their owners all over emigration areas, from Turkish villages to Croatian towns. Some are fully realized, others are only marked out as a piece of property or stagnate in an unfinished state, with concrete pillars and gaping holes instead of windows, standing as material metaphors for a dream put on ice or gone awry.

Having two homes makes for new transnational skills. You learn to find your way in supermarkets, handle plumbers, carpenters, and local bureaucrats in both settings. A constant ordeal is the transportation of stuff back and forth between your two homes. There is also a practical and emotional division of labor that comes with living in two places, a theme that has been explored by the anthropologist Jean-Didier Urbain in his study of French second homes (2002). How do double homes learn to cohabit? There might, for example, be an attempt to create two kinds of domestic aesthetics, the two homes come to "feel different" or are seen as scenes in which different aspects of personality or aspiration can be played out. In a study of Turks in Berlin, Ayse Caglar (2002) noted how the best furniture was saved for the house back in Turkey, it became a dream space in many ways, while one was prepared to live in more makeshift arrangements in the small flat in Kreuzberg. A fancy glass table was meant for Turkey, in Berlin a simple wooden one had to do for the living room.

The various categories of double homes represent transnational mobilities with a different social and economic base. They also contain different dreams and aspirations. It is striking, though, that much of the research on second homes has not compared the various forms of developing such lifestyles. The sun-loving senior citizens who flock from northern Europe to the South are seldom discussed in terms of exile, diaspora, ghettoization, or multiculturalism as other migrants are. The research on various forms of double homes has, however, brought research on tourism and mobility together in new ways, comparing the kinds of transnational or translocal skills developing (see, e.g., Rolshoven 2007; Povrzanović 2008).

Locals, Tourists, and Anti-tourists

Double homes create new European links, logistics, and commitments, but not always strong integration. In EU rhetoric, tourism plays the role as an integrating tool, uniting Europeans in new ways, but reality is a bit more complex. Travel may both open and close the mind.

Often tourism has not been structured to enhance contacts between locals and visitors. It is not always fun to live in a tourist hotspot, where property prices are booming, local streets are congested, and swarms of loud-mouthed and fun-loving visitors invade everyday life. There is also the tendency toward ghettoization. People manage to live for years on the Costa del Sol or Cyprus without developing many local contacts; they are quite content with their tight-knit network of compatriots (Benson and O'Reilly 2009).

A number of studies have explored the kind of "othering" that goes on in communities invaded by tourists (see, e.g., Waldren 1996; Pons 2009). The first tourists are an adventure, a promise of economic betterment. As the influx grows people find out that land that was seen as having next-to-no value can be sold at a good profit. Investors and developers from the outside move in, and all of a sudden development is no longer controlled locally. Multinational chains build hotels, souvenir stores are run by outsiders, guides are flown in by the tour companies. The new wealth is often very unevenly distributed and most locals end up in low-paid service jobs.

The old community disappears, or rather has to retreat, as the tourists take over. The strategy of creating a tourist front and then making sure that there are backstage territories and arenas for local life has been common to many tourist regions.

Tourists are an economic resource but also a source of constant tension, and that is also the case with double homes. The second-home owners look out on a landscape inhabited by local owners. To what extent is one seen as just a visitor or a guest; will one ever become a local? A complex hierarchy may develop, as in holiday settings, where the "old summer visitors" may view themselves as true locals and regard newcomers or renters as an alien influence. In such cases, the old summer guests may come to see themselves as the true guardians of local traditions, taking up central positions in the local heritage movement, or getting involved with the local museum or the politics of preservation and environmental policies.

It is not just locals and visitors that position themselves and judge "the Other." Throughout the modern history of tourism one of the sights most enjoyed is that of other tourists. There is a classic debate separating real travelers from "all those tourists," often described with derogatory metaphors like "herds" or "swarms." It is a polarity that often sneaked into tourist research itself, where tourists often were described as mindless consumers of sights and attractions, easy prey of marketing strategies. Urbain has captured this genre in his classic study *L'Idiot du voyage* (1991).

In order not to fall into the trap of moralizing about profound or shallow experiences, staged or authentic settings, scholars in the 1990s started to study the internal tensions within the tourist collective, looking at the ways tourists label and judge other tourists, often using class-based or ethnic stereotypes, for example in the favorite European stereotype of "the typical American tourist." The phrase "anti-tourist" was coined to capture the ways in which some travelers are eager to disassociate themselves from ordinary tourists. The anti-tourist is constantly searching for the unspoilt and authentic, and has nothing but scorn for *Turistus vulgaris.* During the 1990s the concept of the "post-tourist" was developed to illustrate how some tourists develop an ironic attitude or stand toward the staging of sights and attractions, enjoying the fake and celebrating the kitschy (see the discussion in Löfgren 1999:260ff.).

In the 1990s there also emerged a critique of research perspectives that saw tourists as passive consumers (see, e.g., Franklin and Crang 2001). This led to a stronger emphasis on agency: tourists as producers of their own experiences, which also brought a new emphasis to the role of the senses. First into focus were discussions of the making of the tourist gaze, learning to look and overlook. This often favored a strong semiotic approach. What kinds of signals and messages were sent out and how were they received and interpreted? In later years, studies of the tourist gaze have been broadened to how tourists mediate experiences, sights, and local atmosphere with the help of all kinds of technologies: How do you perform the happy family or the loving couple on vacation in photo albums, videos, diaries, postcards, or Web pages (see Ek et al. 2008)? This analytical shift can be illustrated by comparing John Urry's classic 1990 study *The Tourist Gaze* with the new edition (Larsen and Urry 2010).

The early focus on the tourist gaze soon led to other reactions. Scholars started to ask questions about the rest of the body (see, e.g., the critique in Veijola and Jokinen 1994). The perspective was broadened and other senses brought into play, often with a phenomenological approach. A good example of this shift is a study of "how theme parks happen," where Kirsti Hjemdahl Mathiessen (2003) reacts against the tradition of reading tourist attractions as "cultural texts" and instead explores how they are made by the tourist moving through them – all senses involved. In later years it is perhaps this kind of perspective of tourists as producers that represents the most important contribution of ethnological and anthropological research to the interdisciplinary field of tourism. I am thinking of the ways in which travelers come to take in a landscape, turning a heritage site into a picnic-spot, sharing a fiesta with a friend back home through photos and messages over the cellphone, making an event into a narrative on the back of a postcard or in a blog. What kinds of skills, competences, and forms of multitasking have been developed in this process?

This perspective has also brought back the materialities of the lives of tourists and travelers (Christensen 1999; Haldrup and Larsen 2006; Seidl 2009). Tourist lives call for a lot of body-work, dragging mountains of luggage along, getting sunburned on the beach, drinking or eating too much. They struggle with malfunctioning cameras, get lost in city alleys, or are bored to death waiting for delayed flights. They bring back home not only souvenirs, from miniature Eiffel towers and folklore dolls to reindeer horns or pieces of the Berlin Wall, but also digital images and materials for their travel blogs. They also acquire new tastes for the exotic, start making Greek salads and Spanish paellas, learn about local wines, and bring back strange bottles of liqueurs.

At home the exotic is domesticated in many forms. In his classic study of the Irish village of Ballymenone, Henry Glassie (1982) describes how Mrs Cutler constantly evokes the outside world by lovingly dusting and rearranging the items on her souvenir shelf. The souvenir plates and mugs, the doll in a kilt, and the dippy duck are always on the move, and it is in this haptic relationship that memories are created and travel dreams produced.

Bernhard Pöttler (2009) has analyzed the ways in which souvenirs turn homes into holiday spaces. There is the German couple who spend all their holidays in their beloved Greece and have decided to turn their bathroom at home into a small Greek temple, complete with pillars and ornaments bought from the local hardware store, but also holiday souvenirs and small statuettes. By taking a bath they travel south and back to all their holiday memories.

The European Experience

How has tourism Europeanized Europe and the rest of the world? One very obvious level is that of the standardization of the tourist industry. During the nineteenth century the Swiss taught the rest of the continent how to develop first-class hotels, the Germans invented the Baedeker genre of tourist guides as well as the system of ranking tourist sites with a three-star system, and Thomas Cook demonstrated how a network of local travel agents could create security and assistance for travelers abroad. Over the last two centuries an international grammar toolbox has emerged, with the paradoxical goal of producing local atmosphere by borrowing concepts across borders – from tourist menus and folklore shows to souvenir production and branding strategies. At first this could take the form of creating Little Paris or Little Switzerland all over Europe (and in other corners of the world). Later on there would be attempts at imitating the success formulas of "Swinging London" or "Hip Barcelona." On another level there were also attempts to meet tourists' expectations of "local culture." How can a reliable and well-functioning structure of sights and attractions be developed? If there are no local crafts or interesting folk dances they have to be developed. Thus matrices for sightseeing plans were constantly circulated, borrowed, and adapted from older destinations.

The Europeanizing force, tourism as a special mode and mood of taking in the world, was also seen in the making of American tourism during the nineteenth century. John Ruskin wrote about America: "I could not even for a couple of months live in a country so miserable as to possess no castles" and his laments on the lack of ruins and monuments were echoed by others, although Americans tried to create their own local version of the European Grand Tour in the mid-nineteenth century. In the same way the American wilderness was filtered through the romantic European tourist gaze (see Löfgren 1999:37ff.).

The lessons of Europe are also striking in the twentieth-century making of mass tourism. Turning to 1936, it is possible to see the interwar European experimentations with leisure forms and attitudes as prototypes that later become commonplace and global. One prerequisite of this was the immensely increased mobility during the twentieth century (see Kaschuba 2004). In 1936 the train, the bus, and the bike were the dominating travel technologies. In Sweden, 1 in 6 owned a bike but only 1 in 60 a car – and it is not until the 1950s and 1960s that European automobility became a mass movement. At the beginning of the century a Swede traveled on average around 230 km per year, at the end of the century this figure had grown to 13 000 km, and that figure does not take in account the more than 15 million transnational journeys of a 10 million population. Those journeys include, apart from business travel, numerous charter and low-budget flights to sunny beaches and alpine resorts, as well as weekend trips to cities.

The first legislation for paid holidays in 1936 also marks the start of a European profile. In the United States workers made higher wages a priority, which created a tradition of short vacations. Today, Europeans, and especially the Northerners, have the longest vacations in the world. In the same way the tradition of investing in a second home is much stronger in Europe. In short, many Europeans have chosen to invest much of their time and resources in vacationing and holiday making.

I have argued that a historical perspective shows how tourists learn to experience and become fascinated by certain settings, but also grow tired of them, thus constantly changing the European touristscapes. There are some destinations, from Florence to Blackpool Pleasure Beach (Walton 2008), that constantly manage to reinvent themselves, catering to the appetites of new generations, but there are also many sights and hotspots that have faded into the background. The old European spa culture of the nineteenth century was slowly dying during the next century, only to be reinvented as a successful element in the new Experience Economy (O'Dell 2010).

We may see the European history of tourism as a constant process of learning to handle abroadness and to master transnational movements. In this process adventure may turn into routine, or be revitalized as adventure again, but to understand such processes we need ethnographies of tourism as lived and situated practice. The tourist mode of experiencing the world is framed by preunderstandings and expectations – the new destinations we already know from the media. What is a three-star sight, a picturesque village, a pulsating city, a fantastic panorama, a breath-taking experience? Most tourists travel with a heavy baggage of preunderstandings and expectations, and this baggage has also Europeanized other parts of the tourist world, creating a global tourist mode of seeing, experiencing, and moving.

During the last decades the European continent has become a popular destination, not only for Americans but for the rapidly rising number of middle-class tourists from countries like Japan, India, and China. Their perception of us, their desires and habits will increasingly shape the European tourist landscape: now Europeans are the interesting natives . . .

REFERENCES

Baranowski, Shelly, and Ellen Furlough, eds.
2001 Being Elsewhere: Tourism, Consumer Culture, and Identity in Modern Europe and North America. Ann Arbor: University of Michigan Press.

Bendix, Regina, and Orvar Löfgren
2007 Double Homes, Double Lives? *In* Double Homes, Double Lives. Theme Issue. Ethnologia Europaea 37(1–2):7–16.

Benson, Michaela, and Karen O' Reilly
2009 Lifestyle Migration: Expectations, Aspirations and Experiences. Farnham: Ashgate.

Borelius, Fredrik
1936 Där forntiden lever. Stockholm: Nordstedt.

Black, Jeremy
1992 The British Abroad: The Grand Tour in the Eighteenth Century. New York: St Martin's Press.

Boissevain, Jeremy, ed.
1996 Coping with Tourists: European Reactions to Mass Tourism. Oxford: Berghahn.

Buzard, James
1993 The Beaten Track: European Tourism, Literature and the Ways to Culture, 1800–1918. Oxford: Clarendon Press.

Caglar, Ayse
2002 A Table in Two Hands. *In* Fragments of Culture: The Everyday of Modern Turkey. Ayse Saktanberk and Deniz Kandiyoti, eds. pp. 294–307. London: I. B. Tauris.

Christensen, Olav
1999 The Playing Collective: Snowboarding, Youth Culture and the Desire for Excitement. Ethnologia Scandinavica 29:106–119.

Corbin, Alain
1994 The Lure of the Sea: The Discovery of the Seaside in the Western World, 1750–1840. Berkeley: University of California Press.

De Grazia, Victoria
1992 How Fascism Ruled Women: Italy 1922–1945. Berkeley: University of California Press.

Ek, Richard, Jonas Larsen, Soeren Buhl Hornskov, and Ole Kjaer Mansfeldt
2008 A Dynamic Framework of Tourist Experiences: Space-Time and Performances in the Experience Economy. Scandinavian Journal of Hospitality and Tourism 8(2):122–140.

Franklin, Adrian, and Mike Crang
2001 The Trouble with Tourism and Travel Theory? Tourist Studies 1(1):5–22.

Frykman, Jonas
1993 Becoming the Perfect Swede: Modernity, Body Politics, and National Processes in 20th-Century Sweden. Ethnos 58(3):259–274.

Furlough, Ellen
1998 Making Mass Vacations: Tourism and Consumer Culture in France, 1930–1970s. Comparative Studies in Society and History 40(2):247–286.

Fussell, Paul
1980 Abroad: British Literary Travelling between the Wars. Oxford: Oxford University Press.

Glassie, Henry
1982 Passing the Time in Ballymenone: Culture and History of an Ulster Community. Philadelphia: University of Pennsylvania Press.
Gmelch, Sharon Bohn, ed.
2010 Tourists and Tourism: A Reader. Long Grove, IL: Waveland.
Haldrup, Michael, and Johan Larsen
2006 Material Cultures of Tourism. Leisure Studies 3:275–289.
Hjemdahl Mathiesen, Kirsti
2003 When Theme Parks Happen. *In* Being There: New Perspectives on Phenomenology and the Analysis of Culture. Jonas Frykman and Nils Gilje, eds. pp. 149–168. Lund: Nordic Academic Press.
Kaufmann, Jean-Claude
1995 Corps de femmes, Regards d'hommes. Paris: Nathan.
Larsen, Jonas, and John Urry
2011 The Tourist Gaze, 3.0. London: Sage.
Löfgren, Orvar
1999 On Holiday: A History of Vacationing. Berkeley: University of California Press.
2005 Cultural Alchemy: Translating the Experience Economy into Scandinavian. *In* Global Ideas: How Ideas, Objects and Practices Travel in the Global Economy. Barbara Czarniawska and Guje Sevón, eds. pp. 35–47. Malmö: Liber.
Mai, Ulrich
2007 Paradise Lost and Regained. German Second Home Owners in Mazury, Poland. Ethnologia Europaea 37(1–2):134–139.
Marling, Gitte, and Martin Zerlang, eds.
2007 Fun City. Copenhagen: Danish Architectural Press.
Moser, Johannes, and Daniella Seidl, eds.
2009 Dinge auf Reisen: Materielle Kultur und Tourismus. Münster: Waxmann.
O'Dell, Thomas
2007 Tourist Experiences and Academic Junctures. Scandinavian Journal of Hospitality and Tourism 7(1):34–45.
2010 Spas: The Cultural Economy of Hospitality, Magic and the Sense. Lund: Nordic Academic Press.
Pagenstecher, Cord
2009 "Pixi geht wie ein Sofa über die Prachtstrasse" Das Auto im Tourismus der Nachkriegszeit. *In* Dinge auf Reisen Materielle Kultur und Tourismus. Johannes Moser and Daniella Seidl, eds. pp. 263–280. Münster: Waxmann.
Pons, Pau Obrador, Mike Crang, and Penny Travlou
2009 Cultures of Mass Tourism: Doing the Mediterranean in the Age of Banal Mobilities. Farnham: Ashgate.
Pöttler, Burkhard
2009 Der Urlaub im Wohnzimmer. *In* Dinge auf Reisen Materielle Kultur und Tourismus. Johannes Moser and Daniella Seidl, eds. pp. 119–136. Münster: Waxmann.
Pöttler, Burkhardt, and Ulrike Kammerhofer-Aggermann, eds.
1992 Tourismus und Regionalkultur: Referate der österreichischen Volkskundetagung 1992 in Salzburg. Buchreihe der österreischischen Zeitschrift für Volkskunde, 12.
Povrzanović Frykman, Maja
2008 Beyond Culture and Identity: Places, Practices, Experiences. Ethnologia Europaea 38(1):13–22.
Pemble, John
1987 The Mediterranean Passion: Victorians and Edwardians in the South. Oxford: Oxford University Press.

Rolshoven, Johanna
2007 The Temptations of the Provisional: Multilocality as a Way of Life. Ethnologia Europaea 37(1–2):17–25.
Sallnow, John
1985 Yugoslavia: Tourism in a Socialist Federal State. Tourism Management June 1985:113–124.
Seidl, Daniella
2007 Breaking Out into the Everyday: German Holiday-Owners in Italy. Ethnologia Europaea 37(1–2):107–114.
Urbain, Jean-Didier
1991 L'Idiot du voyage: Histoires de tourists. Paris: Plon.
2002 Paradis verts: Désirs de campagne et passions résidentielles. Paris: Payot.
2003 At the Beach. Minneapolis: University of Minnesota Press.
Urry, John
1990 The Tourist Gaze: Leisure and Travel in Contemporary Societies. London: Sage.
1995 Consuming Places. London: Routledge.
Veijola, Soile, and Eeva Jokinen
1994 The Body in Tourism. Theory, Culture and Society 11:125–151.
Waldren, Jaqueline
1996 Insiders and Outsiders: Paradise and Reality in Mallorca. Oxford: Berghahn.
Walton, John K.
2007 Riding on Rainbows: Blackpool Pleasure Beach and Its Place in British Popular Culture. St Albans: Skelter.
Ward, Colin, and Dennis Hardy
1986 Goodnight Campers! The History of the British Holiday Camp. London: Mansell.
Willim, Robert
2005 It Is in the Mix: Configuring Industrial Cool. *In* Magic, Culture and the New Economy. Orvar Löfgren and Robert Willim, eds. pp. 97–104. Oxford: Berg.
Zadnicek, Franz
1992 Paradiesruinen: Das KdF Seebad der Zwanzigtausend auf Rügen. Berlin: Links.

CHAPTER 21

The Diversity of European Food Cultures

Gisela Welz

What Europeans eat and drink today is to a great extent shaped by European Union (EU) policies. In recent years, tightened food hygiene and consumer safety regulations have had a considerable impact on European food products. European economic policies, regulatory frameworks, and financial support systems tend to privilege large-scale industrial production. This also holds true for food production and for the agricultural sector, where subsidies and funds granted under the umbrella of the Common Agricultural Policy determine what is produced, where, and how much. But the European Commission also champions niche products such as ecologically produced food, rewards small-scale projects of sustainable rural development, and extends special copyright protection to traditional and regional "origin foods." It is the interplay of these sometimes contradictory policies with each other, and with the artifacts and practices of European people that coproduce the European foodscape at the beginning of the twenty-first century.

This chapter will inquire into the effects of Europeanization on food production and consumption in Europe, against the backdrop of the state of the art of the international anthropology of food. The cultural diversity of food has always been of interest to anthropologists. In the 1960s, the sheer range of what humans categorize as edible – and the seeming arbitrariness of declaring certain foods as subject to dietary taboos – gave rise to functionalist explanatory models (Harris 1975) and inspired structuralist anthropology to view food systems as embodying fundamental patterns of order (Lévi-Strauss 1965; Douglas 1971; Tolksdorf 2000).

Most anthropologists engaging in food research today follow a poststructuralist agenda and consider food items and food practices as sites for the construction, negotiation, and contestation of culturally specific meanings (Counihan and Van Esterik 1997; Sutton 2001). More recently, anthropologists have also started to address the political dimensions of food and its integration into processes of

A Companion to the Anthropology of Europe, First Edition. Edited by Ullrich Kockel, Máiréad Nic Craith, and Jonas Frykman.

economic globalization (Watson and Caldwell 2005; Wilk 2006). Anthropological research on food-related practices emphasizes the social agency of consumption, viewing it as an exemplary arena "for cultural production and class differentiation, a location of resistance or complicity" (Paxson 2006:202). Conversely, recent studies also consider food producers as social actors who generate cultural meanings and moral economies (Leitch 2003; Terrio 2005; Grasseni 2008). Valuable insights are offered by other disciplines as well, most prominently by economic history and cultural sociology (Teuteberg 1992). Ethnological food research in Europe developed in the 1970s, building on earlier traditions especially in *Volkskunde* of the German-speaking countries (Bendix and Wierlacher 2008; Teuteberg 2008) and generating numerous studies with a strong social history orientation (Teuteberg et al. 1997; Mohrmann 2008). Within the framework of SIEF, ethnological food research has developed as a lively, international endeavor (e.g. Lysaght 1998).

The Emergence of Food Diversity in Europe

Ecological anthropology and archaeology suggest that in Europe since prehistory, innovations in culturally learned practices of foraging, agriculture, and animal husbandry interacted with meteorological and soil conditions and water supplies to create patterns of subsistence that were well adapted to climatic regions and vegetation zones (Bérard et al. 2005). Ethnobiologists and geneticists also point out that the patterns of resource management and the cultural knowledge that made them possible resulted in the coevolution of regional biodiversity, landscape formation, and human physique. Human geneticists suggest that the physical properties and health dispositions of contemporary European populations have been shaped epigenetically by past nutritional patterns (Niewöhner et al. 2008). Food, then, from the very beginning of mankind's history in Europe, has always incorporated both the organic and the cultural, entailing biological as well as symbolic properties. The first volume of Braudel's economic and social history of the Mediterranean area (1996) maps the primordial distribution of subsistence patterns in Europe, taking into account those environmental conditions that remain unchanged over centuries or even thousands of years.

Cultural historians and sociologists have contributed much to our understanding of the changes in nutrition and culinary practices of European populations since medieval times. The refinement of courtly culinary practices has been followed closely, with the emergence of table manners (Elias 1994), changing tastes, and the regulation of appetite (Mennell 1985) in France and England serving as exemplary cases of the civilizing process shaping the distinctive cultural history of Europe. For the larger part of the population, regional diversity in food consumption – compounded by differences between the rural masses and the comparatively far less numerous urban populations – remained in place throughout most of Europe well into the nineteenth century (Hirschfelder 2001). Also, national cuisines emerged during the eighteenth century, attested to by a growing body of cookery literature, and were consolidated in the nineteenth century. These were invented traditions (Hobsbawm 1992). Often, regional patterns were selected for this purpose, modified, and then taken to represent the culinary practices of an entire nation (Mintz 2003). Those food items and meals that served as national emblems were hardly ever identical with those that people actually consumed on a regular basis; at best, they were enjoyed on holiday and feast-day occasions (Wiegelmann 2006).

Economic historians and anthropologists emphasize the fact that none of the emblematic national cuisines of Europe would have their present shape without considerable input from overseas products that were introduced to European agricultural production from the fifteenth century onward. Most prominently, fruits, vegetables, and grains originating from the Americas were transformed into genuinely European staples, such as potatoes, tomatoes, and maize. In addition, products that colonial powers were cultivating on a large scale overseas – such as coffee, tea, cane sugar, cocoa – became readily available in European societies. Sidney Mintz in his study *Sweetness and Power* (1985) elucidates the link between industrialization in Western Europe and large-scale agricultural production in the New World, relying on slave labor.

It was not until the second half of the nineteenth century that periodic food shortages and widespread malnutrition in Europe became a thing of the past. The dramatic increase in agricultural productivity throughout the nineteenth century was the consequence of a variety of factors, some among them technological and scientific, such as the invention of nonorganic fertilizer and the mechanization of agriculture, others political and economic, such as land reforms and the abolition of serfdom. Commercial trade networks brought food products from far away, and new types of retail establishments catered to the needs of urban residents. Food production increasingly relied on elaborate sociotechnical systems, integrating means of transportation such as railways and steam ships, and new preservation technologies such as canning and refrigeration. Mechanized production methods led to manufactured goods and packaged items dominating the market (Giedeon 1969; Goody 1997).

Industrialization, Scientification, Lifestyle Formation

While the processes of mechanization and rationalization of food production did not proceed at an equal pace in all parts of Europe, and did not have the same effects everywhere, on the whole, as most social historians readily assert, the premodern axes of food cultural differences – namely the contrast between the nutritional patterns of rural and urban populations, and the regional variations of available food products – diminished during the nineteenth century. Instead, the construction of national cuisines led to an assertion of difference that was also economically exploitable in tourism and gastronomy. At the same time, socioeconomic differences in food and eating became decoupled from the rural–urban divide and instead began to mark separate class cultures (Goody 1982). Elite culinary systems such as French haute cuisine also emerged in the nineteenth century, along with a star system of celebrated chefs, the social practice of eating out in restaurants, and related book publications and journals (Mennell 1997). Technical innovations, especially new household appliances, coproduced modern gender roles, and prepared the ground for the advent of the consumer society. Food preferences and meal patterns increasingly were rationalized and became subject to scientific knowledge and expert discourses (Tanner 1999).

The year-round availability of industrially produced, packaged, and branded food and the integration of European agricultural products into global markets both contributed to severing the link between local diet and local farm products – a process that was complete by the second half of the twentieth century. Carole Counihan's ethnographic monograph of the abandonment of domestic bread-baking in the Italian region of Sardinia since World War II is one of many anthropological case studies exemplifying this process (Counihan 1997). Local grain cultivation had decreased and was finally given up when the economic situation and national agricultural policies made subsistence farming untenable by the 1960s. The social ties that had been created and maintained by the collective bread-baking of local women, and also by the habitual exchange of bread between households, became weaker and gradually ceased altogether when individual households resorted to consuming store-bought bread.

However, food products did not become uniform and homogenized throughout Europe. Rather, increasingly specialized demand created the need for ever new and more diverse products (Holm 1997; Tanner 2004). Consumption became a culturally expressive practice. Pierre Bourdieu's (1984) work has made it clear that there is no simple correlation between socioeconomic household status and the quality, variety, and quantity of foodstuffs consumed. Rather, food consumption allows for social distinction and lifestyle formation. To be a connoisseur in matters of food and drink became an important aspect of cultural capital of the educated classes in postindustrial Western societies, the aspiration to the status of a gourmet catered to by a whole industry of publishing, audiovisual media, and educational products as well as specialized food production and marketing. To eat well as well as responsibly in terms of health and ecological implications has become a middle-class lifestyle tenet throughout Europe and the United States (Paxson 2005). Differential food preferences, then, are not simply a means to advertise social status but have turned into a moral issue as well. All of these developments contribute to the segmentation of markets in the food sector that may cross-cut national differences but creates ever finer distinctions between various taste cultures.

Another factor that contributes to the diversity of food systems and cuisines in European countries is the increase in transnational mobility since World War II. Labor migration within the framework of so-called "guest work," the presence of colonial and postcolonial immigrants in those European countries that had been colonial powers, as well as the influx of more recent groups of transnational migrants from regions outside of Europe, have had the effect of making the food sector much more diverse (Harbottle 1997; Bernstein 2010). A wide range of ethnic and national foods and imported culinary products are available in grocery shops, supermarkets, take-aways, and restaurants in most European cities today (Çaglar 1999; Pang 2003). The predilection of consumers to experiment with and become knowledgeable of exotic cuisines makes the appeal of these markets reach far beyond ethnic immigrant clienteles. Lifestyle choices and new types of recreational consumption, especially within the framework of tourism, contribute to this process (Cook and Crang 1996; Römhild et al. 2008). However, discriminatory and racist discourses of majority populations will also often single out culinary preferences of immigrants, with the intention of stigmatizing them.

Some critics claim that European consumption patterns have been massively subverted by US models, and see much evidence for an ongoing "McDonaldization" (Ritzer 1993) of European societies that ultimately will lead to a leveling of cultural difference. However, findings of anthropological food research have also significantly contributed to irritating, simplistic notions of the homogenizing effects of the global food industry, pointing to divergent appropriations and creative responses (Watson 1997). No matter which assessment will be proven accurate in the end, what Australian anthropologist Alison Leitch has observed certainly will hold true, namely that, like the euro, food has become "a single common discursive currency through which to debate Europeanness and the implications of economic globalization at the beginning of the 21st century" (Leitch 2003:442). Leitch comes to this assertion by way of her ethnographic research in metropolitan and rural Italy during the 1990s, charting the rise of food activism under the banners of the "slow food" movement that is ostensibly opposed to the leveling effects of American-type modernization and seeks to create new market opportunities for "endangered" foods and small-scale producers (Petrini 2001). Increasingly, then, the consumption of food and beverages serve as important building blocks for identities of local, national, or transnational scope among Europeans, as Wilson (2006) has emphasized.

Food Safety, Consumer Rights, and Audit Culture

Food hygiene is one of the classic intervention points of the modern nation-state. The safeguarding of sufficient nourishment and healthy living conditions for the state's subjects count among the measures of what Michel Foucault has called "biopolitics," arguing that alongside its beneficial effects, it also serves to discipline and control populations (Foucault 2007). When relations between food producers and food consumers became market-regulated and anonymous in the course of urbanization and industrialization, food safety deteriorated. In the eighteenth and early nineteenth centuries, there was an increasing risk for urban consumers to be exposed to unhealthy, hygienically dangerous products or to adulterated foods of little nutritional value. By the mid-nineteenth century, in England, "the combined contribution of public medical testing, branded goods, and widespread advertising" (Goody 1997:353) managed to minimize food risks. In modern commodity markets where face-to-face contact between producer and consumer is not possible, it is brands and labels that provide consumers with information about products (Cook and Crang 1996). By the twentieth century, building on advances in the natural sciences, European countries had effective systems of state inspection in the veterinary and catering sectors in operation. In what follows, this chapter will focus on more recent developments, with food safety becoming an issue for transnational governance.

Since 2000, the European Union has considerably augmented its restrictive regulations to ensure food safety. With the BSE crisis and the decline of consumer trust in European products, the European Commission was forced to implement structural reforms, tighten hygiene controls, and aim for a new division of responsibility (Halkier and Holm 2006). The European Commission's White Paper on Food Safety (Commission 2000) served as a basis for a new framework legislation which became effective in 2002. It

> revealed a clear shift in political priorities: the principal aim was now consumer protection and health, and the free market had become less important, even if the ultimate justification of food safety regulation was once more presented in terms of market efficiency. (Bergeaud-Blackler and Ferretti 2006:138)

The General Food Law was transposed into national legislation between 2002 and 2005, making food production all over Europe comply with more stringent measures of bacterial hygiene and the avoidance of pollution. This tightened legislation forced businesses – especially those processing meat and dairy products – to upgrade their production facilities. Also, a new program made it mandatory to document the provenance of individual products so that even a single egg could be traced back all the way to the laying battery (European Commission 2004). Critics point out that the implementation of rigid hygiene standards hastens the replacement of traditional artisanal production techniques by industrialized, high-technology mass production. The standardization and rationalization of food production that is supposed to protect the consumer does change the production methods and the products themselves to such a degree that the specific taste, the organoleptic quality, and the variation that consumers expect from an artisanal product are lost (Bérard et al. 2005). There is much evidence that in spite of subsidies being available, the financial burden of complying with the new regulations is often too heavy for small enterprises, forcing artisanal producers to go out of business. The new food safety requirements can be implemented in an economically feasible way only by high-volume mass-producing food businesses (Karn 2009).

Today's exclusive reliance on scientifically based food-safety measures makes us forget that in traditional food production, experience-based judgments and embodied knowledge enabled producers and consumers alike to assess the quality of a food product by its smell, taste, color, texture, and density. Safe cheese or sausages were considered distinguishable from spoiled products. The implementation of modern food safety measures marginalizes culturally learned abilities to discern good from bad products. In addition, the consumer's trust in the quality and safety of a product used to rest on his or her social relationship with the producer, which, in traditional social worlds, was not anonymous and abstract but quite personal, and often embedded in other social relations as well, between kin, between covillagers, or between patrons and clients. Most importantly, it rested on moral judgments: a good person makes good sausages. Wherever modern methods of state-controlled hygienization were introduced, it is state inspectors who visit production units and end-products are submitted to laboratory testing. Modern methods make judgments of food quality impersonal and abstract, based on scientific knowledge and measurement technologies (Welz 2006).

Today, however, we are witnessing another shift in the instituting of food safety, away from the modern regime of top-down, scientifically based state control, and toward a new regime of governmentality where producers are called upon to voluntarily check their own compliance with the rules. The transposition of the EU's General Food Law requires so-called nonprimary food-producing facilities such as dairies, meat packers, or bakeries to adopt quality-control measures such as the "Hazard Assessment and Critical Control Point" (HACCP) protocol. This also often implies the outsourcing of formerly state-run inspection measures to private sector firms of quality control experts, food safety consultants, and hygiene specialists. "These measures were strongly supported by food multinationals and the food industry in general, as they were perceived as a chance to regain consumer confidence by proving the efficiency of the operating traceability systems" (Bergeaud-Blackler and Ferretti 2006:140). Protocols such as HACCP require people working in food production or processing to prove by constant documentation that they are following the proper procedures at all times. The shift from state control to self-regulation is indicative of a new form of noncoercive accountability that some social anthropologists consider typical of the new "audit culture" of the European Union and other neoliberal economic formations (Strathern 2000). Anthropologist Elizabeth Dunn, who did extensive fieldwork in Poland both before and after EU accession, sees the new food hygiene regimes as evidence of what she calls the "normative governmentality" of the EU:

> Normative (or "neoliberal") governmentality attempts to integrate new geographic spaces and populations not by overt coercion, but by instituting a host of "harmonized" regulations, codes, and standards. . . . To ensure food safety, the EU's sanitary and phytosanitary standards specify not only the qualities of the product, but particular production processes and the creation of auditable records. Food processing standards thus illustrate the ways in which normative governmentality claims to reveal truth, to transform economic structures, and to be applicable across geographies with diverse histories and institutions. (Dunn 2005:175)

Both the 2004 and the 2007 accession rounds of the EU have shown that the implementation of EU regulations is to the detriment of many small subsistence farmers and food producers in rural areas. However, national governments in Eastern Europe did little to halt this process, welcoming the opportunity it brought to consolidate and professionalize the agricultural sector and the food industry.

European Quality Labels: Blueprints for the Construction of Commodity-Heritage

Heritage-making is a modern practice that redefines as valuable and worthy of protection vernacular practices and traditional products that would otherwise disappear because they cannot compete against modernized life styles and mass-produced consumer goods. As a consequence, they are transformed into "objects of trade and exhibition" (Herzfeld 2004:196). Many artisanal foodstuffs, produced in rural households and small family-run businesses, have become almost extinct because of the small scale of production and markets. Today they are at risk of disappearing altogether when the older generation of producers abandons production and no successors take over. Other products – especially dairy and meat products such as cheese, sausages, and hams – may survive because they have made the transition to semi-industrial or even industrial food production. Thus, vernacular food in the sense of traditional local food systems had mostly ceased to exist decades ago. At best, "one item in an older farming or culinary system . . . has been selected out by the market, [while] the rest of the local system is largely abandoned and unlamented" (Pratt 2007:298). Today, most artisanal products marketed in European countries have been "generated out of sustained commercial activity, state regulatory systems, and international trade agreements" (Pratt 2007:298).

In 1992, the European Union decided to establish a quality label system for the protection of geographically specific food products. "The creation of a legal framework makes it possible to establish and protect the relationship between a product and a place by reserving the use of a particular name" (Bérard and Marchenay 2007:9). This was supposed to have a positive effect on niche markets for artisanal food products and to safeguard the diversity of food traditions, thereby increasing the EU's competitiveness in global markets (Salomonsson 2002).

The pertinent European regulation distinguishes between two categories of protected names: protected designation of origin (PDO) and protected geographical indication (PGI). The inclusion in the public register of protected product names is marked by a publication in the Official Journal of the EU and also on the Internet (European Agricultural Product Quality Policy 2009). In 2006, the regulation was updated and somewhat modified. To be eligible for the protected designation of origin (PDO), a product must meet two conditions:

> The quality or characteristics of the product must be essentially or exclusively due to the particular geographical environment of the place of origin; the geographical environment is taken to include inherent natural and human factors, such as climate, soil quality, and local knowhow; the production and processing of the raw materials, up to the stage of the finished product, must take place in the defined geographical area whose name the product bears. (Guide to Community Regulations 2004:6)

For protected geographical indication (PGI), the requirements are less stringent. It is sufficient that one of the stages of production takes place in the defined area. In both cases, however, elaborate and very precise product specifications form the basis for the European Commission's decision to include the product in its list of "origin products" and to give the applicants the right to print the certification seal on the product label. Specifications are required to give precise information on the "authentic and unvarying" production methods as well as those physical, chemical, microbiological, biological, and organoleptic characteristics which allow "the objective differentiation of the product from other products of the same category through characteristics conferred on the product by its origin" (Guide to Community Regulations 2004:12). The PDO/PGI system goes beyond protecting the mere provenance of a food product, but engages origin as a category constructed to signify the interdependence between the place of production, the producers and their knowledge, and the historical depth of a tradition (Bérard and Marchenay 2007). It is not particularly difficult to recognize the similarity to the French concept of "*terroir*" at the core of these European regulations. *Terroir* presupposes "specific rural space possessing distinctive physical characteristics . . . seen as the product of the interaction between a human community and the place in which it lives"(Bérard et al. 2005:22). Indeed, the European quality label system of PDO/PGI integrated and superseded the national legislation already in place in France and Italy.

The EU emphasizes the voluntary nature of the PDO/PGI process. It is the producers themselves who embark on the application process. "Producers draw up their own rules, and the discipline required is self-imposed" (Guide 2004:12). Once the product is certified, however, the self-imposed discipline becomes a rigid corset, and the producers themselves are held accountable for the proper implementation of regulations. Breaches are sanctioned with fines and loss of the label. The expectation that food products that have been awarded an EU quality label will fetch higher prices is the main incentive for groups of producers to apply. In most cases, the national agricultural ministry is the body in charge of processing applications, guiding them through a complicated review process and submitting them to the European Commission. The application process and all follow-up costs, such as quality control measures, are paid for by the producers. The transformation of food into heritage requires producers, distributors, local administrators, and agricultural advisors (Grasseni 2005:86) to engage in a huge effort in order to translate an unregulated product into a standardized commodity.

Food is a mobile commodity, especially since cooling, storage, and transport technologies have made global distribution possible. The quality labels of the European Union transform food into a "commodity-heritage"(Grasseni 2005) that may travel great distances. Customarily, traditional food production required skills and knowledge that could not be acquired in formalized training – as a dairy technician or food scientist – but were experience-based and embodied. Also, there was a direct, face-to-face relationship between producers and consumers. It is when the product starts to circulate in translocal markets, or competes domestically with products from elsewhere, that truth-claims as to its origin become decisive in establishing its authenticity as heritage. The type of standardization that occurs with heritage production ostensibly serves the purpose of maintaining distinctly nonstandard artifacts and practices in the face of the kind of homogenization that economic globalization effects. Its goal is to safeguard and highlight the singularity of these objects. This process creates a tension between local forms of traditional knowledge and various types of expert knowledge. In determining the authenticity of food products, the European Commission enlists findings of biochemistry and genetics to bolster cultural claims for singularity. A new type of "microbiopolitics" is emerging in this process (Beck and Scholze-Irrlitz in press).

Managed Diversity, Messy Histories: The Case of Halloumi Cheese in Cyprus

In Europe at the beginning of the twenty-first century, traditional food products are transformed by, and in an important way reshaped or even invented for, global consumption. The culinary diversity of Europe is marketed globally, and traditional food constitutes a growing economic sector within Europe. As a consequence, competition between producers may be fierce, and the need to protect the uniqueness of one's product becomes particularly important. While the procedure of application to the European Commission rests on an agreement, presumably of all producers in a defined region, it is rarely consensual and quite often intensely contested. The link between the product and the area which gives it its name is often complicated to document, and disputes over real or symbolic ownership come to the fore (Leitch 2003; Tschofen 2007). Paradoxical effects occur that may even lead to the exclusion of the original producers from access to the market.

Consider the transformations that the production and marketing of halloumi cheese in Cyprus has undergone. Up until the 1960s, the production of halloumi was a gendered activity that formed part of the subsistence economy of agrarian households. Groups of women would pool the small quantities of milk that they got from the few goats and sheep that each family kept, collectively fill the cheese kettle, and cook halloumi in the cheese kitchen of one of their group. Biochemists claim that "a feature of the production method of this particular cheese is that no starter cultures are used; rather, the flavour and texture depend solely on the indigenous microflora of the milk" (Lawson et al. 2001:45). In addition to known strains of lactobacilli, the research team isolated a hitherto unknown lactic acid bacterium in halloumi cheese.

It was modernization, growing prosperity, and urbanization since the 1970s that turned the traditional collective cheese-making into a more professional and commercialized activity pursued by individual women who became full-time "halloumi ladies." But production still took place in an artisanal fashion, according to traditional recipes, in the village house. In addition to satisfying the village's demand, small-scale producers also delivered to supermarkets in town (Welz and Andilios 2004). Yet, at the same time, halloumi developed into an important mass-market commodity produced by large dairy companies that dominated the national market for cheese and other milk products. Since the 1970s, halloumi cheese production has been industrialized and transposed into high-tech modern factory settings. Industrially produced halloumi from the Republic of Cyprus is available worldwide, with the United Kingdom and United States, as well as the Arab world, as major markets (Welz and Andilios 2004). Halloumi cheese for many years has enjoyed the status of being the most successful export product of the Greek Cypriot economy (Gibbs et al. 2004).

In Cyprus, during the run-up period to the 2004 accession, the transposition of EU regulations into national law was achieved more swiftly and efficiently than in other accession countries. Two years prior to EU accession, the Cypriot government declared the artisanal cheese production in households as well as in small workshops and factories a "public health hazard." The owners and managers of the large industrial companies had anticipated this event and already invested considerable sums of money in order to bring their factories up to date with the most advanced food technology and hygiene measures (Welz and Andilios 2004). In 2003, when the government demanded that all enterprises in the food sector comply with new regulations, the market leaders in cheese production had completed their modernization process. Many small rural production units, however, had to close down when they could not comply with government demands. Many of them were not were able to mobilize expertise and money to embark on the difficult course of reopening their premises. State officials saw the EU hygiene regime as an instrument for effectively weeding out the food sector, leaving only medium-sized and big companies able to compete internationally. In spite of the disastrous impact of these new regulations, a fairly substantial number of individual producers who sell their halloumi directly to consumers who come to their premises continue to operate in Cypriot villages (Welz 2006). Many Greek Cypriots consider the industrial cheese products tasteless and bland and prefer the artisanal product (Papademas and Robinson 2001). Among middle-class urbanites, it has become a mark of social distinction to cultivate a "halloumi lady" in one of the villages. Research conducted in other EU countries also points to an increase of clandestine and informal market activities in food production as a response to tightened EU food safety regulations (Dunn 2005). Illegal or quasilegal operations, however, are vulnerable and precarious, having no recourse to the protection of the law.

With EU accession, the Republic of Cyprus also became eligible for the application process for quality labels for origin products. By that time, many rural production units had been closed down in the food hygiene clampdown. In the wake of these developments, there was little interest in the villages in sharing traditional knowledge with representatives of the ministry when they attempted to collect recipes for applications to Brussels. Research in other European countries also points to the reluctance of some producer groups to submit to the regulatory regimes set up in accordance with EU legislation (Bérard et al. 2005). However, the powerful industrial dairy corporations in Cyprus had not been idle in the meantime. The biggest players in industrial cheese production had invented a new cheese product line, called "village style" halloumi (Welz and Andilios 2004). These products are cleverly devised to comply with the requirements of EU regulations, both for food hygiene, and for the status as certified regionally specific food item. They are made exclusively from sheep's and goats' milk from specified microregions within Cyprus, but produced in factories in urban centers of Cyprus, and fetch high prices in the domestic market.

In addition to this move, the big companies also applied pressure on the government bodies preparing the application for PDO status for halloumi cheese. They wanted the application to the European Commission to include cows' milk in the list of ingredients for the product specification. For the industrial mass-produced halloumi cheese in Cyprus, especially the grade made for export, cows' milk is utilized due to its easier availability all year round and its much lower price. National legislation passed in the 1980s allows for this practice, only specifying that a "substantial amount of goats' and/or sheep's milk" needs to be included in a cheese called "halloumi," without any fixed percentages and threshold levels. Dairy cows were only introduced to Cyprus on a large scale in the 1960s, so the claim that a halloumi cheese that contains a large portion of cows' milk may still be called traditional is hotly contested (Welz 2007). However, it appears that powerful dairy companies who also dominate the Cyprus Cheese-Makers Association were able to champion a definition of the cheese's composition in the application to the European Commission that will allow them to continue using cows' milk while at the same time enabling them to secure the coveted PDO status.

The application to the European Commission was finally submitted in July 2009, after having been stalled for many months. Cheese products like halloumi are not unique to Greek Cypriot food culture. Among the Turkish Cypriot inhabitants of the island, the cheese is known as *hellim*; it is also produced in Turkey and by Turkish dairy corporations in Western European countries with a sizeable Turkish immigrant population. To complicate things further, similar cheese products can be found in Lebanon and Syria. Halloumi is one of the food items of the areas of the former Ottoman Empire that share messy genealogies and lack clearcut territorial connections. Such products – like jelly confections made of fruit juices, rose water, and almonds known variously as *loukoumi* or *lokum* – instil a feeling of cultural belonging but cannot easily be mapped according to the idea of *terroir* that assumes isomorphic relations of product, people, and place.

In 2008, Turkish Cypriot dairy companies went to court in an attempt to halt the process of the halloumi application submitted by the Republic of Cyprus to the European Commission, demanding acknowledgement of the fact that this is not an exclusively Greek Cypriot product. Only when their complaint was judged irrelevant by the Greek Cypriot administrative court, could the application be finalized and submitted to the European Commission. At the date of the writing of this chapter, the decision of the European Commission is still pending. The last chapter in the long saga of safeguarding halloumi as a traditional product has not been written yet.

Conclusion: Material Culture and European Products

As Stefan Beck and Leonore Scholze-Irrlitz recently pointed out, with the PDO/PGI system, the EU is deploying

> [the] idea of cultural diversity as a means to erect a homogeneous space of governance by cultivating these cultural differences and regional traditions; instead of internal homogenisation which was the project of the modern nation state, the EU project is about the harmonisation of preserved cultural difference. (Beck and Scholze-Irrlitz in press:7)

The authors assert that the promotion of diversity serves economic ends while it also helps gain support and wider acceptance for EU policies among European citizens. When "people become Europeans, their identities no longer turn around categories of religion, folk, or national defense but around categories of exchange, difference, and value" (Borneman and Fowler 1997:492). Europeanization challenged anthropology to enter into lively debates on modernity, subjectivity, power, and the state. The anthropology of Europeanization for many years was particularly interested in how the institutional policies from above, prescribing a pan-European identity for a unified European citizenry, are actually received and understood by the population of EU member states. Cultural heritages and cultural policies, notions of belonging, symbols of inclusion, and representations of history and collective memory, both on the national and the European levels, became important topics of studies of European identity formation and identity politics (Bellier and Wilson 2000; Shore 2000). However, the cultural dimension of Europeanization is not to be found only in identity formation and identity politics. The technologies of power that are – in a quite literal sense – at work in Europe in the form of legislation, regulation, and standards come to bear on everyday life. Here, protocols, quality-control mechanisms, and monitoring bodies create new relationships between people and the material world. An anthropology of Europeanization misses its target if it remains restricted to a notion of the cultural as the management of meanings, instituted from above and resisted and subverted from below. The cultural dimension of Europeanization is not to be found only in notions of belonging, symbols of inclusions, or representations of history and collective memory. The culture of the EU's Europe is at least, or perhaps even more so, evident in the material and immaterial artifacts it produces. Children's toys that comply with the EU's consumer safety laws, new Bachelor and Masters degrees at European public universities that measure workloads of students and professors according to the European Credit Transfer and Accumulation System, permitted levels of microdust air pollution that, if superseded, force administrative action prohibiting large vehicle traffic in metropolitan areas, nature conservation areas called Nature 2000 sites listed according to the EU's habitats directive, or cheese awarded with a PDO label, are all European products. They are products that would not exist without the regulatory practices of the European Commission. Far from being standardized across Europe, these are artifacts that have been constructed locally or nationally in compliance with EU legislation, taking different shapes but all affected, or, one might even say, impregnated by the EU. The food sector is far from exempt – indeed, it appears as an exemplary case of the power of European regulatory regimes.

REFERENCES

Beck, Stefan, and Leonore Scholze-Irrlitz

In press Microbiopolitical Regimes and the Co-constitution of the *Homo europaeus*. *In* Imagined Europeans. Matthias Middell, ed. Leipzig: Universitätsverlag.

Bellier, Irène, and Thomas Wilson, eds.

2000 The Anthropology of the European Union: Building, Imagining, Experiencing Europe. Oxford: Berg.

Bendix, Regina, and Alois Wierlacher, eds.

2008 Kulinaristik: Forschung – Lehre – Praxis. Münster: LIT.

Bérard, Laurence, Marie Cegarra, Marcel Djama, Sélim Louafi, Philippe Marchenay, Bernard Roussel, and Francois Verdeauc, eds.

2005 Biodiversity and Local Ecological Knowledge in France. Paris: INRA/CIRAD.

Bérard, Laurence, and Philippe Marchenay

2007 Localized Products in France: Definition, Protection and Value-Adding. *In* From Local Food to Localised Food. Theme issue. Anthropology of Food. S2 March. At http://aof.revues.org/index415.html (accessed December 18, 2011).

Bergeaud-Blackler, Florence, and Maria Paola Ferretti

2006 More Politics, Stronger Consumers? A New Division of Responsibility for Food in the European Union. Appetite 47:134–142.

Bernstein, Julia
2010 Food for Thought: Contested Affiliations of Russian-Speaking Jewish Migrants in Israel and Germany: A Study of Everyday Life and Food Practices. Frankfurt am Main: Campus Verlag.
Borneman, John, and Nick Fowler
1997 Europeanization. Annual Review of Anthropology 26:478–514.
Bourdieu, Pierre
1984 Distinction: A Social Critique of the Judgement of Taste. London: Routledge and Kegan Paul.
Braudel, Fernand
1996 The Mediterranean and the Mediterranean World in the Age of Philip II, vol. I. Berkeley: University of California Press.
Çaglar, Ayse S.
1999 McKebap: Döner Kebap and the Social Positioning Struggle of German Turks. *In* Changing Food Habits: Case Studies from Africa, South America and Europe. Carola Lentz, ed. pp. 263–283. Amsterdam: Harwood Academic.
Commission of the European Communities
2000 White Paper on Food Safety. Brussels, 12 January 2000, COM (1999) 719 final. http://ec.europa.eu/food/food/intro/white_paper_en.htm (accessed December 18, 2011).
Cook, Ian, and Philip Crang
1996 The World on a Plate: Culinary Culture, Displacement and Geographical Knowledges. Journal of Material Culture 1:131–153.
Counihan, Carole
1997 Bread as World: Food Habits and Social Relations in Modernizing Sardinia. *In* Food and Culture: A Reader. Carole Counihan and Penny Van Esterik, eds. pp. 283–295. London: Routledge.
Counihan, Carole, and Penny Van Esterik, eds.
1997 Food and Culture: A Reader. London: Routledge.
Douglas, Mary
1971 Deciphering a Meal. *In* Myth, Symbol, and Culture. Clifford Geertz, ed. pp. 61–82. New York: Norton.
Dunn, Elizabeth C.
2005 Standards and Person-Making in East Central Europe. *In* Global Assemblages. Technology, Politics, and Ethics as Anthropological Problems. Aihwa Ong and Stephen J. Collier, eds. pp. 173–193. Oxford: Blackwell.
Elias, Norbert
1994 The Civilizing Process: The History of Manners and State Formation and Civilization. Oxford: Blackwell.
European Agricultural Product Quality Policy
2009 DOOR Database. Electronic document. http://ec.europa.eu/agriculture/quality/ (accessed November 5, 2011).
European Commission
2004 From Farm to Fork: Safe Food for Europe's Consumers. European Commission, Directorate-General for Press and Communication July 2004. Luxembourg: Office for Official Publications of the European Communities. Electronic document. http://ec.europa.eu/publications/booklets/move/46/en.pdf (accessed November 5, 2011).
Foucault, Michel
2007 Security, Territory, Population: Lectures at the Collège de France. Basingstoke: Palgrave Macmillan.

Gibbs, Paul, Ria Morphitou, and George Savva
2004 Halloumi: Exporting to Retain Traditional Food Products. British Food Journal 106(7):569–576.
Gideon, Sigfried
1969 Mechanization Takes Command: A Contribution to Anonymous History. New York: Norton.
Goody, Jack
1982 Cooking, Cuisine and Class: A Study in Comparative Sociology. Cambridge: Cambridge University Press.
1997 Industrial Food: Towards the Development of a World Cuisine. *In* Food and Culture: A Reader. Carole Counihan and Penny Van Esterik, eds. pp. 338–356. London: Routledge.
Grasseni, Cristina
2005 Slow Food, Fast Genes: Timescapes of Authenticity and Innovation in the Anthropology of Food. *In* Creativity or Temporality. Theme issue. Cambridge Anthropology 25(2):79–94.
2008 Developing Skill, Developing Vision: Practices of Locality at the Foot of the Alps. Oxford: Berghahn.
Guide to Community Regulations
2004 Protection of Geographical Indications of Origin and Certificates of Specific Character for Agricultural Products and Foodstuffs. Working Document of the Commission Services. European Commission, Directorate-General for Agriculture, Food Quality Policy of the European Union. 2nd edition, August 2004. Electronic document. http://ec.europa.eu/agriculture/publi/gi/broch_en.pdf (accessed November 5, 2011).
Halkier, Bente, and Lotte Holm
2006 Shifting Responsibilities for Food Safety in Europe: An Introduction. Appetite 47:127–133.
Harbottle, Lynn
1997 Taste and Embodiment: The Food Preferences of Iranians in Britain. *In* Food Preferences and Taste: Continuity and Change. Helen Macbeth, ed. pp. 175–186. Oxford: Berghahn.
Harris, Marvin
1975 Cows, Pigs, Wars, and Witches: The Riddles of Culture. New York: Random House.
Herzfeld, Michael
2004 The Body Impolitic: Artisans and Artifice in the Global Hierarchy of Value. Chicago: University of Chicago Press.
Hirschfelder, Gunther
2001 Europäische Esskultur: Eine Geschichte der Ernährung von der Steinzeit bis heute. Frankfurt am Main: Campus.
Hobsbawm, Eric
1992 Mass-Producing Traditions: Europe, 1870–1914. *In* The Invention of Tradition. Eric Hobsbawm and Terence Ranger, eds. pp. 263–306. Cambridge: Cambridge University Press.
Holm, Lotte
1997 Food and Identity among Families in Copenhagen: A Review of an Interview Study. *In* Essen und kulturelle Identität: Europäische Perspektiven. Hans Jürgen Teuteberg, Gerhard Neumann and Alois Wierlacher, eds. pp. 356–371. Series Kulturthema Essen, 2. Berlin: Akademie.
Karn, Catharina
2009 Sicher vom Acker bis zum Teller: Die EU-Verordnung zur Lebensmittelsicherheit und ihre alltagspraktischen Auswirkungen auf hessischen Bauernhöfen. *In* Projekte der

Europäisierung. Kulturanthropologische Forschungsperspektiven. Gisela Welz and Annina Lottermann, eds. pp. 163–178. Kulturanthropologie Notizen, 78. Frankfurt am Main: Institut für Kulturanthropologie und Europäische Ethnologie.

Lawson, Paul A, Photis Papademas, Carmen Wacher, Enevold Falsen, Richard Robinson, and Matthew D. Collins

2001 Lactobacillus cypricasei sp.nov., Isolated from Halloumi Cheese. International Journal of Systematic and Evolutionary Microbiology 51:45–49.

Leitch, Alison

2003 Slow Food and the Politics of Pork Fat: Italian Food and European Identity. Ethnos 68(4):437–462.

Lévi-Strauss, Claude

1965 Le Triangle culinaire. L'Arc 2:9–22.

Lysaght, Patricia, ed.

1998 Food and the Traveller: Migration, Immigration, Tourism and Ethnic Food. Proceedings of the 11th Conference of the International Commission for Ethnological Food Research. Nicosia: Intercollege Press.

Mennell, Stephen

1985 All Manners of Food: Eating and Taste in England and France from the Middle Ages to the Present. Oxford: Oxford University Press.

1997 The Culinary Culture of Europe Overseas. *In* Essen und kulturelle Identität: Europäische Perspektiven. Hans Jürgen Teuteberg, Gerhard Neumann, and Alois Wierlacher, eds. pp. 459–464. Series Kulturthema Essen, 2. Berlin: Akademie.

Mintz, Sidney W.

1985 Sweetness and Power: The Place of Sugar in Modern History. New York: Viking Penguin.

2003 Eating Communities: The Mixed Appeals of Sodality. *In* Eating Culture: The Poetics and Politics of Food. Tobias Döring, Markus Heide, and Susanne Mühleisen, eds. pp. 19–34. Heidelberg: Universitätsverlag Winter.

Mohrmann, Ruth E., ed.

2008 Kulturhistorische Nahrungsforschung in Europa: Festschrift für Günter Wiegelmann zum 80. Geburtstag. Theme issue. Rheinisch-Westfälische Zeitschrift für Volkskunde, 53.

Niewöhner, Jörg, Christoph Kehl, and Stefan Beck

2008 Wie geht Kultur unter die Haut – und wie kann man dies beobachtbar machen? *In* Wie geht Kultur unter die Haut? Emergente Praxen an der Schnittstelle von Medizin, Lebens- und Sozialwissenschaft. Jörg Niewöhner, Christoph Kehl, and Stefan Beck, eds. pp. 9–29. Bielefeld: Transcript.

Pang, Ching Lin

2003 Beyond "Authenticity": Reinterpreting Chinese Immigrant Food in Belgium. *In* Eating Culture: The Poetics and Politics of Food. Tobias Döring, Markus Heide, and Susanne Mühleisen, eds. pp. 53–70. Heidelberg: Universitätsverlag Winter.

Papademas, Photis, and Richard Robinson

2001 The Sensory Characteristics of Different Types of Halloumi Cheese as Perceived by Tasters of Different Ages. International Journal of Dairy Technology 54(3):94–99.

Paxson, Heather

2005 Slow Food in a Fat Society: Satisfying Ethical Appetites. Gastronomica 5(1):14–18.

2006 Artisanal Cheese and Economies of Sentiment in New England. *In* Fast Food/Slow Food: The Cultural Economy of the Global Food System. Richard Wilk, ed. pp. 201–217. Lanham, MD: Altamira.

Petrini, Carlo
2001 Slow Food: Le ragioni del gusto. Roma: Editori Laterza.
Pratt, Jeff
2007 Food Values: The Local and the Authentic. Critique of Anthropology 27:285–300.
Ritzer, George
1993 The McDonaldization of Society: An Investigation into the Changing Character of Contemporary Social Life. Thousand Oaks, CA: Pine Forge.
Römhild, Regina, Christian Abresch, Michaela Nietert, and Gunvor Schmidt, eds.
2008 Fast Food, Slow Food: Ethnographische Studien zum Verhältnis von Globalisierung und Regionalisierung in der Ernährung. Kulturanthropologie Notizen, 76. Frankfurt am Main: Institut für Kulturanthropologie und Europäische Ethnologie.
Salomonsson, Karin
2002 The E-economy and the Culinary Heritage. Ethnologia Europaea 32(2):125–144.
Shore, Cris
2000 Building Europe: The Cultural Politics of European Integration. London: Routledge.
Strathern, Marilyn, ed.
2000 Audit Cultures. Anthropological Studies in Accountability, Ethics, and the Academy. London: Routledge.
Sutton, David
2001 Remembrance of Repasts: An Anthropology of Food and Memory. Oxford: Berg.
Tanner, Jakob
1999 Fabrikmahlzeit: Ernährungswissenschaft, Industriearbeit und Volksernährung in der Schweiz 1890–1950. Zürich: Chronos.
2004 The Arts of Cooking: Modern Times and the Dynamics of Tradition. *In* Changing Tastes: Food Culture and the Processes of Industrialization. Patricia Lysaght and Christine Burckhardt-Seebass, eds. pp. 18–35. Basel: Schweizerische Gesellschaft für Volkskunde and Department of Irish Folklore, University College Dublin.
Terrio, Susan J.
2005 Crafting Grand Cru Chocolates in Contemporary France. *In* The Cultural Politics of Food and Eating: A Reader. James L. Watson and Melissa L. Caldwell, eds. pp. 144–162. Oxford: Blackwell.
Teuteberg, Hans Jürgen, ed.
1992 European Food History: A Research Review. Leicester: Leicester University Press.
Teuteberg, Hans-Jürgen
2008 Kulturhistorische Ernährungsforschungen: Ziele, Theorien und Methoden seit dem 19. Jahrhundert. *In* Kulturhistorische Nahrungsforschung in Europa. Festschrift für Günter Wiegelmann zum 80. Geburtstag. Theme issue. Rheinisch-Westfälische Zeitschrift für Volkskunde, 53:17–45.
Teuteberg, Hans Jürgen, Gerhard Neumann, and Alois Wierlacher, eds.
1997 Essen und kulturelle Identität: Europäische Perspektiven. Reihe Kulturthema Essen, 2. Berlin: Akademie.
Tolksdorf, Ulrich
2000[1988] Nahrungsforschung. *In* Grundriß der Volkskunde: Einführung in die Arbeits-fel-der der Europäischen Ethnologie. Rolf Wilhelm Brednich, ed. pp. 171–184. Berlin: Reimer.
Tschofen, Bernhard
2007 Vom Geschmack der Regionen: Kulinarische Praxis, europäische Politik und räumliche Kultur – eine Forschungsskizze. Zeitschrift für Volkskunde 103(2):169–95.
Watson, James L., ed.
1997 Golden Arches East: McDonald's in East Asia. Stanford: Stanford University Press.

Watson, James L., and Melissa L. Caldwell, eds.
2005 The Cultural Politics of Food and Eating: A Reader. Oxford: Blackwell.
Welz, Gisela
2006 Europäisierung als qualkulatives Regime. *In* Turn to Europe: Kulturanthropologische Europaforschungen. Kerstin Poehls and Asta Vonderau, eds. pp. 11–26. Berliner Blätter: Ethnographische und ethnologische Beiträge, 41. Münster: LIT.
2007 Europäische Produkte: Nahrungskulturelles Erbe und EU-Politik. Am Beispiel der Republik Zypern. *In* Prädikat "HERITAGE": Wertschöpfungen aus kulturellen Ressourcen. Dorothee Hemme, Markus Tauschek, and Regina Bendix, eds. pp. 323–336. Studien zur Kulturanthropologie and Europäischen Ethnologie, 1. Münster: LIT.
Welz, Gisela, and Nicholas Andilios
2004 Modern Methods for Producing the Traditional: The Case of Making Halloumi Cheese in Cyprus. *In* Changing Tastes: Food Culture and the Processes of Industrialization. Patricia Lysaght and Christine Burckhardt-Seebass, eds. pp. 217–230. Basel: Schweizerische Gesellschaft für Volkskunde and Department of Irish Folklore, University College Dublin.
Wiegelmann, Günter
2006[1967] Alltags- und Festspeisen: Wandel und gegenwärtige Stellung. Münster: Waxmann.
Wilk, Richard, ed.
2006 Fast Food/Slow Food: The Cultural Economy of the Global Food System. Lanham, MD: Altamira.
Wilson, Thomas M., ed.
2006 Food, Drink and Identity in Europe. European Studies: An Interdisciplinary Series in European Culture, History and Politics, 22. Amsterdam: Rodopi.

CHAPTER 22

Language, Power, and Politics in Europe

Máiréad Nic Craith

"Language" was invented in Europe.

(Gal 2006:14)

While speaking is a natural condition of the human being, the idea that we speak particular, named, recognizable languages such as French, Irish, or German may be a legacy of the European Enlightenment and the concurrent Romantic movement. A process of standardization over the last two centuries has meant that we accept particular forms of speech as standard and legitimate and reject others as "not quite there." In this, we are adopting a "culture of standardization" (Silverstein 1996:285). This European "invention" has generated enormous challenges for organizations such as the European Union (EU) and the Council of Europe – institutional structures themselves heavily reliant on a cultural construct called "Europe." The primary focus in this chapter is on the way these institutional structures deal with concepts of language and the linguistic communities that speak these languages.

The multilingual mosaic is one of the biggest challenges facing the EU today. In 2011, there are currently 23 official and working languages within the organization: Bulgarian, Czech, Danish, Dutch, English, Estonian, Finnish, French, German, Greek, Hungarian, Irish, Italian, Latvian, Lithuanian, Maltese, Polish, Portuguese, Romanian, Slovak, Slovenian, Spanish, and Swedish. This number is likely to increase with each new accession. These languages have emerged from three different language families: Finno-Ugric, Indo-European, and Semitic. There are three alphabets in the EU: Cyrillic, Greek, and Latin. As well as these, there are more than 60 minority, indigenous, or regional language communities in the EU. Some of these, such as Sámi, Sorbian, or Basque, have official status at local level. In addition to these, millions of people speak contested languages and dialects and regularly seek legitimacy and greater "cultural capital" for these languages (Bourdieu 1991). Immigrant communities enrich Europe's linguistic landscape with a range of languages still

A Companion to the Anthropology of Europe, First Edition. Edited by Ullrich Kockel, Máiréad Nic Craith, and Jonas Frykman.

thought of as "non-European" and Europe's cultural bricolage is increasingly complex (Nic Craith 2006).

The overall response of the EU to this challenge is defined by a quest for commonality and a strategy of finding unity in Europe's diversity. However, given the complexity of the picture, this overarching strategy is not easily implemented and is not always welcome. From a positive perspective, the motto "unity in diversity" can be interpreted as an attempt to bring together, recognize, and legitimize the full range of Europe's cultures and languages. From a contrary perspective, a cynic could argue that the strategy is simply an appropriation of power to the center. European culture, in this context, is defined as the "over-arching, encapsulating and transcendent composite of national cultures; a whole greater than the sum of its discordant parts" (Shore 2000:54).

The Herderian Model of Language

National, state languages have had privileged status within the EU since the beginning. In 1958, the first European Community regulation on official languages was passed. It identified four languages, Dutch, French, German, and Italian, as the official and working languages of the Economic Community. These were the national languages of the six member states at that time: France, Italy, Belgium, Netherlands, Luxembourg, and West Germany. Since then the number of official and working languages has increased to 23. As each new nation-state joins, its official language acquires official and working-language status within the EU. However, there are more states than languages in the EU as some states share common languages. These include Belgium where Dutch, French, and German are spoken and Cyprus where the majority of the population speaks Greek which already has official and working status.

This privileging of a "national language" is commonly traced back to the influence of ethnologists and folklorists such as Herder and the Grimm brothers who emphasized the significance of the German *Volk* and their culture. In particular they were interested in the German language and its folk narratives as an expression of German character (Humboldt 1988[1836]). In *Über den Ursprung der Sprache*, Herder put forward the argument that the ancestral tongue of a people was crucial for their sense of well-being. The traditional language was the key mechanism for accessing the core of a group and helped preserve their identity and cohesion. Every nation was unique and that specificity was reflected in its language (Herder 1770). This Herderian model of language contrasts sharply with other models, which focus on language as process rather than object. For scholars such as Gumperez, Hymes, and others, "the (Herderian) category of 'language' is not a natural fact, it is a folk construct, a product of institutional and cultural processes of standardization" (Gal 2006:17).

The standardization of particular languages as legitimate has dominated the linguistic landscape on the European continent. In her *Community and Communication*, the anthropologist Sue Wright (2000) has explored the significance of language in nation-states and the role of these national languages in the process of European integration. Wright's volume explores three European models of nation-building – namely assimilation, blood and belonging, and fragmentation. France is the classic example of the first of these models and the process of assimilation has been very lengthy. Germany and Italy are the standard examples of these models of nationalism which give priority to "'blood' and language" (Wright 2000:41). Fragmentation (or Balkanization) is the third model of nationalism identified by Wright. It is most clearly found in the reconstruction of Europe that occurred after World War I when a number of nation-states emerged from the ruins of the Austro-Hungarian, Russian, and Turkish empires.

When giving official working status to a new entrant, the EU does not consider any linguistic histories, criteria, or credentials. Instead it simply accepts the national status of a state's language and proceeds to reaffirm this legitimacy by conferring official, working status on the new member's national language. Initially this strategy appeared straightforward but difficulties arose with each enlargement and the context became particularly ambiguous with the accession of Ireland along with Denmark and the United Kingdom in 1973.

When Ireland became a member of the European Economic Community (EEC), its government did not seek working status for Irish and proceeded to advise the EC against granting the status of a working language to Irish Gaelic (Ó Murchú 1992; Nic Craith 1994). One can only speculate as to their reasons for this. As almost everybody in Ireland speaks English as their first language, it is possible that Irish politicians did not wish to overburden EEC administrators with translation duties. It is also possible that "cultural cringe" was a factor here. As a postcolonial country, Ireland was still suffering from a sense of shame in its native culture, a byproduct of centuries of colonization. For whatever reason, the Irish request left EU parliamentarians in a quandary and a special status of treaty language had to be invented to accommodate Irish.

This "special status" for Irish seriously diminished its cultural and economic capital in a European context. In the first instance, it represented a loss of employment opportunities in Brussels for Irish-speakers in the field of translation. More significantly, it denied many bilingual speakers in Ireland of EEC job opportunities in other fields as knowledge of two languages, Irish and English, did not fulfil the basic requirement of two official and working languages necessary for employment in these European institutions. Following a vigorous campaign by Irish speakers at the turn of the millennium, the ambiguous position of Irish was revisited and Irish was given the status of an official working language in 2005. This status position has applied since January 2007.

The Irish faux pas of 1973 should be set in the context of another controversy that erupted in relation to Denmark. When Denmark joined the EU at this time, the addition of Danish and consequent increase in the number of official working languages generated concern from certain quarters. Arguments were made for restricting the number of official languages. The Danes agreed to this and the exclusion of Danish from this group on one condition – that no individual parliamentarian was permitted to use his or her mother tongue in EU institutions. This proposal illustrated the genuine difficulties that would be experienced by people operating in their second rather than in their first language. It would ensure that all members were equally disadvantaged. Both the British and the French rejected the idea and Danish was giving official, working status without further controversy (Wright 2000).

With subsequent accessions of new members to the EU, the increase in the number of official working languages has continued to raise hackles. Between 1979 and 1982, a number of individual members of the European Parliament and parliamentary committees reviewed the language issue and expressed alarm at the prospect of additional new working languages within the institutions. Proponents on all sides were probably operating from a position of sincerity with a genuine concern to promote democratic principles. However they differed in their assessment of the principles of democracy. Those arguing for a curtailment on the number of official, working languages were genuinely anxious that European multilingual institutions would collapse under the burden of translation. Those against restricting the number of official languages pointed to the importance of ensuring that such institutions would continue to be relevant for ordinary individuals. This could hardly be achieved if the institutions operated in a language these individuals did not understand (Phillipson 2003).

Official status as EU working languages has major implications for language standing and employment. For this reason, Croatian delegates insisted on official status for Croatian during talks on their country's proposed accession to the EU in 2013. Privately, there were concerns that some members would prefer the admission of a single hybrid language known as BCS (Bosnian, Croatian, and Serbian), which is used in The Hague at the UN's International Criminal Tribunal. However, EU legislation on the issue is clear and the Croatian language will become the 24th official working language on Croatia's entry to the EU.

Language and Power

The process of increasing the number of official, working languages has always proved controversial for speakers of languages designated as "regional" or "minority." The current EU strategy ensures that "smaller" languages such as Estonian, Irish, Latvian, and Maltese benefit from official, working status whereas Catalan, with speakers of many millions, is excluded from this elite club. All of these official working languages enjoy considerably greater status than that of regional or minority languages. In modern society, the national culture has emerged as the "natural repository of political legitimacy" and the national language plays a vital role in that context (Gellner 1983:55).

While the distinction between majority and minority languages in the Western world is often perceived (incorrectly) as referring to relative numerical size, it is more appropriate to think of it in terms of access to power (Nelde et al. 1996: Skutnabb-Kangas 2000). The main, substantive difference between dominant and minority languages relates to rights, privileges, and resources. The primary factor uniting speakers of minority languages is that they do not have majority standing in established nation-states and have not benefitted from centuries of state language planning and investment. In consequence, their position is low and their privileges few.

A small number of anthropologists have conducted separate and independent research on minority language communities. For example, Malcolm Chapman's *The Gaelic Vision in Scottish Culture* explored the major differences between Gaelic and English spheres in the Highlands and Islands of Scotland (Chapman 1978). Chapman examined the confrontation between Highland and Lowland Scotland and gave careful consideration to the understanding of the "folk" in contemporary Gaelic society. Sharon Macdonald (contributor to this volume) conducted a more recent ethnographic investigation of Scottish Gaelic culture and language (Macdonald 1997). Her fieldwork was carried out in the community of "Carnan" (a pseudonym) on Skye and her focus was on the potential for imagining and reimagining Gaelic identity at a time of renewed interest in Gaelic cultural identities. Generally speaking, Gaelic culture is not perceived as a threat to the unity of the British state. It enjoys a position of more benign neglect rather than active promotion or suppression.

More often than not, regional or minority languages are constructed as problematic – as "obstacles to the political project of nation-building – as threats to the 'unity' of the state – thus providing the *raison d'être* for the consistent derogation, diminution and ascription of minority languages that have characterised the last three centuries of nationalism" (May 2005:213). A number of anthropologists and ethnologists have conducted fieldwork in these contexts. Woolard, for example, has explored the politics of ethnicity in Catalonia (Woolard 1989). Kockel (1999), Urla (1993), Echeverria (2003), and others have conducted fieldwork on the Basque situation. One of the more controversial case studies has been the work of Maryon McDonald (contributor to this volume) in Brittany, a context which she has described as bristling "with political sensibilities" (McDonald 1989:1). McDonald's fieldwork investigated Breton identity in the 1980s with particular reference to Breton movements, language, and education.

A number of anthropologists have explored an equally complex case study in Northern Ireland where the nationalist community often uses the phrase "our own language" to denote the importance of Irish for the sense of identity. Since the foundation of the Northern Irish state in the early decades of the twentieth century, speakers of Irish there have suffered varying degrees of neglect, hostility, and sometimes downright suppression. When the "Troubles" began some four decades ago, the Irish language acquired a new profile among activists seeking separation from the United Kingdom. O'Reilly's fieldwork investigated the three different discourses adopted by individuals and institutions in their quest to gain status for the language (O'Reilly 1999).

Although membership of the EU has primarily benefitted official, working languages, there have been some initiatives for promoting regional or minority language policy (Nic Shuibhne 2002). European Parliament resolutions in the field fall into two categories. Before the turn of the millennium, the Parliament offered support funding for initiatives and projects which were designed to promote minority languages. It has also provided support for various organizations such as the European Bureau for Lesser Used Languages and the Mercator information network which are devoted to encouraging speakers of these languages.

Perhaps the most significant initiative in the field has been the Council of Europe's Charter for Regional and Minority Languages (Council of Europe 1992). This charter pertains to languages that are "traditionally used within a given territory of a State by nationals of that State who form a group numerically smaller than the rest of the State's population," and to those that are "different from the official language(s) of the State." It formally came into force in March 1998.

There are two levels of commitment to the charter. A signature commits a member state to principles of respect as set out in the initial sections of the charter. States signing the charter are not necessarily obliged to these principles for every single minority language spoken within national boundaries. Instead they can identify the languages which they wish to support in the first instance and are free to extend the number of nominated languages at a later stage.

A more significant commitment is the ratification of the charter. With ratification, a participating state agrees to implement a number of measures designed to enhance and promote regional and minority languages in the public space. At the time of writing, a total of 33 states have signed or ratified the charter (see Table 22.1). Of these, 25 have actually ratified and brought the charter into force. The remaining 8 have not yet proceeded to this stage – and may not necessarily do so. (Of notable

Table 22.1 Nation-states that have signed or ratified the ECRML (February 2011) (based on http://conventions.coe.int/).

Member state	*Signature*	*Ratification*	*Entry into force*
Armenia	11/05/2001	25/01/2002	01/05/2002
Austria	05/11/1992	28/06/2001	01/10/2001
Azerbaijan	21/12/2001		
Bosnia and Herzegovina	07/09/2005	21/09/2010	01/01/2011
Croatia	05/11/1997	05/11/1997	01/03/1998
Cyprus	12/11/1992	26/08/2002	01/12/2002
Czech Republic	09/11/2000	15/11/2006	01/03/2007
Denmark	05/11/1992	08/09/2000	01/01/2001
Finland	05/11/1992	09/11/1994	01/03/1998
France	07/05/1999		
Germany	05/11/1992	16/09/1998	01/01/1999
Hungary	05/11/1992	26/04/1995	01/03/1998
Iceland	07/05/1999		
Italy	27/06/2000		
Liechtenstein	05/11/1992	18/11/1997	01/03/1998
Luxembourg	05/11/1992		
Malta	05/11/1992		
Moldova	11/07/2002		
Montenegro	22/03/2005	15/02/2006	06/06/2006
Netherlands	05/11/1992	02/05/1996	01/03/1998
Norway	05/11/1992	10/11/1993	01/03/1998
Poland	12/05/2003	12/02/2009	01/06/2009
Romania	17/07/1995	29/01/2008	01/05/2008
Russia	10/05/2001		
Serbia	22/03/2005	15/02/2006	01/06/2006
Slovakia	20/02/2001	05/09/2001	01/01/2002
Slovenia	03/07/1997	04/10/2000	01/01/2001
Spain	05/11/1992	09/04/2001	01/08/2001
Sweden	09/02/2000	09/02/2000	01/06/2000
Switzerland	08/10/1993	23/12/1997	01/04/1998
FYR of Macedonia	25/07/1996		
Ukraine	02/05/1996	19/09/2005	01/01/2006
United Kingdom	02/03/2000	27/03/2001	01/07/2001

interest here are the examples of Caucasian states such as Azerbaijan who have joined this European club!)

The charter offers a measure of linguistic standing for speakers of those regional or minority languages that are included within its terms of reference. It also provides a transnational context for regional speech communities. This international platform offers opportunities for speakers of minority languages to work with language partners across national boundaries. As the European Charter offers some relief from the national context, it is generally viewed as an opportunity rather than a threat.

Rootedness and Territory

The introduction to the charter's explanatory notes focuses on the issue of territory. It states that "many European countries have on their territory regionally based autochthonous groups speaking a language other than that of the majority of the population." This is explained in terms of "historical processes whereby the formation of states has not taken place on purely language-related lines." As a result smaller language communities have been divided and/or surrounded by larger ones.

Minority languages covered by the Charter are primarily those which can be identified as belonging to a specific region or territory. Cultures and languages are usually identified with a particular place but this is not necessarily helpful for groups that have maintained nomadic lifestyles over the centuries and regarded state territorial boundaries as irrelevant. Such groups "could teach us how meaningless frontiers are: careless of boundaries, Romanies and Sinti are at home all over Europe. They are what we claim to be: born Europeans" (Grass 1992:108).

Non-territorial languages are defined in the Charter as those spoken "by nationals of the State which differ from the language or languages used by the rest of the State's population, but which, although traditionally used within the territory of the State, cannot be identified with a particular area thereof." The explanatory notes suggest that there would be a great difficulty in dealing with languages that are not associated with particular places since most of the measures proposed in the Charter require the definition of a territorial or geographical field which is not coterminous with the state as a whole.

While the charter excludes "non-territorial languages" from the category of regional and minority languages, it advocates that languages traditionally used on state territories by citizens of a state could be included on a limited basis and specifically suggests Romani as an example. Although it might prove complicated to apply the provisions of Part III to non-territorial languages like Romani or Cant, there should be far less difficulty in applying the principles of respect and dignity as contained in Part II.

When signing the charter, many countries deliberately included specific non-territorial languages within its terms of reference. Norway and Sweden, for example, incorporated the Sámi languages within the terms of reference of the charter. Several nation-states have afforded formal recognition to the languages of the Roma. These are Austria, Bosnia and Herzegovina, the Czech Republic, Finland, Germany, the

Netherlands, Poland, Romania, Serbia and Montenegro, Slovenia, and Sweden. Yiddish is included within the terms of reference of Bosnia and Herzegovina, the Netherlands, Poland, Romania, and Sweden. Interestingly, Cyprus and Poland take in Armenian under the rubric of "non-territorial" as defined in the charter while Poland also includes Hebrew and Karaim.

In the past, those with nomadic lifestyles were often omitted or neglected in international covenants or charters. Communities are generally perceived to have a "shared location" and those who cannot be identified with a particular place are not necessarily perceived as legitimate. But it would be an error to assume that nomadic peoples such as Travelers lack a sense of community. Instead it seems that their concept of community is different. "All Travellers owe allegiance to the greater 'community' of Travellers" (Binchy 1994:149–50). Travelers themselves make the point that the concept of "Traveler" is essentially one of community. "To be a Traveller is to be part of a community." When settled people focus on the concept of "Traveler," they immediately think of mobility, but that is not the essence of a Traveler. "Although being mobile is part of being a Traveller, it is not what a Traveller is. Being a Traveller means being part of a community that has a shared history, shared culture and an understanding of what it is like to be a Traveller. It's having a family with a support mechanism there" (McDonagh 2000a:28–9).

Nomadism generates a feeling of community rooted in a territory that is physically different from the immediate locale. It "entails a way of looking at the world, a different way of seeing things, a different attitude to accommodation, to work and to life in general" (McDonagh 2000b:34). Travelers employ a concept of mapping that is very different from conventional maps. They have "alternative spatial languages or 'tracings' of kinlines, tradelines and memory lines" and "negotiate a separate identity and sense of place" from the settled community.

Burke suggests that a Traveler's definition of the term "country" is "radically different from that which is understood by sedentary society." Essentially, "country" is understood as "a region characterised by family or cultural unities, not necessarily coinciding with country lines and not necessarily rural." Travelers engage with an alternative mapping system and identify houses with generous occupants for relatives and other Travelers by leaving sticks or rags in a particular manner called *patrin.* "Such non-textual modes of representation challenge sedentarist assumptions of what constitutes script" (Burke 2000:90).

The Sámi also have a singular relationship with the land and nature which provides the resources for both their material and spiritual cultural outlook. Over the centuries, the Sámi people adapted their lifestyle to the seasons of nature and the local natural environment, and their relationship with the land is reflected in their languages which have rich vocabularies for aspects of nature and reindeer in particular: "Dissimilar landscapes and ways of living create different concepts." In the case of reindeer husbandry, for example, one "will find a rich assortment of words and expressions which have arisen from the countryside, equipment and processes related to the work involved" (Valkeapää 1983:78).

For nomadic peoples such as the Sámi, individual ownership of the land has never been relevant and they did not require formal, institutional structures. From medieval times, the Sámi people organized themselves into villages or *siidas*, each with their communal territories. Members of different *siidas* enjoyed a system of fishing and hunting rights as well as feeding rights for the reindeer. Any land rights pertained to the extended family rather than the individual. Ultimately the lack of formal ownership of Sámi land was abused and Sámi land rights were gradually ignored, lost, or forgotten. At the beginning of the last century, Norwegian Sámi were regarded as a "landless" people. They were obliged to pay taxes but enjoyed no privileges – especially in relation to land ownership. "One country even adopted a law, according to which land could be owned only by citizens who both knew and used the Norwegian language" (Seurujärvi-Kari et al. 1997:30). However this situation is being readdressed and the special position of the Sámi people is reflected in their recognition as an indigenous population who existed in the Arctic Circle before the present state borders were established.

The concept of an indigenous people has gradually been marked in various documents to safeguard human rights as well as into national legislation in the Scandinavian states. The Norwegian government formally recognised the Sámi as an indigenous people in 1990 (Seurujärvi-Kari et al. 1997:2). Sámi themselves emphasize the concept of indigeneity in relation to language policy. They insist on the responsibility of Scandinavian national governments to the Sámi as an aboriginal people rather than as speakers of a regional or minority language. "For that reason the governments have a greater responsibility for Sámi language rights than they have for such minorities whose language preservation is based on the situation in their mother country" (Lehtola 2002:85).

On the Importance of Being European

While the territorial issue is a major challenge for the European Europe, the concept of indigenous and European is even more problematic. How does one define the languages of Europe? A non-linguist might innocently point to the Indo-European family of languages. This would include languages such as Proto-Albanian or Proto-Indo-Iranian and exclude languages such as Basque which have no connection with this language group. But I am not a linguist. Moreover, from an anthropological perspective, pointing to Indo-European languages is hardly satisfactory and includes many languages spoken well beyond the boundaries of either the EU or even the Council of Europe.

The issue of whether a language is European or not is important as languages deemed to be "non-European" do not derive any major recognition or resources from either the EU or the Council of Europe. This term "non-European" is frequently applied to languages such as Arabic, Bengali, Chinese (Mandarin, Cantonese, etc.), Hindi, and Urdu, and many other languages that are primarily spoken outside the geographical or political European entity. While there have always been speakers of these migrant languages in Europe, they have only emerged as community languages in recent decades, particularly in countries such as France, Germany, or Great Britain (Extra and Gorter 2001). Yet they are also significant languages spoken within the continent of Europe.

Although these languages are highly significant for a sense of identity among non-European immigrant groups and have recently acquired some limited recognition within various state systems of education, they are often perceived negatively by speakers of dominant languages and policy-makers who view their presence "as obstacles to integration." (This is precisely the argument that is often used against the promotion of minority languages in national contexts.)

Despite their period of residency in Europe, these immigrant groups are usually regarded as foreigners (*étrangers, ausländer*) who have not integrated. The terminology reflects the general assumption that as these people have no roots in Europe, they can hardly become "rooted" in the continent. While they live, work, and raise their children on the European continent, it is assumed that that they will maintain loyalty only to their "home" country. Such assumptions either refuse to recognize the existence of multiple or transnational identities or regard them as an obstacle to national and/or European integration. Yet composite loyalties are a feature of European as well as non-European immigrants in Europe. Research among Turkish and Moroccan communities in Brussels concluded that while immigrants shared a social-contract type of citizenship with Belgians, they also adhered to a more communal type of long-distance citizenship in their countries of origin (Phales and Swyngedouw 2002).

Sometimes it is argued that these are languages *in* but not *of* Europe, that is, they do not belong on the Continent. They belong "elsewhere." They are rooted "elsewhere." Examples here would include Turkish which is Germany's second language and the Sylheti dialect of Bengali which is now Wales' third language (Cheesman 2001:151–152). This argument illustrates the difficulty with Europe as a cultural construct which has always relied on a set of others to define itself. If the "other" is within, where does that leave the concept of Europe? The implication is that "other" will remain outside the cultural boundaries of Europe as they will eventually return home. In this context, Susan Gal (2006) makes an interesting distinction between speech and language communities. She argues that "migrant and diaspora populations are part of a European *speech* community." However, they are not perceived as belonging to the language communities of Europe. Instead "they are members of *language* communities of Hindi, Urdu, Indonesian, Turkish or Yoruba, speakers that have their highly valued, standardizing, centers outside of Europe" (Gal 2006:25, emphasis original).

With time, the criterion of indigeneity becomes increasingly difficult to sustain. As "non-European" languages are spoken by second- and third- rather than first-generation groups, the dividing line between "indigenous" and "non-indigenous" becomes less obvious. How does one define the concept of "European" and is there any point at which a "non-European" becomes part of the "European" family of languages? Can one raise these issues without becoming essentialist? These are questions, not just for anthropologists, but for politicians, policy-makers, and bureaucrats as the conclusions reached have implications for issues of recognition as well as of resources. This must be set in a context where speakers of contested languages and dialects are actively seeking language status and resources at national and transnational levels are stretched.

Non-European immigrants have been a feature of anthropological and ethnological research in Europe. (Nic Craith 2006) However, research on the languages spoken by these migrants is sparse and exceptional. One anthropologist that has addressed these questions is Ralph Grillo, who has explored immigrants and their languages in the United Kingdom and in France (Grillo 1989). A small number of other anthropological publications have focused on the impact of communicative abilities on the education of immigrant children in Europe. Researchers at the Free University of Berlin examined the educational conditions of Turkish migrant children in German schools (Alamdar-Niemannd et al. 1991). The authors conducted research on Turkish labor migrants in Germany and, in particular, on the situation of their children in German schools. They noted the practice of brokerage that had been raised in an earlier context by Grillo. Turkish pupils often regard themselves as competent speakers of the language – even though their language ability is hardly sufficient or appropriate for the purpose of the school curricula. However, their self-perception as competent speakers of German means that "from a very young age they help their parents by acting as translators in important family affairs (i.e., residence permit, authorities)" (Alamdar-Niemanndet al. 1991:157).

Not surprisingly these researchers found a direct link between language performance and educational achievement in schools and in many instances there is also a gender division. Turkish girls are hampered in their language development by lack of contact with German children of the same age. Moreover, it appears that Turkish girls are burdened with housework and strongly encouraged not to assimilate to the host society. At that time, Turkish children had few formal opportunities to learn their "mother tongue" in German schools.

Even where such opportunities are available, they are not necessarily helpful. Barbara Wolber, an anthropologist who conducted fieldwork among returning Turkish migrant families from Germany, found that the form of Turkish that children acquire in German schools is not necessarily appreciated in their country of origin. Language policy in Turkey has forbidden the use of particular expressions and introduced different elements into the language. This has led to a rapid transformation of the Turkish spoken in Turkey. As a result, Wolber found that many returnees to Turkey send their children to remedial classes where they relearn a more acceptable form of Turkish (Wolber 1991). It appears that returnee migrant children suffer a great deal of anxiety regarding language competence and social alienation.

Since these publications some 20 years ago, the occasional anthropologist has featured non-European immigrants and their languages in his or her research. Jan Blommaert has focused on African asylum seekers in Belgium (Blommaert 2001). Gabriele Marranci (contributor to this volume) has penned a number of publications concerning Muslim diaspora communities and their respective languages (Marranci 2003, 2006, 2007). However, there is still much research to be done in the field as a matter of urgency.

THE WAY FORWARD

It would not be possible within a single chapter to draw attention to the range and breadth of anthropological work in the field of languages in Europe and there are many other issues of contested languages and dialects which have been explored by anthropologists and ethnologists alike (Spindler 1973; Nic Craith 2000; Cavanagh 2009). Some fascinating research on contested cultural boundaries has been conducted by Povrzanović Frykman (contributor to this volume). Drawing on her own experiences of living in Sweden since 1998 as well as on her research on identity formations, Povrzanović Frykman contributes new ethnographic evidence on the contestation of Balkan identities and languages among the Balkan diaspora in Sweden (Povrzanović Frykman 2002). She illustrates the significance of language as a marker of identity and specificity among the diaspora. Most interestingly, she points to the quest for recognition of Croatian as a separate language – not just in Croatia but in those places where Croats live. Languages such as Croatian, Ulster-Scots, and others are competing for status, legitimacy, and resources in a transnational context and at an everyday level Europe is teeming with different languages, dialects, and worldviews.

While theoretically the EU regards all of these languages as a gift to humanity, the reality is that a small number of languages have come to dominate institutional proceedings and effectively the status of official, working language has become a two-tiered category. Due to time and budgetary constraints, it is argued that it is not feasible to translate every working document into every official working language. For this reason, the European Commission often employs English, French, and German as what it terms "procedural languages," while the European Parliament offers translation into other different languages when required.

Speakers of the other official languages generally do not object to the concept of "procedural languages" as their "equality" of status is theoretically guaranteed, although "there is a certain dishonesty in maintaining the fiction that the EU gives equal weight and respect to all official languages of the member states if, in reality, the languages which permit access to the European centers of power are one, perhaps two, dominant lingua francas: English and French" (Smith and Wright 1999:9). Effectively, a new hierarchy of state languages has emerged and some official, working languages are deemed more useful than others. However, in principle, the EU remains committed to the idea of multilingualism and pledges to promote mutual recognition and respect for the equal integrity of all national cultures (Habermas 2001).

The EU has highlighted the importance of all of its languages though several initiatives. The European Parliament declared 2001 as the "European Year of Languages." Subsequently, it published its *Action Plan* (2004–2006) which calls attention to the principle of "mother tongue plus two other languages" as the guiding principle for its citizens. The European Commission concluded that the range of foreign languages spoken by Europeans was narrow, and confined primarily to English, French, German, and Spanish. In consequence "member states agree that pupils should master at least two foreign languages, with the emphasis on effective communicative ability: active skills rather than passive knowledge" (Commission of the European Communities 2003:6).

Moreover, the *Action Plan* specified that efforts to acquire new languages should not be confined to the acquisition of official, working languages. Instead "the range on offer should include the smaller European languages as well as all the larger ones, regional, minority and migrant languages as well as those with 'national' status, and the languages of our major trading partners throughout the world" (Commission of the European Communities 2003:9). While new initiatives are laudable, a cynic could view them as a necessary stage before the formal reduction of the number of official, working languages of the EU. As long as citizens are primarily monolingual, the EU will be required to offer services in all national languages. If, however, most citizens are competent in two or three languages, then it might be feasible to reduce the number of official, working languages.

More recently, the EU published a council resolution on multilingualism in November 2008. Among other things, this resolution reaffirmed "linguistic and cultural diversity" as "part and parcel of the European identity." It suggested that multilingualism "is at once a shared heritage, a wealth, a challenge and an asset for Europe." It considered the "promotion of less widely used European languages" as representing "an important contribution to multilingualism." It also encouraged member states to "value and make use of the linguistic competences of citizens with migrant backgrounds, as a means of strengthening both intercultural dialogue and economic competitiveness" (Council of the European Union 2008).

While Europe's "tower of Babel" could be regarded as a distraction from the process of integration, the reality is that it is essential to the democratic process. As long as the EU aims to be a truly democratic organization, it must ensure that all of its citizens are communicated with in a language they actually understand. Otherwise, there will be a democratic deficit that will be insurmountable and the financial cost of multilingualism will seem very small indeed.

REFERENCES

Alamdar-Niemannd, M., D. Bergs-Winkels, and H. Merkens

1991 Educational Conditions of Turkish Migrant Children in German Schools. Anthropology and Education Quarterly 22(2):154–161.

Binchy, A.

1994 Travellers' Language: A Sociolinguistic Perspective. *In* Irish Travellers: Culture and Ethnicity. M. McCann, S. Ó Síocháin, and J. Ruane, eds. pp. 134–154. Belfast: Institute of Irish Studies.

Blommaert, J.

2001 Investigating Narrative Inequality: African Asylum Seekers' Stories in Belgium. Discourse & Society 12(4):413–439.

Bourdieu, P.

1991 Language and Symbolic Power. Cambridge: Polity.

Burke, M.

2000 Hidden like a Religious Arcanum: Irish Writing and Shelta's Secret History. *In* Travellers and Their Language. J. Kirk and D. Ó Baoil, eds. pp. 79–100. Belfast: Cló Ollscoile na Banríona.

Cavanagh, J.

2009 Living Memory: The Social Aesthetics of Language in a Northern Italian Town. Oxford: Wiley-Blackwell.

Chapman, M.

1978 The Gaelic Vision in Scottish Culture. Montreal: McGill-Queen's.

Cheesman, T.

2001 "Old" and "New" Lesser-Used Languages of Europe: Common Cause. *In* Language, Ethnicity and the State: Minority Languages in the European Union. C. O'Reilly, ed. pp. 147–168. Basingstoke: Palgrave Macmillan.

Commission of the European Communities
2003 Promoting Language Learning and Linguistic Diversity: An Action Plan 2004–2006. Brussels: European Commission.
Council of Europe
1992 European Charter for Regional or Minority languages: Explanatory Report. Electronic document. http://conventions.coe.int/Treaty/en/Reports/Html/148.htm (accessed November 5, 2011).
Council of the European Union
2008 Council Resolution of 21 November 2008 on a European strategy for multilingualism. Electronic document. http://eur-lex.europa.eu/LexUriServ/LexUriServ.do?uri=OJ:C:2008:320:0001:01:EN:HTML (accessed November 5, 2011).
Echeverria, B.
2003 Schooling, Language and Ethnic Identity in the Basque Autonomous Community. Anthropology and Education Quarterly 34(4):351–372.
Extra, G., and D. Gorter, eds.
2001 The Other Languages of Europe: Demographic, Sociolinguistic and Educational Perspectives. Clevedon: Multilingual Matters.
Gal, S.
2006 Migration, Minorities and Multilingualism: Language Ideologies in Europe. *In* Language Ideologies, Policies and Practices: Language and the Future of Europe. C. Mar Molinero and P. Stevenson, eds. pp. 13–27. Basingstoke: Palgrave Macmillan.
Gellner, E.
1983 Nations and Nationalism. Oxford: Blackwell.
Grass, G.
1992 Losses. Granta 42:97–108.
Grillo, R.
1989 Dominant Languages: Language and Hierarchy in Britain and France. Cambridge: Cambridge University Press.
Habermas, J.
2001 A Constitution for Europe? New Left Review 11:5–26.
Herder, J.
1770 Über den Ursprung der Sprache. Berlin: Reclam.
Humboldt, W. von
1988[1836] On Language, the Diversity of Human Language: Structure and its Influence on Thememtal Development of Mankind. P. Heath, trans. Cambridge: Cambridge University Press.
Kockel, U.
1999 Borderline Cases: The Ethnic Frontiers of European Integration. Liverpool: Liverpool University Press.
Lehtola, V.-P.
2002 The Sámi People: Traditions in Transition. Inari: Kustannus-Puntsi.
Macdonald, S.
1997 Reimagining Culture: Histories, Identities and the Gaelic Renaissance. Oxford: Berg.
Marranci, G.
2003 "We Speak English." Language and Identity Processes in Northern Ireland's Muslim Community. Ethnologist 25(2):59–77.
2006 Being Muslim in Northern Ireland: Dangerous Symbols and the Use of English. *In* Negotiating Culture: Moving, Mixing and memory in Contemporary Europe. U. Kockel and R. Byron, eds. pp. 167–185. Münster: LIT.

2007 Faith, Language and Identity: Muslim Migrants in Scotland and Northern Ireland. *In* Language, Power and Identity Politics. M. Nic Craith, ed. pp. 167–178. Basingstoke: Palgrave Macmillan.

May, S.

2005 Language Rights: Moving the Debate Forward. Journal of Sociolinguistics 9(3):319–347.

McDonagh, M.

2000a Ethnicity and Culture. *In* Travellers: Citizens of Ireland. Our Challenge to an Intercultural Irish Society in the 21st Century. F. Murphy and C. McDonagh, compiled, and E. Sheehan, ed. pp. 26–33. Dublin: Parish of the Travelling People.

2000b Nomadism. *In* Travellers: Citizens of Ireland. Our Challenge to an Intercultural Irish Society in the 21st Century. F. Murphy and C. McDonagh, compiled, and E. Sheehan, ed. pp. 33–45. Dublin: Parish of the Travelling People.

McDonald, M.

1989 We Are Not French!: Language, Culture and Identity in Brittany. London: Routledge.

Nelde, P., M. Strubell, and G. Williams

1996 Euromosaic: The Production and Reproduction of the Minority Language Groups in the European Union. Luxembourg: Office for Official Publications of the European Communities.

Nic Craith, M.

1994 The Irish Language in a Comparative Context. Oideas 42:52–67.

2000 Contested Identities and the Quest for Legitimacy. Journal of Multilingual and Multicultural Development 21(5):399–413.

2006 Europe and the Politics of Language. Basingstoke: Palgrave Macmillan.

Nic Shuibhne, N.

2002 EC Law and Minority Language Policy: Culture, Citizenship and Fundamental Rights. The Hague: Kluwer Law.

Ó Murchú, M.

1992 "The Irish Language." *In* The Celtic Connection. G. Price, ed. pp. 30–64. Buckinghamshire: Princess Grace Irish Library.

O'Reilly, C.

1999 The Irish Language in Northern Ireland: The Politics of Culture and Identity. Basingstoke: Palgrave Macmillan.

Phales, K., and M. Swyngedouw

2002 National Identities and Representations of Citizenship: A Comparison of Turks, Moroccans and Working-class Belgians in Brussels. Brussels: Centre for Interdisciplinary Studies.

Phillipson, R.

2003 English-Only Europe: Challenging Language Policy. London: Routledge.

Povrzanović Frykman, M.

2002 "Establishing and Dissolving Cultural Boundaries: Croatian Culture in Diasporic Contexts." The Balkans in Focus: Cultural Boundaries in Europe. S. Resic and B. Törnquist-Plewa, eds. pp. 137–188. Lund: Nordic Academic Press.

Seurujärvi-Kari, I., S. Pedersen, and V. Hirvoonen

1997 The Sámi: the Indigenous People of Northernmost Europe. Brussels: European Bureau for Lesser Used Languages.

Shore, C.

2000 Building Europe: the Cultural Politics of European Integration. London: Routledge.

Silverstein, M.
1996 Monoglot "Standard" in America: Standardization and Metaphors of Linguistic Hegemony. *In* The Matrix of Language: Contemporary Linguistic Anthropology. D. Brenneis and R. Macauley, eds. pp. 284–306. Boulder: Westview.
Skutnabb-Kangas, T.
2000 Linguistic Genocide in Education – or Worldwide Diversity and Human Rights? Mahwah, NJ: Lawrence Erlbaum.
Smith, D., and S. Wright
1999 The Turn Towards Democracy. *In* Whose Europe? The Turn Towards Democracy. D. Smith and S. Wright, eds. pp. 1–18. Oxford: Blackwell.
Spindler, G.
1973 Burgbach: Urbanization and Identity in a German Village. New York: Holt, Rinehart and Winston.
Urla, J.
1993 Cultural Politics in an Age of Statistics: Numbers, Nations, and the Making of Basque Identity. American Ethnologist 20(4):818–843.
Valkeapää, N.-A.
1983 Greetings from Lappland: The Sami – Europe's Forgotten People. London: Zed Books.
Wolber, B.
1991 "More than a Golden Bangle" . . . The Significance of Success in School for Returning Turkish Migrant Families. Anthropology and Education Quarterly 22:181–199.
Woolard, K.
1989 Double Talk: Bilingualism and the Politics of Ethnicity in Catalonia. Stanford: Stanford University Press.
Wright, S.
2000 Community and Communication: The Role of Language in Nation-State Building and European Integration. Clevedon: Multilingual Matters.

CHAPTER 23

Europe at the Crossroads of Rights and Culture(s)

Valdimar Tr. Hafstein and Martin Skrydstrup

Is it a "cultural right," an "individual woman's right," or not a right at all to wear a burqa in the neighborhoods, public transportation networks, and classrooms in, say, Paris, Berlin, or Stockholm? Would such collective or individual rights threaten Western constitutionalism as we know it? Is it a "cultural right" for, say, the Somali diaspora in London to have their girls circumcised according to customary practice – or a subordination and bodily mutilation disenfranchising the girls of their human rights? Is it a "cultural right" for, say, the Sámi in Sweden or the Roma in France to demand instruction in their mother tongue to strengthen their cultural identity? Or, if we step outside the European context to gain a broader perspective, the acclaimed PBS documentary *Through Deaf Eyes* (2006) posed the question if it is a "cultural right" for parents to refuse hearing implants for their children with hearing disabilities, because such operations in the longer run would undermine the sign language and ultimately threaten the entire cultural identity of the deaf community.

By now, so-called "multicultural" metropoles like Paris, London, Rome, Berlin, and Stockholm are rather accustomed to and familiar with this set of questions, since they have faced them since the late 1960s and they have been explicated and debated since the 1980s. Of late, such identity claims have been coupled with the loss of natural and cultural resources. Thus, the Sámi have made land claims in the name of "cultural rights" to sustain their livelihoods, such as hunting rights and reindeer herding. But not only "indigenous people" and "minorities" within European nation-states have mounted such claims. Greece has – albeit in a different register – claimed the Parthenon sculptures back from London as their "cultural birthright."

There is more than one way to tell the story of cultural rights. Two hold sway in critical discourse: the one a narrative of liberation and the other a narrative of liberalization. The former recounts a concerted effort to secure human dignity and

A Companion to the Anthropology of Europe, First Edition. Edited by Ullrich Kockel, Máiréad Nic Craith, and Jonas Frykman.

maintain the multiplicity of human culture. The latter is more ominous: it warns that cultural rights have as much to do with political economy as with human dignity; it suggests that rights to culture are a poor substitute for political and economic equality; ultimately, it maintains that cultural rights are a Trojan horse of sorts, that cultural rights talk sneaks the language of neoliberalism into the speech of oppressed peoples. We take both narratives to offer valuable insights into the history and politics of cultural rights, but ultimately we suggest that the story of cultural rights is more complicated than either narrative suggests.

In some ways, cultural rights are the Cinderella of the human rights family. For most of the twentieth century they were an afterthought in human rights debates, playing second fiddle to civil, political, and economic rights. In the last couple of decades, however, cultural rights talk has proliferated and its varieties have multiplied. The language of rights has helped to constitute new ways of making claims to culture and claims based on culture. From the right to participate in cultural life in society to the right to maintain one's own culture, from indigenous rights to copyright to cultural property rights, the international community recognizes certain cultural rights that have taken on increasing importance in societies criss-crossed by migrations, characterized by differences, and composed of multiple minorities.

As this enumeration makes evident, cultural rights have a civil rights aspect as well as a property rights aspect. They are addressed to various actors: some entitle individuals and hold local and national governments responsible for respecting their rights; other cultural rights are collective and entitle subnational, indigenous, and transnational communities while ascribing responsibility to states; finally, there are those cultural rights that states claim for themselves and ask other states to respect. These correspond to distinct legal regimes guaranteed by various laws and conventions and underwritten by a number of different institutions. They sometimes come into conflict with one another and with other human rights: for instance, the cultural right to freely participate in the cultural life of the community can conflict with the cultural rights of communities to maintain their culture and control its circulation; likewise, the rights of minorities to practice their culture in some cases clash with the human rights of women in those minorities. Thus, while the regimes are separate, the practices are of necessity intertwined.

Of course, cultural rights do not exist in the abstract. Their proof is in the pudding – in local struggles where universal concepts like cultural rights, cultural property, cultural heritage, and culture itself are mobilized under particular circumstances that invest them with meaning. On the ground, in a number of different ways, social actors articulate their claims within the terms of rights models and in so doing they vernacularize, reinterpret, resist, and transform these models, concepts, and regimes.

Faced with a wide horizon of different invocations of cultural rights by various actors and agencies in different circumstances and contexts, how should we go about thinking through them, let alone act on them? Seemingly, such questions challenge strongly held – even constitutive – ideas of Western liberal democracies, such as individual rights, secularism, and ultimately what most of us have come to see as modernity. In debates within the academy, "cultural rights" have often been framed as an oxymoron: the tension – even incommensurability – between the concept of "right" and that of "culture." In this optic, rights are seen to represent *sameness* (equality vis-à-vis the law), whereas culture is seen as *difference* (particular and distinct communities). Consequently, the debate has often been framed as a conundrum between the particularities of human collectives bound together by communal forms, such as language, culture, and history set against a notion of rights, which supposedly cut through such holistic entities with enlightened universalism and liberal individualism.

The anthropologist Jane Cowan is one who has steered clear of this impasse and emerged as a leading figure in the debates over these complex issues. Reiterating her key findings, we may say that the state of play in this field is that "cultural rights" are both enabling and constraining, that "cultural rights" are productive of cultural identities, and that the pursuit of rights entails unintended consequences (Cowan 2006:10). In what follows, we shall first respond to Cowan's call to study the institutionalization of the broad register of cultural rights (Cowan 2006:20). Then we shall proceed by mapping the conceptual terrain of "cultural rights," where we see three larger theoretical moves in the literature offering different vistas. Finally, we shall consider the coupling of "cultural rights" with loss in a European context.

TOPOGRAPHIES OF CULTURAL RIGHTS

It is perhaps a truism, but one that bears repeating, that cultural rights only function as rights insofar as they are recognized. Insofar as they are recognized they are recognized within a particular regime, shaped by laws, conventions, treaties, declarations, as well as institutions, experts, authorities, and administrations that the regimes vest with power and knowledge. A variety of such instruments and institutions operate at national and regional levels, but our focus is primarily on international regimes within which cultural rights are lodged and which give them various sorts of legitimacy (we discuss only the more important instruments here, but we attempt to sketch a more complete topography in Table 23.1).

One of the foundation documents of the United Nations is the Universal Declaration of Human Rights, adopted by the UN General Assembly in 1948, three years after 51 states signed the United Nations Charter. Cultural rights appear in the Universal Declaration of Human Rights in Article 27, of which the first paragraph guarantees to everyone "the right freely to participate in the cultural life of the community, to enjoy the arts and to share in scientific advancement and its benefits," while the second paragraph guarantees to everyone "the right to the protection of the moral and material interests resulting from any scientific, literary or artistic production of which he is the author." Already in their first appearance, then, cultural rights manifest a dual aspect, regarding on the one hand the civil right to participate in cultural life and on the other hand the property right to protect moral and material interests in cultural products.

In the following decades, each aspect was developed further through a series of declarations and conventions on cultural rights. The UN General Assembly adopted two instruments in 1966 to complement the Universal Declaration of 1948: the International Covenant on Civil and Political Rights, and the International Covenant on Economic, Social and Cultural Rights. The former guarantees, among other rights, the right of minority populations to "enjoy their own culture, to profess and practise their own religion, [and] to use their own language" (Article 27), whereas

Table 23.1 List of international instruments protecting cultural rights.

Universal Declaration of Human Rights	1948
Convention for the Protection of Cultural Property in the Event of Armed Conflict	1954
Recommendation Concerning the Most Effective Means of Rendering Museums Accessible to Everyone	1960
International Covenant on Civil and Political Rights	1966
International Covenant on Economic, Social and Cultural Rights	1966
Declaration of Principles of International Cultural Co-operation	1966
Recommendation concerning the Preservation of Cultural Property Endangered by Public or Private works	1968
Convention on the Means of Prohibiting and Preventing the Illicit Import, Export and Transfer of Ownership of Cultural Property	1970
Convention concerning the Protection of the World Cultural and Natural Heritage	1972
Recommendation concerning the Protection, at National Level, of the Cultural and Natural Heritage	1972
Recommendation on Participation by the People at Large in Cultural Life and their Contribution to It	1976
Recommendation concerning the International Exchange of Cultural Property	1976
Recommendation for the Protection of Movable Cultural Property	1978
Convention on the Elimination of All Forms of Discrimination against Women	1979
Convention on the Rights of the Child	1989
Recommendation on the Safeguarding of Traditional Culture and Folklore	1989
International Convention on the Protection of the Rights of All Migrant Workers and Members of Their Families	1990
Declaration on the Rights of Persons Belonging to National or Ethnic, Religious and Linguistic Minorities	1992
Convention on Biological Diversity	1994
Convention on the Protection of the Underwater Cultural Heritage	2001
UNESCO Universal Declaration on Cultural Diversity	2001
Convention for the Safeguarding of the Intangible Cultural Heritage	2003
UNESCO Declaration concerning the Intentional Destruction of Cultural Heritage	2003
Convention on the Protection and Promotion of the Diversity of Cultural Expressions	2005
Convention on the Rights of Persons with Disabilities	2006
United Nations Declaration on the Rights of Indigenous Peoples	2007

the latter restates the rights recognized in Article 27 of the Universal Declaration but adds an obligation for states to take the steps "necessary for the conservation, the development and the diffusion of science and culture," to "respect the freedom indispensable for scientific research and creative activity," and to "recognize the benefits . . . of international contacts and cooperation in the scientific and cultural fields" (Article 15).

Taken together, the Universal Declaration from 1948 and the twin covenants from 1966 make up the International Bill of Human Rights and provide the basis for all invocations of cultural rights in their civil aspect (as opposed to their property aspect). An array of other cultural rights instruments adopted since 1966 cite these and inflect the rights that they guarantee with reference to particular social groups or categories of persons. Thus, for example, the UN General Assembly adopted in 1979 the Convention on the Elimination of All Forms of Discrimination against Women. In Article 13(c), it establishes the right of women "to participate in recreational activities, sports and all aspects of cultural life," while Article 5(a) enjoins parties to the convention to "modify the social and cultural patterns of conduct of men and women" in order to eliminate customary practices that reinforce the subordination of women. Ten years later, in 1989, the General Assembly adopted the Convention on the Rights of the Child: in Article 30, it compels states not to deny a child belonging to a minority or indigenous group "the right, in community with other members of his or her group, to enjoy his or her own culture, to profess and practise his or her own religion, or to use his or her own language"; in the following article, states take on the obligation to recognize and promote every child's right to participate freely and fully in cultural life and the arts. Moreover, in the 1990s and 2000s the UN adopted a series of instruments that further build on and develop the civil aspect of cultural rights with regard to specific population groups, including migrant workers and members of their families (1990), national or ethnic, religious, and linguistic minorities (1992), persons with disabilities (2006), and indigenous peoples (2007).

The property aspect of cultural rights was developed in another series of instruments under the auspices of the United Nations Educational, Scientific and Cultural Organization (UNESCO) (founded in 1946), beginning in 1954 with the Convention for the Protection of Cultural Property in the Event of Armed Conflict, often called the Hague Convention for short. "Recognizing that cultural property has suffered grave damage during recent armed conflicts," the Hague Convention begins, and "Being convinced that damage to cultural property belonging to any people whatsoever means damage to the cultural heritage of all mankind," the parties to the convention take on various duties to protect cultural property from theft and destruction. As is evident from these sentences from the preamble, cultural property and cultural heritage both emerged in international law through the Hague Convention, and they are already recognizably distinct: here, cultural property belongs to a people, cultural heritage to mankind. Along with the concept of cultural rights, the concepts of cultural property and heritage were thus coined and canonized in the wake of World War II as part of the new world order institutionalized in the UN.

In the half-century following the adoption of the Hague Convention, UNESCO developed separate legal instruments and bodies for what it terms the protection of cultural property and the safeguarding of cultural heritage. For the former, the Convention on the Means of Prohibiting and Preventing the Illicit Import, Export and Transfer of Ownership of Cultural Property (1970) played a pivotal role along with the Intergovernmental Committee for Promoting the Return of Cultural Property to its Countries of Origin or its Restitution in case of Illicit Appropriation (1978). As the names of the convention and the committee make clear, cultural property is at its inception a national concept, used in the context of claims for the return or restitution of historical artifacts from one state to another.

Cultural heritage, on the other hand, is the preferred term in contexts that stress the general safeguarding of artifacts, buildings, sites, and, most recently, cultural practices. UNESCO is today best known for its 1972 World Heritage Convention and its associated World Heritage List; in 2003, it added to its legal arsenal the Convention for the Safeguarding of the Intangible Cultural Heritage, with a Representative List of the Intangible Cultural Heritage of Humanity. If conflicting national claims and the settlement of international disputes over transfer are the primary focus of conventions for protecting cultural property, then legal instruments for safeguarding cultural heritage organize international cooperation around the common objective of keeping safe those objects and expressions that are considered of value to humanity as a whole, regardless of where they may be located or who may use them. Thus one might say that cultural property belongs to an exclusive "us," whereas cultural heritage belongs to an inclusive "us." Claims staked within both regimes help to constitute collective subjects, but the subject of cultural property is by default exclusive, subject to misappropriation and entitled to restitution; the subject of cultural heritage tends rather to be an inclusive subject, a collective "we" that is entreated to stand together to prevent degradation and loss, rather than theft by another.

Of course, the terms are not unequivocal, and we should be careful not to reify them. In practice, the distinction is often blurred. Actors in the social world participate in new opportunities offered by both concepts, and shape new options in politics and markets that have come to be imaginable through instruments such as inscriptions and lists. The distinction is rather clear-cut, nevertheless, in the international regimes, and one should not underestimate the importance of these regimes in diffusing a conceptual matrix and shaping local practices. The term "cultural property" gained currency worldwide following the adoption of the Hague Convention in 1954, not the other way around, and likewise the ascendancy of cultural heritage in recent decades only gained momentum as a result of the adoption of the World Heritage Convention in 1972. In recent years, intangible cultural heritage exemplifies how international conventions, when successful, can act as catalysts; in spite of its etymological roots in bureaucratese, this term, concocted in the assembly halls of UNESCO in the 1990s, has rapidly gained acceptance following the adoption of the convention dedicated to safeguarding it. Social actors in tens of thousands of scattered places all over the world now use the term to describe their traditional practices, and in so doing make claims that are recognizable with reference to an international regime and validated by a proliferating production of expert knowledge on intangible heritage (Bendix and Hafstein 2009).

The claims that the international regime of cultural property recognizes and validates are claims to objects which colonialism, capitalism, and science have transported in their common luggage. These claims propose now to reverse their trajectories and return the objects to their countries of origin or to their rightful owners within settler colonial societies. Cultural property is claimed in the aftermath of war or colonial rule as an assertion of sovereign powers and an affirmation of cultural integrity vis-à-vis foreign invasion and foreign rule, or else in the face of globalized markets and the universalist aspersions of foreign science. One of the effects of cultural property claims is thus to help form sovereign subjects. In other words, claims to cultural property are a technology of sovereignty (Skrydstrup 2009, 2010).

Conversely, cultural heritage may be said to be a technology of governmentality. Teaching people to have a heritage, to value it, and keep it safe, requires the intervention of outside experts and training of local ones to reform the practices of local populations and reframe their relationships to habitat and habitus in terms of heritage. Populations learn to conceive of buildings and practices as their heritage and to appreciate the need for safeguarding them from change or destruction; through an infusion of expertise and in cooperation with state, nongovernmental, and intergovernmental organizations, they are consequently charged with administering themselves and their cultural heritage. Thus projects of safeguarding connect agendas in political centers to those dispersed sites where operations of power connect with the population; its experts, councils, committees, museums, workshops, and awareness-raising and grassroots organizations help establish lines of communication between the calculations of authorities and the aspirations of free citizens (Kirshenblatt-Gimblett 1998; Rose 1999; Bennett 2000; Mitchell 2002; Noyes 2006; Poulot 2006; Smith 2006; Hafstein 2007; Di Giovine 2009).

One way to make sense of the history of cultural rights in the past six or seven decades – and their recognition within a set of emerging regimes, shaped by a number of new conventions and declarations executed by an expanding array of institutions, experts, and administrations – is as a historical movement from unity and universality to plurality and difference. In 1948, in a United Nations dominated by the victors of World War II and still untouched by decolonization (with 58 members), Article 27 of the Universal Declaration of Human Rights speaks of cultural life in the singular and guarantees the individual's right to take part in it, as well as to protect his individual rights as an author. In 1954, still cleaning up after the war, UNESCO (with 70 members) adopted the Hague Convention, which affirms state sovereignty and recognizes the claims that one state makes on another state in the name of its cultural and historical unity and its property rights in its cultural patrimony. Cultural property rights in the Hague Convention are to the state what author's rights are to individual persons in Article 27 of the Universal Declaration. Cultural property helps to organize states as individuals-writ-large (as Plato would have them be), and both state and individual are recognized in human rights and cultural property regimes as sovereign, unified, and creative subjects, with moral and material interests in their creations.

Moreover, early efforts to institutionalize cultural rights at the international level understood culture in the singular as a universal good to which all individuals have a right but which is distributed unequally among them. Thus, the opening article of UNESCO's constitution from 1945 says it will achieve its purpose of contributing to peace and security by building collaboration, by maintaining, increasing, and diffusing knowledge, and by "giving fresh impulse to popular education and to the spread of culture." In other words, like knowledge and education, culture here refers to something that needs to spread. There is no sign yet here of the sense of culture as difference which has gradually come to the fore in cultural rights debates and instruments (let alone of a plurality of knowledges).

At the other end of the spectrum, instruments of cultural rights from the past two decades have moved effectively away from unity to plurality and from universality to difference. Thus, the UN General Assembly adopted in 2007 the United Nations Declaration on the Rights of Indigenous Peoples, recognizing in the preamble "the right of all peoples to be different, to consider themselves different, and to be respected as such" and affirming "that all peoples contribute to the diversity and richness of civilizations and cultures." A considerable portion of the declaration relates specifically to the cultural rights of indigenous peoples, and importantly these rights are specified as not only individual but also collective rights. The social collectives whose rights the declaration thus recognizes present a serious challenge to the monopoly of states on the moral resources of community; they question the property rights of states in "their" cultural patrimony and complicate underlying narratives of their historical and cultural unity.

To take another recent example, UNESCO's 2003 Convention for the Safeguarding of the Intangible Cultural Heritage defines intangible heritage as "the practices, representations, expressions, knowledge, skills [...] that communities, groups and, in some cases, individuals recognize as part of their cultural heritage" (Article 2). This is perhaps better described as an indefinition; the convention's circular formula begs the question of what the terms "community" and "group" denote. In fact, it requires the definition of the communities and groups with which the convention requires state actors to consult and cooperate. In order, first, to figure out what intangible heritage is and, then, to involve communities in safeguarding it as the convention requires, it is necessary to delimit such communities, to define membership in them, and to designate a mechanism for consultation or cooperation.

Part of the political attraction of communities lies in their apparent naturalness. Nevertheless, like nations before them, communities need to be made up. Boundaries and distinctions have to be put into place. Communities have to be visualized, surveyed, and mobilized. Intangible cultural heritage does just that: it converts cultural practices into resources for administering populations. By defining community, providing it with outside expertise, and conferring official prestige on its marginalized practices and expressions, the communities to which UNESCO's concept of intangible heritage refers itself are positioned squarely as collective subjects within states and subject to states. Their empowerment cements their administrative bonds to central government, even as it loosens their cultural bonds (Yúdice 2004; Littler and Naidoo 2005; Klein 2006; Turtinen 2006; Ashworth et al. 2007; Bortolotto 2008; Kuutma 2009; Smith and Akagawa 2009; Hafstein In press; Kapchan In press).

In this way, the Intangible Heritage Convention serves to illustrate three main points about cultural rights that we have previously credited Jane Cowan with summarizing (2006:10): cultural rights are simultaneously enabling and constraining; like other legal regimes, cultural rights regimes have a constitutive capacity and help to produce new legal and ethical subjects, affinities, and obligations; and the pursuit of cultural rights entails unintended consequences. Together with the UN Declaration on the Rights of Indigenous Peoples, the Intangible Heritage Convention stands as a signpost for how cultural rights regimes have shifted from rights to culture in the singular vested in universal individual subjects (conceived of in the dual form of natural persons and states) toward a conception of culture as difference that is central to subject formation in a new multiple field of identity, allegiance, and rights: a shift from Enlightenment to counter-Enlightenment, from the universal to the particular, from the modern to the postmodern.

These grand narratives open up three major theoretical vistas, which we shall map in the following.

Mapping the Conceptual Terrain

The rights to culture

The Canadian political philosopher Charles Taylor's *The Politics of Recognition* (1994) is credited as one of the most influential essays on the right to culture under the rubric of "multiculturalism." Taylor argues that *mis*recognition of cultural identities is capable of inflicting "grievous wounds," which is why due recognition is a "vital human need" (Taylor 1994:26). Taylor operates here with an essential kernel of identity, developed in his earlier work *Sources of the Self* (Taylor 1989), where he argues against poststructuralist conceptions of subjectivity. His dialogical notion of recognition is indebted to Georg W. F. Hegel's parable *Lordship and Bondage* (*Herrschaft und Knechtschaft*) (Hegel 1952[1807]), which he reads as an affirmative story about the possibility of mutual recognition: "The struggle for recognition can find only one satisfactory solution, and that is a regime of reciprocal recognition among equals" (Taylor 1994:50). However, in his quest to track the vital human need for recognition as a particular sensibility of modernity, he travels further back in the intellectual history on recognition than Hegel. He stops at Johann G. Herder (1744–1803), who, for Taylor, becomes the first articulator of two new discoveries: each individual carries his/her own worth and measure (*eigenes Maass*), and cultural traditions carry their own historicity, authenticity, and uniqueness (*Einmaligkeit*). These two seminal ideas become foundational for cultural relativism, nationalism, folklore, cultural anthropology, and, most importantly for Taylor, *modernity*. According to Taylor, Herder's articulation of this new form of subjectivity brings forth "the conditions in which the attempt to be recognized can fail" (Taylor 1994:35). Herder's two antipodes, in Taylor's view equally important signposts of modernity, are Immanuel Kant and Jean-Jacques Rousseau. Whereas Herder's discourse demands recognition of distinctiveness, Kant and Rousseau are early prominent exponents of a discourse underwritten by the principle of equal entitlements accorded to citizens, the very idea of *rights*.

These touchstones of European intellectual history signal of course the well-known schism between Enlightenment and counter-Enlightenment: equality of rights and respect for distinctiveness, which in Taylor's optic become "two incompatible views of liberal society" (Taylor 1994:60). This brings Taylor to conceive contemporary articulations of "cultural rights" as a strange amalgam of the Herderian and Kantian positions, and leads him to a centrist position: "There must be something midway between the inauthentic and homogenizing demand for recognition of equal worth, on the one hand, and the self-immurement within ethnocentric standards, on the other" (Taylor 1994:72).

Writing in the wake of Taylor's important work, another Canadian political philosopher, Will Kymlicka, delivers an influential defense for what he calls the "right to culture" (Kymlicka 1995:36). This right to culture is grounded in a liberal vision of "individual freedom," which needs to be secured through "multicultural citizenship." This idea is defined as the granting of citizenship on the grounds of cultural identity, which, according to Kymlicka, will let cultural minorities enjoy effective rights and protections. Employing the liberal democratic ideal of self-determination, he argues both for citizenship rights and formal political recognition of cultural difference, that is, for what he calls "a plurality of cultural memberships" within the nation-state (Kymlicka 1995). He contends that within the limits of equality and autonomy, his liberal vision can accommodate indigenous aspirations to cultural flourishing. To further this end, he suggests recognition of extensive rights to indigenous self-government and title to lands, because "such rights render individual freedom meaningful" (Kymlicka 1998). Clinging to the liberal tradition, Kymlicka argues against collective rights for minorities, because indigenous self-determination is satisfied *ipso facto* through individual rights. Kymlicka's vision of "cultural rights" within the context of multiculturalism is both a form of redress for past injustices and a guarantee that no individual belonging to a particular culture is "denied access to whichever culture is their own" (Kymlicka 1995). Thus, as Cowan also has remarked, liberal political theorists such as Kymlicka deploy a conception of culture which is "a take it or leave it thing." From this perspective, "culture" is a personal choice coupled with individual freedom and autonomy (the liberal subject), which is antecedent to, and preexists, political structures. The objective of "cultural rights" is to ensure individuals have the freedom to access and participate in the culture of their choosing, enrich human development, and set the emancipatory potential of culture free.

The recognition of cultural rights

What is then the emancipatory force of cultural rights claims on behalf of subaltern or former subordinated identities on the threshold of the twenty-first century? What is the liberating potential of "law-fare" (Comaroff and Comaroff 2007)? When does "culture" articulated through and as "rights" become production and regulation of identity through law and bureaucracy? When does the legal recognition of "cultural rights" become an instrument of governmentality? Common for the post-Foucaultian cluster of contributions on "rights and culture" is an argument that liberals fail to understand that a "cultural right" is only a right insofar as it is recognized as such by a state. This implicates that "cultural rights" are always and already conditioned and mediated by coercive discursive regimes, which may shape what such rights purport to set free. Thus, "cultural rights" may not be liberating, rather they may be yet another installment of the relations between (neo)liberalism in late modernity and identity formation. Another common denominator of critical theory is that instead of invoking the step stones of Herder, Kant, and Rousseau, they urge us to reconsider Marx's essay "On the Jewish Question," because it resonates with the complex and contradictory consequences of being granted rights on the basis of having a cultural identity.

In "On the Jewish Question" (Marx 1994[1843]), Marx raised the seminal issue of whether Jews wanted political recognition and rights as Jews or as persons: Do Jews seeking emancipation want to be free from Judaism, or free to be Jewish? Should the Prussian secular state recognize Jewish claims to citizenship and political inclusion on the basis of their religion or their humanity? And what does it mean to turn to the state and ask for emancipation *qua* rather than *in spite of* being different? Importantly, Marx distinguishes between *l'homme* (actual man) and *citoyén* (true man):

"Actual man is recognized only in the form of the egoistic individual, and true man only in the form of the abstract *citoyén*" (Marx 1994:49). According to Marx, the state recognizes rights on the basis of a citizenship category, which is an "unreal universality" robbed of actual embedded, sensuous, individual, and immediate life. In Marx's account, the strange power of liberal constitutionalism emanates from the granting of freedom, equality, and representation to abstract categories, rather than concrete subjects. This implies that "rights talk," for Marx, establishes a fictional and hollow sovereignty of the individual and illusions about liberty and equality in the state, which ultimately mystifies, naturalizes, and veils the very powers it is set to challenge. Roughly, for Marx, "cultural rights" is a technology of rule, which encodes rather than emancipates.

Taking their cue from Marx, contemporary political theorists post-Foucault have generally argued that "cultural rights" are more likely to become sites of identity production and regulation coupled with injury than vehicles for emancipation. One of them is Martin Chanock, who argues that historically "cultural rights" emerge from fierce political contestation and it is with this awareness of catastrophic origins that we should approach "cultural rights" in the contemporary world (Chanock 2000:17). He argues that the collapse of Marxism as critical thinking and the babble of globalization theory have naturalized "culture" as an explanatory paradigm. Our question should therefore be when did "culture" assume this importance in describing group difference? What narratives are being replaced by the shift in focus from "class" to "culture"? Chanock suggests that we have to look for the answers to these questions as part and parcel of the intellectual history of Empire. From this perspective, what liberal political theorists say about the politics of *cultural* recognition constitutes different discourses of occidentalizing and orientalizing in a world of globalized symbolic exchange (Chanock 2000:35). Chanock argues that the discursive deployment of "culture" takes place within particular histories of political and intellectual power (2000:19). In these rights discourses, "culture" is invoked as an argument against universalism, but often it is done by local rulers and not those who actually need their rights protected. Seen from this perspective, appeals to rights in Africa should be founded on an appeal to universalism, rather than to local institutions and cultures (2000:31).

David Scott's critique of what Taylor, Kymlicka, and their liberal compatriots are up to runs along somewhat similar lines as Chanock's. In his piece *Culture in Political Theory* (Scott 2003) he levels an incisive generalized critique of the import of the culture concept into contemporary political theory. He calls it for the "contemporary naturalization of the culture concept in political science," and, according to him, it is predicated on "the conceptual Geertz effect" (Scott 2003). Taylor's perspective is a view from nowhere, says Scott, underwritten by a remnant of the Herderian concept of "culture," defined as shared particular cosmologies, constituting the worldviews of discrete, cohesive, and bounded social groups; precisely the notion of "culture" postmodern anthropology has labored to dismantle and ultimately to do away with. Scott's main argument is that this constructionist idiom of culture as symbolic action has been uncritically appropriated by political theory, inaugurating a seemingly new egalitarian era of knowledge relations between the West and the Rest. In this view, most political theory under the rubrics of "cultural rights," "multiculturalism," "claims of diversity," "politics of difference," "politics of recognition," and so on, is inattentive to the ideological history of anthropology's culture concept and thus complicit in its ideological reproduction. Both Chanock's and Scott's critiques of "cultural rights" suggest that they are more oriented to ideological reproduction than social justice.

Povinelli's critique of the "cunning of current forms of liberal recognition" addresses "cultural rights" in ways more fundamental and ethnographically grounded than most other interventions in this cluster. Her radical critique of late liberal reasoning in the shape of Australian multiculturalism from the perspective of the Belyuen community in the Northern Territory is highly acclaimed. Povinelli asks what the Australian nation-state is actually recognizing in court cases such as *Mabo and Others v. Queensland (No. 2)* (1992) when native title and "customary law" is recognized. This profound question serves as *entrée* to a critique of liberal humanism where it seemingly succeeds in accommodating cultural difference in cases such as Mabo. Povinelli reads such seemingly morally courageous court decisions as national responses to its colonial past: "In sum, the court was engaging in and helping to define public debates over the proper affective response of the nation to its settler past" (Povinelli 2002:160). Mabo was about national reparation and reconciliation – successfully staged – but in this act of successful liberal recognition, the state failed to acknowledge the "potential radical alterity of indigenous beliefs" (2002:163). Akin to Marx's project, Povinelli shows "the gaps between abstracted anthropological and legal models and local modes of localization" as "one of the means by which forms of liberal force are extended rather than critically engaged" (2002:267). Ultimately, she argues that the Mabo court decision is not about the preservation of Aboriginal ways of life under the ideology of multiculturalism, but about advancing Australian common law principles, and, in the act, Aboriginal subjects are forced to do the same. Thus, the actual aim of liberal law is "the re-subordination of Aboriginal society and law vis-à-vis European law and society" (2002:181). From this perspective the liberal politics of *cultural* recognition enables liberal law, a technology of state power, to turn emancipation struggles against it into its own legitimization (2002:184). Thus, Povinelli's work is an incisive critique of liberal forms of recognition, not where it fails to recognize cultural difference, but exactly in the court decisions where it seemingly succeeds.

Cultural rights as social debts

What happens to "cultural rights" if ideas about personhood, alienation, and entitlements look radically different from those most Euro-Americans carry around? How well does the Euro-American idea of "cultural rights" travel to places like Papua New Guinea (PNG)? This has partly been explored by British social anthropologist Marilyn Strathern, who has conducted long-term fieldwork on Massim exchange, and generally conceives of her work on cultural and intellectual property rights as being situated "on the periphery of international debate, but at the heart of how people in Papua New Guinea negotiate claims" (Strathern 2004:85). Strathern differs from the earlier perspectives in that her key analytic is to couple rights with the social practice of transactions, rather than the state of discursive regimes:

> Rights, we may say, anticipate transactions. Debts, on the other hand, presuppose them . . . Property-based regimes construct a sphere of social life that lies "beyond" individual claims. In this beyond, communal rights may be imagined as inalienable, in opposition to the alienable rights of property or commodity, and thereby seen to divide gift giving from commercial transactions. By contrast, in a situation of the kind encountered in those Papua New Guinean practices where anything is amenable to transaction, and where debts presuppose enchainment to others (and the reverse), one does not have to specify the conditions under which things are alienable or inalienable. What has to be endlessly, infinitely, specified are the conditions of relationship, for relationships are not of equal weight or value. (Strathern 2004:102)

The subtle implication here is that what figures as an alternative to individual rights in the Euro-American legal imagination, namely "communal or collective rights," does not have much bearing on the social ontologies in PNG. Here, people are indebted to one another, rather than have rights vis-à-vis one another. There is no "free choice of culture" or other artifacts of Euro-American notions of liberalism and personhood. Rather, rights and entitlements cannot be conceived of as something beyond the realm of a specific sociability: "only the particularity of circumstances would define what an entitlement or right might mean in those specific conditions under which people live" (Strathern 2005:232). In its own particular way, Strathern's approach to "cultural rights" represents an alternative to the post-Foucaultian discursive critiques of liberal visions of the "right to culture."

Cultural Rights and Losses

The coupling of cultural rights with notions of loss and alienation has proliferated in the past decade. However, taking Chanock's argument (Chanock 2000:17) seriously, that historically "cultural rights" emerge from fierce political contestation and that it is with this awareness of "catastrophic origins" that we should approach "cultural rights" in the contemporary world, we might sketch two distinct trajectories: the first is claims made to "cultural property" in the aftermath of imperial colonialism, and the second is claims made to "cultural property" in the aftermath of settler-colonialism. The first cluster of claims turn on morals and ethics, where debts are involved; the second cluster of claims hinge on formal entitlements, where rights are involved.

If we consider the first trajectory – morals and debts – we may argue that it took off as colonial demarcations gave way to the birth of postcolonial nation-states. With that followed claims for recovery of the cultural objects amassed during colonial times and kept in museums and private collections in the Western metropoles. With his evocative appeal in 1979, the former Director-General of UNESCO, Amadou-Mahtar M'Bow, came to coin this type of reparative claim: "One of the most noble incarnations of a people's genius is its cultural heritage, built up over the centuries . . . [T]he vicissitudes of history have nevertheless robbed many peoples of a priceless portion of this inheritance in which their enduring identity finds its embodiment . . . [T]hese men and women who have been deprived of their cultural heritage therefore ask for the return of at least the art treasures which best represent their culture, which they feel are the most vital and whose absence causes them the greatest anguish" (M'Bow

1979). In the wake of numerous resolutions in the United Nations General Assembly about the urgency of a response to these claims, the UN assigned the task to UNESCO. The debates in Paris in the late 1960s and 1970s about the scope and justification of these reparations were complex (Ganslmayr and Paczensky 1984; Greenfield 1989). What crystallized was an international convention (UNESCO 1970) and an intergovernmental body (UNESCO IGC) founded on two important premises: (i) A philosophy of government action, which required claims to be filed by state actors – contrary to Jewish reparations, only claims filed through official diplomatic protocol were recognized as legitimate; and (ii) a distinction between *return* and *restitution* – the former term designated cases where objects had left their country of origin during colonial times and was a question of *ad hoc* negotiations between states and subject to voluntary action; the latter term applied to cases of documented illicit appropriation, covering reparation for injury in a judicial sense, turning on formal obligation similar to the Jewish restitutions in the wake of World War II.

If we consider the second trajectory – gravitating toward entitlements and rights – we may argue that since the 1980s, the governments in the United States, Canada, Australia, and New Zealand have begun a process of reparations to indigenous peoples within the limits of the settler–colonial nation-state. These reparative efforts cover a wide range of different kinds of properties and are often enforced by legal regimes. An example is the Native American Graves and Repatriation Act (NAGPRA) passed by Congress in 1990, which has been called the most important piece of cultural policy legislation in the history of the United States (Tweedie 2002). This legal instrument gives Native people a legal mechanism through which they can reclaim specific objects of importance to the tribe. For cultural objects to be repatriated, the claimant must substantiate by the preponderance of evidence that the desired object meet a range of criteria stipulated by NAGPRA.

If we were to look at these two trajectories from the theoretical perspectives outlined in our map of the conceptual terrain above, John Moustakas's piece "Group Rights in Cultural Property: Justifying Strict Inalienability" (Moustakas 1989) would fall within the rubric of "the rights to culture" (the first theoretical move). Moustakas asserts that the nexus between a cultural object and a collective entity such as a community or a nation should be "the essential measurement for determining whether group rights in cultural property will be effectuated to the fullest extent possible – by holding such objects strictly inalienable from the group" (Moustakas 1989:1184). Just as "property for personhood might describe property so closely bound up with our individual identities that its loss causes pain that cannot be relieved by the object's replacement . . . property for grouphood expresses something about the entire group's relationship to certain property . . . essential to the preservation of group identity and self-esteem" (Moustakas 1989:1185). Drawing on the case of the Parthenon sculptures, Moustakas argues that cultural property is constitutive of collective identity and strictly inalienable, because descendants of the makers of such objects would never consent to commodity exchange of objects intimately bound up with their cultural integrity.

In the liberal tradition, the question of "cultural rights" is framed as *failure* to recognize others in virtue of who they are. This notion of cultural identity as an essence which exists prior to political claims is exactly what contributions under the rubric of "recognition of cultural rights" set out to dismantle (the second theoretical move in our conceptual map). Roughly, they would argue that the first question to ponder would be if the discursive register of UNESCO does not form the precepts of nationhood and inalienability, upon which the claim is crafted and advanced. Ultimately, they would contend that the question of "cultural rights" in this domain and specific case turns on a set of artificial questions generated by liberal statecraft, questions that reproduce power rather than challenge it. Finally, the cluster of "cultural rights as social debts" (the third theoretical move) would perhaps raise fundamental ontological questions about whether the concept of "cultural property" invented by the Western legal imagination is adequate to apprehend the issues at stake. Ethnography in the Ministry of Culture in Athens could perhaps tell us something new about what cultural rights struggles look like in bureaucracies, and the value conversions that take place within the hallways and boardrooms of the Greek State.

Europe and Cultural Rights

In the Greek *polis*-state, Kreon was faced with the question whether he should recognize Antigone's claim to bury her brother in Thebes on the basis of her religious beliefs, sense of justice and kinship affiliation. Most of us know the tragedy dramatized by Sophocles and the fatal outcome of Kreon's decision. Outside Europe, authorities seem often to find themselves in the same predicament as Kreon did. In Canberra, museum directors face the question of whether it is a "cultural right" for Aboriginal people to bar female curators access to certain Aboriginal museum objects. In this register of claims we seem to find those who argue that "cultural rights" are a fundamental human right and on the other hand their critics, who claim: "Once human-rights thinking wades into waters as muddy as 'culture,' 'heritage' and 'knowledge,' we face the possibility that the legitimacy of all human-rights standards might be undermined" (Brown 2004:58). We need more ethnography of how the universal concept of "cultural rights" is mobilized, resisted, reinterpreted, vernacularized, and transformed in particular relations if we are to overcome this impasse in the debate.

References

Ashworth, Gregory J., Brian Graham, and John E. Tunbridge
2007 Pluralising Pasts: Heritage, Identity and Place in Multicultural Societies. London: Pluto Press.

Bendix, Regina, and Valdimar Tr. Hafstein
2009 Culture and Property: An Introduction. Ethnologia Europaea: Journal of European Ethnology 39(2):5–10.

Bennett, Tony
2000 Acting on the Social: Art, Culture and Government. American Behavioral Scientist 43:1412–1428.

Bortolotto, Chiara, ed.
2008 Il patrimonio immateriale secondo l'Unesco: Analisi e prospettive. Rome: Istituto Poligrafico e Zecca dello Stato.

Brown, Michael F.
2004 Who Owns Native Culture? Cambridge, MA: Harvard University Press.
Chanock, Martin
2000 "Culture" and Human Rights: Orientalising, Occidentalising and Authenticity. *In* Beyond Rights Talk and Culture Talk. M. Mamdani, ed. pp. 15–36. New York: St. Martin's Press.
Comaroff, Jean, and John Comaroff
2009 Ethnicity Inc. Chicago: University of Chicago Press.
Cowan, Jane
2006 Culture and Rights after Culture and Rights. American Anthropologist 108(1): 9–24.
Ganslmayr, Herbert, and Gert von Paczensky
1984 Nofretete will nach Hause: Europa – Schatzhaus der "Dritten Welt." Munich: Bertelsmann.
Di Giovine, Michael A.
2009 The Heritage-scape: UNESCO, World Heritage and Tourism. Lanham, MD: Lexington.
Greenfield, Jeanette
1989 The Return of Cultural Treasures. Cambridge: Cambridge University Press.
Hafstein, Valdimar Tr.
2007 Claiming Culture: Intangible Heritage Inc., Folklore©, Traditional Knowledge™. *In* Prädikat "Heritage." Wertschöpfungen aus Kulturellen Ressourcen. Regina Bendix, Dorothee Hemme, and Markus Tauschek, eds. pp. 75–100. Münster: LIT.
In press Protection as Dispossession: Folklore on the International Agenda. *In* Intangible Rights: Heritage and Human Rights in Transit. Deborah Kapchan, ed. Philadelphia: University of Pennsylvania Press.
Hegel, G. W. F.
1952[1807] Phänomenologie des Geistes. Hamburg: Verlag von Felix Meiner.
Kapchan, Deborah A.
In press Intangible Rights: Heritage and Human Rights in Transit. Series: Pennsylvania Studies in Human Rights. Philadelphia: University of Pennsylvania Press.
Kirshenblatt-Gimblett, Barbara
1998 Destination Culture: Tourism, Museums, and Heritage. Berkeley: University of California Press.
Klein, Barbro
2006 Cultural Heritage, the Swedish Folklife Sphere, and the Others. Cultural Analysis 5:57–80.
Kuutma, Kristin
2009 Who Owns Our Songs? Authority of Heritage and Resources for Restitution. Ethnologia Europaea: Journal of European Ethnology 39(2):26–40.
Kymlicka, Will
1995 Multicultural Citizenship: A Liberal Theory of Minority Rights. Oxford: Clarendon Press.
1998 Finding Our Way: Rethinking Ethnocultural Relations in Canada. Oxford: Oxford University Press.
Littler, Jo, and Roshi Naidoo
2005 The Politics of Heritage: The Legacies of "Race." London: Routledge.
Marx, Karl
1994[1843] On the Jewish Question. *In* Marx: Early Political Writings. J. O'Malley and R. A. Davis, eds. pp. 28–56. Cambridge: Cambridge University Press.

M'Bow, Amadou Mahtar
1979 A Plea for the Return of an Irreplaceable Cultural Heritage to Those Who Created It. Museum International 31(1):58–58.
Mitchell, Timothy
2002 Rule of Experts. Berkeley: University of California Press.
Moustakas, John
1989 Group Rights in Cultural Property: Justifying Strict Inalienability. Cornell Law Review 74:1179–1227.
Noyes, Dorothy
2006 The Judgment of Solomon: Global Protections for Tradition and the Problem of Community Ownership. Cultural Analysis 5:27–56. Electronic document. http://socrates.berkeley.edu/~caforum/ (accessed November 5, 2011).
Poulot, Dominique
2006 Une histoire du patrimoine en Occident. Paris: Presses Universitaires de France.
Povinelli, Elizabeth A.
2002 The Cunning of Recognition: Indigenous Alterities and the Making of Australian Multiculturalism. Durham, NC: Duke University Press.
Rose, Nikolas.
1999 Powers of Freedom: Reframing Political Thought. Cambridge: Cambridge University Press.
Scott, David
2003 Culture in Political Theory. Political Theory 31:92–115.
Skrydstrup, Martin
2009 Theorizing Repatriation. Ethnologia Europaea. Journal of European Ethnology 39(2):54–66.
2010 Once Ours: The Making and Unmaking of Claims to Cultural Property. PhD dissertation, Columbia University.
Smith, Laurajane
2006 Uses of Heritage. London: Routledge.
Smith, Laurajane, and Natsuko Akagawa, eds.
2009 Intangible Heritage. London: Routledge.
Strathern, Marilyn
2004 Transactions: An Analytical Foray. *In* Transactions and Creations: Property Debates and the Stimulus of Melanesia. Eric Hirsch and Marilyn Strathern, eds. pp. 85–109. Oxford: Berghahn.
2005 Kinship, Law and the Unexpected: Relatives are Always a Surprise. Cambridge: Cambridge University Press.
Taylor, Charles
1989 Sources of the Self: The Making of Modern Identity. Cambridge: Cambridge University Press.
1994 The Politics of Recognition. *In* Multiculturalism: Examining the Politics of Recognition. Charles Taylor and Amy Gutmann, eds. pp. 25–73. New Jersey: Princeton University Press.
Turtinen, Jan
2006 Världsarvets villkor: Intressen, förhandlingar och bruk i internationell politik. Stockholm Studies in Ethnology, 1. Stockholm: Acta Universitatis Stockholmiensis.
Tweedie, Ann M.
2002 Drawing Back Culture: The Makah Struggle for Repatriation. Seattle: University of Washington Press.
UNESCO
1945 Constitution of the United Nations Educational, Scientific and Cultural Organization.

1954 Convention for the Protection of Cultural Property in the Event of Armed Conflict.
1970 Convention on the Means of Prohibiting and Preventing the Illicit Import, Export and Transfer of Ownership of Cultural Property.
2003 Convention for the Safeguarding of the Intangible Cultural Heritage, with a Representative List of the Intangible Cultural Heritage of Humanity.

United Nations
1948 Universal Declaration of Human Rights.
1966 International Covenant on Civil and Political Rights.
1966 International Covenant on Economic, Social and Cultural Rights.
1972 Convention concerning the Protection of the World Cultural and Natural Heritage.
1979 Convention on the Elimination of All Forms of Discrimination against Women.
1989 Convention on the Rights of the Child.
1990 International Convention on the Protection of the Rights of All Migrant Workers and Members of Their Families.
1992 Declaration on the Rights of Persons Belonging to National or Ethnic, Religious and Linguistic Minorities.
2006 Convention on the Rights of Persons with Disabilities.
2007 United Nations Declaration on the Rights of Indigenous Peoples.

Yúdice, George
2004 The Expediency of Culture: Uses of Culture in the Global Era. Durham: Duke University Press.

CHAPTER 24

Corporate Social Responsibility and Cultural Practices on Globalizing Markets

Christina Garsten

Entry Point: Contested Corporate Interests

Corporate social responsibility (CSR) is a concept that has risen to prominence in the pantheon of ideas influencing the governance of global markets. Spurred by economic globalization and recurring financial crises, CSR has come to assume the role of a panacea for the quandaries and challenges related to globalizing corporate powers, addressing the new social and environmental challenges to their operations. It has been celebrated as a way to enhance the ethical reflexivity and sensitivity of corporate actors, as well as a new promising market niche. Today, ethical initiatives, ranging from codes of conduct, certification, and labeling schemes to social and environmental accounting, are omnipresent. Ethical aspects have, by way of the CSR "movement," been instituted into the field of global business, and have merged with liberal market thinking as the arbiter of social concerns and financial gain. New regimes of accountability are being created, aiming to create a more "humane capitalism."

But how can we make sense of CSR? What kind of "anthropological problem," in Paul Rabinow's sense (2005), is brought forward? Whilst it would appear that CSR is a young concept and a novelty, it speaks to classic questions and conflicts regarding the balancing of profit and social accountability. It invites us to reflect on basic questions pertaining to the contributions to society that should be expected from business, the relation of business to civil society, and to the state. CSR is thus a concept that speaks to larger issues related to processes of globalization, and to the relativity or universality of human values and rights.

In the wake of Adam Smith's (2002) notion of "the invisible hand," the conjunction of the forces of self-interest, competition, and supply and demand, we know that

A Companion to the Anthropology of Europe, First Edition. Edited by Ullrich Kockel, Máiréad Nic Craith, and Jonas Frykman.

the primary rationality of corporations is the pursuit of calculated self-interest. The corporation is in essence a social and economic construction aimed at pursuing the self-interest of capitalism and of profit. As a legal entity with an official seal beyond its individual social actors, with the rules and the procedures that constitute it, it is devoid of emotional capacities. Indeed, it is an institution of which we can expect little in the form of social responsiveness, sympathy, or responsibility. As A. F. Robertson (2001) suggests, the Western business corporation instantiates the predatory instinct for greed and self-interest. From this bottom-line priority, the ways in which a corporation relates to the social world at large, to employees as well as to other stakeholders, may vary considerably. From this perspective, the current CSR movement aims to overcome, challenge, or at least balance, opposing and conflicting interests: profit and social responsibility. What the growth of CSR signals, however, is an ongoing attempt to reconfigure or rearticulate the relations of capital and profit to social responsibility and sustainability. The very notion of CSR inspires us to tease out the connections between business cultures and the larger sociocultural contexts in which they operate. Only by careful investigations into the social and cultural nestedness of CSR can we appreciate what the assemblage of ideas, tools, and technologies that together make up CSR, imply.

This chapter will discuss the components of CSR and situate the phenomenon in a broader context of globalization. It will also introduce some relevant and timely anthropological questions that are raised by the development of corporate social responsibility, from the global perspective and more specifically a European horizon.

The Ascendance of an Idea

Corporate Social Responsibility (CSR) can be described as a form of voluntary regulation whereby corporations monitor and ensure their adherence to law, international conventions, and ethical standards. Ideally, it assumes that corporations take responsibility for the impact of their activities on the larger social and natural environment, that is, on employees, communities, consumers, and other stakeholders in society at large. In its more encompassing version, it stipulates a proactive stance on the part of business in encouraging community development and in voluntarily eliminating practices that might harm the public sphere, beyond legal standards. In this way, corporations wish not only to respond to stakeholder pressure but also to project an image of business as not just profit-seeking, but also socially responsible and ethically minded.

CSR, also known as "corporate responsibility," "corporate citizenship," "responsible business," "sustainable responsible business" (SRB), or "corporate social performance," has long-standing roots, deeply entwined with the particularities of the cultural, social, political, and economic contexts and structures of which they are a part. There is no easy way to summarize when and how social responsibility began to take shape. Here I will only sketch the rough contours of a long-term and complex trajectory (for a more detailed historical account, see Carroll 2008).

Investigations into its beginnings generally identify the 1950s as the decade during which CSR began to take hold in the Western industrialized world. Since the 1960s, awareness of CSR has grown significantly among corporate actors, and the idea that corporations had a social responsibility beyond legal compliance gained a firm foothold. During the late 1960s and early 1970s, companies began focusing on specific issues, such as working conditions, industrial relations, urban decay, racial discrimination, and pollution problems. In the following years, corporations also began to take serious management and organizational actions to address CSR issues. Such actions would include altering boards of directors, examining corporate ethics, and making use of social performance disclosures. The decade of the 1960s all in all witnessed a momentous growth in attempts to articulate and formalize what CSR meant. In this period, the intimate connections between corporations and society were being recognized and put forward as a reason for broadening the narrowly circumscribed interests of firms. In a general sense, however, there was still "more talk than action on the CSR front" (McGuire 1963; Carroll 2008:28).

The 1970s marked an acceleration of CSR in the world of business as well as in academic writings. The changing social contract between business and society under the influence of a general recognition of the responsibilities of business called for attention, underscored by an enhanced process of globalization and the uncovering of corporate misdemeanors. The 1970s also saw increasing reference being made to "social responsiveness," signaling the adaptation of corporate behavior to social needs, as well as a more anticipatory and preventive approach. This was also the decade during which many were suggesting the importance of managerial approaches to CSR, implying that corporations should forecast and plan for CSR, organize for CSR, and institutionalize corporate social policy and practice (Carroll 2008:34). Still widely characterized as a field generating "more talk than action," CSR at this point in time was beginning to be seen as a movement to be taken seriously, and one that also spurred organizational and legislative actions.

The diversification and splintering of CSR was enhanced in the 1980s. A range of alternative and complementary concepts and themes emerged, together with new tools, technologies, and professional categories. Alongside corporate responsiveness, "corporate social performance," "business ethics," and "stakeholder theory" were ideas that took hold. Frameworks of principles, processes, and policies were articulated.

The themes and ideas that were developed in the 1980s continued to grow and take center-stage in the 1990s, now complemented with the notions of "corporate citizenship" and "sustainability." Each of these notions, which are to some degree overlapping and complementary, has given rise to its own extensive literature. In a very general sense, corporate citizenship signaled the recognition of the embeddedness of the corporation in a larger social web, with accompanying obligations as well as rights, whilst sustainability embraced concerns for the environment and later the larger social and stakeholder environment. Also, philanthropy expanded considerably during this period, not least in the United States. The expansion of philanthropy was not seen as entirely unproblematic, since these kinds of corporate contributions suggest, at least among critics, corporate generosity and patriarchal gift-giving rather than obligation and responsibility. The 1990s also witnessed a formidable explosion of standards for social responsibility and codes of conduct (see, e.g., Leipziger 2003). The birth of the UN Global Compact in 1999, when the former UN Secretary General Kofi Annan in a speech at the World Economic Forum in Davos challenged the business leaders of the world to help fill the governance voids that the rise of the global economy had brought about, was a significant event. It marked a number of business-based and other initiatives toward CSR. Since its establishment thousands of corporations from all regions of the world have signed up to the UN Global Compact and its principles (7300 businesses in over 130 countries, as of January 2010 (Rasche and Kell 2010)). Since the 1990s, then, CSR has emerged as one of the priorities in the policy documents and yearly reports of corporations.

Around the turn of the millennium, CSR – and its associated set of ideas, tools, and technologies – has not only established itself in management practice and corporate governance, but as an academic area of research in its own right. Empirical research on the topic of CSR has grown considerably in all disciplines across the social sciences. Conceptual approaches have mushroomed as well as been refined, and CSR is now a staple ingredient in academic conferences across disciplines, with established academic publication outlets (such as *Business Ethics*, *Business & Society*, and *Social Responsibility Journal*). Management and legal expertise have been established and there is now a vast body of consultancies addressing the field of CSR.

The idea that business has a broader social responsibility or citizenship role has grown with the globalization of markets (see, for example, Compa and Diamond 1996; Addo 1999; Andriof and McIntosh 2001; Sullivan 2003). First, the globalization of markets has meant that the national state and its legal system have encountered challenges in ensuring that legal norms are upheld in transnational business. Deregulation in both rich and poor countries has opened up the field for the play of market forces across borders, and for mergers and acquisitions that have strengthened corporate power at transnational level. With the gradual dismantling of national regulations and trade barriers and the establishment of flexible and entrepreneurial corporations as the template for organizational design, nation-state governments have been left with a fragmented political authority, with limited power to fashion markets (Palan 2000). Hence, with enhanced globalization of markets and increasing financial interdependencies, governments are facing significant challenges in the regulation of market forces. International standards and conventions have not been able to come to terms with the complex regulatory gaps invoked by the globalization of business. In their place, governance mechanisms that rely on voluntary norm-creation and monitoring have been set up. The multiple CSR standards available, such as the OECD Guidelines, The UN Norms on the Responsibilities of Transnational Corporations and Other Business Enterprises with Regard to Human Rights, ISO 26000, and others, seek to promote the voluntary engagement in CSR by corporations.

Second, the globalization of markets has also spurred the emergence of a new market niche for organizations offering support in developing, implementing, or monitoring ethical standards. A veritable jungle of new positions and consultancies are competing with each other in this new market: ethics managers, ethics officers, CSR officials, ethics consultants, and the like. The growth in such positions and organizations has been further spurred by an increasing emphasis on compliance and a gradual tightening of regulations.

For some 20 years, the CSR movement has been a global phenomenon. It is important to recognize, however, that corporate responsibility in its contemporary version is a distinctively Anglo-American phenomenon. The emergence of CSR on the public scene was intimately linked to the particular corporate governance prevalent in the United States at the time. In the liberal welfare model of the United States, advocating a limited role for the state and legal interference in the obligations of corporations toward society, CSR allowed for a self-regulatory mode of governance, based on voluntary engagement and on liberal values. In the United States, and in the United Kingdom (rather an exception in the European context), the growth of CSR has also been closely tied with business philanthropy. In continental Europe on the other hand, where corporatist welfare models are more prevalent, allowing for a more prominent role for the state in defining the role of business to society, and with a more clearly regulated social contract in terms of its legal structures, CSR did not make a real impact until the 2000s. At this point, the interest in CSR peaked in the European Community and became a major trend in business. It has since become one of the more important topics of discussion among NGOs, trade unionists, politicians, and researchers. In a milestone Communication on CSR (COM 2006) the Commission emphasized the importance of CSR and challenged business to take leadership in this field. The Commission intends to continue to promote CSR as a voluntary concept, with an emphasis on dialogue between stakeholders. In March 2010, the Commission made a commitment to renew the EU strategy to promote CSR as a key element in ensuring long-term employee and consumer trust. CSR is put forward as "more relevant than ever in the context of the economic crisis. It can help to build (and rebuild) trust in business, which is vital for the health of Europe's social market economy" (OCEG 2011).

Across Europe there is considerable variation in how CSR is both conceptualized and implemented in practice. There is a divergence of political involvement and management practice, evident in areas such as labor standards, environment, human rights, and fighting bribery. With a broad stroke of the brush, CSR is most clearly mainstreamed into a wider political debate and into the legal framework in the Scandinavian countries. An ethnologically inspired study (Roepsdorff 2010) situates CSR in Denmark in the context of transforming relations between state and industry, where early models of patriarchal goodwill have given way to a more clearly regulated regime of social responsibility. Continental Europe shows a more diversified and fragmented picture. In the former Eastern bloc, CSR is still a relatively new phenomenon, with yet more limited impact on business practice. Habisch et al. (2005), in a major volume depicting the development and variety of CSR across Europe, situate it as an integral part of a debate around sustainability and globalization. Karolina Windell (2006) explores, with a new-institutional theoretical lens, the interrelationship between ideas, actors, and institutional change, and how and why CSR was constructed and became a widespread idea in Europe. Her findings suggest that CSR was collectively mobilized in interplay and contestations among actor groups that translated it in accordance with their disparate interests. In this way ambiguous forms and meanings for CSR were created, resulting in nonclarification over time. The findings suggest that translation processes are set in motion through contestations that draw attention to an idea.

There are fundamental questions to be asked about the nature and purpose of CSR, how it has been constructed and framed, and by whom. The teasing out of the different discourses of CSR has become an important theme in academic research in recent years. Further, the practice of CSR is subject to a lively debate and criticism.

While proponents argue that corporations can benefit in multiple ways by operating with a perspective that is broader and longer than their own immediate, short-term profits, and that there is a strong business case for CSR, critics argue that it distracts from the fundamental economic role of businesses and enters into the realm of the welfare state. Others argue that it is nothing more than a branding and publicity exercise and yet others argue that it is an attempt to preempt the role of the state and of government as a watchdog over the activities of transnational corporations. There is also a critique against assumptions of universality of human values underlying the ethical norms.

From the above it is clear that the field of CSR constitutes both a broad and varied field of inquiry and practice. What exactly CSR means remains an open question, in academia as well as among practitioners. Few concepts arouse as much controversy and give rise to as much negotiation and contestation as CSR. There is now such an abundance of definitions of the term, both among practitioners and among academics, that we can rightfully conceive of CSR as an "essentially contested concept," that is, a concept "which inevitably involves endless disputes about [its] proper uses on the part of [its] users" (Gallie 1956:169).

On a larger scale, what exactly the CSR movement as a whole means, and how it should be understood, remains as well contested. Whilst many have placed it solidly within the area of global governance and positioned it as a framework for soft regulation (Djelic and Sahlin-Andersson 2006), some see in CSR evidence of corporate actors contributing to development and sustainability (Sherer and Palazzo 2008), whilst yet others see it merely as a management trend (Sahlin-Andersson 2006). From an anthropological vantage point, CSR has primarily been approached as a new articulation of the relations of the large-scale powers of capital to small-scale, local communities, and as a movement creating new geographies of inequality, as well as of inclusion and exclusion (see, e.g., de Neve et al. 2008). Strikingly evident is the vibrancy of this multidisciplinary academic field of inquiry. In a study of the CSR literature over a ten-year period, Lockett et al. (2006:133) concluded that CSR knowledge could best be described as "in a continuing state of emergence." It is thus as a continuously transforming field of inquiry that we should approach the CSR movement.

An Agile Assemblage of Ideas

At the global level, there are now a large number of organizations that seek to advise, guide, or set rules for the conduct of corporations in a global market. In the CSR area, corporations, civil society organizations, and state agencies compete, collaborate, or complement each others' efforts to formulate frameworks for the governance of market actors. A multiplicity of actors are involved: state actors, corporations, nonprofit organizations, professional associations, and intergovernmental organizations, sometimes in networks of private and public actors. Indeed, globalization has created new operational and formal openings for the participation of a variety of organizational actors in regulatory activities. And these organizations are vital in opening up "new sites of normativity" alongside the normative order represented by the nation-state (Sassen 1998:94–95). These "new sites of normativity" to some extent challenge the established authority of the state in regulatory affairs. They also play a vital role in spreading the gospel of CSR, the core normative ideas, as well as diffusing tools and technologies to further their implementation into practice.

Anthropological research has until more recently been more concerned with the normative ideas that are created and disseminated by public organizations and bureaucracies, than those circulated by corporations. As pointed out by Dolan and Rajak (2011), anthropology's reflection on ethics has, until recently, neglected engagement with the corporate "organization" as such, its situated organizational practices and the corporate forms associated with CSR. Recently, however, anthropologists have begun to engage with charting and problematizing the contested morality of the corporate form (see, e.g., Foster 2010). There is a recognized concern to grapple with the myriad configurations of CSR and the meanings, expectations, and frictions the movement is generating. Novel forms of the "ethical economy" in industries around the world, including garments (de Neve 2008), soft drinks (Foster 2008), petroleum (Shever 2008), mining (Welker 2009; Rajak 2010), pharmaceuticals (Ecks 2010), and retailing (Dolan 2007), have been more closely looked at, revealing the various ways in which CSR and ethics in a wider sense are negotiated in corporate settings.

Anthropological studies of CSR take, in general, a critical approach, investigating the social implications of CSR as a dominant discourse and set of practices. An interesting contribution to this end is Welker's study (2009) of the practices of Newmont Mining Corporation on the island of Sumbawa in Indonesia. She devotes analysis to the activities of those who support and defend capitalist development, thereby shedding light on the social dynamics of contemporary capitalism and corporate dealings. She demonstrates how CSR initiatives have "produced fresh zones of struggle and new forms of violence" in addition to productive spaces in which anthropologists can reconsider the pressures capital places upon subjects and the corporate response through such projects as CSR.

Contemporary capitalism shows tremendous versatility in appropriating and rearticulating challenges to critiques of its ways of functioning. In my own research (Garsten 2003, 2004), I have explored the field of CSR as one in which organizational actors discuss and negotiate the relation of "things social" to "things economic." In discussions of CSR, managers try out partly-new ways of conceptualizing the enterprise mission, the meaning of profit, and new ways of combining profit with social accountability. In the process, they negotiate bottom-line reasoning with sustainable futures, markets and moralities. Corporate managers reflexively and flexibly juggle and balance the different priorities they are up against, pragmatically situating CSR within their core business. In doing so, they are able to provide the company with legitimacy in the society of stakeholders. A flexible assemblage of keywords provides the managers with a *lingua franca* that facilitates communication among parties that may represent different interests. Some keywords, such as "transparency" and "accountability," appear frequently but acquire a range of contingent meanings, as used by different actors with differing interests, and when introduced into new areas of operation (cf. Williams 1976; see also Shore and Wright 2000). The strength of this vocabulary is that it has the capacity to disentangle itself from the particularities of local context and to reentangle with new actors in new contexts and situations. Its very abstractness and visionary character facilitates its use across social contexts, across organizations, countries, and cultural boundaries of any sort. Because of the flexible usage of these terms, their supposed neutrality, and not least their visionary appeal, they make up an attractive toolbox for positioning the corporation as socially responsible.

The discourse of CSR, I argue, is far from a neutral vehicle for communication. Those who are exposed to this particular *lingua franca* are also shaped by it, and learn the ways of thinking and acting associated with it. The discourse of CSR is, in other words, performative. It gives direction for daily practice, and prescribes and encourages certain types of behavior, oftentimes supported by various types of practices, such as those of evaluation, reward, and sanctions.

Studying how market keywords are used during conferences and meetings, in presentations, and in documents, and as part of informal conversations in the European and North American context, I was able to discern four metaphoric structures that represent the different ways in which corporate actors position themselves in society (Garsten 2004). Whilst these images or metaphoric constructs are based on interviews and participant observation, they represent my own interpretations and extrapolations of the narratives. The metaphoric structures found to be prevalent among corporate actions were "the entrepreneurial corporation," "the collaborative corporation," "the cosmopolitan corporation," and "the conscientious corporation." These constructs serve the purpose of illustrating different voices in the process of engaging with CSR, and the ways this engagement is perceived in organizational life. They represent different routes through which the role of the corporation in society is negotiated and positioned, slightly different uses of the discursive elements, with some shifts in the emphasis made. The metaphoric construct may be said to work as a model, not only *of* the world (Geertz 1973; Fernandez 1974), but, more importantly, *for* the world. For actors in the field of CSR, they serve as tools for ordering the world, the role of corporations within it, and a device for the structuring of their own thoughts and actions.

Looking more closely at how these discursive strategies work in practice, Garsten and Hernes (2008, 2009) have found that managers actively channel attention so that a favorable impression of the company is created and maintained, in much the same manner as a lightning rod functions to deflect lightning. In their discursive strategies, they are able to combine discursive elements to direct attention to particular, desired values and aspirations of a company, whilst leaving others in the shadow, as it were. In this perspective, CSR may be seen as a discursive structure, and one that is continuously shaped and reshaped by the actors engaged in it. The positions and interests of the actors involved influence the moves and actions, realigning elements of the discursive structure accordingly. Strategic acting may lend the impression that the corporation is acting ethically, while it may, at the same time, remove the need for the company to deal with potentially important ethical dilemmas (Garsten and Hernes 2008).

The role of standards and other technologies in the discursive strategies of organizational managers compels us to look more closely into what they are; how they work; and what the implications of using them are. The area of CSR is ripe with audit technologies, suggestive of their prominent role on the centre stage of CSR performance.

Tools, Technologies, and the Social Life of Standards

Over the past couple of decades, many organizations have made efforts to create specific standards of appropriate ethical conduct for individual as well as corporate actions. Whilst much of this standard-setting is done informally or implicitly, by way of cultural expectations, CSR has sparked an impressive number of explicit codes of conduct and standards. In a general sense, such standards are rules for what the corporation and its employees should do. They are based on normative expectations about what is right and wrong, and what the proper kind of behavior ought to be. Standards may also help to establish and maintain norms, and as such they are performative. Standards, being voluntary by nature and prescriptive in character, are an effective means of coordination in markets (Brunsson and Jacobsson 2002). As noted above, standards experienced a substantial rise in number and usage in the 1990s and 2000s, particularly in large, transnational companies with well-known, sensitive, brands. CSR standards show a considerable variety. They may be issued by international organizations (such as the OECD), or by nongovernmental organizations (such as ISO, the International Organization for Standardization). They may be unilateral (issued by one party), bilateral, or multilateral in their origin. They may be comprehensive (such as the UN Norms on the Responsibilities of Transnational Corporations and Other Business Enterprises with Regard to Human Rights), or they may be issue-focused (such as the UN Global Compact CEO Water Mandate Transparency Framework). Moreover, and importantly, codes of conduct are often pregnant with different interpretations and translate differently into practice. Further, codes of conduct often overlap with each other and can be rather complex (for an overview see, e.g., Leipziger 2003; Crane et al. 2007).

Other tools and technologies in use in the area of CSR are different forms of corporate reporting, formalized into accounting routines, or more informal ones such as ethics hotlines and other reporting channels. Labeling schemes and certification procedures have been developed to ensure and recognize compliance with standards and codes of ethics, and to ensure that the standards are implemented down the line of procurement and production.

Anthropologically, standards may be regarded as "global forms," in Stephen Collier and Aiwa Ong's sense (2005, see also Dunn 2005) in that they have a particularly global character. Although locally produced through series of meetings and negotiations in specific places, they move easily across space, and their range of impact is intended to be global. They communicate easily across local realities, albeit at abstract and distanciated levels. In Collier and Ong's words (2005:11), "[T]hey have a distinct capacity for decontextualization and recontextualization, abstractability and mobility." Lofty and abstract in character, their strength is in their capacity to point to preferred directions, to offer a certain directionality to organizational visions, and to mobilize people around these. A telling case in point is Elisabeth Dunn's study of ISO standards (2005) as a global form in the Polish meatpacking industry. ISO standards, as global forms, are able to assimilate themselves to new contexts, and to operate in similar fashions in various environments. But to function, they require that the work routines and the record keeping procedures change to accommodate for coding in a way that allows for control and valuation. They need to be made "legible" to health inspectors, regulators, and investors in diverse sites. As shown by Dunn, standards work only by the flexible accommodation of the objects and processes under scrutiny. They require that the objects make themselves amenable to cooperation and control.

Standards and codes of conduct can fruitfully be conceived as what Bruno Latour calls "immutable mobiles" (Latour 1987) – technoscientific forms that can be both decontextualized and recontextualized, abstracted, transported, and that aim to produce comparable results in different localities. They carry a potentiality for governance and control that should not be underestimated, but that merits critical scrutiny in the "unpacking" of the assemblage, as it were. Whilst the emergence of such technologies of governance is interesting in its own right, as a means of coordination in markets, they speak to transformation in the forms of control that are being developed for "governance at a distance." Anthropologists have begun to direct interest in the role of standards in the implementation of CSR programs. In this context, Geert de Neve's work on the effects of trade liberalization on export industries in Tamil Nadu, with a particular focus on the social politics of CSR, NGO activism, and corporate governance in the garment commodity chain, is relevant. De Neve's research on the implementation of corporate codes of conduct and labor standards among south Indian garment manufacturers shows how seemingly "innocent" standards play a role in the politics of governance and inequality in the era of neoliberal reform (de Neve 2008).

CSR standards are thus not stand-alone items, but should be seen as particular instantiations of the values and norms underlying their creation. Standards are vessels of communication that embody particular assemblages of ideas and norms. By tracing the processes through which CSR standards and codes of conduct are created and put to work in actual practice, anthropologists are beginning to tease out how standards may embody tensions between different logics and values, and how abstract and seemingly context-independent ideas are rendered social, and thus political.

A large part of the potential of a standard to act as a means of governance resides in its being presented as impersonal, technocratic, and neutral. Hence, the richness both of sociality and of the social and political negotiations that go with implementing CSR standards appear to be rendered obsolete by way of technical procedures and abstract ideals. The contemporary modalities of ethical governance, such as standards, code of conduct, and auditing technologies are increasingly proxies for face-to-face interactions, supplanting sociality with the material artifacts of ethical regulation (Dolan and Rajak 2011). This is aptly illustrated in several ethnographic studies of CSR, as in an article by Jamie Cross pointing to the detachment produced by texts and documents pertaining to CSR in the context of diamond processing in South India (Cross 2011). As a way to get beyond the fiction of economic abstraction, he suggests we view detachment as a relationship, that is, not the absence of a social relationship but as a social relationship in itself, or a way of relating to other market actors. In this sense, it also makes up an ethical stance of a particular sort, but one that runs counter to that of attachment or reconnection. This goes to show how processes of attachment and detachment, abstraction and personalization, are rarely each other's opposite poles, but constantly matters of degree, and of interrelatedness. In a similar vein, Marianne Elisabeth Lien analyzes with detailed sharpness the place of standards, science, and technologies of scale in the construction of Tasmanian Atlantic salmon (Lien 2009). Standards, as global forms, are thus powerful tools in the abstraction and universalization of local and single instance products.

Hence, when studying the organization of accountability tools and arrangements, it is not enough to focus merely on the tools and techniques; we must also pay attention to the more general ideologies, definitions, programs, discourses, strategies, and framings underpinning such tools. The flourishing CSR movement goes far beyond an appreciation of its particular techniques, but must be seen as a broad ideological or cultural commitment to interorganizational regulation, governing, checking, and monitoring (cf. Power 1997; Djelic and Sahlin-Andersson 2006). It is important to examine critically the hegemonic commitment around CSR and investigate the many subpolitical power struggles around the pros and cons of diverse tools and techniques. Revealing such power struggles must simultaneously imply the unmasking of the widespread rhetoric around neutrality and objectivity.

Universalizing Values

The CSR movement should be understood as a contemporary version of how profit and social concerns are to be legitimately balanced and governed. As such, it is an arrangement underpinned by particular sets of values and may be seen as ideologically shaped. The differing trajectories that corporate organizations may take in different contexts and at different times, afford the CSR field a great deal of variety. Even so, CSR emerged largely out of an Anglo-American context in which liberal market ideology was highly influential. Since the 1980s, ideological shifts in the direction of liberalized views on markets more generally have provided further leeway for soft forms of governance. Corporations and their dealings should, in this understanding, preferably be governed mainly by way of voluntary, self-regulatory efforts, than by state law and directives. Thus, underlying CSR is, in a general sense, a liberal and market-oriented ideology advocating soft means of governance, rather than hard law regulation. A key tenet of critical research into CSR is that the activities and ideas of corporate actors are shaped by such ideological strands, which create chains of signification and shape actors' interpretations (Crane et al. 2008). From this perspective, ideologies are implicated in the ideas and practices of CSR, and their presence in the tools and techniques should be recognized.

The area of CSR can be regarded as an example of how contemporary ethical problems related to key questions of human rights, workers rights, and environment, may assume a global form. They become organized by and through organizations that define humanity and social responsibility through a single cultural and political lens. They are as well attached to global technologies designed to produce comparable results in diverse domains and different parts of the world, and that make up what we could call a "standards regime." Marilyn Strathern has shown how allegedly universal values, such as "liberality" and "democracy," are operationalized through the "flexible" ethical forms of the social audit and made to operate in a wide range of environments (Strathern 2005). Moreover, in the abstracting and generalizing ambitions of audit organizations, the very notion of "society," which is commonly implicated in CSR practices and audit practice more generally, becomes desocialized. "The invocation of 'society,'" she argues, "summons the fragility of measurement: What will count as 'society'? Whose views will figure?" (Strathern 2005:476).

In an ethnographic study of a mining-company, Dinah Rajak (2010) has shown how CSR practices are imbued with moralizing claims by corporate managers. Her case shows how traditional corporate philanthropy is rebranded as the company engages in partnership programs with the local community. Enacting their mission in terms of CSR principles, company managers communicate their mission through the various projects they support. She suggests that Mauss's idea of the gift (2000) can enhance our understanding of how CSR works. The gift of support to workers and to projects, Rajak argues, acts to support the authority of the corporation and of management and compels a return gift of loyalty to the corporation and its mission. The moral terms in which CSR is cast assert the asymmetrical, dependent relations between workers and management. Indeed, the phenomenon of CSR, in its manifestations of "giving" through projects such as housing, childcare, social services, or other provisions, may be seen as a gift of sorts, with expectations of reciprocity attached. When basic human or workers' rights are not provided through a public welfare system and by legal sanctioning, the provision of such rights comes to be seen as "gifts" that are to be reciprocated. Employee loyalty and discipline may thus be secured by CSR initiatives, imbued with moralizing concerns and motives. The fact that CSR may contribute to the conservation of dependencies has, not surprisingly, given rise to criticism and reservations about the implications of voluntary forms of corporate governance.

The increasing reliance on voluntary forms of governance, such as CSR standards and codes of conduct, is intrinsically linked to a new ethics of governance. This in turn relies on the inculcation of norms and values positioned as voluntary and benign in nature, and by which external regulatory mechanisms are to transform and monitor the conduct of organizations through "action at a distance" (Miller and Rose 1990:1). As such, they are articulations of a new rationality of government, usually referred to as "neo-liberal governmentality" (Foucault 1991a). In a general sense, CSR is premised on the norms of the free market as the organizing principles of economic life, but also of the activities of corporations in society at large, as well as of the conduct of individuals.

From a critical standpoint, CSR can be apprehended a clear example of the "post-political" nature of contemporary forms of regulation and governance (Garsten and Jacobsson 2008). It assumes that we have reached a stage where antagonisms between "things economic" and "things social," between bottom-line reasoning and social responsibility, can actually be transcended. In the new vocabulary of social responsibility, classical antagonisms, such as those between state and market, welfare and profit, have been eradicated or at least blurred. As with related forms of soft governance, there is instead a discursive emphasis on "partner," "partnership," "commitment," and "agreement." There is little in the way of "interest," "party," or "conflict," except possibly at the grassroots level where the actual consequences of the failures to live up to the codes of conduct are experienced. CSR here bears evidence of what Laura Nader (1990) has termed "harmony ideology," an ideology that is centered on the belief that the existence of conflict is necessarily a bad thing, and that a healthy society is one that achieves harmony between people and minimizes conflict and confrontation.

Moreover, the way to transcend problems or conflicts is to rely on voluntary market-based forms of regulation that stipulate a moral directionality. The call for accountability is a call for morality and represents a "benign" form of power that is hard to resist (Foucault 1991b). Power is regarded as benign insofar as it is exercised in discordant relationships between actors to serve altruistic and/or collective ends and in which the social and political values of democracy, political freedom, and social justice are paramount (McCalla 2002). It presumes actors of goodwill who assume responsibility, or a positive agency, and who also tend to refuse to accept force (as in legislation). CSR discourse, as evinced in the talk and social practices of market actors, posits social responsibility as a general point of reference, but it fails to address power relations. Power, as well as its distribution, tends to be invisibilized and rendered obsolete. We can here see clear parallels to the "anti-politics machine" described by Ferguson (1994). Ferguson analyzes how the institutional framework within which development projects are crafted, and the "development discourse," play out in the implementation of a development project in Lesotho. The development apparatus acts as an "anti-politics machine," Ferguson argues, whisking political realities out of sight, all the while performing, almost unnoticed, its own preeminently political operation of strengthening the state presence in the local region.

Hence, regulatory codes work by taking what is essentially a political problem, removing it from the realm of political discourse, and recasting it in neutral language. Regulatory codes often present themselves as rational, objective, and neutral, based on the sound principles of human solidarity and market dynamics working together to form a humane capitalism. CSR gains legitimacy by enabling corporations to strike a balance, at least theoretically, between profit and greed on the one hand, moral considerations and universal values on the other. Data and practices that are by nature conflictual and political are, in the field of CSR, transformed and come to exist in a moral field. In this transformed moral field, standards, codes of conduct, and related tools achieve a status beyond political contestation, being viewed as morally and ethically sound, and, hence, difficult to question in principle (Garsten 2004:85). Thus, while often of a voluntary nature, CSR regulations are often impossible to critique, since they are seen to advance good and ethical practice.

Looking Ahead

Corporate social responsibility, although it may appear as a new feature on the catwalk, is a worn rag. The basic questions and quandaries addressed by CSR go as far back in history as do market exchange and social organization. Albeit a novelty in its contemporary articulations, CSR raises old issues to do with the balancing of greed and profit on the one hand, and social concern and responsibility on the other. Looking ahead, what are the prospects of CSR for the future? Will it continue to grow and gain in legitimacy in organizations? Or will it wane, like so many other organizational fads?

The global penetration of market-driven corporate enterprise into societies has been accompanied by disruptive and often disastrous social and environmental consequences. The political instability and unrest that have followed in the wake of these processes render the governance of markets increasingly complicated, and all the more important. Wherever markets and corporate enterprise constitute the basis of a society's economic endeavors, CSR is an idea that will probably continue to play a leading role in political and public debates around the role of business in society for some time to come.

The ascent of CSR and its variety of toolboxes – standards, code of conduct, labeling schemes, and so on – on the agenda of organizations during the past two decades points to its mobilizing potential and the high expectations placed on it as a "soft" governance technology tailored to a globalizing capitalist economy. Research into the assemblages of core ideas and how these are underpinned by ideology and values can reveal the sophisticated ways in which dominant powers depict a particular version of reality as legitimate and then diffuse these across the world. The panoply of CSR instruments are flexible and agile, abstract and lofty enough to be impregnated with different sets of meanings as they are instantiated in discourses and put into practice. Rather than constituting a clearly discernible empirical problem, then, CSR opens up a vast problem area for critical studies on the "social contract" between business and society.

How the globalized and abstracted versions of CSR come into view in different social and cultural contexts and respond to local concerns is as well an area that merits further investigation. Comparative research may shed light on how different dominant political ideologies and structures make for different versions of CSR in different regions, industries, and organizations. A closer look at the conflictual meanings evoked as CSR engages with other assemblages of ideas and practices should also contribute to revealing the assumptions embedded in and carried by such global forms as standards and labeling schemes. And by doing so, the force by which soft modes of governance work is manifested.

REFERENCES

Addo, M. K., ed.
1999 Human Rights Standards and the Responsibility of Transnational Corporations. The Hague: Kluwer Law International.
Andriof, J., and M. McIntosh, eds.
2001 Perspectives on Corporate Citizenship. Sheffield: Greenleaf.
Brunsson, Nils, and Bengt Jacobsson
2002[2000] The Contemporary Expansion of Standardization. *In* A World of Standards. Nils Brunsson, Bengt Jacobsson, and associates, eds. pp. 1–17. Oxford: Oxford University Press.
Carroll, Archie
2008 A History of Corporate Social Responsibility Concepts and Practices. *In* The Oxford Handbook of Corporate Social Responsibility. Andrew Crane, Abagail McWilliams, Dirk

Matten, Jeremy Moon, and Donald S. Siegel, eds. pp. 19–46. Oxford: Oxford University Press.

Collier, Stephen, and Aiwa Ong

2005 Global Assemblages, Anthropological Problems. *In* Global Assemblages: Technologies, Politics, and Ethics as Anthropological Problems. Aihwa Ong and Stephen J. Collier, eds. pp. 3–21. Oxford: Blackwell.

COM(2006) 136 final. Brussels

2006 Communication from the Commission, to European Parliament, the Council and the European Economic and Social Committee Implementing the Partnership for Growth and Jobs: Making Europe a Pole of Excellence on Corporate Social Responsibility. Commission of the European Communities.

Compa Lance A., and Stephen F. Diamond, eds.

1996 Human Rights, Labor Rights, and International Trade. Philadelphia: University of Pennsylvania Press.

Crane, Andrew, Dirk Matten, and Laura J. Spence, eds.

2007 Corporate Social Responsibility: Readings and Cases in Global Context. London: Routledge.

Crane, Andrew, Abagail McWilliams, Dirk Matten, Jeremy Moon, and Donald S. Siegel, eds.

2008 The Oxford Handbook of Corporate Social Responsibility. Oxford: Oxford University Press.

Cross, Jamie

2011 Detachment as a Corporate Ethic: Materializing CSR in the Diamond Supply Chain. Focaal 60:34–46.

de Neve, Geert

2008 Global Garment Chains, Local Labour Activism: New Challenges to Trade Union and NGO Activism in the Tiruppur Garment Cluster, South India. *In* Hidden Hands in the Market: Ethnographies of Fair Trade, Ethical Consumption and Corporate Social Responsibility. Theme issue. Research in Economic Anthropology 28:213–241.

de Neve, Geert, Peter Luetchford, Jeffrey Pratt, and Donald Wood, eds.

2008 Hidden Hands in the Market: Ethnographies of Fair Trade, Ethical Consumption and Corporate Social Responsibility. Theme issue. Research in Economic Anthropology 28.

Djelic, Marie-Laure, and Kerstin Sahlin-Andersson, eds.

2006 Transnational Governance, Institutional Dynamics of Regulation. Cambridge: Cambridge University Press.

Dolan, Catherine

2007 Market Affections: Moral Encounters with Kenyan Fairtrade Flowers. Ethnos 72(2):239–261.

Dolan, Catherine, and Dinah Rajak

2011 Introduction: Ethnographies of Corporate Ethicizing. Focaal 60:3–8.

Dunn, Elisabeth C.

2005 Standards and Person-making in East-Central Europe. *In* Global Assemblages: Technologies, Politics, and Ethics as Anthropological Problems. Aihwa Ong and Stephen J. Collier, eds. pp. 173–193. Oxford: Blackwell.

Ecks, Stefan

2010 Near-Liberalism: Global Corporate Citizenship and Pharmaceutical Marketing in India. *In* Asian Biotechnologies. Nancy Chen and Aihwa Ong, eds. pp. 144–166. Durham, NC: Duke University Press.

Ferguson, James

1994[1990] The Anti-Politics Machine: "Development," Depoliticization and Bureaucratic Power in Lesotho. Minneapolis: University of Minnesota Press.

Fernandez, James
1974 Persuasions and Performances: Of the Beast in Everybody and the Metaphors in Everyman. *In* Myth, Symbol and Culture. Clifford Geertz, ed. pp. 39–60. New York: Norton.
Foster, Robert J.
2008 Coca-Globalization: Following Soft Drinks from New York to New Guinea. Basingstoke: Palgrave Macmillan.
2010 Corporate Oxymorons and the Anthropology of Corporations. Dialectical Anthropology 34(1):95–102.
Foucault, Michel
1991a Governmentality. *In* The Foucault Effect. G. Burchell et al., eds. pp. 87–104. London: Harvester Wheatsheaf.
1991b Discipline and Punish: The Birth of the Prison. Harmondsworth: Penguin.
Gallie, Walter B.
1956 Essentially Contested Concepts. Proceedings of the Aristotelian Society, New Series, 56:167–198.
Garsten, Christina
2003 The Cosmopolitan Organization: An Essay on Corporate Accountability. Global Networks 3(3):355–370.
2004 Market Missions: Negotiating Bottom Line and Social Responsibility. *In* Market Matters: Exploring Cultural Processes in the Global Marketplace. Christina Garsten and Monica Lindh de Montoya, eds. pp. 69–90. Basingstoke: Palgrave Macmillan.
Garsten, Christina, and Tor Hernes, eds.
2008 Ethical Dilemmas in Management. London: Routledge.
2009 Beyond CSR: Dilemmas and Paradoxes of Ethical Conduct in Transnational Organization. *In* Economics and Morality: Anthropological Approaches. Katherine E. Browne and B. Lynne Milgram, eds. pp. 189–210. Lanham, MD: Altamira.
Garsten, Christina, and Kerstin Jacobsson
2007 Corporate Globalization, Civil Society and Post Political Regulation: Whither Democracy? Development Dialogue 49:143–158.
Geertz, Clifford
1973 The Interpretation of Cultures. New York: Basic Books.
Habisch, André, Jan Jonker, Martina Wegner, and René Schmidpeter, eds.
2005 Corporate Social Responsibility across Europe. Berlin: Springer.
Latour, Bruno
1987 Science in Action: How to Follow Scientists and Engineers through Society. Milton Keynes: Open University Press.
Leipziger, Deborah
2003 The Corporate Responsibility Code Book. Sheffield: Greenleaf.
Lien, Marianne Elisabeth
2009 Standards, Science and Scale: The Case of Tasmanian Atlantic Salmon. *In* The Globalization of Food. David Inglis and Debra Gimlin, eds. pp. 65–80. Oxford: Berg.
Lockett, Andy, Jeremy Moon, and Wayne Visser
2006 Corporate Social Responsibility in Management Research: Focus, Nature, Salience and Sources of Influence. Journal of Management Studies 43(1):115–136.
Mauss, Marcel
2000[1954] The Gift: The Form and Reason for Exchange in Archaic Societies. London: Routledge.
McCalla, Doreen
2002 A Theoretical Framework of Benign Power in School Sector Decision Making: A Preface. Discourse 23(1):39–57.

McGuire, Joseph W.
1963 Business and Society. New York: McGraw-Hill.
McWilliams, Abagail, Donald S. Siegel, and Patrick M. Wright
2006 Corporate Social Responsibility: Strategic Implications. Journal of Management Studies 43(1):1–18.
Miller, Peter, and Nikolas Rose
1990 Governing Economic Life. Economy and Society 19(1):1–31.
Nader, Laura
1990 Harmony Ideology: Justice and Control in a Zapotec Mountain Village. Stanford: Stanford University Press.
OCEG
2011 EU, European Commission's Site on Corporate Social Responsibility. Electronic document. http://www.oceg.org/resource/eu-european-commissions-site-corporate-social-responsibility (accessed November 5, 2011).
Palan, Ronen
2000 New Trends in Global Political Economy. *In* Global Political Economy: Contemporary Theories. Ronen Palan, ed. pp. 1–18. London: Routledge.
Power, Michael
1997 The Audit Society: Rituals of Verification. Oxford: Oxford University Press.
Rabinow, Paul
2005 Midst Anthropology's Problems. *In* Global Assemblages: Technologies, Politics, and Ethics as Anthropological Problems. Aihwa Ong and Stephen J. Collier, eds. pp. 40–53. Oxford: Blackwell.
Rajak, Dinah
2010 "HIV/AIDS is Our Business": The Moral Economy of Treatment in a Transnational Mining Company. Journal of the Royal Anthropological Institute 16(3): 551–571.
Rasche, Andreas, and Georg Kell
2010 Introduction: The United Nations Global Compact – Retrospect and Prospect. *In* The United Nations Global Compact: Achievements, Trends, and Challenges. Andreas Rasche and Georg Kell, eds. pp. 1–20. Cambridge: Cambridge University Press.
Roberts, John
2001 Corporate Governance and the Ethics of Narcissus. Business Ethics Quarterly 11(1):109–127.
Robertson, A. F.
2001 Greed: Gut Feelings, Growth, and History. Cambridge: Polity.
Roepsdorff, Anne K.
2010 CSR: Virksomheders sociale ansvar som begreb og praksis. Copenhagen: Hans Reitzels.
Sahlin-Andersson, Kerstin
2006 Corporate Social Responsibility: A Trend and a Movement, but of What and for What? Corporate Governance 6(5):595–608.
Sassen, Saskia
1998 Globalization and its Discontents. New York: The New Press.
Scherer, Andreas G., and Guido Palazzo, eds.
2008 Handbook of Research on Corporate Citizenship. Cheltenham: Edward Elgar.
Shever, Elana
2008 Neoliberal Associations: Property, Company and Family in the Argentine Oil Fields. American Ethnologist 35(4):701–716.

Shore, Cris, and Susan Wright
2000 Coercive Accountability: The Rise of Audit Culture in Higher Education. *In* Audit Cultures. Anthropological Studies in Accountability, Ethics and the Academy. Marilyn Strathern, ed. pp. 57–89. London: Routledge.
Smith, Adam
2002[1759] The Theory of Moral Sentiments. Cambridge: Cambridge University Press.
Strathern, Marilyn
2005 Robust Knowledge and Fragile Futures. *In* Global Assemblages: Technologies, Politics, and Ethics as Anthropological Problems. Aihwa Ong and Stephen J. Collier, eds. pp. 464–481. Oxford: Blackwell.
Sullivan, R., ed.
2003 Business and Human Rights: Dilemmas and Solutions. Sheffield: Greenleaf.
Welker, Marina
2009 "Corporate Security Begins in the Community": Mining, the Corporate Responsibility Industry and Environmental Advocacy in Indonesia. Cultural Anthropology 24(1):142–179.
Williams, Raymond
1976 Keywords: A Vocabulary of Culture and Society. Oxford: Oxford University Press.
Windell, Karolina
2006 Corporate Social Responsibility under Construction: Ideas, Translations, and Institutional Change. PhD dissertation, Uppsala University.

CHAPTER 25

Extreme Neo-nationalist Music Scenes at the Heart of Europe

David Murphy

The idea for the title of this chapter derived from a consideration of the various contests for meaning and identity that take place at a micro- and macrolevel in European discourse. Given both the legacy of extreme nationalism in Europe and a perception of increasing homogenization under EU enlargement, the forms of collective effervescence that nationalism once offered no longer hold the same mass appeal. Music scenes in certain instances have formed in a manner that taps into a need among young people for intense forms of belonging, while at the same time transcending traditional local and national ties. Therefore, this chapter can be read as both an endorsement of ethnographic forms of inquiry and a tongue-in-cheek return to a style of anthropological writing which searches for the exotic/other, but in familiar places. Since the decline of communism and the increasing flexibility of EU borders and possibilities offered through cheap travel, countries in Central and Eastern Europe have been largely demystified in the Western gaze. Therefore the references below to a certain novel by Bram Stoker (1897) are intended here in a purely playful spirit in order to provide a measure of descriptive irony and commentary on the ways in which certain regions have been represented in the past.

On August 25, 2007, when Sibiu in Romania was celebrating its status as the European Capital of Culture, an event took place just a few kilometers from the center, in which hundreds of young music fans came together for a Pagan Metal music festival. Although a largely peaceful affair, this quasi-private music festival was an example of the mixing of music and extreme right-wing/neonationalist politics, with hundreds of fans chanting "Sieg Heil" in unison with the bands performing.

Several themes will be merged in this chapter, which is based primarily on the genres of travel writing, ethnographic observation, and the conditions of possibility that meant a music festival with strong neo-Nazi elements could take place, in relatively unchallenged conditions, in Romania. The descriptions in this chapter move back and forth, from observation to reminiscence, to analysis; in order to build up

A Companion to the Anthropology of Europe, First Edition. Edited by Ullrich Kockel, Máiréad Nic Craith, and Jonas Frykman.

a detailed sketch of a type of event, and the sense of expectation felt on the journey to the event. This is undertaken in order to demystify a music scene that is generally only observed online or in print, and to give the reader an insight into the appeal that these events hold for their adherents. The early sections on this chapter also offer a reflection upon the experience and perception of moving across two EU countries, and the expectations of homogeneity and otherness. This chapter also includes snippets of conversation and observations made by a friend from Ireland who accompanied me to Romania.

Having grown up in Ireland, during a time when there was a complete change in the economic and social composition of many parts of the country which was to a large degree spearheaded by the adoption of EU membership, I was curious to see the changes and effects of recent entry into the EU (albeit on as superficial a level that a road trip can ever reveal) on Romania. My previous visit to Romania had been something of a pilgrimage undertaken to visit Poinari Fortress, the former residence of Vlad Tepes (fifteenth-century Voivode and Bram Stoker's inspiration for the novel *Dracula*), on Halloween of 1998.

As in Ireland, the most visible manifestations of EU membership were/are often observable in the roads and infrastructure. Changes in attitude are always much harder to discern, but the fact that such a large national-socialist black metal festival was taking place in Romania seemed to me an indicator that legislation against hate speech and racism was slow to take hold, or at least was not being policed to the degree that it is in the Czech Republic (Murphy 2010). Not that this is necessarily an automatic outcome of EU membership, but it is of relevance, given that the EU project was in part conceived with a view to avoiding the types of extreme nationalist discourse that led to previous conflicts. True, this is only a superficial look at one live event, but at the same time it is worthy of account, as live performances, although fleeting and temporal, can have profound and lasting effects on those participating. This quality in music is recognized and expressed in the following statement by White power activist William Pierce, in an interview during which he discussed the significance of Resistance Records, a label which promotes right-wing music:

> Music speaks to us at a deeper level than books or political rhetoric: music speaks directly to the soul. Resistance Records . . . will be the music of our people's renewal and rebirth. It will be music of strength and joy for our people. It will be music of defiance and rage against the enemies of our people . . . It will be the music of the great, cleansing revolution, which is coming. Enjoy it. (Pierce quoted in Davisson 2010:191)

The Embodiment of Place and Possibilities for Expression

On a lighter note, this trip to the festival in Romania was also an occasion to take a break from Serbia and my main fieldwork (exploring the Serbian black metal scene) and catch up with a close friend from home who was flying to Budapest in order to meet me. We had both been looking forward to meeting up with each other, and were glad of an excuse to rent a big, conspicuous car and take it on a trip through the Transylvanian mountains at a pace that was considerably faster than Jonathan Harker's coach-ride in *Dracula* (Stoker 1897), which route we were inadvertently following.

Arrangements had been made for me to meet Simon, a close friend living in Dublin who managed a motorcycle shop, but who, before that, had been a 1977-era punk from London and a refugee of the poll tax riots, which had necessitated his having to make a hasty exit to Ireland. Having another person with me who was familiar with the metal scene, even if more at home in the punk scene, was useful in terms of asking questions and inviting comparisons that I may not have noticed. Simon has always tended to hold strong anarchistic principles, but at the same time has mellowed enough to be able to enjoy the sound and spectacle of the many black metal concerts I had dragged him to over the past few years, without necessarily judging the bands based on perceived ideologies. I was also glad to have another person with me in case there was any violence, as the NSBM (national socialist black metal) scene was still new to me and something of an unknown variable in terms of whether or not these events were violent. Recent scholarship on the political aspects of NS (national socialist) and skinhead movements in Central and Eastern Europe states that:

> the significance of the skinheads lies not so much in the actions of their organizations as in the threat of its members. In fact the skinhead subculture in these countries has become recognized nationally and internationally as a problem, most notably because of its high level of violence. (Mudde 2005:168–169)

Diversions aside, although Simon is very much an anarchopunk, he actually looks the part of a tough old English skinhead, with barbed-wire neck tattoos and various Indian ink tattoos on his arms and hands. Therefore in the paranoid imaginary scenario I had rehearsed in my head, we both looked as though we would fit in among a crowd of Nazi-skinheads and have enough familiarity with the black metal and Oi-punk scenes to be able to chat to people and ask and answer any questions that arose.

Although all this attention to fitting-in may seem a bit paranoid, it was not without good reason. Frey Faxi Festival is not an event that any ordinary member of the public can simply buy tickets to and attend. In order to attend one must receive an invitation to buy tickets by participating on the Internet forums of the Pagan Front, an organization of indeterminate size with links to extreme right-wing, neonationalist, and national-socialist organizations around Europe and the United States. This convoluted method of researching a subject and obtaining tickets for the Frey Faxi festival produced something of an ethical dilemma, as I am generally of the opinion that people have a right not to be studied. However, scholars have also pointed to the lack of research into extremist politics in central and eastern European areas. Mikenberg (in Mudde 2005:161) has noted that "studying the radical right in transformation countries in Central and Eastern Europe not only resembles shooting at a moving target but also shooting with clouded vision." Mudde also states that there is a poignant lack of reliable information on racist extremism in the region, both academic and nonacademic.

Other factors that have been alluded to in *Neo-nationalism in Europe and Beyond* (Gingrich and Banks 2006:60) are the "mental-hygienic issues to consider in contemplating fieldwork with members of or subscribers to neo-nationalist movements." However, this statement in itself should strike anthropologists as problematic. For example, how often is mental hygiene a consideration when studying any other group of people with strongly held and expressed beliefs? If anything, statements such as the above point to the need for more ethnographic research into the participatory aspects of neonationalist groups, as opposed to relying entirely on published sources. In an article entitled "Confronting Anthropological Ethics," Bourgois addresses the imbalance of power issues inherent in obtaining informed consent for research (2007). Here Bourgois addresses the issue of so-called apolitical anthropology by asking the question, "How does one investigate power relations and fulfill the researcher's obligation to obtain consent from the powerful?" (2007:290). In the case of Frey Faxi the issue is complicated further; consider the fact that extreme right-wing political groups of the kind considered here are in fact a marginal social minority, but one which treats "Whiteness" as a category of being that is inherently privileged and elite. Therefore, in this case, the "end justifies the means" is a weak but cogent argument to put forward to justify engaging in this piece of covert research. It is anticipated that it falls under the "does no harm" category of research, as most identities are protected and those that are not have already provided a good deal of information about their activities on the Internet. Therefore, as a researcher I simply could not let this opportunity to study the recreational side of extremist politics slip by, as events of this type are rare and difficult to access, particularly at such close proximity. The majority of research into national-socialist black metal has tended only to focus on song lyrics, symbolism, Web sites, and media statements, as opposed to understanding the dynamics of interaction and performance as theory in practice.

In part, these scenes are a reaction against moral certainties, particularly so in light of the collapse of mass nationalism and the imagined consensus of communism. Given the degree to which black metal is so vehemently anti-Christian, the humanitarian ethos of older forms of rock music has also become a target. The missionaries of old, the failed dreams offered by communism, and the bewildering array of identity choices offered by mainstream media have all blurred into one common enemy in the eyes of the black metal scene. Individually black metalers donate to charity, rescue stray animals, and occasionally help their fellow humans. But, collectively, an aesthetic stance has developed that seeks to attack anything which promises unity, togetherness, and homogeneity. The moral entrepreneurs such as Bono, Sting, and Geldof (it could be any altruistic pop star but these names seem to crop up most regularly during my fieldwork) who want to "heal the world" are targeted by many in the black metal scene as hypocrites and champagne socialists whose sin has been to mix music with humanitarian proselytizing. In black metal there is generally (NSBM being the exception) a distinction between theory and practice (music and social values), coupled with a strong desire to challenge most forms of political correctness that are seen as the prevailing consensus in mainstream music.

Having secured tickets for Frey Faxi whilst still in Serbia, I then took the overnight train from Beograd and met Simon in Budapest on August 28. Being more interested in live music than typical pubs and clubs we quickly managed to find some gigs to check out.

After a pleasant two nights in Budapest, Simon and I set off for Romania in our rented Chrysler PT Cruiser. We left Budapest early that morning, I was clutching bottles of energy drink and praying to any gods who'd listen for a miracle hangover cure, but Simon the teetotaler (of two years) was alert, curious, and keen to see something of the Hungarian countryside. We made rapid progress across Hungary on one of the main roads toward Romania: an ancient route which eventually terminates in Istanbul. Unfortunately it was difficult to see or experience anything other than speed and efficiency. The motorways keep travelers well out of the towns and at times we could have been in any country in Western Europe. Only the occasional sign or advertisement betrayed the fact that the country we were moving across so rapidly was Hungary.

The drive itself was very straightforward, predictable, and as efficient as one generally expects in most EU countries. There was good road signage, plenty of petrol stations, and adequate information that facilitated the kind of "moving through a non-anthropological space" type of experience that Marc Augé (1995) describes. The traveler's interaction with the landscape and people had certainly changed since Jonathan Harker's genre-defining journey to meet Count Dracula.

Upon crossing the border into Romania, differences between the two countries became apparent immediately. The change of countries was particularly noticeable through the bumpy transition from Hungarian EU efficiency and nonanthropological space, to Romanian roads in disarray, damaged signage, and a funny, frightening, and chaotic approach to driving. Here it became much easier to fantasize about smoky taverns and superstitious peasants. The landscapes and townscapes, too, were so different from the relatively affluent Hungary with its well-marked signs and degree of predictability and efficiency that makes the place "feel" European.

This "feeling" is one that can be described as a kind of quasi-homogeneity, whereby a sense of efficiency and recognizable standards gradually become the norm as a result of EU membership. To many people, these are the most visible markers and signifiers of EU membership, in terms of investment in state infrastructure and other standardized signifiers such as road signage and sameness of "roadscape" that tend to increase in frequency depending on the level of inward investment.

Feeling European and the Limits of Musical Expression

The concept of "feeling" like an EU country also takes into account the possibility of racist action and agitation. Romania is a country where "serious outbursts of racist extremist violence have occurred at a few occasions but overall the level is not that high" (Mudde 2005:173).

In a study of politics and racist extremism in Central and Eastern Europe, Mudde (2005:173) has grouped countries into three specific categories:

1 Countries where racist extremist occurrences are "absent or highly incidental. This group includes the three Baltic states."

2 "Countries where racist extremist violence does occur but is not (yet) frequent or widespread, such as Slovenia." Romania is characterized by more serious outbursts of racist extremist violence occurring on a few occasions "but overall the level is not that high and, importantly, is decreasing."
3 Countries considered to have high levels of racist violence which are thought of as a "structural and long-term problem." These countries include Bulgaria, Czech Republic, Hungary, Poland, and Slovakia. In most of these countries "the skinhead movement is the main perpetrator of racist attacks," with Bulgaria being the exception.

Further afield in Russia the situation of racist extremism seems worse than in Central Europe, as this quote from Davisson illustrates:

> The large number of NSBM and NS affiliated metal bands in Russia could also be reflective of the general population's attitude around race. In the two decades following end of the Soviet Union, Russia's racism became public. The Moscow based Sova Centre for Human Rights reported: In the spring of 2007, radical violence continued to grow. Over the three spring months, xenophobic and neo-Nazi attacks affected at least 137 people, killing 18 . . . there are no reasons yet to report improvement." (Davisson 2010:196)

With Romania being a country in which attacks against Roma and other ethnic minorities are common, and which was chosen as the location for the Frey Faxi festival, I was curious as to what bearing (if any) this would have on the behavior of people at the event. For example, at concerts I have attended in Germany, Holland, and the United Kingdom where there was an NS presence in the crowd, I have never witnessed anyone making Nazi salutes or chants, whereas in Slovenia and Serbia I have witnessed this taking place among some young black metal fans and skinheads, though such actions were not reciprocated or visibly appreciated by the bands to which they were directed. In contrast, at the Dunkelheit festival in Brno in the Czech Republic which I attended after Frey Faxi, it was stated on ticket stubs, that any overt political expressions, badges, or T-shirts (whether fascist or communist) were expressly prohibited and could result in expulsion from the festival and the police being called. So it would appear that in countries which have and enforce antiracist/antifascist legislation, these prohibitions do actually have noticeable effects on the conditions of possibility for extremist expression at concerts.

It must also be taken into account that a reconstituted sense of value which is attached to the breaking of taboos also occurs through their creation. At metal concerts and festivals that I have attended in Serbia and to a lesser extent in Slovenia, a Nazi salute is one of these taboos in which meaning is never an absolute. They are sometimes made jokingly among friends as greetings but also among drunken music fans as gestures of appreciation toward bands. The typical reaction from the rest of the crowd is sometimes to ignore or deride these gestures and expressions (in Serbia and Slovenia). However, in other countries these gestures have led to annoyance and occasionally violence. Therefore the presence of Nazi gestures at a black metal concert is also an indicator of both the success of, or lack of, policies that target and regulate extremist behavior, and the overall level of taboo that these gestures stimulate among black metal fans in any given country.

Meanwhile, Back on the "Thick" EU-Descriptive Carpathian Trail

Many of the towns and villages on the first section of the road from Oradea to Sibiu were surrounded by acres of barren-looking industrial desolation, broken windows, and old communist-era buildings wrapped in tangles of rusted metal and thorn bushes. Though in contrast to these sights, especially as we entered the Carpathians, many of the villages were cheerful and pretty, populated with small colorful houses and the pleasant trappings of Transylvanian rural life. The streets and gardens contained many fruit trees and rural entrepreneurs selling fruit, vegetables, honey, and faux-folk trinkets to the steady stream of trucks passing through.

It took approximately 10 hours to drive from Budapest to Sibiu, and it was dark by the time we arrived. We tried to ask a young man who was sweeping the street for directions, but we couldn't understand each other or the address that I showed to him. He also looked like he was dizzyingly high on glue or some kind of ether or hallucinogen, as he had a nervous but unwaveringly manic, vacant grin on his face. A nearby taxi driver who was watching us with a look of playful derision then took pity on us and intervened, leading us to our destination. We then dropped off the car at our *pensione* and rode in a taxi for several miles outside the town until we arrived at the campsite where the festival was taking place.

At the entrance were three police officers chatting to some skinheads who were checking tickets; the police then searched us in a very thorough manner. When they motioned for us to enter we walked through a heavily wooded area for ten minutes until we reached a terraced amphitheater. This faced on to a huge lake which, even at night, beautifully reflected the surrounding mountains. This was one of the most spectacular concert settings we had ever seen, the audience terrace overlooked a large floating platform on the lake; it was on this platform that the bands were performing.

We first walked over to a small stall where two friendly but tough-looking German skinheads were selling festival T-shirts. They told us that Temnozor (one of the headline bands) were about to start playing. As we moved through the crowd I read people's T-shirts, banners, and flags. It was very much an international gathering, with some skinheads carrying a banner from Sweden, another group wearing Aryan nations T-shirts with American flags, and groups from all over Europe, with English and German being the most commonly spoken languages.

Temnozor conducted a suspiciously short sound-check and then began to play a song from their *Horizons* album. The crowd shuffled down the terraces in order to get closer to the band, and began to cheer loudly, shouting "*slava*" (a Slavic word with multiple meanings, but generally meaning "glory" in this context). There was also a large group of skinheads and metalheads who were quite drunk and raucous. They participated, nervously and unsure at first, by giving furtive Nazi salutes toward the band and shouting "Sieg Heil," testing the water in order to gauge the crowd's reaction. But after glancing around and finding no significant objections they became louder and more fanatical. Upon seeing these guys, a few other groups throughout the crowd also began saluting and chanting "Sieg Heil" until it became the most vocal chant during that part of the concert.

Simon and I looked at each with a growing sense of nervous unease and he whispered, "Fuck me this is all a bit surreal, . . . how the fuck did you talk me into coming along to this?" I jokingly responded "Relax, we'll be fine as long as no one sees the CRASS [an anarcho punk band] tattoo or anarchy symbols on your arm." Later when we were discussing the concert Simon remarked, referring to the Sieg Heils and salutes, "I bet they don't get the chance to do that very often. When it used to happen at gigs in England it was as much about starting a fight with the rest of the crowd as anything else." Simon went on to explain: "Most of the time the bands had nothing to do with it. Just look at any old footage of Sham 69 [a British punk/ skinhead band] and Jimmy [Sham 69's vocalist] pleading with hundreds of skinheads to stop being boneheads. He often finished those gigs in tears, but he always thought it was better to try and include people rather than just ignore the problem." Simon also pointed out that "this was something a bit different, these bands are egging 'em on. . . . the only other time I've seen bands giving Nazi salutes is when they're taking the piss [provocatively using humor]."

At Frey Faxi, the Nazi gestures could be considered an occult use of a symbolic repertoire, which in one sense was impotent and directionless, as despite the diversity of the crowd, I doubt that there were many people attending who would be deeply offended by these gestures. However, what was taking place at Frey Faxi was based on a shared consensus between the band and sections of the crowd. There was a relationship of reciprocity in which taboo gestures in the crowd were acknowledged by the band and responded to positively, encouraging an escalation in behavior.

Depending on the complexity of the song, there were at any given time 6 to 10 musicians onstage performing in Temnozor. The vocalist was a large, heavy, bear of a man, wearing leather trousers, no shirt and a wolf pelt over his shoulders; he had a shaved head and a short goatee beard. The whistle player was tall with a blond Hitler style haircut, wearing a T-shirt and combats tucked into steel-toe-capped army boots. The keyboard player was slightly hidden but playing quite well, driving the overall sound despite the muffled audio quality. The drummer also played skillfully but it was apparent that they were having difficulties with their sound monitors as they kept gesturing to the sound desk for changes. The guitarists and bass player were dressed in a more typical black metal style, in black jeans, boots, and T-shirts. They moved around the stage a lot but didn't communicate very openly with the crowd.

The first few songs sounded OK, the Russian vocals gaining a favorable reaction from the crowd and sounding similar to their recorded work. As the night went on, the section of the crowd giving Nazi salutes moved closer together in the centre of the terrace in front of us. Gradually they formed a cohesive group, all drinking, chanting, and creating a booze- and testosterone-soaked atmosphere that kept spilling over into unwilling groups of people beside them. There was a lot of gesticulating, hugging, raising beers, and shouting encouragement at each other. In any other venue this would probably be the section of the crowd that would initiate and dominate the mosh pit [a frenzied physical form of dancing with lots of punching and shoving between audience members]. But due to the terracing in this venue, there was no possibility of a mosh pit, and the fact that the stage was on a floating platform at the edge of the lake also made it unconducive to moshing.

After a few more songs the rain began to fall and lightning struck several times in the hills surrounding the lake. Visually, this natural pyrotechnic show really enhanced the atmosphere, and it helped to cool down the humid night air. But the break in the weather also served as a cue for a large group of French-speaking people on our left to make their exit. When the crowd had began shouting "Sieg Heil" earlier, this group of French-speakers began to get increasingly agitated, especially some of the girls in the group, and as they were leaving they kept glancing toward some of the skinheads with a look of disgust on their faces. The guys in the group all had long hair and none of them dressed in the genre-mixing style that some NSBM fans adopt (long hair with skinhead-type bomber jackets or shaved heads and clothes emblazoned with NS insignia). As they were leaving, the girls in the group, all of whom looked to be in their early twenties, didn't disguise their looks of disapproval toward the NS section of the crowd.

Temnozor played a few more folksy/ballad type metal songs sung in Russian which sounded really strong and emotive. By now, large sections of the crowd were singing in unison with the band and perhaps due to the layout of the stage, and the fact that it was utterly unconducive to moshing, this seemed to be the high point in Temnozor's performance.

The singer of Temnozor then addressed the crowd, shouting in a growled voice "Heil Romania, it's great to be here," then they launched into one of their most rousing folk/metal ballads, a song called "Fatherland." This song started off powerfully but gradually descended into a musical farce as it became obvious that the crowd had a better knowledge of the lyrics than the singer, who was trying to read them from a piece of paper (through correspondence on the band's myspace.com profile I later found out that the vocalist that night was a temporary replacement from another band (Kroda), as Temnozor's normal vocalist was sick on the night). Though the singer's ignorance of the lyrics didn't seem to deter the band's NS skinhead fans, who, seemed basically to treat the whole occasion as an opportunity to shout "Sieg Heil" and wave their arms in salute. At this point it was also possible to see a divide appearing in the crowd's reaction to the band. An increasing number of the more typical black metal fans (long hair and black clothes, non-skinhead dress styles) became obviously annoyed at the standard of musicianship and poor sound quality, and they wandered off in small groups as the rain and bad weather increased. This is something that I have occasionally witnessed at black metal gigs in Serbia, where quite often musicians from many local bands make up a large section of the crowd. This is usually the section standing in the area of the venue with the best sound quality, listening with what Harris Berger aptly describes as "a powerful, motionless intensity" often standing with arms folded at the edges of the mosh pit (1999:70). It is this group that will generally be the harshest critics of a band's musicianship and technique. The other sections of the crowd with whom a metal band will be engaged in a relationship of deep reciprocity are the headbangers and moshers, who are typically located directly in front of the stage. The layout of a venue is often a critical factor in the failure or success of a metal concert. Berger provides an excellent "sociology of metal audience's attention" by analyzing the architecture and phenomenological effects between crowds and performers (1999:67–73). Therefore, the success of Temnozor's performance at Frey Faxi was unusual given the unorthodox layout of the venue and the inability to mosh and participate in the manner typical of the majority of metal concerts.

When Temnozor played their most famous song "White Thunder Roars" it became painfully obvious that the singer had lost all grasp of the lyrics and timing, mumbling through the main verses and repeating over and over again the line "white thunder roars" wherever he felt it appropriate. This increased the level of frustration in some sections of the crowd as a large number of people on the left side of the terrace made their exit. It was also obvious that the other band members were becoming irritated at the poor sound quality as they glanced angrily toward the singer and each other and looked distracted and less involved in playing as the song progressed. So although there is a tacit tolerance of many forms of intolerance within the wider black metal scene, among the scene members for whom musicianship is more important than ideology or spectacle a band performing in an unprofessional manner is not something that can easily be condoned.

On a few occasions at gigs in Serbia that I had attended and enjoyed with Kozeljnik, the guitarist from bands The Stone and May Result, when we engaged in a postgig analysis I tended to get caught up in the atmosphere and effect on the crowd that bands could evoke. These criteria would usually form the basis for my appreciation of the gig. However for Kozeljnik, these aspects were of only secondary importance to the musicianship of a band, and he was often deeply critical of any mistakes or deviations that to me had been trivial and barely perceptible.

Therefore, Nazi gestures and ideology and the play element (referring to "play" as understood by Huizinga in *Homo ludens* (1938)) that goes along with these taboo displays, is for many of the more serious adherents of black metal simply not enough to provide an attraction and support for a band. So, when Temnozor's musicianship began to falter (though a degree of blame also lies with the sound rig) it was no surprise that so many of the more typical black metal fans decided to make their exit. Whereas, given that bands such as Temnozor and Absurd tend to attract fans from both black metal and Nazi skinhead musical genres, the skinheads tended not to be as bothered about the standard of musicianship and were predominantly concerned with the public reciprocation and verification/performance of their ideologies. This dynamic is one that hasn't managed to cross genres in as successful a manner as other aspects of the black metal/skinhead crossover. The sound structure of music that comes from the skinhead genre is largely based on a punk and Oi musical template from the United Kingdom; therefore it is usually the force of the message, rather than the medium, that is important: attitude overrules technical ability. Contrastingly, in metal, control, displays of power, and musical virtuosity are of paramount importance; most bands will spend many hours a week rehearsing and perfecting their technique. Certainly this was the case with The Stone and May Result in Serbia. As both Walser (1993) and Berger (1999) point out, despite appearances and misconceptions, metal is deeply concerned with the controlled use of power (chords), as opposed to punk, which is premised on getting out of control.

Rather surprisingly the bonehead element of the crowd (Simon's name for the Nazi skinhead section of the crowd) either didn't notice or didn't care about the poor musicianship and sound quality, they became more and more vocal as the songs and beer consumption progressed. They were especially enthused whenever a performer shouted "Juden raus" in between one of the songs as they now had a new phrase to intersperse between their "Sieg Heils."

While waiting for the next band to play I asked Simon what he thought of the festival and everything that was taking place. He said: "This is exactly the same as some of the shit that used to happen at some punk gigs during the early eighties, but more at football matches. . . . I remember when one team signed their first black player and lots of skinheads on the terraces started calling him a monkey whenever he played. . . . This is the same sort of shit, an excuse for a bunch of lads to shout 'Sieg Heil' while they're in a large group that won't get beaten up."

Black Metal Back Story

The final band to play Frey Faxi Festival that night was a German band named Absurd. Absurd were a little-known black metal band, mainly composed of three members, Hendrick Mobus, Sebastian Schauscheill, and Andreas Kirchner, from the town of Sondershausen in former East Germany. When the three were 17 years old they became fascinated by horror, death/black metal and Satanism, and began meeting and conducting Satanic "baptism" ceremonies in an old quarry (Moynihan and Soderlind 2003:273). In 1992 a 14-year-old youth named Sandro Beyer began hanging around with the group and attend their band rehearsals. However they soon began quarreling, and Beyer began a slanderous letter-writing campaign exposing an affair between Schauscheill and an older married woman (Moynihan and Soderlind 2003:274). This culminated in the murder of Bayer by the three members of Absurd, who were quickly apprehended, and there followed a media frenzy in which the crime was depicted as a "Satanic sacrifice" (Moynihan and Soderlind 2003:273–278). Absurd later released an audio cassette of their music with a photograph of Beyer's tombstone on the cover. In 1999 after serving a portion of their murder sentences, Mobus and Schauscheill were released on parole and renewed their contacts with the black metal scene, releasing a four-track CD *Asgardsrei*, which features Rob Darken of Polish national-socialist black metal band Graveland on guest vocals (Moynihan and Soderlind 2003:301). Soon afterwards there was a series of police raids on German record labels, and Absurd's CDs featured prominently among those confiscated. Mobus's parole was later revoked for "political activities" – displaying banned political emblems and giving a Hitler salute at a concert (Moynihan and Soderlind 2003:301). He soon disappeared, only to reemerge in the United States where he spent several weeks hiding out with William Pierce's racialist group The National Alliance. Following his subsequent arrest Mobus sought political asylum. William Pierce began soliciting donations to help fight the case on the grounds of "freedom of speech," since the actions which resulted in the original parole violation were not of a violent nature but rather, political misdeeds which would not be illegal according to US laws (Moynihan and Soderlind 2003:302).

At the time when these events were taking place, Pierce was using his label Resistance Records to sign up black metal bands and bring about a crossover between the black metal and Nazi skinhead scenes. In this he had some partial successes, though in general the NSBM and skinhead scenes tend to merge due more to shared musical tastes than to political action.

Tonight Absurd really managed to live up to their name; they went through a long sound check that drew a large number of people back to the terraces in order to hear them. After a few false starts they began their first songs amid lots of cheering and a few drunken "Sieg Heils." Overall their stage presence, dress, and style was quite underwhelming, the older members looked slightly comical, obese with long scraggy hair at the sides and balding on top. Although I had been aware of the "legacy" of Absurd, I had not seen any recent photos of the band and I couldn't help thinking that they looked at odds with all of the hype that surrounds them. The singer looked particularly cartoonish in his painfully tight leather trousers and some form of male corset that was too big even for his considerable size.

Here my recollections became a bit fuzzy as the effects of the days long drive and beer took hold. Though one particular memory that stands out was a song which Simon and I instantly recognized as "borrowing" the guitar riff from a song called "Strychnine" by an obscure 1960s psychedelic band called The Sonics. The rip-off was so blatant that after a few seconds of the song being played Simon and I glanced at each other and started laughing out loud, simultaneously saying "no way" in recognition of something that sounded so out of place. Simon asked: "How many people in this crowd do you reckon know where they nicked the riff for this song?"

After a few more underwhelming songs and an increase in rainfall we decided to make our exit back to Sibiu, we walked back through the forest and hailed a passing taxi. When we reached the centre of Sibiu, the "Capital of Culture" celebrations were still in full swing, well into the early hours of the morning. We walked past a beautifully preserved/restored medieval tavern which, bizarrely, had traditional Irish music blaring out of the narrow little windows. The scenes of carnival, pomp, and ceremony that were strewn all over the town seemed a world away from the strange drunken attempt to recreate Nuremberg circa 1939 that we had just witnessed. Remembering the scenes of hundreds of people chanting "Sieg Heil" and "Juden Raus" Simon asked: "Did that really just happen?" "Yeah," I replied, "and it's becoming more common in Russia and Ukraine." Urok the bass/keyboard player from Serbian black metal bands The Stone/May Result had told me of a conversation he had with someone from the Russian black metal scene, who told him that in the urban areas where 10 or 15 years ago whole sections of tenements were squatted by punks and hippies, now they were populated by ultranationalist skinheads.

Alter-Europe and the Love of Hate

It seems these changes in musical–political orientation are increasing and spreading across Europe, although in many areas they are being actively challenged, particularly in the West, where these types of bands rarely, if ever, play. In Germany it is a criminal offense to display symbols or promote rhetoric that is in any way associated with National Socialism. These laws are rigidly enforced, to the extent that even black metal bands with absolutely no connection to NS politics have come under the gaze and censure of the state. As a research topic these hidden/occult music scenes present an interesting challenge, namely how something which bears all the symbols of an overtly political movement can be understood as a social rather than a political phenomenon. The use of symbols in these instances are not in support of a specific party, rather they are aspects of a bricolage that seeks to profit on their capacity to shock and confront. Yet, they are so hidden from mainstream audiences that it is an almost directionless form of attack on some vaguely defined sense of imagined political correctness and homogeneity. This is where for many fans the appeal lies: the black metal scene thrives on being an "extreme" form of musical and artistic expression, drawing upon some of the most horrific acts of recent history, wallowing in them and celebrating them to the extent that meaning has become completely recontextualized, rather than viewing the actions as a moral outrage, aimed at the destruction of a particular ethnic or religious group. The types of rage and sentiment being invoked are rendered impotent in terms of how fascism was originally used and instead are energetically channeled into maintaining a scene, drinking, creating, partying, and forging links across Europe and the globe.

Individually, most of the black metalers to whom I have spoken are well aware of the moral hazards and implications of Nazism. "Safely" confined within a music genre, the use of Nazism is at odds with the lifestyle and moral outlook that many of the fans actually practice. Whilst most people will utterly condemn every aspect of the legacy of National Socialism, there are a number for whom the art, esoteric philosophies, and spirit of *völkisch* camaraderie can be separated from the atrocities and partially reimagined in music scenes.

A cursory glance at these phenomena leads many to dismiss the scene as infantile rebelliousness. But there is a good deal more to be observed when studied up close. These is an underlying tension informing these scenes which could be read as deriving from the same difficult-to-articulate tensions that underscore the enlarging European project. At the same time as the EU is becoming increasingly integrated economically, there are many for whom the darker legacies of Europe are both unresolved and strangely alluring. The luster of taboo histories has a powerful hold, particularly for those who have found themselves disenchanted with contemporary modernity and the manifestation of a "culture industry" critiqued by Adorno (2005) and characterized by Orwell (1948). These and similar music scenes could also be understood as a form of reaction against the impersonal overproduction of generic sameness that has come about since the advent of MTV-type media.

To members of the black metal scene, MTV-type media serve as a symbol of all that is banal, mundane, politically correct, multicultural, and therefore boring in the extreme. To many of them, the music genres that have come about since the advent of MTV are seen as a dilution of identity, based on a miscegenated mix of different genres and styles that have led to the production of a Frankenstein's monster – a musical monoculture. To many of its followers black metal provides a sense of order, certainty as opposed to musical flux, an identity rooted in a neoromantic idea of Europe. This is particularly relevant in former socialist countries where the sense of tangible certainty and identity that existed under communism is no more. It is this search for a new certainty, at odds with but utterly enmeshed in modernity, that has found an extreme form of expression in the blood, soil, and mythology ethos of black metal. Many other youth music scenes function as similar alter-political movements, punk most explicitly so. Although punk is generally considered the polar opposite of black metal, both share a similar *zeitgeist* of connectedness, with punk as a quasi-cosmopolitan alternative to mainstream collectivities and black metal as a scene which simultaneously utilizes ideas of nationhood whilst rejecting the contemporary definition of it.

At the heart of Europe is a chimera that is viewed in a multiplicity of ways, all wishing to find some end-destination, some ideal state of Platonic perfection in which utopian fantasies of an identity that is certain and fixed can be realized. This is seen to be preferable to failed political systems and the numbing individualism of a predatory free-market and postsocialist nonsociety that many black metal fans find themselves at odds with. This is the fuel feeding the aesthetic rage that leads young people to grasp for certainties among the Euro flux of change, "development," and rational modernization; in which people find that they are no longer members of a nation but units in an economy. This is one of the reasons that Slavs, Germans, Scandinavians, and even a few Americans came together and found common cause and an occult sense of certainty in these types of festivals. They are an opportunity to openly express and celebrate an outdated concept that has been revitalized in a new context. This is the tragic idea within the NSBM scene that being "White" is somehow an achievement. This is a fantasy of "Whiteness" and a conceptual flexibility that has allowed members of nations formerly at war with one another to come together and attempt to recreate a *zeitgeist* of brotherhood and togetherness. Ironically this is perhaps a similar *zeitgeist* to the one that nationalism and war was so adept at creating in the past. Because of the difficulty and the uncertainty of contemporary modernity (Augé 1995), and conditions of perceived underachievement and lack of opportunity, NSBM scene members are taking pride in and fostering a sense of self-respect based on a tragic fantasy: that the (a?) White race has achieved something to be proud of. So when there is little else to celebrate in life, the occult fantasy of Whiteness is something that is clung to and venerated, leading to these reflexively unreflexive celebrations of hatred and religious intolerance that are only ever intended for the initiates of a hidden and marginal cult.

REFERENCES

Adorno, Theodor
2005 The Culture Industry. London: Routledge.
Augé, Marc
1995 Non Places: An Introduction to the Anthropology of Supermodernity. London: Pluto.
Berger, Harris
1999 Metal Rock and Jazz: Perception and the Phenomenology of Musical Experience. Hanover, NH: Wesleyan University Press.

Bourgois, Philippe
2007 Confronting Anthropological Ethics: Ethnographic Lessons from Central America. *In* Ethnographic Fieldwork: An Anthropological Reader. Antonius and Robben and J. Sluka, eds. pp. 288–291. Oxford: Blackwell.
Davisson, Justin
2010 Extreme Politics and Extreme Metal: Strange Bedfellows or Fellow Travellers. *In* Critical Issues: The Metal Void, First Gatherings. Niall Scott and Imke Von Helden, eds. Oxford: Interdisciplinary Press (ebook).
Gingrich, Andre, and Banks, Marcus
2006 Neo-Nationalism in Europe and Beyond: Perspectives from Social Anthropology. Oxford: Berghahn.
Goodrick-Clarke, Nicholas
2003 Black Sun: Aryan Cults, Esoteric Nazism and the Politics of Identity. New York: New York University Press.
Huizinga, Johan
1938[1971] *Homo ludens*: A Study of the Play Element in Culture. Boston: Beacon.
Kahn-Harris, Keith
2007 Extreme Metal: Music and Culture on the Edge. Oxford: Berg.
Moynihan, Michael, and Soderlind, Didrik
2003 Lords of Chaos: The Bloody Rise of the Satanic Metal Underground. Los Angeles: Feral House.
Mudde, Cas
2005 Racist Extremism in Central and Eastern Europe. East European Politics and Societies 19:161–184.
Murphy, David
2010 The Gift and Collective Effervescence. Irish Journal of Anthropology 13:36–43.
Orwell, George
1948 Nineteen Eighty-Four. London: Secker and Warburg.
Stoker, Bram
1897[1997] Dracula. New York: Tor.
Walser, Robert
1993 Running with the Devil: Power, Gender and Madness in Heavy Metal Music. Middletown: Wesleyan University Press.

CHAPTER 26

Anthropological Perspectives on the European Urban Landscape

Christiane Schwab

Cities condense culture. The density of social life within urban agglomerations favors the formation of cultural elements, such as artifacts, forms of social organization, practices, and norms. City-dwellers leave cultural traces, and the new generations have to deal with adapting, rejecting, or modifying them more or less consciously. Cities are accumulations of culture.

In 2006, approximately 75% of the European population lived in urban areas; in 2020 it will be about 80% (EEA 2006:5). It is not only because of their increasing significance for people and society within the last two centuries, or their cultural intensity, that cities represent a substantial task for the anthropological investigation of and in Europe. Urbanization and the meaningful role of cities within their larger contexts is a significant characteristic of European history, especially in the Mediterranean regions with their long-standing empires throughout the past millennia. In this chapter, I first introduce the changing relations anthropologists have had, and continue to have, with cities and the theoretical and methodological responses they have developed in exploring them. Then I will discuss a recent research approach in urban anthropology that deals with the investigation of the uniqueness of particular cities, followed by a short overview of the most important concepts and contentious issues within this discussion. Finally, I will summarize the main points of the chapter and conclude with a plea for the commitment of anthropologists to the fact that cities matter, and they matter as *particular* places.

FACING THE CITY

There is no academic discipline that could do justice on its own to such a difficult phenomenon as a city. Owing to the complexity of urban life, its exploration is a priori an interdisciplinary undertaking, and consequently the history of

---

A Companion to the Anthropology of Europe, First Edition. Edited by Ullrich Kockel, Máiréad Nic Craith, and Jonas Frykman.

anthropologically orientated urban studies shows a continuous influence of other academic disciplines.

In the nineteenth century and at the beginning of the twentieth, anthropologists commonly considered cities as destroyers of traditions and social communities. In contrast to rural forms of life, the city was characterized by anonymity, separation, economically based relationships, and the whirligig of time. This binary perspective in urban studies was established, among others, by the German sociologists Ferdinand Tönnies (1855–1936) and Georg Simmel (1858–1918). Simmel had a strong impact on the work of Robert Ezra Park (1864–1944), who was one of the founding members of the Chicago School of Sociology. In Chicago, for the very first time, researchers dedicated themselves empirically and systematically to the exploration of city life. For the Chicago researchers, in conceiving cities as quasi-biological systems, city quarters represented "natural areas" of distinct social groups that were thought to coexist relatively independently one from another. According to this conception, many of the Chicagoan works focused on group-specific urban life, especially of marginal groups, such as Louis Wirth's *The Ghetto* (1923) about Jewish community life, or William F. Whyte's *Street Corner Society* (1943) about the Italian Americans of Boston. In dividing the city into small and manageable groups and areas, the researchers were able to transfer the anthropological method of participant observation with its holistic perspective to urban contexts. In the introductory essay of the trend-setting work *The City*, Park suggested accordingly:

> Anthropology, the science of man, has been mainly concerned up to the present with the study of primitive peoples. But civilized man is quite as interesting an object of investigation, and at the same time his life is more open to observation and study. Urban life and culture are more varied, subtle, and complicated, but the fundamental motives are in both instances the same. The same patient methods of observation which anthropologists like Boas and Lowie have expended on the study of the life and manners of the North American Indian might be even more fruitfully employed in the investigation of the customs, beliefs, social practices, and general conceptions of life prevalent in Little Italy on the lower North Side in Chicago, or in recording the more sophisticated folkways of the inhabitants of Greenwich Village and the neighborhood of Washington Square, New York. (Park 1967[1925]:3)

The works and conceptions of Park and the Chicagoan scholars had a lot of influence on further urban anthropology in the United States, and, giving direction to the setting of urban life and cities as research objects in the social sciences, they are to be considered of high relevance for the development of urban anthropology and urban studies in general. Still, they continue to offer many incentives to reflect on methods and theory in exploring cities and city life.

Another important milestone in anthropological urban studies was marked by British social anthropology. From the 1930s onward, the rampantly growing cities in the African colonies provoked the anthropologists' interest, particularly in the rural exodus and migration into cities, as well as in interracial relations. The so-called Manchester School developed and applied innovative research methods, such as situational and network analysis (cf. Mitchell 1969), and in doing so, they faced the challenge to manage the dichotomy between small groups on the one hand and a larger context (urban, regional, national, or global) on the other. In order to approach urban development, they separated situational and social entities from the heterogeneous and apparently unmanageable city and put them into urban and colonial contexts. Just like their Chicagoan predecessors, they constructed particular points of access to apply anthropological concepts and research methods. Consequently, both schools have given us ideas of how to face the methodological and conceptual problem of mediating between the micro- and the macro-level, which seems to have been one of the most exigent problems in urban anthropology to this day.

During the 1960s and 1970s, the focus on small entities pursued by major parts of urban anthropology was increasingly questioned by sociological paradigms. Influenced by the "city-as-context" debate (cf. Rollwagen 1975) and the Marxist French urban sociology (cf. Castells 1973), urban phenomena were increasingly considered in their interdependencies with the whole city, or with the national or even the global context. Furthermore, the rising field of research on global cities focused on cities as junctions within the global flows of capital, information, migrants, and goods (cf. Sassen 1991). One important step to reopen theoretical debates about the contextualization of anthropological research in cities on the one hand, and the specificity of urban existence on the other hand, was Ulf Hannerz's book, *Exploring the City: Inquiries Toward an Urban Anthropology* (Hannerz 1980). Hannerz, having revised and criticized several theoretical approaches of urban anthropology, suggests considering cities not as an accidental "locus" of anthropologically interesting phenomenon, but to develop new perspectives for urban anthropology. The suggestions made by Hannerz are mainly based on role and social network theories. For instance, he divides urban life into five domains, where the people's networks are located (household and kinship, provisioning, recreation, neighboring, and traffic). Hannerz criticizes that most investigations in urban anthropology remain stuck in those domains instead of taking them as points of departure to explore urban systems as a whole:

> There is obviously nothing wrong in principle with domain ethnographies [...]. Ethnography must begin somewhere and end somewhere, and the institutions, groups, or more loosely constituted networks which fall within domain boundaries are often natural foci. We come back here, however, to the question whether they are anthropology of the city, or only in the city. The study of traffic relationships can perhaps hardly help belonging in the former category, to the extent that one is ready to regard these as just about intrinsically urban phenomena. As far as the others are concerned, we may feel that they are only urban anthropology in the strict sense when they give a reasonable measure of attention to the fact that they deal with entities which are somehow integrated parts of a differentiated urban social system; when they are not "blind to overlap and connection," as we may remember that a critic of the early Chicago studies put it, but contribute to an understanding of the ways this system both segments and coheres. (Hannerz 1980:248)

Apparently, since *Exploring the City*, there has been no significant advance within the theoretical framework of urban anthropology, although the number of studies *within* domain boundaries has proliferated. With reference to editions of the journal *City and Society* published by the American Anthropological Association from June 2008 until June 2010, we may observe the most recurrent themes in recent research in urban anthropology: urban heritage, migration, space-making, kinship, neighborhood, politics, transport and infrastructure, applied urban anthropology, collective urban identities, urban myths and urban images, gentrification, and racial discrimination. Those anthropological case studies reveal a variety of topics, concepts, and methods. What lacks, however, is a synthetic view, a comparative evaluation of the abundance of data and observations we have accumulated (cf. Antweiler 2004:288–289). Our theoretical knowledge about cities and the "urban being" has not increased significantly. "Thus, urban anthropology, although inspired in its earlier years by theories of urbanism, now examines social life in the city as it exists for the people who live in it, rather than the city itself" (Merry 2006:480).

Anthropologizing Cities?

The demand for theorizing cities brings us forcefully to the question of whether it should be the province of social and cultural anthropologists to express far-reaching statements about cities at all. Furthermore, are the familiar concepts and methods of anthropologists suited to such an undertaking? And, above all, how appropriate would those general categories be? If we, hypothetically, postulate social anonymity as a basic feature of cities, would we encounter the same quality of anonymity in Frankfurt as we have it in Palermo? Probably not. Frankfurt *is not* Palermo, although it has nearly the same amount of inhabitants. But evidently, besides population, there are a multitude of factors that influence the conditions of life within a determined city.

The recent debate of an anthropology of specific cities is based precisely on this understanding. It claims to focus on the city neither as an accidental context of domains, cultural phenomena, or social groups nor as mere junctions of social developments on a national or even global level. Concomitant with the topographical turn in the humanities (cf. Warf and Arias 2010), it tries to discuss ways of research that do not neglect the concrete place, where sociocultural phenomena occur. Consequently, cities are perceived as quasi-anthropomorphic entities, with a specific cultural imprint. They have their own biography, which renders a particular overlapping of different temporal layers in geographical spaces, and in interaction with changing internal and external conditions cities develop their specific character, their atmosphere, and their way of responding to challenges.

Several objections may be raised to the suggestion to conceive cities as unique entities. First of all, the progressive urbanization seems to be evening out the frontiers and the differences between urban agglomerations and their hinterland. This process calls into question whether we can seriously assume qualitative differences between cities, suburbs, villages, and the countryside. One could still argue that there exist neat administrative borders, but it is debatable if administratively delineated places should be considered as anthropological entities. Nevertheless, the overall-urbanization argument seems much less suited to describe European conditions than those in other regions of the world, where the process of intensified urbanization started after the emergence of modern transport systems. Another point of critique is the standardization-through-globalization argument. It seems that even the traditional shopping streets in European cities become more and more similar in adapting to a globalized economy and consumer culture. Also, the public transport systems, cultural events, sports, and economies seem to be nearly the same in every major city. If there is still something particular about cities, according to the globalization argument this will probably be leveled soon. A further valid objection we could mention is the heterogeneity of cities. Cities consist of very diverse groups, places, and representations that often conflict with each other. Consequently, it would not be appropriate to conceive them as distinct items or to suppose urban landscapes of taste with "systemic" or even "harmonic" patterns. Finally, as anthropologists, we must take into consideration the implications of essentialization. In conceiving cities as spatial-cultural entities, we run the risk of naturalizing and essentializing cultural identity. Hence, we could fall into the mistake of considering symbolic attributions as inseparable from the material world. In this regard, for instance, Pierre Bourdieu has shown how the inculcation of social structures in spatial orders provokes them to be perceived as quasi-essential objectivities (Bourdieu 1989).

New approaches

Keeping some direct responses to these objections for the conclusion, I will now introduce several investigations on particular cities. All of them share one basic assumption: cities are places with a distinct character, and all studies on urban culture are requested to take into consideration a city's particular sociocultural imprint. This claim is especially valid for urban studies within Europe, as most European cities have a particular and compact historical setting developed long before the emergence of private transportation and the suburban sprawl.

One trend-setting article was written by Martyn Lee, who warned about the increasing omission of the spatial in favor of the purely cultural in the field of human geography. Lee claimed to consider place as a "historical determined site upon which the effects of prior social relations produce a complex array of meanings" (Lee 1997:127). Consequently, a city should be regarded as "a relatively coherent and autonomous social domain which exercises a certain determinacy upon both the population and the social processes located upon its terrain" (Lee 1997:127). Drawing upon Bourdieu's concept of the habitus, Lee conceives cities as autonomous structures with "relatively enduring cultural orientations which exist and function relatively independently of their current populations" (Lee 1997:132). The habitus of a city would encompass the distinct forms of perception and the evaluation of facts, as well as the local reactions to these, which Lee considers as the "*practice* of the city" (Lee 1997:133).

A convincing point about the conception of the habitus is its explanation of the *longue-durée* of cultural orientations of cities, but also the changes they are running through in time. When a city is confronted with modified conditions, it will not only react according to its habitus but also adapt its particular patterns to the new situation. In responding to altering contexts and challenges, the city changes its structure of unconscious dispositions, capacities, and practices. Lee assumes internal facts (climate, physical geography, economical structures of the city, and so on), as well as external facts (for example, regional, national, and global economy, demography, politics, migration) to provoke changes on a city's habitus. In this conception, he manages to reconcile the supposition of a city's autonomy with that of the existence of external influences.

The conception of the habitus was also applied by the sociologist Martina Löw, who has significantly advanced the city-centered approach within the German-speaking social sciences. With regard to the idea of cities' uniqueness, she uses the term "intrinsic logic of cities." Löw proposes to sharpen the conception of the habitus and to distinguish between "habitus" and "doxa" as different realms of scientific approach. "Doxa" then would refer to the pre-reflective processes of sense-making and common beliefs of a city, whereas the term "habitus" directs the research perspective on the incorporations of the same:

> The habitus concept accordingly operationalizes the region of the doxa that relates to the perception of place qualities and which implants the qualities of a city in the flesh (the faster or slower walking pace in this or that city, different practices of personal exhibition during a Sunday afternoon promenade or early evening stroll, etc.). Doxa, in contrast, refers to the structures of an urban meaning context, articulated in local rules and resources and thus realized just as much in talk as in architecture, technologies, urban planning, associations, etc. The dichotomous concept doxa/habitus presupposes structured sociality and concentrates attention on the structures of the specific place. (Löw 2010:3)

Löw advocates a comparative approach and a coordination of monographic studies that deal with the uniqueness of cities and their structuring features. Proceeding from this base, urban studies should aim to disclose parameters that determine their intrinsic logics. Following the example set by research on individual biographies, urban studies could then discern groups of similar cities and try to understand the processes of differentiation and the patterns of similarities (Löw 2008:100–102).

Criticizing the ahistorical and leveling perspective of the global cities approach, the sociologist Janet L. Abu-Lughod pursued a comparative study on the development of New York, Chicago, and Los Angeles (Abu-Lughod 1999). According to Abu-Lughod, even though all three cities are global cities, each consists of a unique history and of distinctive patterns, according to which it has responded, and continues to respond, to the effects of globalization. The sample of three global cities seems particularly appropriate to differentiate between local and global factors of development. Among others, Abu-Lughod (1999) specifies the following points of urban differentiation:

1 their natural geographic settings [...];
2 their spatially specific links to an external world [...];
3 their original economic functions, political sponsorships, and first settlers, which to some extent helped to define cultural patterns that left lasting marks;
4 the moments of their most dramatic physical expansion [...] during which the basic template for the future form of the particular city was established;
5 the timing of their growth spurts and the changing sources of their immigrant populations, which framed their subsequent racial and ethnic compositions and their persisting political structures and practices;

> 6 the technologies of transport during initial phases that generated armatures of passage […];
> 7 the social and technological organization of production and communication over time that shaped the imperatives of land, location, and scale in unique ways; and
> 8 the interclass and political relations that gave to each region its own modus vivendi: characteristic patterns of power relations, conflict, and modes of conflict resolution – what I shall refer to as its distinctive *civic culture*. (Abu-Lughod, 1999:4)

Abu-Lughod pays particular attention to spatial patterns, which are often completely neglected within the global city approach. She assigns them an overriding impact on the development of cities, because apart from being the "most visible 'signatures' of their individual characters" (Abu-Lughod 1999:422), spatial patterns significantly determine a city's social order: "Spatial patterns are deeply associated with variations in social life, and the relationship among residents, and it is these social relations that yield differences in the patterns of urban living that give to each city its quintessential character" (Abu-Lughod 1999:3).

In her search for parameters that influence the character of cities, the method of comparison turns out to be a suitable heuristic resource, which should be exploited to a greater extent. More specifically, the categories of urban differentiation pointed out by Abu-Lughod, and also the emphasis on the significance of spatial patterns may provide heuristic perspectives for further comparative research on all kinds of urban agglomeration. This latter understanding is particularly relevant for research in European cities with their long-standing and compact cores.

Another comparative examination in urban sociology deals with the cities of Manchester and Sheffield (Taylor et al. 1996). Ian R. Taylor, Karen Evans, and Penny Fraser pursued "a detailed comparative study of two cities, which ostensibly share a great many general characteristics but which on closer inspection reveal significant differences, especially at the cultural level" (Taylor et al. 1996:xiii). The British sociologists aimed to disclose the cities' characteristic features by examining their different strategies in coping with recent structural change in Northern England. The research scrutinized variables such as shopping, transport, the health service, the labor market, and criminality. In order to grasp an integrated whole beyond those features, the researchers applied the category "structures of feeling" to both Sheffield and Manchester. Despite several objections to this application of a concept that Raymond Williams developed primarily for "national societies," Taylor et al. (1996:5–6) affirm its heuristic value: presupposing that cities have their specific structures of feeling, the researchers assume that all the routinized and taken-for-granted social practices within a city point to a holistic structure beyond. The practices, emotions, and interpretations within the examined domains should be seen not as "a set of unconnected, distinct practices, but as elements of a complex, organized whole: they were part of a given 'ensemble' of social relations, exercising enormous power over individual behavior and belief […]" (Taylor et al. 1996:5). In the end the researchers offer an interpretation of how local emotions differ in the face of restructuration and social change – despite geographical and economical similarities. Furthermore, they emphasize the meaningful role of emotions within the specificity of places. The interesting point of this investigation is about how it manages the (re-)location of global effects and how the category "structures of feeling" is used as an attempt to approach the cities' intrinsic logics. It turns the gaze on emotional conditions and – just as the terms habitus and doxa – it enables us to imagine an underlying structure beyond cultural practices and formations.

In cities, different historical layers, social groups, institutions, the mass and the individual, different scales from global to local, media, bodies, material structures, smells, and much else intermingle. However, when talking about cities, both the process of research and theory building and the form of scientific representation pose special challenges. One of the most accomplished works on a particular city is Mike Davis's Marxist interpretation on the development of Los Angeles. *City of Quartz* (Davis 1990) is not a monographic investigation in a narrow sense; it is rather an assemblage of several urban reports that deals among other topics with local history and myths, racial and social discrimination, politics, power, and spatial patterns. What I want to point out here is not so much the content of the work as the method of representation pursued by Davis. In an essayistic spirit, the sociologist focuses on discursive representations as well as materiality, social structures, and practices. Taking advantage of the essayistic digression, he manages to mix true-to-life examples and anecdotes with larger contexts and theoretical considerations in a witty and illustrative way.

Davis's successful portrayal of Los Angeles points clearly to the suitability of the essayistic form for urban anthropologies. If we have to represent a city's character within the limits of our linear language – what can be more appropriate to grasp this complex entity than the "methodically unmethodically" (Adorno 1984[1958]:161) operating essay? The essay neglects formal conventions and its invitation to digression permits a circulation without restraint between the different realms and scales a city encompasses. Furthermore, the essay seems not only to be an appropriate form of *representing* cities, but also a method of *understanding* them. In "The Essay as Form," Theodor Adorno deals with the essayistic approach as a model of thinking. In that respect, within the multi-perspective essay, "concepts do not build a continuum of operations, [and] thought does not advance in a single direction, rather the aspects of the argument interweave as in a carpet. The fruitfulness of the thoughts depends on the density of this texture" (Adorno 1984[1958]:160). Adorno opposes the Cartesian supposition that objects could be perceived and represented completely and treated with a logical, continuous train of thought. The essay is the medium for a different, more open-minded approach to reality: "It thinks in fragments just as reality is fragmented and gains its unity only by moving through the fissures, rather than by smoothing them over. The unanimity of the logical order deceives us about the antagonistic nature of that on which it was jauntily imposed" (Adorno 1984[1958]:164). When we assume cities to have an underlying habitus, a doxa or a structure of feeling, we have to circumscribe them departing from the fragmented signs they offer on their distinctive surface. To do justice to a city's complexity, its signs have to be examined carefully; they have to be rubbed against each other in different constellations in order to light up each other and to lead into a higher level of understanding. The essayist is not very distant from that idea. Despite shrinking back from general ideas, he does not reject the existence of over-arching concepts. Yet his method to reach them does not follow a strict thread but rather a "groping intuition": "The essay must let the totality light up in one of its chosen or haphazard features but without asserting that the whole is present" (Adorno 1984[1958]:164). Its inductive modesty, its digressive structure, and its awareness of unfinishedness designate the essay to be an appropriate form to represent a city's character. With our linear language, we will never be able to grasp cities in totality. All we can do is to approximate them in more and more contracting circles and give way to catch a glimpse of their character.

The symbolic realm

Up to this point, I have discussed several approaches and concepts that consider cities as distinct characters, proceeding rather from sociological and geographical backgrounds. When considering the city as a social phenomenon the disciplinary differences largely vanish, although we can still determine a special perspective, which is mainly pursued by anthropologists. In this respect, ethnographical methods of observation and representation and the emic exploration of urban contexts have turned out to be particularly suitable in researching cities and city life. Ethnological methods of approach mean that the researcher will be in touch both with the physical as well as the imagined realities of the city-dwellers, but also open to the multiplicity of voices and forces competing within a city.

Social and cultural anthropology focuses on culture as a dynamic and contested semiotic system. In its capacity of treasuring significations, culture is empirically accessible only via its representations in myths, rituals, language, art, practices, material formations, and so on. Applying this idea to particular cities, we may conceive them as symbolic webs with particular patterns of thinking, feeling, and acting. They are semiotic textures with densely interrelated significations. Considered as cultural systems, cities have their particular "structures of feeling," their prevailing topics and emotions, their particular concerns and self-reflexive accounts.

One of the first social scientists who pointed to the fruitfulness of investigating the symbolic realm of cities was Anselm Strauss (1916–1966). According to the assumptions of symbolic interactionism, he postulated that every city-dweller needs to develop a simplified idea about his environment in order to arrange his life within it. Through the local press, personal conversations, and sensory impressions of the city, the city-dweller is "exposed to a persuasive propaganda about its distinctive attributes" (Strauss 1961:5). Since it is not possible to grasp the city in its totality, "any individual citizen, by virtue of his particular choices of alternatives for action and experience, will need a vocabulary to express what he imagines the entire city to be" (Strauss 1961:13). To reduce spatial and social complexity, "he builds up a set of associations which prepare him to accept and appreciate a shorthand symbolic characterization of the place" (Strauss 1961:5–6). In his book *Images of the American City* (1961), Strauss examines the rise of American city images and tries to define some of their basic features. His main sources are popular texts: urban legends, historical books, travel literature, newspaper articles, and novels. According to Strauss, one important characteristic of urban images is their systemic interconnectedness. The collective representations "form a characteristic system of symbolism; they do not merely constitute a bunch of discrete images" (Strauss 1961:32). A city is collectively represented in various dimensions, as space, economy, social order, and time. Taking the historical dimension as an example, some historical periods have more weight in the collective memory than others, whereas others again are completely neglected. Furthermore, temporal categories such as progress, nostalgia, and change may have different connotations and relevance in cities. Accordingly, on how a city deals with change, Strauss stated: "Whether the dominant set of images about change is one that pictures change as growth, development, discontinuity, or no change at all, anyone who makes temporal statements about a city necessarily is ordering a tremendous mass of events into a complex symbolic system" (Strauss 1961:24). And it is apparent that the significance of temporal categories varies even more significantly between different regions of the world.

Apart from his accentuation of the symbolic realm of cities, Strauss was one of the first to postulate a historical perspective in urban studies. The "system of symbolism" (Strauss 1961:32–33) is historical and changeable, because

> it develops out of the contributed perspectives of various important sectors of the city's population, as they have experienced this city during its past. Today's populations inevitably redefine the old terms, using them in new ways, thinking about the city anew but using old symbolism. They also add, in their own turn, elements of imagery to the city's total symbolism. Likewise, today's populations may stress or select certain particular images from among the total set, ignoring or denigrating the others – as some may wish to represent, for instance, their city as progressive and to disregard its slums. (Strauss 1961:32–33)

Conceiving cities as symbolic systems, and taking the citizen's collective representations as a point of departure, Strauss pursued a classical anthropological perspective. It is remarkable that it was an American sociologist who pointed to the historical dimension of urban imaginaries. If considering that the changing images of Chicago tell us much about the city and the lives of its inhabitants, how enriching would such a perspective be for examining cities like Rome or Thessaloniki with their uncountable architectonical and cultural layers mixed up within one urban landscape?

Regrettably, despite offering a treasure of inspiration for further research, Strauss' symbolic approach was followed by few social scientists. One exception was made by Gerald Suttles, who in 1984 published an article suggesting a methodology to approach the "cumulative structure of local urban culture" (Suttles 1984). Referring to the ideas introduced by Strauss, Suttles aimed to detect general patterns of how local culture accumulates in time and how it is passed on in collective representations. He proposed to concentrate on physical and fixed representations (as monuments, songs, festivals, parks, engravings, libraries), since those confer stability and duration to local culture. According to Suttles, a city's basic topics derive from its predominant economic regime (e.g. the dream-factory of Los Angeles or the financial sector of New York). The main actors in the production of urban representations are "formulaic journalists" and "local boosters" (Suttles 1984:296), who, in stereotyped and repetitive comments on cities, render "a selective reading of the present in the light of a believable past" (Suttles 1984:302). Considering the conditions of persistence of particular urban topics, it is the "mnemonic relatedness and assumption of characterological unity [that] are part of the reason for the fixity of local culture" (Suttles 1984:296). However, Suttles does not deny temporal change. He points to the constant accumulation *and* variation of local culture. In building on each other, these different cultural representations are attuned to each other. Nevertheless, when cities adapt to new conditions, their representations may change color (cf. Suttles 1984:298). At this point we are reminded of Lee's concept of the city habitus, which also focuses on temporal change as a response to altered conditions. In considering collective representations of local culture, Suttles assumes three "sets" to be found in any city: founders and discoverers; representations of local entrepreneurs and politicians; and songs, artifacts, and narrations that tell of the "local character" of a place (Suttles 1984:288–289). Suttles proposes to take the most recurrent and distinctive representations of local culture as a basis for further research. Even though those representations do not define a city exhaustively, "they are a good starting point because they seem the most general items in local culture" (Suttles 1984:288). In the end, Suttles suggests an organizing perspective on local culture. His conceptions of "texture," "set," and "accumulation" are promising items for the analysis of the collective representations of cities. With his analytical and, at the same time, interpretive symbolic approach, urban anthropology can be inspired to cultivate and to refine research on the symbolic realm of particular cities.

Besides the incentives offered by Strauss and Suttles, the volume *Urban Mindscapes of Europe* (Weiss-Sussex and Bianchini 2006), which is based on an interdisciplinary conference held at the University of Leicester, offers very interesting perspectives on the symbolism of cities. Drawing upon the assumption that every city has a particular "image-bank" (Bianchini 2006:14), the volume gathers several chapters pursuing a symbolic approach. It is divided into three sections, which deal with the methodology of investigating urban mindscapes, methods of application (as for city marketing or tourism), and several case studies of collective representations of cities. Matthew Reason introduces his research through the narratives of Glasgow illustrated in local newspaper cartoons. Dealing with the failed intentions of reimaging the city as the "European Capital of Culture" in 1990, he points to the principle of accordance within urban representations. Reason shows how the "official" images of a dynamic and cosmopolitan city, proposed by the initiators of the event, were contrary to the city's "self-narratives"; this "needs to be seen in the light of the city's nostalgia for the lost heavy industries" (Reason 2006:192). The study again shows the systemic and the emotional qualities of cities' collective representations. Another exemplary study is about urban material culture and its symbolical positioning. Levente Polyák analyzes the two bridges of Budapest as crystallization points within the city's narratives (Polyák 2006). He shows, among other things, how the role of being a symbol of the city was passed from one bridge to the other as a result of political discourse and representation. Polyák's work is an example of how the material and the discursive intermingle within a symbolic system, and how those relations may be approached methodically.

Having touched on symbolic approaches to cities, I will now present two works which seem to be the first attempts to portray particular European cities as a whole, deriving from urban anthropology. In 2006, Rolf Lindner and Johannes Moser published a volume about the city of Dresden, aiming at disclosing the city's particularities via an ethnographic approach. They propose to take the collective images or stereotypes on cities as a starting point, because, as the authors argue, first, they result from a certain tinting of human reality, and second, they influence the perception of reality and the way of handling it (cf. Lindner and Moser 2006:13). Proceeding from the typified representations and clichés about Dresden, Lindner and Moser pursue an "anthropology of the city, in which the city as a whole is the effective object of research" (Lindner and Moser 2006:15). They focus on the capital of Saxony as a "landscape of taste," as a local texture made of elements that interact with each other, and that reemerge from one another (Lindner and Moser 2006:21). This is the case, for instance, when special industries or services are attracted by an environment that offers possibilities of synergy. Furthermore, the term "landscape" points to an established harmony of aesthetic choices and conventions (see Fischer in this volume). The final goal is to circumscribe a city habitus, which, according to the authors, enables an individual to conceive of a preconditioning unity, a structuring pattern beyond the diverse sociocultural manifestations. Lindner and Moser suggest that the habitus of Dresden has been, and is, strongly determined by the expansion and development of the city to a baroque royal town (Lindner and Moser 2006:15–20). When the court was the predominant economical and social factor, the whole city tended to act in accordance with its demands and habits. This effect promoted the emergence of a particular landscape of taste, where the categories of representation, refinement, and beauty play a primary role. The volume contains different case studies on the most diverse realms of the city. Ethnographically they illustrate how Dresden's past as a royal seat still has its material, discursive, and emotional effects on consumerism, leisure activities, settlement of enterprises, political concerns and actions, collective representations, tourism, and so on.

To my knowledge, the first monographic study in the explicit sense of an anthropology of a city was Lutz Musner's study of Vienna (Musner 2009). Musner's major concepts are "habitus" and "landscapes of taste." Referring to Lee, Lindner, and Moser, he focuses on the city habitus as mediating "between traditions and current challenges, just as between history and the present time. The city habitus expresses the diverse interdependencies between the parameters of a city (geography, climate, demography, economy, politics) in its translocal, economical and cultural general conditions (national state, national economy, globalization)" (Musner 2009:46). Musner considers the city habitus to manifest itself in urban landscapes of taste. "The city habitus is substantially imprinted by the interaction between history and the historical memories, and it shows itself in landscapes of taste, whose canon of images makes the city unmistakable and expresses both real as virtual realms" (Musner 2009:260). In the introduction, Musner refines the concept of "landscapes of taste," defining them as "historically shaped topographical formations [...] where the symbolical capital of a place and the subsequently shaped representations of social and economical conditions, do not only find a particular cultural-spatial expression, but also a specific imago, that may become an economically exploited 'branding' of the city" (Musner 2009:24). The suitability of the concept comes from its complexity, because it represents material places and sociocultural phenomena as well as the symbolic staging and (re-)presentation of these. In landscapes of taste, the real and the virtual become blurred. Being partly spatial and physical, they have ideological potential in the sense of their quasi-natural appearance. In examining and artistically bringing together the most diverse points of crystallization within the urban landscape of taste – such as images, leisure practices, monuments, city marketing, debates about architecture, political processes, the topos of the "Music City," and so on – Musner advances to disentangle the intricate, dynamic, and generating patterns of Vienna.

Conclusion

The goal of this chapter was to introduce briefly the history and the main focus areas of urban anthropology, which due to the dense and long-standing urbanization in Europe has to be considered as a fundamental branch within any anthropology of Europe. After having explored certain presuppositions of urban anthropology, I presented the city-centered approach as one which conceives of cities as distinctive cultural formations. The advantage of assuming the individuality of cities prevents the loss of the specific urban context, which is often the problem with anthropological investigations of social, spatial, temporal, and other entities *within* cities. Moreover, it enables us to pay attention to singular socio-spatial conditions within our globalizing societies, and – in terms of "spacing history" – it allows us to catch the presence of historical processes and decisions in coexistent spatial formations.

Following a spatial approach, we always have to consider its propensity of naturalization and its neglect of the constructive character of significations, which are seen to be integral (and ahistorical) parts of the material world. Such constructivist objections are epistemologically relevant, but at the same time we have to recognize a distinct ontological reality of physical conditions, which becomes particularly relevant for the long-standing cities in Europe with their historical cores. The city's layout, its buildings, but also monuments and parks, its statues and commemorative plaques have a different durability and perceptibility than the ephemeral anecdote – unless they become part of a stylized, collective representation appearing in written, pictorial, or material form. The distinct ontology of physical appearances and of all stylized cultural forms induces Gerald Suttles to focus on representations or elements that "take on physical or *stylized* form. Indeed, one of my contentions is that these objective artifacts give local culture much of its stability and continuing appeal" (Suttles 1984: 284). Physical and stylized representations of urban culture are durable crystallizations of collective imagination. Future generations will inevitably have to deal with them, adapting, reinterpreting, or rejecting them. As tradition needs stylized forms, stylized forms also force tradition.

For the purpose of an anthropology of distinctive cities we can draw on several concepts and approaches proposed by exemplary studies. In view of the complexity of the task, we have to recognize that it is necessary to draw on sociological and geographical knowledge, for mere "classical" anthropological methods as fieldwork and interviewing are not sufficient to grasp cities in their macroeconomical, macropolitical, and macrocultural relations. However, urban anthropology does not need the backing of sociological and geographical theory merely as conceptual instruments and as a support for positioning its own investigations. By communicating with other disciplines in urban studies, the specific potentialities of anthropological approximations are accentuated and social and cultural anthropology can highlight its special virtues: its conceptual and methodological openness, its close-to-life approaches, and its capacity for interpreting complex systems.

With its focus on cultural patterns, urban anthropology can easily counter objections to an anthropologization of cities: looking at the symbolic realm of cities in stylized representations and in the human imaginaries reveals the existence of particular cities as an empirical fact. Multitudinous representations in paintings, literature, music, city-lore, jokes, and biographical accounts tell us about the uniqueness of cities. Over and above, people put their lives and themselves into a city's textures. As such, local representations are adapted as a part of individual and collective identities and become eminently emotional and meaningful for individuals and social groups. Furthermore, collective representations of cities draw on the scope of thinking and acting of the city-dwellers. How we move and feel in a city, how we deal with public space, and how we position ourselves within the city's social order is widely determined by the conceptions and images we have in mind. Hence it is valuable to take the symbolic realm as a starting point when investigating the uniqueness of cities.

The same argument is put forward by Martina Löw, when she argues that in successful city-images, as they crystallize in paintings, rituals, monuments, architecture, or tourism brochures, we have a reference to the topics that seem specific for this or that city or town (cf. Löw 2008:86). Images are successful only when they are assimilated by future generations and become part of a city's cumulative texture. Then we may considerate the representation as a "practical densification and verbalization or as a pictorial expression of the urban doxa" (Löw 2008:86). Löw therefore proposes to take successful images of a city – its "branding" – as a point of departure to analyze its intrinsic logic.

Reflexivity is another specific quality of social and cultural anthropology to be realized and introduced in investigations of particular cities. Since the crisis of representation, anthropologists have developed a certain uneasiness concerning cultural homogenization and essentialization. The perspective on a city as a more or less harmonic texture of interacting elements arouses suspicions of being at the cost of agency and disguising inner conflicts and fractions. Thus, anthropology needs a critical perspective on synthesizing conceptions, such as habitus, structures of feeling, doxa, texture, and landscapes of taste. They are of great heuristic value; however, they may block the view on a city's inner struggles. These must be tracked down by intensive fieldwork and thick descriptions. Referring to such a complex subject as a city, the ideal of research should be the total immersion in city life and the continuous questioning of every perceptible phenomenon as a source. Only through an emic, ethnographical approach and the establishment of direct relationships will research uncover the city's inner contradictions and find out about the coexistence and interweaving of different ways of life, significational processes, and social strategies within the distinct conditions of a city. Thus, the ethnographical approach, although it was developed in very different contexts, appears not only to be appropriate for exploring inductively the uniqueness of cities, it is indeed indispensable to grasp their "heterogenous unity" as well as their identitary functions for people.

The city-centered approach, in turn, may render new perspectives for urban anthropology in general and set a new course of investigation. Taking space seriously, and focusing on cities' characteristic features, city-centered studies will advance theory construction and favor interdisciplinary investigation. They will also provide new foundations for participatory approaches. If, for example, we want to promote municipal environmental protection, a long-term and sustainable policy will only be successful if the city's particularities, including its opportunities and its vices, are taken into account.

Furthermore, the anthropologization of cities implies a new geographical scale for the purpose of an anthropology in and of Europe. This is an eminently important point, considering that the increased mobility and connectivity within Europe has altered the relations between cities, regions, and national states. Moreover, the importance of nation-states is a very recent phenomenon, considering most European cities in their course of time. By challenging the category of national societies as all-determining contexts, the city-centered approach goes down to a local scale of social life, trying to come to grips with the locally operating regional, national, or global influences. This innovative focus on urban life may bring forth a more differentiated perspective on European cities and the Europeans living in them.

REFERENCES

Abu-Lughod, Janet L.
1999 New York, Chicago, Los Angeles: America's Global Cities. Minneapolis: University of Minnesota Press.

Adorno, Theodor
1984[1958] The Essay as Form. New German Critique 32:151–171.

Antweiler, Christoph
2004 Urbanität und Ethnologie: aktuelle Theorietrends und die Methodik ethnologischer Stadtforschung. Zeitschrift für Ethnologie 129(2):285–307.

Bianchini, Franco
2006 Introduction: European Urban Mindscapes: Concepts, Cultural Representations and Policy Applications. *In* Urban Mindscapes of Europe. Weiss-Sussex, Godela and Franco Bianchini, eds. pp. 13–31. European Studies, 23. Amsterdam: Rodopi.

Bourdieu, Pierre
1989 Social Space and Symbolic Power. Sociological Theory 7(1):14–25.

Castells, Manuel
1973 La Question Urbaine. Paris: Maspero.

Davis, Mike
1990 The City of Quartz. London: Verso.

EEA (European Environment Agency)
2006 Urban Sprawl in Europe: The Ignored Challenge. EEA Report 10. Luxembourg: Office for Official Publications of the European Communities.

Hannerz, Ulf
1980 Exploring the City: Inquiries Toward an Urban Anthropology. New York: Columbia University Press.

Lee, Martyn
1997 Relocating Location: Cultural Geography, the Specificity of Place and the City Habitus. *In* Cultural Methodologies. Jim McGuigan, ed. pp. 126–141. London: Sage.

Lindner, Rolf, and Johannes Moser
2006 Dresden: Ethnografische Erkundungen (in) einer Residenzstadt. *In* Dresden: Ethnografische Erkundungen einer Residenzstadt. Rolf Lindner and Johannes Moser, eds. pp. 11–34. Leipzig: Leipziger Universitätsverlag.

Löw, Martina
2008 Soziologie der Städte. Frankfurt: Suhrkamp.
2010 The Intrinsic Logic of Cities. Electronic document. http://www.sss7.org/Proceedings/02 Invited Papers/I03_Low_Intrinsic_Logic_of_Cities.pdf (accessed December 29, 2011).
Merry, Sally E.
2006 Urban Anthropology. *In* The Dictionary of Anthropology. Thomas Barfield, ed. pp. 479–480. Oxford: Blackwell.
Mitchell, James Clyde, ed.
1969 Social Networks in Urban Situations: Analyses of Personal Relationships in Central African Towns. Manchester: University of Manchester Press.
Musner, Lutz
2009 Der Geschmack von Wien: Kultur und Habitus einer Stadt. Frankfurt am Main.: Campus.
Park, Robert
1967[1925] The City: Suggestions for the Investigation of Human Behavior in the Urban Environment. *In* The City: Suggestions for Investigation of Human Behavior in the Urban Environment. Robert Park, Ernest W. Burgess, and Roderick D. McKenzie, eds. pp. 1–46. Chicago: University of Chicago Press.
Polyák, Levente
2006 Drifting Bridges: Semantic Changes of the Bridge Metaphor in Twentieth Century Budapest. *In* Urban Mindscapes of Europe. Godela Weiss-Sussex and Franco Bianchini, eds. pp. 197–210. European Studies, 23. Amsterdam: Rodopi.
Reason, Matthew
2006 Cartoons and Comic Exposure of the European of the European City of Culture. *In* Urban Mindscapes of Europe. Godela Weiss-Sussex and Franco Bianchini, eds. pp. 179–196. European Studies, 23. Amsterdam: Rodopi.
Rollwagen, Jack
1975 The City as Context: The Puerto Ricans of Rochester. Urban Anthropology 4:53–59.
Sassen, Saskia
1991 The Global City: New York, London, Tokyo. Princeton: Princeton University Press.
Strauss, Anselm
1961 Images of the American City. New York: Free Press.
Suttles, Gerald
1984 The Cumulative Texture of Local Urban Culture. American Journal of Sociology 90:283–304.
Taylor, Ian, Karen Evans, and Penny Fraser
1996 A Tale of Two Cities: Global Change, Local Feeling and Everyday Life in the North of England: A Study in Manchester and Sheffield. London: Routledge.
Warf, Barney, and Santa Arias, eds.
2010 The Spatial Turn: Interdisciplinary Perspectives. London: Routledge.
Weiss-Sussex, Godela, and Franco Bianchini, eds.
2006 Urban Mindscapes of Europe. European Studies, 23. Amsterdam: Rodopi.
Whyte, William F.
1943 Street Corner Society: The Social Structure of an Italian Slum. Chicago: University of Chicago Press.
Wirth, Louis
1923 The Ghetto. Chicago: University of Chicago Press.

PART V Disciplinary Boundary Crossings

CHAPTER 27

Medical Anthropology and Anthropological Studies of Science

Maryon McDonald

This chapter offers a brief exploration of some of the studies of Europe that would classify as (i) medical anthropology and (ii) anthropological studies of scientific practice. It also includes works that have influenced or helped to shape these areas in Europe, even if such works are neither European in origin nor anthropological. The outline presented here is, I would stress, not exhaustive and it draws principally on studies published in English, although others are included.

We can start with a quick tour through two sets of spatial metaphors that have been very common in Europe. First, as the contents of this companion illustrate well, in the moral topography of Europe, the focus of anthropologists has gradually moved in from the edge, looking now at supposed centers as much as peripheries, and examining this construction itself. Anthropological preoccupations initially located an excess of culture around the edge of Europe – where "meaning comes in barrowloads," as one anthropologist cheekily reflected in the 1980s (Chapman 1982). By the 1990s, this "culture" was located in the more central areas, where science and medicine have more obviously flourished. At the same time, another topographical edifice was awaiting deconstruction. A product and victim of European priorities and preoccupations, anthropology has lived for a long period in a world stacked in layers, like floors in a building: "nature" has been the basic, ontological rock on which all else rests, then perhaps the "economy" above this, then "society" resting on its economic base, and finally "culture" on the top floor where clouds float past the windows. The further down the stack, into the depths, that one could reach, the more "real" and "material" it has felt and the more "scientific" the practice required (and the more likely you have been also to get the research funding). The general picture here has not been unfamiliar in much of Europe. In recent decades, anthropology has turned its ethnographic attention to this construction and, instead of taking it for granted, has taken on the layers, examining them one by one. It was then time to take certain categories out of the analytical toolbox and deal with them

A Companion to the Anthropology of Europe, First Edition. Edited by Ullrich Kockel, Máiréad Nic Craith, and Jonas Frykman.

ethnographically instead – whether "the economy" or "science," to give but two examples. It has taken quite a long time – but ethnographic treatments of the constitution, practices, regulation, and effects of both medicine and science mean perhaps that anthropology is finally coming home.

This home-coming, if it is such, began in very particular circumstances. Within the span of historical Europe, we can look back to the eighteenth century and then put on hundred-year boots to stride forward again, past the construction of new national, imperial, and post-national boundaries in Europe, past the construction of disciplines within the universities, and into that world familiar with nature and culture, with society and the economy, and with both historiographical pasts and modern futures, all with their myriad specialists. In the twentieth century there were also two world wars and then the Cold War. "Scientists," familiar figures since the nineteenth century especially, now gained a high public profile in physics and military science particularly. This public profile was not unproblematic. The 1960s became an important historical (and historiographical) pivot. Amidst demographic changes, the reinvention of the category of "youth" and increased studentification, a new "generation" was self-consciously establishing itself in contra-distinction from its parents. Old certainties such as progress, reason, positivism, and the whole project of modernity were put in question. "Top-down" was to be replaced by "bottom-up" and both the "workers" and the "grass roots" gained new significance. This was a time when a world of cultural diversity was reinvented, a time of civil rights marches and of decolonization and counter-cultures, a time when the alternative worlds of regionalism and relativism appealed, and when new nationalisms and new identities, ethnic and national, began to crowd the map in Europe and beyond (McDonald 1989).

In the 1960s some of this dissent inevitably turned to anger against a science and technology that was apparently external to and threatened "society" – as it had done already in two world wars. Until the last decade of the twentieth century, the focus of concern was largely developments in physics but with new developments in genetics particularly, this focus shifted to the biological sciences. This became the age of biotechnology, an age of new bodies – and new concerns have ensued (Brodwin 2000). Where the weapons of mass destruction had threatened national or human society, now the new genetics and biotechnology seemed to be messing with bodies, with the very stuff of persons or individuals.

It was not long after the 1960s, with "medic-bashing" accompanying the rage against science, that criticism and dissent created a space in which both medical anthropology and then a new "science studies" (particularly science and technology studies, known as STS for short) were born. In parts of Europe, both medicine and science were now meant to be ready to listen to the "social" (Nowotny et al. 2001), and even if they were not ready, the space was there for anthropology to jump in where it had not done so already. We will look first at medical anthropology and then at anthropology's science studies, and then finally at some of the two together.

Medical Anthropologies

In the United Kingdom, medical anthropology developed in the 1970s, largely combining the work of Evans-Pritchard on witchcraft and Victor Turner on healing ritual with a growing influence from the self-consciously "medical anthropology" work of medical practitioners who had become anthropologists – such as Byron Good and, later, Arthur Kleinman in the United States (Frankenberg 2007). Kleinman had appropriated and refined an explicit focus on what he termed "explanatory models" and an "illness/disease" distinction that had already appeared in medical texts in the United States. The combination of such influences became a distinctly anthropological, grass roots, or bottom-up intervention formulated through theoretical tendencies within anthropology at the time toward semantic and phenomenological concerns. The General Medical Council in the United Kingdom was already calling for attention to the patients' perspectives – calls that have persisted. In what external critics had loudly chastised as a patriarchal and imperial medicine, it was these realities that were seen as having been ignored. A medical doctor constructs or diagnoses "disease" but acceptable or successful intervention, medical or otherwise, can depend on the patient's experience: how does he or she understand and live "illness," including what it is that has been caused and what or who caused it and how ("explanatory model")? These were the same questions that medical anthropologists had posed, and were posing, in their ethnographies elsewhere in the world.

An anthropological study of cancer sufferers in East Anglia in the United Kingdom was a pioneering work in this direction published in 1976 – in the first UK-published volume with "medicine" as well as "anthropology" in its title (Loudun 1976). It was social anthropology *and* medicine, however, not medical anthropology nor yet an anthropology of medicine. Work on spiritualism and healing in Wales also appeared in this volume – as "ethnomedicine." The editor explained that this meant "systems of thought and practice" outside "cosmopolitan medicine" and might naturally include "witchcraft, sorcery and magic" (Loudun 1976:35). These last topics were eventually excluded from the volume solely because so much had already been recently published on them. The editor, Joseph Loudun, and five of the contributors, including Gilbert Lewis, were – like several of their American counterparts at the time – both physicians and anthropologists. Lewis's own contribution in the volume hinges on the illness/disease distinction, citing a medical text (not Kleinman) on this. In order better to grasp "ethnomedicine" in New Guinea, Lewis begins to examine aspects of the disease model of his own UK medical training. The introduction to the volume makes use of Foucault's work on the birth of the clinic, recently translated into English (Foucault 1973). "Cosmopolitan medicine" was beginning to come within the anthropological gaze – but the main focus was elsewhere.

Developments in medical anthropology studies of the United Kingdom were given further impetus by the AIDS/HIV epidemic at the beginning of the 1980s. It was similar in other parts of Europe (Saillant and Genest 2007a; and later in the former Eastern Europe: R. Goodwin et al. 2003). Anthropologists became involved in studies related to epidemiology and public health in the United Kingdom and began examining activities such as drug use and prostitution (McDonald 1994; Day 2007; Frankenberg 2007). Some hoped that such research, when linked to understanding the spread of AIDS, might raise the profile of anthropology as responsible and even "useful" (Frankenberg 1995). Other UK studies at this time went further in examining some of the assumptions of medicine (still often singular) – but in psychiatry particularly, an area metaphorically closer to "culture" than other specialties (Frankenberg 2007:194ff; Helman 2007). An interest in self-care and in Internet medicine also grew in the United Kingdom and in Europe more generally (Oudshoorn and Somers 2007).

In France, medical anthropology emerged in the 1980s, with three broad schools developing: one, which took the label "medical anthropology," was intellectually attached to epidemiological studies and aimed to add the "socio-cultural" element to medicine's sciences; another devoted itself to "ethnomedicine," which largely meant pharmacopoeias. A third set of interests, closest perhaps to the developments in the United Kingdom but initially keen to distinguish itself from French "medical anthropology" and "ethnomedicine" alike, became known as the "anthropology of illness," headed by Marc Augé. Again, this was influenced by the work of Evans-Pritchard and Turner. Whilst the "anthropology of illness" and "medical anthropology" thus delineated two different sets of preoccupations in France, the term "medical anthropology" was gradually taken on by all, under external pressure from international publications in the field. Favret-Saada's 1977 work on witchcraft in Normandy, influenced by Evans-Pritchard and seen at the time in France as a work on religion and magic, had by 2000 become "medical anthropology" (Benoist 2002). The anthropology of illness, which brought such earlier works within the historiographical fold, paid special attention to explanatory models. One well-known example offers comparisons between parts of Africa and France and concludes that whilst, in Africa, blame for illness might be lodged with close relatives or acquaintances, in France it was predominantly the impersonal "modern life" or "society" that was blamed (Fainzang 1989). Health-seeking behavior and "medical pluralism" are examined in this work and tended to become stock themes in medical anthropology as it developed in France and elsewhere in Europe. Medical anthropologists in France feel they have struggled – and struggle still – to come to the "conclusion that Western medicine itself is an object for anthropology" rather than being "simply a scientific discourse that cooperates with anthropology in examining illness" (Fainzang 2007). This can seem very odd in a country that had long since produced Foucault, but the hierarchical nature of all French education and the compartmentalization of individual research centers, together with a prolonged anthropological focus on rurality, peripheries, and alterity, meant that these worlds rarely met. French political anthropology nevertheless injected new life into an examination of health and illness. This was not seeking to delineate the "political" but, with both Foucault and Latour in the analytical toolbox, sought to understand pervasive relations of power (see Fassin 2007:253–256 for a summary and exemplary insight into lead poisoning in France, inspired by this perspective.)

Medical anthropology in Spain took some direct early influence from France – but more readily took on investigations of the clinic within a national context in which healthcare became a central matter of political concern, debate, and reform. An earlier Spanish anthropology looking at "lay medicine" was launched in the 1970s – by a student of Evans-Pritchard, looking at connections between witchcraft and illness in Galicia (e.g. Lisón 1979). Studies of internal minority identities that followed, while seen as paying welcome attention to "ethnomedicine," have more recently been criticized for paying little attention to mainstream medicine in local life (Comelles et al. 2007). It was in 1980 – in the heat of debate about reform of the Spanish healthcare system – that a joint work by a sociologist and an anthropologist both launched and took stock of "medical anthropology" in Spain (Kenny and de Miguel 1980). This work included an encouragement to "applied anthropology" in clinical settings, which became a reality in the following decade. Studies of the institutional realities of health-care centers, emergency rooms and intensive care followed, along with studies of drug use, the deinstitutionalization of psychiatry, and death management, in a stream of attention to a context of changing healthcare practices. Feminism – together with the influence of theorists from Goffman to Foucault – has been apparent (Comelles et al. 2007).

In Italy, medical anthropology took on an earlier and rather different shape. It developed through the political commitment of anthropologists working alongside doctors on health promotion and education from the 1950s onward. This was largely an interventionist, Marxist and Gramsci-inspired project. Italian medical anthropology found echoes in Latin America, and thence back in Europe again, in Spain. It has been noted that, throughout much of Southern Europe particularly, medical anthropology tended to develop through the politics of care and the national struggles for, and structures of, its provision (Comelles 2002).

Studies of Europe developed in part along the lines of those already carried out by medical anthropologists from Europe elsewhere in the world: from "folk" healing and "ethnomedicine" to "patients" perspectives' within the doctor–patient relationship. Variations of an "applied anthropology" and a politically inspired "critical medical anthropology" are also found. Gradually the medical world itself became an object of study. Although often US-led, several anthropological collections focusing on the assumptions of medicine – becoming "biomedicine" in the titles – were already published in English in the 1980s and 1990s (including Lock and Gordon 1988; Johnson and Sargent 1990). By the end of the first decade of the second millennium, the French medical anthropology that had previously been hesitant was engaging in the hospital ethnography for which Foucault had done part of the analytical groundwork. Indeed, ethnographies in and of the hospital had become more common in Europe, examining relations, organization, and some of the assumptions at work (e.g. Van der Geest and Finkler 2004). However, hospitals are not islands. Tanassi's ethnography of practices in an Italian hospital shows how women patients, echoing a world of personalized relations outside the clinic, made deliberate use of apparent "compliance" requirements as a strategy toward motherhood and better care (Tanassi 2004). Similarly, Vermeulen's study of difficult decisions about continuing or withdrawing treatment in a neonatal ward in Amsterdam suggests the implication of wider Dutch practices of mediation and bargaining (Vermeulen 2004). In the meantime, the sometimes constitutive, sometimes cross-cutting practices of different specialties through "biomedical platforms" had been examined – a platform being a specific configuration of instruments, persons, entities, and activities held together by standard reagents and protocols (Keating and Cambrosio 2003). As critiques have become less shrill, new prospects and problems of a "collaborative anthropology" in the clinic have also been aired (Fainzang et al. 2010). The more we get into the practices of hospitals now, however, the more we have joined up with science studies. Medicine seems already to have become "biomedicine" by the 1970s, and a study of a hospital complex in Europe may now have to sweep through molecular biology to hands-on medicine, and from normal cell maturation to pathology, and through a variety of technologies, institutions, biotechnology companies, instrument makers, metrologies, and the clinic (Keating and Cambrosio 2003).

Anthropologies of Science

Prior to World War II, the dominant historiography and philosophy of science in Europe tended to stress science as an acme of achievement, an apparently perfect way of knowing – one that was the outcome of historical refinement and a careful approach to, and use of, logic and language. Through World War II and then the early Cold War, human reason became "rationality," assumed to exist in mathematics, economics, and science but ideally in all behavior. Such ideals, through the construction of disembodied logics and alterities, often engaged in debates with themselves. In anthropology, the so-called "rationality debates" of the 1970s resulted in part from an unsettling appeal within philosophy to the work of Wittgenstein and Evans-Pritchard in an attempt not only to relativize "rationality" but also to insert "meaning," a venture that was then followed by assertive reactions from the rationality modelers (e.g. Lukes and Hollis 1983). Evans-Pritchard's 1930s work on witchcraft inspired, we have seen, a great deal of work in medical anthropology from the 1970s, posing questions about both causality and remedy, and it was summoned here again – but it had left "science" intact. Science was still science for all sides in these debates, a disembodied arbiter and its practice a black box that took a while to open.

A few decades after World War II, and led by the United States, science had become an object of study across several disciplines. Conferences, journals, centers, and associations were launched (including, for example, the European Association for the Social Study of Science and Technology, or EASSST), with three main types of projects recurring: STS (science and technology studies), plus ethics, and policy. In their early days, these assumed a science or technology or medicine *and* "society" (Traweek 1993:5–6). "Science and society" was a rallying banner alongside concerns about "the public understanding of science," which had been one of the early reactions to 1960s criticisms of science and scientists (Jasanoff et al. 1995; Hackett et al. 2008). Anthropologists would now tend, analytically, to de-reify and collapse the two terms – science and society – while perhaps watching them being resurrected ethnographically as a distinction salient in some form to the people studied (Lambert and McDonald 2009).

Boys with Toys

Amongst the first attempts to link science and society in a way that was potentially critical of any idealized rationality of science, on the one hand, or any separate world of "society" on the other – and that instead made science a social activity – was work influenced by the American thinker Thomas Kuhn. Kuhn had been inspired by others such as Fleck, Polanyi, and Lakatos, and he in turn encouraged more critical reflection from thinkers such as Feyeraband and then Fuller, Hacking, and Longino: these philosophers have now become part of the historiography of a social study of science and technology, with attention drawn to their conclusion that "facts" are made through social processes of adjudication (Traweek 1993:8). In Europe, studies of science and technology developed that put more empirical flesh on these philosophical bones. This work was done primarily by sociologists in the first instance; they drew a commitment to ethnography from anthropology – but initially took their inspiration for the kind of ethnography they did from the work of the phenomenology-inspired "ethnomethodologists" (notably the American, Harold Garfinkel). Amongst these sociologists were Karin Knorr (later Knorr Cetina) from Austria, and John Law and Steve Woolgar in the United Kingdom. Woolgar joined up with Bruno Latour from France for their pioneering work, *Laboratory Life* (Latour and Woolgar 1979).

The real-life laboratory in these studies is seen to have taken the place of the ideal experiment in the earlier historical and philosophical studies of science. Science was reborn as plural practices, a cultural activity for some (e.g. Traweek 1993; Knorr Cetina 1995:143), and apparently capable of being localized in place and time. The laboratory studies posed interesting empirical questions about the claims and procedures of science as standardized and universal, and they have made clear that scientific results are not weakened by attention to local configurations; rather, it is always through what might count as local "circumstances" that results are generated and their robustness assured (Latour and Woolgar 1979:239; Knorr Cetina 1995).

One striking, early conclusion drawn from the ethnographic work seems to have been that scientists and engineers produced their experimental designs, ideas, arguments, and papers in seemingly mundane face-to-face interactions (Traweek 1993:8). Whilst it was worth drawing attention to this for all the anthropologists who had previously left science untouched, Latour and Woolgar felt that these same conclusions seemed almost a disappointment to the scientists themselves (a point noted in their "Postscript" to the second edition of *Laboratory Life* in 1986). These studies nevertheless helped to fuel excitement in some predictable "science wars" that followed in the 1990s (Franklin 1996), in which the boundaries of science were defensively redrawn as a space purified of all that was deemed personal, emotional, artistic, political, social, or partisan – and these proclivities were then simplistically poured together into various damnable recensions of non-science that, equally predictably, gathered themselves together and fought back. A mutual constitution of "science and society" here, colored by associations of C. P. Snow's "two cultures" and by other well-worn dualities such as gender differences and many others familiar from the old rationality debates, has, of course, left any such "wars" without solution in these terms.

The ethnographic studies of science and technology that have since grown into the very large and American-fed beast known as "STS" developed mostly in Europe initially – but the American and the anthropological influences were always strong. Students of Garfinkel such as Michael Lynch inspired attention to visual images (Lynch and Woolgar 1990); Lucy Suchman, a linguistic anthropologist inspired by Garfinkel, encouraged attention to machine–human communication; and it was Jean Lave, a cognitive anthropologist, along with Edwin Hutchins, who encouraged attention to practical reasoning in laboratories and an understanding of "distributed cognition" (Traweek 1993:8; Hutchins 1996). These ideas have been cited, detected, or emulated in much of the work in STS and its uptake in medical anthropology. Whilst some laboratory studies have seemed heavily influenced by Geertzian ideas of "culture" (e.g. Traweek 1988, Gusterson 1996), most studies of science, especially those that went on to find themselves under the label of "STS," have been shaped by a very different source – that of actor network theory (ANT) and various "assemblage" theories (e.g. Ong and Collier 2005). Much of this, through the metaphoric of networks, construction, devices, assemblages, platforms, and a proliferation of "technologies," can seem like boys with toys, from meccano and train sets to motorbikes and embedded computers. These ideas have nevertheless encouraged a renewed focus on post-Saussurian realities and reinjected materiality into ethnographic studies.

The anthropological force of the approach that developed was, ideally, to be rigorously and radically ethnographic (or "symmetrical" in the language ANT borrowed from earlier Edinburgh-based "Sociology of Scientific Knowledge" exponents such as David Bloor). Analytically, everything could be deemed to be "social," rendering this term superfluous, but when dealing with the world ethnographically, "science," "facts", "society," "social," "social relations," and so on, might all become interesting objects of inspection (although many of the sociological and ANT studies fail to be as rigorous ethnographically here as anthropologists might want them to be). No "society" is the a priori "context" for science; instead science and society became definitional and co-constitutive realities, accomplished in micro-practices that could be studied (Latour 1991). Within the laboratory as beyond it, everything – human and non-human – has "agency." Scientific practices are seen to involve mutual articulations of objects, instruments, humans, and the non-human, indeed of everything available ("circumstances"), with everything involved reconfigured – well-behaved nature, working objects, instruments, and workable scientists. Relationality gained a new materiality in heterogeneously composed networks of relations or became emergent "assemblages." Nothing could be taken for granted – from a drawing to a door. These studies departed from the idea that scientific facts were to be accounted for in terms of the material reality they claimed to represent; instead, they were accounted for in terms of the processes of their construction. Attempts to "represent" nevertheless reappear as ethnographically important. It may be that, ethnographically, a specific diagram, design, or plan is a representation of a train, for instance – but in very particular ways, according to autonomous and selective conventions (e.g. geometry, technical drawing). The train and drawing have different ontological qualities: the train will rust, for example; the drawing has not drawn – and cannot draw – everything together (Latour 2007). In an important sense, it may be a diagram that a train driver will drive nevertheless and, in the event of a crash, hitherto unknown "actants" may be summoned in an inquiry.

Clearly, as ethnography got hold of science it also got hold of some central assumptions held dear in Europe; at the same time, science was taken apart, both unity and disunity demonstrated, and ontological issues pushed to the fore again in anthropology. It is often difficult to untie European and American concerns; written by a Frenchman and an Englishman, the pioneering work was a study of a neuroendocrinology laboratory in the United States, and the "actor network" approach that then developed and cohered under that banner in Europe fed back into general anthropology in both the United States and Europe more widely. This approach has given rise to several criticisms, partly for its evocations of scientific practice as quasi-military engagement – and there has been a feeling at times that the ANT/STS complex was forging autonomous debates that appeared to ignore the necessary entanglement of matter and meaning, and a great deal more of anthropology (Barad 2007; Navaro-Yashin 2009). It also seemed as if important insights into national difference were being left to policy concerns (e.g. Jasanoff et al. 1995; Jasanoff 2005; Hackett et al. 2008).

Difference and comparison were not ignored, however. Knorr Cetina's study (1999) of "epistemic communities" compared and contrasted the different assumptions and practices of two disciplines in Europe – high-energy physics and molecular biology – suggesting how the meaning of the empirical changes as different ontological objects and machineries of fact production are constructed and deployed in different fields. When we then put together anthropology, STS, and different disciplinary practices, and move to the Netherlands, we find a medical student-turned-philosopher using ethnography in the 1990s to show the classification of one disease (atherosclerosis) becoming different ontological objects through the practices of different hospital specialties, and the body similarly made "multiple" (Mol 2002). This last work does not set out to draw attention to anything particularly "Dutch" about the practices involved but scientific objects, practices, and theories have elsewhere been located within the comparative cultural framework of different national traditions (e.g. Traweek 1988; Franklin 1995:175–176; Hess 1995; Harding 1998) – with a reminder that differences can cause problems at international meetings and have also provided the conditions historically for particular kinds of theory and research interests, as in 1930s Germany (Harwood 1993). Other suggestive work for comparison has been done as more studies of scientific practice have moved beyond the laboratory. In particular, Latour's historical study of the work of Pasteur (1984), suggestively entitled *The Pasteurization of France* in English, shows how the germ theory of disease gained adherence in France, with micro-organisms empowered to reshape the social world in new policies and practices of hygiene and sanitation. The laboratory becomes here an agent of change but this is effected only by eliciting the cooperation of a range of "actants" in the particular circumstances of French farms, other people and objects – notably microbes – and reconstituting in an extra-mural world the conditions that pertain in a laboratory in order to make facts or results reproducible.

Paul Rabinow's work *French DNA* (1999) further highlights the circumstances of France – but more as a lived national identity in knowledge production. This short book, which followed previous work by Rabinow on biotechnology in the United States, offers interesting insights into French nationalist protectionism, with resentful French scientists in the biotechnology industry summoning up a protection of French families who had donated DNA in order to fend off US competition. Americans were not to steal and profit from "French DNA." This is a work that links up issues ranging from blood donation, venture capital, and genomic assemblages to different modes of doing anthropology and biotechnology alike. One chapter (Chapter 4) in particular throws into relief some of the moral, monetary, and legal differences between the United States and France in the production and handling of human biological material. We are once more in a merging world here of medical anthropology, STS, and more general anthropology.

Rabinow's work more generally takes us back to the terrain of a Foucauldian attention to scientific knowledge and relational power effects, and has been seen as gathering together an analysis of contemporary biosciences and the conceptual history of the life sciences in France exemplified by the work of Canguilhem (Franklin 1995:177). Rabinow's "biosociality" and the Foucauldian "biopolitics" have been put to a great deal of work where medical anthropology, science studies, and other social concerns meet – whether teamed with the insights of Giorgio Agamben to look both sensitively and critically at "humanitarian" interventions in areas of trauma such as the post-communist Balkans (Pandolfi 2002), for example, or to examine biosciences outside the laboratory, suggesting some of the ways in which we have come to live, in Europe and beyond, the facts and practices and spillages of the biosciences and of other technologies, from the practical imaginations of governance to the identities and practices of our daily lives in governmentalities and our regulated, corporeal selves (e.g. Franklin 1995: 177–178; Rabinow and Rose 2006; Rose 2006; Gibbon and Novas 2007). Such studies outline the ways in which genetic testing and other screening results, and associated "risks," are lived and embodied by those whom they shape – or they trace corporeally based claims to entitlement, which Petryna's careful study of the aftermath of the Chernobyl disaster refers to as "biological citizenship" (Petryna 2002). Drawing on earlier ideas of "genetic citizenship," this idea has been taken up by other scholars and contrasted across national borders. The general claim here is that "new subjectivities, new politics and new ethics" are taking shape in Europe in "the age of rapid biological discovery, genomics, biotechnological fabrication and biomedicine" (Rose and Novas 2005:458). Studies of new subjectivities are growing – and those of genetic screening particularly, its perception and its effects, generating new classifications of diseases and of persons, are many in Europe, some of them interestingly comparative (e.g. Beck and Niewöhner 2009; Lock and Nguyen 2010:26; ch.12).

Women Throw Out Nature

With only a few deviations, we have so far tended to follow a historiography of science studies that privileges both ANT and STS. There has been another route into science studies for anthropology, however. This route has generally been drawn through reflections on the more traditional domains of gender and kinship, driven largely by the impetus of feminism as well as – like ANT/STS – the insights of post-Saussurian studies in British and French social anthropology.

A shift from sex to gender, as if it were a shift from nature to culture, had seemed to be both analytically exciting and politically radical in anthropology in the 1970s but the excitement left the biology behind initially, as nature and its scientific pursuit were deemed irrelevant or indeterminate at best. It then became necessary to take into account also the important point that – through the preoccupations of an eighteenth-century Europe that had required nature as an ontological rock for normative appeal as well as for experimentation – sex had been gendered (e.g. Laqueur 1990). Biology, as both nature and a science that pursued it, was therefore up for grabs. Anthropological deconstructions of "nature," and of so much else, happened largely from the 1960s to the 1990s, throwing any nature/culture dichotomy or recensions of it out of the respectable analytical toolbox. The "nature" that had been available for so long to be "discovered" by a bioscience apparently innocent of anything that might be deemed social or, worse, cultural was now – well, what was it? It was an interesting metaphor (Latour 1991; Franklin 1995). The world that had been comfortably stacked in layers for so long was now, less comfortably, an interesting object of examination. Layers were flattened, available for critical inspection.

As anthropology engaged with other science studies, it showed its strength in challenging "common-sense biologisms" (Franklin 1995:168). "Real" kinship, "real" families, "blood relatives" and the like were being challenged at this time not only by feminism but also by other social changes in Europe involving new reproductive technologies (or assisted conception/reproduction) and gamete donation. It was in this context in the United Kingdom that the notion of a "natural family" was shown in anthropology to have been a relatively new, post-Darwinian artifact; it seemed to have been constructed in the nineteenth century in the United Kingdom through the borrowing of "genealogy" from statements of social ties and status to depict instead life as a system organized through natural selection. In turn, the loan was "read back" and genealogy naturalized (Strathern 1992a, 1992b). This may have been a vulgarity for Victorians for whom the family was a moral institution rather than a part of nature – but it became a certainty in the twentieth century against which early public concerns about new reproductive technologies and other unnaturalities could be framed. "Real" parents were "biological" parents. Other anthropologists also engaged with assisted reproduction technologies and then with other new technologies that attended the beginning of life, such as prenatal, genetic screening (Franklin 1997; Edwards 2000; Franklin et al. 2003; Gibbon and Novas 2007; Lock and Nguyen 2010: ch.10).

Like the British anthropologist Marilyn Strathern, the American biologist-cum-historian-of-science, Donna Haraway, has encouraged the examination of nature as a foundational metaphor, with Haraway emphasizing, in stridently feminist analyses, the gendered aspects of scientific metaphors and practices (e.g. Haraway 1997). When we bring these interventions together, we see a picture in which, analytically, there is no a priori universal nature "out there" any more for normative appeal – nor waiting to be "discovered." Instead, a complex of circumstances or persons, objects, technologies, and practices – a network of "actants" for some – produce facts through evidence that has to be witnessed and accepted as valid. Whereas this witnessing process might once have been effected through the first-hand observation of gentlemen scholars in the seventeenth century, the increasing sequestration of science in purpose-built laboratories and then clinics has meant that credibility has increasingly been effected through academic affiliation and consensus among other scientific practitioners – for example, through peer review – and, where appropriate, an openness about methodology. It is this garnering of credibility, this winning of allies, this publication (journals, conferences) that constructs the apparent universality of scientific facts and thereby constructs the universality of "nature" or of any natural fact that it claims impartially to represent. In Europe generally, this impartial construction of facts has joined up with medicine and is very much a part of biomedical practice.

Anthropologies of Biomedicine(s)

"Biomedicine" can denote a complex of medical practices across Europe that are seen to have developed historically through different approaches at different times but which may now sit side-by-side. These would include biographical and scientific medicine, personal relations and objectivity, both analytical or classificatory understandings and experimental approaches (with measurement and calibration progressively important), the technologies of disciplines and pedagogies, plus models as prototypes alongside models of nature. This has become a world of wider "technoscientific" practices that include pharmaceutical companies, clinics as proving grounds, engineering, and industrial and university research laboratories. Diagnosis involves overlapping analyses much of the time now, with apparently technical, social, commercial, and regulatory aspects, and with professionals, cells, and machines inhabiting both particular clinics and wider global networks (Keating and Cambrosio 2003).

As one might expect, "biomedicine" has become "biomedicines" for many anthropologists. Whilst "cosmopolitan" or "western" medicine had previously remained a relatively unexamined unity against which various "ethnomedicines" and "patients' perspectives" could be constructed and examined, biomedicine has now – whether analytically in the plural or in the singular – definitely become an object of anthropological examination. This is not new in itself – but analyses that venture to announce "biomedicine as culture" now may also include, as in one recent example, a sub-title such as "Instrumental Practices, Technoscientific Knowledge, and New Modes of Life" (Burri and Dumit 2007). Significantly, although the chapters of this volume offer an exemplary range of what might now be deemed "medical anthropology" in Europe (from medicalization to the "epistemic practices" and "material cultures" of diagnosis, therapy, biopolitics, and more), several of the contributors might not think of themselves as medical anthropologists at all. Scholars who might always have thought of themselves as medical anthropologists will now find themselves keeping company with historians, Foucauldian and STS social scientists, and other anthropologists who simply find that scientific medicine and other issues of health and illness or suffering and remedy can no longer be bracketed out of their field sites.

There are important challenges built into the burgeoning field of medical anthropology broadly conceived. Political, moral, epistemological, and ontological issues are regularly grappled with. This is a world of life and death, and of redefinitions of both (Franklin and Lock 2003). It is a world where difficult moral decisions have to be made about the beginnings and ends of life (e.g. Vermeulen 2004; Kaufman and Morgan 2005; McDonald 2011). It is here, too, that we need to understand how "the human body" that some might once have imagined to be there, really, beneath the cloud of a diversity of "cultural representations," has itself been constructed and standardized in Europe through Anatomy, population statistics and the development of the "norm" – and standardized such that randomized control trials can extrapolate across the globe in ways that potentially carry serious harm (Petryna 2009) and produce the facts and "evidence" on which medical practitioners in Europe, and those whom they treat, are then increasingly required to rely (Lambert 2006).

Scientific facts incorporated into modern biomedicine are standardized partly through documentation, not simply textbooks but law or codes of practice and guidelines, from which local protocols may be constructed. These standardization practices tend to hide the elements and processes of their own construction. Objectivity has been an important accomplishment in Europe (Daston and Galison 2007) and, for better or for worse, its shadows and recensions have been embodied in scientific and medical specialties – some more than others – and in medical training. Objectivity incorporated into medicine has marked its limitations in generating contested illnesses (Dumit 2006; Kilshaw 2008), as well as a proliferation of, and interest in, "alternative" or "complementary" approaches – and a range of more general problems (Sharma 1992; Saillant and Genest 2007b; Lock and Nguyen 2010: esp. 53–54). The new "regulatory objectivity" (Cambrosio et al. 2006) of clinical governance that is found in evidence-based medicine, guidelines, and protocols has been criticized for its limitations, and its impositions and constraints on clinical practice. Empirical studies have suggested that any standardization is always at most a "local universality," that formal plans are always underspecified and rely on a great deal of "tacit knowledge," "tinkering," and "instabilities" for their achievement, and that – drawing further on STS studies – standards of a kind are in any case ubiquitous in healthcare (Timmermans and Berg 1997; Bowker and Star 2000). At the same time, in an ethnographic study of anaesthetic practitioners and procedures in an operating theatre in the United Kingdom, we are shown how anaesthesia "configures a relationship between humans, machines and devices that transforms and distributes agency" and how this contrasts with and challenges the implicit "rational, intentional agent" of the guidelines (Goodwin 2009:26, 167). One of the concerns here is that so much of the professional "discretion" and relational, distributed agency on which safe practice and care depend may be "obscured or driven underground" by an ever more rigid coupling of safe practice to the implementation of guidelines.

This is one of many ethnographies that have tried to show how healthcare practitioners and their patients or clients work in concert with each other but also with a variety of devices and technologies, including technologies of evidence (Casper and Berg 1995; Lock et al. 2000; Lambert et al. 2006). This approach can point to new subjectivities or "more bodies" for the patients where otherwise objectification and reductionism might have been a concern (e.g. Mol 2002). The consequences, in medicine and more widely, of developments in imaging have gained in attention (Edwards et al. 2010). This links up with a growing anthropological interest in the senses. Objectivity has generally encouraged, and been effected through, occulocentric technologies and new attention has been paid to the development of "skilled vision" in professional practices as well as to the older medical technologies of touch and to the emblematic, auditory technology of the stethoscope (Grasseni 2007; Rice 2010). Given the cultural importance attached to "the brain," just what is being "represented" and how, and with what clinical and social effects, is seen as especially interesting in the field of neuroscience (Vidal 2009). Claims that neuroscience and brain scanning will aid the diagnosis and classification of diseases may well renew medical anthropology attention to definitions of the normal, disease classification and stigma (Lambert in press); at the same time, neuroscience is also of interest as another field having difficulty in getting outside or beyond the cultural divisions of mind and body, or mind and brain, or beyond thinking and "neural correlates."

The objectivity of scientific biomedicine had seemingly left the "social" dancing round the edges but, with the wide protests and contestations of science and medicine after World War II, the social has come back in force – not only in critique but in the growing "ethics" industry. "Bioethics" organizations and committees have grown around biomedicine, and anthropology has helped to tease out some of the assumptions and problems (e.g. Simpson 2001). One of these is the strong ideal that exists in parts of Europe of an individuated embodied person as an autonomous self with a will and choice. This individuated body-self emerged historically in Europe alongside, and then at the expense of, previous ideas of permeability, and is marked in the medical arena by explicit or informed consent. "Informed consent" is one key element of modern bioethical governance. It has been incorporated more widely and is everywhere problematic but generally involves technologies that can appear to bring forth the very self that it assumes – subjects that are required to reflect and decide (Hedgecoe 2010; Reubi 2010). It is felt that attention to regulatory mechanisms and the institutions that enact them is likely to grow in medical anthropology (Lambert in press).

One area in which ethical and legal issues have arisen strongly concerns body parts or "biologicals" and fears about their "commodification," initially in the face of a perceived "organ shortage" for transplantation (e.g. Sharp 2000). The sale of organs and tissue is rigorously excluded in European legislation. Projects such as "biobanking," the construction of genetic databases, and the creation of human biologicals such as cell-lines and stem cells for commercial use and profit, have generated anthropological interest in their construction and use but also in the particular concerns they raise (e.g. Brodwin 2000; Franklin and Lock 2003; Hoeyer 2004, 2009; Ong and Collier 2004; Landecker 2007). A dominant legal view has been that intellectual property can be claimed from work, discovery, or invention to do with body parts, but there are otherwise no property rights in the unworked parts themselves. The distinction between person and object operative here – like that of gift and market, which pervades this field – is culturally achieved and has to be worked at. While there may be control rights of various kinds in Europe, bodies are ideally not property that can be bought or sold. This is an ideal which, in European governance, has forged and sustained notions of "human dignity" as a "European" value, constructing "commodities" on the one hand and what it is to be human on the other.

Conclusion

So where are we now? Science studies and medical anthropology in Europe cannot easily ignore each other. In studying Europe, it also feels as if science and medicine, innovation, illness and health, and related issues, ought to be part of many ethnographies anyway. Given the many specialist courses, journals, conferences, networks, workshops, and other publications available now, however, there is no fear that either studies of science or medical anthropology will go away soon, and it might be clear from the survey given in this chapter – albeit necessarily highly selective – that both have been thriving. I would stress again that there are many other areas, works and issues that could have been included (not least, biosecurity, for instance, Collier et al. 2004, or much more on the anthropology of engineering, nanotechnology, finance, or climate change, on some of which see Jasanoff et al. 1995; Hackett et al. 2008). Only an apology for these and other omissions could properly be brief.

Cellular technologies and molecular bodies have raised important issues and attracted anthropological attention, from genetics to genomics (Gaudillière and Rheinberger 2004; Lock and Nguyen 2010: chs. 12–13). These developments of a "molecularized universe" have feasted on an "economy of hope" for future healthcare in Europe and beyond – but have also brought ontological shifts away from "the gene" and eclipsed genetic determinism (Lock and Nguyen 2010:334–335). The new "epigenetics" that has replaced determinism can seem to be genetics hungry for the social; epigenetics means embodying the social in ways that render both embodiment and the social seriously inadequate analytically, not least in their distinction. Social or cultural anthropologists separated themselves from – or jettisoned – biology and biological anthropology long ago, whether making themselves theoretically beholden to a Durkheimian world or because fearful of various biological determinisms, and they have left themselves largely spectators of the biosciences. Having thrown the baby out with the bathwater, some anthropology has been struggling to bring corporeality back (for some examples in the United Kingdom, see the papers and bibliographies collected in the *Journal of the Royal Anthropological Institute*, Marchand 2010); for other parts of Europe, some indication of historic links and separations can be found in Saillant and Genest 2007b). Such attempts might profitably join forces with the studies of "local biologies" launched in medical anthropology (Lock and Kaufert 2001). Medical anthropology encouraged empirical studies of "embodiment" and important new insights have continued here (e.g. Fassin and d'Halluin 2005) but key aspects of embodiment theory have been held up for critical inspection (e.g. Vilaça 2009). One requirement now would seem to be new empirical understandings of how human corporeal beings constitute each other in, with, and through the "circumstances" of their daily lives.

REFERENCES

Barad, Karen

2007 Meeting the Universe Halfway: Quantum Physics and the Entanglement of Matter and Meaning. Durham: Duke University Press.

Beck, Stefan, and Jörg Niewöhner

2009 Translating Genetic Testing and Screening in Cyprus and Germany: Contingencies, Continuities, Ordering Effects and Bio-Cultural Intimacy. *In* The Handbook of Genetics and Society: Mapping the New Genomic Era. P. Atkinson, P. Glasner, and M. Lock, eds. pp. 76–93. London: Routledge.

Benoist, Jean

2002 Petite bibliotheque d'anthropologie médicale: Une anthologie. Theme issue. Bulletin d'AMADES 6 (Paris).

Bowker, Geoffrey, and Susan L. Star

2000 Invisible Mediators of Action: Classification and the Ubiquity of Standards. Mind, Culture and Activity 7(12):147–163.

Brodwin, Paul, ed.

2000 Biotechnology and Culture: Bodies, Anxieties, Ethics. Bloomington: University of Indiana Press.

Burri, Regula, and Joseph Dumit, eds.
2007 Biomedicine as Culture: Instrumental Practices, Technoscientific Knowledge, and New Modes of Life. NewYork: Routledge.
Casper, Monica, and Marc Berg
1995 Constructivist Perspectives on Medical Work: Medical Practices and Science and Technology Studies. Science, Technology and Human Values 20(4):395–407.
Cambrosio, Albert, Peter Keating, Thomas Schlich, George Weisz
2006 Regulatory Objectivity and the Generation and Management of Evidence in Medicine. Social Science and Medicine 63(1):189–199.
Chapman, Malcolm
1982 "Semantics" and the "Celt." *In* Semantic Anthropology (ASA Monograph 22). D. Parkin, ed. pp. 123–144. London: Academic Press.
Collier, Stephen J., Andrew Lakoff, and Paul Rabinow
2004 Biosecurity: Towards an Anthropology of the Contemporary. Anthropology Today 20(5):3–7.
Comelles, Josep M.
2002 Writing at the Margin: Medical Anthropology in Southern Europe. Anthropology and Medicine 9(1):7–23.
Comelles, Josep M., Enrique Perdiguero, and Angel Martinez-Hernaéz
2007 Topographies, Folklore and Medical Anthropology in Spain. *In* Medical Anthropology: Regional Perspectives and Shared Concerns. F. Saillant and S. Genest, eds. pp. 103–121. Oxford: Blackwell.
Daston, Lorraine, and Peter Galison
2007 Objectivity. New York: Zone.
Day, Sophie
2007 On the Game: Women and Sex Work. London: Pluto.
Dumit, Joseph
2006 Illnesses You Have to Fight to Get: Facts and Forces in Uncertain, Emergent Illnesses. Social Science and Medicine 62:577–590.
Edwards, Jeanette
2000 Born and Bred: Idioms of Kinship and New Reproductive Technologies in England. Oxford: Oxford University Press.
Edwards, Jeanette, Penny Harvey, and Peter Wade, eds.
2010 Technologized Images, Technologized Bodies. Oxford: Berghahn.
Fainzang, Sylvie
1989 Pour une anthropologie de la maladie en France: Un regard africaniste. Paris: Editions de l'Ecole des Hautes Etudes en Sciences Sociales.
2007 Medical Anthropology in France: A Healthy Discipline. *In* Medical Anthropology: Regional Perspectives and Shared Concerns. F. Saillant and S. Genest, eds. pp. 89–102. Oxford: Blackwell.
Fainzang, Sylvie, Hans-Einer Hem, and Mette-Bech Riser, eds.
2010 The Taste for Knowledge: Medical Anthropology Facing Medical Realities. Aarhus: Aarhus University Press.
Fassin, Didier
2007 The Politics of Life: Beyond the Anthropology of Health. *In* Medical Anthropology: Regional Perspectives and Shared Concerns. F. Saillant and S. Genest, eds. pp. 252–266. Oxford: Blackwell.
Fassin, Didier, and Estelle d'Halluin
2005 The Truth from the Body: Medical Certificates as Ultimate Evidence for Asylum Seekers. American Anthropologist 107(4):597–608.

Favret Saada, Jeanne
1997 Les mots, la mort, les sorts: La sorcellerie dans le bocage. Paris: Gallimard.
Foucault, Michel
1973 The Birth of the Clinic. London: Tavistock. (Translation of La Naissance de la Clinique. Paris: Presses Universitaires de France. 1963.)
Frankenberg, Ronald
1995 Learning from AIDS. *In* The Future of Anthropology: Its Relevance to the Contemporary World. A. Ahmed and C. Shore, eds. pp. 110–133. London: Athlone.
2007 British Medical Anthropology: Past, Present and Future. *In* Medical Anthropology: Regional Perspectives and Shared Concerns. F. Saillant and S. Genest, eds. pp. 183–211. Oxford: Blackwell.
Franklin, Sarah
1995 Science as Culture, Cultures of Science. Annual Review of Anthropology 24: 163–184.
1996 Making Transparencies: Seeing through the Science Wars. Social Text 46/47: 141–155.
1997 Embodied Progress: A Cultural Account of Assisted Conception. London: Routledge.
Franklin, Sarah, and Margaret Lock, eds.
2003 Remaking Life and Death: Toward an Anthropology of the Biosciences. Oxford: James Currey.
Gaudillière, Jean-Paul, and Hans-Jörg Rheinberger, eds.
2004 From Molecular Genetics to Genomics: The Mapping Cultures of Twentieth Century Genetics. London: Routledge.
Gibbon, Sahra, and Carlos Novas, eds.
2007 Biosocialities, Genetics and the Social Sciences: Making Biologies and Identities. London: Sage.
Goodwin, Dawn
2009 Acting in Anaesthesia: Ethnographic Encounters with Patients, Practitioners and Medical Technologies. Cambridge: Cambridge University Press.
Goodwin, Robin, Alexandra Kozlova, Anna Kwiatkowski, Lan Anh Nguyen Luu, George Nizharadze, Anu Realo, Ahto Külvet, and A. Rämmer
2003 Social Representations of HIV/AIDS in Central and Eastern Europe. Social Science and Medicine 56:1373–1384.
Grasseni, Cristina, ed.
2007 Skilled Visions: Between Apprenticeship and Standards. Oxford: Berghahn.
Gusterson, Hugh
1996 Nuclear Rites: A Weapons Laboratory at the End of the Cold War. Berkeley: University of California Press.
Hackett, Edward J., Olga Amsterdamska, Michael Lynch, and Judy Wajcman, eds.
2008 The Handbook of Science and Technology Studies. 3rd edition. Cambridge, MA: MIT Press.
Haraway, Donna
1997 Modest Witness: Feminism and Technoscience. London: Routledge.
Harding, Sandra
1998 Is Science Multicultural? Postcolonialisms, Feminisms and Epistemologies (Race, Gender and Science). Bloomington: Indiana University Press.
Harwood, Jonathan
1993 Styles of Scientific Thought: The German Genetics Community 1930–33. Chicago: Chicago University Press.

Hedgecoe, Alan
2010 Bioethics and the Reinforcement of Socio-technical Expectations. Social Studies of Science 40(2):163–186.
Helman, Cecil
2007 Culture, Health and Illness. 5th edition. London: Hodder and Arnold.
Hess, David
1995 Science and Technology in a Multicultural World: The Cultural Politics of Facts and Artifacts. New York: Columbia University Press.
Hoeyer, Klaus
2004 Ambiguous Gifts: Public Anxiety, Informed Consent and Commercial Genetic Biobank Research. *In* Genetic Databases: Socio-Ethical Issues in the Collection and Use of DNA. R. Tutton and O. Corrigan, eds. pp. 97–116. London: Routledge.
2009 Tradable Body Parts? How Bone and Prosthetic Devices Acquire a Price Without Forming a "Market". Biosocieties 4:239–256.
Hutchins, Edwin
1996 Cognition in the Wild. Cambridge, MA: MIT Press.
Jasanoff, Sheila
2005 Designs on Nature: Science and Democracy in Europe and the United States. Princeton: Princeton University Press.
Jasanoff, Sheila, Gerald E. Markle, James C. Petersen, and Trevor J. Pinch, eds.
1995 Handbook of Science and Technology Studies. London: Sage.
Johnson, Thomas, and Carolyn Sargent
1990 Medical Anthropology: A Handbook of Theory and Method. New York: Greenwood. (Revised and expanded in 1996).
Kaufman, Sharon, and Lynn Morgan
2005 The Anthropology of the Beginnings and Ends of Life. Annual Review of Anthropology 34:317–341.
Keating, Peter, and Alberti Cambrosio
2003 Biomedical Platforms. Cambridge, MA: MIT Press.
Kenny, Michael, and Jesús M. de Miguel, eds.
1980 La Antropologia Médica en España. Barcelona: Anagrama.
Kilshaw, Susie
2008 Gulf War Syndrome: A Reaction to Psychiatry's Invasion of the Military? Culture, Medicine and Psychiatry 32(2):219–237.
Knorr Cetina, Karin
1995 Laboratory Studies: The Cultural Approach. *In* Handbook of Science and Technology Studies. S. Jasanoff, G. E. Markle, J. C. Petersen, and T. J. Pinch, eds. pp. 140–166. London: Sage.
1999 Epistemic Cultures: How the Sciences Make Knowledge. Cambridge, MA: Harvard University Press.
Lambert, Helen
2006 Accounting for EBM: Notions of Evidence in Medicine. Social Science and Medicine 62:2633–2645.
In press New Medical Anthropology. *In* ASA Handbook of Social Anthropology (Section 4: Futures). London: Sage.
Lambert Helen, Elisa J. Gordon, and Elizabeth A. Bogdan-Lovis
2006 Introduction: Gift Horse or Trojan Horse? Social Science Perspectives on Evidence-Based Healthcare. Social Science and Medicine 62:2613–2620.
Lambert, Helen, and Maryon McDonald, eds.
2009 Social Bodies. Oxford: Berghahn.

Landecker, Hannah
2007 Culturing Life: How Cells Became Technologies. Cambridge, MA: Harvard University Press.
Laqueur, Thomas
1990 Making Sex: Body and Gender from the Greeks to Freud. Cambridge, MA: Harvard University Press.
Latour, Bruno
1984 Les Microbes: Guerre et Paix, suivi de Irréductions. Paris: Editions A. M. Métailié. (Trans. as The Pasteurization of France, Followed by Irreductions: A Politico-Scientific Essay. Cambridge, MA: Harvard University Press, 1988.)
1991 Nous n'avons jamais été modernes: Essai d'anthropologie symétrique. Paris: La Découverte. (Trans. By C. Porter, We Have Never Been Modern. Cambridge, MA: Harvard University Press, 1993.)
2007 Can We Get Our Materialism Back, Please? Isis 98:138–142.
Latour, Bruno, and Steve Woolgar
1979 Laboratory Life: The Social Construction of Scientific Facts. London: Sage. (Republished in 1986 as Laboratory Life: The Construction of Scientific Facts. Princeton: Princeton University Press.)
Lisón, Carmelo
1979 Brujera, estructura social y simolismo en Galicia. Antropologia cultural en Galicia. Madrid: Akal.
Lock, Margaret, and Deborah Gordon
1988 Biomedicine Examined. Dordrecht: Kluwer.
Lock, Margaret, and Patricia Kaufert
2001 Menopause, Local Biologies, and Cultures of Aging. American Journal of Human Biology 13:494–504.
Lock, Margaret, and Vinh-Kim Nguyen
2010 An Anthropology of Biomedicine. Oxford: Wiley-Blackwell.
Lock, Margaret, Allan Young, and Alberto Cambrioso, eds.
2000 Living and Working with the New Medical Technologies. Cambridge: Cambridge University Press.
Loudun, J. B., ed.
1976 Social Anthropology and Medicine (ASA Monograph13). London: Academic Press.
Lukes, Steven, and Martin Hollis, eds.
1983 Rationality and Relativism. Cambridge, MA: MIT Press.
Lynch, Michael, and Steve Woolgar
1990 Representation in Scientific Practice. Cambridge, MA: MIT Press.
Marchand, T., ed.
2010 Making Knowledge: Theme issue. Journal of the Royal Anthropological Institute.
McDonald, Maryon
1989 We Are Not French! Language, Culture and Identity in Brittany. London: Routledge.
2011 Deceased Organ Donation, Culture and the Objectivity of Death. *In* Organ Transplantation: Ethical, Legal and Psycho-Social Aspects. Vol. 2. W. Weimar, M. A. Bos, and J. J. Busschbach, eds. pp. 267–273. Eichengrund: Pabst.
McDonald, Maryon, ed.
1994 Gender, Drink and Drugs. Oxford: Berg.
Mol, Annemarie
2002 The Body Multiple: Ontology in Medical Practice. Durham and London: Duke University Press.

Navaro-Yashin, Yael
2009 Affective Spaces, Melancholic Objects: Ruination and the Production of Anthropological Knowledge. Journal of the Royal Anthropological Institute 15(1):1–18.
Nowotny, Helga, Peter Scott, and Michael Gibbons
2001 Rethinking Science: Knowledge and the Public. Cambridge: Polity.
Ong, Aihwa, and Stephen Collier, eds.
2004 Global Assemblages: Technology, Politics and Ethics as Anthropological Problems. Oxford: Blackwell.
Oudshoorn, Nelly, and André Somers
2007 Constructing the Digital Patient: Patient Organizations and the Development of Health Websites. *In* Biomedicine as Culture: Instrumental Practices, Technoscientific Knowledge, and New Modes of Life. R. Burri and J. Dumit, eds. pp. 205–222. New York: Routledge.
Pandolfi, Mariella
2002 Moral Entrepreneurs, Souverainetés Mouvantes et Barbelés: La Biopolitique dans les Balkans Post-communistes. *In* Politiques et Jeux d'Espaces. M. Pandolfi and M. Abélès, eds. Theme issue. Anthropologie et Sociétés 26(1):1–24.
Petryna, Adriana
2002 Life Exposed: Biological Citizens after Chernobyl. Princeton: Princeton University Press.
2009 When Experiments Travel: Clinical Trials and the Global Search for Human Subjects. Princeton: Princeton University Press.
Rabinow, Paul
1999 French DNA: Trouble in Purgatory. Chicago: University of Chicago Press.
Rabinow, Paul, and Nik Rose
2006 Biopower Today. BioSocieties 1:195–218.
Reubi, David
2010 The Will to Modernize. International Political Sociology 4(2):142–158.
Rice, Tim
2010 Learning to Listen: Auscultation and the Transmission of Auditory Knowledge. Journal of the Royal Anthropological Institute 16:S41–S61.
Rose, Nik
2006 The Politics of Life Itself: Biomedicine, Power and Subjectivity in the Twenty-First Century. Princeton: Princeton University Press.
Rose, Nik, and Carlos Novas
2005 Biological Citizenship. *In* Global Assemblages: Technology, Politics and Ethics as Anthropological Problems. A. Ong and S. Collier, eds. pp. 439–463. Oxford: Blackwell.
Saillant, Francine, and Serge Genest, eds.
2007a Medical Anthropology: Regional Perspectives and Shared Concerns. Oxford: Blackwell.
2007b Introduction. *In* Medical Anthropology: Regional Perspectives and Shared Concerns. F. Saillant and S. Genest, eds. pp. xviii–xxxiii. Oxford: Blackwell.
Sharma, Ursula
1992 Complementary Medicine Today: Practitioners and Patients. London: Routledge.
Sharp, Lesley
2000 The Commodification of the Body and its Parts. Annual Review of Anthropology 29:287–328.
Simpson, Bob
2001 "Making 'bad' deaths 'good'": The Kinship Consequences of Posthumous Conception. Journal of the Royal Anthropological Institute 7(1):1–18.

Strathern, Marilyn

1992a After Nature: English Kinship in the Late Twentieth Century. Cambridge: Cambridge University Press.

1992b Reproducing the Future: Anthropology, Kinship and the New Reproductive Technologies. Manchester: Manchester University Press.

Tannassi, Lucia

2004 Compliance as Strategy: The Importance of Personalised Relations in Obstetric Practice. Social Science and Medicine 59(10):2053–2069.

Timmermans, Stefan, and Marc Berg

1997 Standardization in Action: Achieving Local Universality through Medical Protocols. Social Studies of Science 27:273–305.

Traweek, Sharon

1988 Beamtimes and Lifetimes: The World of High Energy Physicists. Cambridge, MA: Harvard University Press.

1993 An Introduction to Cultural and Social Studies of Sciences and Technologies. Culture, Medicine and Psychiatry 17:3–25.

Van der Geest, Sjaak, and Kaja Finkler

2004 Hospital Ethnography: An Introduction. Social Science and Medicine 59(10): 1995–2001.

Vermeulen, Eric

2004 Dealing with Doubt: Making Decisions in a Neo-Natal Ward in the Netherlands. Social Science and Medicine 59(10):2071–2085.

Vidal, Fernando

2009 Brainhood: Anthropological Figure of Modernity. History of the Human Sciences 22(1):5–36.

Vilaça, Aparecida

2009 Bodies in Perspective: A Critique of the Embodiment Paradigm from the Point of View of Amazonian Ethnography. *In* Social Bodies. H. Lambert and M. McDonald, eds. pp. 129–147. Oxford: Berghahn.

CHAPTER 28

Uses of the Internet in European Ethnographic Research

Elisenda Ardévol and Adolfo Estalella

Internet and Digital Technologies Everywhere

Since the mid-nineties, the Internet and digital technologies have increasingly extended around the globe, capturing, at the same time, a growing anthropological interest, along with an increasing concern in the discipline for many other cutting edge technologies, such as biotechnology or life technologies, which have highlighted key anthropological questions, such as the "nature versus culture" debate and the role of technology in human societies, and a renewed debate around methodological issues.

The Internet is, in itself, an object of study for anthropologists, and a subfield known as cyberanthropology (Budka and Kremser 2004). However, for others, it is just a powerful tool that, with other digital technologies, enhances our methods for data gathering, storage, retrieval, analysis, and representation – digital methods or hypermedia ethnography (Mason and Dicks 2001; Pink 2006). Contemporary cultural and social practices are deeply mediated by networked infrastructures that combine different digital media like mobile devices, text-based, voice and visual artifacts, and different Internet technologies. They are currently so deeply implicated in people's everyday lives that it is difficult to ignore them when studying any contemporary social or cultural phenomena. Even in parts of the world that are digitally disconnected, these technologies are present by their meaningful absence.

The ethnographical study of the Internet has posed many methodological challenges to anthropologists in the last 20 years and is still a source of both controversy and inspiration. While the initial conceptions of the Internet as a "virtual" space – disembodied, disembedded, nonspatial, and ageographical – constituted it as a world

A Companion to the Anthropology of Europe, First Edition. Edited by Ullrich Kockel, Máiréad Nic Craith, and Jonas Frykman.

apart, fieldwork over recent years has shown that the Internet is not as "virtual" as it was previously assumed. On the contrary, Internet technologies are nowadays deeply interwoven with other digital technologies and mediated in common daily practices that do not necessarily take place in front of the computer screen.

Communication and information technologies have been incorporated in the everyday life of individuals and corporations around the world. At any time during fieldwork, any anthropologist could be prompted to expand his or her fieldwork to the Internet, or to incorporate different digital technologies used by their informants as part of the fieldwork. The key point is that these technologies mobilized enormous numbers of actors – individuals and collectives, material infrastructures, and technological designs – that force us to decide how we incorporate these technologies into our anthropological inquiry. Even more, the Internet is also used for academic collaboration and interchange, opening up new avenues for exploration in every step of the anthropological practice.

For more than 10 years we have been involved in this field of research, doing studies about first text-based Internet interactions, like chats and electronic forums, later extended to other Internet technologies, such as online dating sites, video and photosharing social networks and blogs, among others. Dealing with the Internet has encouraged us to explore interdisciplinary approaches from the field of computer mediated communication, media studies, and science and technology studies (STS). Our discussion will draw mainly on two of our field studies in the European context, one dealing with online dating practices and the other focused on intensive blogging practices. In our discussion we want to take advantage of our fieldwork experience for reflecting on two fundamental issues raised by doing Internet research.

The first concerns the methodological debates around conducting "virtual ethnographies." The Internet as a research object brings back to the arena questions about culture, community, and identity related to the concept of fieldsite as defined by geospatial boundaries, a debate that has been taken place in anthropology since the 1980s.

With our second topic, we try to present an argument in favor of a twofold dimension of the Internet, as a field for conducting research and as a research instrument. This second issue concerns the affordances opened by the Internet and digital technologies for producing knowledge, that is, how reflexive practices in using the Internet as a research tool are shaping the ethnographic practices of knowledge production.

From Virtual to Connective Ethnographies

The process by which the Internet has become a legitimate object of study for anthropological research has been relatively slow, but the ethnographic approach in computer mediated communication and Internet studies has played an important role.

The first ethnographical studies on the Internet were conducted by scholars from different backgrounds – mostly from communication theory – and were based on the idea that the Internet could be conceptualized as a culture in its own right (Porter 1996; Jones 1997). This led to the development of an extensive amount of literature focused on the study of Usenet, chats, virtual communities, and multiuser online games, mainly focusing on the social and cultural dynamics within these collectives (Baym 1998; Markham 1998). The phenomenon of central interest was how individuals come together via computer mediated interaction and develop common rules, norms and values, and a sense of belonging or group identity in cyberspace (Jones and Kucker 2001:217).

Over the course of the 1990s, these ethnographical approaches to the Internet demonstrated that computer-mediated interactions were socially significant and were fully loaded with meaning for the participants (Reid 1991). This was a first step for legitimating the social and cultural study of these phenomena given that previous conceptions considered computer mediated communication to be socially weak or second-class communication.

Whether or not such work has been conducted by anthropologists, Bronisław Małinowski's work has been repeatedly quoted as a point of reference and Margaret Mead's culture and personality approach has been used to some extent to describe virtual communities as if they were a kind of new "tribes," and indeed sometimes described as the new world of "Cyberia" (Escobar 2000), as the "cyberothers" (Mayans 2002), or as "natives of the Internet Islands" (Bakardjieva 2005).

This holistic approach to Internet "others" is an argument for the anthropological study of Internet social and cultural phenomena, and the notion of cybercultures as separate worlds can be found in more recent works, such as *Coming of Age in Second Life* (2008) by Tom Boellstorf. This author begins his study paraphrasing Małinowski's (1922) famous description of arriving on the Trobriand Islands. The very title of the book is also a transposition of the famous book by Mead, *Coming of Age in Samoa* (1928). With these canonical anthropological references, the Second Life site is legitimated as an anthropological site and it is justified to conduct fieldwork entirely inside its boundaries, without contacting the company that owns and manages it or to follow avatar actors in their activities outside the virtual world. By emphasizing the tropes of entry and exit, a radical separation of "the field" from "home" is posited and an anthropologist's differentiated identity performed in front of the studied "others." Second Life becomes, then, a well-defined location, an exotic isolated place where relations with the outside world are not negated, but mitigated in front of a relative homogeneous and autonomous culture – where "real" or canonical fieldwork can be conducted.

For many years, the virtual nature attributed to the Internet led to the virtualization of ethnographic methodology. The Internet as cultural phenomenon has been built over the metaphor of "cyberspace," which has been broadly used to define "where" online interactions take place. Cyberspace acts as a unifying field to describe all kinds of technologies developed on the Internet, aligning different artifacts, uses, and practices under the same category of "virtual." Cyberspace has contributed to the idea of the Internet as a unified object with inherent characteristics and properties, leading to a set of dichotomies that define cyberspace as a special kind of "place," which can be considered relatively autonomous or, on the contrary, embedded in daily social life.

Virtual ethnographies have been largely based in the a priori attribution of properties to the Internet that has been translated in a limitation of the fieldsite, or in prior assumptions about time, space, and the differentiated nature of online culture, online identity, and online social ties, establishing the terms of comparison with the physical world experience and face to face relationships.

This dichotomy between the virtual and the real life has been maintained by different authors throughout the years to the present to legitimate their claims for applying ethnographic methods to online research and in order to describe the particular traits and patterns of cybercultures. However, other authors have been inclined toward the study of the Internet as part of everyday life, demonstrating that it is possible and legitimate to conduct ethnographic research in online contexts without necessarily assuming the Internet as a world apart.

The ethnographic works that broke the division between the ethnography of online interaction and the ethnography of physical communities or, indeed, of media practices were Daniel Miller and Don Slater's study of Interent use in Trinidad (2000) and Christine Hine's (2000) study of the media coverage of the Louise Woodward case, which concerned a young English au pair convicted of the involuntary manslaughter of a baby while he was in her care in Massachusetts, USA. Miller and Slater's research is focused on Trinidadians' appropriations of the Internet in everyday life, that is, how the Internet is used and signified in multiple ways by Trinidadians. They found that, among other more or less prosaic practices, the Internet can function as an important venue for performing national identity. For these authors, what is surprising is the practice of treating the Internet as a "world apart" from the rest of people's lives, which is something that needs to be explained, rather than assumed as the starting point of ethnographic research. Hine approaches Louise Woodward's case through the analysis of different Web pages on the case as well as their links with the mass media system. This ethnography breaks with the ideas of community and place as central for the definition of the ethnographic field, as she situates the Internet and traditional media practices as the locus for her social analysis. Hine also discusses the question of authenticity in online social interaction as something that is negotiated and sustained by the social actors themselves. For example, she found that the Web page that was considered more authentic and reliable for the case by their respondents was the site administered from Louise Woodward's village in the United Kingdom. Again, she demonstrates that place and geographical location matters for online interaction, and that it is difficult to prove otherwise.

Christine Hine was one of the first to reflexively apply the ethnographic paradigm of the constructed nature of the field in anthropology (Marcus 1995; Gupta and Ferguson 1997; Amit 2000) within Internet studies, systematizing her "principles for virtual ethnography" from a multi-sited and connective notion of ethnography (Hine 2000:62). As Hastrup and Olwig have argued, instead of viewing the field as a "site" it is better to understand it as a set of relations, focusing on the connections between multiple locations where actors engage in activity; "ethnography in this strategy becomes as much a process of following connections as it is a period of inhabitance" (Hastrup and Olwig 1997:8).

Internet ethnographers have developed different strategies regarding the online/offline dichotomy. Leander and McKim also point out that this polarity cannot be an assumption of the ethnographer but that we must be concerned with describing the participants' practices to create, bound, and articulate social spaces. Their shift, therefore, is to identify "siting" as a productive social process, instead of identifying "sites." This "unbounding" ethnographic practice from location (physical or virtual) does not suggest that location does not matter, but rather, that it cannot be used as a pre-defined self-evident boundary for fieldwork (Leander and McKim 2003:214).

Following global anthropologists' open concept of "fieldsite," these authors propose the concept of a "connective ethnography" for studying what people do with the Internet. That implies the development of combined online/offline methodologies, for example the position adopted by Dirksen et al. (2010), who consider connective ethnography as one methodology to address the issue of integrating research across online and offline situations, therefore, blending traditional with online research methods. Fields and Kafai (2008) also use the notion of a "connective ethnography" for focusing on how gaming expertise spreads across a network of youth at an after-school club where they simultaneously participate in a multiplayer virtual environment, drawing on online and offline participant observation, interviews, video recordings, online tracking and chat data. And Hine (2007) uses it for studying what she calls e-science practices; departing from the influential laboratory-based ethnographies that initially helped to understand science as a constitutively social practice, she opens the field to study a multi-sited science characterized by multidimensional practices which solidify new communication regimes and infrastructures.

For Jenna Burrell (2009), connective ethnography is not only a question of mixing methods and combining online and offline strategies, but to deal with the notion of fieldsite in a constructive way (Amit 2000). For her, instead of thinking of the fieldsite as a "place," it can be defined as a network and as a strategy for locating ethnographic research. Constructing the fieldsite as a heterogeneous network allows one to map out the social relationships of the subjects, but also their connections to material and digital objects and to physical locations.

Usually, Internet studies, whether they follow social actors only online or also in offline encounters (Orgad 2005), have centered the focus on the analysis of a "community" linked to a "place" in the sense of doing ethnography of a determined platform, community or social network, for example, a virtual community (Baym 2000; Carter 2005) an online game or virtual world (Nardi and Harries 2006) or a social network like Friendster (Boyd 2004). As Postill (2008) noted, using the Internet as a field method does not imply using the notions of community or social networks, but to understand that there are different forms of sociality mediated by Internet networks. Methodologically, it renders the online versus offline distinction itself problematic if taken as opposite modes of social communication.

Thus, we shall develop research methodologies that look at different, related Internet practices that do not just favor the analysis of a single platform or social network, but that cover more comparative and cross-site studies. This methodological shift is especially relevant if we consider that people practices and relationships extend across multiple Internet technologies. For example, people who interact in social networks like MySpace may also use instant messaging, texts, Tweets, email, and other sites like Facebook, YouTube, or Vimeo for different purposes and for relating to each other in different ways that also may include mobile phone calls and face to face encounters. By decentering structural elements of the Internet such as sites or platforms, we want to focus the analytical lens on the processes and practices that interweave material objects, technological procedures, bodies, and discourses. This deliberate repositioning also enables us to bypass some of the polar oppositions (such as offline/online) that limit the conceptualizations of identity, agency, and subjectivity to the properties of the medium. Thus, Internet mediated research is broader than the study of online communities, including social practices that are mediated by different artifacts and technologies.

Making geography on the Internet

Internet research is always situated in geopolitical and cultural terms. Thus, despite the fact that the Internet works through global infrastructures, its very materiality is locally situated, through Internet practices, users, and researchers. Our intention, then, is to examine how "place making" works, that is, how geography is made present through the Internet.

Our ethnographic fieldwork about Internet practices can be considered within the broader context of European anthropology, thus contributing to the situated anthropological knowledge developed in European countries. Livingstone (2003) points out the advantages and disadvantages of cross-national comparison; the aim of improving the understanding of one's own country (e.g. Livraghi and Monti 2002) and the possibility of examining transnational processes across different contexts (e.g. Hanafi 2005; Wilding 2007) is in contrast with the difficulty of balancing similarities and differences when the units compared are not homogeneous.

It may be useful to compare quantitative data about Internet use in Europe (Räsänen and Kouvo 2007), but to understand specific appropriations and practices we need to base our research in ethnographic methods; we cannot presuppose a cultural homogeneity, and generalizations must be done in relation to those particular practices that usually cross-cut national borders and identities.

In our research cases, Europe is our locale, but it does not constitute our unit of analysis, nor Spain or Catalonia, although they form part of the research context where our research actions are taking place. We are aiming to identify not national or ethnic similarities and differences in Internet use, but how particular cultural practices are shaping Internet technologies and are themselves being shaped by them.

Internet technologies are designed today in many ways with geopolitical and language sensitivities. As an example, the Internet Corporation for Assigned Names and Numbers (ICANN), responsible for managing the assignment of domain names and IP addresses, finally accepted in 2006 the domain .cat as a top level domain name for Catalonia. Such domain names had initially been reserved for countries recognized by the UN, multiorganizations, and other categories. However, the acceptance of the .cat domain was recognition of Catalan culture and language, although Catalonia is a nation under the Spanish rule. A year earlier, the ICANN approved the domain .eu for Europe, in response to the European Union political agenda, and recently, following pressure from non-English speaking countries, the Internet became open to the development of Internationalized Domain Names (IDNs), which could contain letters or characters from non-ASCII scripts (e.g. Arabic or Chinese, but also European language characters such as ç and ñ).

Locating the Internet geographically is not only a question of users' convenience, but is also relevant for designers, political institutions, and corporations. Contrasting with initial characterizations of the Internet as disembodied, ageographical, and globalized, it is evolving into a powerful tool for geospatial localization.

Internet infrastructures mediate not only practices that take place in front of the screen, not only social interactions and the production and consumption of informational objects, but also many social practices that take place further away from the computer. Thus, instead of exploring the interconnections and discontinuities between cyberspace and geographical space, presupposing the separation of regimes of place which confront or hybridize each other, we propose to examine how geography is mediated and enacted by Internet technologies and practices.

Look, for example, at a mundane practice such as dating. The search for new relationships is one of the most popular and widespread uses of the Internet and there are many services that offer an opportunity to seek sexual partners, to "flirt," or simply to find companionship. By the time Ardévol began her research on dating practices in 2004, the match.com service was a multilingual site connected to instant message services based in the United States that claimed to have more than 15 million subscribers worldwide and more than one million in Spain (Ardévol 2005). In those days, accessing match.com meant literally gaining direct access to user profiles all over the world, just by selecting language and country. Today, match.com redirects Spanish IP visitors to the Spanish version of the site. However, the site offers the option of signing up to sites from other countries, but limited to Europe. Obviously, for dating-site users, language and geographical location is top-level information, but this geographical access limitation technologically performs in the European space at the level of the user.

Because of the importance of language and geographical location, match.com has put these as the first options for searching for partner, besides sex and age range. Dating sites offer a gallery of individual profiles people can look at, but to get in contact with the user, the system usually requires registration; that is, to fill in a profile and become one more "option" in the catalog. But, to understand what is happening in match.com it is not enough to watch what is happening on the screen and gallery profiles. Although not all users have the aim of finding the partner of their dreams, the main purpose is to take initial online contacts to a physical encounter. The process may be more or less original, but usually follows a pattern that goes through sending pictures, talking by mobile phone, chatting on instant messaging, and so on, until the physical date. The same person may do this several times, gaining some expertise about tacit rules, risks to avoid, and precautions to take (see match.com "Dating advice"). For match.com users, online and offline relationships make a difference that matters – until the first meeting. There is no sense of a *match* community, nor can we talk about *match* as a shared cyberspace, although we can speak about a Spanish match.com site and a European space building through the technological design decisions of match.com. These decisions also take into account "cultural" variations; for example, while the item "race" was very important in the North American first versions, it has been substituted by "ethnic origin" in the current European versions and is left blank by many users.

The results of this research cannot be generalized to other online dating services, nor to all online dating practices. In a comparative study of a gay online dating site (Enguix and Ardévol in press), one of the most significant differences we found between both sites refers to the interconnections between online interactions and geographical places. On bearwww.com, the gay Web service, the connection of the social network with gay venues is explicit and central to shaping the site. For example, the top of the home page includes banners advertising clubs and special events in the chosen locality and the main menu offers a list of the most important events for the bear community worldwide. In this case, the establishment of social ties between users goes beyond the individual contact. Although bearwww.com cannot be considered an online community, in many senses it is more than a dating Web site; it has merged the functions of a traditional medium with the interactive practices of the Internet, blending online and offline contexts in creating an extended setting of homosocial interaction. In this case, the Web designers have stressed the sense of a global gay community through its international character and advertising, while at the same time taking care to highlight local events, clubs, and bars. While match.com design policy stresses the Spanish and European geopolitical space, bearwww.com plays with the tension of the global and the local for characterizing the gay community this site addresses. Thus, the same technological artifact – a dating Web site – for the same purpose – getting to know people for physical contact – performs place and geography in different ways and for different purposes, not only by the users, but also by the designers of each site.

As we have seen in these two examples of online dating sites, the notion of cyberspace is not useful to explain Internet practices, and online versus offline relationships are relative to users' social contexts, not a property of the technology. What is more, geography is present in both sites, and participants are strongly localized – they need to know where the other is located; but this does not necessarily mean that we can standardize online dating practices across different collectives or communities.

The same criticisms we have made with regard to notions of cyberspace as a homogeneous "place" with inherent properties can be applied to Europe as a geographical unit that can be studied as a "bounded community" with specific cultural traits that are inherently different from other geographical locations. That does not mean that Europeanist anthropology must disappear, as Internet studies are still quite useful and alive, but other conceptual grounds must be looked for. And just as globalization studies help illuminate how to deal with defining fieldsite in Internet studies, maybe Internet studies will also help us to develop new approaches for studying Europe.

The Internet is an open and flexible technology, changing with its design, uses, and appropriations. It is a global communication system crossed by transnational technologies and practices, whose meaning is locally negotiated by every cultural agent. Thus, an ethnographic understanding of the Internet is enriched by a twofold perspective: that of the social shaping of technology as an approach to understand how technology is created (Bijker and Law 1994), and the domestication theory approach to highlight users' agency in the innovation process and how technology is creatively appropriated by users (Silverstone et al. 2003), not simply "used." But, at the same time, the Internet can be understood as a heterogeneous network, within which various elements are equally able to act on one another. This approach emphasizes the relationship between material and narrative practices – the meanings of things and their materiality – to understand the everyday shaping of the inextricable network of human and non-human actors (cf. Latour 1999). Networks are dynamic processes or achievements rather than fixed structures or entities, and this notion can raise meaningful questions about "Europe" better than understanding it as a geographical, cultural, or however else defined entity.

Experiencing Technology in Everyday Ethnography

The incorporation of digital technologies in everyday ethnographic work opens a space for reflecting and renewing classical debates in anthropology. Engaging with digital technologies in our fieldwork led us to intervene in long-debated issues, such as the ethical responsibility and the value of the anthropologists' experience. Indeed, some of the issues raised by the incorporation of Internet technologies into the ethnographic fieldwork, like the problematization of the field construction, bear a strong resemblance to the debates on the ethical and methodological implications of the camera in visual anthropology (Estalella and Ardévol 2010).

The consequences of incorporating digital technologies into the epistemic practices of scientists are much more than simply deploying new instances for producing empirical data. STS has shown since the 1980s that the incorporation of technologies into the epistemic practices of researchers is fraught with values, methodological assumptions, and social relations (Latour and Woolgar 1986; Rheinberger 1997; Knorr-Cetina 1999).

Drawing on our empirical work, we want to discuss some of the possibilities that digital technologies offer for articulating ethnographic research by briefly reflecting on three key issues that we have faced during our fieldwork: the value of the anthropologist's experience when he or she is engaged with the same technological practices as their research subjects; the ethical dilemmas posed by recording information published on the Internet; and third, and by way of a conclusion, the destabilization of some of the methodological fundamentals of ethnography.

The fieldworker's experience

Using and experiencing the same technology that the ethnographer is researching has been argued as a way to gain insight on the culture and practices under research (Hine 2000; Miller and Slater 2000). Moreover, reflexive ethnography conceives fieldwork experience not only as a way of producing data but as the very moment for producing anthropological knowledge (Guber 2004). Applying this to the research of Internet-mediated phenomena, the ethnographic approach means that we have to get involved with the same infrastructures and artifacts as our research subjects.

In an 18-month-long ethnography focused on the study of intensive bloggers in Spain, Estalella combined fieldwork in face-to-face contexts with Internet-mediated practices. These intensive bloggers blog almost every day, writing entries about their daily life, work, and projects. Most of them publish and share an enormous amount of information on the Internet – not only posts on their blogs but images, videos, bookmarks, or music, posted on many other platforms. They are intensive users of

Internet and digital technologies but also, and most importantly, they deeply believe in the capacity of blogs to transform society.

A large part of Estalella's daily fieldwork practice consisted of reading and registering informants' blogs and the images and videos that they published. This was combined with attendance at bloggers' conferences and informal meetings. Estalella himself blogged extensively during his fieldwork: sharing information with his informants via his own blog as well as adding to their blogs (Estalella 2008). By disclosing information about himself the way his informants did, the ethnographer gained their confidence and established a close relationship with most of them. Blogging was, moreover, a strategy to interrogate the technology reflexively, or, to go even further, let the technology interrogate him, and experience what it means to be a blogger. Finally, it allowed him to make bloggers aware of his presence in the field, which was also a way to articulate ethical concerns. Blogging turned out to be a key methodological strategy in sustaining his field copresence and relationships, a process of socialization that was combined with meetings, emailing, chatting, and phoning.

As Estalella's blogging practice grew during his fieldwork, he found that the more he blogged the more face-to-face events he needed to attend at the instigation of many of his correspondents. As his bloggers wrote almost every day from Monday to Sunday, he felt prompted to blog every day too. Blogging dictated the temporal rhythm of his fieldwork, as it was necessary to read blogs in the morning, write a new entry related to what others were writing in the evening, and write some answers to the comments posted in his blog at night. It was precisely experiencing this particular way of blogging that gave him access to the heavy burden of blogging every day; a quote from his field diary said: "I have been a few days without posting and I have a strange feeling [. . .] it lets me realize how much effort I need to sustain the blog going on" (Estalella 2008).

There is something slightly singular in researching bloggers using a blog: to conduct his research, the researcher is using the same technology as his research subjects. If engaging with technology is understood as a way for embodying the cultural practices under study, then experiencing technology is not simply using technology but participating in it in particular ways. In this case, intensive blogging practice was a way for the anthropologist to spend time as an intensive blogger himself. His blog was a key element in the construction of the field. Moreover, his blog became part of the fieldsite.

Ethical dilemmas and methodological tensions

Estalella's intensive blogging posed hard ethical issues during his fieldwork. Part of his activity as researcher was publicly exposed, as were his connections to key informants, informants' comments, and debates. There was no way to guarantee informants' anonymity. Moreover, as the blogs studied were open access, it was difficult to know when it was proper to freely record data from the Internet and when and how the ethnographer should ask for informed consent.

The production of data on Internet-mediated contexts poses ethical dilemmas that are not easy to answer drawing on the conventional guidelines of ethics in anthropology. This has led academic organizations to elaborate specific guidelines for researching the Internet (NESH 2001; AoIR 2002). Research on the Internet has particular characteristics in this regard, as a large part of the ethnographer's information is generated from the study of digital objects produced by the subjects (blogs, text, photographs, videos), and a good part of the interaction in the field is recorded in users' files, which may even be accessed by people who have not directly participated in the research. Ethical action is thus not limited to direct interaction between subjects and the researcher, but also concerns the type of information produced by the online interaction and the recording techniques used.

Distinguishing what is public and what is private has been, to a large extent, the basis for dictating a wide range of ethical decisions when anthropologists record data from the Internet; however, it is a highly controversial issue. While sometimes what is directly accessible on the Internet (without a password, for instance) is considered "public," different authors have shown that even in accessible mediated contexts, participants have certain expectations of privacy that do not coincide with researchers' conception of what is private and public (King 1996; Bakardjieva and Feenberg 2001). This controversy is not solved by assessing the characteristics of a particular technology. We have explored ways of reconciling opposing views and practices around privacy and publicity, arguing in favor of a dialogic ethic that tries to explore the values of the participants (Estalella and Ardévol 2007). Here again, the anthropologist's field experience has become a source of knowledge for understanding what these values are and how they are put into practice by our research subjects. This uncertainty on how the informant understands and, more importantly, performs values such as privacy, intimacy, and publicity in practice reinforces the need for formulating the domain of a dialogic ethnographic research ethic, not focused on the search for aprioristic principles, but as a domain that should be focused on questioning the epistemic practices of anthropologists in the light of how research participants understand and put into practice certain values.

Ethnography: Fundamentals and Transformations

As we briefly pointed out in the first section of this chapter, the incorporation of the Internet and digital technologies into the epistemic practices of anthropologists and other social scientists has led to the production of a whole series of research techniques.

Although, initially, these online methods were developed for researching the Internet as a cultural artifact or as the locus for emerging cybercultures, they have since been incorporated by researchers focusing on other research objects than the Internet itself. We are referring here to a process in which digital techniques decenter the Internet as their research object and make the Internet a research instrument. For instance, this is the shift involved in making the chat into an instrument for interviewing about mothering, away from research focused on chat culture. What is important to note here is that chat rooms can be used for many research interests.

The use of the Internet in general anthropological research has already been discussed in the literature, although mainly focusing on the possibilities that arise for experimenting with and testing new forms of hypertextual and interactive representation (Banks 2001; Pink 2006), as was tried some years earlier with CD-ROMs (Farnell 1995; Biella 1996). Much less attention has been paid to the possible use of the Internet during any kind of anthropological fieldwork. We are referring specifically to cases where digital techniques are incorporated into empirical data production practices.

For example, digital methods like email, chatting, and instant messaging have all been used to conduct interviews (Mann and Stewart 2000; Bampton 2002) and the Internet survey is another technique that has been extensively applied. Forums and similar technologies have been used to establish discussion groups on a variety of issues (Hewson et al. 2003). As well as these techniques, inspired by their conventional counterparts, others have been developed based on the exploration of the connected lattice-like nature of the Internet, mainly through the study of hyperlinks (Hine 2007).

Annette Markham (2004; Markham and Baym 2008) has analytically drawn the *double face* of the Internet as a method: it can be considered just as a research tool for collecting, analyzing, and presenting results, or also as the field for conducting research; that is, the context of interaction where the subjects and the researcher meet and interact. For those researchers interested in the Internet as an object of study, the object, the tool, and the fieldsite collapse in many ways, but as mentioned earlier, this analytical division may be useful for those interested in incorporation of the Internet in their field methods, even if they do not want to become "cyberanthropologists."

When using Internet methods, the geographic distribution of participants is no longer a practical problem; in fact, the Internet allows us to construct objects of study that are dispersed over a broad geographical area. However, one of our risks is to uncritically assume that the nature of online interaction is essentially different than face to face encounters. The space-time conditions and the communication modality may differ allowing for extremely variable modes of interaction, which does not imply any kind of pre-given "online" sociability. Another trapdoor is to presume that our object of study has nothing to do with the Internet. Even if we only use the Internet as a research tool, our subject of study may bring us to Internet practices. As a matter of fact, household Internet access in European countries ranged from 30% in Bulgaria to 90% in the Netherlands, with the number of homes connected in Spain being around 54% (Eurostat 2009); for Europeanist anthropology, these simple data bring out the need to include the Internet in almost every research topic.

Nowadays, there is a wide variety of practices that are transformed by incorporating digital media. For example, Ardévol's interest in audiovisual popular practices such as home-video production has brought her to work on self-produced videos on YouTube (Ardévol and San Cornelio 2007). We cannot ignore how Internet practices are transforming home video practices in Europe and everywhere. Internet technologies take part in shaping the materiality of the visual object itself and its sociality. The Internet and its particular technologies mediate in the production of the visual object, in the kind of content registered, in the circulation of the image, its audience, and its consumption. Home videos are not only private family memories anymore, as studied by Richard Chalfen (1987), but are part of media-circulating products (VanDijk 2009; Ardévol et al. 2010), thus reshaping all the dimensions of the anthropological analysis and the object of the research itself. The same happens with other subjects such as immigration in Europe, and how Internet and new media practices are bringing new research insights about integration processes, community cohesion, and ethnic and national identities (Hanafi 2005; Van den Bos and Nell 2006), participation in political and social movements, or how digital media articulates racist and hate speech but also new cultural and creative freedoms in East Europe, or even new media practices among European youth (Hasebrink et al. 2009).

Another object of study of anthropologists has been enhanced to embrace contemporary societies and globalization processes, so digital methods are not dissolving but, rather, enhancing ethnographic objects and methods. Online research practices are transforming conventional methods for the production of knowledge within social research (Wouters et al. 2007).

The Internet has, therefore, become just another digital technology that anthropologists and other social scientists have incorporated into their practices to produce knowledge. The distinction we initially established between the Internet as a research tool and the Internet as an object of study is an attempt to demonstrate to what degree the use of the Internet in fieldwork can be – and has been – removed from the study of the Internet. This dual aspect corresponds to extreme cases of the articulation of the Internet in anthropological research. This analytical distinction is useful to identify the set of specific problems that they pose and the opportunities that they create when ethnographic research makes use of Internet methods.

The Internet and related digital technologies open up new research fronts as objects of study, as part of our fieldsites, and as methodological tools. But by doing so, we shall consider its consequences, not just for the kind of knowledge we produce, but also for the type of reality we bring into existence through our research practices.

REFERENCES

Amit, V. ed.
2000 Constructing the Field: Ethnographic Fieldwork in the Contemporary World. London: Routledge.

AoIR
2002 Ethical Decision-Making and Internet Research: Recommendations from the AoIR Ethics Working Committee. Compiled by C. Ess. Association of Internet Researchers.

Ardévol, E.
2005 Dream Gallery: Online Dating as a Commodity. EASA Media Anthropology Network e-Seminar. Electronic document. http://www.media-anthropology.net/ardevol_dreamgallery.pdf (accessed November 5, 2011).

Ardévol, E., and G. San Cornelio
2007 Si quieres vernos en acción: YouTube.com. Prácticas mediáticas y autoproducción en Internet. Revista Chilena de Antropología Visual 10:1–29.

Ardévol, E., A. Roig, G. San Cornelio, R. Pagès, and P. Alsina
2010 Playful Practices: Theorising New Media Cultural Production. *In* Theorising Media and Practice. B. Bräuchler and J. Postill, eds. pp. 259–280. Oxford: Berghahn.

Bakardjieva, M.
2005 Internet Society: The Internet in Everyday Life. London: Sage.

Bakardjieva, M., and A. Feenberg
2001 Involving the Virtual Subject: Conceptual, Methodological and Ethical Dimensions. Journal of Ethics and Information Technology 2(4):233–240.
Bampton, R., and C. Cowton
2002 The E-Interview. Forum: Qualitative Social Research 3(2), art. 9. Electronic document. http://www.qualitative-research.net/index.php/fqs/article/viewArticle/848/1842 (accessed November 5, 2011).
Banks, M.
2001 Visual Methods in Social Research. London: Sage.
Baym, N.
1998 The Emergence of On-line Community. *In* CyberSociety 2.0: Revisiting Computer-Mediated Communication and Community. S. Jones, ed. pp. 35–68. Newbury Park, CA: Sage.
2000 Tune In, Log On: Soaps, Fandom, and Online Community. London: Sage.
Beaulieu, A.
2004 Mediating Ethnography: Objectivity and the Making of Ethnographies of the Internet. Social Epistemology 18:139–163.
Biella, P.
1996 Interactive Media in Anthropology: Seed and Earth – Promise of Rain. American Anthropologist 98:595–616.
Bijker, W., and J. Law
1994 Shaping Technology/ Building Society: Studies in Sociotechnical Change. Cambridge, MA: MIT Press.
Boellstorff, T.
2008 Coming of Age in Second Life: An Anthropologist Explores the Virtually Human. Princeton: Princeton University Press.
Boyd, D.
2004 Friendster and Publicly Articulated Social Networks. Conference on Human Factors and Computing Systems (CHI 2004). Vienna: ACM, April 24–29.
Budka, P., and M. Kremser
2004 CyberAnthropology – Anthropology of CyberCulture. *In* Contemporary Issues in Socio-Cultural Anthropology: Perspectives and Research Activities from Austria. S. Khittel, B. Plankensteiner, and M. Six-Hohenbalken, eds. pp. 213–226. Vienna: Loecker. At http://www.philbu.net/budka_kremser_cyberanthro.pdf (accessed November 5, 2011).
Burrell, J.
2009 The Fieldsite as a Network: A Strategy for Locating Ethnographic Research. Field Methods 21:181–199.
Carter, D.
2005 Living in Virtual Communities: An Ethnography of Human Relationships in Cyberspace. Information, Communication and Society 8(2):148–167.
Chalfen, R.
1987 Snapshot Versions of Life. Bowling Green: Bowling Green State University Popular Press.
Dirksen, V., A. Huizing, and B. Smit
2010 "Piling on Layers of Understanding": The Use of Connective Ethnography for the Study of (Online) Work Practices. New Media & Society. Published online before print, January 19:1–19.
Enguix, B., and E. Ardévol
In press Enacting Bodies: Online Dating and New Media Practices. *In* Gender, Sexuality/ies and the Media. Karen Ross, ed. Oxford: Blackwell.

Escobar, A.
2000 Welcome to Cyberia: Notes on the Anthropology of Cyberculture. *In* The Cybercultures Reader. D. Bell and B. Kennedy, eds. pp. 56–76. London: Routledge.
Estalella, A.
2008 Blogging as Fieldwork: More Than Producing Knowledge, Performing Reality in Ethnography. Paper presented at the "In the Game" Preconference, 9th Annual Conference, AoIR, Copenhagen, Denmark.
Estalella, A., and E. Ardévol
2007 Ética de campo: Hacia una ética situada para la investigación etnográfica de internet. Forum: Qualitative Social Research 8(3). Electronic document. http://www.qualitative-research.net/index.php/fqs/article/view/277 (accessed November 5, 2011).
2010 Internet: Instrumento de investigación y campo de datos para los antropólogos visuales. Revista Chilena de Antropología Visual 15:1–21.
Eurostat
2009 Database. Electronic document. http://epp.eurostat.ec.europa.eu/portal/page/portal/eurostat/home/ (accessed November 5, 2011).
Farnell, B., and J. Huntley
1995 Ethnography Goes Interactive. Anthropology Today 111:7–10.
Fields, D., and Y. Kafai
2008 A Connective Ethnography of Peer Knowledge Sharing and Diffusion in a Tween Virtual World. International Journal of Computer-Supported Collaborative Learning 4(1):47–68.
Guber, R.
2004 El salvaje metropolitano: Reconstrucción del conocimiento social en el trabajo de campo. Buenos Aires: Paidós.
Gupta, A., and J. Ferguson
1997 Culture, Power, Place: Explorations in Critical Anthropology. Durham: Duke University Press.
Hanafi, S.
2005 Reshaping Geography: Palestinian Community Networks in Europe and the New Media. Journal of Ethnic and Migration Studies 31(3):581–598.
Hasebrink, U., S. Livingstone, and L. Haddon
2009 Comparing Children's Online Opportunities and Risks across Europe: Cross-National Comparisons for EU Kids Online. Electronic document. http://www.eukidsonline.net (accessed November 5, 2011).
Hastrup, K., and K. F. Olwig
1997 Introduction. *In* Siting Culture. K. Olwig and K. Hastrup, eds. pp. 1–14. London: Routledge.
Hewson, C., P. Yule, D. Laurent, and C. Vogel
2003 Internet Research Methods. Sage: London.
Hine, C.
2000 Virtual Ethnography. London: Sage.
2007 Connective Ethnography for the Exploration of e-science. Journal of Computer-Mediated Communication 12:618–634.
Jones, S. G.
1997 Virtual Culture, Identity and Communication in Cybersociety. London: Sage.
Jones, S., and S. Kucker
2001 Computer, the Internet and Virtual Cultures. *In* Culture in the Internet Communication Age. J. Lull, ed. pp. 212–225. London: Routledge.

King, S.
1996 Researching Internet Communities: Proposed Ethical Guidelines for the Reporting of Results. The Information Society 12(2):119–129.
Knorr-Cetina, K.
1999 Epistemic Cultures: How the Sciences Make Knowledge. Cambridge, MA: Harvard University Press.
Latour, B.
1999 Pandora's Hope: Essays on the Reality of Science Studies. Cambridge, MA: Harvard University Press.
Latour, B., and S. Woolgar
1986 Laboratory Life: The Construction of Scientific Facts. Princeton: Princeton University Press.
Leander, K., and K. McKim
2003 Tracing the Everyday "Sitings" of Adolescents on the Internet: A Strategic Adaptation of Ethnography across Online and Offline Spaces. Education, Communication & Information 3(2):211–240.
Livingstone, S.
2003 On the Challenges of Cross-National Comparative Media Research. European Journal of Communication 18(4):477–500.
Livraghi, G., and A. Monti
2002 The Network Society as Seen from Italy. The Information Society 18:165–179.
Malinowski, B.
1922 Argonauts of the Western Pacific. Prospect Heights, IL: Waveland Press.
Mann, C., and F. Stewart
2000 Internet Communication and Qualitative Research: A Handbook for Researching Online. London: Sage.
Marcus, G.
1995 Ethnography in/of the World System: The Emergence of Multi-Sited Ethnography. Annual Review of Anthropology 24:95–117.
Markham, A.
1998 Life Online: Researching Real Experience in Virtual Space. London: Altamira.
2004 Internet Communication as a Tool for Qualitative Research: Theory, Methods, and Practice. D. Silverman, ed. pp. 95–124. London: Sage.
Markham, A., and N. Baym
2008 Internet Inquiry: Conversations about Method. London: Sage.
Mason, B., and B. Dicks
2001 Going Beyond the Code: The Production of Hypermedia Ethnography. Social Science Computer Review 19(4):445–457.
Mayans, J.
2002 Género Chat: O cómo la antropología puso un pie en el Ciberespacio. Barcelona: Gedisa.
Mead, M.
1928 Coming of Age in Samoa: A Psychological Study of Primitive Youth for Western Civilization. New York: Morrow. (Trans. Adolescencia y Cultura en Samoa. Barcelona: Paidós Studio, 1995.)
Miller, D., and D. Slater
2000 The Internet: An Ethnographic Approach. Oxford: Berg.
Nardi, B., and J. Harris
2006 Strangers and Friends: Collaborative Play in World of Warcraft. Proceedings of the 2006 20th Anniversary Conference on Computer Supported Cooperative Work, pp. 149–158. Banff, Alberta, Canada.

NESH
2001 Guidelines for Research Ethics in the Social Sciences, Law and the Humanities. Oslo, Norway: National Committee for Research Ethics in the Social Sciences and the Humanities (NESH).
Orgad, S.
2005 From Online to Offline and Back: Moving from Online to Offline Relationships with Research Informants. *In* Virtual Methods: Issues in Social Research on the Internet. C. Hine, ed. pp. 51–65. Oxford: Berg.
Pink, S.
2006 The Future of Visual Anthropology: Engaging the Senses. London: Routledge.
Porter, D., ed.
1996 Internet Culture: New York: Routledge.
Postill, J.
2008 Localizing the Internet Beyond Communities and Networks. New Media & Society 10(3):413–431.
Räsänen, P., and A. Kouvo
2007 Linked or Divided by the Web? Internet Use and Sociability in Four European Countries. Information, Communication & Society 10(2):219–241.
Reid, E.
1991 Electropolis: Communications and community on Internet Relay Chat. Honors thesis, Department of History, University of Melbourne. Electronic document. http://cyber.eserver.org/reid.txt (accessed November 5, 2011).
Rheinberger, H.-J.
1997 Toward a History of Epistemic Things: Synthesizing Proteins in the Test Tube. Stanford: Stanford University Press.
Silverstone, R., E. Hirsh, and D. Morley
2003 Information and Communication Technologies and the Moral Economy of the Household. *In* Consuming Technologies: Media and Information in Domestic Spaces. R. Silverstone and E. Hirsch, eds. pp. 15–31. London: Routledge.
Van den Bos, M., and L. Nell
2006 Territorial Bounds to Virtual Space: Transnational Online and Offline Networks of Iranian and Turkish–Kurdish Immigrants in the Netherlands. Global Networks 6(2):201–220.
Van Dijk, J.
2009 Users Like You? Theorizing Agency in User-Generated Content. Media Culture Society 31:41–58.
Wilding, R.
2007 Transnational Ethnographies and Anthropological Imaginings of Migrancy. Journal of Ethnic and Migration Studies 33(2):331–348.
Wouters, P., K. Vann, A. Scharnhorst, M. Ratto, I. Hellsten, J. Fry, and A. Beaulieu
2007 Messy Shapes of Knowledge – STS Explores Informatization, New Media and Academic Work. *In* The Handbook of Science and Technology Studies. E. J. Hackett, O. Amsterdamska, M. Lynch, and J. Wajcman, eds. pp. 319–352. Cambridge, MA: MIT Press.

CHAPTER 29

Visual Culture, Ethnography, and Interactive Media

Terence Wright

Although pictorial images have formed an integral part of human cultural history from earliest times, the traditional relationship between anthropology and the visual arts has not been easy. Where nineteenth-century theorists of "recapitulation" took a social evolutionary perspective, making much of superficial similarities between the pictorial images of "primitive" cultures and those of children, the post–World War II rise of the "social" in anthropology made a clear demarcation between the *visual* and a primarily *language-based* anthropology. By and large, in this context, visual culture (alongside objects of "material culture") was consigned to the museum where it remained until the latter part of the twentieth century.

More recently, an increased interest in the status and role of visual phenomena has witnessed the emergence of the new discipline of visual culture which, as a subject area, has proved problematic to characterize. Not only are there almost as many definitions of visual culture as there are writers to write about it, but it is also a field of study that extends its territory into a number of established disciplines and has become parasitic upon them. It has encroached upon the resources and methodologies of the arts and sciences alike, the humanities and the social sciences: anthropology being a case in point. As a new area of study, visual culture has spawned a regular stream of publications (Jenks 1995; Mirzoeff 1999; Sturken and Cartwright 2000 to name a few); a flood of approaches to visual research methodology (e.g. Prosser 1998; Banks 2001; Pink 2001; Sullivan 2010); together with a deluge of debates and applications: *Tokyo Cyberpunk: Posthumanism in Japanese Visual Culture* (Brown 2010); *Islamic Art and Visual Culture* (Ruggles 2011); *The Visual Culture of Chabad* (Katz 2010); *Visual Culture in Organizations* (Styhre 2010); *Global Image Wars: Geopolitics and Post-9/11 Visual Culture* (Andén-Papadopoulos in press); *For All the World to See: Visual Culture and the Struggle for Civil Rights* (Berger 2010); *Ophelia and Victorian Visual Culture* (Rhodes 2008). All of these are indebted to the great-granddaddy of them all (though not all care to admit it) – John Berger's *Ways of*

A Companion to the Anthropology of Europe, First Edition. Edited by Ullrich Kockel, Máiréad Nic Craith, and Jonas Frykman.

Seeing (1972), a publication which, together with the accompanying BBC Television series, paved the way for a radical reconsideration of the role visual imagery plays in society.

This chapter begins by singling out a number of common elements to help provide a succinct, digestible definition and a summary of key points. A fundamental one is that visual culture as a subject area recognizes the centrality of visual imagery in contemporary culture, it does not acknowledge a hard and fast distinction between forms of popular "low" culture and those of elitist "high" culture. At the same time, visual culture is not considered to be exclusively "visual" – rather like film studies, it often comprises a combination of image, text, and sound, and even extends its domain to tactility (in a regard for the experience of objects and place) and to the architectural. To some extent, this inclusive approach represents the underlying synaesthetic tendency found in the arts of the modern age. For example, in literature, James Joyce brings "different forms of art, high and low, old and new into proximity . . . *Ulysses* endeavours to cater to the eye and the ear, continuously supplying the quasi-ideal senses of sight and hearing with sublime pleasures . . . By incorporating newspaper headlines and musical scores, *Ulysses* even attempts to offer the textual equivalent of tactility" (Danius 2002:185). Perhaps Danius's approach to Joyce (from her perspective on technology and aesthetic modernism) is indebted to visual culture's influence upon textuality. Nevertheless, it does bring into focus another aspect of visual culture – that of a holistic and wide-ranging attitude to visual phenomena, placing them in the context of their specific cultural settings: especially pertinent to the visual representation (and representations) of "other" cultures which are crucial to the study of anthropology.

Despite the temptation to consider it essentially a modern phenomenon, visual culture is not only relevant to the present day. In one form or another, it has always been with us: "Pictures . . . now seem likely to be a defining characteristic of our species" (Cutting and Massironi 1998:137). It also has an inexorable bearing on how we view the past. Visual representation not only plays a significant role in our conceptualization of history, but in the formation of community identity and in fostering social cohesion – outcomes studied by historians and anthropologists alike. And finally, particularly in light of its synesthetic dimensions, visual culture has strong associations to another new field – that of "performance studies." This area brings into congruence the visual with the performative, theatre with ritual, and music with decoration of the body, among other sutures, visual culture and Performance Studies both draw upon the discipline of Anthropology.[1] Both fields consider the production and reception of diverse media forms within their specific localities, as well as in an overall global context. It almost goes without saying that the characteristics and rapid expansion of the Internet and the World Wide Web reflect and parallel these developments and their tendency toward interdisciplinarity and "sutured" studies.

During the formative period of this moving closer of approaches, Banks and Morphy, in their *Rethinking Visual Anthropology* (1997), set out to expand the range of inquiries in their area. From an initial conflation of the two subdisciplines, visual anthropology and the anthropology of art, traditionally concerned with film and photography of "other" cultures and the art of "other" cultures respectively, they widen the scope of the field to include much of visual culture's domain: television, electronic representation, and material culture. This results in a broad sweep across a variety of visual systems under the umbrella of cross-cultural representation, founded on the rationale that "an understanding of the nature of representational processes across cultures is . . . integral to the overall objectives of anthropology" (Banks and Morphy 1997:2). It soon becomes apparent that this enterprise, whereby "the properties of anthropologists own representational and visual systems need to be considered, as well as those of the other cultures studied" (Schneider and Wright 2006:21) has much in common with the multi-faceted nature of visual culture that "focuses on the cultural construction of visual experience in everyday life as well as in media, representations and visual arts" (Mitchell 1995:540).

In 1998, Mirzoeff defined visual culture as "an idea in the making" (1999:6), and since the 1990s the expansion of visual studies has continued apace. For example, in common with Danius's work in literary studies, Pink et al. (2010:4) are currently involved in re-situating the visual in "the multi-sensoriality of everyday contexts." Such a move constitutes a significant innovation to visual culture and reintroduces the significance of what psychologist James Gibson termed "perceptual systems" (1966) when applied to visual anthropology and to visual representation (see Wright 1992:21–4, 1997:28–30) as well as to "mainstream" anthropology (Ingold 2000:166–168, 260–265). Gibson's scheme of things removes the central focus of perception from the traditional five senses, or the purely "visual," in favor of the total active body experience of the environment. This not only establishes a key role for psychology in the arena, but sets the stage for applying visual culture, like performance studies, research to the development of the immersive interactive computer-based experience (see Ryan 2001:69–72, 290–5, her sections "Baroque Art and Architecture" and "Ritual" are especially relevant in this context). Visual culture in the twenty-first century positions itself to embrace innovative practices in visual representation, wider perspectives on the production of visual culture and alternative approaches to research, exhibition, and dissemination, for example, via the Internet and other electronic media forms. On this basis, the fieldwork studies discussed in this chapter cover many of the areas identified here in the introduction, and include visual representation by means of computer-based media, interactivity, and performance. The multidisciplinary visual-cultural environment also places an emphasis on the interactive role of the viewer and has important consequences for issues of narrativity, often conceptualized as the option of alternative endings to stories:

> [I]f novelists truly wanted to simulate the delta of life's possibilities, this is what they'd do. At the back of the book would be a set of sealed envelopes in various colours. Each would be clearly marked on the outside: Traditional Happy Ending; Traditional Unhappy Ending; Traditional Half-and-Half Ending; Deus ex Machina; Modernist Arbitrary Ending; End of the World Ending; Cliffhanger Ending; Dream Ending; Opaque Ending; Surrealist Ending; and so on. You would be allowed only one, and would have to destroy the envelopes you didn't select. *That's* what I call offering the reader a choice of endings . . . (Barnes 1985:99–100)

The case study which follows aims to show how the multifaceted approach of visual culture can illuminate a rather more complex and compelling case for a variety of fluid narratives.

CASE STUDY: *INTERACTIVE VILLAGE* (BRICOLAGE WITH INTENT)

As Sergei Eisenstein said: "A place must be prepared in consciousness for the arrival of new themes which, multiplied by the possibilities of new techniques, will demand new aesthetics for the expression of these new themes in the marvellous creations of the future" (1949:44). The *Interactive Village*,[2] a computer-enabled ethnography which employs interactive multimedia tools, is one such project. It was developed as part of the European research project NM2: New Media for a New Millennium (http://www.ist-nm2.org). The interactive production offers a documentary-style profile of the Czech village Dolní Roveň, enabling participant viewers to piece together an individual viewing narrative of village life and activity, based on their own interests and choices. These can be selected interactively through a graphical user-interface (GUI), which simulates navigating through the village determining the subject and depth of the information desired. Based on the belief that the "documentary" genre can "give voice to those, generally outside established elites, who [are] able to speak to the nature of daily life in a particularly compelling manner" (Jordanova 2006:92), the documentary-approach taken in *Interactive Village* intends to address "human interest" stories. Its purpose is not to offer a kind of television program formula or format as such, but rather to test out a variety of strategies that could easily be adapted to future real-life scenarios in television, Internet, or mobile production and delivery.

The location of Dolní Roveň in Eastern Bohemia, Czech Republic, was chosen for the production for a number of practical reasons. The village had been the subject of a number of academic studies since 1937, which provide a depth of historical insight and factual credibility and offer unique historical perspectives from which the present-day village can be viewed. The studies had covered extensive social and political change from Czechoslovakia's First Republic (1919–1938) and Second Republic under Nazi occupation (1938–1945); the Communist period to the Prague Spring through to the Velvet Revolution of 1989–1992; up to the final Dissolution of Czechoslovakia (1993), marked by its split with Slovakia and the establishment of the Czech Republic; and in May 2004 (just before shooting for *Interactive Village* began) the Czech Republic's membership of the European Union. Not only could we resort to considerable historical insight on which to base the production (e.g. Galla 1939), but also the ongoing research of contemporary anthropologists (Novotná 2004; Skalník 2004) who worked closely with the *Interactive Village* production.

In order to design and compile *Interactive Village*, I visited the location on a regular basis over a period of three years with anthropologists from the University of Pardubice, in order to identify and collect relevant information. This included the gathering of purpose-captured visual material using video according to a screen-grammar of establishing shots, interviews, local scenes, cutaway images, and other components used in ethnographic and documentary movies, together with the products of local visual culture (i.e. archive images, pictures of historic objects, still photographs, and paintings made by the village children). Local people were invited to a series of public screenings of work in progress. These were followed by lively

Figure 29.1 A village feedback session. Photograph © Terence Wright. (Reproduced courtesy of the author.)

debate and suggestions as to how the project could be improved, as well as recommendations for future "photo opportunities" (see Figure 29.1). Such discussions included enthusiasm for the future potential for villagers to incorporate their own personal video diaries and image-capture, using camcorders and/or mobile devices, plus the inclusion of an added dimension whereby the villagers could discover, create, and access family and local histories.

The anthropologists first secured the necessary cooperation with the villagers to enable shooting the footage, thus establishing a useful precedent for return visits and video shooting. They also made contact with specialists who were consulted to help explain specific local cultural phenomena, importantly Martina Bromová, who provided detailed information and commentary on the footage of the annual village masquerade.

We gathered information with a view to the fact that conceptually linked but disparate material elements could best be fully realized by enabling the viewer to navigate the village as do its inhabitants and as did the documentary team. Such an approach not only mirrors the exploratory nature of the shooting process, but develops a virtual landscape in which visitors can explore the village in an effortless interactive interface. So, rather than shooting a definitive storyline, we looked for "narrative potentials" – a process analogous to the procedures of investigative journalism. An interactive explorable program is not a "story" that has to be finally "written-up": it is up to participant viewers to develop the narrative building-blocks provided by the authors into the "story" of their own choice via the media tools. The "Shapeshift" production tools, developed by the NM2 project, provided the environment for making such a user-navigable production. In *Interactive Village*, participant viewers can choose the character who narrates the ethnography – so they might opt for an "unofficial" view of the village from Mr Zevl, the newsagent, or the "official" view of the mayor, Mrs Vinarova. However, visitors may prefer the expert "outsider's" view to either of these interested parties, and so select anthropologist Petr Skalník, who comments on recent social and political change from an informed critical standpoint. Alternatively, or as a complement, yet another view of the village can be selected – the perspective of anthropologist Hana Novotná, who considers the central role of Mr Zevl in the village community.

The *Interactive Village* production represents a new kind of formula as an alternative to existing documentary and ethnographic genres, offering a range of unique interactive experiences. It also enables participant viewers to "telescope" their chosen narratives, which operate on a sliding scale, from a headline-news style of presentation to in-depth documentary, or from automatic presentation to participant viewer-explored/contributed ethnography, using a pool of audio-visual material accessible from different perspectives of interest. An unmediated viewing or a commentated view presented by an expert can be chosen at will. Each configuration of the visual material provides a personalized interactive experience, where the "Shapeshift" media tools edit together the source sequences seamlessly in real time, following frameworks formulated by the author(s) and labeled with metadata by the editor, to suit the personal wishes and needs of individual participant viewers.

In a research experiment like *Interactive Village*, which employs the sutured approach of visual studies, one of the advantages of a sustained (historic) study – as opposed to the documentary "snapshot" of the synchronic approach – is that change can be documented as it happens. Besides major structural changes (such as the ongoing road-improvements that took place throughout the village during the process of the filming), personal changes occurred in the lives of individuals. To take the case of Mr Zevl, the village newsagent: when filming started in 2003, his thriving business not only proved a viable commercial enterprise, but was the unofficial center of the village. Situated next to the railway station, it fulfilled a vital social role, attracting daily visits from most of the village characters and the gossip that accompanied them. Toward the conclusion of the research project in 2007, Mr Zevl had given up the business. Interviewed again (in 2007), he took the opportunity to reflect on the changes in his life and explain the reasons for his decision to quit. A man well into his 70s, he admitted: "I was simply exhausted . . . owing to my state of health, it wasn't good." Having already seen himself on screen describing an earlier period of his life provided the context and structure for this current spontaneous narrative. From a wider perspective, Mr Zevl's individual experience may parallel the closure of small businesses, run by the recently retired elsewhere in Europe, helping to identify as well as document for social and cultural anthropology a larger phenomenon with significant personal and social implications. The ability to call out and compare thematically linked or role-related reminiscences, using the topics and situations offered by the GUI, which (crucially) takes the form of images (rather than the word-based menus generally employed by search-engines) – enables viewers to focus easily on such relationships between issues. Using the metadata to configure each playout, the links are made behind the scenes, so every story is presented smoothly in a continuous narrative, rather than in fragments, as would be the case using a conventional data search-engine (for details see Ursu et al. 2007, 2008). The more the material is explored, the more linked narratives are likely to be elicited, to be added to the collection ad infinitum, in a continual process of revelation and association. Central to these processes emerged the villagers' reliance upon their visual culture – images and objects of memorabilia. The extent to which visual perceptions underlie thematic and character-based links is strikingly apparent throughout *Interactive Village*, but it is most exuberantly obvious in the preoccupation with the village Masquerade. Even a brief review of this event, as part of the *Interactive Village* case study, provides a good example of the way lowering the barriers between visual culture and performance studies, using visual means to capture and help interpret a performance-based cultural phenomenon, offers new insights and new knowledge.

Carnival

At the outset, in compiling visual information for the *Interactive Village* project, we identified key village organizations and institutions which would act as the "nuclei" of the ethnography. While obvious centers of influence would include the mayor's office, the church, the school, and other public venues, the village's volunteer fire brigades presented something of an intriguing challenge. Not only did it appear unusual that a village of 1800 population should be served by four brigades (comprising some 250 volunteer members in all), but the village had experienced only one fire in the last six years. Furthermore, when asked how volunteers could cope with modern-day hazards such as air disasters or chemical spillages, I was informed that these emergencies were left to the "professionals" – as it turned out, yet another local fire brigade. While one of the volunteer brigades appeared equipped and quite capable of dealing with a serious "traditional" fire, other brigades perform an essentially social/ceremonial role. They all maintain small archives of historical memorabilia, organize sports activities within the village, and provide fire-fighting training (along semi-military lines) for the village children. Indeed, the camaraderie, structure, and methodology of a fire-fighting team is relied upon to act as a vehicle for wider social activity.

> The firemen never considered their membership in the brigade as more than honourable service to their community. They considered their service as an occasion to demonstrate their ties to the local community. Nonetheless, showing themselves off in their dress uniforms in front of their fellow countrymen must have bought pride and personal satisfaction. The firemen entertained well too, and enjoyed being with their friends, the rustic countrymen and fellow citizens of their village. (Pospíšilová 2004)

Along with the confessed rivalry between the four volunteer brigades, this tradition of service has much in common with a Maussian scheme of things: it combines a sense of rivalry with acts of generosity to the community (Mauss 1969:37).[3] During a video interview, Messrs Slezák and Třasák, of the Horní Roveň fire station, outline the main activities of their organization: "We organise a lot of events: the Fireman's Ball, a masquerade parade through the village . . . We collect scrap metal, burn witches (along with a paper lantern procession). And fireworks!" Of these, for the inhabitants of Dolní Roveň, the village masquerade is one of the most visual phenomena in the social calendar. Taking place at the beginning of Lent, it is associated with carnival/Mardi Gras festivities taking place at this time of year throughout Europe, and by extension, elsewhere.[4] Turner notes the way pagan late-winter and early spring celebrations (such as the Saturnalia, December 17–23) coincide with events in the Christian calendar, such as the pre-fasting (pre-Lenten penitence) "Mardi Gras" (Shrove Tuesday) carnivals, running between Epiphany (Twelfth Night, January 6) and culminating the day before Ash Wednesday (now usually mid-February):

> The wide diffusion . . . of carnival customs is perhaps due first to the spread of the Roman Empire which introduced such antistructural rites as Saturnalia and Lupercalia to its distant provinces, and secondly to the spread of the Catholic Church which took with it around the world not only a common liturgy and liturgical year, but also a host of popular feasts and customs representing in some cases "baptised" circum-Mediterranean pre-Christian rituals. (Turner 1987:134)

While the "traditional" Czech Lenten carnival, celebrated between Epiphany (*Den tří králů*) and Ash Wednesday (*Popeleční středa*), can be traced back to the thirteenth century, in Roveň it was a late-nineteenth-century reinvention.[5] Despite the general disruptions to the traditional culture of war and the communist era, carnival has been subject to a revival of interest since the 1989 revolution, with the fire brigades playing a key role. The general format of the activity was derived from people's memories and information that could be gained from the chronicles.[6] Originally the Lenten carnivals were "agrarian in nature" (Bakhtin 1984:8). In the Czech case, modifications were made to old masks, and new ones were introduced, reflecting the decline of farming over the last 50 years. The new pace of modern life has resulted in celebrations being shortened from three days to one day (traditionally carnivals could last several days) along with a move to Saturday in deference to the modern working week. The participants maintain that the masquerade strengthens bonds and establishes local identity. It celebrates the coming season: spring, and the end of winter: "the century-old celebrations: the gay farewell to winter, to Lent to the old year, to death; and the gay welcome to spring, to Shrovetide, to the slaughtering of cattle, to weddings, and to the new year" (Bakhtin 1984:99).

The perambulatory nature of this Czech *Masopust*[7] (see Figure 29.2) removes it from the stage of the formal theatre, but it has much in common with the tradition of the English mummers, in that the actors "make a series of visits (in England to pubs and private houses) so that the audience must wait for the play to come to them" (Axton 1974:36).

But then there is no real "audience" in the conventional sense. A handful of "observers" (and one or two anthropologists) follow the procession around the village, but the complete masquerade "experience" is to be had by the masqueraders themselves, and the householders who take on a participatory role, welcoming them with food and drink, joining in the play-acting (e.g. dancing with the bride and groom who are perennial characters) and bawdy banter. As Bakhtin puts it "[C]arnival does not know footlights . . . Carnival is not a spectacle seen by people: they live in it, and everyone participates" (1965:7). This form of categorization sets

Figure 29.2 Michał Elwiro Andriolli's 1876 illustration of the Polish *Zapust* which follows a similar format to the Czech *Masopust* (original kept at Biblioteka Narodowa).

the *Masopust* aside from "processions." Like London's Notting Hill (Mardi Gras style) Carnival,[8] it follows a set route, with little variation from year to year, but unlike the carnivals of New Orleans or Notting Hill, the route is not lined with spectators: its primary function is participation, not spectatorship. Despite its preoccupation with the visual and the performative, one would not be tempted to describe the Roveň carnival as a "spectacle" (until, of course, it is committed to video). Following the ceremonial authorization when the mayor gives her permission for the masqueraders to visit the houses in the village, the character "Laufr" scouts ahead of the parade and negotiates the hospitality. He is followed by the bride and groom (see Figure 29.3), whose differences are the reverse of conventional modern European expectations: the bride is taller with masculine features (the year of filming "she" was played by a man); the groom, smaller and more feminine, can, we were informed, be played by a woman, offering examples of the world-upside-down gender exchange found in a number of carnivalesque situations. Axton (1974:15) cites similar acts of transvestism taking place in Greece and, according to a sixteenth-century book, in the Shrovetide celebrations in Elizabethan England:

> Both men and women change their weede, the men in maydes array,
> And wanton wenches drest like men, doe trauell by the way.
>
> (Axton 1974:15)

Figure 29.3 Bride and groom, Dolní Roveň masquerade. Photograph © Terence Wright. (Reproduced courtesy of the author.)

In addition to the wedding party, other traditional elements in the Roveň masquerade include a performing bear (costume) and keeper with drum; chimney sweeps – who blacken bystanders faces for luck (see Figure 29.4); clowns, and a team of butchers.[9] According to informants, while the bear and his keeper are deemed to provide a form of sympathetic magic for a better harvest to come, in an act with sexual innuendo, the bear (if it takes his fancy) sometimes rolls a woman in the snow. Hawkers and peddlers offer the villagers second hand goods with explicit sexual significance – for example, offering women's underwear at cheap prices (see Figure 29.5). As an example of a contemporary iconography being integrated into the proceedings, there are two characters dressed as traveling toilet-sellers (see Figure 29.6). Wheeling a mobile toilet captioned "Your relief is our business," they encourage onlookers to sit on the seat. When they do so, a "whoopee" cushion provides the appropriate sound effects and (with great hilarity) plastic feces lurking under the toilet seat are revealed to all. This "performance" could be a parody of commercialization and concern for market forces that have been infiltrating Czech society following the fall of the communist regime. More controversially, some of the masqueraders dress as Jews and gypsies. While the Jews symbolize wealth and prosperity for the oncoming year, both groups are also intended to represent the margins of society. The masquerade is accompanied by a small brass band whose music deteriorates during the course of the day's perambulation as the drink takes its effect.

Out of these basic ingredients, the ethnographer/detective can find underlying patterns that are shared by a number of European folk customs (and it would be

Figure 29.4 Bear and chimney sweeps, Dolní Roveň masquerade. Photograph © Terence Wright. (Reproduced courtesy of the author.)

Figure 29.5 Hawkers, Dolní Roveň masquerade. Photograph © Terence Wright. (Reproduced courtesy of the author.)

Figure 29.6 The toilet salesman, Dolní Roveň masquerade. Photograph © Terence Wright. (Reproduced courtesy of the author.)

quite possible to build these variations on a theme into the computer-delivered ethnography of *Interactive Village*): "A number of 'primitive' plays and ceremonies observed by anthropologists at the beginning of this century have served since then as archetypal models for interpreting folk dramas" (Axton 1974:35). Axton continues by citing the work of Jane Harrison (1921) which (though based in Greece) describes events similar to the Dolní Roveň carnival, involving perambulatory masqueraders. The Greek carnival also featured a bride and groom and a significant amount of cross-dressing. Another variation of the subversion of expectation in masquerade displayed in the appearance and role reversal of the Czech bride and groom is described in the eighteenth-century English journal, *Connoisseur*: "one gentleman above six foot high . . . came to the Masquerade drest like a child and leading-strings, attended by another gentleman of a very low stature, who officiated as his nurse" (May 1, 1755, quoted by Castle 1986:22). While Axton interprets the carnival wedding-performance in European folk-performance as sympathetic magic "in which the life of the year, and the fertility of the grain are assured by mimetic human action," it is also "entertaining – absurd, knockabout bawdy fun" (Axton 1994:35), an attribute it shares with another Europe-wide carnival theme: that of the "world turned upside down." "This topos of *mundus inversus* is an ancient and widespread one,

Figure 29.7 Hunter's funeral, painted beehive front board. (Reproduced by permission of the Beekeeping Museum Radovljica, Slovenia.)

found very extensively in popular art and literature throughout Europe from classical times" (Donaldson 1970:22). As part of this topsy-turvy world, in addition to "reversals in the normal relationships between people" (1970:23), there are also "reversals in the normal relationships between animals and men" (1970:22). For instance, referring to the wider field of visual culture reveals Slovenian beehive paintings including this theme, for instance, animal/human reversal in "The animals burying a hunter" (see Figure 29.7); while Russian popular folk imagery (e.g. eighteenth-century *lubok* prints) also portrays animal/animal reversals with a similar theme: such as depicting a funeral procession where the mice are burying a cat.

The topos of masking, clowning, and the grotesque was incorporated by Czech film-maker Miloš Forman in his feature film *The Firemen's Ball (Hoří, má panenko)*,[10] which provided an inspiring frame of reference to the *Interactive Village* project. In his fictional account, using non-professional actors – the firemen themselves – he takes into the cinema Bakhtin's idea of the manifestation of the carnivalesque (made in the context of the novel), where disguise, grotesquerie, and the subversion of the natural order dominate:[11]

> Forman has assembled an impressive ensemble of grotesque types and fantastic faces. The movie's droll naturalism occasionally flirts with cuteness, but its deadpan comedy is darkened by an unwaveringly clear-eyed view of human stupidity and deception
>
> . . . The ball is a series of small catastrophes, absurd ceremonies, and inane intrigues – these rendered all the more ridiculous by the firemen's tendency toward self-important official rhetoric and coercive authoritarianism. Just about everything that can go wrong does. Decorations fall from the ceiling. The brass band misses its cues. The lottery prizes are pilfered by those assigned to watch over them. The reluctant participants in a beauty contest run for cover and, in the confusion, a fat middle-aged lady happily crowns herself the winner. (Hoberman 2002)

Menus and bricolage

Forman worked with the linear, fixed-edit movie form. But the participatory nature of the Czech carnival with its subversive tendencies makes it an ideal subject for representation via interactive media. On one level, participant viewers can choose individually the style of ethnographic rendition – for example, either "observational" or "didactic" (Wright 2003:166). On another level, they can select the type of information – deciding whether to watch the interviewee as "talking head" or to select "cutaways," showing items and events referred to in the narrative. Interviews can be played out at longer or shorter length, depending on individual wishes; and selection can be made from a range of presenters, giving voice-over commentaries. The metaphor of a restaurant menu offers an analogy to the full range of the selections available to the participant viewer of *Interactive Village*. A conventional menu may offer 3 starters, 3 main courses, and 3 desserts – giving diners 27 possible eating permutations. A choice of wine, other beverages, and side dishes multiply the range of possibilities. While a number of possible variations are available, the outcome (i.e. number and type of courses in any individual meal) is relatively predictable. However, *Interactive Village* aims for a more fluid, open experience – more akin to the dining experience offered by the Seafood Market and Restaurant ("If it swims, we have it") in Bangkok:

> Once you enter, you will pass an active fish market and you can select your entrée from dozens of large fish tanks. Next, you enter a small market area where a clerk helps you select salads and vegetables. Now, choose a bottle from the wine and spirit area. Give instructions on how everything should be cooked to the captain. Then sit at your table and wait for your meal to arrive. (Seafood Market, http://www.seafood.co.th/index.php)

In this context, not only are the ingredients chosen, but also the sizes of the portions and the cooking style. Translated into *Interactive Village* terms, the participant viewer chooses a location-based subject area (e.g. the Litětiny fire station), makes a selection of clips (interview, general scenes, cutaway shots) and decides on length of engagement and the style of ethnography (observational, didactic, or journalistic). However, in moving away from the gastronomic to folk culture, with the potential for much more participative viewers adding their own material to the database, a fairer analogy emerges: namely between this style of ethnography and Lloyd's description of the folk ballad, like the folk-play or village masquerade, "made by individuals and subsequently reshaped to some extent by the mass of people in the course of being handed on" (1967:129) – a phenomenon constantly in touch with its environment. In a parallel observation, Bakhtin describes the *grotesque realism* of the carnival as being integrated into, not separated from, the rest of the world: "It is not a closed, completed unit; it is unfinished, outgrows itself, transgresses its own limits" (1984:26).

This succinct description of the central characteristic of carnival can be used as a metaphor for the Internet itself: "It belongs to the borderline between art and life. In reality, it is life itself, but shaped according to a certain pattern of play" (Bakhtin 1984:7). Indeed, Murdock expands upon this analogy, describing the Internet as a resilient and resistant place:

> where initiatives designed to reconfigure it as a centralized system of distribution and surveillance are countered by horizontal networks of peer-to-peer exchange and ribald mockery of power. As simultaneously both a space of deliberation and a continuous carnival, the Net presents a substantial challenge to anyone wishing to explore the interplay between political and cultural public spheres or examine the relations between deliberation conducted on- and off-line. Bakhtin and Habermas remain essential starting points for anyone wishing to analyse the implications of this emerging communicative space for the future of democracy and cosmopolitan citizenship. (Murdock 2004:288)

Cosmopolitan citizenship may seem a far cry from tribal organization, but in this context it is perhaps closer than at first appears. In his *La Pensée Sauvage* (The savage mind) Lévi-Strauss (1966) proposed that tribal cultures operate to a different kind of logic from that developed in Western civilizations. And it was to explain the character of this type of thought that Lévi-Strauss coined the metaphor of "bricolage" – *whereby* everyday objects are taken up and appropriated, in an improvised fashion, to serve the task in hand. He contrasts this approach to creativity with our concept of the "engineer," who follows a pre-ordained plan and proceeds in a methodological manner, guided by Western rationality.

While the Czech carnival has a tendency to take objects and instances of the everyday and reverse or reconfigure them for purposes of personal entertainment, the method of gathering information for the *Interactive Village* project likewise did not operate to a precise plan: audio-visual material was put together in a piecemeal fashion, based on a rough estimate that it might have some use or relevance to a participant-viewer-defined narrative. Rather than following the rules of a conventional linear moving-image-based ethnography – where at some stage the author/producer has to draw a line under the work achieved thus far and declare it "finished" – the existing *Interactive Village* shapeshifting project can be extended at any time to incorporate additional material. This could be based on the village itself, or include other villages in the vicinity or (in a more ambitious scenario) create a Europe-wide network of interactive villages. While such a format could offer the participant viewer opportunities to compare and contrast many types of material from a range of perspectives, it could also enable disparate villagers to communicate, identify common aims, and engage in problem-solving.

The overall NM2 project (of which *Interactive Village* formed part) developed the Shapeshift software in tandem with the productions being worked on, in order to ensure that the tools served the needs of real producers. So, not only could we review our progress beside the other NM2 productions tackling other genres of storytelling and adopt successful strategies, but as theoretical and practical demands emerged during the *Interactive Village* fieldwork, requests were made to design and implement certain helpful features on a day-to-day basis. The similarity of the process of bricolage is clear in Hawkes's summary of Lévi-Strauss' metaphor:

> The process involves a "science of the concrete" (as opposed to our "civilized" science of the "abstract") which, far from lacking logic, in fact carefully and precisely orders, classifies and arranges into structures the *minutiae* of the physical world in all their profusion by means of a "logic" which is not our own. The structures, "improvized" or "made up" (these are rough translations of the process of *bricoler*) as *ad hoc* responses

> to an environment, then serve to establish homologies and analogies between the ordering of nature and that of society, and so satisfactorily "explain" the world and make it able to be lived in. (Hawkes 2003:36)

So while the various multimedia elements are analogous to the raw materials of the bricoleur, the storytelling itself (as handled by the software according to frameworks authored by the visual ethnographer, anthropologist, or producer) can be effectively illuminated by this analogy. Indeed, an interesting case for author as bricoleur has been put forward by Conville (1997). He examines a passage from James Agee's 1941 book, *Let Us Now Praise Famous Men*, made with photographer Walker Evans (expanded not from an academic study but from a 1936 journal article on US sharecroppers), in a way which enables Conville to paint Agee as something of an anthropologist:

> he the outsider, in a car, dressed like he was from the city; they the indigenous peoples . . . Agee could not be the engineer in this episode. He must be the bricoleur. Given no time to carefully plan a response to this (to him) bizarre circumstance, Agee was obliged to use only ad hoc materials, those readily to hand, bricolage to craft the relationship that ensued with his captors. (Conville 1997:378)

Here, the Lévi-Straussian notion of bricolage moves smoothly into the realm of photojournalism, a primary area of study for visual culture. Its usage can equally be seen as representative of the convergence between anthropology and interactive media, as well, potentially, as continuing to act incisively as a metaphor for the interdisciplinary dimension of visual culture:

> The "bricoleur" is adept at performing a large number of diverse tasks . . . [His task] is to be defined only by its potential use or, putting this another way and in the language of the "bricoleur" himself, because the elements are collected or retained on the principle that "they may always come in handy." . . . They each represent a set of actual or possible relations; they are "operators" but they can be used for any operations of the same type. (Lévi-Strauss 1966:17–18)

The open-ended nature of *Interactive Village* with its "story potentials" – which remain largely unresolved until engaged with by the participant viewer – goes beyond the Lévi-Strauss concept of bricolage, to reinforce his claim that mythical thought can reach "unforeseen results on the intellectual plane" (1966:17). Lévi-Strauss also describes bricolage as an alternative approach to that of western scientific inquiry. Rather than taking a "top-down" approach in which information and items are ordered to pre-ordained schema, the bricoleur assembles by piecing together a collection of *objets trouvés* into a kind of collage. Unlike the traditional, edited, linear ethnographic film, *Interactive Village* has created a repository of information, parts of which will be seen by individual participant viewers, but much of which may remain dormant: lying in wait for the appropriate viewing context. From this collection, the computer program, working within parameters designed by expert authors (visual ethnographers) and prompted by participant viewers, collates and reconfigures the linked groups of material (video footage, sound bites, archive documents, still photographs) into many and various whole coherent narrative playouts.

CONCLUSION

By the 1970s, "bricolage" was a well-established term in the art-school vocabulary. Also in the art context, Fry and Willis have used it, where they note how indigenous peoples are adopting television technology as part of a process of cultural regeneration: "Making a new culture which knowingly embraces the future is a more viable form of cultural *bricolage* (by this we mean the making of a culture by a process of the selection and assembly of combined and recombined cultural forms)" (quoted in Ginsberg 1991:97). Updating the analogy to embrace the computer software designer as bricoleur, Turkle and Papert (1990) actually enlarge it with reference to the act of painting itself – culturally, a visual activity. Rather than establishing and conforming to a rigid plan, they suggest that the software bricoleur masters associations and interactions like the painter "who stands back between brushstrokes, looks at the canvas, and only after this contemplation, decides what to do next. For planners, mistakes are missteps; for bricoleurs they are the essence of a navigation by mid-course corrections" (Turkle and Papert 1990:136).

In the final analysis, this description reflects both the putting together of the *Interactive Village* program in the way the information was gathered; and in its realization; and its enjoyment, in the way that participant viewers can choose "jumping-off" points from one narrative to another as they explore the virtual village, or by impulsively extending or contracting the length of the narrative as the mood takes them. "We tend to think of interactivity as a phenomenon made possible by computer technology, but it is a dimension of face-to-face interaction that was shut off by manuscript and print writing and reintroduced into written messages by the electronic medium, together with several other features of oral communication" (Ryan 2001:204). As this case study of *Interactive Village* demonstrates, the type of interactivity brought about by computer technology may be creating an innovative twenty-first century form of engagement with the artwork, and indeed revising modes of perceiving the world, but this is not the first time that the dynamics by which it operates have come into play. As referred to in the introduction to this chapter, Danius showed in the context of early twentieth-century modernism, already in the novels of James Joyce, Thomas Mann, Marcel Proust, "a variety of technoscientific configurations are a vital part of the inner logic of these works, including their narrative structures, thematic obsessions, and formal procedures" (Danius 2002:196), which laid down models for digital creativity. Even before the modernist movement, the American photographer Albert Sands Southworth enthused in 1871 over photography's ability to revitalize the study of art, by enabling art historians to hold up side-by-side photographs of different objects or paintings from different locations and periods, and thus make unprecedented comparisons: "The treasures of the artistic world are laid upon our tables: ancient and modern art we can study at our leisure" (Southworth 1871:531), endorsing, before its time, the practice of bricolage in visual culture.

Some 70 years later, André Malraux, while sharing Albert Sands Southworth's excitement, remains a little sceptical of the *Museum without Walls*: "Reproduction has disclosed the whole world's sculpture. It has multiplied accepted masterpieces, promoted other works to their due rank and launched some minor styles – in some cases, one might say, invented them" (1953:44). Despite the sting in the tail of this comment, offering a word of caution, the contemporary promise and potential of the interactive ethnography remain extensive and enticing. As the example of *Interactive Village* shows, digital bricolage where the framework is provided by experts who mediate the parameters within which the process is carried out not only provides an umbrella under which diverse cultural phenomena can be compared and contrasted, but also allows for a variety of depths of engagement, to suit individual users, thus widening the scope of ethnography and extending the range of the term "visual culture." The commonality of approach offered by Lévi Strauss' inclusive concept of "bricolage" already unites the study of art and the practice of folk performance. This chapter has, I hope, shown how it can also productively link Bakhtin's illuminating work on carnival with ethnography and interactive digital media, to bring them onto the shared firm ground of visual culture.

NOTES

1 Throughout his essay *Interdisciplinarity and Visual Culture*, Mitchell (1995) cites the interdependence between visual culture and anthropology.

2 I am grateful to Petr Skalník and Hana Novotná, University of Pardubice, for their help and support in the production of the *Interactive Village* and to the villagers of Dolní Roveň for their cooperation, hospitality, and openness to share their experiences.

3 In his video interview for the *Interactive Village* project, Mr Vobratilek, chief fireman of the Litětiny Brigade, speaks of the rivalry between brigades and the a sense of competitive giving to the community. For example, the hunters donate a deer to one of the village balls.

4 Barden (1998) for example describes the manifestation of the Czech *Masopust* festival among the Czech community in Winconsin.

5 Issues of the nature of Czech revivals of folk traditions have been addressed at length by Lass (1989) and Tufnell (1924) describes some variations on Czech and Slovak perambulatory Lenten festivities.

6 Early Czech literature contains significant carnivalesque elements: "Cleverly punning, drastic medieval humour is exemplified by the 14th-century Czech dramatic text known as Mastičkář, a version of a comic episode added to the Easter story in which a Quack-Salver purveys ointment to the three Marys visiting Jesus' tomb. Not only does it contain coarse references to masturbation, monkly fornication, and so on, but there is also a mock resurrection, achieved by the anointing of one Isaac's backside. Humorous, satirical or parodic poems, often associated one way or another with University life, include 'The Groom and the Scholar,' 'The Dispute of Water and Wine,' and Czech-Latin macaronic verses" (Naughton 2004).

7 Like the English word "carnival" ("good-bye to meat"), the term *masopust* ("meat fasting") also suggests the pre-Lenten period when butchering and feasts were held.

8 The Notting Hill Carnival, a deliberate initiative made in 1959 by Trinidadian activist Claudia Jones to improve race relations, had by 1976 taken on many characteristics of

Afro-Caribbean celebration from local inhabitants of the Notting Hill area, to become a national institution in the twentieth century.

9 According to Bakhtin (1984:202) it was a French custom to lead an ox "through the streets during carnival season . . . it was the sacrificial meat, to be chopped up for sausages and patés" – true carnival imagery.

10 See also: The Eccentric Carnival – Valerie and her Week of Wonders (on Czech New Wave) at http://www.sensesofcinema.com/2007/cteq/valerie-week-wonders/.

11 "In spite of their variety, folk festivities of the carnival type, the comic rites and cults, the clowns and fools, giants, dwarfs, and jugglers, the vast and manifold literature of parody-all these forms have one style in common: they belong to one culture of folk carnival humor" (Bakhtin 1984:4).

REFERENCES

Andén-Papadopoulos, Kari
In press Global Image Wars: Geopolitics and Post-9/11 visual culture. London: Routledge.

Axton, Richard
1974 European Drama of the Early Middle Ages. London: Hutchinson.

Bakhtin, Mikhail
1984 Rabelais and His World. Trans. Helene Iswolsky. Bloomington and Indianapolis: Indiana University Press.

Banks, Marcus
2001 Visual Methods in Social Research. London: Sage.

Banks, Marcus, and Howard Morphy
1997 Rethinking Visual Anthropology. New Haven: Yale University Press.

Barden, Thomas E.
1998 The Yuba, Wisconsin, Masopust Festival. *In* Wisconsin Folklore. James P. Leary, ed. pp. 352–361. Madison: University of Wisconsin Press.

Barnes, Julian
1985 Flaubert's Parrot. London: Picador.

Berger, John
1972 Ways of Seeing. London: Penguin.

Berger, Maurice
2010 For All the World to See: Visual Culture and the Struggle for Civil Rights. New Haven: Yale University Press.

Brown, Steven T.
2010 Tokyo Cyberpunk: Posthumanism in Japanese Visual Culture. London: Palgrave Macmillan.

Castle, Terry
1986 Masquerade and Civilization: The Carnivalesque in Eighteenth-Century English Culture and Fiction. Stanford: Stanford University Press.

Conville, Richard L.
1997 Between Spearheads: Bricolage and Relationships. Journal of Social and Personal Relationships 14:373–386.

Cutting, James E., and Manfredo Massironi
1998 Pictures and Their Special Status in Perceptual and Cognitive Inquiry. *In* Perception and Cognition at Century's End: History, Philosophy, and Theory. J. Hochberg, ed. pp. 137–168. San Diego: Academic Press.

Danius, Sara
2002 The Senses of Modernism: Technology, Perception, and Aesthetics. Ithaca, NY: Cornell University Press.
Donaldson, Ian
1970 World Upside-Down: Comedy from Jonson to Fielding. Oxford: Oxford University Press.
Eisenstein, Sergei M.
1949 About Stereoscopic Cinema. Penguin Film Review 8:35–44.
Galla, Karel
1939 Dolní Roveň: Sociologický obraz české vesnice. Prague: Spolek péče o blaho venkova.
Gibson, James J.
1966 The Senses Considered as Perceptual Systems. Boston: Houghton Mifflin.
Ginsberg, Faye
1991 Indigenous Media: Faustian Contract or Global Village? Cultural Anthropology 6(1):92–112.
Harrison, Jane Ellen
1921 Epilegomena to the Study of Greek Religion. Madison: University of Wisconsin Press.
Hawkes, Terence
2003 Structuralism and Semiotics. 2nd edition. London: Routledge.
Hoberman, J.
2002 The Firemen's Ball. The Criterion Collection. February 11. Electronic document. http://www.criterion.com/current/posts/187-the-firemens-ball (accessed November 5, 2011).
Ingold, Tim
2000 The Perception of the Environment: Essays on Livelihood, Dwelling and Skill. London: Routledge.
Jenks, Chris
1995 Watching Your Step: The History and Practice of the Flâneur. *In* Visual Culture. C. Jenks, ed. pp. 142–160. London: Routledge.
Jordanova, Ludmilla
2006 History in Practice. 2nd edition. London: Hodder.
Katz, Maya Balakirsky
2010 The Visual Culture of Chabad. Cambridge: Cambridge University Press.
Lass, Andrew
1989 What Keeps the Czech Folk "Alive?" Dialectical Anthropology 14:7–19.
Lévi-Strauss, Claude
1966 The Savage Mind. Chicago: Chicago University Press.
Lloyd, Albert L.
(1967) Folk Song in England. London: Lawrence & Wishart.
Malraux, André
1953 The Voices of Silence. Trans. S. Gilbert. New York: Doubleday and Co.
Mauss, Marcel
1969 The Gift. London: Routledge.
Mirzoeff, Nicholas
1999 An Introduction to Visual Culture. London: Routledge.
Mitchell, W. J. T.
1995 Interdisciplinarity and Visual Culture. Art Bulletin 77(Dec):540–544.
Murdock, Graham
2004 Theatres without Footlights: Deliberative Democracy and Creative Engagement. Current Sociology 52(2):281–289.

Novotná, Hana
2004 Global versus Local: Share of Global Culture on the Village Culture. *In* Dolní Roveň: Research at Half-Time. P. Skalník, ed. pp. 179–206. Pardubice: University of Pardubice.
Naughton, James
2004 Czech Literature up to the Hussite Wars. Electronic document. http://users.ox.ac.uk/~tayl0010/lit_to_hus.htm (accessed November 5, 2011).
Pink, Sarah
2001 Doing Ethnography: Images, Media and Representation in Research. London: Sage.
Pink, Sarah, Phil Hubbard, Maggie O'Neill, and Alan Radley
2010 Walking across Disciplines: From Ethnography to Arts Practice. Visual Studies 25(1):1–7.
Pospíšilová, Jana
2004 Sulkovec – Polom: Voluntary Fire Brigades. Trans. Irena Přibylová. Brno: T.D.V. Electronic document. http://www.iach.cz/uef/sulkovec/doc/EN06%20-%20Voluntary%20Fire%20Brigades.pdf (accessed November 5, 2011).
Prosser, Jon D.
1998 Image-Based Research; A Sourcebook for Qualitative Researchers. London: Falmer Press.
Rhodes, Kimberly
2008 Ophelia and Victorian Visual Culture: Representing Body Politics in the Nineteenth Century. Farnham: Ashgate.
Ruggles, D. Fairchild
2011 Islamic Art and Visual Culture. Oxford: Wiley-Blackwell.
Ryan, Marie-Laure
2001 Narrative as Virtual Reality: Immersion and Interactivity in Literature and Electronic Media. Baltimore: Johns Hopkins University Press.
Schneider, Arnd, Chris Wright
2006 Contemporary Art and Anthropology. Oxford: Berg.
Skalník, Petr, ed.
2004 Dolní Roveň: Research at Half-Time. Pardubice: Univerzita Pardubice.
Southworth, Albert Sands
1871 The Early History of Photography in the United States. British Journal of Photography 18(Nov.):530–532.
Sturken, Marita, and Lisa Cartwright
2000 Practices of Looking: An Introduction to Visual Culture. New York: Oxford University Press.
Styhre, Alexander
2010 Visual Culture in Organizations: Theory and Cases. London: Routledge.
Sullivan, Graeme
2010 Art Practice as Research: Inquiry in the Visual Arts. 2nd edition. London: Sage.
Tufnell, Blanche O.
1924 Czecho-Slovak Folklore. Folklore 35(1):26–56.
Turkle, Sherry, and Seymour Papert
1990 Epistemological Pluralism: Styles and Voices within the Computer Culture. SIGNS: Journal of Women in Culture and Society 16(1):128–157.
Turner, Victor
1987 The Anthropology of Performance. New York: PAJ.
Ursu, Marian F., Maureen Thomas, Mika L. Tuomola, Terrence Wright, and Vilmos Zsombori

2007 Interactivity and Narrativity in Screen Media. *In* Proceedings of the IEEE Symposium on Multimedia Systems, pp. 227–232. Taichung, Taiwan, December 10–12, IEEE Computer Society.

Ursu, Marian F., Maureen Thomas, Ian Kegel, Doug Williams, Mika Tuomola, Inga Lindstedt, Terence Wright, Andra Leurdijk, Vilmos Zsombori, Julia Sussner, Ulf Maystream, and Nina Hall

2008 Interactive TV Narratives: Opportunities, Progress and Challenges. ACM Transactions on Multimedia Computing, Communications and Applications 4(4), Article 25:1–39.

Wright, Terence

1992 Photography: Theories of Realism and Convention. *In* Anthropology and Photography 1860–1920. Elizabeth Edwards, ed. pp. 18–31. New York: Yale University Press.

Wright, Terence

1997 The Photography Handbook. London: Routledge.

Wright, Terence

2003 The "Creative Treatment of Actuality": Visions and Revisions in Representing Truth. *In* Architectures of Illusion: From Motion Pictures to Navigable Interactive Environments. Maureen Thomas and François Penz, eds. pp. 165–194. Bristol: Intellect.

CHAPTER 30

Hybrid Worlds of Europe: Theoretical and Practical Aspects

Elka Tschernokoshewa

Hybridity

On April 24, 2008, *Die Zeit* published a voluminous article on Pulitzer Prize winner Michael Chabon. The headline was "The Messiah of Zemenhof" and the subtitle was "The Hybrid Poet." The focus of the report was the author's new novel *The Yiddish Policemen's Union* (2007). The author is introduced this way: "Of course one can simply praise him for his wit, his intelligence, and, above all, for his language, in which he adds a glaring sound of his own to the sound of our time, which is formed by elements of the present and the past, of invented Yiddish and invented worlds. He is the hybrid poet for our hybrid time. Chabon lives in Berkeley, California – and he drives a hybrid car from Toyota" (Diez 2008, translation author's own).

Notions such as "hybrid poet," "hybrid times," or "hybrid worlds" come even more to the center of public debates in articles, art events, and culture of the twenty-first century. This is of no surprise to us, because many things around us bear traces of mixtures, the overlapping and coming together of different references. This applies not only to works of art such as modern novels, jazz music, or collages in paintings, where goal-oriented mixtures already belong to the specifics of that genre. It also concerns the character of everyday life today, as well as the whole organization of society. A walk through town, a glance at the stores' exhibits or commercial posters, reading papers, listening to the radio, or watching TV – they all show an astonishing multiplicity of cultural references in comparison to past decades.

The trend I am highlighting here is, moreover, no longer a phenomenon of the cities, of the youth, or of artistic elites. Even in the most remote villages of the Balkan mountains, old women have their cell phones in the fields ready to communicate with children and grandchildren hundreds of miles away. Then they watch the evening news to see how weather, workers' strikes, stock quotations, or other universal events interact with the lives of their loved ones. The next day they comment

A Companion to the Anthropology of Europe, First Edition. Edited by Ullrich Kockel, Máiréad Nic Craith, and Jonas Frykman.

upon this to their neighbors and wait eagerly for the next phone call. They feel that somehow everything is connected to everything, and that no event happens on its own – and that their life is changed by events that happen at the other end of the world. But they have to deal with these events; their room for action has become completely pervious.

The tendency toward delimitization and pluralization of cultural connections and individual drafts of life are the most outstanding signs of culture today. This statement appears to be plausible, and yet it seems to be beyond dispute. The question which has to be posed, however, is: Which approaches do we have in anthropology and cultural studies to observe these processes analytically and to describe them logically? How can we describe ambiguities, mixtures, and transitions without imposing important experiences, sensitivities, and competencies, which are connected to such a life? With which perspective of observation can we conduct our research in such a way that the structures of power and institutional frames of reference can also be discussed? Moreover: What ways of dealing with diversity are there: at the level of discourse, of practice, and of politics?

The hybridological approach is situated within this complex of questions. The notion "hybrid" means that something is brought together which had not been together before: two forms of art, two cultural references, two technologies. Hybridology is the approach that analyzes the hybrid. It is an approach and research methodology, which puts this multiplicity deliberately into the center of research interest. Here we are interested in cultural diversity and ways of dealing with it. Knowledge from diverse subjects and schools of thought flows into this research perspective. Hybridology is a cross-disciplinary subject, hybrid in itself, an attempt not to cling to the common fragmentation of subjects and disciplines. Its goal is to study, on the one hand, the emergence of new forms of art and cultural practices, and, on the other hand, the possibilities of minorities, migrants, and marginal people, and explicitly to explore the options of organizing society according to the principle of a "shared diversity."

Situation of Departure

When I came to Germany from Sofia, Bulgaria, in September 1992 and became head of the Department of Empirical Cultural Studies/Ethnology at the Sorbian Institute in Bautzen, the word "hybrid" was not part of the arsenal of cultural studies. According to old subject traditions, it was customary to analyze Sorbian culture and German culture separately. In these studies the specifically "own," the peculiar, was at the center of research interest, and for these peculiarities, criteria were sought and found: peculiar language, peculiar traditions, peculiar habits, peculiar territory. The relation between Sorbian and German was not the object of research. Neither were the various overlappings, multiple identities, and syntheses. With regard to cultural differences, research until the 1990s concentrated predominantly on the notion of cultural differentialism. In anthropology, this is the perspective of cultural relativism and the view of cultures as single entities. The notion of culture as an island, and cultural research as "island-research," dominated the imagination of Sorbian culture. This lineage goes back to the Romantics such as Herder. It implies a kind of "billiard ball" model of cultures as separate units. Elsewhere I have described the development of Sorbian ethnology/cultural research from "island-research" to the "analysis of relationships" in a study (Tschernokoshewa 2008).

A second observation followed in the early 1990s, when I prepared a survey of current investigations of aspects of Sorbian culture in cultural studies and ethnology at the federal level. The findings showed that there were rarely explicit studies. The reasons for this were rather diverse. Ethnology in Germany (*deutsche Volkskunde*) during the 1970s and the 1980s made a decisive turnaround by focusing on social aspects of popular cultures (Bausinger et al. 1989). "Social aspects" here meant class-specific (especially lower strata), generation-specific (especially youth cultures), and later also gender-specific ways of life. The notion of ethnicity was either completely circumvented or used only critically, that is, in the context of a critique of the instrumentalization of concepts such as people, ethnicity, or nation in nationalist ideologies and practices. This was also the time of intellectual confrontation with the heritage of National Socialism. In the academic realm, this was an important discussion, which founded the democratization of the subject and its establishment as a part of the social sciences.

Another reason for the relative neglect of ethnic characteristics of human socialization and life in the anthropological cultural studies of the time is a sociological tradition linked to Max Weber. According to Weber, adherence to ethnic principles in social organization processes indicates a low degree of rationalization. He held this view for valid conceptual reasons (the emphasis is on rational social technologies), but his position was uncritically perpetuated by his successors and resulted in ethnic aspects being denigrated for decades both within the social science and in public discourses. Weber's school of sociology subscribes to a model of modernity that is insensitive toward ethnic differences. This perspective combines ideas from the Enlightenment, the idea of a single-track universal process of evolution through which all societies – some faster than others – are progressing, and the idea of a universalism that downgrades cultural diversity.

Within anthropological research on Germany since the end of the 1990s there has been a new interest in problems of differences. The discussion ranged from the assertion of a "fear of difference" (Schiffauer 1996) to the question: "May ethnic groups exist?" (Kramer 1996). Problems of differences were mentioned anew in the sociology and philosophy of the time by commentators such as Luhmann (1997), Beck (1997), and Nassehi (1999). The decisive impulse came, however, from those fields of research which addressed questions of cultural practice and cultural politics in respect to minorities (Räthzel 1997). Above all there was the research of postcolonial studies, which decisively posed anew the question of difference. Quite openly a positive conception of the ethnicity of the margins, of the periphery, was suggested. A great deal of work was done to decouple ethnicity, as it functions in the dominant discourse, from nationalism, imperialism, racism. Stuart Hall, for example, developed his thoughts following Derrida's distinction between *différence* that makes a radical and unbridgeable separation and *différence* that is positional, conditional, and conjunctural. Derrida used for this second meaning the term *différance*. In Hall these thoughts emerged in direct connection with cultural-practical and cultural-political discussions on Black film in British cinema:

> That is to say, a recognition that we all speak from a particular place, out of a particular history, out of a particular experience, a particular culture, without being contained by that position as 'ethnic artists' or film-makers. We are all, in that sense, *ethnically* located and our ethnic identities are crucial to our subjective sense of who we are. But this is also a recognition that this is not an ethnicity which is doomed to survive, as Englishness was, only by marginalizing, dispossessing, displacing and forgetting other ethnicities. This precisely is the politics of ethnicity predicated on difference and diversity. (Hall 1997:227)

Talking about Others and Otherness

This was the professional situation. In addition, there was my personal story and the everyday experience of being an "alien woman" and an "alien scholar." That was my motivation to study deliberately the way of talking about Others and Otherness. Thus, I took the German-language press as an object of research and observed the way it spoke about Sorbs, and Sorbian culture, but also in general about Others and Otherness. My sources ranged from tabloids such as *Bild* and Germany's regional press to quality papers like *Die Zeit*, *Frankfurter Allgemeine Zeitung*, and *Süddeutsche Zeitung*. The time span of the analysis was from New Year's Day 1994 to the same date in 2000. The material encompassed 4400 pages in total and the results of this research have been published in the book *Das Reine und das Vermischte* (Tschernokoshewa 2000). This was also the foundation of the series *Hybride Welten* with Waxmann publishers.

That study showed a strong presence of the well-known position of cultural differentialism and thinking in dichotomies. Sorbs and Sorbian culture in Germany were presented as a distinctive culture with a pronounced dualistic character. The dualistic way of thinking poses oppositions, counter-worlds, which have clear borders that exclude each other. Consequently, something on one side cannot be on the other side as well; Sorbian culture can only exist as an antagonism to German culture. Characteristic of this way of thinking is that the counter-worlds are imagined as being homogenous. I call this the "dream of purity." Here are some typical phrases from the press: "The Sorbs – a life against time," "Yesterday is here," "The Sorbs have always been farmers," "The Sorbs are like a large family," "The Sorbs are presently responsible for upholding established traditions," "There is no place in Germany where one can see such beautiful, old, authentic costumes as in Lusatia," "Here one can see old, authentic, unbroken tradition," or "The Sorbs are most Sorbian when they sing and pray in Sorbian."

I want to stress: it is for the purpose of distinction that Sorbs or Sorbian culture are presently forced into a "pre-modern," folkloristic, often rustic corner by the majority – the latter, so to speak, makes the sole claim to progress and modernity. This distinction is also often thought of in a hierarchical way, thus going hand-in-hand with the placement of ethnic minorities in the lower stratum of society. The folklorization of minorities like the Sorbs is part of a comprehensive national power construct. It is a product, and it more or less openly accompanies the idea of homogenous national culture, which is historically *passé* and has been for a long time.

This way of thinking in Europe has a long historical tradition, as we know. Since the middle of the eighteenth century and especially in the nineteenth and twentieth centuries, a paradigm prevailed in Europe, in which the relationship of own versus foreign was thought of as an opposition of good versus evil. This paradigm acquired a structural impulse as a result of the economical and political development of the nation-state. Indicative of this mode of thought is its dualistic and excluding character. For this the term purity was also activated; simultaneously, as counter pole, impurity, filth, or trash, were drawn into the argumentation. Concealed behind the term "purity," there is always, in the final analysis, a conception of the unity and self-containedness of the community itself, which demands the exclusion, or rather eradication, of differences.

In regard to the Sorbian–German relationship, the Sorbian component has experienced a double exclusion: first as a distinctive culture within the German Empire, second as part of the Slavic East. As we know, the external demarcation – in the west to France, in the east to the Slavic region – was fundamental for the emergence of the German nation-state, which was the primary reason why these enemy images were produced on such a scale. The historian Wippermann has analyzed the development of anti-Slavism in Germany and posed the question: "Have the Sorbs been persecuted for racist reasons?" Wippermann has taken into consideration texts by prominent thinkers such as Hegel, Schlegel, or Reitemeier to describe this general process. Thus, for example, the historian Reitemeier maintained in his *History of the Prussian State*, published 1801–1805, that the Slav is rather primitive, lazy, and distinguished by "uncleanliness" (Wippermann 1996:513).

Philosophers, historians, and ethnographers were instrumental in the development of this way of thinking. In regard to purity, we can find comparable notions in the fathers of German *Volkskunde* such as, for example, in Jahn's publication *Deutsches Volkstum*. We read there: "The more pure a people, the better; the more mixed, the more like a rabble" (Jahn 1813:26, translation author's own). Constitutional doctrine and state educational practice were also based on this paradigm, as was the notion of democracy, as it was substantially conceived by Carl Schmitt at the beginning of the twentieth century: "Every actual democracy is based upon this, that not only equivalent is treated equally, but, with unavoidable consistency, that non-equivalent is unequally treated. Thus, democracy necessarily requires, firstly, homogeneity, and, secondly – should the need arise – the exclusion or elimination of the heterogeneous" (Schmitt 1923:13). In this interpretation of the Weimar Constitution, ethnic nationalism is given the status of public law. Habermas explains in detail how homogeneity is conceived by Schmitt as normality, and as a fundamental principle, which logically leads to repressive politics, be it the "compulsory assimilation of foreign elements, or the maintenance of the purity of the people through apartheid and cleansing" (Habermas 1997:169).

At this point I wish to draw attention to the following observation: the dualistic principle pure versus impure, thought of as good versus evil, as it became generally accepted in connection with national or ethnic belonging in Europe, follows the dualistic principle of the Christian religion. The separation of holy and unholy, as is well known, is grounded in the terms "purity" and "filth"; based on this opposition, communities and enmities were founded. As Braun (1996) points out, from the Christian ideal of purity, which above all meant sexual renunciation, would later derive, in the secular context, a form of chastity which refers precisely to the corporation. A form of "post-Christian" purity emerges, which does not require sexual abstinence but rather forbids intercourse with "foreigners." As an example for the maxim of keeping pure – where the religious and the national clearly connect – von Braun provides the first of the 10 German commandments from the *Antisemiten-Katechismus*, by Theodor Fritsch (1887): "First commandment: You shall keep your blood pure – regard it as a crime to spoil your people's noble Arian race through the Jewish race. Then know, the Jewish blood is indestructible and forms body and soul according to the Jewish race, until the furthest generations" (von Braun 1996: 9).

Interestingly, the speakers of the minority often responded within the same patterns of thinking. When they were debating their own culture, traditions, language, and territory, they argued with purity as well. The elites of interpretation go back to this vocabulary until this day (Tschernokoshewa 2000, 2008). It is remarkable how stubbornly this traditional pattern of thinking in dichotomies survives and is reproduced constantly in the region.

The relationship between Sorbian and German was thought of for a long time as the juxtaposition of self versus other or good versus evil. This "either–or" notion exists also today. It is a dualistic way of thinking, which we know well from other domains. Siegfried Schmidt, who founded radical constructivism to overcome it, describes the starting manoeuvre of dualistic philosophy: frameworks of interactive dependencies are broken up into components by means of these very frameworks; these components are then separated from their constitutive frameworks and treated as independently existing entities – from which the basis of philosophical thinking takes off. Due to this unreflected starting maneuver, dualistic philosophical thinking generates the dichotomies it has been toiling with for centuries. In European thought, the problems in question definitely possess the status of "grand" philosophical problems (Schmidt 2007).

The hybridological approach is an attempt to go beyond this dualistic way of thinking. Overcoming the dualistic way of thinking gives us the possibility to question relationship stories and multiple lives anew, in order to discuss discrimination experiences, but also the desire to be different and the possibility of multiple existences. A replacement of the "either–or" notion by a "both, and" notion of handling cultural diversity is suggested. The suggestion takes place at first on the level of discourse, but also has structural consequences in regard to the handling of cultural diversity by society as a whole. At last there is the question of how to prevent processes of exclusion, or how to use and develop the different cultural resources in community life.

Hybridology as a Theoretical Concept

Here I would like to offer my brief definition of "hybrid," keeping in mind that my main interest in the hybrid is as a research approach and methodology. The question that guides me is: What kind of problems can we analyze with this concept?

In everyday language, hybridity and hybridization convey the idea of mixture or mixing. As an analytical category, hybridization questions boundaries. It refers to the combining, or doing both, or the in-betweens of cultural phenomena that have been separated by historical circumstances or social differentiation. It can, in that sense, be approached as a Hegelian *Aufhebung* of thesis and antithesis by synthesis, though not in the sense of harmony or reconciliation between opposites, and without conjuring up something stable or enduring or invariable. Indeed, the assembling along those lines can be a momentary event, yet it implies a reconfiguration of an entire field of meanings. In other words, hybridization does not mean that differences disappear; it merely suggests that boundaries become more permeable. It means that the one element is implied in the other. It is premised, in conceptual terms, on a desire to challenge and relativize dualistic models of thought.

The term "hybridization" refers to the simultaneous presence of two or more phenomena, which are, in some respects, assumed to be diverse. Without a sense of difference we could not meaningfully talk about processes of combining. The question of difference can thus be considered the *first key research question* of the hybridological approach. The nature of the differences varies considerably. They can be of a social kind, such as ethnicity, gender, age, occupation, or socioeconomic status, and can be rendered in distinctions of technologies, structures, fields, ideas. From the hybridological perspective, categories like ethnicity, gender, or age are not treated as fact of nature, not as anthropological fixed points, but as social and historical constructs. Within this paradigm, we concentrate on the questions of how realities arise in our actions and what we can and may do with them.

This is a basic consideration in the development of the hybridological approach. For instance, if we talk about Sorbs and Germans: this is not about stating that they are different, but to ask whether they have achieved different experiences, sensitivities, and competencies. Or as well when and how they were treated "differently" – by the majority, the state, or the press. Similarly, gender research doesn't show that women and men *are different*, but that women and men often *live differently* and have developed different experiences, sensitivities, and competencies. It is just the point to study these different experiences. This is the first methodological consideration of the hybridological approach.

Practicing anthropology shows that it is still difficult to research cultural diversity without getting into issues of homogenization and the essentialization of ethnic/national differences. Therefore these differences often tend to be rather concealed, to avoid the well-known and theoretically widely critiqued pitfalls of homogenization/essentialization. Often, however, this means that the specific experiences and aspirations of minorities are ignored. If differences are not questioned, a kind of "increasing sameness" is suggested without reflection; this is somewhat reminiscent of the old universalism, but this framework is hardly suitable for analyzing the cultural processes of the present times. The hybridological approach, by contrast, deals with the recognition of different experiences (in respect to ethnicity, generation, occupation, gender, etc.), without wishing to explain everything in the life of a person (or a community) by this, or putting somebody into an ethnic container. New concepts may lead out of the old dilemma, such as the reflections by Brubaker (2004) about "ethnicity without groups," or Geertz's (2000) thoughts on culture without consensus: "It is the faults and fissures that seem to mark out the landscape of collective selfhood" (2000:250).

Moreover, as a concept for analyzing links between disparate elements, the hybridological approach implies that the focus of enquiry should be on relationships, especially relationships and encounters between previously separate phenomena. This is the *second key research question* or methodological consideration of the hybridological approach. Within this kind of theoretical framework, different kinds of hybrid spaces and events can be categorized, on the one hand, according to the kinds of relationships (different styles and types of mixing, overlapping, and multiplicity), and, on the other hand, according to the power constellations. It is one thing to mix between equally powerful parties and another thing altogether to mix or put together unequal ones. The mix when opera greats like Pavarotti sing with pop and rock stars is an example of a mix of equals. An unequal mix can be seen in some tourism marketing of Otherness. For example, the cultural resources of otherwise marginalized minority-communities were exotic ingredients for the campaign "Zu Gast bei Freunden" [As a guest at a friend's] during the soccer world championship in Germany 2006, but were repressed again after the campaign and were not integrated in other areas.

These asymmetries are taken in the focus of the hybridological approach. After all, it is necessary to differentiate between hybridity as a process of cultural subversion and subaltern resistance and hybridity as an industrial conception for marketing the margins. Commercial cultural hybridity comes often as exoticism, leading to the cultural commoditization of certain stylish images of Black and immigrant people. While the first understanding of hybridity is based on everyday cultural practices, on ambivalent ways of artistic expression and the ongoing identity-formation processes of marginalized groups, the second conception of hybridity allows the dominant White self to extend his/her range of self-definition by consuming and appropriating fashionable and permitted forms of Otherness (Nghi Ha 2005).

For this reason, hybridization is a different experience for ethnic minorities, colonized populations, or migrant workers than it is for the majority or the societal mainstream. Certainly, even within these two broadly identified groups (i.e. minority and majority), there is a need to make distinctions. The evaluation of power relationships and power asymmetries is a key consideration in investigations of hybridization processes, applying as much to the spheres of economics and politics as to the symbolic sphere.

Finally, with the hybridological notion our attention shifts from objects to processes and their contexts and premises. This is what I consider the *third key research question* or methodological consideration of the hybridological approach. This is about *understanding* intercultural and interethnic as well as intergender relations as open and fluent and to acknowledge these processes not only as changing but as a mutual negotiation of belongings, solidarities, and frames for action.

Thus an empirical study about the Sorbian minority which we conducted with students of the University of Bremen from 1999 to 2003 demonstrated how hybridity functions as everyday practice and how identity, the meaning of life, or possibilities of action are constantly negotiated anew. We asked young people, workers, employees, jobless people, multicultural couples, people born here and new immigrants, artists, cultural practitioners, as well as political decision-makers. The Sorbian component showed itself as "the joy of being different," as "a millstone around the neck," again as freedom and solidarity with the Slavic east, many times as multiple competency, then as a constraint and restriction, and ultimately as "living many worlds." (Tschernokoshewa et al. 2005). The hybridological approach made it possible for us to talk about some contradictions, thus addressing ethnic aspects, but showing them as fluent and negotiable.

The hybridological approach and its derivations help us to reflect on both the construction and the crossing of boundaries. Indeed, the spaces in-between, the crossovers, and overlaps become the real object of our research. The concept of hybridity gives us a grasp of the simultaneity of the non-simultaneous, of the life-long efforts to assemble our different biographies. Human action and the conditions of such action are of interest here. More than this, hybridization in that sense allows us to recognize the power aspect in encounters between different elements and in the interplay of cultural traditions, and it also forces us to engage with this power element. I can say more generally that this approach allows us to develop a better understanding of contemporary human lives because all biographies are characterized by intersections of different strands of tradition or chains of meaning, and by the use of different discourses and technologies in the production of stories, actions, and strategies of coping with life that feature patchwork and collage. These general thoughts do not invalidate the existence of distinctive social differences in the "hybrid" field, but they lead directly to posing the question of the conditions of participation in social wealth anew.

It was at the end of the twentieth century when the notion of hybridity gained particular prominence in debates about ethnic and national identities in postcolonial settings. It is closely associated with the work of Hall, Said, Bhabha, and Appadurai. Hall's use of the concept (1991) reflects the sense in which it was developed by members of minority communities in the immediate aftermath of anticolonial and antiracist struggles. Their underlying objective was to expose the increasingly untenable binary mode of identity (in theory, as well as in cultural politics) and to show that identity is the product of more than one discourse. Bhabha (1994) notes that it is "displaced and diasporic peoples," that is, groups who were marginalized by hegemonic powers and acts of purification, who are returning to the "centers" today, bringing with them their own perspectives and serving as a constant reminder to the post-Imperial West of the hybridity of its mother-tongue and the heterogeneity of its national space. Bhabha uses hybridity as an "in between" term, referring to a "third space" and "blended worlds."

Scholars of various backgrounds within the humanities and social sciences have been developing arguments in support of this approach for a number of years. Here ideas of poststructuralism, constructivism, gender, and systems theory pour in. In theoretical terms, the hybridity notion is closely linked to the globalization debates. Relevant discussions have also been stimulated by certain economic and political changes: increasingly globalized economics and the creation of supranational structures.

Currently, this research perspective is gaining in importance within anthropological research in Germany. The anthropologists themselves turn more and more into "hybrid anthropologists" – as the prominent anthropologist Ina-Maria Greverus (2002:26) has acutely observed.

The notion of hybridity is relevant in this context because it captures effectively that very complex, interlaced, and contradictory process of identity and culture that is the hallmark of our age. This was the crucial point for new theoretical departures, though the term "hybridity" already existed in the fields of aesthetics and cultural studies, particularly in relation to the novel and with specific reference to the phenomenon of carnival and its culture of laughter as described by Bakhtin in his book on Rabelais (1984[1965]). What attracted Bakhtin to carnival and the culture of laughter is the fact that whatever is experienced as monolithic, unchangeable, and incontestable in "normal life" can be relativized in those contexts and the potentiality of an "entirely different world," of "another order," "another way of life" can be disclosed. Offering an unfamiliar perspective on objects, structures, and people, the principle of laughter can thus be said to constitute a tool for human liberation. Bakhtin's book contains a plethora of thoughts that are highly relevant to the development of a non-normative type of aesthetics and challenge the opposition of "high arts" and "low arts." Elsewhere, Bakhtin (1981) engages with language as a cultural and aesthetic phenomenon and defines "hybridization" as a mixture of two social languages within the limits of a single utterance, an encounter within the arena of an utterance between two different linguistic consciousnesses that are separated from one another by an epoch, by social differentiation, or by some other factor.

The way in which the hybridological approach is to be understood in the present text draws on both of these lines of enquiry. It is based on the assumption that the concept of hybridity can be applied in such a sense to ethnic groups and national cultures, to gender distinctions and generational or spiritual categories of belonging, but also to the vast field of artistic creativity, the enjoyment of artistic products, the emergence of new types of art, and in analyses of media techniques. We can recognize multiple connections between these fields, while the concept of hybridity provides us with a specific focus.

Minority Research and Hybridity

Debating hybridity discloses an elusive paradox – as Pnina Werbner has stressed in her text *The Dialectics of Cultural Hybridity*:

> Hybridity is celebrated as powerfully interruptive and yet theorized as commonplace and pervasive. (. . .) But what if cultural mixings and crossovers become routine in the context of globalising trends? Does that obviate the hybrid's transgressive power? And if not, how is postmodernist theory to make sense, at once, of both sides, both routine hybridity and transgressive power? Even more, what do we mean by cultural hybridity when identity is built in the face of postmodern uncertainties that render even the notion of strangerhood meaningless? (Werbner 1997:1–2)

This paradox is an enduring contentious point for supporters and critics of the hybridity paradigm. Often this argument is discussed somewhat abstractly; often new dichotomies of thought emerge. In the framework of minority research, the paradox may already appear solved once the everyday practices of minorities are described as pioneering global modernity, and so as trendsetters for all human beings and for a reorganization of community. With such a turnaround of perspectives, which also aims at a turnaround of power relations, commonplace routine and transgressive power coincide.

We can offer this turnaround because minority research has collected strong evidence of how a life with several languages and several cultural references is conducted. Let me cite the well-known researcher of Roma and Traveler communities, Judith Okely: "The Roma have always been bricoleurs: they have taken things out of the systems in their environment and changed their meaning according to what suited them. They made some things their own, whereas they rejected other things. . . . And they have, reciprocally, given form to the surrounding dominant cultures" (2006:36).

Minorities, people of the periphery, are true experts in a multiple hybrid life. As far as language is concerned, the special feature of the Sorbs in Germany is not that they speak Sorbian, but that they speak Sorbian and German, in other words, that they are multilingual. The people here have knowledge of both languages and change languages several times daily, sometimes within one conversation. They switch between both languages according to need: depending upon the circle of communication, or topics of discussion, for pragmatic considerations, or just for fun.

Yet, the multiplicity does not concern the language only. Migrants and minority people combine disparate elements in their everyday lives. They use cultural experiences, expressions, knowledge of their own minority background and their own majority background, and other hinterlands, developing a multiple perspective. If we understand culture as a program, as a complex framework of interactive dependencies and sense-generating mechanism (Schmidt 2004), then minorities have double, even multiple programs. They develop several competencies in the process of their life. Our empirical research around the Sorbian minority in Lusatia produces evidence for this repeatedly: people there grow up with the good and bad spirits of two or more cultural references. Although they can tell a number of stories about discrimination coming from the "German side," they have lots of friends there. They know that the familiar and the unfamiliar are not diametrically opposed to one another, because one can appear within the other, familiar and foreign elements merge and become inseparable. They know what it means to be simultaneously an insider and an outsider, different and alike, world and counter-world. The people here are in a position to look at a problem from more than one angle; they know that there is more than one truth. Thus people develop in their concrete living multiple strategies of coming to terms with this life.

Migration research gives comparable observations. "I speak many languages" – this sentence, written in seven languages, opens the impressive volume *Projekt Migration* (2006), which documents the exhibition of the same title. "I am not half and half, but both, double, or something else," Irena tells me, as I speak with her during my field research on women with immigrant backgrounds in Bautzen during April to October 2010. Irena left Russia for Germany at the age of 43, had to be retrained, stayed out of work for a long time, changed from Rostock to Bautzen, now she tries to be self-employed in the service sector. In a conversation with her I get to know how she thinks, who she is, after each conversation with her mother in Russia or with her two daughters, who went to study far away from Bautzen. Then there are permanent negotiations with offices, structures, laws. She reports how she is learning something new all the time, then questioning the learned elsewhere, also comparing, being amazed, being silent. "Because, who cares?" Often she is only expected to become like the others here – she says.

In other words, migration as lived experience stands for change by fusion, change by co-joining, which results in something new. Something, that is neither here nor there. Something, that transcends the binary opposition of here and there, of us and the others, ours and theirs. A life of migration creates a "third space." There is no firm ground in this third space, there are no stops and there is no endpoint. It is a permanently fluid relationship of negotiation. The life of the migrant has, at its core, the following process: to be different while remaining part of the whole, to be different yet similar at the same time.

I want to say it quite explicitly: studies of minorities – whether they are "old" minorities like the Sorbs and the Roma or "new" minorities with a migration background – are significant vanguards in overcoming the dualistic mode of thought and in the development of a hybridological perspective.

Practical and Political Implications

Today basically three notions exist, or three ways of seeing cultural diversity: cultural differentialism, cultural convergence, and sharing diversity. Each of these positions involves particular theoretical precepts and as such they are paradigms. Each paradigm represents a different politics of diversity, a different politics of multiculturalism (Nederveen Pieterse 1996).

Cultural differentialism

Cultural differentialism is the first way of seeing cultural diversity. It is closely connected with the notion of cultural relativism. Cultural differentialism translates into a policy of closure and apartheid. Following the well-known "methodological nationalism" (Beck 1997, 2006) often territorial (spatial) separation is being thought of here.

The differentialism concept is still widely spread in the practice of representation, as we have seen in the example of the discourse on Sorbs and Sorbian culture in German-language press. Reports about migrants from Turkey, Russia, or Vietnam show this imprint, for instance the talk about "parallel societies" or "ghettos." Here these "separate worlds" are produced in discourse and consolidated politically. The differentialist approach showed clearly its political tendency when Huntington proclaimed in an essay a *Clash of Civilisations*: the clash between the West and non-Western civilizations and among non-Western civilizations. Here difference became a concrete address as danger and threat: "While Muslims pose the immediate problem in Europe, Mexicans pose the problem for the United States" (Huntington 1996:206). After 9/11 this mode of thought became especially strong. The separation of "the

Muslim" and "the Christian" world was formulated as a desirable goal. In this context of thinking the "axis of evil" was constructed and localized, new enemy images were produced, from here political and military actions were legitimized and led. This is the extreme case of thinking in counter-worlds.

In local cultural policy differentialism can have different imprints. It attempts to keep cultural communities separated. The idea of multiculturalism, sometimes known as "the human mosaic," belongs to the framework of differentialism as well. Also, those ideas which pretend to strive for the development of the local – in tourism, ecological networks, or museums – but define the local as nostalgic and conservationist, belong here. Media politics with the slogan "Sorbian television for Sorbs" show mosaic-thinking. The imagery of the mosaic is biased in the first place, as Hannerz (1992) points out, because a mosaic consists of discrete pieces whereas human experience, claims and postures notwithstanding, is open ended. The way out of mosaic-thinking – in case the community wants recognition of diversity – would not be "no Sorbian television." One way out would be – to stay with this example – "Sorbian television for all who are interested in it." The regional broadcaster MDR has had that discussion for a long time (Tschernokoshewa 2004).

Cultural convergence

Cultural convergence is the second way of seeing cultural diversity. This second paradigm translates into a politics of assimilation. In theory this second perspective has a long tradition. It continues some ideas of well-known universalism, but it is also present in new imprints, such as the McDonaldization thesis by Ritzer (1993). Often certain cultural developments are reflected in the context of the impact of multinational corporations, to detect then a growing sameness. The problem with this perspective is not only that striking power asymmetries between regions, strata, and human beings are not addressed, but that it legitimizes a new policy of colonization and assimilation.

In integration policy and practice in Germany, this paradigm is dominant to a large extent. The German-Turkish author Şenocak questions this type of politics in an essay collection with the title "Tongue Removal": "Integration of aliens is nearly always defined as assimilation of the alien into the home-grown. But can this adaption be successful, if it happens on the basis of the negation of biographies?" (Şenocak 2001:29). This kind of integration reminds us of that model in gender politics, in which equality of the sexes was understood as a minimalization of differences and women were challenged to "be like men."

We find examples for assimilation politics in museum work, schools, media as well as in the realm of art. In 2000 to 2004, the Museum of European Cultures in Berlin, together with museums from six European countries, prepared an exhibition with the theme "Migration, Work and Identity." During the project, the museums realized that their collections did not have enough material to present the theme adequately. Migrant culture was to a large extent nonexistent in the store of their collections. There were also very few objects relating to their "own" or "traditional" minorities (Neuland-Kitzerow 2005). The policy of integration as assimilation leads to the invisibility of different experiences, sensitivities, and competencies. The dramatic scarcity of teachers from a migration background is a fact in Germany. The curriculum of the schools contains few materials which express different views. To question the situation in the area of theatre, the Institute for Cultural Policy at the University of Hildesheim organized a symposium in June, 2010, because the state of things is alarming – to quote the announcement for the symposium: "Theatre in Germany is rather monocultural in regards to personal! Theatre in Germany is aesthetically and from its contents sparsely intercultural! Theatre in Germany is still one-sidedly fixated on the German educated middle classes in its viewer orientation!" (Kulturwissenschaften & Ästhetische Kommunikation 2010, translation author's own).

Sharing diversity

The hybridological approach is the third way of seeing cultural diversity. This third paradigm translates into polities of sharing diversity, unity of diversity, or society of societies. That means: integration without assimilation, sharing of common space. Here the spectrum is broad. Unity in diversity. These politics are about the presence of different elements or experiences in a dynamic balance within a larger community or structure. It is a new politics of integration without the need to give up identity, while cohabitation is expected to result in new cross-cultural patterns of difference.

These politics are on the one hand about the recognition of differences, on the other hand about claims to equality, equal rights, equal treatment. In other words: a common universe of diversity. The possibility to be different while remaining part of the whole. Here difference is taken seriously, but it is not presented as something absolute. It is treated as something that can be crossed and transcended. This is, in a nutshell, what politics of the hybridity perspective are all about: the simultaneous acknowledgment and transcending of lines of difference. These politics have many names: cosmopolitan vision (Beck 2006), transculturality (Welsch 1999), interculturalism (Khan 2006), or hybridization (Nederveen Pieterse 1996). Also intercultural dialogue, especially if it is not understood as dialogue between individual states, but within states, regions, and institutions.

This policy was tested in 2008, named as the Year of Intercultural Dialogue by the European Commission. In preparation of the year an investigation was made about "National Approaches to Intercultural Dialogue in Europe." While doing this study (ERICarts 2006–2008) we adopted the following definition: "Intercultural dialogue is a process that comprises an open and respectful exchange or interaction between individuals, groups and organizations with different cultural backgrounds or worldviews. Among its aims are: to develop a deeper understanding of diverse perspectives and practices; to increase participation and the freedom and ability to make choices; to foster equality; and to enhance creative processes" (ERICarts 2008).

The question of shared space concerns on the one hand big structures and institutions such as schools, media, museums, on the other hand smaller establishments, associations, and projects. In order to achieve these, enormous changes will be necessary, because many structures try to continue functioning monoculturally, even though this is hardly possible in global modernity. Often examples of "good practice" can be found precisely in smaller projects, at the base level, there, where people of different backgrounds or worldviews come together, develop joint projects, and work on them with a long-term perspective: the lay theatre group "Kultur-Kontakt" at the Frauenzentrum Bautzen, the youth project Pontes in the Germany/Czech Republic/Poland triangle, a Roma exhibition at the Sorbian Museum Bautzen 2009, or when a mixed band with the name "The Moslems" appears at the youth center "Steinhaus" in Bautzen, even though nobody in the band is of Islamic belief.

Conclusion

The hybridological approach in anthropology/cultural studies is a specific way of seeing, observing, and thinking about cultural processes. Sure, there is no pure culture. This has to be stated very explicitly, because misunderstandings often emerge. This means not that cultures are pure, but that there are models of thinking and colloquialisms – in the media, at the regular's table, sometimes also in scholarly texts – looking for purity and continuing the dream of purity. There are political aspirations of trying to postulate homogeneity, to draw firm borders, mostly to pursue power interests. And there are structures, for which different experiences, sensitivities, and competencies are hard to permit. Integration, not as uniformity of style but as equality of opportunities, is something which does not happen on its own. Here I see the responsibility, but also the creative potentials of our research.

Here is one description how a "shared space" can emerge: reflecting on the example of a museum in North London Naseem Khan writes

> For these artists, tradition has been the tap root, even though their later relationship with it raised questions. They have a very particular way of working, using their own hinterland to refract on their immediate circumstances, and in that way they create a language. Transition is the catalyst and the outcome is a form that allows both past and present to have a voice. The layering is rich; its resonances travel beyond the limitations of ethnic frontiers. In this exercise, neither side loses identity, but brings something special and distinctive to the mix. And in that way, they can transcend as well as honour ethnicity, and bring a new cultural language to the overall mix. (Khan 2006:54–55)

The hybridological approach aims not only at the political and practical responsibility of our research, but it makes anthropology more challenging as well.

ACKNOWLEDGMENT

A special thanks to Volker Gransow and Hristio Boytchev for help in preparing this text for publication.

REFERENCES

Bakhtin, Mikhail

1981 Discourse in the Novel. *In* The Dialogic Imagination: Four Essays, Michael Holquist, ed. pp. 259–422. Austin: University of Texas Press.

1984 Rabelais and His World. Bloomington: Indiana University Press.

Bausinger, Hermann, Utz Jeggle, Gottfried Korff, Martin Scharfe
1989 Grundzüge der Volkskunde Darmstadt: Wissenschaftliche Buchgesellschaft.
Beck, Ulrich
1997 Was ist Globalisierung? Irrtümer des Globalismus – Antworten auf Globalisierung. Frankfurt am Main: Suhrkamp.
2006 The Cosmopolitan Vision. Cambridge: Polity.
Bhabha, Homi K.
1994 The Location of Culture. London: Routledge.
Braun, Christina von
1996 Zum Begriff der Reinheit. Metis 6(11):6–25.
Brubaker, Rogers
2004 Ethnicity without groups. Harvard: Harvard University Press.
Diez, Georg
2008 Der Messias von Zamenhof. Die Zeit 18 (April 24). Electronic document. http://www.zeit.de/2008/18/L-Chabon (accessed November 5, 2011).
ERICarts
2008 Sharing Diversity: National Approaches to Intercultural Dialogue in Europe. Electronic document. http://www.interculturaldialogue.eu (accessed November 5, 2011).
Fritsch, Theodor
1887 Antisemiten-Katechismus. Leipzig: Herrmann Beyer.
Geertz, Clifford
2000 Available Light. Anthropological Reflection on Philosophical Topics. Princeton: University Press.
Greverus, Ina-Maria
2002 Anthropologisch Reisen. Münster: LIT.
Habermas, Jürgen
1997 Die Einbeziehung des Anderen: Studien zur politischen Theorie. Frankfurt am Main: Suhrkamp.
Hall, Stuart
1991 Old and New Identities, Old and New Ethnicities. *In* Culture, Globalization and the World-System: Contemporary Conditions for the Representation of Identity. Anthony D. King, ed. pp. 41–68. Basingstoke: Palgrave Macmillan.
1997 New Ethnicities. *In* The Post-Colonial Studies Reader. Bill Ashcroft, Gareth Griffiths, and Helen Tiffin, eds. pp. 223–227. London: Routledge.
Hannerz, Ulf
1992 Cultural Complexity. New York: Columbia University Press.
Huntington, Samuel P.
1996 The Clash of Civilizations and the Remaking of World Order. New York: Simon & Schuster.
Jahn, Friedrich Ludwig
1813 Deutsches Volkstum. Lübeck: Niemann und Comp.
Khan, Neseem
2006 The Road to Interculturalism: Tracking the Arts in a Changing World. Stround: Comedia.
Kramer, Dieter
1996 Dürfen Ethnien sein? Zur Diskussion um das Recht auf Anderssein. Info-Blatt der Gesellschaft für Ethnographie 11/12:54–65.
Kulturwissenschaften & Ästhetische Kommunikation
2010 Symposium: Theater und Migration. Electronic document. http://kulturpraxis.wordpress.com/2010/06/20/symposium-theater-und-migration/ (accessed November 5, 2011).

Luhmann, Niklas
1997 Die Gesellschaft der Gesellschaft. Frankfurt am Main: Suhrkamp.
Nassehi, Armin
1999 Differenzfolgen: Beiträge zur Soziologie der Moderne. Opladen: Verlag für Sozialwissenschaft.
Nederveen Pieterse, Jan
1996 Globalization and Culture: Three Paradigms. Economic and Politica Weekly, June 8:1389–1393.
Neuland-Kitzerow, Dagmar
2005 "Ich lebe zwei Heimaten." Eine Projektskizze zum europäischen Ausstellungsprojekt "migration, work, identity." *In* Auf der Suche nach hybriden Lebensgeschichten. Elka Tschernokoshewa and Marija Jurić-Pahor, eds. pp. 281–289. Münster, Berlin: Waxmann.
Nghi Ha, Kien
2005 Hype und Hybridität. Bielefeld: transcript.
Okely, Judith
2006 Kontinuität und Wandel in den Lebensverhältnissen und der Kultur der Roma, Sinti und Kále. Berliner Blätter 39:25–41.
Projekt Migration
2006 Kölnischer Kunstverein. Cologne: DuMont. Electronic document. http://www.signandsight.com/features/424.html (accessed November 5, 2011).
Räthzel, Nora
1997 Gegenbilder: Nationale Identität durch Konstruktion des Anderen. Wiesbaden: Opladen.
Ritzer, George
1993 The McDonaldisation of Society. London: Pine Forge/Sage.
Schiffauer, Werner
1996 Die Angst von der Differenz: Zu neuen Störungen in der Kulturanthropologie. Zeitschrift für Volkskunde 1(92):20–31.
Schmidt, Siegfried J.
2004 Kultur als Programm: jenseits der Dichotomie von Realismus und Konstruktivismus. *In* Handbuch der Kulturwissenschaften, vol. 2. Friedrich Jaeger and Jürgen Straub, eds. pp. 85–100. Stuttgart: Metzler.
2007 Histories and Discourses: Rewriting Constructivism. Exeter: Imprint Academie.
Schmitt, Carl
1923 Die geistesgeschichtliche Lage des heutigen Parlamentarismus. Berlin: Duncker & Humblot.
Şenocak, Zafer
2001 Zungenentfernung: Essays. Munich: Babel.
Tschernokoshewa, Elka
2000 Das Reine und das Vermischte: Die deutschsprachige Presse über Andere und Anderssein am Beispiel der Sorben. Münster, Berlin: Waxmann.
2004 Constructing Pure and Hybrid Worlds: German Media and "Otherness." *In* Communicating Cultures. Ullrich Kockel and Máiréad Nic Craith, eds. pp. 222–242. Münster: LIT.
2008 The Hybridity of Minorities: A Case-Study of Sorb Cultural Research. *In* Everyday Culture in Europe. Máiréad Nic Craith, Ullrich Kockel, and Reinhard Johler, eds. pp. 133–147. Aldershot: Ashgate.
Tschernokoshewa, Elka, Johannes Huxoll, Ute Allkämper, Susanne Schatral, Britta Höhne-Porsch, Anna Hoppe, and Jens Töpert
2005 Empirische Forschung: Hybride Lebensgeschichten im Umfeld der sorbischen Minderheit in Deutschland. *In* Auf der Sucher nach hybriden Lebensgeschichten. Elka Tschernokoshewa and Marija Jurić-Pahor, eds. pp. 113–233. Münster, Berlin: Waxmann.

Welsch, Wolfgang

1999 Transculturality: The Puzzling Form of Cultures Today. *In* Spaces of Culture: City, Nation, World. Mike Featherstone and Scott Lash, eds. pp. 194–213. London: Sage.

Werbner, Pnina

1997 Introduction: The Dialectics of Cultural Hybridity. *In* Debating Cultural Hybridity: Multi-Cultural Identities and the Politics of Anti-Racism. Pnina Werbner and Tariq Modood, eds. pp. 1–26. London: Zed Books.

Wippermann, Wolfgang

1996 Sind die Sorben in der NS-Zeit aus "rassischen" Gründen verfolgt worden? Lětopis 43(1):32–38.

CHAPTER 31

An Anthropological Perspective on Literary Arts in Ireland

Helena Wulff

"Can writing be taught?" is the provocative issue hovering around creative writing programs at universities and non-academic workshops. Yet many leading writers have graduated from creative writing programs, and many continue to teach this topic. This type of issue now also concerns anthropology. For a few decades now, anthropologists have been more reflexive in relation to their writing than before, and more interested in the craft of writing.

Originating in the United States almost a century ago, master and doctoral degrees in creative writing increased as a part of the postwar expansion of higher education (McGurl 2009). The most known MFA (Master's in Fine Arts, including writing among other arts) at the Iowa Writers' Workshop, was started in 1936, and with time fostered a number of successful fiction writers, not only American but also European writers, such as Irish man John Banville, who went back to their own countries. It would take quite some time before creative writing courses were set up at European universities. Britain's first program was at the University of East Anglia in 1970. Another Irish writer, Anne Enright, is a graduate of this program. In Ireland, the teaching of writing in workshops goes back to the annual Listowel Writers' Week in the early 1970s, which was followed by numerous other non-academic workshops. It was not until the late 1990s that creative writing was offered at universities in Ireland. Like in the rest of Europe, creative writing is now widespread in Ireland with degree programs at all major universities. Creative writing tends to grow out of English departments which supports the notion that "the discipline is on the way to becoming a globally Anglophone phenomenon" (McGurl 2009:364). In Europe, however, there are now creative writing courses and workshops in other languages as well, such as in Swedish in Sweden, in German in Germany, and in French in France.

John Banville and Anne Enright are among the writers figuring in my anthropological study of the social organization of the world of contemporary fiction writers

A Companion to the Anthropology of Europe, First Edition. Edited by Ullrich Kockel, Máiréad Nic Craith, and Jonas Frykman.

in Ireland and their English-language writings: novels, short stories, plays, poetry (Wulff 2008). Methodologically, I conduct the study through participant observation at writers' festivals and retreats, literary conferences, book launches, prize ceremonies, readings, and creative writing workshops (taught by the writers in the study). I also spend time with writers informally and collect additional data from in-depth interviews with writers, as well as publishers, editors, and agents, in order to find out how works are selected to be published. Texts by the writers, as well as newspaper features and reviews about their work, are also central for this study.

These writers work to a great extent in relation to the rest of Europe, especially to Britain (where they often publish), negotiating Ireland's postcolonial situation and their own sense of living on the edge of Europe. Contemporary writers build on the rich literary tradition in Ireland, which has been identified as a factor contributing to Ireland's movement toward political independence. In this chapter, I will explore creative writing as practice and product among contemporary Irish writers in a European context. This leads over to an engagement with the question of the legitimacy of literature as a resource for anthropology. When Irish writers comment on Ireland in their writings, these texts can be used as ethnographic fiction by an anthropologist, as one way to collect data. Ethnographic fiction is fiction built around real social, political, and historical events and circumstances (Fogarty 2003; Wulff 2009). Writers of ethnographic fiction prepare their fiction writing through research, even fieldwork-like observations, interviews, and archival work.

The first thing to note about Irish literature in a European context is that it keeps being mixed up with English literature, or rather included in it, as if it did not have any distinct characteristics such as a sense of rhythm or certain recurring topics. In line with this, Irish writers from Oscar Wilde to John Banville are taken to be English, and in book shops and libraries outside Ireland their work is more often than not to be found on shelves for English literature. One postcolonial comment in Dublin's literary world about this tendency is that the former colonizer appropriates Irish writers taking the credit for their success, rather than allowing the Irish their independence, and to shine in their own right. This brings to mind Samuel Beckett's much-quoted reply to the question (in French as he was living in exile in Paris): "Monsieur, est-ce que vous êtes Anglais?" To which Beckett is reputed to have retorted: "Au contraire!"

Creativity, Craftsmanship, Collaboration

With its creative vein, Ireland has long been famous for storytelling, literature, music, and dance (Wulff 2007; Cashman 2009). Strong creativity is often analyzed in social theory as a result of resistance against political suppression. The fact that Ireland was colonized for 400 years seems to fit in here, but there are instances of storytelling and literary accounts before that. Contemporary creative writing in Ireland can roughly be divided into Irish and non-Irish topics. The latter can be located in New York, Scandinavia, Spain, and Greece among many other places and feature topics such as politics, religion, art, relationships emerging from these places. Irish topics tend to relate to the history in Ireland, the conflict and post-conflict in Northern

Ireland, the postcolonial situation, and to the role of the European Union in Ireland, the economic boom in the late twentieth century, the so-called Celtic Tiger, and to the downturn thereafter. Connected to these social observations are emigration and exile, other classic Irish topics as illustrated by Colm Tóibín in *Brooklyn: A Novel* (2009), set in a small town in 1950s Ireland. The novel traces the trajectory of a young woman, Eilis, who has to emigrate. She goes to Brooklyn in search of a job which she gets in a department store. She falls in love with an Italian man, but is suddenly called home to Ireland when her sister dies. In the end, Eilis decides to go back to Brooklyn and make her life there. The painful pivot of the novel is the legacy of leave-taking in Ireland. But Ireland is not only an emigration country; now it is also an immigration country. The new immigration to Ireland is beginning to appear in literary accounts such as Roddy Doyle's collection *The Deportees and Other Stories* (2007). In the "Foreword," Doyle (2007:xi) describes how the new Ireland came about quite suddenly as he "went to bed in one country and woke up in a different one": "It was about jobs and the E.U., and infrastructure and wise decisions, and accident. It was about education and energy, and words like 'tax' and 'incentive,' and about what happens when they are put beside each other. It was also about music and dancing and literature and football. It happened, I think, some time in the mid-90s" (Doyle 2007:xi).

Following up on the opening question of this chapter ("Can writing be taught?"), I asked John Banville this question in an interview in February 2010 in Dublin, and his was a succinct response: "You can be taught what *not* to do. But not what is needed – dedication, ruthlessness, love of language, insight of tips you don't really think about."

If dedication, ruthlessness, and love of language can be said to be included in an innate personality repertory, writers (including Banville) and other artists know that those qualities have to be nurtured in order to blossom. In art and performance worlds, even in sports, there is an indigenous dichotomy between on the one hand "a natural talent" or "a good body" and "the right mentality" or "determination" on the other. In the highly competitive ballet world, for example, both types of qualities are needed in order to succeed: it does not suffice with "a good body," "the right mentality" meaning determination has to be there as well. It does happen, however, that dancers who do not possess the right physicality for ballet, through regimented training and diet schemes, to the astonishment of ballet directors and coaches, manage to position themselves among the leading dancers, if not at the very apex (Wulff 1998:104). Considering the significance of having a body of specific proportions for athletes and pianists, ethnomusicologist John Blacking (1977:23) observed that "a mysterious quality such as determination or will may help a less adequate body to perform better than expected."

So if determination and willpower seem to connect artistic and athletic work, writing and dancing, there is yet another part of the work process in the ballet world that can shed light on the making of creative writing. Ballet and dance are evaluated by ballet people, ranging from dancers and choreographers to critics and audience, by way of two criteria: technique and artistry. A rehearsal process in ballet takes place in a studio with mirrored walls. The mirrors are there to assist the dancers in what the steps they are learning look like when they are doing them. The dancers learn what it feels like when a step is executed correctly, they can then check in the mirror how their bodies look. This is how they learn the technique of a certain ballet. But when the time of performance is getting close, a curtain is drawn in front of the mirror concealing it. Now the dancers are supposed to forget what they look like, the technique, and start expressing themselves through their steps. This is when new artistry happens, especially later on stage, not at every performance, rarely throughout a full-length three-hour performance, but in the form of occasional zones of sudden artistry (Wulff 1998:8). An experience of art cannot happen if the artist or the audience, let alone critics, are aware of the technique, busy deconstructing how a ballet (or a book) is put together.

It seems likely that creative writing programs and workshops can provide the technique of writing from practical matter-of-fact tips such as to start writing in the morning without checking emails to acquiring an editorial eye for style and structure, the craftsmanship of writing – but not necessarily the artistry. Leaving the issue of taste aside at the moment, there are "natural writers," while others can train to become relatively good writers. Mastering the technique of creative writing does not, however, automatically release original textual artistry. This is why the issue of whether creative writing can be taught remains. And it raises the question of what exactly creativity is. In *Creativity and Cultural Improvization* (2007), Hallam and Ingold discuss how to define creativity. Going back to early twentieth-century philosophical thought, they suggest that creativity can be seen "on one hand as the production of novelty through the recombination of already extant elements, or on the other, as process of growth, becoming and change" (Hallam and Ingold 2007:16). For such "recombination of extant elements" to be put together in a creative way in writing, which possibly includes adding one or two new elements, the craftsmanship, the technique, has to be honed – and the elements carefully chosen in order to fit a certain time and context.

Creativity has often been connected with individual talent, skill, and even "genius." Writing fiction professionally requires long working hours on one's own. This is the private side of a writer's career. It is intertwined with the public side which importantly is organized around the literary texts, novels, collections of short stories or poems, and plays. First, this is where marketing occurs which consists of readings that writers do of their own work, media interviews and panel discussions they take part in, prize ceremonies, and book launches. Second, the public side of a writer's career is the social life among writers which unfolds at events at writers' organizations such as the Irish Pen (especially its annual dinner and prize ceremony in Dublin) and Aosdána, the Irish Arts Academy, as well as at small informal gatherings at restaurants, bars, and in homes. These small gatherings of writer friends are typically formed on the whole according to level of fame: writers with an international reputation move in one circle, writers with a national reputation and some international experience of publishing and/or lecturing in another circle, and aspiring, often young, writers with a degree in creative writing and one book tend to stick together in a third circle of friends. Unsurprisingly, there are power struggles and competition: writers review each other in newspapers and magazines, which can produce enmities. When Anne Enright rather unexpectedly, but certainly well deservedly, won the Man Booker prize in 2007 for her novel *The Gathering* (2007), this was at first met with much pride among her writer friends and colleagues in Dublin. After all, this is the most prestigious literary prize a citizen of the Commonwealth or the Republic of Ireland can get (except for the Nobel Prize in literature which is not limited to certain citizenships). Awarded at a black tie ceremony at the Guildhall in London in front of live television, the Man Booker prize comes with £50 000 and worldwide marketing of the book. Like at the Oscars ceremony, and many literary award ceremonies, the short-listed writers are present, but they do not know who will win the prize until the very moment it is announced. This is causing much anxiety among the writers in Ireland who are short-listed now and then, and occasionally win the Man Booker. John Banville's *The Sea* (2005), which details the development of a new widower's grief, was shortlisted in 2005, but as Banville described it for me: "I tried to avoid the four hours Booker dinner, it's pure hell. But my publisher said I had to be there." He continued looking back: "When I had finished The Sea, and sent it off to the publisher, I thought this is not going to be accepted, they are going to say 'we wait for your next book' – and then it was short-listed!" Banville's Man Booker prize was a major success for the Dublin literary world, more so than when Anne Enright won the prize. Just a few days after this news had hit Dublin, in October 2007, critical voices denounced the fact that Enright had won the prize on the grounds that she had written an article in *London Review of Books* where she took the McCann parents, whose daughter Madeleine had disappeared on a family holiday in Portugal, to task for being bad parents. It is unclear how the ensuing media campaign against Enright broke out, but it is not entirely unlikely that it was initiated by an envious colleague. Ireland's strong focus on family may have mattered too. The campaign faded out after Enright had apologized to the McCann's. But while it was going on, literary Dublin was divided: Enright's friends and admirers supported her, wrote cards, and called her, while her competitors were aggressively against her, behind her back.

Like all artists, literary writers collaborate. They do not co-author texts, but they collaborate in other ways: they comment on each other's drafts, or support each other by offering compliments for a book, a review, or a television appearance. They sympathize when a writer friend has had a bad reception of a book. They are invited to do readings together, which usually are occasions for a great sense of community (Wulff 2008). And they advise each other about how to get published. Those who are close friends convey contacts with agents, editors, and publishers. There is a group of writers in Dublin, born in the mid-1950s, who have been friends since they went to university: Anne Enright, Colm Tóibín, Dermot Bolger, and Roddy Doyle are some of them, as well as leading cultural critics and publishers. Éilís Ní Dhuibhne, is connected to this group and she has written a satire of Dublin's literary world, the novel *Fox, Swallow, Scarecrow* (2007). The novel circles around Anna, an aspiring, but amateur, middle-class popular fiction writer, and reveals exploitation and emotion among writers and publishers against a backdrop of a greedy Celtic Tiger economy.

Another literary case of a Dublin writer, a playwright, is the protagonist in the novel *Molly Fox's Birthday* (2008) by Deirdre Madden. As the *New York Times* review with the headline "Method Writing", says:

> Here's an exercise for the blocked writer: Write what you don't know about what you know. That's the approach the unnamed narrator of Deirdre Madden's ninth novel

> chooses. She takes her friend of 20 years and revisits memories from their times together, wondering whether she truly knows her. And in doing so, she conquers her writer's block and creates this novel, "Molly Fox's Birthday." (Vanasco 2010)

The playwright has created roles for her friend, Molly, for many years. The novel poses questions about writing and acting in relation to family, friendship, and love over time. Also Colm Toíbín's *The Master* (2004), a biographical fiction about the American writer Henry James, deals with a decline in a writing career and the ensuing upswing. In the novel, Henry James lives in London where his play *Guy Domville* premieres. But the reception is disappointing, the reviews are bad. James escapes to Ireland "since it was easy to travel there and because he did not believe it would strain his nerves" (Tóibín 2004:22). His friends in Dublin have not seen his play, and eventually he is able to put the failure behind him. Like James, Tóibín is a prolific writer. He writes in different genres from fiction to literary essays on art and politics and travel journalism for newspapers and magazines in Ireland, Britain, and the United States such as the *Irish Times*, the *New Yorker*, and the *London Review of Books*. Tóibín has a house in Dublin but spends a few months in Spain and the United States every year. This is partly an extension of the international side of Dublin's literary world as he meets Irish writers and friends abroad, as well as others, as he says: "Some writers are in France, the United States, all you want is three writers who share the same jokes."

The analytical point here, about Banville, Tóibín, Enright, Ní Dhuibhne, and Madden among others, is that a writer's creativity does not spring up in isolation. This illustrates Howard Becker's (1984) influential insight that all artists, writers included, are part of art worlds where not only the artists but a variety of people contribute to the production of the art work. In Dublin's literary world, other writers, agents, publishers, and critics, as well as readers, are among these people who can be said to contribute to how creative writing is composed.

Another aspect of Dublin's literary world is the life and work of Colum McCann who was born in Dublin, but moved to New York as a young adult. He frequently goes back to Ireland for readings and other events at literary festivals. McCann's acclaimed novel *Let the Great World Spin* (2009) opens and closes in Dublin, but spends most of the time in New York. The point of departure in this ethnographic fiction is a real event: in New York on August 7, 1974, Philippe Petit walked on a tightrope between the twin towers of the World Trade Center. This event is the focal point of fictional stories in the novel about people from different positions in the social structure of New York whose lives connect through the tightrope event, some just fleetingly by standing in the same crowd in the street 110 floors below, others developing close relationships. The novel moves from Corrigan, an Irish monk, who works with prostitutes such as formidable Tillie, in the Bronx, to Claire, an Upper West Side housewife who has lost her son in Vietnam, and Fernando, a teenage photographer, looking for underground graffiti. According to McCann in an interview, this novel is about 9/11. The tightrope walker is the connector to the Twin Towers that do not exist anymore, the Iraq war becomes the Vietnam War. "Set against a time of sweeping political and social change" it says on the back cover, this is "a time that hauntingly mirrors the present." Like many ethnographic fiction novels, *Let the Great World Spin* has acknowledgments, which supports the argument that writers work in a community of many people who contribute to the texts in different ways. As McCann says:

> This particular story owes enormous thanks to many – the police officers who drove me around the city; the doctors who patiently answered my questions; the computer technicians who guided me through the labyrinth; and all of those who helped me during the writing and editing process. The fact of the matter is that there are many hands tapping the writer's keyboard. (McCann 2009:351)

Teaching Creative Writing

It goes without saying that writers who teach creative writing would not question whether it is possible to teach writing or not, even though they sometimes have to confront the issue especially when some students are not doing all that well, while other students admittedly reveal a natural flair for writing. Many Irish writers teach creative writing, both in Ireland and abroad, mainly in the United States. They are invited to residencies at universities, and workshops at conferences. Some writers have university positions as fellows or lecturers, even professors in creative writing. A standard university syllabus would cover literary genres such as the novel, short stories, drama, and poetry. At non-academic workshops, the Listowel Writers' Week, for instance, this list of genres would be expanded to popular fiction, screenplay, songwriting, crime writing, storytelling, freelance journalism, memories into memoir, and writing funny.

There is moreover a Writers-in-School Scheme, funded by the Arts Council of Ireland and the Department of Education and Science. Writers who have published at least one book can apply to the scheme, organized by Poetry Ireland, a national organization which arranges festivals, readings, and writing competitions, and publishes literary journals. The scheme started in 1977, and engages more than 250 writers and storytellers. There are two types of visits: one is a visit for about 3 hours, the other type is a residency lasting for 8–10 weeks when the writer returns once a week to the same class of about 20 pupils. The scheme includes all literary genres from short stories and novels to poems, drama, even storytelling by professional storytellers, as this oral tradition impacts on written literary genres in Ireland.

In Dublin, there is also a relatively recent creative writing center, Fighting Words, which was set up by Roddy Doyle in 2009 in collaboration with schools. Supported by his success as a writer (a number of his novels have been made into acclaimed films, one of them *The Commitments*), with his working-class background, and driven by his strong sense of making the skill of writing widely available, Doyle's idea is to provide tutoring in creative writing for free. There are storytelling fieldtrips for primary school pupils, creative writing workshops for secondary students, and workshops for adults. The emphasis is on "character development, dialogue, plot, and on the importance of editing – editing as a form of, and help to, creativity" (http://www.fightingwords.ie/secondary). Professional writers teach there, as do secondary school teachers (some retired), journalists, and students as volunteers.

Generally, teaching creative writing is a way to make a living as a writer, but it is not unimportant for marketing writers' books. Students are an interested, captive audience that has to read books, discuss them, and write about them in their papers in order to pass an exam. And they might well return later to these books, or other ones by the writer that taught them. Graduates of creative writing programs are educated for the literary world. Not everyone ends up as writer but many can be found in literary journalism or publishing. For a writer, teaching is moreover an opportunity for inspiration in his or her writing, as lecturing and comments from students can bring out new ideas. And a university milieu can trigger new topics to write about. It is quite common that contemporary Irish fiction includes university people outside the university, less common that an entire novel is devoted to a university class, especially on creative writing at Trinity College Dublin! This is the case in *All Names Have Been Changed* (2009) by Claire Kilroy, who was a student of creative writing at that very university. In a lukewarm review in the *Guardian* (2009), Greenland writes:

> Michaelmas Term, 1985. Dublin languishes in a fug of tobacco and poverty. Chucking in his factory job in Leeds and sneaking back without telling his ma, Declan joins the Trinity College creative writing class run, in theory, by his idol, the appalling genius Patrick Glynn. There are eight of them, "a shower of messers" all in awe of the great Glynn, all vying for his erratic approval. Declan, narrating, tells us how their year wears on. Much Guinness is drunk, much whiskey. Souls are bared, hearts are broken. Novels are begun, savaged, abandoned. The weakest fall by the way. (Greenland 2009)

This is a satire not only of creative writing at universities, but of academia in general, as well as of writing as a profession. Contrary to many Irish novels and short stories, this novel does not make use of humor. Otherwise, even dark drama in Ireland, of which there is plenty, tends to be lighten up by wit and warmth. Creative wit is highly valued in Ireland, according to Éilís Ní Dhuibhne, especially among men. With a PhD in Irish folklore, Éilís Ní Dhuibhne is sometimes invited to contribute to academic volumes. This is why she was encouraged to write an article "The Irish" (1999). In this article, Ní Dhuibhne holds up loquacity as a general trait among people in Ireland, which is reflected in the strong storytelling tradition. But there is a "a moroseness which lurks not far beneath the skin of many Irishmen" Ní Dhuibhne (1999:54) says, and this is mellowed through funny conversation, and writings could be added, as wit is included in fiction, novels, and short stories, even those that deal with hardships. Ní Dhuibhne exemplifies with Irish plays "the literary form which is most closely modeled on conversation" (Ní Dhuibhne 1999:54). Irish plays are usually tragicomedies, not either comedies or tragedies, they are one expression of how a "fusion of creative wit and dark drama forms a vital vein running through Irish culture" (Wulff 2007:72). This is confirmed by Banville when he in an interview identifies "an Irish tone of voice" in fiction and drama as "grim comedy."

One instance of the numerous creative writing groups in Dublin was referred to as the "Writers Group," and run by Éilís Ní Dhuibhne in the winter of 2006.The group, which met once a month to discuss each other's essays and poems, had started as a part of the creative writing course Ní Dhuibhne taught at Trinity College Dublin when she was Writer Fellow there for a year. At the meetings of the Writers' Group, nine people, six men and three women, most of them in their 40s and 50s, a couple in their 20s, took turns commenting on each other's writings, which they had read in advance. The last to comment was Ní Dhuibhne, which she did in an encouraging tone yet with suggestions for improvement. Like in most creative writing workshops, this one was attended by some writers with publications, but the majority of the participants had not yet found their outlet. One of the students in this group was Kevin McDermott, who used to be a secondary school teacher. McDermott now works with Navan Educational Centre, a governmental secondary level support service, and organizes courses for English teachers called "The Teacher as Writer" where one emphasis is on oracity, on storytelling, as "this is still a very oral culture, people make jokes, people tell stories." According to an interview I did with McDermott, "the best writers have an ability to recreate the way people speak." Referring to the fact that English teachers come to their profession out of a "love of literature," he went on to say that: "We try to encourage teachers to think of writing in a conversational way, a craft to be learnt, not as something magical." This points, again, to the importance of learning and developing writing as a craftsmanship.

Anthropology and Creative Writing: Blurred Genres

A concern with forms of writing has been a theme of debate in anthropology since Clifford Geertz, in his influential book *The Interpretation of Cultures* (1973:19), famously asked (in the idiom of the time): "What does the ethnographer do? – he writes." Geertz (1988) later considered the anthropologist as author (such as Malinowski, Benedict, Evans-Pritchard, and Lévi-Strauss), and in the late twentieth century a substantial "writing culture" debate was stimulated by the volume edited by Clifford and Marcus (1986, see also Marcus and Fischer 1986). In Britain, more than elsewhere in European anthropology, the writing culture approach was regarded with certain reservations such as by Dawson, Hockey, and James (1997), while the recent volumes by Waterston and Vesperi (2009), Barton and Papen (2010) and Zenker and Kumoll (2010) confirm the enduring impact of this approach, more than 20 years after it was introduced. As Ulf Hannerz points out in his *Anthropology's World* (2010:13): "No wonder that the complexities of writing – the purposes, the risks, the successes, the failures, the sheer styles and techniques – can become a preoccupation once we start thinking about them."

In the early 1990s, Eduardo Archetti (1994:13) formulated an anthropology of the written by arguing that "a literary product is not only a substantive part of the real world but also a key element in the configuration of the world itself." Analyzing the role of fiction in anthropological understanding, Archetti identifies three different types of fiction: "the realistic historical novel that attempts to 'reconstruct' a given period in a given society; the totally imagined story set in a historical period; and the essays devoted to an interpretation of a nation, its characteristics and creed" (Archetti 1994:16). It is easy to agree with Archetti (1994:16, 17) when he states that "some kind of historical and sociological knowledge is important in fiction," which is a point where the act of writing fiction comes close to that of writing anthropology. According to Archetti, it is likely that a novelist is unaware that he or she employs cultural topics. Such fiction, he continues, is "ethnographic raw material, not as authoritative statements about, or interpretations of, a particular society."

An anthropological interest in creative writing brings together not only anthropology of writing, and text (Barber 2007), as well as cultural literacy (Street 1997), but also important inspiration from literature which has been an area in anthropology for a long time. In the 1970s, Victor Turner (1976:77–78) argued that African ritual and Western literature could be "mutually elucidating." Handler and Segal (1990) thought of Jane Austen as an ethnographer of marriage and kinship in her time and class in England, which revealed different social realities within this culture. In Nigel Rapport's (1994) fieldwork in Wanet, a village in England, the writer E. M. Forster was a significant fellow ethnographer, as Rapport compared Forster's literary writings with his own research about the village.

The volume *True Fiction* (1990a), which was edited by the Dutch anthropologist Peter Kloos, discusses similarities and differences between literary fiction and anthropology. "Is anthropology a science or is it an art?" is Kloos's rhetorical question in the introduction. His view is that "it is both": "After all, any science is a combination of creative imagination, primarily associated with the artist, and methodological rigour, usually believed to be the trademark of the scientist" (Kloos 1990b:1) Categorizing the texts of science and art in two main genres, with literary texts as "the novel, the short story, the poem, the essay," Kloos (1990b:1, 2) characterizes anthropology in terms of "monographic account or ethnography, the theoretical treatise, the specialized article, the introductory text, and again the essay." He suggests that the novel and the ethnographic account are not easily separated into different genres, as "boundaries between the two are ambiguous." In fact, he continues, from an artistic perspective ethnographies would tend to be boring, while from a scientific perspective, novels are seen as uncertain concerning reliability. Novels do not report on the research process. But as Kloos says, it is not only novels that lack "independent replications." Ethnographic accounts do, too. Juxtaposing artistic and scientific representations of reality, Kloos observes three results: first, both representations display the same piece of information; second, they differ as the scientist regard the artistic representation as incorrect; and third, the artistic account reveals data that the scientist has failed to notice. Kloos maintains that "novelists have something to offer that is often sadly absent in scholarly work: a sensitivity to important currents and values in actual life . . . why is it that scholars often fail to notice these things?" (Kloos 1990b:5). By contrast, Kloos sees how the scientist offers "systematic and explicit description . . . and explanation . . . general statements that explain what can be observed: theories, if you like." Finding it intriguing, Kloos yet finishes by saying that "an artistic description often rests on what is not said at all!" (Kloos, 1990b:5). In the article "Ethnography and Fiction: Where Is the Border?" (1999), Kirin Narayan argues that the border between ethnography and fiction often is fuzzy, yet that there are important distinctions between the two genres such as ethnography's disclosure of process, generalization, representations of subjectivity, and accountability.

Inspired by ethnography, anthropologists write pure fiction. Paul Stoller's *Jaguar: A Story of Africans in America* (1999) is one among many anthropological novels drawing on the author's research. Some anthropologists prefer writing detective stories based on ethnographic experiences (White 2007). Ruth Behar makes the persuasive case for the importance of literature in anthropology in her article "Believing in Anthropology as Literature" (2009). This is creative writing authored by anthropologists. A sister genre to creative writing, which has had a recent upsurge among anthropologists (primarily in the United States), is creative non-fiction (Cheney 2001). Going back to the New Journalism in the late 1960s, creative non-fiction is a literary movement which reports on facts in a fictionalized style. Narayan (2007) urges that "attention to the craft of creative nonfiction is potentially useful to ethnography. I present a few practical tools that may help ethnographers seeking to shape the materials of fieldwork: story, situation, persona, character, scene, and summary" (Narayan 2007:130). To Narayan's advice can be added that while writing anthropology it is useful to think of the text as taking place on stage: just like in the theatre, how a text is perceived depends on entrance and exit – they should be carefully crafted. And in order to keep the reader's interest throughout the text: suspense and surprise are needed. There is no doubt that a literary style is useful, even crucial, for conveying anthropology, even when it is not about writers or writing, but for any type and topic in the discipline. Complex analytical discussions do not benefit from being inaccessible, to argue that is nothing but academic hype. Complex analysis including the interplay of theory and ethnography can, and should, be expressed in an accessible way. This does not equal popular scholarship which is yet another genre. To write accessible academic texts requires training, however, and this should be provided to students and young scholars, which is not always the case today. Just like creative writing can indeed be taught to a certain extent, so can lucid academic writing.

Moving toward the end of this chapter, it is time to consider the relevance of creative writing in a conceptual sense for anthropological inquiry. In particular, literature has, again, been included in the anthropological agenda for a long time, but also writing. My anthropological study of writers in Ireland and their literary products referred to in this chapter, is different, however, as the focus is on the people, the writers. Their fiction matters too, as does fiction they recommend. Conversations in the field often consist of the meaning of recent fiction. This is an opportunity for me to check the ethnographic validity of what is in the texts. Such content also triggers new research questions that can be investigated during participant observation and interviews.

In line with a growing trend in anthropology, this study of writers in Ireland is taking place by way of "yo-yo" fieldwork (Wulff 2007) on a number of visits (back and forth from Stockholm) to Ireland funded by a grant. Like many other contemporary field studies, this study demands recurrent visits over more than the traditional uninterrupted year in the field. To be able to cover pivotal points from book launches to writers' festivals that occur regularly but occasionally in Ireland, this study unfolds during week-long stints mainly about every third month over a three-year period, and subsequent follow-up visits.

The study of writers also connects to another current development in anthropology: that of studying people who in some sense are the anthropologist's colleagues and counterparts (Holmes and Marcus 2005). This is different from classic anthropology. For this study, I share the task of writing (and incidentally teaching writing) with the writers as "I as anthropologist, and they as fiction writers, comment on contemporary Irish society" (Wulff 2008:110). There is an intellectual companionship, even though I by definition tend to have more insight into the writers' work than vice versa. Following Hannerz (2004:4) in his research on foreign correspondents, this is an example of studying sideways.

Looking back on this chapter, it is clear that creative writing and literature capture a central concern in Ireland from migration to economic ups and downs. For the purpose of this chapter, a number of instances of fiction about fiction – about writers and writing – have been discussed. The considerable institutional initiatives to teach creative writing to children and teenagers in Ireland are noteworthy, as is the growth in workshops and university programs in creative writing. It also turns out that in Ireland not only professional writers write fiction, so do many other people. Despite being categorized as English literature in certain contexts outside Ireland, the Irish literary voice is prominent in the larger literary conversation. All this explains why a study of the world of contemporary Irish writers contributes to broader understandings of Ireland and its connections to the rest of Europe, and shows how Ireland is finally one thriving piece in the anthropology of Europe.

ACKNOWLEDGMENTS

I wish to thank Dorle Dracklé and Hélène Neveu Kringelbach for useful comments on this chapter.

REFERENCES

Archetti, Eduardo P.
1994 Introduction. *In* Exploring the Written: Anthropology and the Multiplicity of Writing. pp. 11–28. Oslo: Scandinavian University Press.

Banville, John
2005 The Sea. London: Picador.

Barber, Karin
2007 The Anthropology of Texts, Persons and Publics: Oral and Written Culture in Africa and Beyond. Cambridge: Cambridge University Press.

Barton, David, and Uta Papen, eds.
2010 The Anthropology of Writing: Understanding Textually-Mediated Worlds. London: Continuum.

Becker, Howard S.
1984 Art Worlds. Berkeley: University of California Press.

Behar, Ruth
2009 Believing in Anthropology as Literature. *In* Anthropology off the Shelf. Alisse Waterson and Maria D. Vesperi, eds. pp. 106–116. Oxford: Wiley-Blackwell.

Blacking, John
1977 Towards an Anthropology of the Body. *In* The Anthropology of the Body. John Blacking, ed. pp. 1–28. London: Academic Press.

Cashman, Ray
2009 Storytelling on the Northern Irish Border: Characters and Community. Bloomington: Indiana University Press.

Cheney, Theodore A. Rees
2001 Writing Creative Nonfiction: Fiction techniques for Crafting Great Nonfiction. Berkeley: Ten Speed.
Clifford, James, and George E. Marcus, eds.
1986 Writing Culture: The Poetics and Politics of Ethnography. Berkeley: University of California Press.
Dawson, Andrew, Jenny Hockey, and Allison James, eds.
1997 After Writing Culture: Epistemology and Praxis in Contemporary Anthropology. London: Routledge.
Doyle, Roddy
2007 The Deportees and Other Stories. London: Jonathan Cape.
Enright, Anne
2007 The Gathering. London: Jonathan Cape.
Fogarty, Ann
2003 Preface. *In* Midwife to the Fairies: New and Selected Stories by Éilís Ní Dhuibhne. pp. ix–xv. Cork: Attic.
Geertz, Clifford
1973 The Interpretation of Cultures. New York: Basic.
1988 Works and Lives: The Anthropologist as Author. Stanford: Stanford University Press.
Greenland, Colin
2009 "All Names Have Been Changed" by Claire Kilroy. *The Guardian*, August 8. Electronic document. http://www.guardian.co.uk/books/2009/aug/08/all-names-have-been-changed (accessed November 5, 2011).
Hallam, Elizabeth, and Tim Ingold, eds.
2007 Creativity and Cultural Improvisation: An Introduction. *In* Creativity and Cultural Improvisation. pp. 1–24. Oxford: Berg.
Handler, Richard, and Daniel Segal
1990 Jane Austen and the Fiction of Culture: An Essay on the Narration of Social Reality. Tucson: University of Arizona Press.
Hannerz, Ulf
2004 Foreign News: Exploring the World of Foreign Correspondents. Chicago: University of Chicago Press.
2010 Anthropology's World: Life in a Twenty-First-Century Discipline. London: Pluto.
Holmes, Douglas R., and George E. Marcus
2005 Cultures of Expertise and the Management of Globalization: Toward the Re-Functioning of Ethnography. *In* Global Assemblages. Aihwa Ong and Stephen J. Collier, eds. pp. 235–252. Oxford: Blackwell.
Kilroy, Claire
2009 All Names Have Been Changed. London: Faber and Faber.
Kloos, Peter
1990a True Fiction: Artistic and Scientific Representations of Reality. Amsterdam: Vrije Universiteit University Press.
1990b Reality and Its Representations. *In* True Fiction: Artistic and Scientific Representations of Reality. Peter Kloos, ed. pp. 1–6. Amsterdam: Vrije Universiteit University Press.
Madden, Deirdre
2008 Molly Fox's Birthday. London: Faber & Faber.
Marcus, George E., and Michael M. J. Fischer
1986 Anthropology as Cultural Critique: An Experimental Moment in the Human Sciences. Chicago: University of Chicago Press.

McCann, Colum
2009 Let the Great World Spin. London: Bloomsbury.
McGurl, Mark
2009 The Program Era: Postwar Fiction and the Rise of Creative Writing. Cambridge, MA: Harvard University Press.
Narayan, Kirin
1999 Ethnography and Fiction: Where Is the Border? Anthropology and Humanism 24(2):134–147.
2007 Tools to Shape Texts: What Creative Nonfiction Can Offer Ethnography. Anthropology and Humanism 32(2):130–144.
Ní Dhuibhne, Éilís
1999 The Irish. *In* Europeans: Essays on Culture and Identity. Åke Daun and Sören Jansson, eds. pp. 47–66. Lund: Nordic Academic Press.
2007 Fox, Swallow, Scarecrow. Belfast: Blackstaff.
Rapport, Nigel
1994 The Prose and the Passion: Anthropology, Literature and the Writing of E. M. Forster. Manchester: Manchester University Press.
Stoller, Paul
1999 Jaguar: A Story of Africans in America. Chicago: University of Chicago Press.
Street, Brian V.
1997 Cross-Cultural Approaches to Literacy. Cambridge: Cambridge University Press.
Tóibín, Colm
2004 The Master. London: Picador.
2009 Brooklyn: A Novel. New York: Scribner.
Turner, Victor
1976 African Ritual and Western Literature: Is a Comparative Symbology Possible? *In* The Literature of Fact. Angus Fletcher, ed. pp. 45–81. New York: Columbia University Press.
Vanasco, Jeannie
2010 Method Writing. The New York Times Sunday Book Review, May 23 (online May 21). Electronic document. http://www.nytimes.com/2010/05/23/books/review/Vanasco-t.html (accessed November 5, 2011).
Waterston, Alisse, and Maria D. Vesperi, eds.
2009 Anthropology Off the Shelf: Anthropologists on Writing. Oxford: Wiley-Blackwell.
White, Jenny
2007 The Sultan's Seal. New York: W.W. Norton.
Wulff, Helena
1998 Ballet across Borders: Career and Culture in the World of Dancers. Oxford: Berg.
2007 Dancing at the Crossroads: Memory and Mobility in Ireland. Oxford: Berghahn.
2008 Literary Readings as Performance: On the Career of Contemporary Writers in the New Ireland. Anthropological Journal of European Cultures 17:98–113.
2009 Ethnografiction: Irish Relations in the Writing of Éilís Ní Dhuibhne. *In* Éilís Ní Dhuibhne: Perspectives. Rebecca Pelan, ed. pp. 245–265. Galway: Arlen House.
Zenker, Olaf, and Karsten Kumoll, eds.
2010 Beyond Writing Culture: Current Intersections of Epistemologies and Representational Practices. Oxford: Berghahn.

CHAPTER 32

Toward an Ethnoecology of Place and Displacement

Ullrich Kockel

Calls for a "new" anthropology are voiced frequently in the course of critiques of contemporary culture. This meditation engages with some such critiques that have emerged since the second half of the last century, exploring what interdisciplinary approaches arising from them might potentially contribute to the development of an eco-anthropology of Europe.

Displacement: Three Stories

Suvi-Sárá-Ainá-Ann

Once upon a time there was a Sámi woman. She was young and strong, and she was used to roaming far and wide with her reindeer. One day, a young nobleman stepped into her tent, accompanied by an elder from her community. The young man told her that he had bought 12 reindeer and was going to take them to a faraway place south of the Snowy Mountains. He wished her to come with him to look after the animals. The young Sámi woman reluctantly agreed to the proposal, saying to herself that she would surely find the way back home to her community. And so they went on their way south together. For many weeks they crossed dark forests and great seas; the journey went on and on, and the reindeer suffered greatly. At long last the company arrived in a wood with huge broadleaf trees. On a hill rising above the trees was a mighty stone-built house with tall turrets. The people spoke a strange language and behaved curiously. The Sámi woman and her reindeer were eyed with suspicion. But what hurt the woman more than anything was that her beloved reindeer grew ever weaker. As winter approached, they could not find the mosses and lichens they liked so well back home, and the dried grass and other winter feedstuff made them sicker and sicker. Oh, how she longed to be back in the wide tundra and the deep woods of her homeland. It broke her heart but there was nothing she could do – one by one, her animals died. The loss

A Companion to the Anthropology of Europe, First Edition. Edited by Ullrich Kockel, Máiréad Nic Craith, and Jonas Frykman.

> caused the woman great sorrow, and although the people at the big house made every effort to cheer her up, she could not be happy any more. She tried to tell the people of her sorrow, but they simply could not understand. And so, one day, the sorrowful young Sámi woman went away. They say she followed her reindeer.

Freely translated from the Web page of Brigitte and Uwe Kunze's *Renrajd Vualka* (Kunze 2010), meaning "a trail [of Sámi with their reindeer] setting out," this tale is based on a true story that happened in 1580, when Count Wilhelm IV of Hessen-Kassel had a 1.5 sq km "wild park" created at the foot of the Sababurg, his hunting lodge in the Reinhardswald forest, and asked the Swedish scientist Tycho Brahe to arrange acquisition of some reindeer. Twelve animals were purchased, and sent to the Reinhardswald accompanied by a Sámi woman who was to look after them. However, the animals that survived the long journey died within a short time after arrival, and the woman disappeared, her fate unknown. The Sababurg, reputedly the home of the original "Sleeping Beauty," is now on a tourist trail known as the *Deutsche Märchenstraße* – German Fairy Tale Road – that connects locations associated with the Brothers Grimm and the material they gathered for their books of folk tales two centuries later. This is not the point at which to ask why the Sámi woman and her story did not make it into their collection, although that would certainly be an interesting question to pursue on another occasion. In 2003, two shamans came to the Reinhardswald, to help her spirit come home. They gave the woman the names Suvi-Sárá-Ainá-Ann, representing the four countries – Norway, Sweden, Finland, and Russia – in which the Sámi live.

The Heath is Green

> At a rural summer festival, in the Lüneburg Heath area of West Germany in the early 1950s, local people are coming together with refugees and expellees from Germany's "lost territories" in the East, especially from Silesia. One of these incomers, Lüder Lüdersen, is rising from his seat to say his farewell to the community where he had found refuge and "a second homeland." Once the owner of an estate in East Prussia from where he fled toward the end of the World War II, Lüdersen is finding it difficult to adapt to his changed circumstances and has decided to move on to an urban environment:
>
> "Never shall I forget the days that I have been allowed to spend here with you on the Heath – the Heath, which has become for me, too, a second homeland. Do not make it difficult for those people who have found refuge here. . . . I know we have not always been as we ought to be. But we have been punished the hardest. . . . I was on the verge of losing myself, but through the kindness and understanding that has been extended towards me here, I have found myself again."[1]
>
> Addressing the refugees and expellees, many of whom are wearing traditional costume for the festival, the local mayor introduces a traveling minstrel who strikes up a tune "from your homeland," and they join in an emotional rendition of Riesengebirglers Heimatlied, a Silesian regional anthem.

The 1951 movie *Grün ist die Heide* (Deppe 1951; English version: *The Heath is Green*), a remake of a successful 1932 version based on a story by Hermann Löns, was only the second *Heimatfilm* produced after World War II. It became the biggest grossing German film of the 1950s, with some 19 million viewers. Critics have focused on the obvious kitsch elements in the film, and treated its representation of refugees and expellees as a successful strategy to increase the popular appeal of the movie. These groups, more than 10 million people in total, made up a large portion of postwar society in West Germany, and thus the commercial argument appears persuasive. But why, then, was this theme of displacement picked up only rarely in postwar movies, and with rather limited success (albeit with occasional critical acclaim)? Relations between the "locals" and the incomers were full of tensions, as Lüdersen's speech indicates. The original story, and the first film of 1932, did not include comparable characters or plot lines. The festival takes up quite a large amount of time in the 1951 film, making it a central piece of the narrative, with Lüdersen's speech very much at the heart of it, making that speech conceivably the key point of the film. Were the characters of Lüdersen and his daughter Helga's friend Nora, another expellee, introduced in 1951 to highlight those tensions and use the medium of kitsch cinema to convey a critical moral message to both "locals" and "incomers"? A conclusive answer to this question has to wait for another occasion. As a former estate owner, Lüdersen does not represent the majority of refugees and expellees, who appeared as folk-dressed "extras" in the festival sequence in the film, invoking their lost homeland in song.[2]

Gorleben: The Dream of Something

In the early hours of the morning, the village is surrounded by several battalions of riot police with armoured cars and some companies on horse-back, supported by helicopters that whirl up the ubiquitous sand. The villagers try to protect their faces with scarves, which is interpreted as a sinister gesture by the authorities. For a few hours, village life continues as almost normal while the forces are closing in. A group of young people play a game of bowls in front of a dense line of shields and helmets; a middle-aged man plays his accordion surrounded by rolls of barbed wire guarded by armed police; an old man with a walking stick sits down in the center of the village, staring defiantly at the invaders. From the watchtower, the community radio now uses loudspeakers to broadcast news updates and music. For several hours very little happens. At 11:04 am, the police begin to remove villagers, who refuse to leave. Force is used – judiciously and only where inevitable, according to the authorities; excessive and unjustified, say the villagers and their supporters. The radio plays a song by the drama troupe Theaterwehr Brandheide, written to the tune of Pink Floyd's "Another Brick in the Wall, Part II," and the villagers join in, their voices straining against the noise of the helicopters:

> Der Kampf um unsre Heimat ist mehr als nur ein Wort.
> Das Wendland ist befreit. Wir gehen hier nicht fort![3]

Three hours later, most of the villagers are rounded up behind the police lines, where their photographs and fingerprints are taken. About 6 pm, the top of the watchtower is lifted off by a crane. The group that had held out there offers the police wine and chocolate. It seems the Free Republic of Wendland is no more. But over the following weeks, expelled villagers and their supporters set up refugee camps and agencies of a Wendland government-in-exile up and down the country, and even some abroad. A documentary film, *Der Traum von einer Sache*,[4] is produced by a local cooperative. In

> a defining scene, a local figure approaches the barrier across an opening in a barbed wire fence, quietly but defiantly singing to the armed guards a verse from the Bible (Hebrews 13, 14) that speaks of the impermanence of our home in this world, and of our anticipation of the home yet to come.

Three decades later, the Free Republic of Wendland remains a tangible yet elusive actuality. In 2010, the regional broadcaster Norddeutscher Rundfunk produced a series of programmes documenting 30 years of resistance to the nuclear waste disposal site in Gorleben, where for 33 days, from May 3 until June 4, 1980, a broadly based social movement established an alternative republic (NDR 2010). It does not matter here what, if any, the constitutional implications of that republic might have been, and for the present purpose its political ramifications for today are of only marginal importance.

Displacement: Forms, Experiences, Narratives

Alienation has been a theme for social research across the disciplines at least since Marx and Engels diagnosed it as quasi an existential condition of capitalist society. Displacement as a specific form of alienation – the (often forceful) removal of someone from his or her place of belonging – has almost become an existential condition of late and post-modernity, and therefore has been described in terms of "challenges for the 21st century" (McDowell and Morrell 2010). The three vignettes above relate to different forms of displacement, to different modes in which displacement is experienced, and to different styles in which the story of that displacement is told. The narratives offered share a basically romantic outlook, and as such they are likely to be contested, regardless of any factual content they might have. Any intellectual period has its hierarchy of acceptable representations, and in the currently hegemonic discourse, "romantic" as a genre tends to be placed way down the rank order of acceptability, not least because of the political uses to which romantic representations have been put (or lent themselves) in the past. Moreover, while much has changed since Leach (1984) challenged the anthropological canon by suggesting that any observer will inevitably encounter something in the field that nobody else can see there – a projection of the observer's own personality – and the "writing culture" (Clifford and Marcus 2010) debate has opened up the field for exploration of alternative modes of anthropological writing, a certain uneasiness persists as, like the medieval monastic orders, some alternatives are embraced by the canon whereas others remain heresies. Hugh Beach (see Chapter 3 in this volume) has argued that "[w]e must try to grasp alternative cosmologies in terms that make sense to us, not only as strange superstitions that make sense to others." I will come back to these issues later.

The first vignette, in the manner of a fairy tale, tells the story of an individual removed from her ecological context for putatively benevolent reasons – a wildlife park was to be established and the well-being of a group of animals ensured through having them looked after by a person with the appropriate knowledge. The endeavor failed miserably because, among other factors, the early modern gentleman-scholar

Figure 32.1 *Die wilde Lappenfrau* sculpture at Tierpark Sababurg, Germany. Photograph © Ullrich Kockel. (Reproduced courtesy of the author.)

did not heed his scientist-friend's advice that a radical change of place was going to have detrimental effects on the health of animals and herder alike. Four centuries later, reindeer have been reintroduced to the Reinhardswald, now redeveloped as a landscape park stocked with rare breeds and "wild" animals, and a Sámi center has been established at the park, where visitors can experience Sámi "life and culture" on certain days. The center, attached to a project called Renrajd Vualka, has been set up by a couple who live and work both locally and in Sápmi, the land of the Sámi, and who have been campaigning for Sámi causes. In 2003, a memorial to the Sámi woman of the story was erected next to an oak tree in the center of the park (see Figure 32.1).

In the second vignette, a clip from a popular movie, we meet a range of people from different social backgrounds and with different experiences of displacement, although the primary focus is clearly on the former estate owner. For much of the postwar period, individuals from Lüdersen's background (e.g. Dönhoff 2009) satisfied the market for autobiographical accounts of life in Germany's "lost territories," and of flight and expulsion at the end of World War II. In recent years, however, this genre has expanded exponentially with the addition of autobiographical narratives by "ordinary" people, written either by themselves or with the help of others (e.g. Lachauer 2000; Hirsch 2004). There has also been a growing literature emanating from the "second generation" who have experienced flight and expulsion only through the lived memories of their parents' and grandparents' generations, and whose coming to terms with these memories takes a range of literary forms, from travelogue (e.g. Reiski 2002) to semi-autobiographical novel (e.g. Treichel 2005). Once World War II was officially concluded after unification of the two postwar German states, a debate began to emerge that involved the rather tricky question of whether perpetrators can be victims (see, e.g., Niven 2006; Schmitz 2007). In recent years, proposals for the establishment of a "center against expulsions" have deeply divided public opinion in Germany (Benz 2008; Völkering 2010). Major new TV productions, such as *Die Flucht*, dealing with the flight of Germans from East Prussia, are seeking to develop a differentiated picture of the events. While arguably a necessary element of societal mourning and coming to terms with the past, these respresentations remain part of a process of the aestheticization of loss, and a power discourse in the public domain (Köstlin 2010).

The third vignette gained fresh significance at the time of writing, when an earthquake damaged nuclear reactors at Fukushima in Japan and thereby indirectly contributed to the unexpected sweeping into office of the first Green prime minister in the German state of Baden-Württemberg, just as the Wendland affair contributed to the first success of the Green party in German federal elections at that time. The occupation of prospecting site 1004, one of the locations where the safety of the Gorleben salt caverns for nuclear waste disposal was to be tested, and its subsequent clearing by the state and federal authorities, has entered the folklore of the groups and social movements involved, both locally and further afield. Led by local pressure groups and supported by villagers from across the local region, the people of the Free Republic of Wendland came from all over West Germany and West Berlin. "For those not originally from the Wendland, it offered, not least through its passports that are 'valid as long as the bearer can still laugh,' a sense of belonging and at-home-ness in a state that many at the time perceived as cold, hostile, and teetering on the brink of the next World War" (Kockel 2010:172). Whether an actual attempt at secession or a clever political joke, the Republic at the time reflected strong local resistance. Although bulldozed after little more than a month, the Republic retains a spiritual existence, evident in a continuous stream of broadcasts, publications, and "other grass-roots political actions expressing opposition to the nuclear dump" (Kockel 2010:172), as well as in many songs and ballads extolling the virtues of the Wendland and celebrating the struggle to protect it from what are perceived as remote political interests. While this emphasis that "members of local pressure groups" place on "the uniqueness or Otherness of place as a unique piece of cultural capital to be maintained" is perhaps not surprising, as Tilley (2006:14) observed in a different context, the Wendland has over the past three decades become a countercultural iconic landscape that projects quirkiness, rather than Arcadia, against a background of emblematic grass-roots resistance that recreates through practice the Wendland republic as a place of ideological belonging for many who are not from there.[5]

The Sámi woman, lured away from her home by persuasion, may have moved out of a sense of duty toward the reindeer that needed looking after in a strange environment. Isolated in her new location, she may have tried to reach her home when the animals died, or she may have suffered the fate of Kasper Hauser, slain by locals suspicious of her unfamiliar appearance – we do not know, and her story has been integrated into the broader narrative of the "Fairy Tale Road" that runs through central Germany. The voice of the narrator comes from the present; living centuries after the events, the narrator has no immediate, first-hand knowledge of what happened. In fact, we do not even know whether, as the tale suggests, she was actually lured away more or less gently, or forcefully removed.

The Silesian Germans fled from the advancing Red Army or were later expelled as Polish settlers moved into their home region. Few stayed behind, and one could surmise that this makes the move of those who left voluntary, a matter of choice as in the case of the Sámi woman – but that was not how those affected experienced their situation. In their new locations, mostly in West Germany, the refugees and expellees were often less than welcome (see, e.g., Frantzioch 1987; Connor 2007; Kossert 2009). Like the Sámi woman (according to the story), they longed for their lost homelands, and many hoped for a long time that they would one day return. The narrator was a contemporary of the characters in the story and may or may not have shared a fate similar to theirs.

Many of the counter-cultural Wendlanders may not actually have been from the Wendland, but they found in the Republic a kind of spiritual home and local roots that they were missing, for whatever individual reasons, in their everyday life. By joining the Free Republic of Wendland, they gained opportunities to develop and experience an intentional community with reference to a particular, meaningful place. They also set themselves up for ultimate expulsion, thereby – more or less consciously – laying the foundations for the subsequent mythologizing of their experience. Thus they may not be considered comparable to the other examples. The narrator appears to have been personally involved in the events, in whatever capacity, and thus has first-hand knowledge of the events, but because of this immediacy may not be able to view them with the level of detachment considered appropriate for academic accounts.

My concern here is not primarily with displacement in its various forms, but with issues of place: sense of, and attachment to, place, and the possibilities and implications of replacing ourselves. The vignettes that I used in the opening sequence highlight different instances of disconnecting people and places, and thus point toward placelessness as an existential condition to which we may seek, and find, cultural responses. In the remainder of this meditation, I will consider aspects of place, and some responses to the – real or perceived – loss of place, drawing largely but not exclusively on material related to Germany. My approach reflects an academic trajectory that traversed several disciplines before settling with ethnoanthropology, and from that basis has proceeded across a few more boundaries since then, toward an integrated, interdisciplinary perspective for European ethnology as a philosophically grounded applied regional science that specializes in the local (Kockel 2009), closely connected to art practice (Kockel 2011) and human ecology (Kockel 2012).

Belonging In and Out of Place

Hannah Arendt (1992) argued that any thinking and action must have its place in the world to which it belongs. This suggests the local contingency of thinking and action, an idea that seems to sit uneasily with the hegemonic interpretation of the universalist paradigm generally attributed to Immanuel Kant's philosophy. Marc Augé (1995) has argued that

> at the very same moment when it becomes possible to think in terms of the unity of terrestrial space, and the big multinational networks grow strong, the clamour of particularism rises; clamour from those who want to stay at home in peace, clamour from those who want to find a mother country. As if the conservativism of the former and the messianism of the latter were condemned to speak the same language: that of land and roots. (1995:34–35)

Kantian universalism is often seen as the Enlightenment's polar opposite to Herderian particularism, which is thus portrayed – and despised – as its antithesis; but is that juxtaposition correct? The homogenizing force of "reason," waging what Bauman (1995) characterizes as a merciless war on tradition, seeks to supplant any particularizing authorities like the shaman that stand in the way of "progress"; this is perhaps why artists like Joseph Beuys have been cast in the role of the shaman (e.g. White 1998; cf. Walters 2009) invoking a lost connection between people and place. However, the emphasis on place and the associated concern with essences, found in approaches such as Kenneth White's "geopoetics" or Joseph Beuys's "expanded concept of art," are deeply problematic – both have been thoroughly discredited by political developments in the nineteenth and the first half of the twentieth century. Much of contemporary discourse tends to highlight space and spaces, struggling to find any meaningful way of dealing with issues of place and belonging that is not politically suspect. And yet, the "reappearance of place" began already with Kant, as Casey (1998) has traced, thereby refuting the popular juxtaposition noted earlier. In a dictionary of anthropology published the same year as Casey's philosophical history, place has been defined as "a space made meaningful by human occupation or appropriation and . . . a cultural concept fundamental to describing human beings' relations with their environment" (Lawrence 1997:360), suggesting that the concept has at least some validity in anthropology. But there are problems and dangers with the close association of "place" and "culture," just as with their dissociation – what the sociologist Willke (2001) calls "atopia." This raises the questions of whether we can afford to replace culture, and whether and why we should want to do so in the first instance, as I have argued elsewhere (Kockel 2012).

The disregard, if not contempt, for place as a theoretical concept has not been unanimous across the disciplines. Lawrence (1997:360) notes that while "place has been historically devalued or ignored in the social sciences, especially in the social and cultural anthropology . . . Geographers, by contrast, have focused on place and its essential moral qualities but have often confused it with community." There is indeed no chapter on "place" in the second edition of a book on key concepts in social and cultural anthropology (Rapport and Overing 2007), although there are

28 entries in the index, most of these only cursory references. European ethnology, by contrast, has historically had what some might regard as an obsession with place and community, which became unfashionable in the postwar decades, but has been making a comeback of sorts in the twenty-first century, as the proceedings of major conferences indicate (e.g. Paládi-Kovács 2004; Binder et al. 2005), albeit from within a different hegemonic perspective.

Lawrence (1997:361) sums up the hegemonic view at the end of the twentieth century: "Actual mobility of . . . peoples through contemporary migrations makes presumptions of 'authenticity' of place-based culture impossible to sustain." Notwithstanding any wider issues with the concept of "authenticity" that have been well acknowledged (e.g. Bendix 1997), geographers like Bonnemaison (2005) would not necessarily agree with that assessment, and I recall another geographer – without being able to pinpoint a full reference from memory – who asserted at a conference in the 1990s that the vast majority of people still die within a few miles of where they were born. There may well be "a tendency to universalize by portraying the experience of some people as the experience of all" (Dwyer 2005:21), as Bausinger (1997) noted with regard to the distinctly American appearance of the "global village." We may have become so captivated by certain manifestations that we exclude or disregard other possibilities – what Weiner (2001:8; emphasis original) describes as "the power of *nescience*, not-knowing." Thus most "city-dwelling northerners experience everyday living in a way that fundamentally mis-recognizes the ecological dependencies of our situation" (Scott 2011:57).

Place and its alleged destruction by globalization have become key concerns, in academic and political debate as much as "on the ground," in everyday lived experience. Research on these issues is therefore of crucial importance, but must be carried out with a high level of critical awareness. Anthropologists and ethnologists are challenged to develop ethnographically inflected understandings of place that contest conventional divisions between culture and nature (cf. Ellen et al. 2000; Ingold 2000). Macdonald (Chapter 14 in this volume) has pointed out that place research often focuses on material aspects of "place memory," such as "when everyday knowledge and memory become recorded into official memorials and heritage." She also notes "a flourishing of work on migration, displacement, border-crossing, and diaspora" (see also the chapters by Byron, Horvat, Wilson, Straczuk, Kopf, and Löfgren in this volume), which is where much of my own work over the past two decades has been focused (Kockel 2010).

Connecting "place" with "space," Rodman (2003:206) distinguishes two types of sense of "place" in anthropological thought – as "an anthropological construct for 'setting' or the localization of concepts," and as "socially constructed spatialized experience." She argues that "places come into being through praxis, not just through narrative" (2003:207); consequently, one should not simply assume consistency between the discourses of the researchers and the researched, or indeed that the views of all the members of each group are necessarily similar. Entrikin (1991:134) diagnosed a divide "between the existential and naturalistic conceptions of place" which "appears to be an unbridgeable one . . . that is only made wider in adopting a decentered view." Arguing that an overemphasis on objectivity loses valuable insights and understanding, he suggested "addressing both sides of this divide . . . from a point in between, a point that leads us into the vast realm of narrative forms," of different ways of telling a story: "From this position we gain . . . a sense both of being 'in a place' and 'at a location,' of being in the center and being at a point on a centerless world." The geographer's diagnosis pointed in a similar direction as Leach's (1984) assertion that anthropological observers ought to expect always to recognize in the field their own subjective projections.

Munn (2003) connects issues of space, place, and landscape with aspects of morality and cosmology expressed or found in and through the land. Her concept of "relative spacetime," as Johnson (2010:10) rightly observes, bears a resemblance with Ingold's (2000) concept of "journeying." Munn (2003:93) contrasts the "locale," where events take place, with "locatedness," which is an expression of "mobile action rather than things." Realization that this "locatedness" of "mobile action" can take place anywhere, in any space and along any trajectory, led me some time ago to surmise that territory was being replaced by trajectory as the main way of rooting spatial identities (Kockel 1999). While that conclusion remains broadly tenable, it takes too little account of different meanings of place. In an introduction to "ethnology" intended to cover both social anthropology and European ethnology, Haller (2005:124) differentiates six types of place:

locality – geographical extension with name and boundaries
utopian locality – imagined, non-geographical extension with name and boundaries
place [German: "Ort"] – utilization of a locality by a social group as their field of interaction
imagined place – utilization lies in the past or the future
territory – claim to ownership of a place
imagined territory – possession lies in the past resp. future

These distinctions between location, territory, and place are a useful reminder that, while the footloose postmodern world may well dispose of the nation-state as the primary basis for political identity, there is more to place, identity, and belonging than the narrow analysis of identity politics recognizes. The concept of trajectorial identities defined by events along an individual's life-path is closely aligned with the concept of hybridity (see also Tschernokoshewa, Chapter 30 in this volume). Hybridity has been described by the poet and anthropologist Michael Jackson (2000) as being at-home-in-the-world neither here nor there. However, this is not the disembedded, rootless existence celebrated at the hight of postmodernism. Rapport offers a useful "working definition for charting the morass of ambiguities and fluidities of contemporary identity" (Rapport and Overing 2007:176) in terms of "home" as the locale "where one best knows oneself" (Rapport and Dawson 1998), taking "best" to mean "most," but not necessarily "happiest."

While not every place will be, or indeed can be, such a "home," every "home" in this sense is clearly a place with a defined meaning, not merely an open space of unlimited possibilities. In an "unhomely" (Bhabha 1994) world, the "generalized elsewhere" (*generalisiertes Anderswo*) detected by Meyrowitz (1998) becomes a "generalized anywhere" (*generalisiertes Irgendwo*), atopic contingency, which still permits locale, *Heimat*, village, and all that, but makes it arbitrary where and with which members such primary spaces of community-building are realized (Willke 2001:105). Social theory, in these circumstances, is like an Odyssey, seeking to localize viable places for the Self, although, as Willke (2001:209) points out, it remains rather unclear what the constitutive characteristics of this "Self" might be in the face of radical societal dissolution, and what places might be viable under conditions of radical deterritorialization: real places of engagement with people, imaginary places of engagement with gods, or atopic, hybrid places of engagement with oneself? Around the turn of the century many of us expected a "future of intense deterritorialization"; that expectation may simply have resulted from a failure to observe "the different ways in which people and identities take place on new arenas and in novel forms"(Löfgren 1996:166).

However, that does not invalidate Willke's more general diagnosis of rampant atopia. Rauschenbach (2001:241) notes, especially with reference to Marc Augé's (1995) work, that the newer sociology, examining contemporary places, discovered the phenomenon of "non-places," which correspond to the disposable reality of an omnipresence that brings forth and standardizes the dominant *Dasein* as a way of existence for users of networked transitory spaces and routes. The information superhighways finally liberate us from the resistiveness of matter and the time-consuming drudgery of crossing mountains, rivers, and oceans (Rauschenbach 2001:242; see also Ardévol and Estalella, Chapter 28 in this volume). With reference to German film maker Edgar Reitz's TV-epics *Heimat* and *Zweite Heimat*, Rauschenbach (2001:240–241) notes that the first *Heimat* did pass, not because a young generation left, but because the Moloch Modernity during the 1960s and 1970s discovered the hiding places of the old days and modernized them; the second *Heimat* is past since the visions of arrival in another *Heimat* have scattered under the jeers of an all devouring post- and hypermodernity; from a contemporary perspective, the 1970s with their siren songs and alternative dreams of escaping in a soft praxis of settlement appear as a burlesque episode of a fugitive generation, inspired by utopias and disturbed by the abstractions of class struggle in the metropoles. The destruction of the Free Republic of Wendland was a physical expression of that scattering of visions.

Envisioning a time when the whole earth may become a single place, Augé (1995:120) seems to say – in a way reminiscent of Hebrews 13, 14 – that until this happens there can be no actual place on earth, and any "community of human destinies is experienced in the anonymity of non-place"; he ends his analysis by postulating "an ethnology of solitude." Whereas Augé, in a sense, sees place as a utopian "Not-Yet," Paul Virilio (1992) coins the term "dromology" (Greek *dromos*: "race") to describe the destruction of time-space, brought about by the total mobilization associated with modernization, as a frenzied standstill that ultimately suspends the ground of all experience, putting place – and identification by belonging – beyond reach.

When we raise, as we must, anthropological questions about these processes and conditions we need to be acutely aware of the snares of a shallow essentialism (Kockel 2012). As anthropologists we recognize cultural ascriptions as relative and specific, but their incidence as universal. The process is social in the sense of societal location, but we are nevertheless dealing with a cultural system of meaning that can be regarded as place-specific, and indeed often makes sense only if understood in this specificity (Basso 1996; Weiner 2001). We need to understand the relationships and references in their entirety as well as in isolation, not merely one or the other, as shallow essentialists and their critics do. One of the simplest examples of this that I can think of is the eloquence of "Irish Energies," a 1974 art work by Joseph Beuys combining peat briquettes with butter, thereby saying perhaps more about 1970s Ireland than volumes of painstakingly detailed ethnography.

Healing the Wounds of Memory

Macdonald (Chapter 14 in this volume) has used the concept of "past presencing" to avoid "the problematic distinction between 'history' and 'memory.'" Some consider history "the established and verified past relative to memory's individual and relatively fallible accounts," while others would regard it as "the canonical and thus relatively untrustworthy other to memory's subjective veracity." The artist Joseph Beuys has long been seen, and indeed projected himself, as a mediator of history and memory, especially in the context of his native Germany but also other places, not least in the Gaelic regions of Europe (Lerm Hayes and Walters 2011). A number of recent doctoral theses have considered the artist's work in this regard from a broadly ethnological perspective. Walters (2009) examines examples of Beuys's practice with special reference to his Irish and Scottish explorations in the 1970s, arguing that the artist's creative engagement with pre-Christian symbols in Ireland might be seen in relation to his broader interest, especially in the German context, in rehabilitating symbols through a reflective process that attempts to come to terms with history and memory and circumvents potential problems in the future. Fritz (2007:9) understands the works of Joseph Beuys as (in a Weberian sense), an "aesthetic re-enchantment" and seeks to locate this practice from an ethnological perspective in the context of academic debates on discourses of memory and cultural theories of remembering. In Fritz's analysis, Beuys appears as a bearer of the cultural memory who, with religio-pedagogic intentions, activates mythical and magical traditions in his memory art (*Erinnerungskunst)* in order to reconstruct the damaged national memory of the Germans (Fritz 2007:13).

It might seem as if memory that no longer has any cultural form and societal function has taken refuge in art (Assmann 1999:359). However, artists involved in landscape/place-oriented art practice, such as those active in the "Land^2" network (www.land2.uwe.ac.uk), would not necessarily see this as memory taking refuge. With particular emphasis on the sense, spirit, and wisdom of place, the work by Iain Biggs (2004, 2007), for example, blends visual and textual genres with creatively deployed insights from a range of academic disciplines in an exploration of place that contributes significantly to the shaping of the kind of aesthetic anthropology postulated by Greverus (2005). Like the work of Beuys, this aesthetic anthropology is an attempt to heal a (part of the) world that is perceived as wounded and broken.

From a different yet related perspective, a new anthropology to heal a broken world has been postulated by the poet Kenneth White (2004:145), who compares Beuys to "a shaman dancing on the glacier" (White 1998). The relationship between anthropology and literature as forms of representation has been examined at least since the "writing culture" debate, but White's postulate points beyond literariness (cf. Rapport and Overing 2007:269–278) as a genre of anthropological representation, toward "a new experience of the earth and of life" (White 2004:22), and therefore a new way of practicing ethnography poetically. White coined the term "geopoetics" to describe this remaking of the world through poetic practice in the "nomadic spirit" (White 1987), which he deems necessary to overcome the radical atopia (cf. Willke 2001) or loss of place that characterizes contemporary society.

Similar concerns are expressed in what may be termed "a hermeneutically-oriented philosophical theology of place" (Clingerman 2011:142). An ecotheology of place is evolving, inspired partly by the work of Jürgen Moltmann (e.g. Bergmann 2006), but especially by indigenous cosmologies (e.g. Wallace 2005; Deffenbaugh 2006) with regard to the relationship of human beings with the land. In this context, being "indigenous" does not refer to essential attributes acquired through blood-lines, but is a matter of "having the right to belong and to have a say," which "is established through demonstrating an ability to care for ones [sic] own interests in a way that sustains rather than harms others" (Kenrick 2011:201; see also MacKinnon 2008). As Clingerman (2011:147) points out, "memory of place is a dialectic of personal and communal memory," and only by a joint effort can we "build and inhabit place from individual reminiscences" (2011:149). This theology of place is therefore linked to the idea of "rekindling community" (McIntosh 2008b) – between human beings and the places where they belong – through a process of healing by "re-membering what has been lost, re-visioning how we could live, and re-claiming what is needed to achieve that vision" (McIntosh 1998). It can thus be conceived of as a kind of ecologically grounded liberation theology (McIntosh 2008a) that seeks ways of "dwelling beyond dualistic tensions" (Campbell 2011) between Nature and Culture, Past and Future. Place is not only a spatial category, but also a temporal one. However, "our vision is distorted with an emphasis on the present" (Clingerman 2011:151; see also Scott 2011).

Dwyer uses the term "ethnoecology" to describe an approach to ecology as experienced by cultural groups, arguing (2005:13) that "people are embedded within local environments and that knowledge of the natural world arises through their engagement with those environments." Clingerman (2011:150) has defined memory of place as "a form of knowing"; through "holding a place in time," it works "against the environmental amnesia that confronts us." A similar view of people – place relationships underpins *Heimatkunde*, or ethnotopology, as revisioned in Kockel (2012).

Dwyer (2005:13) argues that classical approaches to ethnoclassification "sacrificed the relational foundations and ecological embeddedness of all knowledge in favour of devising formal schemes divorced from human agency." Moreover, "human engagement with the world, and the persons unfolding through that engagement, are always and necessarily grounded in metaphor, in tropes, in the imagination" (Dwyer 2005:21). Quoting Hornborg (1996:45), Dwyer argues that contemporary approaches have a tendency "to prioritize our interpretations of the experience of those who we judge to be the least disembedded, the experience of those who live in societies where 'local and implicit meanings' prevail." But, he points out, there are many societies in which "those local and implicit meanings" have become disembedded and to some extent "subordinated to 'abstract, totalizing systems' and to understandings and practices that, so often, are guided by entrenched polarities" – the same polarities that are among the causes for environmental amnesia through "a lack of engagement with nature in daily life" (Clingerman 2011:150), and which authors like Campbell (2011) or Kenrick (2011) seek to transcend through what one might call "ethnoecological appreciation" (Dwyer 2005:21).

Geographers have long maintained, not surprisingly, that in order adequately to understand cultural difference it needs to be placed in its geographical context. However, "in the English-speaking world . . . cultural geography often seems indistinguishable from a larger field of cultural studies in which space and place hardly figure at all except metaphorically" (Agnew 2005:xii). A major reason for this is the danger of determinism and essentialism, widely perceived as inherent to any treatment of space and place as other than metaphoric and representational. In contrast, Bonnemaison (2005:29) argued that "[t]he best form of anti-determinism is culture, for culture is the very essence of unpredictability." Places and landscapes are created by human beings making use of their ecological settings (Bonnemaison 2005:30; see also Fischer, Chapter 19 in this volume). Cultural expressions, such as language, customs, and beliefs establish and maintain connections between individuals and leave material traces; thus landscape "becomes the matrix of identity as well as its imprint" (Bonnemaison 2005:33; see also Clingerman 2011:146), a connector between past and future that can both remember and forget (cf. Harrison 2004). Bonnemaison (2005:68–69) argued that the idea of "progress" implies and indeed necessitates continuity between past and future, that progress requires a link with a people's roots and continuity of its traditions; he defines the word "custom" as "progress with the past." That even applies to modernity, usually seen as pitched against tradition: "Founding myths underlie traditions – and the modernity that aims at replacing tradition. In traditional cultures, the golden age often lies in the past . . . In modern cultures, the golden age is the myth of progress and therefore lies in the future" (Bonnemaison 2005:81).

Replacements

Memories establish and maintain relationships with places; they "replace" us (Clingerman 2011:151). Place emerges "out of activity that does not have the 'production of place' as such as its avowed goal" (Weiner 2001:15), but this does not mean that it is a random creation. Rather, place and its community can be regarded as work of art, as Weiner indicates, pointing (2001:105) to Heidegger's "concern with the role of . . . aesthetic, form-inducing processes in human social and cultural life in general and not just with respect to . . . artwork narrowly conceived." Thus place and community are, in a Beuysian sense, "social sculpture" (see also Walters 2009).

Writing at about the same time as Marc Augé (1995) proposed his ethnology of solitude, Keith Basso (1996) argued that

> it is simply not the case . . . that relationships to place are lived exclusively or predominantly in contemplative moments of social isolation. On the contrary, relationships to places are lived most often in the company of other people, and it is on these communal occasions – when places are sensed *together* – that native views of the physical world become accessible to strangers. (1996:109, emphasis original)

The festival in *Grün ist die Heide* and the brief spring of anarchy in the Free Republic of Wendland were such communal occasions when places are sensed together, as was the homecoming ceremony performed by two shamans in the Reinhardswald. All three instances highlight the metaphysical, transcendental aspect of place. Nina Afanasjeva, a Kildin-Sámi from the Kola peninsula and member of the Sámi Council, has experienced expulsion in her own life. In 2003 she led the healing and homecoming ceremony for the nameless Sámi woman in the Reinhardswald, offering salt for the reindeer and comforting the woman's spirit before calling her "rediscovered sister, mother and friend" home to Sápmi (Kunze 2010). On the Lüneburg Heath, as the refugees join the minstrel in a hymn to their homeland, the camera pans over the crowd and then steeply upward, lingering on a piece of blue sky for several seconds before cutting to the minstrel for the refrain. Kürsten (2010:264) interprets this sequence as symbolizing the situation of the refugees: the song, rather than expressing some irredentist ideology, signifies a *lieux de memoir*, a lifeworld reference to a past that has been irretrievably lost in material terms. The image of the sky which, as the only place-related constant, stretches over both old and new homeland can be read not only as a religious symbol, but rather as a sign of the – however idealized – connection between the different localizations (Kürsten 2010:265). In the story of Gorleben, too, there is an element of religious symbolism, most clearly expressed in the scene at the barrier. In the days after the village had been razed, citizens of the Free Republic gathered in "refugee camps" all over West Germany and West Berlin. Outside a tent pitched by the Jungfernstieg, a bridge in the center of Hamburg, sat a small group rehearsing the lyrics of a song one of them had written to the tune of Phil Coulter's popular anthem to his home town of Derry, "The Town I Loved So Well," the new words closely mirroring the invocation of place in the original, ending with a defiant vision of song and laughter defeating the powers that destroyed the village, but could not crush "the dream of something."

Basso (1996:145; emphasis original) notes that "sense of place may gather unto itself a potent religious force, especially if one considers the root of the word in *religare*, which is 'to bind or fasten fast.'" The crucial question with sense of place is "not where it comes from, or even how it gets formed, but what . . . it is made with." Its character "emerges from the quality of its ingredients." Place is not just spatial but also, and importantly, temporal. Clingerman (2011:148), arguing that "individual memory is transformed when it enters into shared memory," highlights a "forward-looking, eschatological" dimension of such shared memory, which "contains the anticipation of a 'new world': a just, sustainable and flourishing future that is built upon a narrative sense of the past or tradition." Thus the place for which we feel homesick may be a place requiring an act of *poiesis*, a social sculpture yet to be created. The philosopher Höffe (2005:39) suggests that *Heimat*, the place to which belonging is projected, cannot be simply a "gift from Heaven," nor can it be seen as merely the duty of others to provide. While a person who fails to find a new *Heimat* even after many years in a place of residence does not need to feel guilty, he or she should not simply blame "the others" for that failure. *Heimat* is not something that we simply find, without us having an active input. Memories of place as lived experience in space and time can engage and replace us (Clingerman 2011:151), but successful replacement requires more than passive remembering, and is not a matter of scale and reach. "The scale of space-as-experienced," Bonnemaison (2005:50) has argued, "has no relation to cultural space. Paradoxically, travelling can close rather than open one's mind, thereby destroying cultural space." This is also noted by Basso (1996:147) when he describes young Apaches who may be traveling far away from their local area but, "reluctant to appear old-fashioned before their watchful peers," tend to travel much less extensively around that area, therefore learning "smaller bodies of cautionary narratives" and subscribing "with mounting conviction to the imported belief that useful knowledge comes mainly from formal schooling." The alternative cosmologies (see Beach, Chapter 3 in this volume), transmitted via such narratives through processes other than formal schooling, are lost to tradition as a result, and environmental amnesia sets in – a continual failure to remember place rightly: "Remembering place rightly . . . means more than having nostalgia for the pristine wilderness of some mythic past" (Clingerman 2011:154). The "complex affinities" of place are a matter of community engagement more than geography; the "social and moral force" of a sense of place "may reach sacramental proportions, especially when fused with prominent elements of personal and ethnic identity" (Basso 1996:148). Remembering rightly is an ethical challenge, therefore, particularly for groups that may have to come to terms with a past of nationalism and colonialism.

Höffe (2005:40), considering *oikos* as the Greek word for *Heimat* and combining it with *poiesis*, creation, speaks of an act of *oikopoiesis*: through appropriate perception and adaptation we can deal with the strange and often threatening aspects of a new place and turn it into a place of belonging and well-being. However, this happens in the knowledge that elements of "otherness" and brokenness will inevitably remain. Successful *oikopoiesis* also depends on the willingness to take on the work required, and this needs time. An interesting case study in this regard is the negotiation of place identities over successive generations of the *Deutsche Jugend des Ostens*, founded in 1951 – between a "backward" glance at lost homelands and a "forward" embracing of European "unity in diversity." Established to draw together youth organizations of refugees/expellees from areas of German settlement in Eastern Europe, it was perceived during its early decades as "cadre-forge" of nationalism. Reconstituted in 1974 as djo-Deutsche Jugend in Europa, a part of the European movement, it later became an umbrella organization for immigrant youth groups. Although its transformation revolves around key concerns of contemporary social and cultural studies – migration, belonging, and integration – in terms of concepts, policy and practice, there is a surprising dearth of research on this organization. Issues that such research could usefully address include the appropriation of place, beliefs and practices of belonging, and patterns and processes of experiencing what some describe as a *Heimat Europa* (Kockel 2010:173–174). The vast majority of refugees and expellees, and especially their children and grandchildren, are not concerned with blame and restitution, but with grieving for the places they lost and recovering the roots of their belonging (Hirsch 2004:251).

Ethnologists and anthropologists are called upon to develop ethnographically inflected understandings of place that help rekindled communities to remember rightly. Such research requires ethical sensitivity, and a finely honed sense of discernment to guard the researcher against serving the ever-ready jack-boots of a shallow essentialism (Kockel 2012). It studies in particular understandings based on ecologically grounded beliefs and practices, and the traditions from which these draw inspiration – in urban (cf. McIntosh 2008b) as much as in the more customary rural contexts, because a critical ethnotopology is nothing if its approach is not holistic.

NOTES

1 Lüdersen's speech from the film as transcribed by Kossert (2009:269–270) (translation by Ullrich Kockel).
2 The extras were actual refugees from Silesia, some 1000 of whom had been housed in the village of Bleckede, where the film was shot.
3 Translates as: "The struggle for our home place is more than just a word. The Wendland is liberated. We will never leave here!"
4 Translates as: "The dream of something." (Bolbrinker et al. 1981).
5 This even finds expression in the growing genre of *Regionalkrimis* (regional detective stories); for example, see Cibach (2004:31).

REFERENCES

Agnew, J.
2005 Introduction to the English edition. *In* Culture and Space: Conceiving a New Cultural Geography. J. Bonnemaison, ed. pp. xi–xxi. London: Tauris.
Arendt, H.
1992 Vita activa oder vom tätigen Leben. Munich: Piper.
Assmann, A.
1999 Erinnerungsräume: Formen und Wandlungen des kulturellen Gedächtnisses. Munich: Beck.
Augé, M.
1995 Non-Places: Introduction to an Anthropology of Supermodernity. London: Verso.
Basso, K.
1996 Wisdom Sits in Places: Landscape and Language among the Western Apache. Albuquerque: University of New Mexico Press.
Bauman, Z.
1995 Life in Fragments: Essays in Postmodern Morality. Oxford: Blackwell.
Bausinger, H.
1997 Intercultural Demands and Cultural Identity. Europaea III–1. Electronic document. http://www.h-net.org/~sae/europea/1997iii1.html (accessed November 5, 2011).
Bendix, R.
1997 In Search of Authenticity: The Formation of Folklore Studies. Madison: University of Wisconsin Press.
Benz, W.
2008 Zur Debatte: Flucht, Vertreibung, Versöhnung. Bundeszentrale für politische Bildung. Electronic document. http://www.bpb.de/themen/XMHIB5.html (accessed November 5, 2011).
Bergmann, S.
2006 Creation Set Free: The Spirit as Liberator of Nature (Sacra Doctrina: Christian Theology for a Postmodern Age). Grand Rapids, MI: William B. Eerdmans.

Bhabha, H.
1994 The Location of Culture. London: Routledge.
Biggs, I.
2004 Between Carterhaugh and Tamshiel Rig: A Borderline Episode. Bristol: Wild Conversations.
2007 Debatable Lands. Vol. 1. Bristol: Wild Conversations.
Binder, B., S. Göttsch, W. Kaschuba, and K. Vanja, eds.
2005 Ort, Arbeit, Körper. Ethnografie Europäischer Modernen. Münster: Waxmann.
Bolbrinker, N., R. Ziegler, B. Westphal, and K. Seybold, dirs.
1981 Der Traum von einer Sache. Produced by Wendländische Filmcooperative.
Bonnemaison, J.
2005 Culture and Space: Conceiving a New Cultural Geography. London: Tauris.
Campbell, L.
2011 The Foyle River Catchment Landscape: Connecting People, Place and Nature; Dwelling Beyond Dualistic Tensions. Unpublished PhD thesis, University of Ulster.
Casey, E.
1998 The Fate of Place: A Philosophical History. Berkeley and Los Angeles: University of California Press.
Cibach, A.
2004 Rat der Raben. Kassel: Prolibris.
Clifford, J., and G. Marcus
2010 Writing Culture: The Poetics and Politics of Ethnography. 25th Anniversary Edition. Berkeley: University of California Press.
Clingerman, F.
2011 Environmental Amnesia or the Memory of Place? The Need for Local Ethics of Memory in a Philosophical Theology of Place. *In* Religion and Ecology in the Public Sphere. C. Deane-Drummond and H. Bedford-Strohm, eds. pp. 141–159. London: T & T Clark.
Connor, I.
2007 Refugees and Expellees in Post-war Germany. Manchester: Manchester University Press.
Deffenbaugh, D.
2006 Learning the Language of the Fields: Tilling and Keeping as Christian Vocation. Cambridge, MA: Cowley.
Deppe, H. dir.
1951 Grün ist die Heide. Produced by Berolina.
Dönhoff, M.
2009 Namen, die keiner mehr nennt: Ostpreußen – Menschen und Geschichte. 2nd edition. Reinbek b. Hamburg: rororo.
Dwyer, P.
2005 Ethnoclassification, Ethnoecology and the Imagination. Journal de la Société des Océanistes 120–121:11–25.
Ellen, R., P. Parkes, and A. Bicker, eds.
2000 Indigenous Environmental Knowledge and Its Transformations: Critical Anthropological Perspectives. Amsterdam: Harwood.
Entrikin, N.
1991 The Betweenness of Place: Towards a Geography of Modernity. Baltimore: Johns Hopkins University Press.
Frantzioch, M.
1987 Die Vertriebenen: Hemmnisse und Wege ihrer Integration. Berlin: Reimer.

Fritz, N.
2007 Bewohnte Mythen: Joseph Beuys und der Aberglaube. Nuremberg: Verlag für moderne Kunst.
Greverus, I.
2005 Ästhetische Orte und Zeichen: Wege zu einer ästhetischen Anthropologie. Münster: LIT.
Haller, D.
2005 dtv-Atlas Ethnolgie. Munich: Deutscher Taschenbuchverlag.
Harrison, S.
2004 Forgetful and Memorious Landscapes. Social Anthropology 12:135–151.
Hirsch, H.
2004 Schweres Gepäck: Flucht und Vertreibung als Lebensthema. Hamburg: edition Körber-Stiftung.
Höffe, O.
2005 Europas Entdeckung und Erfindung: Die Vision eines Philosophen. *In* Europa – Mythos und Heimat: Identität aus Kultur und Geschichte. K. Kufeld, ed. pp. 25–41. Freiburg and Munich: Karl Alber.
Hornborg, A.
1996 Ecology as Semiotics: Outlines of a Contextualist Paradigm for Human Ecology. *In* Nature and Society: Anthropological Perspectives. P. Descola and G. Pálsson, eds. pp. 45–62. London: Routledge.
Ingold, T.
2000 The Perception of the Environment: Essays in Livelihood, Dwelling, and Skill. London: Routledge.
Jackson, M.
2000 At Home in the World. Durham, NC: Duke University Press.
Johnson, L.
2010 Trail of Story, Traveller's Path: Reflections on Ethnoecology and Landscape. Edmonton: Athabasca University Press.
Kenrick, J.
2011 Scottish Land Reform and Indigenous Peoples' Rights: Self-determination and Historical Reversibility. Social Anthropology 19:189–203.
Kockel, U.
1999 Borderline Cases: The Ethnic Frontiers of European Integration. Liverpool: Liverpool University Press.
2009 Wozu eine Europäische Ethnologie – und welche? Österreichische Zeitschrift für Volkskunde LXIII/112(3):39–56.
2010 Re-Visioning Europe: Frontiers, Place Identities and Journeys in Debatable Lands. Basingstoke: Palgrave Macmillan.
2011 Morphogenetic Fieldwork and the Ethnologic of Toposophy: Meditation on a Coyote Wandering on Rannoch Moor. *In* Beuysian Legacies in Ireland and Beyond: Art, Culture and Politics. C. Lerm Hayes and V. Walters, eds. pp. 195–219. Münster: LIT.
2012 Being From and Coming To: Outline of an Ethno-Ecological Framework. *In* Radical Human Ecology: Intercultural and Indigenous Approaches. L. Williams, R. Roberts, and A. McIntosh, eds. pp. 57–71. Aldershot: Ashgate.
Kossert, A.
2009 Kalte Heimat: Die Geschichte der deutschen Vertriebenen nach 1945. Munich: Pantheon.
Köstlin, K.
2010 Eine Ästhetik des Verlusts. *In* Zur Ästhetik des Verlusts: Bilder von Heimat, Flucht und Vertreibung. E. Fendl, ed. pp. 7–23. Münster: Waxmann.

Kunze, B.

2010 Renrajd Vualka. Electronic document. http://renrajd.com/volk-der-sami/sami-in-deutschland/sami-in-deutschland.html (accessed November 5, 2011).

Kürsten, A.

2010 Wie klingt Heimat? Musik/Sound und Erinnerung. *In* Zur Ästhetik des Verlusts: Bilder von Heimat, Flucht und Vertreibung. E. Fendl, ed. pp. 253–277. Münster: Waxmann.

Lachauer, U.

2000 Ostpreußische Lebensläufe. Reinbek b. Hamburg: rororo.

Lawrence, D.

1997 Place. *In* The Dictionary of Anthropology. T. Barfield, ed. pp. 360–361. Oxford: Blackwell.

Leach, E.

1984 Glimpses of the Unmentionable in the History of British Social Anthropology. Annual Review of Anthropology 13:1–23.

Lerm Hayes, C., and V. Walters, eds.

2011 Beuysian Legacies in Ireland and Beyond: Art, Culture and Politics. Münster: LIT.

Löfgren, O.

1996 Linking the Local, the National and the Global: Past and Present Trends in European Ethnology. Ethnologia Europaea 26(2):157–168.

MacKinnon, I.

2008 Crofters: Indigenous People of the Highlands and Islands. Kyle of Lochalsh: Scottish Crofting Foundation.

McDowell, C., and G. Morrell

2010 Displacement Beyond Conflict: Challenges for the 21st Century. Oxford: Berghahn.

McIntosh, A.

1998 Deep Ecology and the Last Wolf. Aisling Magazine 23. Electronic docment. http://www.aislingmagazine.com/aislingmagazine/articles/TAM23/Deep.html (accessed November 5, 2011).

2008a Some Contributions of Liberation Theology to Community Empowerment in Scottish Land Reform. Unpublished PhD thesis, University of Ulster.

2008b Rekindling Community: Connecting People, Environment and Spirituality. Schumacher Briefings 15. Dartington: Green Books

Meyrowitz, J.

1998 Das generalisierte Anderswo. *In* Perspektiven der Weltgesellschaft. U. Beck, ed. pp. 176–191. Frankfurt am Main: Suhrkamp.

Munn, N.

2003 Excluded Spaces: The Figure in the Australian Aboriginal Landscape. *In* The Anthropology of Space and Place: Locating Culture. S. Low and D. Lawrence-Zúñiga, eds. pp. 92–109. Oxford: Blackwell.

NDR

2010 Gorleben (1) – Das Hüttendorf. NDR Mediathek. http://www.youtube.com/watch?v=fgpJXvFKhbg (accessed November 5, 2011).

Niven, B, ed.

2006 Germans as Victims: Remembering the Past in Contemporary Germany. Basingstoke: Palgrave Macmillan.

Paládi-Kovács, A., ed.

2004 Times – Places – Passages: Ethnological Approaches in the New Millennium. Budapest: Akadémiai Kiadó.

Rapport, N., and A. Dawson, eds.
1998 Migrants of Identity: Perceptions of Home in a World of Movement. Oxford: Berg.
Rapport, N., and J. Overing
2007 Social and Cultural Anthropology: The Key Concepts. 2nd edition. London: Routledge.
Rauschenbach, B.
2001 Heimat im Übergang: Erbschaft dieses Landes, dieser Zeit. *In* Grenzgängerin: Bridges between disciplines; Eine Festschrift für Irmingard Staeuble. C. Kraft Alsop, ed. pp. 229–251. Heidelberg and Kröning: Asanger.
Reiski, P.
2002 Ein Land so weit: Ostpreußische Erinnerungen. Berlin: List.
Rodman, M.
2003 Empowering Place: Multilocality and Multivocality. *In* The Anthropology of Space and Place: Locating Culture. S. Low and D. Lawrence-Zúñiga, eds. pp. 204–224. Oxford: Blackwell.
Schmitz, H., ed.
2007 A Nation of Victims? Representations of German Wartime Suffering from 1945 to the Present. Amsterdam: Rodopi.
Scott, P.
2011 Right Out of Time? Politics and Nature in a Postnatural Condition. *In* Religion and Ecology in the Public Sphere. C. Deane-Drummond and H. Bedford-Strohm, eds. pp. 57–75. London: T & T Clark.
Tilley, C.
2006 Introduction: Identity, Place, Landscape and Heritage. Journal of Material Culture 11(1/2):7–32.
Treichel, H.
2005 Der Verlorene. BasisBibliothek 60. Frankfurt am Main: Suhrkamp.
Virilio, P.
1992 Rasender Stillstand. Munich: Piper.
Völkering, T.
2010 Die Musealisierung der Themen Flucht, Vertreibung und Integration: Analysen zur Debatte um einen neuen musealen Gedenkort und zu historischen Ausstellungen seit 1950. *In* Zur Ästhetik des Verlusts: Bilder von Heimat, Flucht und Vertreibung. E. Fendl, ed. pp. 71–124. Münster: Waxmann.
Wallace, M.
2005 Finding God in the Singing River. Minneapolis: Augsburg Fortress.
Walters, V.
2009 The Language of Healing: Joseph Beuys and the Celtic Wor(l)d. Unpublished PhD thesis, University of Ulster.
Weiner, J.
2001 Tree Leaf Talk: A Heideggerian Anthropology. Oxford: Berg.
White, K.
1987 L'Esprit nomade. Paris: Bernard Grasset.
1998 A Shaman Dancing on the Glacier. *In* On Scottish Ground: Selected Essays. pp. 35–48. Edinburgh: Polygon.
2004 The Wanderer and His Charts: Exploring the Fields of Vagrant Thought and Vagabond Beauty. Edinburgh: Polygon.
Willke, H.
2001 Atopia: Studien zur atopischen Gesellschaft. Frankfurt am Main: Suhrkamp.

CHAPTER 33

A Tale of Two Disciplines: European Ethnology and the Anthropology of Europe

Jonas Frykman

A palette rich in aspects of European culture is displayed in this book. Here you will find studies of pastoral culture in the Mediterranean area and reindeer husbandry in the North; hormone-packed rock music in Rumanian forests and authors on a creative writing course in Ireland; post-Yugoslavian war atrocities and peaceful days in doctors' surgeries and laboratories. Not to mention the culture that has developed among bureaucrats in Brussels or the treatment of the many migrants seeking a future inside the walls of the European Union (EU). The contributors all specialize in the academic subjects of Ethnology and the Anthropology of Europe. In a world where many are occupied with similar issues – sociology, cultural studies, history, and political science – we might wonder what it is that makes people feel immediately at home with ethnological and anthropological studies.

Anthropology is the comparative study of society that attempts to draw generalized conclusions about *anthropos*, mankind. It was established during the nineteenth century as the study of primitive civilizations in far-off lands and has belonged to the social sciences for a long time. Ethnology belongs to the humanities and is regarded as the historical study of *ethnos*, people – mainly Europeans – and their spiritual, material, and social culture. But such definitions cannot easily capture the contributions to this volume. As will become evident, this is a mix in which ethnology has been anthropologized, and vice-versa, where new impulses have come from neighboring disciplines and where radical changes have taken place over time.[1] Since the 1970s ethnologists could probably say that they have changed the discipline from antiquarian-oriented research to *cultural analysis* with historical perspectives (Bausinger 1972) and that anthropology works just as well "at home" as abroad.

It is in fact easier to capture their distinctive characters on the basis of how they work, because here they are most alike and at the same time different from other disciplines. As Ullrich Kockel (2008:9) writes in the journal, *Ethnologia Europaea*,

A Companion to the Anthropology of Europe, First Edition. Edited by Ullrich Kockel, Máiréad Nic Craith, and Jonas Frykman.

"European ethnology is how European ethnologists do things." And behind this seemingly circular statement there is a history of two academic disciplines that throughout the years have focused on people's everyday lives in different societies and have worked with qualitative methods, "unlike sociologists and historians . . . their interest in society was not concerned with formal institutions and macro-structures" (Löfgren 2008:124). With ears pressed closely to the ground their theories have kept pace with social change. The art of pursuing ethnography has become their characteristic feature and most important export commodity.

In the following we will see what the differences have been and what has united them, how they have arrived at this diversity, and how they can be recognized by "the way in which they do things." The story of the two disciplines is a fascinating one of how two relatively marginal members of the academic community have become key disciplines for understanding the world. Although the interest in culture was something of an oddity from the beginning, it has now become everyone's property.

The word "culture" has spread like an epidemic throughout academia and society alike. Indeed, we can see how economists, political scientists, sociologists, doctors, architects, journalists, and media experts have diligently borrowed concepts and methods and added them to their own courses. The ethnographic way of working has become public property in marketing, the tourist industry, and social planning. Considering the wide acceptance it could be said that ethnology and anthropology have simply been too victorious; that their ways of working have proved to be useful in so many fields, yet as disciplines they have not been growing to the same extent. Students have not been rushing into the lecture theaters and the disciplines have remained relatively small in terms of numbers. The impact says something important about the benefits of being a small discipline. It can mean having room in which to maneuver simply because – unlike so many other academic fields – there is little dependency on administrative or professional expectations, as is the case with schools, public administration, the church, the marketplace, or healthcare. Ethnologists and anthropologists can now be found in a variety of professional fields in society. It is rightly maintained that the disciplines work heuristically – with a wide range of methods and theoretical openness. Such positions are permissible if "customer requirements" are somewhat vague.

The Two Triangles

At the beginning of the 1990s, Roger Abrahams, Professor in Folkloristics at the University of Pennsylvania, gave a seminar at the institute in Bergen, Norway, where I was then working. The theme was the difference between ethnology and folkloristics on the one hand and anthropology on the other – from an American perspective. He maintained that for much of the twentieth century the frontiers had been closely guarded and that the academic quarreling that took place during this period may even have been necessary for the formation of the disciplines; neither of which had been fully scientifically established. The decisive factor was that both dealt with the same theme – culture – and that the differences thus had to be exaggerated. The risk of confusion has been ever present, but there's much more to it than that. Anthropology was English-based and dominated by American and English universities, while ethnology was national; whereas ethnologists used archives, worked historically, and were oriented toward things and verbal sources, anthropologists worked with synchronized social investigations and used participant observation as a data collection method.

These were well-known differences and I nodded in agreement. It was even a bit comical when Abrahams likened the subjects to two triangles. Anthropology stood on its point of fairly limited empirical data, but had a strikingly strong theoretical superstructure. With the aim of developing "Grand Theories," the starting point was often individual fieldwork in locally confined communities. Ethnology, on the other hand, was a contextually rich discipline with both legs firmly planted in its empirical soil. Throughout the years it had been characterized by rather vague interpretive models, which in itself was completely natural, given that it was the detailed knowledge about people – usually one's own country's inhabitants – that was thought to motivate researchers. The two fields had created different working methods and their scholars developed a different habitus. There was something in their approach that sustained the differences.

I sat at the seminar table self-consciously drawing triangles with flat bases and points and was struck by how well this tallied with the changes I had witnessed during the 30 years that I had been involved with the discipline. The renewal of European ethnology had been necessary during the 1960s. It was a science that had got stuck in its antiquarian and descriptive perspectives. What were ingrained concepts to an older generation jarred against the reality we encountered at that time. Inspiration definitely came from the more theory-conscious anthropology and flowed along channels like Fredrik Barth's interactionism, Edmund Leach's and Mary Douglas's empirical structuralism and Lévi Strauss' linguistically inspired structuralism. It also came from historians and philosophers like Norbert Elias, Michel Foucault, and E. P. Thompson, and gradually also from poststructuralism and phenomenology. And those of us who read about studies in more exotic countries than Europe constantly asked ourselves why the theories often dealt with far-flung civilizations when they could throw so much light on our own!

It probably took about a generation for ethnology to shed its skin and develop new tools, which to adopt Bausinger's (1972) words ranged from *Altertumsforschung* [antiquarian perspective] to *cultural analysis*. The readjustment process was more turbulent within my own discipline than within anthropology – and it was that story that the two triangles told.

The Making of an Ethnologist

When I began my studies in ethnology at Lund University in the mid-1960s my professor, Sigfrid Svensson, announced to the seminar participants – albeit with a glint in his eye but still with personal conviction – that "the most important thing for an ethnologist was to be born somewhere." That made those of us who belonged to the baby-boom generation sit up and take notice, because we immediately felt disqualified. We had an urban background. The issues that concerned us related to the 1960s and to class and social structures, to solidarity with undeveloped countries, the relation between town and country, equality and the rapid demise of "the affluent society."

We had been born into a world of movement and dismantled frontiers. We had no memories of a densely populated countryside, of horse-drawn carts, local shops, and junior schools where the teacher rang a bell to call the children inside. Instead of winding dirt roads with gates and wooden fences, we worshipped asphalt and new makes of car. Suburban houses, living rooms with contrast wallpaper and TV, working mothers, and nursery schools were our home environments. But Svensson's own background was the Scanian village. As a youngster he had mucked out the stables and worked in the fields. At home he heard older people talk about their childhood practices, traditions, and imaginings about what life was like before there was a school or village shop – and about the excitement of seeing the first train roll across the plain. He sat in the kitchen on many an evening and "celebrated twilight" while waiting for the paraffin lamp to be lit at the fade of day. It was then that the stories flowed and the past was temporarily rekindled.

After secondary school in the nearby town, he took the train to the center of learning Lund where he began his academic career. Like his fellow students in folkloristics, as the subject was then called, he spent his summers cycling around remote villages in order to discover and document the traces of the old world that were still visible. In order to earn his living he worked periodically as a journalist and became a skilled writer. This proved to be good experience, since at that time communication with readers was a matter of course among folklorists, and the readership was much wider than it was in academia. This fostered a special kind of essayistic style in him that is still prevalent today in Swedish ethnological literature.

Like many of his generation, Sigfrid Svensson knew what the dramatic shift from a rural and traditional community to an industrialized urban culture both meant and implied. As an ethnologist you are always too late. The theme that he constantly returned to was what had happened "when modernity arrived" – and solidarity with those who had experienced the heavy toil and poverty of living and working on the land. His political bent was toward social democracy. Without developing his engagement into theory, he held on to a kind of historical materialism.

After writing his doctoral thesis on folk costumes in Scania (Svensson 1935), he worked for many years at the Nordiska Museet [the Nordic Museum] in Stockholm – Sweden's leading museum. Together with his colleague Gösta Berg, he wrote the exemplary book about Swedish peasant culture, *Svensk bondekultur*, in 1934. In lay terms it describes the customs, religious, and material culture in the world that we now refer to as "the old peasant culture". Here culture was characteristically carved into sections like dwelling, society, customs and beliefs, handicraft and arts, narration and poetry, and so on. In other disciplines within the humanities the epoch was the founding principle, and in the anthropology of the time social relations was the point of departure (cf. Löfgren 1988, 2008).

When a professorship became vacant in Lund he made his way back to the province. His period of service also included management of the large Folklife Archive at Lund University – or was it perhaps the other way around? The archive's collections certainly had an impact on the research that he and those who worked in the department carried out. Since its establishment in 1913 different sides of life in pre-modern peasant society had been systematically documented: its religious and narrative traditions, buildings, and artifacts. Even though the subject of ethnology had become well established, as an academic discipline it was still in its infancy.

The Class Defector's Dilemma

What kind of habitus was then fostered within the discipline? Sigfrid Svensson's career path can serve as an example of how prior to the 1960s ethnology was established as "normal science" in terms of methods, theories, and field of activity – and the world's expectations of what an ethnologist might master. The orientation toward rural society and popular culture in one's own country was obvious, as was the historical perspective; the connection with museums and documentation served as professional preparation. It was now clear that ethnology paved the way for work in museums.

Growing up in a rural area was something that Svensson shared with many of his colleagues. He talked readily about the pragmatism that he had inherited from home; something that prevented him from making too many circumstantial speculations. Ethnology attracted many social climbers: they entered the world of university with simple habits and often felt that the academic cap and gown clamped down on life.

The French sociologist Pierre Bourdieu has written about his experiences – the boy from the countryside who easily worked his way through the school system but who constantly regarded himself as an outsider; someone who longs for home but cannot imagine himself returning (cf. Reed-Danahay 2005). The home environment was much too suffocating and the strains and stresses of work claimed all his attention. How could he perform his tasks with the same abandon as scholars born into the privilege of intellectual excellence? Bourdieu regarded himself as a class defector; someone who had betrayed his social origins but was at the same time unable to free himself from them. In his case this gave rise to reflections about how tied the social climber can be to the dominant culture, at the same time as it trains him to be extremely sensitive to its rules. The reaction was of course to be both competent and conscientious in his profession.

Circumstances thus provided him with a solid base when it came to observing and drawing conclusions about culture and society. Being able to look at one's own background in an unbiased way and at the same time remain an outsider in the environment to which you belong – this is and remains the class defector's special privilege and curse. This position was decisive for Bourdieu's own research on French society in general and for the study of academia in particular.

For many of the scholars who were drawn to ethnology there were lots of opportunities for identification. It was after all a discipline that reflected their own experiences – and at the same time deepened and universalized what they already knew. A habitus was formed here that clearly differed from that of contemporary scholars – doctors, lawyers, and architects who often came from well-to-do milieus – and also from that of anthropologists. Even though it was possible to find social climbers among the latter, it was unusual for anyone to have family ties with or experiential knowledge of the societies that they would later study. Instead, we have the impression that the education and the fieldwork were tickets for getting as far away from home as possible. Indeed, much of the representation critique that Marcus and Fisher (1986) initiated during the 1980s with *Anthropology as Cultural Critique* was about how the heritage of home colored the description of the unfamiliar and foreign.

Discovering the People

When Anthony Jackson (1987) edited the classic volume *Anthropology at Home* it had become a matter of course for anthropologists to carry out fieldwork in their own countries. The close cooperation between his own discipline and European ethnology was also developing. In the preface he muses on the different public appeal of the two subjects: "why was ethnology so popular with the general public?" and "why social anthropology is not" (1987:4). His answer was that it was probably to do with people's need to belong that afflicted so many nations. This explanation is good enough, but is more characteristic of his own era and search for roots than the historical period when ethnology appeared on the scene. In actual fact, for well over a century people had been brought up to regard ethnological knowledge as knowledge about themselves. Ethnology was a result of the classic triad of the nineteenth century: industrialization and urbanization, nation-building, and the democratic breakthrough. This is where *Altertumsforschung* played it most important role.

At the turn of the last century three-quarters of the population of Europe still lived in the countryside and the majority of them earned their living from the land. Industrialization tipped the balance and many of the new era's workers and proletariat flocked to the towns. Grown men and women still had strong family ties with rural life – both culturally and economically. If they lost their jobs they could always return home.

The European nations were faced with an enormous educational project: the democratic breakthrough had meant that political legitimacy had to be sought among the people – an insight that was not always enthusiastically received by those in power. People obviously needed to be educated in order to live up to expectations – in the countryside as well as in the town. As Camillo di Cavour is credited with saying after Italian unification in 1861, "we have created Italy – now we have to create Italians."[2] Behind his remark lay the fact that Italy was divided into a number of states or provinces, that the dialects that were spoken at one end of the country were almost unintelligible to those living at the other, and that the majority didn't even know what Italy was. As Eugen Weber (1976) depicted, the latter part of the nineteenth century was regarded as the time to turn reluctant French peasants into proper Frenchmen. The elementary school, the conscript army, the newspaper press, and the railway were – together with ethnology – all tools for making citizens out of peasants (Anderson 1983; Gellner 1983).

Ethnology and folkloristics could answer the question about who "the people" actually were and which traditions they had bequeathed. Historians could testify to a glorious military past; but rarely about that which spoke to the heart – the home, the hearth, father and mother, the land, and the many memories – matters which Michael Herzeld called *cultural intimacy* (1997). Together with the folklorists, ethnologists could breathe life into the emotional aspects of the nation. Logically enough the subject came to be called *Folklivsforskning* [Folklife research] in Sweden and, with the same meaning, *Volkskunde* in Germany, or *narodnoznanstvo* in some of the Slavic languages. The terms illustrated that it was a mapping of the majority of people's lives, traditions and origins that was on the agenda. And, naturally enough, such knowledge was included in what was taught at school.

In the majority of European countries knowledge about these things contributed to the cultural homogenization process of each nation. Generation after generation was thus brought up to understand itself as inheriting its nation's popular past, which in a surprisingly short time resulted in "the inclusion of nationally delineated peasants and lower classes into the circle of what each nation defined as its own version of civilised human society" (Hage 2003:15).

National engagement distinguished ethnology from the majority of academic disciplines at that time and shook its already precarious scientific foundations. The subject was actually part of a mass movement that attracted professionals and amateurs whose agenda included the national, regional, and local. People's lives and the nation's peculiarities had become favorite themes of music, art, and literature – not to mention the number of local folklore associations and popular organizations, all of which had their own cultures in mind. The discipline was also influenced by what the general public expected from research. Being in constant contact with the fields they studied and the readers who had a keen interest in the resulting research were additional factors.

The broader interface outside academia and the discipline's political mandate led to ethnology adopting national characteristics in the different countries. In several of the new states formed after World War I, like Finland, the Balkan countries, and Central Europe, the issue of race – which is another way of describing people's origins – was an obvious concern and associated with the nation's self-knowledge. However, in the post–World War II socialist countries, ethnology was reduced to dealing with politically neutral issues. The Croatian ethnologist, Dunja Rihtman Auguštin (2004), wrote that socialism was all about building a better world, and thus having problems with the notion of tradition. The matter of descent had now become both obsolete and antiestablishment. "Our appeals for the nurture of heritage came across as a lamentation and as an anachronism. Ethnology was often accused of being conservative. To be frank, it was so in part . . ." (2004:61). In other countries, such as England and France, the emergence of colonies meant that attention shifted away from one's own country's borders and that anthropology totally dominated the scene.

Documentation

The popularity that Anthony Jackson wondered about was cemented by the accessibility to information about this "folk culture". From the end of the nineteenth century and onward an intensive collection of objects by archives and museums took place, and a stream of scientific publications about one's own folk culture saw the light of day. Being out in the field with notebook in hand was important for the discipline, but even more important was what was in the archives. In country after country this unique combination of academic discipline and accompanying archive collections was reproduced. Lists of questions also flowed out to a diverse network of local informants from the archives. Area after area of popular culture was dealt with, with the ambition of documenting everything that reflected the different aspects of traditional culture and that covered the regional variations.

Invaluable information was thus collected about how ordinary people had worked and lived and about what they had believed and related: covering everything from bringing up children and taking care of the elderly to celebrating annual and seasonal festivals. Interestingly, comparable knowledge about anonymous people's lives – from the early nineteenth century and beyond – can only be found in folklife archives in Europe. When *oral history* emerged as a subdiscipline of history in England in the 1970s it should be remembered that a similar activity had been zealously taking place for decades as a result of ethnological collection.

The archives served as a watershed between ethnology and anthropology. Ethnologists asked their anthropological colleagues if they could really see beyond the knowledge that had been gathered in boxes and behind the headings. Anthropologists, on their part, wondered whether ethnology had become a too retrospective and material-oriented science as a result of their collections and could no longer see society for the records.

Apart from the historically valuable nature of the collections, the role they played for the development of the discipline was often overlooked. It was not simply that they directed attention toward the past – they also fetishized the written word. This might seem strange in a science that attached so much importance to the spoken word. In line with Bruno Latour (1999), it could be said that the objects of scientific study were socially constructed in the actual archives, in that a culture took shape that defined a system of practices about how to translate the results from the field to the finished study. The archival system became what he referred to as *actants*, together with the researcher's parts of the network that produced results and scientific legitimacy. Important concepts like "record," "source criticism," "provenance," and "accession number" were powerful elements in this chain of translations.

Already during his anthropological studies and his immersion in the participant observation method, Pierre Bourdieu (1977) asked what happens when knowledge is acquired and compiled by means of interviews – or records. What the researcher then does is to transfer the task of translation of events to the informant. The result is that rules and structures are easily emphasized instead of practice and agency. What was once embodied practice and experience then appears to be part of a rationally planned course of events. Although this observation might seem persnickety, it highlights a characteristic feature of European ethnology, namely the existence of "an old peasant society." The collection format has emphasized regularity and structure. The method itself has supported the idea of the existence of an old peasant culture. And that people with good memories were the "carriers" of this. This does not nullify the value of the collections, but rather indicates a systematic tweaking of how they have been understood. It also separated ethnology and anthropology by "how they were doing things."

The cultural and political implications of this are more than familiar. "The folklorization" of the past has adopted many different formats – from socialism's ideas about how "ethnicity" belonged to a lost world and therefore had to appear in folk costumes in specific arenas, to the tourist industry's love of the popular and colorful. Peasant culture differed from place to place – which was particularly apparent from the costumes. The places in which people lived were also connected with and manifested in their "national character." *Blut und Boden* was a theory that was very easy to gain support for if you only looked for it in the archives, long before it became a leitmotif within fascism. Naturally enough, it is this theme that has been debated over and over again within the discipline since the end of World War II – particularly in Germany and Austria (Dow and Bockhorn 2004). The break with tradition in German ethnology, *Abschied von Volksleben* (Geiger et al. 1970), actually took place during the 1960s and was preceded by the way in which ethnology was made use of in the Third Reich.

Whereas anthropology has had to dust off its colonial past, ethnology still has a lot of cleaning work to do. Today's political xenophobia has breathed life into dreams about the people and a longing for an original and clearly defined national territory. Extreme right-wing movements have a long history of unrequited love of the idea of "folk culture." Critical studies of nationalistic currents have also developed into a specific theme among ethnologists and anthropologists alike, with Europe as a speciality.

What we should not forget within the subjects when the hair shirt is donned is how notions about people have also served as a moral weapon against different claims for power. The anthropologist Anthony Cohen (1996) has shown how the idea of the national also contains an empowerment of the individual and can make him or her speak out for rights and justice. As the Australian anthropologist Ghassan Hage points out, national identity can work as a kind of everyday magic. "The national 'we' magically enables the 'I' of the national to do things it can never hope to do as an individual 'I'. The child uttering 'we are good at football' sets himself or herself on the road of 'trying to be good at football' " (Hage 2003:13). Being able to see one's own life in the light of belonging to a nation – whether this relates to football or political activity – opens up much more than simply safeguarding who you are and what you have.

The long period of acclimatization that is necessary to become a "people" has also created a common platform for the European nations. There is a discourse, a host of conceptions about what it is that differentiates Frenchmen from Spaniards, Italians from Slovenians, Germans from Poles, and so on. A broad narrative tradition has developed here that today serves as coinage and contact point in encounters between Europeans. The Europeanization "from below" that takes place today is largely facilitated by the fact that people already know so much about each other. Stereotyping also serves as a door opener (Frykman and Niedermüller 2003).

The Different

The history of the anthropology of Europe is much shorter and less bound up with interest groups, staked out careers, or national projects. The organization EASA, the European Association of Social Anthropologists, was established in 1989 and has about a thousand registered members. Its counterpart on the ethnology side is SIEF, Société Internationale d'Ethnologie et de Folklore, which dates back to 1928. While EASA is simply an interest organization that arranges conferences every other year and publishes the *Social Anthropology* journal, SIEF had more ambitious goals, few of which have actually been realized. After World War II many countries produced different maps of the spatial spread of their material and spiritual cultures. A common European project was launched in the 1960s with the intention of mapping different aspects of folk culture. The comparison thus related to the distribution of individual cultural elements rather than comparisons between different societies. However, as the use of such activities was no longer considered relevant, the project was aborted (Rogan 2008). Today EASA and SIEF can be regarded as organizations for collegial collaboration – anthropologists are invited to speak at ethnologists' meetings and vice versa. At their respective conferences in 2008 they both got to grips with their historically inherited sins – ethnology's preoccupation with history and heritage and anthropology's engagement with its colonial past (Povrzanović Frykman 2008).

It wasn't until the late 1960s that the European branch of general anthropology started to grow and become comparable with that in other parts of the world. When Deborah Reed-Danahay, later president of the Society for the Anthropology of Europe, first visited France in the 1970s to begin her studies of the educational system, she found to her surprise that there "was precious little French ethnography undertaken by French anthropologists, most of whom had not yet 'discovered' France as a terrain of fieldwork" (2005:8). "Real anthropologists" went to other places.

In his review of North European anthropology, Reginald Byron (2002) writes: "As late as 1950, a certain British university denied a PhD to a candidate at least partly on the grounds that since the fieldwork for the thesis had been carried out in Scotland, it could not be considered as an appropriate work of social anthropology. Anthropology 'at home' had not yet become generally accepted."

In addition to Europe not giving credit for a continued career, the territory simply did not feel fresh, complex as it was and mortgaged by ethnology and folkloristics. But as Christian Giordano writes in this volume, the world changed and after World War II several of the classic grounds were closed to researchers. Anthropologists from the United States and Europe were no longer welcome in the countries that had ceased to be colonies, while Europe was wide open – even if no-one actually wanted to go there. When "anthropology at home" (Jackson 1987) was established as a concept, it was also a result of the need to take complexity and globalization seriously – not to mention the new themes like state, governance, and diversity that had appeared at the top of the list of important research projects.

But it was difficult to stop being drawn to what was exotically different – or at least comfortably different. Setting out for the renowned "field" was and became the "*rite de passage*" to a promising career; fieldwork undertaken without malaria tablets was actually a compromise (Hannerz 2006). As late as the 1990s, the number of anthropologists in the Mediterranean area was twice that in other areas. Britain and Ireland vied for second place, and after the fall of the Berlin Wall a wave of researchers made their way toward Eastern Europe and Russia.

The preference was to explore inaccessible and besieged areas at the continent's periphery – those that had not yet attracted much attention from society or ethnology. As Reginald Byron (2002) pointed out, European mountain areas, remote villages, native populations like the Lapps and the Celts, and island and fishing communities were better described by anthropologists than ethnologists. What, then, did anthropology contribute in terms of knowledge about these communities, more than to increase the exoticization of Europe? An example of pioneer work can serve as a distant mirror.

The Making of an Anthropologist

While Sigfrid Svensson lapped up the accolades for his innovative thesis on regional folk costumes from the eighteenth century and beyond, the anthropologist Conrad Arensberg was in Ireland doing fieldwork. He was part of a mixed American expedition with the striking name of "Harvard Irish Mission." For his part the work resulted in the thesis entitled *The Irish Countryman* (1937), which after three years was followed by a book that paved the way for what was later developed into the anthropology of Europe, namely the classic *Family and Community in Ireland* (1940), co-authored with colleague and close friend Solon T. Kimball, also an anthropologist and member of the same expedition.

If ethnologists' research-habitus was at that time shaped by expectations within the antiquarian field in which they worked, the backgrounds and the educational routes of anthropologists were somewhat different. Conrad Maynadier Arensberg grew up in an upper-class family in Pittsburgh.[3] His father was a respected lawyer of German stock and eventually became the president of the Pennsylvania Bar. His mother's ancestry could be traced back to the immigration of French Huguenots in the seventeenth century – hence the middle name of Maynadier. As a child and adolescent he found his best friends in the world of books, which also led to the family realizing that their son's future lay in academic studies. As for many gifted students with a secure social background, his period of study at the prestigious Harvard University offered rich grazing in many different fields of knowledge. He felt completely at home among the many disciplines. Before finally deciding on anthropology he had dabbled in history, languages, the social sciences, economy, and literature. He actually learned to speak several European languages, including German, French, Italian, Spanish, some Dutch, and a little Russian – all of which seemed essential for someone who would eventually devote himself to comparative cultural research. In the obituary, Lambros Comitas (1999) mentions that Arensberg suffered from a stammer – except when speaking a foreign language. It was there, among the strange and the unfamiliar, that he felt himself most at ease. It was also anthropology that contained the most attractive challenges and searched for answers to the bigger questions way beyond the national boundaries: the history and science of mankind.

His studies in Ireland became a stepping stone in his career as a researcher – following a path off the beaten track. During World War II he served as an air force intelligence agent. As he knew so much about Europe, he was charged with studying the efficiency of mass bombings on Germany – and arrived at the conclusion that the results did not live up to expectations. When the war ended he obtained a post in sociology, and in 1952 was given a professorship at Columbia University, where he remained until his retirement. After a long and successful professional life that included "applied anthropology," different "community studies," and studies of historical empires and contemporary markets together with the economist Karl Polanyi, on his retirement he was given a commemorative volume with the fitting title of *Culture and Community in Europe* – the theme that had been close to his heart for many years.

With Ireland as Model

In addition to anthropologists, members of the "Harvard Irish Mission" also included experts in the subjects of archaeology and physical anthropology. The goal was ambitious and somewhat hazardous, namely to investigate "a distinctive and characteristic variant of western European civilization, a long, relatively unbroken tradition dating back to pre-Christian and pre-Roman times" (Lysaght 2002). In effect it meant a return to the ancient world and observing it with new methods and fresh eyes. In the preface to *Family and Community,* the authors also emphasized how revolutionary the enterprise actually was in relation to what their colleagues did – those who believed that they had to go to India or New Guinea in order to carry out research: "Their failure to study our own society has not been mere oversight, and not entirely because the subject attracted young men who found in it an excuse for faraway adventure among exotic peoples" (Arensberg and Kimball 1940:xi). Nevertheless, it must have felt like a more unproven field than setting out for the South Pacific and following in Bronisław Malinowski's footsteps.

The investigation did not differ methodically from the already established model for a community study – apart from its proximity to the European civilization. When Robert McGill Thomas, the famous journalist for the New York Times, wrote Arensberg's obituary in 1997 he emphasized that the book "was hailed as a landmark and only partly because it was the first study of a European culture in a field that had previously concentrated on people in loincloths."

In practice the researchers settled for several years in the town of Ennis and the surrounding countryside of County Clare, where they took part in the everyday activities of the farms – routines as well as shared tasks. They identified key informants for interviews and made use of interpreters in order to immerse themselves in the language. Although English was common, the Gaelic that was spoken also revealed specialist knowledge. As a reader of their work we can follow what everyday life on the land was like, the seasonal changes, what the farms looked like, which tasks were carried out by men, women and children, how the elderly were cared for, and how legacies were allocated.

It was here that Arensberg and Kimball also encountered an already established scientific tradition and collaborated with it. Irish folkloristics and ethnology had for many years maintained contact with the Scandinavian scene. Collection methods and filing principles were the same as those practiced at the Folklife Archive in Lund – and in Uppsala. In other words, the system had been borrowed from Sweden.

Strangely enough, the anthropological way of working was regarded as completely different from that which today is a sister-discipline. When the folklorist Séamus Ó Duilearga was doing fieldwork in the same area at that time, it was also in the capacity of Arensberg's assistant. Patricia Lysaght (2002) has described how Ó Duilearga helped him to get to the area that was "still largely steeped in tradition yet not untouched by modernity," because they were also looking for traditional ways of life. While the folklorist collected the informants' oral narratives and traditions, Arensberg studied the community through interactions among members of the household. The collection of stories was eventually archived at the Irish Folklore Commission, where they constitute invaluable material for the study of Irish cultural heritage. Séamus Ó Duilearga became Professor of Folklore at University College in Dublin.

The Irish study was carried out in the functionalistic spirit of Malinowski and Alfred Radcliffe-Brown, which implied that theory generated the relevant questions. Society was seen as a system supported by its institutions, of which family and kinship were the most important. Knowledge about them gave a deeper insight into politics, economics, and other relations between groups. Indeed, Radcliffe-Brown regarded his subject as the natural science of society and was deeply sceptical of historical or genetic interpretations. Events should be explained on the basis of the functions they had in the time to which they belonged.

This approach may have appealed to Arensberg, who had a great interest in the natural sciences. In practice it meant that he tried to identify basic patterns of culture and behavior based on social interactions within the household framework, which is why family structures, marital strategies, authority-relations between relatives, land rights, and inheritance were so important to him. Even the large-scale emigration to the United States was regarded as a safety valve for keeping family structures intact. For the European anthropology yet to be, the model became a royal road, based on something as concrete as family and village life. It was also something that scholars could study by living in the places they had chosen for fieldwork, immersed like a fly on the wall.

The study of Ireland "helped open up Europe to ethnographic studies," as his colleague Lambros Comitas (1999) wrote on Arensberg's death; both through choice of subject and the methods that were applied. As Patricia Lysaght (2002) writes in a review, the books "became classics on the basis of their theoretical and methodological strengths in the studies of local communities in the Old World, and the richness and evocativeness of the descriptions of local life in country and town which they contained."

Criticism of Arensberg and Kimball from the historically related disciplines was not unexpected. When the study was conducted, Ireland as a nation was barely 10 years old. Not only did that give rise to a call for its own history, it was also a country that was deeply characterized by its colonial experiences. Did people really want to be the objects of a "mission" from another great power wanting to describe the exotic inhabitants' lives? And was it not only a limited knowledge that could be extracted from a study that was "moored as it is to a functionalist view of society . . . seem to float in a time-less void isolated from the perturbations of modern history" (Birdwell-Pheasant 1992:205)?

Closing Up and Reinventing

It is fascinating to follow how community studies became directional for anthropologists with Europe as their speciality, but also its impact on ethnology when it began to be anthropologized during the radical years of the 1960s and 1970s. Remote communities also enticed ethnologists to fieldwork in fishing villages, islands, industrial communities, working-class and depopulated areas. The people who lived there were no longer carriers of the traces of a past culture, but were regarded as alternatives to the social development that so many people were critical of. Orvar Löfgren writes that the people who lived in these places had a close interaction – face to face – with each other: "Ethnologists became champions of the 'little people' and the 'little community'" (2008:124). The new generation were on the outlook for "alternatives to modernization, urbanization, industrialization, exploitation, alienation – and not least the fickleness of character that was said to characterize post-modern society" (Frykman et al. 2009:17).

The great undertaking that the generations after Svensson were engaged with was nothing less than reinventing the discipline. The tale of the two triangles was to be turned into history. In this process anthropology appeared to have a greater advantage in terms of clinging to its roots and traditions, while ethnology had to scan the contemporary scene in order to find new moorings. Which new methods could be used to describe this society; which theories could best explain the development? Inspiration from community studies served as a starting point and helped to contour the arenas with alternatives. More were added over time. Methodologically, something crucial was added that was more a question of tradition within the discipline than influence from neighboring disciplines. This was the chronological perspective, and an opportunity to use the rich source-material in the archives. This made it possible to conduct comparisons over time. For a long time the study of historical processes was to brand European ethnology in most countries. To some extent this also applied to the anthropology of Europe, which by "coming home" had widened its contextual knowledge. Nowadays it is not unusual to include the ethnological research that already existed – something that Chris Hann points out in this volume.

Added to local perspectives in ethnology from the 1980s onward were the study of different hyphenated cultures: women, the working class, the bourgeoisie, children, ethnic groups, and migrants. Matters concerning identity were then explored in the 1990s, when the previous paradigm of culture became intensively challenged. In a famous text by Gupta and Ferguson from the beginning of the 1990s they did away with the notion of "the spatial distribution of peoples, tribes, and cultures" and the idea that "space itself becomes a kind of natural grid on which cultural differences, historical memory and societal organization is inscribed" (1992:7). Identity in the plural was so much easier to talk about in a runaway world.

At present the picture is even more complex with the many studies that border on disciplines dealing with the media and communication. Surprisingly, one of the strongest trends seems to be precisely the very nexus of ethnological studies of old, namely material, culture. For over a generation expertise in objects was looked on as part of the antiquarian training, connected as it was to remnants of peasant culture.

Now, as can be seen in many of the contributions, the agency of things – whether these are found in kitchens or medical clinics or are farming implements – is just as interesting.

The most constant trait over the years has been ethnology's public appeal. The German ethnologist Konrad Köstlin has pointed out how ethnologists have developed some kind of expertise in the art of cultural interpretation: "Ethnologists are the storytellers of our time. They explain why we are like we are. And their material – taken from individuals (interviews and archive materials) as the most genuine sources – creates a kind of face-to-face authenticity . . ." (Köstlin 2010:170).

This rings a familiar bell, and again has been achieved by researchers devoting most of their attention to the national arena. Consequently – or ironically – the reinvention of ethnology meant that Europe as a field of interest often gravitated out of sight. It was not until the 1990s, and following the expansion of the EU, that the focus was again on the comparative perspective: the consequences of national borders, how new EU regimes affect everyday life and production, the creation of new elites and the rewriting of history. These are all things that are described and explained by many authors in this volume.

The Way of Doing Things

Are we then talking about two disciplines and two different ways of approaching a common area? To some extent, yes, but no longer based on the social background of the researchers. There is a deep well to fathom if you want to collect narratives about the professional habitus within the two disciplines though. Ethnologists have often grumbled about having their toes trampled on, while anthropologists have hardly feigned their existence. As bearers of "Grand Theories" coming into foreign sites they have expected "'the natives' from the remote periphery to play the role of Herderian nationalist ethnographers" (Baskar 2008:77). Based on his Polish experience, the professor of anthropology Michał Buchowski has explained what it felt like to meet anthropologists "from elsewhere" who now wanted to do their fieldwork in Eastern Europe. The local ethnologists were regarded by the visitors as some kind of "retarded anthropologists" who happened to have a good command of English (Povrzanović Frykman 2008).

The bickering between the two disciplines continues to this day – it is part of their history. But it takes place over a crack, not a chasm. They both want to explain and formulate narratives and analyses of the reality that people in today's Europe share. This has sometimes been called the tradition of "studying down" and sometimes the creation of a "grassroots perspective" – both of which seem equally natural for the two disciplines. It is "the way they do things" – the qualitative methods used – that has ultimately come to unite the subjects. This has often meant researchers going out into the field; ethnography presupposes that you use yourself as the examination instrument. When the anthropologist Ulf Hannerz (2006) reflected on the different fieldwork that he had done since the 1960s – none of which had taken place in Europe – he was struck by the deep personal experience they had all offered. He remembered informants who had become close friends, and places that would always be his own. He wanted to be "out there," with all his senses open, immersed in the site: "Fieldwork of the immersion type can be an intellectual, emotional and aesthetic pleasure, the kind of experience we feel makes both our minds and our hearts grow" (2006:34). As Michael Jackson (2005) has pointed out, as a researcher you have the possibility to temporarily become the Other, thus erasing the difference between oneself and the object being studied. Borrowing from Maurice Merleau-Ponty he calls this "lateral displacement" and from Hannah Arendt "visiting imagination." In both cases it means that you do fieldwork with your feet and use your empathy in order to break into new worlds. It becomes the solid ground on which you stand and from where you can gather more information from archives, directories, and public statistics.

The essence of ethnography is "being there." This leads to insights about how to capture an environment as it appears to the informant – who might be one of the arriving refugees, patients in a doctor's surgery, bureaucrats in Brussels, young writers on Facebook, makers of Halloumi cheese in Cyprus, Muslim women in Europe, or civilians who trying to cope with the acts of war in post-Yugoslav countries, all of which are presented in different chapters in this book. As the European reality becomes all the more complex, people are studied with regard to their different experiences, beliefs, expectations, and conditions; the ethnology and anthropology of Europe have assumed the task of interpreting what is happening and presenting it to both European citizens and to a variety of academic audiences. Each chapter in this volume emphasizes the complexity of the specific topics taken up, the value of insights gained through ethnographic fieldwork, and the many study paths that are worthy of further exploration. The readers, on their part, might try to engage in the difficult – but perhaps futile – task of discerning the original disciplinary belonging of the authors in this book, who all contribute to the effort of understanding Europe.

NOTES

1 Today the difference between departments covering the same subject is greater than the difference between the two disciplines. In many of the former socialist states ethnology has – as Michał Buchowski writes in Chapter 5 of this volume – been renamed as anthropology or cultural anthropology in order to emphasize the difference between the previous control of science by the state, while in other countries *Kulturwissenschaft* or *cultural studies* has become a collective name.
2 These words were actually attributed to the artist and author Massimo d'Azeglio.
3 The backbone of this presentation is the obituary written by Professor Lambros Comitas (1999).

REFERENCES

Anderson, B.
1983 Imagined Communities: Reflections on the Origin and Spread of Nationalism. London: Verso.
Arensberg, C.
1937 The Irish Countryman: An Anthropological Study. Waveland: Illinois.

Arensberg, C., and S. Kimball
1940 Family and Community in Ireland. Cambridge, MA: Harvard University Press.
Baskar, B.
2008 Small National Ethnologies and Supranational Empires: The Case of the Habsburg Monarchy. *In* Everyday Culture in Europe: Approaches and Methodologies. M. Nic Craith, U. Kockel, and R. Johler, eds. pp. 65–80. Aldershot: Ashgate.
Bausinger, H.
1972 Volkskunde: Von der Altertumsforschung zur Kulturanalyse. Darmstadt-Berlin: Carl Habel.
Berg, G., and S. Svensson
1934 Svensk bondekultur. Stockholm: Bonnier.
Birdwell-Pheasant, D., and D. Lawrence-Zúñiga, eds.
1999 House Life: Space, Place and Family in Europe. New York: Berg.
Bourdieu, P.
1977 Outline of a Theory of Practice. Cambridge: Cambridge University Press.
Byron, R.
2002 The Anthropology of Northern Europe. *In* Encyclopedia of Social and Cultural Anthropology. A. Barnard and J. Spencer, eds. pp. 318–320. London: Routledge.
Cohen, A.
1996 Personal Nationalism: A Scottish View on some Rites, Rights and Wrongs. American Anthropologist 23(4):804–815.
Comitas, L.
1999 Arensberg, Conrad Maynadier. American Anthropologist 101(4):810–817.
Dow, J., and O. Bockhorn
2004 The Study of European Ethnology in Austria. Aldershot: Ashgate.
Frykman, J., and P. Niedermüller, eds.
2003 Articulating Europe: Local Perspectives. Copenhagen: Museum Tusculanum.
Frykman, J., M-M. Hammarlin, K. Hansen, B. Rothstein, H. Olofsdotter, and I. Schierenbeck
2009 Sense of Community: Trust, Hope and Worries in the Welfare State. Ethnologia Europaea 39(1):7–46.
Geiger, K., U. Jeggle, and G. Korff, eds.
1970 Abschied vom Volksleben: Untersuchungen des Ludwig-Uhland-Instituts 27. Tübingen: Tübinger Vereinigung für Volkskunde.
Gellner, E.
1983 Nations and Nationalism. Oxford: Blackwell.
Gupta, A., and J. Ferguson
1992 Beyond "Culture": Space, Identity and the Politics of Difference. Cultural Anthropology 7(1):6–23.
Hannerz, U.
2006 Studying Down, Up, Sideways, Through, Backwards, Forwards, Away and at Home: Reflections on the Field Worries of an Expansive Discipline. *In* Locating the Field: Space, Place and Context in Anthropology. ASA Monographs 42. S. Coleman and P. Collins, eds. pp. 23–41. Oxford: Berg.
Hage, G.
2003 Against Paranoid Nationalism: Searching for Hope in a Shrinking Society. Annandale: Pluto.
Herzfeld, M.
1997 Cultural Intimacy: Social Poetics in the Nation-State. New York: Routledge.

Jackson, A.
1987 Anthropology at Home. ASA Monographs 25. London: Tavistock.
Jackson, M.
2005 Existential Anthropology: Events, Exigencies, and Effects. New York: Berghahn.
Kockel, U.
2008 Liberating the Ethnological Imagination. Ethnologia Europaea 38(1):8–12.
Köstlin, K.
2010 European Ethnology: What Does It Mean? Deciphering the Self-Evident. *In* Ethnology in the 21st Century: Transnational Reflections of Past, Present and Future. J. Lehtonen and S. Tenkanen, eds. pp. 161–173. Turku: Kansatiede.
Latour, B.
1999 Pandora's Hope: Essays on the Reality of Science Studies, Cambridge, MA: Harvard University Press.
Löfgren, O.
1988 Ett ämne väljer väg: Folklivsarkivet i Lund 1913–1988. Nils-Arvid Bringéus, ed. Skrifter från Folklivsarkivet i Lund 25:144–166.
2008 When is Small Beautiful? The Transformation of Swedish Ethnology. *In* Everyday Culture in Europe: Approaches and Methodologies. M. Nic Craith, U. Kockel, and R. Johler, eds. pp. 149–163. Aldershot: Ashgate.
Lysaght, P.
2002 Review of Family and Community in Ireland. By Conrad M. Arensberg and Solon T. Kimball. With a new introduction by A. Byrne, R. Edmondson, and T. Varley. Ennis, County Clare: CLASP Press, 2001. Bealoideas, Journal of the Folklore of Ireland 70.
Marcus, G., and M. Fischer
1986 Anthropology as Cultural Critique: An Experimental Moment in the Human Sciences. Chicago: University of Chicago Press.
Povrzanović Frykman, M.
2008 Beyond Culture and Identity: Places, Practices, Experiences. Ethnologia Europaea 38(1):13–22.
Reed-Danahay, D.
2005 Locating Bourdieu. Bloomington and Indianapolis: Indiana University Press.
Rogan, B.
2008 The Troubled Past of European Ethnology: SIEF and International Collaboration from Prague to Derry. Ethnologia Europaea 38(1):66–78.
Rihtman-Auguštin, D.
2004 Ethnology, Myth and Politics: Anthropologizing Croatian Ethnology. Aldershot: Ashgate.
Svensson, S.
1935 Skånes folkdräkter: en dräkthistorisk undersökning 1500–1900. Stockholm: Nordiska museet.
Thomas, R.
1997 Conrad Arensberg, 86, Dies: Hands-On Anthropologist. New York Times, February 16: 51.
Weber, E.
1976 Peasants into Frenchmen: The Modernization of Rural France. Stanford: Stanford University Press.

Index

A Companion to the Anthropology of Europe, First Edition. Edited by Ullrich Kockel, Máiréad Nic Craith, and Jonas Frykman.